DATE DUE

Demco, Inc. 38-293

WILLIAM FAULKNER

A TO Z

WILLIAM FAULKNER

A TO Z

The Essential Reference to His Life and Work

A. NICHOLAS FARGNOLI
and
MICHAEL GOLAY

Facts On File, Inc.

William Faulkner A to Z

Copyright © 2002 by A. Nicholas Fargnoli and Michael Golay

Facts On File, Inc.
132 West 31st Street
New York NY 10001

Library of Congress Cataloging-in-Publication Data

Fargnoli, A. Nicholas.
William Faulkner A to Z : the essential reference to his life and work /
A. Nicholas Fargnoli and Michael Golay.
p. cm.
Includes bibliographical references and index.
ISBN 0-8160-3860-0 (alk. paper)
1. Faulkner, William, 1897–1962—Encyclopedias. 2. Novelists, American—
20th century—Biography—Encyclopedias. 3. Yoknapatawpha County (Imaginary place)—
Encyclopedias. 4. Mississippi—In literature—Encyclopedias. I. Golay, Michael, 1951– . II. Title.

PS3511.A86 Z459 2001
813'.52—dc21
2001023821

Facts On File books are available at special discounts when purchased in bulk quantities
for businesses, associations, institutions, or sales promotions. Please call
our Special Sales Department in New York at (212) 967-8800 or (800) 322-8755.

You can find Facts On File on the World Wide Web at http://www.factsonfile.com

Cover design by Cathy Rincon
Family trees by Jeremy Eagle

Printed in the United States of America

VB Hermitage   10 9 8 7 6 5 4 3 2 1

This book is printed on acid-free paper.

To Harriett and Julie
and in memory of Jenny

CONTENTS

ACKNOWLEDGMENTS

Acknowledgments are due to Don Bowden; Matthew J. Bruccoli; Winnie Chen; Cynthia Cox; Joan Crane; Christina Deane; Kathleen Duffy; Alessandro Fargnoli; Gioia Fargnoli; Giuliana Fargnoli; Harriett Fargnoli; Sister Elizabeth Gill, O.P.; Joel Greenberg; Gregory A. Johnson; Robert Kinpoitner; Robert Martin; Trisha O'Neill; Regina Rush; and Norman Weil and to the Reference Department at the Great Neck Library, Great Neck, New York, and Rockville Camera, Rockville Centre, New York.

Special thanks must be given to Anne Savarese, our editor at Facts On File, Inc., for her gracious patience and sharp eye; to Brian Quinn at Molloy College, for many dynamic and insightful hours of discussion on Faulkner's texts; to Robert W. Hamblin, Director of the Center for Faulkner Studies at Southeast Missouri State University, for his invaluable comments on the manuscript and for generously providing a number of Faulkner photographs; to the Committee for Faculty Scholarship and Academic Advancement at Molloy College, for research and travel grants to Charlottesville, Virginia, and Oxford, Mississippi, and for funds to help defray the cost of photos and permissions; and to Larry Donato, for having magically retrieved an almost lost document.

Eva Weber of Northampton, Massachusetts, contributed entries on 39 of Faulkner's short works from *Collected Stories* and *Uncollected Stories*.

INTRODUCTION

William Faulkner A to Z presents to the general reader and nonspecialist a clear and organized supplement to the reading of William Faulkner's works. Considered one of the most important literary figures in American literature and recognized worldwide as a stylistic innovator, Faulkner can be confusing and bewildering at times because of his complex prose style and narrative techniques. Understanding his plots, themes, and characters, too, can be difficult for the first-time reader. The primary goal of this volume is to assist readers and students of Faulkner in their quest to understand, enjoy, and situate the works and life of this great American writer and Nobel Prize laureate. It is also our intention to provide those already familiar with Faulkner's works a convenient one-volume reference source that can be used to refresh the memory.

Faulkner's published writings span a period of more than 40 years and include poems, short stories, novels, essays, speeches, screenplays, and letters. His literary works contain well in excess of a thousand named characters, some of whom appear in several different works. Unfortunately for the reader, there are times when Faulkner is inconsistent with either the names of his characters or with their spellings. For instance, the surname McCallum first appeared as MacCullum, and the character V. K. Ratliff was first called V. K. Suratt. The reader might bear in mind that Faulkner himself seemed unconcerned about such discrepancies. "What I am trying to say is, the essential truth of these people and their doings is the thing," he once told an editor.

Faulkner's works have endured for several reasons, but—to adapt a concept from Aristotle—primarily because the highest achievement of art is an expression of the human spirit and of the universal element of life. Faulkner catches the imagination as well as the emotions of his readers, and he can be at once serious and comic as he portrays the struggles of the human heart in conflict with itself.

We are indebted to the many scholars and critics who, through the insights and ideas in their writings, have provided us with valuable historical and critical information. Like all major writers whose works are characterized by complexity and depth of purpose and meaning, William Faulkner is an author one must read in communion with others. Faulkner's mythic Yoknapatawpha County—his "little postage stamp of native soil," as he referred to it—occupies a permanent place in the world's literary geography and conjures up a world with boundless interpretative possibilities. If Faulkner drew much of his inspiration from his native Mississippi, he also wrote of what he knew best, and he was not indifferent to trying new narrative techniques that he thought best expressed his characters and themes. His works are peopled with vivid and memorable characters—too numerous to list in this brief introduction—who often face the harshest of conflicts and struggles. Many of Faulkner's major works, such as *The Sound and the Fury, As I Lay Dying,* and *Absalom, Absalom!,* are viewed as exemplary modernist texts and precursors to postmodernism. Faulkner's "little postage stamp" has grown to planetary size. He is translated and read in many languages throughout the world, and his literary influence on later writers endures.

Alphabetically arranged, the entries in this guide provide critical information on a wide range of topics directly related to the study of Faulkner's life and works. Included are names and places (both historical and fictional), events, and ideas. This reference book, like all reference guides, is not a substitute for the enjoyment of reading Faulkner; it is meant to aid and enrich the experience. With the exception of *Soldiers' Pay* (New York: Liveright Publishing Corporation, 1997), *Mosquitoes* (New York: Boni & Liveright, 1927), *Knight's Gambit* (New York: Random House, 1949), and *Sartoris* (Random House, 1956), citations from Faulkner's writings are from the Vintage editions of his works.

Abe Character in *SARTORIS*, a black employee of the elder Dr. PEABODY. Peabody's surgeon son, young "Loosh" (Lucius PEABODY), skillfully repairs the leg of a hunting dog Abe had shot by accident.

Absalom, Absalom! Considered a masterpiece of 20th-century American literature, this novel brought to a close a seven-year burst of creativity in which Faulkner produced *The SOUND AND THE FURY* (1929), *AS I LAY DYING* (1930), *LIGHT IN AUGUST* (1932), and other works. Some critics rate *Absalom, Absalom!* Faulkner's finest work, the peak of his achievement.

The novel chronicles the rise and fall of the YOKNAPATAWPHA COUNTY planter Thomas SUTPEN, a West Virginian of obscure origins who comes into northern Mississippi in the 1830s to fulfill a grand aristocratic design. He buys a hundred square miles of virgin land from a CHICKASAW INDIAN chief, builds a mansion and plantation with the enforced labor of Haitian slaves and a captive French architect, marries the most respectable girl in JEFFERSON, MISSISSIPPI, and attempts to complete his design by establishing a family dynasty.

A work of structural and technical complexity, *Absalom* is an inquiry into the nature of truth. "The whole novel is 'about' the inextricable confusion of fact and fiction, of observation and interpretation, involved in any account of human experience," the critic Michael MILLGATE wrote in his study *William Faulkner.* Closer to the bone, it is an intense, demanding, difficult and often painful exploration of the themes of guilt, shame, and the inability of whites to allow blacks an equal measure of humanity.

The story is simple enough. Sutpen arrives in Jefferson from parts unknown on a Sunday in June 1833. He acquires the land through questionable means and with his half-wild slaves hacks out a plantation he calls SUTPEN'S HUNDRED. In 1838 he marries Ellen Coldfield (SUTPEN), the daughter of a Jefferson merchant. She bears him two children, Judith and Henry SUTPEN. Over Christmas 1860 Judith falls in love with her brother's UNIVERSITY OF MISSISSIPPI friend, Charles BON. Sutpen forbids the marriage. Henry and Charles go off together to fight in the Civil War; Sutpen separately goes to war at the head of a Mississippi volunteer infantry regiment. Ellen dies in 1863. In 1865, at the war's end, Henry kills Bon at the gates of Sutpen's Hundred and disappears. In 1869, Sutpen's factotum, the squatter Wash JONES, kills Sutpen for seducing and then abandoning his 15-year-old granddaughter Milly JONES.

"These facts are never in doubt," Millgate observes. "What is always in doubt, however, and always open to interpretation or conjecture, is the inner meaning of these observable events and the whole intricate sequence of cause and effect which links them to one another."

Faulkner tells the story through Quentin COMPSON, the doomed Harvard undergraduate of *The Sound and the Fury.* It opens on a September afternoon in 1909 as Quentin prepares to call upon Miss Rosa COLDFIELD, an embittered old spinster who has chosen to pass on to him the story of her monstrous brother-in-law, Sutpen. Quentin's father, Jason COMPSON, has heard some of the Sutpen story through his own father, General Jason Lycurgus COMPSON II, Sutpen's only friend; Mr. Compson passes on what he knows to Quentin. As the novel runs its course, Quentin and his Harvard roommate Shrevlin McCannon (see MACKENZIE, SHREVLIN) together reconstruct the Sutpen story.

The novelist supplies three different, sometimes conflicting interpretations of Sutpen. Miss Rosa regards him as a demon. Mr. Compson's version is balanced; it fails to account for the power of Sutpen's obsession. In his frigid dormitory room in Cambridge, Massachusetts, Quentin collates information from both informants to move closer to what Millgate calls a "poetic truth," piecing together his own version of the tale in a long conversation with Shreve.

Absalom, Absalom! had its beginnings in the short story "WASH" (1933). The story introduces Wash Jones, a feckless poor white man who looks after Sutpen's estate while he is away with Lee's army. Sutpen returns to find his wife dead, his son dead, his plantation in ruins. He seduces Wash's granddaughter in hopes of producing an heir. When she bears him a daughter, he repudiates her. Wash then cuts him down with a rusted scythe, kills Milly and the baby, and burns down the fishing shanty that had been their home.

Harper's magazine bought "Wash" in November 1933, paying $350 for it. On a sheet of manuscript dated February 11, 1934, Faulkner began the novel that would become *Absalom, Absalom!* At first he titled it

Dark House, which he earlier had used provisionally and then discarded for *Light in August.*

Faulkner promised his publisher, Harrison SMITH, the manuscript for the autumn of 1934. With money difficulties and other worries to distract him, he would miss the target by 18 months. He did, at least, find a title he liked: "*Absalom, Absalom!;* the story is of a man who wanted a son through pride, and got too many of them and they destroyed him" (*Selected Letters,* p. 84). The biblical Absalom, the third of King David's 17 sons, avenges the rape of his sister by her half brother Amnon, and later rises against his father and attempts to seize his throne.

Faulkner interrupted *Absalom* to return to Hollywood to write film scripts, and he broke off work on the big book entirely late in 1934 to turn out the novel *PYLON,* published in 1935. By March 1935 he had returned to *Absalom.* On March 30 he wrote the title at the top of a sheet of paper, underlining it twice, and after a couple of false starts he opened with Quentin and Miss Rosa in her dark room on a "long still hot weary dead September afternoon" in 1909, just before Quentin heads north to Harvard.

Miss Rosa, Mr. Compson, and Quentin slowly assemble the story of the parvenu Sutpen and the working out of his design. Long flashbacks recount Sutpen's childhood; his first marriage, in Haiti, to Eulalia Bon (see SUTPEN, EULALIA BON), a planter's daughter with a taint of black blood, and the birth of their son Charles; his coming to Yoknapatawpha County. There are vivid and dramatic scenes, as toward the end of chapter 1 when Rosa narrates Sutpen's "raree show," the master stripped to the waist to fight one of his Haitians while his little son Henry and his daughters Judith and Clytemnestra (Clytie, whose mother was a slave) SUTPEN look on.

As Faulkner's biographer Joseph BLOTNER has observed, the introduction of Quentin was a master stroke. Quentin's own complex feelings for his sister Caddy (see COMPSON, CANDACE) in *The Sound and the Fury* make him imaginatively alert to the incestuous triangle of Henry, Judith, and their half brother Bon. Quentin listens quietly, though his nerves are jangling. Rosa's tone is frenzied.

The language of the opening chapter is complex and confused, the atmosphere violent. In chapters 2 and 3, Mr. Compson calmly fills in details of the history of the house of Sutpen as he and Quentin sit on the front gallery in the cigar smoke- and wisteria-scented twilight: the arrival of Charles Bon, the coming of the war and Sutpen's role in it, Sutpen's father-in-law Goodhue COLDFIELD's withdrawal and slow suicide, Henry's and Bon's early war service, Ellen's deathbed request of Rosa to look after Judith. At the end of chapter 3, Wash rides to Jefferson, 12 miles distant, to summon Miss Rosa to Sutpen's Hundred.

Faulkner withholds the reason for Wash's errand to develop more of the history of Henry, Charles, and Judith. Mr. Compson speculates that Sutpen had found evidence of Bon's involvement with a New Orleans octoroon woman and used it as a pretext for forbidding the marriage of Bon and Judith. Henry refused to accept the explanation and broke with his father out of love for Bon. But Mr. Compson seems to find his theory inadequate to explain events. What he does not know is that Bon is Sutpen's son by the racially mixed Haitian wife he had renounced.

Faulkner again takes up Wash's summons at the end of Chapter 4: Wash tells Miss Rosa that Henry has shot and killed Bon.

Again beset with money troubles, Faulkner broke off work on *Absalom* in the summer of 1935, returning to California for another eight-week term writing for the movies. By mid-October he was back in Oxford, launched into chapter 5 of the novel. Miss Rosa again takes up the story, with Quentin as her listener. Judith directs the building of Bon's coffin; after his burial, she, Rosa, and Clytie begin the hard labor of restoring the plantation. The section, mostly flashbacks, ends with Rosa's eerie revelation to Quentin that something is alive in the house: "Something living in it. Hidden in it. It has been out there for four years living hidden in that house" (*Absalom,* p. 140).

In chapter 6, Quentin, now at Harvard, takes over the story. In a letter dated January 10, 1910, Mr. Compson informs his son of Miss Rosa's death and burial. Faulkner here introduces a new character, the Canadian Shreve McCannon, who provides an outsider's detachment as the last of the tale unfolds. The action advances beyond the time of the short story "Wash" and the killing of Thomas Sutpen. Judith and Clytie raise Charles Bon's son by his octoroon mistress, Charles Etienne St. Valery BON. Part black himself, the younger Charles marries a full-blood African American; their child is the feeble-minded Jim BOND, Sutpen's last heir. Judith nurses Charles Etienne through a yellow fever outbreak in 1884; they both die of the disease at Sutpen's Hundred. The chapter ends with Quentin preparing to drive to the mansion with Miss Rosa to flush out whoever is in hiding there.

Faulkner began writing chapter 7 in a state of deep grieving for his younger brother Dean (see FAULKNER, DEAN SWIFT), who was killed in an airplane crash on November 10, 1935. He worked away at the manuscript at his mother's house, where he had moved temporarily to care for her and Dean's pregnant widow. Quentin continues the story with occasional interruptions from Shreve. It is early material: work on the mansion at Sutpen's Hundred, a liveried slave's dismissal of the boy Sutpen from the front door of a Virginia plantation—the initial motivation for Sutpen's design. Quentin reconstructs Sutpen's arrival in Haiti, his marriage to Eulalia Bon, and his abandonment of her when he learns of her taint. (Their son Charles's courtship of Judith will be her revenge.) Sutpen explains his flight from Eulalia to General Compson, his only friend: She could not be part of his plan, so he left her behind.

The chapter concludes with Wash's killing of Sutpen, much of it lifted from the short story, and with Quentin's disclosure to Shreve, withheld almost until the end, that Milly's child had not been the heir Sutpen wanted, but a girl.

So it ends for Sutpen. He never understands where he has gone wrong. General Compson thinks Sutpen's trouble is a sort of innocence of the nature of reality, an inability to fully reckon the consequences of his actions.

By December 1935 Faulkner could see ahead to the tale's conclusion. By mid-month, however, he was in Hollywood again, though he was able to work on chapter 8, which concerns Quentin's relentless exploration of the Henry-Bon-Judith triangle. Bon still wants to marry Judith; even more, he wants Sutpen to acknowledge him as his son. In the end, Henry is prepared to accept incest, but not miscegenation. Quentin and Shreve recreate Henry's last interview with his father in an army bivouac in North Carolina in late winter, 1865. Chapter 8 closes with Shreve's imagined account of the shooting at the gates of Sutpen's Hundred.

In chapter 9, the novel's last and shortest, Quentin relates his night journey with Miss Rosa to the gaunt mansion at Sutpen's Hundred. Quentin follows her upstairs and catches a glimpse of the "something" living there—the spectral Henry, who has come home to die. In the final sequence, he again takes up his father's letter and reads of the death of Rosa, and of Henry and Clytie, and of the destruction of the great house by fire.

Absalom, Absalom! ends on a note of anguish:

> "Why do you hate the South?" Shreve asks Quentin Compson.
> "'I dont hate it,' Quentin said quickly, at once, immediately; 'I dont hate it,' he said. *'I dont hate it* he thought, panting in the cold air, the iron New England dark: *I dont. I dont! I dont hate it! I dont hate it!'"* (*Absalom*, p. 303).

Faulkner finished the draft in Hollywood early in January 1936. Then he began to drink heavily, even though he told friends and acquaintances that he felt good about the book. He returned to Oxford before the end of January and continued to tinker with the manuscript. Finally he appended a date to the last page: "31 Jany 1936."

With many revisions, Faulkner sent the typescript along to his new publisher, RANDOM HOUSE, which had absorbed SMITH & HAAS at the beginning of 1936. Hal SMITH, now at Random House, received the concluding pages in June. Faulkner continued revising up to the last minute. He added, too, a chronology of events, a geneal-

ogy of characters, and a hand-drawn map of Yoknapatawpha County, with identifications of 27 places that had figured in his novels and short stories up to then.

He read and corrected the galleys in August. The official publication date, with 6,000 copies printed, was October 26. Random House soon followed with a second printing of 2,500 copies and a third, in mid-November, of another 1,400. The early reviews, as ever with Faulkner, were mixed. In *The New Yorker*, Clifton FADIMAN famously called *Absalom* "the most consistently boring novel by a reputable writer to come my way during the last decade." *Time*, in an unsigned review, called it "the strangest, longest, least readable, most infuriating and yet in some respects the most impressive novel that William Faulkner has written." Bernard De Voto, in the *Saturday Review*, treated the new work with grudging respect tinged with sarcasm.

"It is now possible to say confidently that the greatest suffering of which American fiction has any record occurred in the summer of 1909 and was inflicted on Quentin Compson," De Voto wrote. That is when, in *The Sound and the Fury*, "he made harrowing discoveries about his sister Candace," while only a month or so later in the new work he "had to watch the last act of doom's pitiless engulfing of the Sutpens, another family handicapped by a curse."

De Voto noted that Faulkner, as usual, had borrowed melodramatic devices and scenes from earlier works: hammering on a coffin, as in *As I Lay Dying*; the incest theme from *The Sound and the Fury*; the intolerable agonies that beset a mixed-race character, as when Charles Etienne Bon endures "cruelties almost as unceasing as those that made Joe Christmas [of *Light in August*] the most persecuted child since Dickens."

Reviewers complained of the novel's technical complexity, of the improbabilities of the characters' actions ("Just why," De Voto wondered, "did not Thomas Sutpen, recognizing Charles Bon as his mulatto son, order him off the plantation, or bribe or kill him, or tell Judith either half the truth, or Henry all of it?"), and of long patches of apoplectic prose.

"In the first paragraph of the novel," Graham Greene observed pedantically in the *London Mercury*, "there are forty-one adjectives in twenty-seven lines qualifying only fifteen nouns."

The novelist probably saw only a few of the notices, and he doubtless shrugged off the ones he did read. "Faulkner is probably the one man in the world who doesn't give a damn what the rest of its inhabitants might think, so long as he has a place to sleep, eat and write, with an occasional jug of corn thrown in for recreational hours," Laurence Bell remarked in *Literary America*. In any case, later critics, taking a longer view, would right the balance.

The critic Cleanth BROOKS called *Absalom* the greatest and least well understood of Faulkner's works. The difficulty of the writing, he argued, "is the price that has to be paid for the novel's power and significance." Millgate viewed *Absalom*'s structural complexity as fundamental to its meaning. Irving Howe agreed, and found *Absalom* the most nearly structurally perfect of all Faulkner's novels.

"Faulkner's greatest risk, *Absalom, Absalom!* is never likely to be read widely; it is for aficionados willing to satisfy the large and sometimes excessive demands it makes upon attention," Howe concluded. "Wild, twisted and occasionally absurd, the novel has, nonetheless, the fearful impressiveness which comes when a writer has driven his vision to an extreme."

Frederick Karl, a Faulkner biographer, judges *Absalom* the "Everest" of Faulkner's achievement, one of the great novels of modernism and the only American work of fiction that can stand with those of Proust, Mann, Kafka, Conrad, Woolf, and Joyce.

For further information, see *Faulkner in the University,* pp. 34–35, 36, 46–7, 71, 73, 74–77, 79–81, 93–94, 97–98, 119, 273–75, and 281; *Selected Letters,* pp. 92, 94, 96, and 280; and *Faulkner at Nagano,* pp. 142–43.

Acarius, Mr. Main character in the short story "MR. ACARIUS." In order to experience the depths of humanity and to be one with it, which includes its debasement, Mr. Acarius convinces his doctor to admit him to a clinic for alcoholics. While there, he is disillusioned by his fellow drunks and their machinations. He leaves the clinic and vows never to drink again.

Acey Character in GO DOWN, MOSES ("Pantaloon in Black"). A black hand at the JEFFERSON, MISSISSIPPI sawmill where RIDER works, he tries to console Rider over his wife's death.

Adams (Mr.) Minor character in *The TOWN.* He is the mayor of JEFFERSON, MISSISSIPPI, before losing to Manfred DE SPAIN in the 1904 election.

Adams, Mrs. Minor character in *The TOWN.* The old fat wife of Mayor ADAMS, she is referred to by some as "Miss Eve Adams."

Adams, Theron Minor character in *The TOWN,* the youngest son of Mayor ADAMS. When the older Adams, running for reelection, tries to smear Manfred DE SPAIN's character, de Spain challenges Theron to an axe fight as a way of defending his honor.

"Ad Astra" *(Collected Stories)* Short story that explores the senselessness of war, set in France on November 11, 1918, the day World War I ended. To celebrate the peace, a group of military men drive to a bar in Amiens. Accompanying the nameless narrator are two American aviators in British uniform, the southerners

Gerald BLAND and Bayard SARTORIS (4), along with the Irish aviator COMYN and an Indian officer of forces under British command. Stopping for a drink, they meet up with another American aviator, Buck MONAGHAN. With him is the German aviator he shot down that morning.

As the level of inebriation increases, Bland jokes about an illusory wife; Comyn fantasizes about girls and offers to fight the others; Monaghan rants about his own Irish immigrant background; and Sartoris reveals the death of his twin brother and his revenge on German fliers. The French patrons of the Cloche-Clos greet the presence of the German prisoner with hostility. After the Indian and German discuss music and art, the German tells his life story and of his rejection of a noble inheritance. A brawl erupts and the group is evicted into the town square, where they tend to the beaten German. In the end, Comyn and Monaghan go off to a brothel, dragging the German with them. The Indian, who periodically comments on the paradoxes of war and peace, predicts their future as former soldiers: They will be the walking dead.

This story first appeared in *American Caravan* (March 25, 1931) and also was included in *These 13* (1931). "HONOR" is its sequel.

"Adolescence" *(Uncollected Stories)* A short story with many poetic passages and a somewhat fairy tale–like plot of a young girl growing up with her grandmother after the death of her mother and subsequent remarriage of her father. Juliet BUNDEN, the heroine, finds living with her grandmother to be peaceful and satisfying after the tumult of her four brothers, indifferent father, and hateful stepmother, and she increases the pastoral happiness of her life when she befriends Lee HOLLOWELL, a boy about her own age of 13 when they first meet. The imagery of a bucolic setting is highly suggestive of the untainted Garden of Eden. Lee happens upon Juliet while she is swimming nude in a brook or river. He strips off his clothes and they swim together in all innocence, an innocence that lasts throughout their relationship. They remain in this idyllic friendship for nearly four years, until Juliet's grandmother discovers them lying together in a blanket. Assuming that she has come upon a scene of lust and uncleanliness, GRAMMAW Bunden chases Lee away and then castigates Juliet for having ruined herself and lost her virtue to a no-good, lazy Hollowell. She orders Juliet home, where the grandmother threatens her; but Juliet seems oblivious. Finally, the grandmother admits that she has told Juliet's father, Joe BUNDEN, about Juliet's wrongdoing and that he is arranging a marriage for her. Juliet, angered and upset, swears not to marry any man chosen by her hated father. That night after a heated confrontation with her grandmother, Juliet makes a mysterious trip to town. A few days later she learns that her father, as well as Lee's father, Lafe HOLLOWELL, both moonshiners, have been killed by federal Revenue agents. When she takes a lonely walk to the creek where she first met Lee, she sees a figure walking toward her and mistakenly thinks it is Lee, but it is her little brother, Bud BUNDEN. After comforting him and giving him a parcel of food and all her savings—just a few dollars—she watches him leave for good. A melancholy wistfulness comes over her as she finally realizes that life must go on.

Written around 1922, "Adolescence" was published posthumously in *Uncollected Stories of William Faulkner.* Faulkner used some of the scenes and ideas from this short piece, however, in his novels *SOLDIERS' PAY* and "The Wild Palms." (For further information, see *Uncollected Stories of William Faulkner,* p. 704). Not unlike "MISS ZILPHIA GANT" and "FRANKIE AND JOHNNY," "Adolescence" is a short story about the conflict between a parent-figure and her daughter, a theme that Faulkner employed in a few of his early short pieces. In "Adolescence," this conflict—handled through the device of an adversarial, possessive, and destructive mother figure—is seen first between Juliet and her stepmother, then between Juliet and her grandmother. In the case of "Adolescence" and "Miss Zilphia Gant," the parent figure comes upon the daughter with a boy in compromising circumstances and the interference disturbs the tranquil relationship that the young ones have worked out between themselves.

"Afternoon of a Cow" *(Uncollected Stories)* A tongue-in-cheek short story that Faulkner passed off as the work of Ernest V. TRUEBLOOD. The story generates interest because it uses Faulkner himself as a character, much in the manner of a postmodernist writer such as Paul Auster. The story reports on a frightened cow that has fallen into a ditch during a fire. The character Faulkner, along with OLIVER, a black butler, and Ernest Trueblood, the first-person narrator of the tale, rush to rescue the cow, but they are at first unsuccessful. In its fear and distress, the cow empties its bladder and bowels upon Faulkner, shattering the dignity of the scene. The story ends with Faulkner stripping in the door of the stable and washing. Later, wrapped in a horse blanket, he and his friends drink to the cow.

Faulkner intended the story to be taken as a joke, and he himself thought it was particularly funny (see *Selected Letters of William Faulkner,* p. 246). "Afternoon of a Cow" was first published in a French translation, "L'Après-midi d'une Vache," by Maurice Edgar COIN-DREAU in the June/July 1943 issue of *Fontaine* (27–28). Faulkner read the story to Coindreau when the latter was visiting Faulkner in Hollywood in late June 1937 to discuss the French translation of *The SOUND AND THE FURY.* The original English version was first published in 1947 in *Furioso* II, 5–17, and reprinted in *Parodies: An Anthology from Chaucer to Beerbohm—and After,* edited by

Dwight Macdonald (New York: Random House, 1960) and in *Uncollected Stories of William Faulkner.* For more information, see *Selected Letters of William Faulkner,* pp. 224, 245, 246, and *Uncollected Stories of William Faulkner,* pp. 702–03.

Aiken, Conrad (1889–1973)   Poet and writer, born in Savannah, Georgia, and reared in Cambridge, Massachusetts. Aiken's work was an early influence on Faulkner, particularly his verse novel *The Jig of Forslin* (1917) and the collection of tone poems titled *The House of Dust* (1920).

Faulkner praised Aiken's experimental *Turns and Movies* (1916) in an essay in the *Mississippian* for February 16, 1921: "He, alone of the entire yelping pack, seems to have a definite goal in mind."

Aiken published an appreciation of Faulkner's much-criticized style in the *Atlantic Monthly* in 1939. Though he conceded Faulkner's obscurity, he went on to observe that readers willing to tackle his intricacies and patches of overwriting were in for great rewards.

Ailanthia   Character in "ELLY" (in *Collected Stories*). She is Elly's grandmother. Aware that Elly's lover Paul has black blood, Ailanthia is deeply disturbed by the connection. Elly hates her grandmother and urges Paul to kill her. In the end, Elly causes the car crash that takes the old woman's life.

Akers   Character in *ABSALOM, ABSALOM!* A coon hunter, he treads accidentally on one of Thomas SUTPEN's "wild negroes" buried in swamp mud.

Alabama Red   *See* RED.

Albert (1)   In *AS I LAY DYING,* the fountain clerk in MOSELEY's drugstore in Mottson (MOTTSTOWN). Albert tells Moseley about the townspeople's reaction to the stench of Addie BUNDREN's decaying body coming from the Bundrens' wagon, which is stopped in front of GRUMMET's hardware store, and how the marshal insisted that the Bundrens move on because no one could stand the smell any longer. (By this time, Addie Bundren had been dead for eight days.)

Albert (2)   Character in "TURNABOUT" (in *Collected Stories*). A British military policeman in France in 1918, he takes charge of Midshipman L. C. W. HOPE from the American MPs who have picked him up out of the street.

Albert (3)   A minor character in *The MANSION.* A member of Brother Joe C. GOODYHAY's religious community, Albert drives the truck containing the lumber to build a chapel, but the owner of the property has changed his mind.

Alec, Uncle Character in *GO DOWN, MOSES* ("PANTALOON IN BLACK"). An African American, he is the husband of RIDER's aunt, who looked after him when he was a boy. When Rider's wife dies, the aunt tries to persuade him to come home.

Alford, Dr. Character in *Sartoris,* a physician in his thirties with "a face like a mask—a comforting face, but cold" (96). He diagnoses old Bayard SARTORIS's wen (a cyst), but when he suggests that it be removed immediately, Sartoris testily objects. Later, however, Dr. Alford accompanies Sartoris to a specialist in Memphis. He shows an interest in the widowed Narcissa SARTORIS. Dr. Alford is referred to in *AS I LAY DYING;* in that novel, his office is upstairs from the JEFFERSON, MISSISSIPPI, drugstore to which Dewey Dell BUNDREN goes for help.

Algonquin Hotel Faulkner's usual stopping-place in New York City, this medium-sized, unpretentious hotel at 59 West 44th Street attracted a loyal clientele of actors, writers, and others associated with the arts. It was famous in the 1920s and 1930s for its Round Table gatherings of Franklin P. Adams, Robert Benchley, Heywood Broun, Dorothy Parker, Alexander Woollcott, and other writers. The host, Frank Case, went out of his way to cater to artistic types.

Faulkner began staying at the Algonquin in the early 1930s, after he had made a name for himself with *The SOUND AND THE FURY* and *SANCTUARY.* He remained loyal to the Algonquin through the 1940s and 1950s. He worked on the final typescript of *The REIVERS* at the Algonquin in late 1961 and put up there for the last time in May 1962, when he traveled to New York to accept the National Institute of Arts and Letters' Gold Medal for fiction.

Alice (1) Character in *LIGHT IN AUGUST.* A 12-year-old girl, she takes care of Joe CHRISTMAS in the orphanage. Alice wakes him up to say good-bye when she wins her release.

Alice (2) Character in *The REIVERS.* She is Miss BALLENBAUGH's African-American cook.

"Al Jackson" *(Uncollected Stories)* Short piece in the form of two letters written in 1925 by Faulkner to Sherwood ANDERSON. In NEW ORLEANS together, the two writers vied to outdo each other in creating a series of tall tales about the imaginary Al JACKSON, a "fish-herd" and surviving descendant of President Andrew Jackson. Here Faulkner relates what was told to him of Al Jackson's remarkable family members by a riverboat pilot. His father, old man Jackson, tried to raise sheep on swampy pastureland, but the sheep were transformed into aquatic creatures. In trying to catch the sheep, Al's brother Claude JACKSON gradually turned into a shark

that chased women swimmers. In the second letter, Faulkner tells what he has learned of Al's sister Elenor, who eloped with a tin peddlar and of his brother Herman, who died of brain convulsions after reading all of Walter Scott's works. Al felt responsible for this because he had helped Herman invent a system of making pearl buttons from fish scales, the profits from which enabled Herman to obtain an education.

Similar Al Jackson anecdotes also appear in *MOSQUITOES,* related by the character Dawson FAIRCHILD, who is based, at least in part, on Anderson. Faulkner wrote this material at the time of the early prose later assembled in *NEW ORLEANS SKETCHES.*

Allanovna, Myra Character in *The MANSION.* She owns a men's tie store in New York City. When V. K. Ratliff is in New York for Linda SNOPES's wedding, Allanovna, who also designs the ties, gives Ratliff one.

Allen Character in "FOX HUNT" (in *Collected Stories*). He is a wealthy Yale student. The neglected Mrs. BLAIR is interested in Allen, and when he marries, she turns for solace to Steve GAWTREY instead.

Allen, Bobbie Character in *LIGHT IN AUGUST.* She is a waitress at a cheap restaurant who doubles as a prostitute. In the eyes of Joe CHRISTMAS, she has a "musing, demure" appearance.

At 17, Joe has a love affair with Bobbie Allen. The stern Simon MCEACHERN, Joe's foster father, confronts them at a dance; Joe attacks him with a chair when he calls Bobbie a harlot. But she rejects Joe and leaves town with her Memphis employers, Max and Mame CONFREY.

Allison, Howard Character in "BEYOND" (in *Collected Stories*). The 10-year-old son of Judge ALLISON, he is killed while riding his pony. The judge seeks the boy's spirit in The Beyond.

Allison, Judge Character in "BEYOND" (in *Collected Stories*). Ailing and elderly, he has never gotten over the accidental death of his 10-year-old son, Howard ALLISON. On his deathbed, the judge's spirit soars to The Beyond to learn about immortality.

Allison, Miss Character in *The MANSION.* A relative of Manfred DE SPAIN, Miss Allison is a retired old-maid school teacher from California. She returns to JEFFERSON, MISSISSIPPI, with her mother to live in the de Spain mansion that Flem SNOPES had bought from Manfred. After Flem's death, Linda Snopes KOHL gives the house back to the de Spain family as a partial vindication of the past.

Allison, Sophia Character in "BEYOND" (in *Collected Stories*). She is the indulgent mother of Judge ALLISON, long in her grave at the time of the story.

"All the Dead Pilots" *(Collected Stories)*   Short story set in France in the last years of World War I. Framing the story is a melancholy elegy for all the dead aviators, including those who survived the war to grow older in a kind of living death. The nameless narrator is a British officer who now works as a censor; he tells the tragicomic tale of Johnny SARTORIS, an American flyer in the British ROYAL AIR FORCE. Sartoris obsessively seeks revenge on his morally bankrupt British squadron leader, SPOOMER, who stole first Sartoris's London sweetheart and then his Amiens girlfriend. As Amiens comes under German fire, Sartoris tracks Spoomer to a tryst and steals his uniform. He dresses a drunken ambulance driver in the uniform and puts the man into Spoomer's bed at the airbase. Spoomer is caught when he sneaks back the next morning disguised in women's clothing; he is demoted and sent back to England. Sartoris himself is demoted for dereliction of duty and courageously dies in combat over German lines on July 4, 1918. The censor learns this when he opens the flyer's final letter to his aunt, the official letter announcing his death, and a parcel of his pathetic personal effects. The narrator reflects that a life of such reckless intensity could not, by its nature, last long.

This story first appeared under the title "Dead Pilots" in *Woman's Home Companion* (April 23, 1931), was included in *These 13* (1931), and was revised for *Collected Stories* (1950).

"Ambuscade"   *See The* UNVANQUISHED.

Ames, Dalton   Character in *The* SOUND AND THE FURY. Dalton is Caddy COMPSON's lover, whom her brother Quentin COMPSON, obsessed with the ideal of honor and the idea of incest, unsuccessfully threatens. Self-possessed and physically stronger than Quentin, Dalton easily defends himself against his ineffective assault. Knowing that Quentin is incapable of beating him up, Dalton hands him a pistol, but Quentin cannot use it. Dalton is the probable father of Caddy's daughter, whom Caddy names after Quentin; Quentin commits suicide before the baby is born.

Anderson, Elizabeth Prall   *See* PRALL, ELIZABETH.

Anderson, Sherwood (1876–1941)   Ohio-born author of *Winesburg, Ohio,* a well-regarded collection of short stories; the novel *Dark Laughter;* and other works. Faulkner was already an admirer of Anderson's stories when Anderson's wife, Elizabeth PRALL, introduced them in NEW ORLEANS in the autumn of 1924. The two men hit it off at first, in spite of the more than 20-year difference in their ages.

Anderson used Faulkner for the basis of the main character in his short story "A Meeting South," in which a bordello madam befriends a young southerner.

The friendship cooled quickly. Faulkner wrote an essay highly critical of aspects of Anderson's work in 1925; perhaps the older writer read and resented it. Faulkner came to regard Anderson as "a one- or two-book man" who ought to have stopped writing after *Dark Laughter* (1925), a judgment that many critics share.

All the same, Anderson treated Faulkner generously. He read at least part of Faulkner's first novel in progress, SOLDIERS' PAY, and recommended it to his publisher, BONI & LIVERIGHT, although evidently he never finished reading it. Faulkner claimed to have heard from Elizabeth Prall that Anderson would recommend the book as long as he didn't have to read it.

In any case, Boni & Liveright published *Soldiers' Pay* in February 1926.

Faulkner returned the favor by dedicating SARTORIS to Anderson in 1929. "TO SHERWOOD ANDERSON," the dedication read, "through whose kindness I was first published, with the belief that this book will give him no reason to regret that fact."

Andrews   Character in "FOX HUNT" (in *Collected Stories*). He is a servant of the wealthy Englishman Harrison BLAIR.

Angeliqué   Character in *A FABLE*. A blind woman, she leads a crippled man and takes a child from MARTHE. She accuses Marthe's half brother STEFAN (the Corporal) of murdering Frenchmen. Although it is not entirely clear from the text, it appears that the child is related to Angeliqué, and not to Marthe or her sister MARYA.

Angelo   Character in "A PORTRAIT OF ELMER" (in *Uncollected Stories*). A hard-bitten World War I veteran, he is the Italian friend of the American artist Elmer HODGE.

Annual Faulkner and Yoknapatawpha Conference   Yearly Faulkner conference sponsored by the Center for the Study of Southern Culture and the English Department at the University of Mississippi. Held in Faulkner's home town of OXFORD, MISSISSIPPI, the conference is normally scheduled for the last week of July. It was first held in 1974. In addition to papers and panel discussions on various issues related to Faulkner studies, there are tours of Oxford and the surrounding area. The winner of the Faux Faulkner contest for the best imitation of Faulkner's stylistic mannerisms is also announced at this time (for examples, see *The Best of Bad Faulkner: Choice Entries from the Faux Faulkner Competition*, edited with a preface by Dean Faulkner Wells [San Diego: A Harvest/HBJ Original, 1991]). Conference proceedings are published each year and include topics on race, women, humor, religion, gender, and postmodernism.

In 1987, the United States Postal Service issued a commemorative first-class stamp bearing Faulkner's likeness. (Stamp Design © 1987 U.S. Postal Service. Reproduced with permission. All rights reserved.)

Anse   In *The SOUND AND THE FURY,* the marshal of a town near Cambridge, Massachusetts, who arrests Quentin COMPSON. On the day of his suicide, Quentin is wrongly accused of kidnapping a little girl from an immigrant Italian family. Anse takes Quentin in for a hearing, which ends in his favor.

Armstead   Family name in *INTRUDER IN THE DUST.* The Armsteads are YOKNAPATAWPHA COUNTY farmers.

Armstid, Henry   A poor farmer who lives in the vicinity of FRENCHMAN'S BEND, he appears in *AS I LAY DYING* (he narrates the 43d chapter, "Armstid"), *LIGHT IN AUGUST,* and *The HAMLET,* but the portrayal of his character in the first two novels (where only his surname is used) differs considerably from that in the latter work. He also appears in the short stories "SPOTTED HORSES" (which was revised for *The Hamlet*) and "SHINGLES FOR THE LORD."

   In book 4 of *The Hamlet,* Armstid is presented as a selfish, greedy, foolish, and impetuous person who ends up making a spectacle of himself. At the auction of the wild ponies that Flem SNOPES and Buck HIPPS transported from Texas, Armstid takes his wife's hard-earned money to buy a horse he cannot afford and breaks his leg trying to catch it. By the end of the novel, he mortgages all he owns and, with V. K. RATLIFF and Odum BOOKWRIGHT, purchases the OLD FRENCHMAN place, a worthless piece of property that Flem tricks the three into buying. Armstid goes mad in his futile attempt at digging up the treasure rumored to be buried there, and eventually he is put away in an insane asylum in Jackson.

   In *As I Lay Dying* and *Light in August,* he is portrayed as a kind and considerate person who helps both neighbor and stranger. In *As I Lay Dying,* Armstid gives overnight shelter to the Bundrens, whose mishap while crossing the flooded river causes them to lose their mules. In *Light in August,* at the risk of his wife's displeasure, he again provides overnight shelter, this time for the stranger Lena GROVE, and the next day takes her in his wagon to VARNER'S STORE, where she can catch a lift to JEFFERSON, MISSISSIPPI. In "Shingles for the Lord," he helps put out the Whitfield church fire that consumes the old, dried-out building. In *The TOWN* and *The MANSION,* he is an off-stage character living in the Jackson asylum.

Armstid, Ina   Referred to in the short story "SPOTTED HORSES." Mrs. ARMSTID's oldest child, she bars the door when her mother has to leave at night and sleeps with an ax for protection.

Armstid, Lula   *See* ARMSTID, MRS.

Armstid, Martha   *See* ARMSTID, MRS.

Armstid, Mrs. (Henry)   The wife of Henry ARMSTID, an impoverished farmer in the area of FRENCHMAN'S BEND. In addition to long hours and heavy manual work (there are times when she pulls a plow with her husband), she earns money by weaving at night. At the auction in book four of *The HAMLET,* she unsuccessfully tries to prevent Henry from bidding her five dollars on one of the wild ponies Flem SNOPES and Buck HIPPS transported from Texas. When Flem pockets the money, she brings suit against him but loses. In *LIGHT IN AUGUST,* her first name is Martha. In this novel, when her husband takes in the travel-weary Lena GROVE, she taps her small store of egg money to see Lena on her way to JEFFERSON, MISSISSIPPI. Although indignant about Lena's pregnancy, Mrs. Armstid is sympathetic too. In

AS I LAY DYING, where Mrs. Armstid is called Lula, she helps Cash BUNDREN, whose leg is broken. Mrs. Armstid, with no given first name, also appears in the short story "SHINGLES FOR THE LORD." (For further information, see *Faulkner in the University,* pp. 30–31).

Arthur The black servant of the family in the short story "SEPULTURE SOUTH: GASLIGHT" who, along with his wife, LIDDY, feels he must leave the household upon the death of the grandfather.

"Artist at Home" *(Collected Stories)* Short story that satirizes the lives of artists and the process of creating art. The moderately successful novelist Roger HOWES has isolated himself and his family comfortably in rural Virginia. This does not deter numerous artist friends from visiting unexpectedly to freely partake of his food and clothing, annoying his wife and upsetting his neighbors.

Having been unable to write anything for some two years, Roger invites John BLAIR, a frail and penurious but promising poet, to stay. Roger's wife, Anne HOWES, at first is dismayed by this unwelcome guest; but she gradually comes to sympathize with him, and she eventually enters into an intimate relationship with him. The triangle between Anne, John, and Roger results in a series of dramatic and emotional scenes. After each, Roger turns to his typewriter to work with renewed energy.

The implication is that Roger invited the poet for precisely this purpose—to provide material and inspiration for a new novel. One rainy night, John, who has moved out of the house and into a village hotel, gazes longingly at Anne's window. Then he leaves and sends Anne the poem he was inspired to write. It is a masterpiece, and Roger sells it to a magazine for him. By this time, John has died from his exposure in the rain. Roger's own book about these events sells so well that he helps pay for John's hospital and funeral debts, and he buys Anne a fur coat. This she passes on to a neighbor, because it reminds her of John's death.

This tale first appeared in *Story* (August 1933).

As I Lay Dying One of Faulkner's shortest novels, but one of his most significant. In it, he presents the story of the death and burial of Addie BUNDREN, as told in individual voices by her husband, her children, neighbors, passing strangers, and even (in one of the more moving and important passages) by Addie herself, apparently speaking five days after her death. In what Faulkner himself called a "tour de force" of writing, *As I Lay Dying* is told in 59 monologues of varying length. Most of these monologues represent the thoughts of the Bundrens themselves, but 16 chapters are told by eight nonfamily members. These punctuate the story told by the Bundrens and comment upon it, giving the outsiders' perspectives on what might seem like a foolish odyssey—foolish because it takes 10 days in the July

heat to accomplish. Some critics have called the journey heroic, because it is the fulfillment of a pledge made by Addie's husband, Anse BUNDREN, to the woman he loves (p. 114).

As the novel opens, Addie awaits death from some unspecified cause. Although she cannot be much more than 50, if anything she seems to welcome her approaching death as the fulfillment of her father's prophecy: "the reason for living was to get ready to be dead a long time" (169). At last, she feels, she will have a rest. Her husband certainly has afforded her no rest in the years of their marriage. Incompetent, lazy, hunchbacked, but shrewd in getting others to do for him, Anse seemingly never has given a thought to Addie's feelings. Now, as she is dying, he seems still to be more concerned with the inconvenience of her coming death rather than grieved by it.

Her children—Cash, Darl, Jewel, Dewey Dell (her only daughter), and Vardaman—each react differently to the impending death. Cash, the oldest son and a carpenter by trade, is fashioning Addie's coffin in the yard outside the room where Addie lies dying. He holds up each board for Addie to see before he nails it into the box. This is his character trait: to do what needs to be done in a workmanlike, unemotional manner. Darl, the next son, is driven by a painful, apparently unreturned, love for his mother, and a deep jealousy of Jewel, Addie's favorite. Darl is the smartest of the Bundrens, and apparently the most imaginative, but he is driven by his hatred of Jewel. Darl manipulates Jewel into going with him to deliver a load of lumber for a fee of three dollars so that Jewel will not be with Addie when she dies. Darl imagines the scene he has left behind, and he taunts his younger, more favored brother, telling him that their mother is dead.

Jewel is selfish, independent, cruel, and direct. His response to his mother's final illness is to deny its finality. He says that if it were not for all the rest of the Bundrens waiting for her to die, Addie wouldn't die at all. He would protect her from death. He goes off with Darl almost in defiance of death.

The delivery of lumber that begins the novel while Addie lies in her bed prefigures the delivery of the dead Addie Bundren. Darl implies that he had promised to make the lumber delivery; Anse had promised to bury Addie with her people in JEFFERSON, MISSISSIPPI, when her time came. Darl appeals to his father's greed by repeating again and again that the family can "use that three dollars." This appeal is like Anse's thought that going into Jefferson will enable him to get some "store-bought teeth" to replace his lost teeth.

Rain begins to fall almost as soon as Darl and Jewel begin their delivery of the lumber, and this slows them considerably. Worse yet, the wagon slips off the road into a ditch and one of the wheels is smashed. Knowing that by now their mother probably has died, Darl and Jewel must repair the wagon and return as quickly as possible so that the family can begin the "hard day's drive" into Jefferson to bury Addie. They have no choice in the matter, for Anse Bundren counts his promise as a solemn pledge, the last act he can do for his wife.

Anse made that promise to Addie right after Darl was born. But that promise, to her, was a meaningless act. She hated "her people," especially her father "for having ever planted me" (p. 170), and demands that Anse make the promise as a revenge upon him for having planted Darl within her. Addie Bundren is incapable of love, it would seem. She contemptuously refers to "love" as a "word like all the others: just a shape to fill a lack" (p. 172). She takes another revenge on Anse, too, refusing to be intimate with him after Darl's birth. Yet a third revenge is that she begins a brief but passionate affair with the preacher WHITFIELD. Here, too, she thinks of her actions as just words, but she is thrilled that the word average people would use to describe this would be "sin." She gets a sexual thrill, it would seem, more from the idea of having intercourse with a man "dressed in sin" than from the act itself. It is akin to her feelings about the students she once taught. She felt a kinship with them only while she was thrashing them for some slight infraction.

Her affair with Whitfield produced Jewel, and led her to have two more children with Anse—Dewey Dell and Vardaman—to make up for her transgressions.

The claim Addie has placed upon Anse by her foolish, spiteful promise leads to the 10-day indignity of her funeral odyssey. Because Anse has forsworn burying her at New Hope, three miles from their farm, his family must take her decomposing body all the way to Jefferson, 15 miles away, for interment. The rains that delayed Darl and Jewel have now swept away the only two bridges that lead easily to Jefferson. When the Bundrens attempt to ford the Yoknapatawpha River, the wagon overturns again. The mules are drowned and Cash's leg, already broken once by a fall from a church steeple, is fractured again. The coffin and Cash's tools are saved, but the loss of the mules delays the Bundrens again. Anse trades Jewel's beloved horse for another span of mules and the horrific journey continues. The coffin is now followed by buzzards, drawn by the awful stench of Addie's body.

There are other motives for making this journey, too. Anse has already coveted new teeth, available only in Jefferson. Cash has the idea of buying a gramophone. Vardaman, only a child and a simple-minded one, has his heart set on a toy train he saw once in Jefferson. Dewey Dell, too, has a secret object. She is pregnant, and LAFE, her boyfriend, has told her that a druggist can give her something to abort the fetus. When she makes her first attempt to buy an abortifa-

cient, however, she is rebuffed by a pharmacist who tells her to marry Lafe and raise the baby.

By the time of this incident, the Bundrens have been traveling for five days with Addie's body. The odor from the body has caused the townspeople to cover their faces with handkerchiefs and demand that the Bundrens move on. Anse Bundren resists their entreaties, and buys a small amount of cement to set Cash's leg. They finally continue their journey and stop that night at the farm of a man called GILLESPIE (1). They store the coffin in Gillespie's barn. That night, the barn catches fire. Gillespie and his son, along with Jewel and Darl, rush into the flames to save the livestock. Jewel returns and single-handedly brings his mother's coffin out of the inferno, getting badly burned in the process. The fire, however, is not an act of God as was the flood: Darl has set it in an attempt to end the farce of his father's burial march.

In *As I Lay Dying*, horror is piled on top of horror, indignity on top of indignity, absurdity on top of absurdity; in this respect, the novel may be more mock-heroic than heroic. The "love" and "devotion" Anse seems to be showing may, from his point of view, be genuine, yet Addie had despised him for years, calling him empty and dead. The promise she asked of him had no meaning for her, except as a cruel and capricious trick. Even Anse's performance in carrying out the promise seems flawed. Although the Bundrens have traveled for 10 days to bury Addie, for example, they have not brought a shovel to accomplish this most basic act. Each member of the Bundren family appears intent on almost anything other than burying Addie; even Darl and Jewel mostly seem to be working out their hatred for each other in ways somewhat parallel to their mother's destructive request.

At the close of the novel, Dewey Dell (who has learned from Vardaman that Darl set the fire) and Jewel gang up on Darl and turn him over to the Jefferson police. At Gillespie's insistence, and with Anse's compliance, Darl is arrested and sent to a mental institution for his act of arson. He has, in fact, become mentally deranged. Dewey Dell again fails in trying to obtain a drug to abort her baby; she has been swindled and sexually molested by the soda jerk Skeet MACGOWAN, who pretended to be a druggist. Anse steals the money that Dewey Dell had saved for her abortion drug and with it buys "them teeth." After he returns the shovels he has borrowed, he apparently goes courting. In the last line of *As I Lay Dying*, he introduces his children to a duck-shaped woman whom he calls "Mrs. Bundren."

As I Lay Dying, Faulkner's fifth novel, dedicated to Hal SMITH, was first published on October 6, 1930, by Jonathan Cape and Harrison Smith (see CAPE & SMITH) of New York. It is the first of Faulkner's novels in which he identifies by name his fictional YOKNAPATAWPHA

COUNTY. For further information, see *Selected Letters of William Faulkner* and *Faulkner in the University.*

Adaptations of *As I Lay Dying* include a dramatized version of the novel by Jean-Louis Barrault in 1935; Valerie Bettis's ballet with music by Bernardo Segall and costumes by Kim Swados, first performed by Choreographers' Workshop at Hunter College in New York City on December 19, 1948; a CBS *Camera Three* television version on October 7, 1956; and Robert Flynn's play first performed in 1960 at Baylor University in Waco, Texas. Faulkner recorded a selection from the novel on Caedmon Records (TC-1035) in 1954.

Atkins, Miss   Character in *LIGHT IN AUGUST.* A dietician in the orphanage where Joe CHRISTMAS lives, she panics when she suspects that Joe has overheard her making love with an intern named CHARLEY. She fears Joe will betray her to the matron.

As it happens, Joe had been too sick from eating the dietician's pink toothpaste to notice anything. But Miss Atkins does not know this, and she decides to tell the matron that Joe is an African American, in the hope that the authorities will deliver him to the "nigger" orphanage. The matron arranges for Joe's adoption by Simon MCEACHERN and his wife.

Atkinson   Minor character in PYLON; Matt ORD's business associate. Atkinson and Ord manufacture airplanes.

Atlantic, Monthly, The   Long-running monthly magazine of literature, the arts, and politics, established in Boston in 1857. Initially reflective of New England regional culture, it later published a wide spectrum of authors and became national in content.

Faulkner in the 1920s attempted without success to sell short stories to the *Atlantic.* The poet and critic Conrad AIKEN introduced Faulkner to the magazine's readership in November 1939 with his essay "William Faulkner: The Novel as Form."

In September 1940, the *Atlantic* accepted the Faulkner short story "All Is Not Gold," paying $300 for it. In the magazine's August 1946 issue, an essay by the French philosopher and writer Jean-Paul Sartre, "American Novelists in French Eyes," assessed the impact of American fiction, particularly that of Faulkner and John Dos Passos, on French culture.

Faulkner sold an essay on Sherwood ANDERSON ("Sherwood Anderson: An Appreciation") to the *Atlantic* for $300; the piece appeared in June 1953. In August of that year, the magazine published Faulkner's speech to his daughter Jill's graduating class at Pine Manor Junior College in Massachusetts. The *Atlantic* paid $250 for the speech, titled "Faith or Fear."

Aunt Etta   *See* BURCHETT, MRS.

Avant, Jim   Character in *The REIVERS.* He is mentioned briefly as a hound specialist from Hickory Flat, Mississippi, who attends the Grand National trials in Parsham, Tennessee.

Ayers, Major   Character in *MOSQUITOES.* A florid Briton with ill-fitting false teeth, he is one of Dawson FAIRCHILD's drinking companions on Mrs. Patricia MAURIER's yacht *Nausikaa.* In the novel's epilogue, Major Ayers consults with the businessman Mr. REICHMAN about selling salts (a laxative) to Americans, for he thinks "all Americans are constipated" (p. 304).

B

Backhouse, Philip S. Character in "MY GRANDMOTHER MILLARD AND GENERAL BEDFORD FORREST AND THE BATTLE OF HARRYKIN CREEK" (in *Collected Stories*). A young Confederate officer, he is so infatuated with Bayard Sartoris's cousin MELISANDRE that he becomes a hazard in the field. She, however, is put off by his name. General FORREST and Rosa MILLARD concoct a fiction in which Lt. Backhouse is killed in battle and an equally dashing officer, Philip St-Just Backus, emerges in his place. The lieutenant, actually the same man with his last name sanitized, marries Melisandre soon after.

Backus, Melisandre (1) *See* MELISANDRE, Cousin.

Backus, Melisandre (2) *See* STEVENS, Melisandre Backus Harriss.

Backus, Mr. The father of Melisandre Backus in *The MANSION*. A widower, he spends his time drinking whiskey in the summer and reading Horace in the winter. Rumor has it that Backus died of a broken heart when Melisandre, his only child, married a wealthy New Orleans bootlegger by the name of Harriss.

Backus, Philip St-Just *See* BACKHOUSE, PHILIP S.

Baddrington, Harold (Plex, Plexiglass) In *The MANSION,* a World War II pilot whose plane is shot down over Germany. Charles MALLISON is one of the crew members. Although Plex manages a one-engine landing, the crew are rounded up by the Germans and taken to the prisoner-of-war camp at Limbourg. Because Baddrington is obsessed with cellophane (which he calls plexiglass), he is nicknamed Plex or Plexiglass.

Baird, Dr. Physician in *SOLDIERS' PAY*. Dr. Baird is a specialist from Atlanta called in to examine the severely wounded Donald MAHON after the latter comes home to Charlestown, Georgia, at the end of World War I. Dr. Baird tells Mrs. Margaret POWERS that there is little hope for Mahon's recovery and suggests that the ex-soldier is hanging on to life only because of some task he had set himself before he was wounded but since has forgotten. The impetus of that self-appointed goal keeps Mahon going.

Baird, Helen (unknown) Faulkner met this Tennessee-born artist and sculptor in NEW ORLEANS in 1925. She was 21 years old, barely five feet tall, and dark. Faulkner seems to have fallen in love with her right away. She barely responded, and sometimes appeared merely to tolerate his company.

Faulkner courted her during the summer of 1926 in PASCAGOULA, MISSISSIPPI, where the family of his friend Philip Avery STONE kept a summer place. Despite her mother's objections, Baird encouraged Faulkner's attentions, at least to the point of accepting poems and other gifts from him, including *Helen: A Courtship,* a series of poems. The volume was published after Faulkner's death.

Faulkner resumed the courtship in Pascagoula in the summer of 1927. While staying with the Stones, he worked on the manuscript of his novel *MOSQUITOES,* modeling the character of Patricia ROBYN on Helen Baird. She also shared some of the physical characteristics of Charlotte RITTENMEYER in "The Wild Palms" in IF I FORGET THEE, JERUSALEM.

Mosquitoes was published in April 1927 with a dedication "To Helen." In early May Helen Baird married Guy Lyman, a longtime suitor, in New Orleans. In later years, Faulkner and the Lymans met occasionally as old friends.

Ball, Albert (1896–1917) British World War I flying ace referred to in *A FABLE*. Ball, BARKER, BISHOP, MCCUDDEN, MANNOCK, and RHYS DAVIDS, were real persons mentioned in the novel, but neither he nor they appear as characters. The French aviators FONCK and GUYNEMER, and the German flyers BOELCKE, IMMELMANN (Faulkner spells it *Immelman*), RICHTHOFEN, and VOSS are also cited (see pp. 73–74). Ball was killed before the Royal Flying Corps (RFC) of the British Army was renamed the Royal Air Force (RAF) in 1918. See also FAULKNER AND FLYING.

Ballenbaugh (1) Character in *The REIVERS*. He becomes the proprietor of Wyott's Ferry on the TALLAHATCHIE RIVER before the Civil War just as mule- and ox-drawn wagons are replacing riverboats as freight and cotton carriers on the Vicksburg-to-Memphis run.

Ballenbaugh (2) Character in *The REIVERS*. He is the son of the proprietor of the old tavern and ferry at Wyott's Crossing, and succeeds his father in 1865. When Colonel

SARTORIS's railroad drives the mule-team freighters out of business, the younger Ballenbaugh sets up a still and converts the place into a resort for drunks, fiddler, gamblers, girls, and sinful characters of all sorts.

For a generation or so, successive sheriffs leave Ballenbaugh's tavern alone. Finally, in the summer of 1886, the crusading Baptist parson Hiram HIGHTOWER cleans up Ballenbaugh's by force.

When Lucius PRIEST, Boon HOGGANBECK, and Ned William MCCASLIN stop there on the way to MEMPHIS in 1905, Ballenbaugh's is a placid inn catering to hunters and fishermen.

Ballenbaugh, Boyd Character in KNIGHT'S GAMBIT ("Hand upon the Waters"). Knowing that his older brother Tyler BALLENBAUGH is the beneficiary of Lonnie GRINNUP's insurance policy, he kills Grinnup in order to collect the insurance. Boyd is killed at the hands of JOE (5), a deaf and mute orphan whom Grinnup had adopted.

Ballenbaugh, Miss Character in The REIVERS. A sober maiden of 50, she succeeds the uproarious younger BALLENBAUGH (2) as owner of the inn at Wyott's Crossing on the TALLAHATCHIE RIVER. Under her ownership it becomes a popular spot for hunters and fishermen.

Lucius PRIEST, Boon HOGGANBECK, and Ned William MCCASLIN spend a night at Miss Ballenbaugh's on their way to MEMPHIS in May 1905.

Ballenbaugh, Tyler Character in KNIGHT'S GAMBIT ("Hand upon the Waters"). The older brother of Boyd BALLENBAUGH and a farmer with a reputation for self-sufficiency and violence, he insures Lonnie GRINNUP's life on a $5,000 policy with a double indemnity for accidental death.

The Ballenbaughs are thus suspects in Grinnup's murder. When Tyler confronts Boyd about it, Boyd shoots him; a moment later, the deaf and mute orphan JOE (5) shoots and kills Boyd, avenging his foster father, Grinnup.

Ballenbaugh's Ferry Fictional place, the successor to Wyott's Crossing, on the TALLAHATCHIE RIVER in northern YOKNAPATAWPHA COUNTY on the wagon road to MEMPHIS. An "ancestryless giant" named Ballenbaugh took the ferry over from Wyott before the Civil War. His son succeeded him in the enterprise, converting it into a roaring dormitory, eating place, distillery, casino, and dance hall. A Baptist minister named Hiram HIGHTOWER shuts the resort down in 1886, and by 1905 the younger Ballenbaugh's only child, a prim, severe 50-year-old spinster, runs a small store and resort for hunters and fishermen there.

Ballott, Mr. Character in The REIVERS. He is the day foreman of Maury PRIEST's livery stable in JEFFERSON, MISSISSIPPI. When Mr. Ballott leaves for the day, Boon HOGGANBECK is in charge.

Barbour Character in "UNCLE WILLY" (in Collected Stories). He is Uncle Willy CHRISTIAN's Sunday school teacher.

Barger, Sonny Character in "UNCLE WILLY" (in Collected Stories). He is a storekeeper in JEFFERSON, MISSISSIPPI.

Barker, William (1894–1930) Historical aviator referred to in A FABLE. (See BALL, ALBERT.)

"Barn Burning" (Collected Stories) Short story in which Colonel Sartoris SNOPES (Sarty, named after the legendary Civil War hero Colonel John SARTORIS), the 10-year-old son of a sharecropper, finds himself pitted against his own emerging sense of honesty and his poor and embittered father, Ab SNOPES, who tends to settle disputes with his landlords by burning down their barns. The story opens with Ab being charged by Mr. HARRIS. The justice of the peace does not convict him, for lack of evidence, but tells Ab to leave the area and never come back. Ab and his family move on to a two-room tenantfarmhouse owned by Major DE SPAIN (1). But even before Ab starts farming the land, he causes a problem for himself by soiling de Spain's expensive new rug, then makes matters worse by further damaging the rug after de Spain orders him to clean it. When a judge rules against him, Ab Snopes takes revenge by burning down de Spain's barn that night. Though Sarty tries to warn de Spain, he is too late. As he flees from the de Spain mansion, Sarty realizes he cannot return home. After spending the night outdoors, he leaves for good and never looks back. (Some readers might speculate that the shots Sarty hears after de Spain rides past him are not only directed at the boy's father but may have actually killed him, as the boy may have unconsciously hoped for but kept suppressed. The interpretation that Snopes was shot, however, has no conclusive textual basis. Since Ab Snopes appears later in The HAMLET, evidence shows that he was not killed or even, as the 1985 film adaptation depicts, wounded by de Spain.)

The critic Cleanth BROOKS considers "Barn Burning" one of the finest examples of Faulkner's great theme of the human heart in conflict with itself (William Faulkner: First Encounters, p. 19). Old enough to understand and sympathize with his father's anger and lot in life, Sarty's conflict, as Brooks points out, is being "caught between loyalty to his father . . . and his own sense of honor and decency" (p. 17). Variations on the theme of loyalty and conflict are found in many of Faulkner's works.

The 1980 film version of "Barn Burning" (part of an educational series on American short stories produced by Learning in Focus, Inc.) used Rowan Oak, Faulkner's home, as the home of Major de Spain (played by Faulkner's nephew Jimmy Faulkner). Sarty (Shawn Wittington) and his father, Al Snopes (Tommy Lee Jones), walk up the path to the house. (Harriett and Gioia Fargnoli)

Considered by many as one of Faulkner's best short stories, "Barn Burning" was first published in *Harper's Magazine* 179 (June 1939), 86–96. Faulkner had originally planned to use it as the opening chapter of *The Hamlet*, where a slightly different version of the story appears— one that is less sympathetic toward the Snopeses by the elimination of Sarty's character. "Barn Burning" was reprinted in *A Rose for Emily and Other Stories*, in *Collected Stories of William Faulkner*, in *The Faulkner Reader*, and in *Selected Stories of William Faulkner*. On August 17, 1954, a television adaptation of the story by Gore Vidal, starring E. G. Marshall, James Reese, Beatrice Straight, Charles Taylor, and Peter Cookson, aired on the CBS dramatic series *Suspense*. In 1985, a film version of the story, starring Tommy Lee Jones, Diane Kagan, Shawn Wittington, and Faulkner's nephew, Jimmy FAULKNER, was produced by Learning in Focus, Inc., an educational series on American short stories hosted by Henry Fonda.

For more information, see *Selected Letters of William Faulkner*, pp. 108, 116, 197, 202, 274, 275, 278, and Diane Brown Jones, *A Reader's Guide to the Short Stories of William Faulkner*, pp. 3–32.

Barnett, Ned (1865?–1947) By Falkner family tradition and Barnett's own probably fanciful account, Ned Barnett had been born into slavery and served Faulkner's great-grandfather, William Clark FALKNER. Barnett later came to OXFORD, MISSISSIPPI, to work for the "Young Colonel," J. W. T. FALKNER, as butler, factotum and chief of staff—or so the story ran. More probably, Barnett was born in August 1865, after Emancipation and Confederate defeat, and he passed most of his life as a Tippah County tenant farmer.

As an elderly man, Barnett was a tenant on Faulkner's GREENFIELD FARM. He also served as butler in the Faulkner household at ROWAN OAK. The Faulkners referred to him as Uncle Ned. He regarded himself as an adviser to Faulkner as well as a retainer. "He's a cantankerous old man, who approves of nothing I do," the novelist once said of him.

Ned Barnett died in 1947 in Ripley, Mississippi, his native place. Something of him seems to have gone into the character of SIMON (1), old Bayard SARTORIS's coachman in *SARTORIS*.

Barr, Caroline (184?–1940) Faulkner's "second mother," born into slavery in Mississippi. Small, thin, and neat, four times married, she came to OXFORD, MISSISSIPPI, to help Maud FALKNER with her three young sons in 1902. The boys knew her as Mammy Callie; and she lived to help raise Faulkner's daughter, Jill FAULKNER.

Faulkner's brother Johncy (*see* FALKNER, John Wesley Thompson III) left this description of Callie Barr: "I remember her small and black (she weighed only ninety-eight pounds), standing unobtrusively to the side, always with a head rag and some sort of bonnet on, a snuff stick in her mouth, and always in a fresh-starched dress and apron and soft-toed black shoes" (*My Brother Bill*, p. 48).

Elements of Caroline Barr appear in several memorable Faulkner character: as Mammie Cal'line Nelson in *SOLDIERS' PAY*; as Dilsey GIBSON, the Compsons' cook, in *The SOUND AND THE FURY*; and as Molly Beauchamp in *GO DOWN, MOSES*.

Barr died at ROWAN OAK in January 1940 at close to 100 years of age. Faulkner delivered Caroline Barr's eulogy, remembering her as "a fount not only of authority and information, but of affection, respect and security." He wrote this epitaph for her gravestone:

Callie Barr Clark, 1840–1940, MAMMY
Her white children bless her

Faulkner dedicated *Go Down, Moses* to Caroline Barr in 1942:

To MAMMY
Mississippi
[1840–1940]

Who was born in slavery and who
gave to my family a fidelity without
stint or calculation of recompense
and to my childhood an immeasurable
devotion and love

Barron, Homer Character in "A ROSE FOR EMILY." A Yankee road construction foreman, he has an affair with Miss Emily GRIERSON, then tries to break it off. Miss Emily poisons him and keeps his corpse in her bridal chamber.

Barron, Jake Character in *The MANSION*. A convict with Mink SNOPES at Parchman, the state penitentiary in Mississippi, he is killed by a guard when he tries to escape in 1943. A fellow prisoner who does escape, Shuford H. STILLWELL, holds Mink responsible for Barron's death because Mink did not go along with the plan.

Bascomb, Maury L. (Uncle Maury) Mrs. Caroline COMPSON's brother in *The SOUND AND THE FURY,* uncle to Quentin, Candace (Caddy), Jason and Benjamin (Benjy) COMPSON. A freeloader off the Compson family who freely drinks his brother-in-law's whiskey, he is described by Faulkner in the appendix to the novel as "a handsome flashing swaggering workless bachelor who borrowed money from almost anyone, even Dilsey [the Compsons' black housekeeper]." He is romantically involved with Mrs. PATTERSON, to whom he sends love letters until he is beaten up by her husband when he finds out. (For further details, see the entry for Benjamin in Faulkner's appendix to the novel in Appendix IV.)

Basket, Herman Character in "A JUSTICE" (in *Collected Stories*). A Chickasaw Indian, he is a friend of CRAWFISHFORD, the father of Sam FATHERS. He relates the story of Doom's return from NEW ORLEANS and his campaign to seize the chiefship.

Basket, John Character in "A BEAR HUNT" (in *Collected Stories*). He is the leader of the Indians who cures Luke (Lucius Priest [also Lucius PROVINE]) HOGGANBECK of the hiccups by scaring him.

Battenburg Fictional place on the road between JEFFERSON, MISSISSIPPI, and MEMPHIS. In *KNIGHT'S GAMBIT,* a Memphis gangster runs down a child in Battenburg on his way back to Memphis from a "job" in Jefferson.

Beale, Colonel In *A FABLE,* the British army officer who identifies the French army corporal STEFAN as a British soldier called Boggan, whom Beale had seen killed at the Battle of Mons in 1914, four years before the setting of the novel. Beale is one of three men who confuse Stefan with other soldiers who had been already killed and buried during World War I. In this, Faulkner seems not to suggest that Stefan is immortal; instead, he seems to imply that Stefan is an Everyman, a soldier who is like all other soldiers in the ranks, even to the extent of exactly resembling three others.

Bean, Captain Character in "UNCLE WILLY" (in *Collected Stories*). A flying instructor at the JEFFERSON, MISSISSIPPI, airport, he refuses to give Willy CHRISTIAN flying lessons without permission from his doctor.

"The Bear" *See* GO DOWN, MOSES.

Beard Minor character in *The SOUND AND THE FURY.* He rents his lot to the visiting circus to pitch its tents.

Beard, Mrs. Character in *SARTORIS.* She is the wife of the JEFFERSON, MISSISSIPPI, grist mill owner Will C. BEARD and the mother of the simple-minded Virgil BEARD, who takes down Byron SNOPES's obscene letters to Narcissa SARTORIS.

In *LIGHT IN AUGUST,* Mrs. Beard operates the boardinghouse where Byron BUNCH has a room. Lena GROVE boards with her when she first arrives in Jefferson.

Beard, Virgil Character in *SARTORIS.* He is the son of Will C. BEARD, who owns the grist mill in JEFFERSON, MISSISSIPPI. A somewhat simple boy, with straw-colored hair, bland eyes, and a secretive mouth, Virgil takes down Byron SNOPES's love letters to Narcissa SARTORIS. As payment, Byron promises him an air gun.

Beard, Will C. Character in *SARTORIS,* father of Virgil BEARD, accomplice of Byron Snopes in sending obscene letters to Narcissa SARTORIS. He owns W. C. Beard's Mill in a black section of Jefferson.

His wife owns the boardinghouse where Byron BUNCH and Lena GROVE stay in *LIGHT IN AUGUST.*

"A Bear Hunt" *(Collected Stories)* Short story, a comic tale of revenge in the oral storytelling tradition. The nameless narrator introduces the events, which occurred at Major DE SPAIN's hunting camp during the annual bear hunt. Nearby is the sinister and ancient Indian mound where de Spain camped as a boy. The narration then is taken over by V. K. RATLIFF, the itinerant sewing machine salesman (a central figure in the SNOPES TRILOGY) who participates in the tricking of the shiftless Lucius "Buck" PROVINE.

Ratliff stops in at the hunting camp to find that Provine, suffering from a horrendous case of hiccups, is keeping his companions awake and scaring away the game. The hiccups have resulted from Provine's gluttony, and all the usual remedies have failed. Ratliff suggests that Provine seek a cure from the Indian healer John BASKET, who lives near the mound. De Spain's black servant, Old Man Ash, overhears this advice and precedes Provine to the site. He warns Basket that a revenue man is on the way and needs a good scare. When Provine arrives, the Indians tie him to a pyre as if to burn him alive, and then let him escape. The terrified Provine indeed does lose his hiccups, but thrashes Ratliff for his role in the prank. Ratliff elicits the rest of the tale from Old Man Ash: Decades earlier, Provine had burned off his exceptionally fine celluloid collar. Ash at last has exacted his revenge and regained his dignity.

"A Bear Hunt" appeared in three versions; the version in *Collected Stories* was the second. In the earliest, published in the *SATURDAY EVENING POST* (February 10,

1934), Ratliff was named V. K. SURATT and Old Man Ash was Old Man Bush. In the last version, for *BIG WOODS* (1955), Provine became Lucius HOGGANBECK, a part Indian, and the first narrator was identified as Quentin COMPSON.

Beat Four   Fictional district in YOKNAPATAWPHA COUNTY northeast of JEFFERSON, MISSISSIPPI. (Mississippi counties are divided into "beats" for administrative purposes; the actual LAFAYETTE COUNTY has five.) Beat Four is "a region of lonely pine hills dotted meagerly with small tilted farms and peripatetic sawmills and contraband whiskey kettles" peopled by White hill clans such as the Gowries of *INTRUDER IN THE DUST*.

In *Intruder*, Lucas BEAUCHAMP, an African American, is alleged to have killed Vinson GOWRIE at FRASER'S STORE in Beat Four.

Beauchamp, Amodeus McCaslin   Character in *GO DOWN, MOSES* ("The Bear"). The son of the slaves Tomey's Turl and Tennie BEAUCHAMP, he dies the day of his birth.

Beauchamp, Bobo   Character in *The REIVERS*. He is Lucas BEAUCHAMP's cousin, reared by Aunt Tennie. Bobo finds work as Mr. VAN TOSCH's groom and manages to fall $128 in debt, payable on Monday, to a MEMPHIS White man.

Bobo confides his troubles to Ned William MCCASLIN in a Memphis barroom and so unwittingly sets in motion the elaborate scheme in which Ned "borrows" Mr. Van Tosch's horse Coppermine (later Lightning) and leaves the Priest automobile with Bobo's creditor.

Beauchamp, Henry   Character in *GO DOWN, MOSES* ("The Fire and the Hearth"). The son of Lucas and Molly BEAUCHAMP, he and Isaac MCCASLIN, the scion of an old planter family, are childhood friends.

Henry first confronts the South's rigid racial code at about age seven, when Ike (Isaac) suddenly refuses to share a pallet on the floor with him, and later eats alone at the Beauchamp table, served by Henry's mother.

Beauchamp, Hubert   Character in *GO DOWN, MOSES* ("Was"). The bachelor owner of an estate just over the edge of the next county from the McCaslins, his leading ambition is to marry off his sister Sophonsiba. When Theophilus MCCASLIN—Uncle Buck—blunders into her bed by mistake, Mr. Hubert sees his chance.

A poker game seals the engagement. Uncle Buck's low hand means he will marry Sophonsiba and buy the slave Tennie BEAUCHAMP, whose lover, the McCaslin slave Tomey's Turl, chronically steals away to the Beauchamp place to see her.

Buck's twin Amodeus—Uncle Buddy—arrives and persuades Hubert to play another hand of stud poker. More skilled at cards than his brother, he wins Uncle

Buck's release for the engagement and gets Tennie for free into the bargain.

Beauchamp appears in two other stories in *GO DOWN, MOSES,* "The Bear" and "Delta Autumn." In "The Bear," he deposits 50 gold pieces into a silver cup as a gift for his nephew Isaac MCCASLIN on his 21st birthday. When Ike reaches his majority and opens the gift, he finds IOUs for the gold pieces and a coffeepot in place of the cup.

In "Delta Autumn," the part African-American woman with whom the McCaslin descendant Carothers EDMONDS is involved mentions Hubert Beauchamp as the man who lost Tennie in a card game.

Beauchamp, James Thucydus (Tennie's Jim)   Character in *GO DOWN, MOSES*. He is the son of the slaves Tomey's Turl and Tennie BEAUCHAMP. In "The Fire and the Hearth," he leaves home before he comes of age, heads north, and doesn't stop until he has crossed the Ohio River.

In "The Old People," Tennie's Jim is a servant in the hunting camp of Major DE SPAIN. He reprises that role in "The Bear," with the special duty of looking after the camp dogs. He vanishes on his 21st birthday, leaving his $1,000 legacy unclaimed. In "Delta Autumn," he is the grandfather of Roth EDMONDS's mistress.

Tennie's Jim also appears in *The REIVERS*.

Beauchamp, Lucas Quintus Carothers McCaslin   Character in *GO DOWN, MOSES, INTRUDER IN THE DUST,* and *The REIVERS*. An important figure in the YOKNAPATAWPHA COUNTY cycle, he is the grandson of old Lucius Quintus Carothers MCCASLIN, a planter and slaveholder, and a slave woman and is fiercely proud of his mixed racial heritage. In his view, his descent from old Cass sets him above his Edmonds landlords, to whom Isaac MCCASLIN has passed the estate, for they are "woman-made," connected to the founder only on the female side.

Born in 1874, he is the youngest of the children of Tomey's Turl and Tennie BEAUCHAMP, who is old Cass's daughter by a slave. Lucas is presented as the oldest living McCaslin descendant on the hereditary land.

In "The Fire and the Hearth," Lucas confronts Zack EDMONDS over his wife Molly's long stay as a nurse in the Edmonds home, and he bests the white man in a violent confrontation at dawn. Later in the story, he defies Roth EDMONDS, Zack's son and heir, by distilling illegal whiskey on the plantation. His overarching pride nearly leads to tragedy; his greed—he is obsessed with the notion of buried treasure—nearly costs him his marriage. In the end, Molly and Edmonds persuade him to give up his hopeless search for wealth.

In "The Bear," Lucas, the only one of the Beauchamp children to remain on the McCaslin plantation, appears in Isaac McCaslin's doorway on his 21st birthday and demands his $1,000 legacy from old Cass.

He may have stayed behind on the old place, but he is nonetheless independent for that.

Lucas Beauchamp dominates *Intruder in the Dust*, leaving the other characters, particularly the windy, speechifying Gavin STEVENS, in the shade. He is an old man in the novel, still farming on the Edmonds estate, proud as ever of his descent from Carothers McCaslin, sturdy, dignified and unintimidated by—even contemptuous of—Yoknapatawpha's rigid racial conventions.

When he is wrongly charged with murder, he learns "what every white man in that whole section of the country" had been thinking about him for a long time:

"We got to make him be a nigger first. He's got to admit he's a nigger. Then maybe we will accept him as he seems to intend to be accepted" (*Intruder,* p. 18).

The victim is a white man, Vinson GOWRIE, a member of a large hill country clan. Beauchamp discovers that Crawford GOWRIE has been stealing timber from brother Vinson and his partner, Sudley WORKITT. To protect himself, Crawford kills Vinson and makes it seem as if Lucas is the murderer. The authorities jump to that conclusion, and Beauchamp is arrested and jailed.

Innumerable Gowries mobilize and threaten to lynch Beauchamp. From the Jefferson jail, he gains the help of young Chick (Charles, Jr.) MALLISON, Chick's friend Aleck SANDER, and the elderly spinster Eunice HABERSHAM (a childhood friend of his wife, Molly) in opening Vinson's grave as a means of proving his innocence: he claims his gun was not the one that killed the victim.

The Jefferson sheriff keeps the lynch mob at bay, Vinson's body is exhumed, the real murderer is revealed at last, and Lucas goes free.

Beauchamp is present offstage in *The Reivers*. The narrator's grandmother recalled descriptions of old Carothers McCaslin from her mother; Lucas, she said, "looked (and behaved: just as arrogant, just as iron-headed, just as intolerant) exactly like him except for color" (*Reivers,* p. 229).

Lucas Beauchamp is Faulkner's personification of the South's tortured racial history, with its patterns of intimacy, for better and mostly for worse, of blacks and whites. He is a rarity in mainstream American fiction of the time, a fully developed African-American male character who is proud, haughty, and courageous.

Beauchamp, Molly (Aunt Molly; Mollie) Character in *GO DOWN, MOSES* ("The Fire and the Hearth," "Delta Autumn," "Go Down, Moses"). The wife of Lucas BEAUCHAMP, she is a longtime loyal servant of the Edmonds family.

In "The Fire and the Hearth," a young Molly nurses her son Henry BEAUCHAMP and the motherless Carothers EDMONDS (Roth) as though they were brothers, and stays on at Zack EDMONDS's place long after the death of Edmonds's wife—too long, in her husband's

view. Lucas finally confronts Edmonds, and Molly returns to their cabin on the Edmonds plantation.

Later in the same story, the elderly Molly moves, with Roth Edmonds's help, to obtain a "voce" (divorce) from her husband, who has become obsessed with a search for buried treasure. Lucas agrees to abandon his quest, and the suit is withdrawn.

In "Go Down, Moses," the novel's title story, Mollie (Faulkner has varied the spelling of her name) has a premonition that disaster has visited her petty criminal grandson, Samuel Worsham BEAUCHAMP (Butch), and she wants him back in JEFFERSON, MISSISSIPPI. Gavin STEVENS, the county attorney, learns that Butch has been convicted and executed for killing a Chicago policeman. With the help of Stevens and Miss Belle WORSHAM, Mollie recovers his body and insists on a proper burial at home, with flowers, a hearse, and a notice in the Jefferson newspaper.

Molly also appears in retrospective scenes in *INTRUDER IN THE DUST.*

Beauchamp, Philip Manigault Character in *A FABLE*. An African-American private from Mississippi who has ambitions to become an undertaker, he is the third of three soldiers who volunteer for an unknown mission in exchange for which they will be issued a three-day pass to Paris. A proud man, he reacts quickly to BUCHWALD's use of the derisive "Sambo" for him, telling Buchwald that his name is pronounced "Mannygo" but spelled Manigault. The mission they are sent on is the execution of Major General GRAGNON. Manigault is described as strong and graceful. It is he who holds Gragnon while Buchwald pulls the trigger.

Beauchamp, Samuel Worsham (Butch) Character in *GO DOWN, MOSES* ("Go Down, Moses"). The grandson of Mollie (Molly) BEAUCHAMP, he is a small-time criminal who is finally tried, convicted, and executed for killing a policeman in Chicago.

With the assistance of the YOKNAPATAWPHA COUNTY attorney, Gavin STEVENS, his grandmother brings his body home to JEFFERSON, MISSISSIPPI, for burial.

Beauchamp, Sophonsiba (1) (Sibbey) Character in *GO DOWN, MOSES* ("Was"). A spinster, pretentious and silly, she fancies herself the mistress of "Warwick," her name for her bachelor brother Hubert BEAUCHAMP's plantation. Mr. Hubert's great ambition is to see Miss Sophonsiba married; her choice settles on Theophilus MCCASLIN, familiarly known as Uncle Buck.

Sibbey wears jangling earrings and beads and heavy perfume, and roaches her hair under a lace cap. Her most vivid characteristic, though, is a roan tooth that flicks and glints fascinatingly between her lips.

Through a misadventure at a hand of cards, Uncle Buck becomes engaged to Miss Sophonsiba. His twin brother, Amodeus MCCASLIN—Uncle Buddy—wins back Buck's freedom in a hand of stud poker with Hubert, but he eventually marries her anyway.

Beauchamp, Sophonsiba (2) (Fonsiba)   Character in *GO DOWN, MOSES.* She is the daughter of the slaves Tomey's Turl and Tennie BEAUCHAMP. In "The Fire and the Hearth," she goes away to live in Arkansas.

In "The Bear," Isaac MCCASLIN tracks Fonsiba down in Arkansas to give her a $1,000 legacy. He finds her married to a black small farmer and living in near destitution. Ike arranges for the money to be delivered to her in monthly installments of three dollars so that she will always have a subsistence.

Beauchamp, Tennie   Character in *GO DOWN, MOSES.* The slave of Hubert BEAUCHAMP in "Was," she moves to the McCaslin place, home of her lover, Tomey's Turl, when Amodeus MCCASLIN acquires her in a card game in 1859.

In "The Fire and the Hearth" Tennie has married Tomey's Turl; their children are James, Sophonsiba, and Lucas BEAUCHAMP. Tennie also appears in "The Bear" and "Delta Autumn."

Beauchamp, Terrel   *See* BEAUCHAMP, TOMEY'S TURL.

Beauchamp, Tomey's Turl   **(1)** Character in *GO DOWN, MOSES.* In "Was," he is a slave of the brothers Amodeus and Theophilus MCCASLIN and the lover (later husband) of Tennie (BEAUCHAMP).

Beauchamp, Tomey's Turl   **(2)** A minor character in *The TOWN* (and in the short story "CENTAUR IN BRASS," where he is referred to as Turl). He is one of two African-American firemen at the power plant in JEFFERSON, MISSISSIPPI, in 1910. Tomey's Turl works at night under Mr. Harker. His counterpart, Tom Tom BIRD, works during the day. When Flem SNOPES becomes superintendent of the plant, he exploits both men in his attempt to steal the solid brass safety valves. When Flem orders Tomey's Turl to retrieve the brass that Tom Tom is hiding on his property, the 30-year-old Tomey's Turl begins an affair with Tom Tom's much younger wife and is caught. After a struggle between Tomey's Turl and Tom Tom, both men realize what Flem is up to and decide to throw the brass in the water tank.

Beck, Warren (unknown)   Writer, critic, and teacher. Beck was one of the first academic admirers of Faulkner's work. In the spring of 1941 he published three essays that acknowledged Faulkner's ethical perspective as well as his daring narrative technique and prose style.

In a 1941 correspondence, Faulkner wrote candidly to Beck about his stylistic excesses and shortcomings, confessing that he was "an old 8th grade man"—that is, largely self-taught.

Beck's *Man in Motion,* a book-length appraisal of Faulkner's fiction, appeared in 1962.

Bedenberry, Brother   Character in *LIGHT IN AUGUST.* After Joanna BURDEN's murder, Joe CHRISTMAS tries to "snatch him outen the pulpit" as he preaches (*Light,* p. 323). When Brother Bedenberry's grandson tries to avenge him, Joe fractures his skull with a bench leg.

Benbow, Belle Mitchell   Character in *SARTORIS* and *SANCTUARY.* In *Sartoris,* Belle is the wife of Harry MITCHELL and the illicit lover of Horace BENBOW. She later divorces Mitchell and marries Benbow. In *Sanctuary,* there are obvious differences between her and Benbow, especially in relation to the rearing of her daughter, Little Belle MITCHELL. Benbow attempts to leave Belle at the beginning of the novel, and she herself departs for Kentucky, where her mother lives. By the novel's end, she returns when Benbow's sister, Narcissa Benbow SARTORIS, informs her that Benbow is coming home after his miserable failure in defending the innocent Lee GOODWIN.

Benbow, Cassius Q. (Uncle Cash)   Character in *The UNVANQUISHED.* A former slave, he flees to the Yankees during the Civil War. When he seeks election to the post of marshal of JEFFERSON, MISSISSIPPI, after the war, Colonel John SARTORIS and his White associates violently oppose him.

Benbow, Francis   Character in *SARTORIS.* He is the grandfather of Horace BENBOW and Narcissa Benbow SARTORIS. He brought home a Barbados lantana in a top-hat box in 1871 and planted it in a fence corner of the Benbow lawn.

Benbow, Horace   Character in *SARTORIS* and *SANCTUARY,* brother of Narcissa Benbow SARTORIS. Like his father, he attended Sewanee (the University of the South) where he distinguished himself as a student and later became a Rhodes Scholar at Oxford University in England. When he came back to JEFFERSON, MISSISSIPPI, he entered the family law practice more from a sense of duty than predilection. During World War I, he served a tour in France with the YMCA. A sensitive and artistic person "with an air of fine and delicate futility" (*Sartoris,* p. 163), Benbow is a contrast to his sister's furious and despairing husband, young Bayard SARTORIS. In *Sartoris,* where he first appears and where he is occasionally called Horry, Horace carries on an affair with Belle Mitchell (BENBOW) in the face of Narcissa's disapproval. He marries her after her divorce and takes an active but ineffective role in the upbringing of her daughter, Little Belle MITCHELL.

Horace is one of Faulkner's intellectual and idealistic characters who are often in conflict with the moral world around them. Well educated, philosophical, talkative, and committed to justice as a guiding principle in human affairs, Horace, like his fictional counterpart Gavin STEVENS at the end of *The MANSION,* confronts in himself the bitterness of reality and moral compromise. Horace is a defeated man at the end of *Sanctuary,* where he painfully discovers the pervasiveness of evil and his impotence against it. When the novel opens, he has left his wife and stepdaughter and is on his way from Kinston to Jefferson. After he stops at a spring for a drink of water near OLD FRENCHMAN PLACE, he encounters the bootleggers POPEYE and Lee GOODWIN. Horace later defends Goodwin against false charges of murder and rape, but loses the case when his principal witness, the rape victim herself, Temple DRAKE, lies under oath. When Goodwin is pulled from his jail cell the evening of his conviction and burned to death by a mob, Horace also is attacked, but escapes. Two days later, Horace leaves Jefferson and returns to his wife, resigned and defeated.

Benbow, Judge Character in *ABSALOM, ABSALOM!, The UNVANQUISHED,* and *The HAMLET.* As the executor of Goodhue COLDFIELD's estate in *Absalom,* Benbow sells the remains of the family store for Coldfield's daughter, Miss Rosa COLDFIELD. She refuses to accept money for the sale, so the judge leaves baskets of provisions on her front porch at night and pays down the debts she contracts in local stores. Judge Benbow also pays for the $200 headstone Miss Rosa ordered for the grave of her niece, Judith SUTPEN.

In *The Unvanquished* ("An Odor of Verbena"), Judge Benbow handles the transaction when Colonel John SARTORIS buys Ben REDMOND's share of the railroad the two jointly own. In the narrative description of Will VARNER in *The Hamlet,* a Judge Benbow is mentioned as having said of Varner that a milder-mannered man never bled a mule or stuffed a ballot box.

Benbow, Julia Character in *SARTORIS.* The wife of Will BENBOW and mother of Narcissa Benbow SARTORIS and Horace BENBOW, she died when Narcissa was a little girl.

Benbow, "Little" Belle Mitchell Character in *SARTORIS* and *SANCTUARY,* she is the daughter of Harry and Belle MITCHELL. Her mother neglects her and finds her a nuisance as she (the mother) carries on her love affair with Horace BENBOW.

Benbow, Narcissa *See* SARTORIS, NARCISSA BENBOW.

Benbow, Percy Character in *ABSALOM, ABSALOM!* The son of Judge BENBOW, he discovers after his father's death that the judge had kept an accounting of his bets on Memphis horse races and credited the winnings to Miss Rosa COLDFIELD's mythical account.

Benbow, Will Character in *SARTORIS.* The father of Narcissa Benbow SARTORIS and Horace BENBOW. He dies not long after Horace returns home from Oxford, England, where he had studied law, and is buried near his wife.

Benjy *See* COMPSON, BENJAMIN.

Berry, Ben Character in *KNIGHT'S GAMBIT* ("An Error in Chemistry"). He is the deputy sheriff of doubtful competence who searches the house of murder suspect Joel FLINT.

Berry, Louis Character in "RED LEAVES" (in *Collected Stories*). A CHICKASAW INDIAN, he helps track down one of the dead chief ISSETIBBEHA's runaway slaves, who by tribal tradition must be caught and put to death before the chief can be buried.

Best, Henry Minor character in *The TOWN.* Best is an alderman in JEFFERSON, MISSISSIPPI, and is present at the bonding meeting investigating the missing brass fittings at the power plant.

"Beyond" *(Collected Stories)* Short story. "Beyond" begins with the death of Judge Howard ALLISON, as witnessed by his servants CHLORY and JAKE (2) and attended by Dr. Lucius PEABODY. In a dreamlike journey, the judge sets out on a quest for truth. Among a crowd of strangers he sees his old friend MOTHERSHED, with whom he often discussed philosophy and religion: Mothershed was an atheist and the judge an agnostic. Since Mothershed was a suicide, the judge now recognizes that he himself is dead.

As he continues his inquiry with the enigmatic Ingersoll (Robert Green Ingersoll, a noted late 19th-century orator and proponent of agnosticism), the judge reveals his past life. The judge then meets a mother and child (Christ as a boy) and is offered the chance to see his own son, who died at age 10 in a horse riding accident. The judge does not pursue this; he realizes he is content with his emotional life and beliefs as they are. Leaving the gathering, he passes his JEFFERSON, MISSISSIPPI, courthouse, visits his son's grave next to the one newly excavated for himself, and hurries home to rejoin his laid-out corpse.

Faulkner explained in a letter that the judge turns down the chance to see his dead son because he "prefers the sorrow with which he has lived so long . . . [which] is perhaps even a pleasure, to the uncertainty of change. . . ." (*Selected Letters,* pp. 71–72).

This story originally was titled "Beyond the Gate." It first appeared in HARPER'S (September 1933) and then in DOCTOR MARTINO AND OTHER STORIES (1934).

Bezzerides, Albert Isaac (1908–) Scriptwriter. Born in Turkey of Greek-Armenian parents, Bezzerides studied engineering at the University of California at Berkeley before finding his way into motion pictures. WARNER

BROTHERS filmed his novel of truck drivers, *The Long Haul*, as *They Drive By Night*, starring Humphrey BOGART.

Warm and emotional, Buzz Bezzerides proved a good friend to Faulkner in Hollywood during the 1940s. He and his wife put Faulkner up for a long stretch at their house near Santa Monica. Bezzerides often drove him to work at the studio and kept a protective eye on him while there. He also curtailed more than one of Faulkner's self-destructive drinking binges.

Bidet, General Group commander of the portion of the French Army that contains the regiment that mutinies in *A FABLE*. Bidet is described as being overly preoccupied with the excretory functions of the soldiers in his command, but he is nonetheless a good soldier. He ranks just below the OLD GENERAL. Bidet denies Major General GRAGNON's demand to have all the 3,000 men of the regiment executed for mutiny.

Bidwell Character in "HAIR" (in *Collected Stories*). He is a storekeeper in Division, the town on the Mississippi-Alabama line where the Starnes family lives.

Big Bottom Fictional place. Modeled on the jungly bottoms of the actual TALLAHATCHIE RIVER, it is a wilderness of gum, cypress, and oak trees. The Big Bottom is the site of the decrepit hunting and fishing cabin Wash JONES and his granddaughter inhabit in *ABSALOM, ABSALOM!* Major Cassius DE SPAIN eventually acquires the camp and the scenes of "The Bear" (in *GO DOWN, MOSES*) are enacted there.

SARDIS LAKE, a reservoir filled in the 1930s, now covers the Big Bottom country.

"The Big Shot" *(Uncollected Stories)* Short story. It is written as a retelling by an unnamed narrator who reports the words of his friend Don REEVES about Dal MARTIN, a Memphis political boss and contractor. Martin is an uneducated yet shrewd and successful multimillionaire. The story also concerns POPEYE, the bootlegger and murderer in the novel *SANCTUARY*. "The Big Shot" centers on Popeye's arrest for running a stop sign and nearly killing a pedestrian while transporting a carload of bootleg whiskey to Martin's house. Reeves tells Martin's history, delving back into his childhood as a sharecropper's illiterate son who pulled himself into financial and political prominence through sheer will and desire. But Martin's money and connections cannot push his daughter, Wrennie (Miss Laverne) MARTIN, onto a higher social plane, which is his deepest desire. Martin attempts to bribe Dr. BLOUNT, one of the city's distinguished citizens, into including his daughter in the next Chickasaw Guards debutante ball. At first Dr. Blount turns Martin out for offering him a cash bribe. But he relents when Martin returns several weeks later with the offer to build an art gallery in honor of Dr. Blount's grandfather. Blount

comes to regret his action, however, and tries to renege; when Martin does not allow him out of the bargain, Blount commits suicide. Martin's social triumph is tragically obliterated at the end of the story when his daughter is run over and killed by Popeye, now freed from jail and rushing Martin's liquor to his house.

In this story (and its revision, "DULL TALE"), Faulkner touches upon themes that resonate in his later fiction, such as the unscrupulous quest for power, rapacity, and the need for social respectability or approbation. The character traits of Popeye and Wrennie Martin, respectively, anticipate Popeye and Temple Drake (see Temple Drake STEVENS) in *Sanctuary*; Dal Martin foreshadows Thomas SUTPEN in *ABSALOM, ABSALOM!* and Flem SNOPES in the SNOPES TRILOGY. Written around 1929, "The Big Shot" was first published posthumously in *Uncollected Stories of William Faulkner*. For more information, see *Uncollected Stories of William Faulkner*, p. 707.

Big Woods Random House bought out this collection of four of Faulkner's previously published hunting pieces in 1955. Faulkner wrote four brief prose narratives linking the stories, together with a coda. Edward Shenton, who had done the drawings for *The UNVANQUISHED*, supplied the illustrations.

The four stories are "The Bear," "The Old People" (see *GO DOWN, MOSES*), "A BEAR HUNT," and "RACE AT MORNING." Faulkner omitted Part Four of "The Bear," which reveals the guilty heritage of the twins Theophilus (Buck) and Amodeus (Buddy) MCCASLIN. As the biographer Frederick Karl notes, the excision converts the story into "an adventure piece—a commercialization of the inner tale." There were only minor changes to the other pieces. Lucius PROVINE becomes Lucius HOGGANBECK, Boon HOGGANBECK's 40-year-old son, in "A Bear Hunt." Faulkner added a dozen or so lines to "Race at Morning."

The introductory narratives for *Big Woods* are drawn from previous work, including *REQUIEM FOR A NUN*, the essay "MISSISSIPPI," and several short stories. They are elegiac, the 58-year-old Faulkner's mournful tribute and farewell to the vanished wilderness. The epilogue ends on a bitter note: "No wonder the ruined woods I used to know don't cry out for retribution. The very people who destroyed them will accomplish their revenge" (*Big Woods*, p. 224).

The publication date was October 14, 1955. The reviews were mostly favorable, although as the critic Malcolm COWLEY observed, "the virtues of *Big Woods* have been achieved too much at the cost of other books from which the material was taken by right of eminent domain."

Biglin, Luther Jailor in JEFFERSON, MISSISSIPPI, in *The MANSION*. During the day, Luther takes care of the jail and its prisoners; at night he sits outside Flem SNOPES's window to protect his life from any threat that the newly released convict Mink SNOPES might pose. Ironically, Luther is not at his post when Mink enters the house to kill Flem.

Biglin, Mrs. Luther (Miz Biglin) Character in *The MANSION*. After coming home from the movies (anytime between 7 and 10 P.M.), she wakes her husband, Luther, who protects Flem SNOPES by sitting outside his window.

Bilbo, Theodore Gilmore (1877–1947) Mississippi-born politician, governor of Mississippi (1916–20 and 1928–32) and United States senator (1935–47). A champion of the state's rural White population, he came to power on the tide of Mississippi's "redneck revolt" of populist hill country small farmers.

Bilbo captured the nomination for the governorship in 1915 and won office with Lee RUSSELL, J. W. T. FALKNER's law protegé, as his running mate. Bilbo's successful effort to control UNIVERSITY OF MISSISSIPPI patronage cost Murry FALKNER his job as business manager there in 1930.

Bilbo was corrupt and opportunistic, a virulent racist and White supremacist, a supporter of the liberal New Deal who violently opposed legislation aiding blacks. A hero to the state's poor whites, he was an anathema to his enemies.

The fictional Flem SNOPES is the Faulknerian apotheosis of the Bilbo man. Faulkner modeled the corrupt governor in the short story "Monk" (see *KNIGHT'S GAMBIT*) after Bilbo; one of the redneck Gowrie brothers in *INTRUDER IN THE DUST* is named for him.

Binford, Dewitt Minor character in *The TOWN*. Married to a Snopes, he and his wife take in Byron SNOPES's four wild and unruly children until Binford fears for his life. The children are sent back to Byron.

Binford, Mr. (Lucius) **(1)** Character in *The REIVERS*. The "landlord" or front man for his lover Miss Reba RIVERS's MEMPHIS brothel, he handles the money, deals with the tradesmen and distillers, settles the tax bill, bribes the police, and enforces strict house rules.

Mr. Binford is honest and meticulous, but for one flaw, a weakness for betting on horses. He offers to take 15-year-old OTIS, the visiting nephew of one of the girls, to the zoo, but they end up at the track instead. When Otis discloses that Mr. Binford has lost $40 on a "horse and buggy," Miss Reba threatens to throw him out.

He is referred to in *SANCTUARY* and, as Lucius Binford, in *The MANSION*.

Binford, Mr. **(2)** One of Reba RIVERS's dogs, named after her late lover and landlord, Lucius BINFORD. The other, Miss REBA, she named after herself. In the chapter he narrates in *The MANSION*, Montgomery Ward SNOPES characterizes them as "two damn nasty little soiled white dogs" (p. 72).

Binford, Mrs. **(1)** The name Miss Reba RIVERS uses when she signs in at the hotel in Parsham; it is the last name of her business associate and lover.

Binford, Mrs. **(2)** Minor character in *The TOWN*. She is Deewit BINFORD's wife.

Bird, Tom Tom Character in *The TOWN* and in the short story "CENTAUR IN BRASS," which Faulkner revised for the novel. Tom Tom is the African-American fireman who reads the gauges at the power plant in JEFFERSON, MISSISSIPPI, on the day shift. He is married to a young woman, his fourth wife (third in "Centaur in Brass"), whom he keeps in seclusion. When he catches his night-shift counterpart, Tomey's Turl (BEAUCHAMP), sneaking into his house, he chases him with a butcher knife until they fall into a ditch. Once they realize their unwitting role in Flem SNOPES's scheme to steal the solid brass fittings at the power plant, Tom Tom and Tomey's Turl put the fittings into the town's water tank. (In the short story, Tom Tom appears as "Tom-Tom," with no last name.)

Bird, Uncle Character in *Sartoris*. He calls on Simon STROTHER, the church treasurer, for an accounting of the church funds. As it happens, Strother has been giving church money to an alluring young mulatto woman named Meloney HARRIS.

Birdsong Character in *GO DOWN, MOSES* ("Pantaloon in Black"). The night watchman at the sawmill in JEFFERSON, MISSISSIPPI, where RIDER works, he runs a rigged craps game and has been cheating the hands out of their wages for 15 years.

The grieving Rider, who has been steadily drinking whiskey, confronts Birdsong about his crooked dice. When Birdsong reaches for his pistol, Rider cuts his throat.

Birdsong, Preacher Minor character in *The TOWN*. He learned to box in France during World War I, and is good enough to fight Linda SNOPES's beau, Matt LEVITT, who won the Golden Gloves in Ohio.

Bishop, Ephriam (Eef) Character in *The MANSION*. He is Jefferson's sheriff when Flem SNOPES is killed. Eef alternates his term as sheriff with old Hub HAMPTON and then later with Hub's son, Hub Jr.

Bishop, William ("Billy") (1894–1956) Historical aviator, referred to in *A Fable*. He was Canada's top ace fighter pilot in World War I. See also BALL, ALBERT.

Black Character in "DEATH DRAG" (in *Collected Stories*). He is the driver of the car that brings the aviators into JEFFERSON, MISSISSIPPI, from the rudimentary airfield on the edge of town.

"Black Music" *(Collected Stories)* A comic short story that concerns a mythical metamorphosis in a 20th-century Virginian arcadia. The tale is revealed through a dialogue between the protagonist and the nameless, at times sarcastic, narrator, who has traveled to the Latin American port town of Rincon. There he hears of a mysterious old American expatriate, Wilfred MIDDLE-STON, who is poor and, above all, happy. Other disreputable American exiles, including one who apparently had to flee his homeland because of thievery, attribute a similar past to Midgleston. The narrator treats the old man to a hearty breakfast and learns the truth.

Midgleston is content with his simple life, sleeping under a roll of tar paper in a rat-infested attic over a cantina. He tells of the event that altered his life. Once a Brooklyn draftsman, he was sent to Virginia to deliver architectural blueprints to wealthy Park Avenue matron, Mrs. Carleton (Mathilda) VAN DYMING, who was building a vacation compound with classical-style structures and an outdoor Greek theater in a vineyard run wild. On the journey, he saw a faun's head with goat's horns and beard suspended outside the window of the train. He collapsed, and was revived by alcohol. When he arrived at the station, he bought a tin flute, continued to imbibe on the wagon ride to the construction site, and was transformed into a faun. In a modern reenactment of a Dionysian orgy, he played the flute while chasing Mrs. Van Dyming through the old vineyard, together with the prize bull he had released.

The Van Dymings consequently abandoned their plans for the property and Midgleston disappeared. To prove that the event, which he believes was ordained by the pagan gods, actually happened, Midgleston produces several yellowed newspaper clippings, including one headlined "Maniac at Large in Virginia Mountains." Since he later was presumed dead, his generous life insurance policy went to his wife, who then moved to Park Avenue and married a more socially acceptable fellow. For Midgleston, his temporary transformation radically changed his life to one he has found more spiritually amenable.

This tale first appeared in *DOCTOR MARTINO AND OTHER STORIES* (1934).

Blake, Jim Character in *KNIGHT'S GAMBIT* ("Hand upon the Waters"). He helps carry Lonnie GRINNUP's body away from the coroner's office for burial.

Blair, Harrison Character in "FOX HUNT" (in *Collected Stories*). A wealthy Englishman and the owner of a large country place, he is married to a woman he doesn't love and can't respect, in part because she is an inept horsewoman. Blair is barely civil to his wife, driving her to seek out other men for affection.

Blair, John Character in "ARTIST AT HOME" (in *Collected Stories*). A down-at-heels poet, he comes to the Howes as a houseguest and falls in love with Anne HOWES. With this affliction, his scruples bar him from entering the house again and he spends a night out in the rain before taking his leave. Roger HOWES later sells a poem of Blair's. By then, though, the lovelorn poet is dead.

Blair, Mrs. Character in "FOX HUNT" (in *Collected Stories*). She is the neglected wife of a wealthy Englishman, Harrison BLAIR. A fine horseman himself, he derides her for her inability to ride gracefully. Mrs. Blair allows Steve GAWTREY, whom she detests, to make love to her after she learns that the man in whom she is interested, ALLEN, has married a showgirl.

Bland Character in "AD ASTRA" (in *Collected Stories*). A handsome American Southerner in the British Royal Flying Corps, he is attractive to women; men dislike him. Although Bland has been flying on the Western Front for five months, no one has yet found a bullet hole in his airplane, suggesting that he is not the most aggressive of combat pilots.

Bland, Gerald Character in *THE SOUND AND THE FURY*. A Kentuckian, he is one of Quentin COMPSON's classmates at Harvard. At the picnic his wealthy mother has for him when she is visiting, Bland beats up Quentin when the latter starts a fight. (The picnic is on the afternoon of Quentin's suicide; his mental state impaired, Quentin momentarily confuses Bland with his sister Caddy's seducer, Dalton AMES, the person against whom he failed to defend Caddy's honor.)

Bland, Mrs. Character in *The SOUND AND THE FURY*. The wealthy mother of Gerald BLAND, she is proud of her son's looks and boastful of the women in his life. Mrs. Bland is present when ANSE places Quentin COMPSON in custody.

Bledsoe Character in *IF I FORGET THEE, JERUSALEM* ("The Old Man"). He looks after the mules at PARCH-MAN prison in Mississippi.

Bledsoe, Sergeant Character in *A FABLE*. A British soldier, he attempts to prevent the RUNNER from reaching the front lines and seeking to further the cause of Corporal STEFAN. The runner uses the flat of a pistol to dispose of Bledsoe without having to kill him. The runner also uses the pistol on HORN and Lieutenant. SMITH.

Faulkner's biographer, Joseph Blotner (left), pictured with Faulkner (center) and Frederick Gwynn. Blotner and Gwynn edited Faulkner in the University. (William Faulkner Collection, Special Collections Department, Manuscripts Division, University of Virginia Library. Photo by Ralph Thompson.)

Bleyth, Captain   Character in Faulkner's first novel, *SOLDIERS' PAY*. He is a Royal Air Force pilot traveling with the cadet Julian LOWE when the novel opens.

Blotner, Joseph (1923–)   Scholar and Faulkner biographer, born in Plainfield, New Jersey. An Army Air Force veteran of World War II, he was educated at Drew University, Northwestern University, and the University of Pennsylvania. He and Faulkner met in 1957 at the University of Virginia, where Blotner was an assistant professor of English and the novelist was writer-in-residence.

With a colleague, Frederick Gwynn, Blotner acted as Faulkner's gatekeeper. A close friendship developed between Blotner and Faulkner, and they were much together during Faulkner's later years.

The family chose Blotner as Faulkner's authorized biographer shortly after the novelist's death in 1962. His two-volume *Faulkner: A Biography* appeared in 1974. Blotner published a revised one-volume edition of the biography in 1984.

"Faulkner could hardly have left his reputation as a writer and as a man in better hands," the historian and later Faulkner biographer Joel Williamson wrote.

With Gwynn, Blotner edited *Faulkner in the University* (1959), a record of the novelist's views on literature as expressed to University of Virginia students. He also published *Selected Letters of William Faulkner* in 1977. Blotner moved from Virginia to the University of North Carolina at Chapel Hill (1968–71) and the University of Michigan (1971–93).

Blount, Dr. Gavin Character in the short stories "THE BIG SHOT" and "DULL TALE." Dr. Blount whose grandfather had been killed in the Civil War riding with Nathan Bedford FORREST, the Confederate calvary general, is a member of MEMPHIS's old aristocracy. It is Dr. Blount's role to invite young women to make their debuts into Memphis society at the annual Chickasaw Guards Ball. He is bribed by Dal MARTIN, the nouveau riche contractor and political boss, to add Wrennie (Miss Laverne) MARTIN—Martin's daughter—to the exclusive list in exchange for the building of an art gallery dedicated to Dr. Blount's grandfather. When Dr. Blount rethinks his position, he asks to be let out of the bargain, but Martin refuses. Dr. Blount, all honor gone, commits suicide.

The short story "Dull Tale" is a reworking of the material of "The Big Shot," with many of the same plot machinations. Dr. Blount's character in these two short stories is essentially the same and prefigures other Faulkner characters such as Gail Hightower in *LIGHT IN AUGUST* and Horace BENBOW in *SARTORIS* and *SANCTUARY*.

In "A RETURN" (in *Uncollected Stories*), Dr. Blount is the grandnephew of a senior officer killed in the Civil War. Dr. Blount romanticizes the war and idealizes the war widow Lewis RANDOLPH, but she rejects Blount's rosy view of the past by throwing soup in his face.

Blum, Major Character in *A FABLE*. Blum identifies Corporal STEFAN as the man who took the winnings from a group of gambling American soldiers and gave it to a pair of newlyweds. This is the third time that Blum has seen the corporal perform a generous deed: Stefan also found the money to save the sight of a young girl, and raised money to send an old and grief-stricken man home to his relatives.

Boelcke, Oswald (1891–1916) Historical German aviator referred to in *A FABLE*. See BALL, ALBERT.

Bogard, Captain H. S. Character in "TURNABOUT" (in *Collected Stories*). An American aviator in France during World War I, he takes a young British naval officer, L. C. W. HOPE, aloft and impresses him with his coolness and courage. In turn, Bogard then accompanies Hope on a torpedo boat mission and is likewise impressed.

Bogart, Humphrey (1899–1957) American actor, best known for his role as a cynical, heroic loner in *Casablanca* (1942) and other films. Faulkner met Bogart in Hollywood in the 1940s when Faulkner wrote film scripts for the WARNER BROTHERS story department.

Faulkner and Bogart became friends on the set of *To Have and Have Not* in early 1944. Bogart played the lead role in the adaptation of the Ernest Hemingway novel opposite his future wife, Lauren Bacall. At one stage of the filming, Faulkner, whose scriptwriting instincts were poor, prepared a six-page-long speech for Bogart, at which the actor balked.

Boggan Character referred to in *A FABLE*. Colonel BEALE of the British Army saw a soldier named Boggan brutally killed during the 1914 Battle of Mons, yet he identifies Corporal STEFAN as being the same man. Stefan is one of three avatars of the "ubiquitous corporal" (p. 236) who has supposedly died. Another is BRZEWSKI, who was buried at sea in 1917. These references underscore the theme of humanity's resurrection from its own brutality and centers on the main character of *A Fable* through which Faulkner enunciates his vision of the futility of conflict and war and announces his belief in the spirit's constant urging for peace and brotherhood.

Bolivar, Uncle Dick An old diviner in *The HAMLET* who helps V. K. RATLIFF, Odum BOOKRIGHT, and Henry ARMSTID search for the treasure rumored to be buried at OLD FRENCHMAN PLACE. Using a forked peach branch as a divining rod, Uncle Dick Finds only the three sacks of coins Flem SNOPES used to salt the worthless property. For his service, Ratliff pays him a dollar. Uncle Dick is said to eat frogs, snakes, and bugs. He also appears in the short story "LIZARDS IN JAMSHYD'S COURTYARD," which Faulkner incorporated into this section of *The Hamlet*.

Bon, Charles Character in *ABSALOM, ABSALOM!* Ignorant of his father's identity, Bon leaves New Orleans at age 28 at the encouragement of his revenge-seeking mother, Eulalia SUTPEN, to attend the UNIVERSITY OF MISSISSIPPI in OXFORD, MISSISSIPPI. There he falls in with Thomas SUTPEN's son Henry SUTPEN. As Eulalia Bon had hoped and planned, Charles goes to SUTPEN'S HUNDRED with Henry, meets Henry's sister (and his own half sister) Judith SUTPEN, and causes her to fall in love with him.

When Bon discovers that Thomas Sutpen is his father, he offers to give up Judith in return for Sutpen's acknowledgment that Bon is his son. Sutpen refuses. Bon insists he'll marry Judith; in response, Sutpen tells Henry that Bon is his half brother, hoping that Henry will somehow settle the matter. Instead, Henry repudiates his father and his birthright, but agonizingly decides to accept the relationship between Bon and Judith.

At the outbreak of the Civil War, Henry and Bon enlist together in the Confederate UNIVERSITY GREYS. Four years of war do not soften Bon's resolve, and Judith waits for him patiently. As the conflict nears its end, Sutpen, now a colonel in a Mississippi infantry regiment, raises the stakes again. He sends an orderly with a summons for Henry in his camp in a North Carolina pine grove. He tells Henry that Bon must not marry Judith because Bon's mother is "part negro," not of Spanish descent as he had once thought.

Henry cannot countenance miscegenation. After the Confederate surrender, the Sutpens return to Mississippi. Bon refuses to give up Judith, and Henry kills him at the gates of Sutpen's Hundred on May 3, 1865.

Bon, Charles Etienne St. Valery   Character in ABSALOM, ABSALOM! The son of Charles BON and his octoroon mistress, he comes to SUTPEN'S HUNDRED as an orphan at age 12. Although Judith SUTPEN and the servant Clytemnestra (see SUTPEN, CLYTEMNESTRA) try to shield him from knowledge of his Black blood, he figures it out on his own. Embittered, he marries a mentally retarded Black woman, "coal black and ape-like," and lives hermit-like with her and their son, Jim BOND, in one of the slave cabins at Sutpen's Hundred. He dies of yellow fever in 1884.

Bond, Jim   Character in ABSALOM, ABSALOM! The son of Charles Etienne St. Valery BON and his feeble-minded wife, he lives in solitude in a cabin behind the haunted mansion at SUTPEN'S HUNDRED. Bond is, like his mother, mentally deficient. He disappears when the old house burns down in 1910.

Boni & Liveright   Publishing firm, based in New York City, an early publisher of Faulkner's works. Founders Albert Boni and Horace LIVERIGHT established the Modern Library with $25,000 in 1917. During the 1920s, Boni & Liveright published such authors as Sigmund Freud, Ezra Pound, Eugene O'Neill, T. S. Eliot, Ernest HEMINGWAY, and Theodore Dreiser.

On Sherwood ANDERSON's recommendation, the firm brought out Faulkner's first novel, SOLDIERS' PAY, on February 25, 1926, and followed up with his second novel, MOSQUITOES, in 1927. Saying it lacked plot and character development, Boni & Liveright rejected Faulkner's third offering, FLAGS IN THE DUST, and urged him to withdraw it altogether. Harcourt, Brace published this novel in 1929 as SARTORIS.

With the rejection of *Flags in the Dust*, Faulkner broke off relations with the firm.

Bookwright   A family name common in the FRENCHMAN'S BEND region. The name appears in "BY THE PEOPLE," a short story Faulkner revised for *The* MANSION, a later work in which several Bookwrights with first names appear. In "Tomorrow," the fourth section of the novel KNIGHT'S GAMBIT, a well-off farmer, husband, and parent by the name of Bookwright (with no first name) turns himself in at four in the morning to Will VARNER and admits to having killed the brawling, swaggering Buck THORPE for eloping with his 17-year-old daughter. The jury is deadlocked and the case put down for retrial. In INTRUDER IN THE DUST, the Bookwright name is included with the early settlers of the area Frenchman's Bend. In *The* TOWN, a passing reference is made to a road near Bookwright's property.

Bookwright, Calvin (Cal)   A bootleg whiskey–maker in *The* MANSION and *The* REIVERS. In *The Mansion*, Bookwright is an old man who sells only to a select few people, of whom V. K. RATLIFF is one. In *The Reivers*, Boon HOGGANBECK gives the stable hand LUDUS two dollars for a gallon of Uncle Cal's fine liquor; Ludus returns with an inferior whiskey instead. (In editions previous to the 1961 Vintage paperback edition of *The* TOWN, Bookwright is the father of Letty Bookwright, [see HOUSTON, LUCY PATE] whom Jack HOUSTON marries.)

Bookwright, Herman   One of Eula Varner's suitors referred to by V. K. RATLIFF in *The* MANSION. Bookwright and Theron QUICK leave town one night once it is known that Eula is pregnant.

Bookwright, Homer   Minor character in *The* MANSION. He believes that Mrs. TUBBS, like everybody else, wants to know about Montgomery Ward SNOPES's pornographic pictures. He also appears in the short stories "SHINGLES FOR THE LORD," where he arrives early to help shingle the church, and "SHALL NOT PERISH," where he owns a cattle truck and gives the father of the deceased Pete GRIER a lift to town for supplies.

Bookwright, Letty   *See* HOUSTON, LUCY PATE.

Bookwright, Mrs. Odum   *See* BOOKWRIGHT, ODUM.

Bookwright, Odum   In *The* HAMLET, a bachelor farmer in the area of FRENCHMAN'S BEND. With V. K. RATLIFF and Henry ARMSTID, he is tricked by Flem SNOPES into buying OLD FRENCHMAN'S PLACE, a worthless piece of property believed to contain buried treasure. This episode is also referred to in *The* MANSION. (Although presented as a bachelor, at one point Bookwright refers to his wife in a remark he makes to Ratliff; see *The Hamlet*, p. 76.)

Bory   *See* SARTORIS, BENBOW.

Bouc, Pierre (Piotr)   Character in *A* FABLE. Pierre Bouc is the false identity assumed by one of the twelve followers of Corporal STEFAN. He pointedly denies knowing the corporal three times and begs to be removed from the cell where the group is held. The corporal produces a regimental order that identifies Piotr as "Pierre Bouc," and asserts that the man was included by mistake. After Stefan is questioned by the OLD GENERAL, however, Piotr demands to be reincluded with the 12 and admits his true identity. He is one of the four ZSETTLANI in the group.

Bowden, Matt   Character in *The* UNVANQUISHED. A member of Major GRUMBY's bushwacker group, he turns against Grumby after the killing of Rosa MILLARD and helps Bayard SARTORIS and Ringo Strother exact their revenge.

Bowman, Mr. The appositive title character in the short story "A DANGEROUS MAN." Willing to defend the honor of southern womanhood and the rights of southern husbands at the smallest provocation, Mr. Bowman is volatile, vain, impetuous, brave, and thoughtless. He works as the agent in an express office, a sinecure he received as the result of having disarmed and killed a robber when he was stationed in an office in a small town. Blinded by his own dangerousness and pride, Mr. Bowman is unaware that his wife, who actually runs the office where they work, is carrying on an affair while he is attending to the business of delivering packages. Faulkner depicts Mr. Bowman as partially deaf, perhaps symbolic of his never hearing about the affair.

Bowman, Mrs. The stout, bad-tempered wife of Mr. BOWMAN in the short story "A DANGEROUS MAN." Mrs. Bowman takes care of the inner workings of the express office she and her husband manage, while he delivers packages throughout the town and surrounding region. Mr. and Mrs. Bowman argue and bicker frequently. She uses his absences as the opportunity to carry on an affair with WALL, a traveling insurance salesman.

Boyd Character in "THE BROOCH" (in *Collected Stories*). A "traveling man," he marries the daughter of a rich merchant and abandons her six months after their child, a boy named Howard (see BOYD, HOWARD), is born.

Boyd, Amy Character in "THE BROOCH" (in *Collected Stories*). The wife of Howard BOYD, she is the object of her mother-in-law's disapproval. Amy's loss of a brooch, the gift of the elder Mrs. BOYD, leads to her dismissal from the house. The marriage collapses when Howard refuses to leave with her.

Boyd, Howard Character in "THE BROOCH" (in *Collected Stories*). He is completely in thrall to his elderly, embittered invalid mother, who rules every aspect of his life. Howard's inability to escape her influence leads to the breakup of his marriage and to his suicide.

Boyd, Mrs. Character in "THE BROOCH" (in *Collected Stories*). An embittered, aging invalid, she rules her son, Howard BOYD, with an iron hand. Mrs. Boyd's attempt to dominate Howard's wife, Amy BOYD, eventually destroys their marriage.

Bradley Character in *IF I FORGET THEE, JERUSALEM* ("The Wild Palms"). A cottager at the Wisconsin lake retreat of Harry WILBOURNE and Charlotte RITTENMEYER, he leaves provisions for the couple when he closes up his place for the winter. Bradley's familiar

manner suggests that he knows Harry and Charlotte are not married.

Bradley, Mrs. Character in *IF I FORGET THEE, JERUSALEM* ("The Wild Palms"). She is the wife of BRADLEY, the lake cottager who leaves supplies with Harry WILBOURNE and Charlotte RITTENMEYER when he closes up the place for the winter.

Brandt, Dr. Character in *SARTORIS*. He is the Memphis specialist to whom Dr. ALFORD refers old Bayard SARTORIS, whose wen Alford believes to be cancerous. Old Bayard has been using old Will FALLS's folk remedy for the wen and it comes off cleanly at Dr. Brandt's touch.

Breckbridge, Gavin Character in *The UNVANQUISHED*. The fiancé of Drusilla Hawk (SARTORIS), he is killed at the battle of Shiloh in 1862.

Bridesman, Major In *A FABLE*, a British fighter pilot commanding the group to which LEVINE belongs; he is one of three flyers who are issued blank machine-gun ammunition and who escort the German GENERAL to the conference with Allied generals. Bridesman knows that the incident was fixed to allow the German to arrive safely, but he is too cautious to investigate why.

Briggins, Lycurgus Character in *The REIVERS*. The grandson of Uncle Parsham HOOD, he collaborates with Ned MCCASLIN in preparing the horse Lightning (Coppermine) for the race against Colonel LINSCOMB's horse. Brisk and efficient, young Briggins tracks Otis with his uncle's hounds and forces him to return the gold tooth he stole from MINNIE.

Briggins, Mary Character in *The REIVERS*. She is Uncle Parsham HOOD's daughter and the mother of Lycurgus BRIGGINS.

Britt, Commander One of three flight commanders in the short story "WITH CAUTION AND DISPATCH." His flight squadron includes Second Lt. (John) SARTORIS (1), who manages to crash three separate times on the short flight from England to France, wrecking three Camel fighter planes in the process. Sartoris is apprehensive that his squadron mates will suspect him of cowardice, but Britt seems to relieve that fear when he greets Sartoris after his third crash at the French aerodrome. As Sartoris emerges from his fighter, which is on its back near the mess tent, Britt hands a pair of flying goggles and wryly tells him to get another Camel and see if he can crash it before teatime.

Brix Last name of the mountain guide in the short story "SNOW." He and Emil HILLER guide the amateur German mountain climber VON PLOECKNER. Soon after

Brix is killed in an accident, his wife leaves the village with von Ploeckner.

Brix, Mrs. The newly married bride of the mountain guide BRIX in the short story "SNOW." Mrs. Brix accompanies Brix, his partner Emil HILLER, and the amateur mountain climber VON PLOECKNER. On that climb, however, an accident occurs, causing Brix's death. Mrs. Brix leaves the village with von Ploeckner. Years later, she stabs von Ploeckner to death.

Brodsky, Louis Daniel (1941–) Poet, scholar, and curator of the Brodsky Collection at Southeast State Missouri University. The collection, which Brodsky acquired over a period of about three decades before transferring ownership to the university in 1988, is one of the major collections of Faulkner material. It includes books, letters, holograph and typescript manuscripts, galley proofs, art work, movie scripts, photographs, and biographical material. In addition to publishing his own poetry, Brodsky is the author of *William Faulkner: Life Glimpses* (Austin: University of Texas Press, 1990) and, with Robert W. HAMBLIN, has edited the five-volume work *Faulkner: A Comprehensive Guide to the Brodsky Collection* (Jackson: University Press of Mississippi, 1982–1988).

"The Brooch" *(Collected Stories)* Short story portraying Howard BOYD, a man who allows his mother to control his life and to wreck his marriage. He rouses himself from his apathy to decide that the only appropriate solution is his own suicide. His mother was deserted by her husband shortly after Howard's birth. Left in comfortable circumstances, Mrs. BOYD devoted herself to Howard, even following him to college. After returning to their Mississippi hamlet, Mrs. Boyd suffered a stroke and was confined to bed, but continued to exert her domineering power.

In a temporary revolt, Howard married the rather unsuitable Amy (see BOYD, AMY), but refused Amy's plea to move out of his mother's house. Mrs. Boyd presented Amy with the old family brooch, which Amy later lost. The couple lost a baby and afterward Howard, who preferred to stay home, helped Amy sneak out to dances on her own. On the night of the story, a telephone call reveals Amy's betrayal of Howard and Mrs. Boyd orders her to leave. Amy asks Howard to go with her, but he refuses. After she departs, Howard meditates on the novel *Green Mansions*, which he sees as a template for his own life. Taking elaborate care not to disturb his sleeping mother, he prepares to kill himself with a pistol.

This story first appeared in *SCRIBNER'S MAGAZINE* (January 1936).

Brooks, Cleanth (1906–1994) Literary critic. Born in Murray, Kentucky, Brooks was a professor at Yale University from 1945 to 1976 and a leading practitioner of the New Criticism of the 1940s and 1950s, which emphasized structural analysis of works of literature.

Brooks wrote important works on Milton, Thomas Percy, and Faulkner. Notable are *William Faulkner: First Encounters* (1983), *William Faulkner: Toward Yoknapatawpha and Beyond* (1978), and *William Faulkner: The Yoknapatawpha Country* (1963).

In *Faulkner: First Encounters,* he asserted that Faulkner's vision of reality is large enough to encompass both tragedy and comedy, and that a reader will often find both in the same novel. "What the reader will not find," Brooks wrote, "is mawkish sentimentality or mere farce, nor will he find special pleading for a thesis or a cause."

Broussard Character in *MOSQUITOES*. He owns the New Orleans restaurant that the novelist Dawson FAIRCHILD patronizes.

Brown, Joe *See* BURCH, LUCAS.

Brownlee, Percival (Spintrius) Character in *GO DOWN, MOSES* ("The Bear"). When Theophilus MCCASLIN acquires Brownlee from the slave trader Nathan Bedford FORREST, he finds that Brownlee cannot do plantation work and tries to set him free; for a long time, Brownlee refuses to leave. He later turns up as a prosperous brothel-keeper in NEW ORLEANS.

Brummage, Judge In *The MANSION*, the presiding judge at Mink SNOPES's murder trial. He gives Mink a life sentence.

Brzewski In *A FABLE*, one of the three avatars of Corporal STEFAN. Captain MIDDLETON identifies the living Stefan as Brzewski, an American soldier who died of flu on a transport ship and was buried at sea in late 1917. *See also* BOGGAN.

Brzonyi In *A FABLE*, the last name that Captain MIDDLETON uses to refer to Corporal STEFAN when Middleton tells of burying the American soldier BRZEWSKI at sea in 1917. Middleton's use of the surname Brzonyi could indicate Corporal Stefan's last name as it was known in the French Army.

Buchwald In *A FABLE*, one of the three American soldiers (along with Philip Manigault BEAUCHAMP and Sergeant WILSON) in World War I who execute Major General GRAGNON. Buchwald is described as a hard-faced man who is at least somewhat aware that the duty he and the others volunteered for (with the offer of a three-day pass in Paris as an inducement) will be a shameful act. Buchwald actually fires the German pistol that kills Gragnon. (He uses a German pistol to make it look like the enemy killed Gragnon.) After the war, Buchwald becomes a bootlegger and crime lord in America.

Buck (1) Character in *SARTORIS*. The sober, good-natured, horse-faced town marshal of JEFFERSON, MISSISSIPPI, he obeys a call from Virginia DU PRE (Aunt Jenny) and takes young Bayard SARTORIS into protective custody when Sartoris and two friends, MITCH and HUB, carry out a drunken serenade beneath Narcissa Benbow's window (see SARTORIS, NARCISSA BENBOW). Buck sends Mitch and Hub home and gives up his bed in the jail-keeper's quarters to Bayard, who had been shaken up in a fall from a wild stallion earlier in the day.

Buck (2) *See* HIPPS, BUCK.

Buckner (Buck) Character in *IF I FORGET THEE, JERUSALEM* ("The Wild Palms"). He manages the Utah mine where Harry WILBOURNE finds work as a doctor. Buckner leaves when he realizes the owners will no longer meet the payroll.

Before he leaves, Buckner persuades Wilbourne to perform an abortion on his wife. Charlotte RITTENMEYER helps BUCKNER talk Wilbourne into agreeing to the operation.

Buckner, Billie Character in *IF I FORGET THEE, JERUSALEM* ("The Wild Palms"). She is the wife of Buckner, the Utah mine manager. Harry WILBOURNE performs a successful abortion on her.

Buckworth Character in *IF I FORGET THEE, JERUSALEM* ("The Old Man"). The deputy warden at PARCHMAN prison, he reports the CONVICT dead, drowned in the flood. The convict's eventual voluntary return poses a paperwork problem that threatens to embarrass the warden; he resolves it by transferring Buckworth to the highway patrol.

Bud, Uncle In *SANCTUARY*, a young boy, about five years old, from a farm in Arkansas. He is with Miss MYRTLE when she and Miss LORRAINE visit Miss REBA (see RIVERS, REBA) shortly after RED's funeral. As the women drink, cry, and commiserate with one another, Uncle Bud sneaks himself some beer, gets sick, and vomits.

Buffaloe, Mr. Character in *The TOWN, The MANSION,* and *The REIVERS*. A mechanical genius, he keeps the JEFFERSON, MISSISSIPPI, steam-driven electric plant running and builds an automobile of his own that one afternoon on the Square, causes Colonel SARTORIS's matched carriage horses to bolt.

Buford In *LIGHT IN AUGUST*, a deputy sheriff assigned to the Joanna BURDEN murder case. Joe CHRISTMAS briefly escapes from Buford's custody before Percy GRIMM tracks down and kills him.

Bullitt, Mrs. In *PYLON*, the wife of the pilot Bob BULLITT.

Bullitt, Bob (R. Q.) Minor character in *PYLON*. Bullitt is one of the pilots competing in the air shows celebrating the opening of Feinman Airport in New Valois, Franciana.

Bull Run, first battle of The first major clash of the Civil War, known to Confederates as the first battle of Manassas. Union and Confederate forces massed near the sluggish stream of Bull Run in mid-July 1861. The battle opened early in the morning of July 21 with a Union attack on the Confederates near Sudley Spring.

After several hours of hard but inconclusive fighting, a Confederate attack forced a Union withdrawal toward Washington that rapidly turned into a rout. Federal casualties for the day were 2,645 killed, wounded, and missing. The Confederates lost 1,981 men and claimed a great victory.

Colonel William C. FALKNER, Faulkner's great-grandfather, commanded the 2nd Mississippi regiment of infantry with distinction at Bull Run. In the thick of the fight, the Old Colonel had two horses shot out from under him; around 100 of his men were killed or wounded. In his after-battle report, the Confederate cavalry commander J. E. B. STUART commended Falkner for his gallantry. Falkner's regiment soon voted him out of the colonelcy, however, and he returned embittered to Mississippi.

Bunch, Byron Character in *LIGHT IN AUGUST*. Hardworking, upright, and devout, he befriends the outcasts Lena GROVE, Joe CHRISTMAS, and Gail HIGHTOWER. Bunch works at the planing mill in JEFFERSON, MISSISSIPPI, and on Sundays he rides 30 miles out of town to lead the choir of a country church.

Bunch is the disgraced and solitary Hightower's only link with the world; they meet and talk only at night. He encounters Lena by the accident of his name, which is close to that of her seducer, Lucas BURCH. Falling in love with her almost at once, Bunch finds her a home, talks Hightower into delivering her baby, and finally tracks down Burch for her.

Lena seems unaware of Bunch's attentions, and he prepares to leave Jefferson. In a final encounter, Burch (Joe Brown) pummels him and then jumps a freight train to make a final escape from his responsibilities. Byron Bunch stays on after all, resuming his role as Lena's protector.

Bunden, Bud Younger brother of Juliet BUNDEN in the short story "ADOLESCENCE." Bud seeks out Juliet, who helps him after their father is killed by Revenue agents.

Bunden, Joe Father of Juliet BUNDEN, the heroine of the short story "ADOLESCENCE." Joe's first wife, Juliet's mother, dies, leaving Joe with four sons and a daughter. When Joe remarries, his daughter and new wife quickly come to despise each other, forcing him to send Juliet to live with her grandmother. Joe and his partner Lafe HOLLOWELL are shot dead at the moonshine still by Revenue agents apparently tipped off by Juliet herself.

Bunden, Juliet The heroine of the short story "ADOLESCENCE." Juliet is the oldest child and only daughter of Joe BUNDEN. After Juliet's mother dies, her father remarries a woman whom Juliet comes to hate, and Juliet is sent to live with her grandmother. Juliet spends her summers swimming and fraternizing with Lee HOLLOWELL, a neighbor, and is falsely accused by her grandmother of immoral sexual behavior with her confidant. Afraid that her father is about to force her to marry a man of his choosing, Juliet makes a mysterious trip into town. The following night, her father and Lafe HOLLOWELL, Lee's father, are both killed by Revenue agents, who raid their secret moonshine still. The text clearly hints at Juliet's involvement in alerting the agents.

Bundren, Addie The first wife of Anse BUNDREN and the mother of Cash, Darl, Jewel, Dewey Dell, and Vardaman BUNDREN in *AS I LAY DYING*. (Jewel is not Anse's son, but the product of an adulterous affair with the preacher WHITFIELD.) Addie's death precipitates the 10-day odyssey to bury her putrefying remains in JEFFERSON, MISSISSIPPI, with "her people." Anse treats her request to be buried in Jefferson as a solemn vow. In "Addie," the 40th chapter, which Addie posthumously narrates (it is set five days after her death), Addie remembers that her father used to say "the reason for living was to get ready to stay dead a long time" (p. 169). A former schoolteacher, she hated her students and always looked forward to the times when they did something wrong so she could whip them.

Mrs. Bundren is referred to as a potential customer by the unidentified first person narrator of the short story "SPOTTED HORSES"; this narrator is most certainly is V. K. SURATT, the sewing machine salesman who is planning to sell her a machine.

(For further information, see *Faulkner in the University*, pp. 109, 110–11, 112, 113, 114–15, 263.)

Bundren, Anse A farmer in *AS I LAY DYING*. When his wife Addie dies, Anse, to fulfill a promise made long ago to her, undertakes a 10-day journey to bury her in JEFFERSON, MISSISSIPPI. He is characterized as a lazy and selfish farmer. Part of his motivation for going to Jefferson is to obtain "store-bought teeth." He also takes a second wife the same day that he buries his first. He claims that if he sweats he will die, a belief that dates back to a case of apparent sunstroke when he was 22. He is the father of Cash, Darl, Dewey Dell, and Vardaman BUNDREN, but not of Jewel BUNDREN. Anse narrates chapters 9, 26 and 28. (For further information, see *Faulkner in the University*, pp. 109, 110, 111, 112, 114, and 265.)

Bundren, Cash Oldest son of Anse and Addie BUNDREN in *AS I LAY DYING*. Cash is a carpenter by trade who constructs his mother's coffin before she dies. He builds the coffin in the yard outside her window, showing his dying mother each piece of lumber before he sets it in place. He once suffered a broken leg from a fall from a church roof; the same leg is broken, on the journey to bury his mother when the Bundrens attempt to ford the flooded Yoknapatawpha River and overturn the wagon. Cash has a secondary motive in wanting to go to JEFFERSON, MISSISSIPPI, where his mother had insisted on being buried: he wants to obtain a gramophone (which he calls a "graphophone"). Cash narrates chapters 18, 22, 38, 53, and 59. (For further information, see *Faulkner in the University*, pp. 114–15 and 121.)

Bundren, Darl The second son of Anse and Addie BUNDREN in *AS I LAY DYING*. Darl is imaginative and jealous. He maneuvers his brother Jewel away from their mother's bedside when she is near death because he knows that Jewel is Addie's favorite. Darl is the Bundren most affected by the horror and growing absurdity of the 10-day journey to bury Addie in JEFFERSON, MISSISSIPPI, as she requested. On the fifth day of the journey (the eighth day after Addie's death), he sets fire to GILLESPIE's barn in order to cremate his mother's putrefying remains. His brother Vardaman witnesses Darl's act of arson and tells their sister, Dewey Dell. Later Dewey Dell, who fears that Darl will reveal that she is pregnant, and Jewel, who hates his brother, turn Darl in to the Jefferson police. Darl is insane at the end of *As I Lay Dying*.

In a course Faulkner gave on American literature at the University of Virginia, he was asked whether Darl was out of his mind all through *As I Lay Dying* or whether the insanity resulted from the events of the journey. Faulkner answered, "Darl was mad from the first. He got progressively madder because he didn't have the capacity—not so much of sanity but of inertness to resist all the catastrophes that happened to the family" (*Faulkner in the University*, p. 110). Darl narrates 19 chapters in the novel, more than any other character: 1, 3, 5, 10, 12, 17, 21, 23, 25, 27, 32, 34, 37, 42, 46, 48, 50, 52 and 57. (For further information, see *Faulkner in the University*, pp. 112–13, 115, 121, 263–64.)

Bundren, Dewey Dell The only daughter of Anse and Addie BUNDREN in *AS I LAY DYING*. Dewey Dell, a teenager, is pregnant and seeks "something" (she is not sure what, but her boyfriend, LAFE, has given her $10 and told her to ask for help at drugstores) to abort the pregnancy before anyone discovers her condition. She first requests this "something" from MOSELEY and is rebuffed sternly. In the final day of the novel, she asks for help from MacGowan (see MCGOWEN, SKEETS), a clerk in a pharmacy in JEFFERSON, MISSISSIPPI, thinking that he is a doctor. He gives her a dose of a phony medicine that "smelled like turpentine" (p. 247) and tells her to return at 10 o'clock that night for the rest of the medicine and the operation. While her brother Vardaman waits outside, MacGowan takes Dewey Dell to the basement and has sex with her, telling her the "hair of the dog" (p. 247) is part of the treatment. Because she knows that her brother Darl is aware of her pregnancy, Dewey Dell helps subdue him for the Jefferson police. Her father, Anse, takes the $10 Lafe gave her and buys himself new teeth with it. Dewey Dell narrates chapters 7, 14, 30, and 58 of the novel. (For further information, see *Faulkner in the University*, pp. 112–13.)

Bundren, Jewel   Son of Addie BUNDREN in *AS I LAY DYING*. Jewel is the result of Addie's adulterous affair with the preacher WHITFIELD, but this fact is unknown to Jewel or his putative father, Anse BUNDREN. Only his half brother Darl BUNDREN suspects Jewel's otherness, and he taunts him with it. Jewel has bought a half-tamed horse from Flem SNOPES by working nights. He is his mother's favorite, although she appears to be harder on him than on her other children. Jewel at first denies the imminence of his mother's death and accompanies his brother Darl on a misadventure to deliver a load of lumber. Addie dies while they are off with the wagon. Later, Jewel insists on fording the swollen Yoknapatawpha River rather than detouring to another bridge, and this impetuosity (a character trait) leads to the drowning of the mules and to Cash's broken leg. To obtain a replacement span of mules, Anse trades Jewel's beloved horse. Jewel rushes into the burning GILLESPIE (1) barn to save his mother's body from the flames, and later helps turn in Darl for starting the fire. Jewel narrates the fourth chapter of the novel. (For further information, see *Faulkner in the University*, pp. 109, 110, 113, 125, and 126.)

Bundren, Mrs.   A JEFFERSON, MISSISSIPPI, woman in *AS I LAY DYING* who lends Anse BUNDREN two shovels so that he can bury his deceased wife, Addie BUNDREN. Anse chooses her house to ask for the loan because he hears a gramophone playing there. She is described as "duck-shaped." In the last line of the novel, Anse introduces her to his children as "Mrs. Bundren"; she is his new wife. (For further information, see *Faulkner in the University*, p. 111.)

Bundren, Vardaman   Youngest son of Anse and Addie BUNDREN in *AS I LAY DYING*. Vardaman cannot accept the fact of his mother's death, and is afraid she will suffocate when she is laid in her coffin. The night after her death, Vardaman drills holes in the top of the coffin, inadvertently ripping into her face. He is confused by the journey to bury his mother and horrified by the buzzards that follow the putrefying corpse. During the journey Vardaman suffers delusions: at one point he

thinks Dr. PEABODY killed his mother, and later, in the famous short chapter of five words (chapter 19), he states, "My mother is a fish." An observant child, Vardaman sees his brother Darl BUNDREN set fire to GILLESPIE's barn. On his mind throughout the journey to bury his mother is a toy train he once saw in a JEFFERSON, MISSISSIPPI, store; he is disappointed when it is no longer there. Vardaman narrates chapters 13, 15, 19, 24, 35, 44, 47, 49, and 56. (For further information, see *Faulkner in the University*, pp. 110–11, 115, 139.)

Burch, Lucas (Joe Brown)   Character in *LIGHT IN AUGUST*. He is Lena GROVE's seducer, but when she becomes pregnant, Burch leaves DOANE'S MILL, ALABAMA, for Mississippi, saying he will send for her later. Six months pass with no word from him, and she strikes out on foot for the west.

Burch finds work in a JEFFERSON, MISSISSIPPI, planing mill under the name Joe Brown, but soon leaves the job to go into the bootlegging trade with Joe CHRISTMAS. He is later found lying drunk in Joanna BURDEN's burning house and is taken into custody as a suspect in her murder. He persuades the authorities that Christmas, whom he exposes as black, is the real killer and claims the $1,000 reward.

Before Burch can collect, Byron BUNCH brings him to Lena. Desperate to escape this complication, he gives up his claim to the reward money and hops a freight train for parts unknown.

Burchett   In the short story "HAIR" (in *Collected Stories*), the couple with whom Susan REED lives. The exact relationship between Susan and the Burchetts is uncertain, causing some people to question its character. Mr. Burchett also appears in the short story "MOONLIGHT," where he is identified as the uncle and guardian of Susan, who in this story has no last name. Mr. Burchett catches Susan and her young beau fumbling and kissing in the hammock and drives the boy off with kicks and blows.

Burchett, Mrs.   Character in "HAIR" (in *Collected Stories*). She and her husband, BURCHETT, take Susan REED into their home. (The familial relationship between the Burchetts and Susan is unclear.) In the story, Mrs. Burchett treats Susan harshly and even beats her for wearing makeup. Mrs. Burchett also appears in the short story "MOONLIGHT," in which Susan (who has no last name in the story) refers to her as Aunt Etta. Susan tells her aunt that she is going to a show with her friend SKEET when she actually plans to meet her boyfriend, whom she has been told not to see again.

Burden, Beck   Character in *LIGHT IN AUGUST*. She is one of three daughters of the elder Calvin and Evangeline BURDEN.

Burden, Calvin (the elder) Character in *LIGHT IN AUGUST*. The youngest of 10 children of Nathaniel BURRINGTON (1), a New Hampshire minister, he ran away to California at age 12, calling himself Burden because he couldn't spell his real name.

In his early 20s, Burden migrated eastward to Missouri, where he met and married his wife, Evangeline (BURDEN). In Missouri he learns to hate slavery, and he kills a man in a dispute over the question. He teaches his children, three daughters and a son, to hate it too. A skirmish with Kansas pro-slavery guerrillas costs him an arm in 1861. After the Civil War he moves to JEFFERSON, MISSISSIPPI, to promote black suffrage. Colonel John SARTORIS shoots him dead in an election dispute there.

Burden, Calvin (the younger) Character in *LIGHT IN AUGUST*. The son of Nathaniel and Juana BURDEN and grandson of the Missouri abolitionist Calvin BURDEN (the elder), he was ringbearer at his parents' wedding as a 12-year-old.

Colonel John SARTORIS kills Calvin, age 20, and his grandfather in a JEFFERSON, MISSISSIPPI, boardinghouse in a Reconstruction-era dispute over black voting. His half sister Joanna BURDEN is born 14 years after his death.

Burden, Evangeline Character in *LIGHT IN AUGUST*. She is the wife of the elder Calvin BURDEN and the mother of Nathaniel BURDEN.

Burden, Joanna Character in *LIGHT IN AUGUST*. She is the daughter of Nathaniel BURDEN and his second wife, and the granddaughter of the murdered abolitionist Calvin BURDEN (the elder). Although she is a native of JEFFERSON, MISSISSIPPI, the white community treats her as an outcast for her support of schools and colleges for African Americans throughout the South. She allows Joe CHRISTMAS to live in one of the tumbledown cabins on the old Burden place.

Joanna looks 30 by candlelight when she and Joe Christmas become lovers, but she is actually 40, or so she tells him. They barely talk, and Joe feels he hardly knows her, but their nighttime lovemaking is savage, sometimes hard and brutal on Joe's part, frantic and furious on hers.

Something shifts in Joanna, and she abruptly turns to the religion of her Calvinist ancestors. She furiously attempts to convert Christmas, whom she now envisions as a missionary to African Americans. When he resists and refuses to pray with her, she aims an ancient pistol at him. It misfires; Christmas attacks her with a razor, slashing her throat. He sets the house afire, but Hamp WALLER, passing by, saves her body from the flames.

Joanna Burden is a powerful, disturbing figure, endowed "with pathos and tragic dignity," wrote the critic Cleanth BROOKS.

She (or, rather, her mailbox) is referred to in *The MANSION*.

Burden, Juana Character in *LIGHT IN AUGUST*. The Spanish wife of Nathaniel BURDEN, she bears so close a resemblance to the elder Calvin BURDEN's late wife that he calls out "Evangeline!" when he first meets her.

Burden, Nathaniel Character in *LIGHT IN AUGUST*. The son of the elder Calvin BURDEN, he runs away from home at 14 and stays away for 16 years, though his family hears of him twice by word of mouth: once from Colorado, later from Mexico. Nathaniel finally returns to find a minister to marry him to the mother of his son, 12-year-old Calvin BURDEN (the younger).

Nathaniel Burden comes to JEFFERSON, MISSISSIPPI, to bury his father and son, victims of Colonel John SARTORIS's determination to prevent Reconstruction-era blacks from voting. He is buried near them in his turn on a cedar knoll in a pasture a half mile from the Burden house.

Burden, Sarah Character in *LIGHT IN AUGUST*. She is one of three daughters of Calvin and Evangeline BURDEN.

Burden, Vangie Character in *LIGHT IN AUGUST*. She is one of three daughters of Calvin and Evangeline BURDEN.

Burgess In *The SOUND AND THE FURY*, the father of the girl whom Benjamin (Benjy) COMPSON almost violates. Burgess hits Benjy with a fence picket and knocks him out.

Burgess, Mrs. Burgess's wife in *The SOUND AND THE FURY*. She is the mother of the girl whom Benjy COMPSON tries to molest.

Burk One of Gerald David LEVINE's tent mates in *A FABLE*. He is an aviator.

Burke Character in "FOX HUNT" (in *Collected Stories*). An Irish maid in Harrison BLAIR's household, she assists the valet ERNIE in arranging Steve GAWTREY's affair with Mrs. BLAIR.

Burney, Dewey In *SOLDIERS' PAY*, a boy from the Charlestown, Georgia, area who had been caught stealing sugar. A former friend of Donald MAHON before World War I, Dewey was permitted to enlist in the American army instead of being sent to jail. While in France he panics and kills Lieutenant Richard POWERS, the husband of Mrs. Margaret POWERS. Later killed in the war, Burney is thought of as one of the honored dead in Charlestown.

Burney, Mr.   Carpenter in SOLDIERS' PAY. He is the father of Dewey BURNEY.

Burney, Mrs.   Mother of Dewey BURNEY in SOLDIERS' PAY. She basks in the reflected glow of her son's "heroic" death in France during World War I, which gives her social standing in Charlestown, Georgia. She speaks cruelly to Mrs. Margaret POWERS; ironically, both are unaware that Dewey Burney went berserk while in combat and killed his lieutenant, Richard POWERS, Margaret's husband.

Burnham, Lieutenant Frank   Minor character in PYLON. One of the pilots competing in the air shows celebrating the opening of Feinman Airport in New Valois, Franciana, Burnham is the first fatality of the events. He burns to death when his rocket plane crashes.

Burrington, Nathaniel   (1) Character in LIGHT IN AUGUST. A New England minister, he is the father of the elder Calvin BURDEN, who runs away from home at age 12.

Burrington, Nathaniel   (2) Character in LIGHT IN AUGUST. Joanna BURDEN's nephew, he lives in Exeter, New Hampshire. He offers a reward of $1,000 for the capture of Joanna's killer.

Burt   Character in "TURNABOUT" (in *Collected Stories*). A boatswain's mate in the British Royal Navy's torpedo boat X001, he is killed in a World War I action, along with the rest of the crew.

Bush, Lem   Character in LIGHT IN AUGUST. A neighbor of the Hineses, he takes Milly HINES to the circus in his wagon. He returns alone, however, for Milly elopes with a member of the troupe.

Butch   Character in "DRY SEPTEMBER" (in *Collected Stories*). He tries to inflame the men in MAXEY's barbershop against Will MAYES, who is accused of attacking 40-year-old Miss Minnie COOPER.

Butler, Charles Edward (1849–unknown)   Faulkner's maternal grandfather. Born around 1849, he was descended from one of the earliest settler families of LAFAYETTE COUNTY, MISSISSIPPI. Butler married Lelia Dean Swift (BUTLER) in 1868. They produced two children: a son, Sherwood, and a daughter, Maud (see FALKNER, MAUD BUTLER), both born in OXFORD, MISSISSIPPI.

In April 1876, Butler won election to the office of Oxford town marshal, a paid post involving police work and tax collection. In May 1883, he shot and killed S. M. Thompson, the editor of the OXFORD *EAGLE*, on the town square as he attempted to arrest him for drunkenness. A jury acquitted Butler of manslaughter in May 1884.

Butler served as town marshal for 12 years. In December 1887 he disappeared, taking as much as $3,000 in town funds with him. According to family legend, the stolen money financed his elopement with the "beautiful octoroon" companion of a prominent local woman.

Maud Butler was 16 at the time of her father's disappearance. Faulkner never knew him.

Butler, Joe   Byron SNOPES in SARTORIS uses this name as addressee for his obscene letters to Narcissa SARTORIS. This way, Virgil BEARD, who writes the letters for Snopes, will not know that they are intended for Narcissa.

Butler, Lelia Dean Swift (unknown–1907)   Faulkner's pious, stern maternal grandmother, known to him as "Damuddy." Born in Arkansas, she married Charles BUTLER of LAFAYETTE COUNTY, MISSISSIPPI, and came to live in OXFORD, MISSISSIPPI. Her husband abandoned the family, which included their grown son, Sherwood, and their daughter, Maud, in the late 1880s and never returned.

Lelia Butler painted well enough to be offered a scholarship in 1890 to study art in Rome but she declined, saying she couldn't leave her daughter. She came to live with the Murry Falkners after their move to Oxford in 1902. Clever with her hands, she made Billy Faulkner a nine-inch doll dressed as a policeman. He named it Patrick O'Leary.

Damuddy is the nickname the COMPSON children use for their grandmother in *The SOUND AND THE FURY*.

Lelia Butler died in June 1907 after a long, painful illness, probably uterine cancer.

Byhalia, Mississippi   North Mississippi town 50 miles from OXFORD, MISSISSIPPI. Byhalia was the home of Wright's Sanatorium, a small, private hospital where Faulkner sometimes went to recover from severe alcoholic poisoning.

Dr. Leonard Wright, a Tennessean, operated the sanatorium in three white clapboard houses a mile outside of town. Estelle Faulkner (see FAULKNER, LIDA ESTELLE OLDHAM) first took her husband there in January 1936 when money pressures, his brother Dean's death, and the completion of ABSALOM, ABSALOM! touched off a major drinking bout that ended in alcoholic collapse.

Faulkner returned to Byhalia and its regimen of vitamins, drugs, nourishment, and rest in October 1953 and again in January 1960. Dr. Wright admitted him to the sanatorium for the last time at 6 P.M. on July 5, 1962. He died there of heart failure in the early hours of July 6.

"By the People" (*Collected Stories*)   Short story first published in the October 1955 issue of *Mademoiselle*. Faulkner revised it to be included in chapter 13 of *The*

MANSION. The story was also published in *Prize Stories 1957: The O. Henry Awards,* selected and edited by Paul Engle and Constance Urdang (Garden City, N.Y.: Doubleday, 1957), and in *40 Best Stories from Mademoiselle, 1935–1960,* edited by Cyrilly Abels and Margarita G. Smith (New York: Harper, 1960). Told from the point of view of Charles MALLISON, Gavin STEVENS's nephew, this amusing and comical story concerns V. K. RATLIFF's scheme to defeat Clarence Eggleston SNOPES, a bigoted and self-serving Mississippi legislator, in his bid to win a congressional election against a wounded Korean War veteran, Colonel DEVRIES. A Congressional Medal of Honor winner, Devries was in charge of a unit of African-American troops. In his plot to assure that Uncle Billy (Will VARNER), the biggest landowner in FRENCHMAN'S BEND and Snopes's sponsor, will become angry enough to withdraw his support and force Snopes to step down, Ratliff arranges for two boys to artfully scent Snopes's trouser legs with damp switches from a dog thicket that cause dogs to trail, sniff, and urinate on him, thus making him look foolish. To Uncle Billy, Snopes becomes too much of an inept embarrassment to represent the citizens of Frenchman's Bend and BEAT FOUR.

As Joseph BLOTNER points out, when writing the story Faulkner drew ideas from the commencement speech he gave at his daughter Jill's high school graduation on May 28, 1951 (see *Faulkner: A Biography,* p. 592). In his analysis of the story, Robert W. HAMBLIN comments that in addition to being a tall tale "in the southwestern yarn-spinning tradition," "By the People" "pits a concern for a democratic ideal of government . . . against the political machinations and ethical abuses of a demagogue like Senator Snopes" and has roots in the American tradition of political satire that "reaches back to such early works as Hugh Henry Breckenridge's *Modern Chivalry* (1792–1815)" (*A William Faulkner Encyclopedia,* edited by Robert W. Hamblin and Charles A. Peek, p. 57). For further information, see *Selected Letters of William Faulkner,* p. 373.

C

Caddy *See* COMPSON, CANDACE.

Cain A storekeeper in JEFFERSON, MISSISSIPPI. In *The HAMLET*, Cain sells Ab SNOPES a milk separator for Snopes's wife, Vynie.

Cajan, the Character in *IF I FORGET THEE, JERUSALEM* ("The Old Man"). An alligator hunter who lives deep in a Louisiana bayou, he befriends the CONVICT and the WOMAN and her child. He and the convict become hunting partners even though they cannot communicate in words.

The men work together for 10 days, and the convict temporarily abandons his goal of returning to prison. But the Cajan's alligator hide business is flooded out when a levee is blown up for flood control, and the convict resumes his prisonward journey.

Caldwell, Sam Character in *The REIVERS*. A railroad flagman who is kin to a high railroad official, he is a customer and admirer of Everbe Corinthia (HOGGANBECK)—Miss Corrie, one of Reba's (see RIVERS, REBA) girls.

At Corrie's request, Sam arranges for rail transportation of Ned MCCASLIN and the horse Lightning (Coppermine) from MEMPHIS to PARSHAM. His contributions are essential to the success of Ned's scheme to race Lightning and win money to pay off Bobo BEAUCHAMP's debt. Ned graciously thanks him for his help.

Caledonia Chapel Fictional place in rural BEAT FOUR in northeastern YOKNAPATAWPHA COUNTY, nine miles from JEFFERSON, MISSISSIPPI. The name suggests the Scots or Scots-Irish background of the hill people of Beat Four. In *INTRUDER IN THE DUST*, the Gowrie clan bury its dead in the graveyard at Caledonia Chapel.

Callaghan (1) Character in "FOX HUNT" (in *Collected Stories*). A riding instructor, he gives lessons to Mrs. BLAIR, who is not an apt pupil. Callaghan tells Mrs. Blair's husband, himself a skilled horseman, that she will never learn to ride well.

Callaghan (2) Character in *IF I FORGET THEE, JERUSALEM* ("The Wild Plams"). The dishonest owner of a worthless Utah mine, he hires Harry WILBOURNE as the mine

doctor. This allows Callaghan to observe the letter of the law while he continues to sell stock in the operation.

Callaghan, Miss Character in "UNCLE WILLY" (in *Collected Stories*). A JEFFERSON, MISSISSIPPI, schoolteacher, she leaves her desk and takes a seat as a pupil for an April Fool's joke.

Callicoat, Buster (unknown) A stablehand who worked in Murry FALKNER's livery stable around 1909, he was a member of a large OXFORD, MISSISSIPPI, family. Young Billy Falkner sought out his company.

Faulkner reportedly modeled the character of Boon HOGGANBECK, who appears in *GO DOWN, MOSES*, *The REIVERS*, and elsewhere, on Buster Callicoat.

Like the fictional Boon, Callicoat drew the errand of journeying to MEMPHIS to replenish the whiskey supply of the autumn hunting camp in the Delta. Billy Falkner accompanied him on that urgent mission on one occasion.

Callicoat, David Character in "A JUSTICE" (in *Collected Stories*). He is captain of the steamboat that makes four trips a year up the river along which Doom's Chickasaw people live.

Callie, Aunt Character in *The REIVERS*. An African American and a longtime servant of the Priest family, she nurses each Priest infant in turn, beginning with Maury PRIEST Sr., Lucius PRIEST's father.

Camus, Albert (1913–1960) French novelist, playwright, and essayist. A journalist in Algiers, he was active in the Resistance during World War II. In his postwar work, Camus became an existentialist exponent of disillusion.

Faulkner's style influenced the young Camus, who remained an admirer of the American's fiction. He once called Faulkner "the greatest writer in the world." Camus's novels include *The Stranger* (1942) and *The Plague* (1947); *The Rebel* (1951) is a collection of philosophical essays. He won the Nobel Prize in literature in 1957.

Faulkner and Camus met in Paris in 1955 but did not manage to connect: Faulkner shook Camus's hand rather distantly at a reception, and Camus shyly withdrew. Camus's adaptation of Faulkner's *Requiem for a Nun* was performed in Paris on September 20, 1956.

In a tribute published after Camus's death in an automobile accident, Faulkner wrote that in spite of denying the existence of God, the French writer had spent his life "demanding of himself answers which only God could know" (Blotner, *Faulkner: A Biography*, Volume 2, p. 1756).

Canova, Signor (Joel Flint)   Character in KNIGHT'S GAMBIT ("An Error in Chemistry"). An illusionist (his advertising slogan is "He Disappears While You Watch Him"), he is in fact Joel FLINT, the Yankee murder suspect.

Cape & Smith   New York City publishing firm, Faulkner's fourth publisher. Harrison SMITH, Faulkner's editor at HARCOURT, BRACE, left Harcourt in late 1928 to found his own firm, allying with the English publisher Jonathan Cape.

On February 28, 1929, Cape & Smith signed a contract to publish *The SOUND AND THE FURY,* giving Faulkner a $200 advance. The new publishing house brought out what would become Faulkner's best-known novel on October 7, 1929.

Cape & Smith published AS I LAY DYING in 1930 and SANCTUARY in 1931. Financial strains caused the breakup of the firm in 1931; the partners went into bankruptcy owing the chronically hard-up Faulkner some $4,000 in royalties. With Robert HAAS, Smith went on in 1932 to found SMITH & HAAS, with Faulkner as one of the house's prize authors.

Carberry, Dr.   The physician in the short story "TWO DOLLAR WIFE." He saves the life of Mrs. HOUSTON's son, who has almost swallowed a needle that Maxwell JOHNS carelessly left in a chair.

"Carcassonne" (Collected Stories)   Short piece, similar to a prose poem, in which Faulkner employs dreams and fantasies in a meditation on the creation of art and on the divided psyche of the artist. The visionary content, with allusions to religion, history, and literature, contrasts with the dreamer's physical existence. His body lies beneath tar paper in the rat-infested attic of a cantina in the port city of Rincon. Mrs. WIDRINGTON (1) wife of the Standard Oil Company manager, allows him to sleep over the cantina and expects him to become a poet. Just as the viewpoint shifts between the real and the imaginary, the tone shifts between despair and transcendence.

This story first appeared in *These 13* (1931). Faulkner also included the attic scene in "BLACK MUSIC."

Carl   Character in "DIVORCE IN NAPLES" (in *Collected Stories*). A young messboy on a merchant ship, he has his first sexual experience in a Naples brothel. Fearing

Meta Carpenter met Faulkner in late 1935 while working as a secretary in Hollywood.

the disapproval of his older friend GEORGE (1), the cook, Carl returns reluctantly to the ship.

Carpenter, Meta (1908–1994)   A Mississippi native, raised in MEMPHIS, Carpenter was working in Hollywood as secretary to the director Howard HAWKS when she met Faulkner in late 1935. She was 28 years old, recently divorced, tall, thin and blonde, and within a few weeks she and the novelist were involved in a love affair that would endure, on and off, for 15 years.

When they met, Faulkner was still grieving for his brother Dean FAULKNER, who had been killed in a plane crash, and had suspended work on ABSALOM, ABSALOM! to make money in Hollywood. He fell deeply in love and began to contemplate the breakup of his marriage.

Estelle Faulkner (see FAULKNER, LIDA ESTELLE OLDHAM) refused to grant him a divorce. Meta, distraught, broke off the affair and married the Austrian concert pianist Wolfgang Rebner. Faulkner tried to keep the affair going.

Meta divorced Rebner and became Faulkner's lover again when Faulkner returned to Hollywood in 1942. They parted for a third time in 1945. Meta remarried Rebner, but they were no happier together than before, and she and Faulkner restarted their long affair in 1951. It ended after only a few weeks, and Faulkner never saw her again.

Her memoir, *A Loving Gentleman: The Love Story of William Faulkner and Meta Carpenter* (1976), chronicled their long, sometimes tortured relationship.

Carruthers, Miss   Character in *LIGHT IN AUGUST*. The organist in the Rev. Gail HIGHTOWER (2)'s Jefferson, MISSISSIPPI, church, she has been dead for 20 years when Hightower imagines her at her usual place in the organ loft for Sunday and Wednesday services.

Carter   Character in "BLACK MUSIC" (in *Collected Stories*). He is the architect for whom Wilfred MIDDLESTON works when he has the strange experience that causes him to believe he is a faun. Under this delusion, Midgleston chases Mrs. VAN DYMING through the woods of her Virginia estate.

Caspey   Character in "THERE WAS A QUEEN" (in *Collected Stories*). The husband of the Sartoris family cook ELNORA, he is in prison for theft.

Casse-tête   One of the two thieves in *A FABLE* executed on either side of Corporal STEFAN. Also called Horse, he is apparently brain-damaged or possibly retarded. Able to speak only the word "Paris," he is executed without even knowing what is about to happen to him. He is a companion of LAPIN, who is honorably loyal to him. Just before he and Lapin are killed, Corporal Stefan tells the anxious Casse-tête, "It's all right. . . . We wont go without you" (p. 325). This comment can be seen as a parallel to Christ's biblical remark on the cross to the repentant thief.

Catalpa Street   Fictional street in MEMPHIS, site of Miss REBA's brothel in *The REIVERS*. (The actual Catalpa Avenue is several miles distant from the Memphis Tenderloin district.) In Lucius PRIEST's description, Catalpa is "a sidestreet, almost a back alley, with two saloons at the corner and lined with houses that didn't look old or new either, all very quiet" (p. 97).

Cavalcanti   Family name in "MISTRAL" (in *Collected Stories*). Giulio FARINZALE's aunt, who keeps a wineshop on the edge of town, is a Cavalcanti.

Cayley, Miss   Character in *KNIGHT'S GAMBIT* ("Knight's Gambit"). A country girl, she is the daughter of Hence CAYLEY. Max HARRISS gives her an engagement ring, but her father disapproves of him and she refuses to wear it.

Cayley, Hence   Character in *KNIGHT'S GAMBIT* ("Knight's Gambit"). The father of Miss Cayley, he disapproves of

Max HARRISS, a well-off young man from NEW ORLEANS who courts her.

"Centaur in Brass" *(Collected Stories)*   Short story about Flem SNOPES's prolonged but unsuccessful attempt at stealing brass safety valves from the power plant in JEFFERSON, MISSISSIPPI. The story opens with a brief summary of Flem's immediate past and his arrival in Jefferson with his wife and her infant daughter, but soon turns to Flem's appointment as plant superintendent and his unscrupulous greed. To accomplish his ends, Flem adulterously exploits his wife's erotic appeal to Major HOXEY, the town's rich bachelor mayor, and then plays Tom-Tom ([BIRD]the day fireman at the power plant) against Turl ([BEAUCHAMP]the night fireman). But Flem's scheme backfires when he orders Turl to recover the brass that Tom-Tom is in fact hiding on his property for Flem. Instead of finding brass, Turl finds Tom-Tom's much younger wife alone during the day. Once Flem suspects why Turl is not delivering the wares, he alerts Tom-Tom to what Turl is doing. Just before sundown one evening, Tom-Tom puts on one of his wife's nightgowns and lies in wait on a cot in the back porch for the unsuspecting Turl. Tom-Tom chases Turl with a butcher knife until the two men fall exhausted in a ditch and realize what Flem has done. To get even with Flem, the two men decide to dump the brass in the water tank.

The themes of sexual and economic opportunism vividly play off each other in "Centaur in Brass," a story which, according to John T. Matthews, "suggests that the age-old economic foundation of erotic desire takes on particular clarification in capitalism's transition to mass market practices" ("Shortened Stories: Faulkner and the Market" in *Faulkner and the Short Story*, p. 29). The story is also a foreshadowing of Flem's unscrupulous greed that dominates the SNOPES TRILOGY.

First published in *American Mercury* 25 (February 1932), 200–210, "Centaur in Brass" was revised for publication in *Collected Stories of William Faulkner*; Faulkner revised it further and used it as the first chapter of *The TOWN*, the second novel in the trilogy. For more information, see *Selected Letters of William Faulkner*, pp. 197, 274, and 278, and Diane Brown Jones, *A Reader's Guide to the Short Stories of William Faulkner*, pp. 154–69.

Cerf, Bennett (1898–1971)   Publisher, born in New York City. A marketer of the classics under the Modern Library imprint, he cofounded RANDOM HOUSE with Donald KLOPFER in 1927 and headed the firm for 40 years.

Cerf became interested in Faulkner after reading *SANCTUARY* in 1931. He pursued Faulkner for several years, first publishing a limited edition of *The SOUND AND THE FURY* in 1933, for which the author received $750. In the autumn of 1935 Cerf met with Faulkner and suggested that the author could name his terms with Random House.

Random House absorbed Faulkner's former publisher SMITH & HASS in 1936, taking on Harrison SMITH and Robert HAAS as partners. On October 26, Cerf and company published ABSALOM, ABSALOM! in a first printing of 6,000 copies.

Random House was reasonably generous with advances when Faulkner found himself short of money in the 1940s. By 1954, his works were making money. Cerf tried to persuade him to be the subject of a cover story in *Time* magazine, saying it would boost sales of his new novel, *A FABLE*. The intensely publicity shy author replied with a telegram: "I protest whole idea but will never consent to my picture on cover. Estimate what refusal will cost Random House and I will pay it."

Along with running a major American publishing house, Cerf compiled humor anthologies, wrote a syndicated newspaper column, and, as a far more outgoing personality than his most celebrated author, appeared regularly on television.

Chance, Vic Minor character in *PYLON*. Chance wants to build a plane for Roger Shumann, one of the competing pilots in the air meets at Feinman Airport, but neither Shumann nor Chance has the money.

Charley (1) Character in *LIGHT IN AUGUST*. An intern at the orphanage, he makes love to the dietician Miss ATKINS while Joe CHRISTMAS is hiding in her clothes closet. She worries that Joe will expose them, but he has become too ill from eating her pink toothpaste to notice anything.

Charley (2) Character in *The REIVERS*. A railroad worker, he helps Boon HOGGANBECK and Sam CALDWELL move the boxcar so the horse Lightning (Coppermine) can be loaded for the short train trip from MEMPHIS to PARSHAM, TENNESSEE, for the races.

Charley, Uncle Character in "DOCTOR MARTINO" (in *Collected Stories*). He is the black porter at Lily CRANSTON's summer resort.

Charlie In *The SOUND AND THE FURY*, one of Candace (Caddy) COMPSON's boyfriends. He appears in the first chapter of the novel, which is narrated by Benjamin (Benjy) COMPSON.

Chatto & Windus English publishing house, the publisher of Faulkner's works in the United Kingdom. The Welsh novelist Richard Hughes brought Faulkner to the attention of the London firm, which published *SOLDIERS' PAY* in June 1930 (with an introduction by Hughes), *The SOUND AND THE FURY* in 1931, and other works as they appeared. In later years, Faulkner customarily called on this venerable publisher whenever he traveled in Europe.

Chickasaw Indians A Native American hunter and warrior tribe with permanent settlements in northeast Mississippi, the Chickasaw ranged over hunting grounds in Mississippi, Alabama, Tennessee, and Kentucky. By the beginning of the 19th century, with most of the game driven out of the country, the Chickasaw had turned to farming, growing cotton with the forced labor of as many as 1,000 black slaves.

With the Cherokee, Choctaw, Creek and Seminole, the Chickasaw were one of the so-called Five Civilized Tribes removed to Indian Territory (now Oklahoma) in the 1830s. King Ishtehotopah signed the Treaty of Pontotoc on October 22, 1831, ceding six million acres of Chickasaw lands in northern Mississippi to the United States government. The tribe began the westward migration in 1835, opening the way for mass white settlement of the region.

Chickasaw Indians resettled in Oklahoma fought for the CONFEDERATE STATES OF AMERICA during the Civil War, 1861–1865.

Colonel Robert Shegog of OXFORD, MISSISSIPPI, built his house, later Faulkner's ROWAN OAK, on land purchased from a Chickasaw Indian. In the short story "RED LEAVES" (1930), Faulkner explored Chickasaw history and culture through the fictional characters ISSETIBBEHA and MOKETUBBE. Sam Fathers in "The Old People" (published in 1940, reprinted in GO DOWN, MOSES, 1942) is the son of the Chickasaw chief IKKEMOTUBBE and a slave mother. In the same story, JOBAKER is a full-blooded Chickasaw leading a solitary life deep in the big woods.

In "The Bear" (1942, included in *Go Down, Moses*), Ikkemotubbe sells part of the BIG BOTTOM wilderness to the empire-building planter Thomas SUTPEN, the principal character in the novel ABSALOM, ABSALOM! (1936).

Chlory Character in "BEYOND" (in *Collected Stories*). She is Judge ALLISON's African-American cook.

Christian, Mrs. Character in "UNCLE WILLY" (in *Collected Stories*). A MEMPHIS prostitute, she is briefly Uncle Willy CHRISTIAN's wife. The townspeople persuade her to leave by giving her Uncle Willy's car and a thousand dollars, and she returns to her MANUEL STREET brothel.

Christian, Uncle Willy Character in "UNCLE WILLY" (in *Collected Stories*) and other works. He is an old JEFFERSON, MISSISSIPPI, drugstore proprietor, a great favorite of the local boys, with a drug habit and an affinity for airplanes. When meddlesome church people try to cure him of his addiction, he takes to his airplane in a bid to escape them and perishes in a crash near Jefferson.

In *The TOWN*, Uncle Willy's use of morphine greatly improves his otherwise misanthropic personality. A burglary of his drugstore and the theft of the morphine stock thus has unfortunate consequences. In *The MAN-SION*, two thieves rob the drug cabinet in his store when the night watchman is up the alley enjoying Montgomery Ward SNOPES's peep show.

Uncle Willy appears in *The REIVERS* as the owner of the drugstore below Dr. PEABODY's office on the Square.

Christian, Walter   In *The TOWN*, he is the African-American janitor in Uncle Willy CHRISTIAN's pharmacy. The grandson of a slave who belonged to Uncle Willy's grandfather, Walter helps himself to the alcohol locked in the store cabinet whenever Uncle Willy turns his back after putting the key down.

Christmas, Joe   Character in *LIGHT IN AUGUST*. The illegitimate son of Milly HINES and a dark-skinned man rumored to be part African American, he passes his first five years in the orphanage where his grandfather left him on Christmas night (hence his name). He then goes to live with adoptive parents, the harsh and puritanical Simon MCEACHERN and his wife, on their hard-scrabble Mississippi farm.

He endures the strict discipline of McEachern with stoicism. The old man whips him for not polishing his boots to his satisfaction and for failing to memorize his catechism. Joe accepts this, and coldly resists his foster mother's attempts at tenderness.

Joe rebels finally, going his own way at age 17 in pursuit of the waitress and prostitute Bobbie ALLEN. He assaults McEachern with a chair when McEachern confronts the couple at a dance hall. Afraid Joe has killed McEachern and will bring her trouble with the police, Bobbie drops him later that night. One of Max CONFREY's thugs beats and robs Joe before the Confreys and their entourage leave Mississippi for Memphis.

The episode leads to a 15-year period of wandering for Joe Christmas. He migrates aimlessly, west to Missouri and Oklahoma, south to Mexico, north to Chicago and Detroit, then back to Mississippi. He is bitter, defiant, proud, and in conflict about his identity. He moves back and forth between black and white worlds, courting trouble, brawling, insulting and abusing women, seeming to live only to inflict pain and to be hurt in his turn.

Christmas drifts to JEFFERSON, MISSISSIPPI, and becomes the lover of Joanna BURDEN, the white spinster outcast whose abolitionist half brother and grandfather paid for their support of Black suffrage with their lives. He works for a time in a planing mill, then leaves to become a full-time bootlegger. He and Joanna quarrel over her sudden religious mania. She attempts to shoot him; he slashes her throat with a razor, sets her house on fire, and flees.

His ambiguities outrage the community, which hates and fears him as much for who he is as for what he has done.

A lynch mob headed by the aptly named Percy GRIMM finds Christmas in sanctuary in the house of Gail HIGHTOWER, the failed minister. Hightower attempts to shield Joe, but Grimm finds his quarry in the kitchen and empties his automatic weapon into him. Just before Christmas dies, Grimm castrates him with a butcher's knife.

Christmas dominates *Light in August*. His story is a tragedy, set against Lena GROVE's comedy. He shows Faulkner's concern with race and identity. Like a lost child, Christmas wanders aimlessly, drawn to life but unable to connect with it, and fated to die.

A student once asked Faulkner if he intended any Christ symbolism in Joe Christmas. He said no, and he also refused to characterize Joe as a bad man, in spite of his horrific crime.

"I don't think he was bad, I think he was tragic," Faulkner said. "And his tragedy was that he didn't know what he was and would never know, and that to me is the most tragic condition that an individual can have—to not know who he was." (*Faulkner in the University*, pp. 117–18)

Church, Mrs.   Character in "THAT WILL BE FINE" (in *Collected Stories*). A JEFFERSON, MISSISSIPPI, lady, she calls on Mrs. PRUITT, the wife of the president of the Compress Association, and spreads the word that Pruitt does not wear corsets and has liquor on her breath, outraging Jefferson's values.

Cinthy   Character in *LIGHT IN AUGUST*. She is the African-American cook for the first Gail HIGHTOWER and retails his Civil War exploits to his grandson and namesake. The older Hightower is a Civil War casualty, shot dead with a fowling piece in a raid on a JEFFERSON, MISSISSIPPI, henhouse. The story haunts the younger Gail's imagination.

Clapp, Walter   Character in *The REIVERS*. Mr. VAN TOSCH's horse trainer, he suspects that Ned MCCASLIN might be trying a ruse in order to win the PARSHAM horse race.

Clay, Sis Beulah   An offstage character in *The SOUND AND THE FURY*. DILSEY's daughter FRONY mentions that Sis Beulah Clay was mourned for two days at her funeral.

Clefus   Minor African-American character in *The TOWN* who sweeps the law office of Gavin STEVENS.

Clytemnestra   *See* SUTPEN, CLYTEMNESTRA.

Cochrane, Dr. Ab   Medical doctor with a wry sense of humor in the short story "MR. ACARIUS." Dr. Cochrane admits the title character into a clinic for alcoholics at his own request to identify with humanity's suffering souls. Upset with what he finds, the idealist Mr. Acarius flees from the hospital, and when he is stopped by the police, Dr. Cochrane intervenes and takes his patient home, where Mr. Acarius admits to his misconception about humanity.

Cofer   Character in *IF I FORGET THEE, JERUSALEM* ("The Wild Palms"). A real estate agent, he rents the doctor's Mississippi gulf coast cottage to Harry WILBOURNE and the ailing Charlotte RITTENMEYER.

Coindreau, Maurice Edgar (1892–1990)   A French-born professor at Princeton, Coindreau introduced literary France to Faulkner's work in 1931 with an appreciative article in the *Nouvelle Review Francaise* after reading *AS I LAY DYING* and *The SOUND AND THE FURY*.

Coindreau translated Faulkner's work for the French publisher Gallimard, beginning with *As I Lay Dying*. Faulkner answered many questions for him when Coindreau translated *The Sound and the Fury* in 1937.

Colbert, David   Character in "A COURTSHIP" (in *Collected Stories*). He is the "Chief Man" of the Chickasaws in the Yoknapatawpha district.

Coldfield, Goodhue   Character in *ABSALOM, ABSALOM!* A Tennessee-born storekeeper in JEFFERSON, MISSISSIPPI, he breaks up his business partnership with his son-in-law, Thomas SUTPEN, over a question of mercantile ethics.

Goodhue argues against secession in 1860. When war comes in 1861 he shuts down his store and withdraws from affairs in protest of its waste. After Confederate troops ransack his store, he locks himself away in his attic.

For a while, Coldfield subsists on food his daughter Rosa (COLDFIELD) hoists up to him. He starves himself to death in 1864.

Coldfield, Rosa   Character in *ABSALOM, ABSALOM!* She is the younger daughter of the JEFFERSON, MISSISSIPPI, storekeeper Goodhue COLDFIELD and sister of Ellen Coldfield SUTPEN. Rosa blames her father, as the agent of the pregnancy, for her mother's death in childbirth with her, but dutifully takes over the management of the household when the spinster aunt who reared her elopes with a mule trader. Rosa supplies her father with food after he nails himself in his attic to hide from the Confederate provost marshals.

After the deaths of her father and of Ellen, who is 27 years her senior, Miss Rosa goes to live at SUTPEN'S HUNDRED to look after her niece, Judith SUTPEN. She had long regarded her brother-in-law Thomas SUTPEN as an ogre, but she believes the war has changed him, and she allows herself to consider what appears to be his offer of marriage.

The offer, it turns out, is conditional. Sutpen insults Rosa by proposing that they marry only if they first produce a son to replace Henry SUTPEN, who has disappeared after killing Judith's suitor, Charles BON. Furious, Rosa returns to her father's old home, surviving on unacknowledged handouts from Judge BENBOW.

One evening in September 1909, Miss Rosa sends for young Quentin COMPSON and narrates her version of Sutpen's history. She has kept her hatred for Sutpen alive over the years, and she wants Quentin to tell the story.

Miss Rosa persuades Quentin to escort her to Sutpen's Hundred, which she has not seen since 1866. She knows "there is something living in that house," and when they discover the invalid Henry in a room upstairs, she sends for an ambulance. Thinking Rosa has called the police, the servant Clytemnestra sets fire to the old, rotted mansion. Clytie and Henry perish in the flames, and Rosa dies soon afterward.

Coleman, Mrs.   In *SOLDIERS' PAY*, Mrs. Coleman is one of the leading women of the village of Charlestown, Georgia, and a friend of Minnie SAUNDERS.

Collected Stories of William Faulkner   Published in 1950, this volume brought together 42 short stories written over a period of two decades. (See entries for individual stories.)

Albert ERSKINE, an editor at RANDOM HOUSE, began preparations for the collection in early 1948, making up a list of stories to be included and passing it along to Faulkner's longtime editor, Robert HAAS. By November, Haas, the editor Saxe COMMINS, and Faulkner himself had chosen the 42 pieces to be arranged in six sections: "The Country," "The Village," "The Wilderness," "The Wasteland," "The Middle Ground," and "Beyond." Faulkner arranged the order of the stories but he did not write a foreword, as Malcolm COWLEY had suggested, to illustrate the volume's themes and connections.

Collected Stories contains much of Faulkner's best short fiction, including "A ROSE FOR EMILY," "BARN BURNING," "DRY SEPTEMBER," "RED LEAVES," "THAT EVENING SUN," and "UNCLE WILLY." Notably absent from the omnibus are the seven stories of *The UNVANQUISHED*, the seven stories of *GO DOWN, MOSES*, and four stories, including "SPOTTED HORSES," that Faulkner wove into *The HAMLET*.

Random House published the *Collected Stories* on August 21, 1950. The early reviews were mostly enthusiastic, always respectful. Harry Sylvester, writing in the *New York Times Book Review*, did not like the "Beyond" section, in which four of the six stories contained supernatural elements, but praised the volume overall and classified Faulkner as a great writer.

"One thing remains to distinguish him above all American writers since James and perhaps since Melville—he simply knows so much more than they," Sylvester wrote.

The poet and critic Horace Gregory, in an essay in the *New York Herald Tribune Weekly Book Review,* ranked Faulkner with James, Kafka, Dostoyevsky, Joyce, and D. H. Lawrence. Writers of such stature are not bound by the ordinary rules, he suggested, and even their failures have value.

"The first impression that the book conveys is one of an Elizabethan richness: here is the variety of life itself, its humors, its ironies, its ancient tempers, its latest fashions, its masks of horror, its violence, its comedy, its pathos," Gregory wrote. "It is gratuitous to say that the stories are uneven in depth, quality and interest."

In March 1951, Faulkner won a National Book Award for *Collected Stories.*

Collier   Character in "TURNABOUT" (in *Collected Stories*). He is a mandolin-playing American aviator in France in 1918. Lieutenant McGinnis suggests that Collier provide the music on one of Midshipman L. C. W. HOPE's torpedo boat missions, which he wrongly regards as pleasure cruises.

Collins, Carvel (1912–1990)   Professor of English, critic, and editor. Collins taught at Harvard, Massachusetts Institute of Technology, and the University of Notre Dame, among other colleges and universities. One of the first important figures in Faulkner scholarship, which was characterized by close reading and perceptive analysis of Faulkner's works, Collins edited and introduced several of Faulkner's works: NEW ORLEANS SKETCHES (1958; revised and expanded, 1968), WILLIAM FAULKNER'S UNIVERSITY PIECES (1962), WILLIAM FAULKNER: EARLY PROSE AND POETRY (1962), MAYDAY (1977; revised, 1980), and HELEN: A COURTSHIP (1981). Collins also wrote introductions to *The UNVANQUISHED* (Signet Books, 1959), *William Faulkner: The Cofield Collection* (a collection of photos, 1980), and other works.

Collyer   British Royal Air Force officer, adjutant to Gerald LEVINE's squadron in *A FABLE.* Collyer orders the hangars and airfield shut down in preparation for the arrival of the German GENERAL.

Commercial Hotel   Fictional place, established around the time of the Civil War as rival to JEFFERSON, MISSISSIPPI's, leading hostelry, the HOLSTON HOUSE. It did not quite rise to the handsomely turned-out Holston. It later becomes the Snopes Hotel; in *The REIVERS,* set in 1905, Boon HOGGANBECK lives in a rented room there.

Commins, Saxe (1892–1958)   Faulkner's sometime editor at RANDOM HOUSE beginning in 1937, and a loyal friend to the author and his wife. A nephew of the political radical Emma Goldman, Commins practiced as a dentist for a time; the playwright Eugene O'Neill,

one of his patients, helped lead him into a new career as an editor.

Commins knew Faulkner's work before they met. He had written a volume titled *Psychology: A Simplification* in the 1920s, and when a package that should have contained his author's copies arrived from his publisher, Horace LIVERIGHT, he found copies of Faulkner's MOSQUITOES inside. Some scholars believed Commins may have worked on *Absalom, Absalom!,* which would date their first association to 1936.

As an editor, Commins was solicitous and unfailingly encouraging. The two men were friends as well as literary associates, and Faulkner often visited Commins at his home in Princeton, New Jersey. Working with measurements from Estelle FAULKNER, Commins bought the dress suit the novelist wore for his Nobel Prize acceptance in 1950. He also made travel arrangements and booked hotels for Faulkner, helped him to recover from his alcoholic binges, and listened to his troubles with Estelle.

Commins put in hard editorial work on A FABLE and on *The TOWN,* the second novel in the SNOPES TRILOGY, reconciling discrepancies between that book and the opening volume, *The HAMLET.* He died of a heart attack at home in Princeton in July 1958, age 66.

Compson   Family name in YOKNAPATAWPHA COUNTY. A Compson with no first name is referred to in "Skirmish at Sartoris" (*The UNVANQUISHED*) as the crazy husband of Mrs. COMPSON. Sometime during the Civil War, he was locked up for shooting sweet potatoes off the heads of little black children. (See Appendix IV.)

Compson, Benjamin (Benjy)   In *The SOUND AND THE FURY,* the idiot son and the fourth and youngest child of Jason Richmond COMPSON and his wife, Caroline Bascomb COMPSON, born on April 7, 1895. Named after Mrs. Compson's brother Maury BASCOMB, Benjy's name was changed when it became evident that he was retarded. He narrates the first chapter of the novel and is referred to in *The MANSION,* in which he dies when he sets his house on fire. The day of the chapter he narrates is Benjy's 33rd birthday.

Circumscribed by present sensations, Benjy's world is virtually timeless. Although he does not differentiate between the present moment and moments of the past, he is able to represent the past through associations in the present; for example, the smell of leaves and trees recalls his sister Candace (Caddy) COMPSON, who is no longer physically present in his life. To help the reader distinguish time shifts in Benjy's narrative, Faulkner intended to use different colors of ink, but his publisher thought it too costly; italics were used instead (see *Selected Letters of William Faulkner,* pp. 71 and 74). After breaking loose from his yard one afternoon and chasing a few neighborhood schoolgirls who are passing by, one of whom he tries to molest, Benjy is castrated. When, while undressing later, he sees that his testicles are missing, he cries. Benjy's impatient and self-centered brother Jason COMPSON IV tries to have him institutionalized in Jackson after their brother Quentin COMPSON commits suicide and their father dies, but their mother will not allow it. (In Faulkner's appendix to *The Sound and the Fury* [See Appendix IV], Benjy is committed to the state asylum in Jackson in 1933, the year that Mrs. Compson dies. However, in *The Mansion,* Mrs. Compson is still alive when Benjy is sent to the asylum; she insists that her son Jason have Benjy brought home. According to Jason in *The Mansion,* "his mother whined and wept" [p. 322] until he gave in. Less than two years later, Benjy burns the house down.)

In 1928, (when three of *The Sound and the Fury*'s four chapters are set), Benjy is 33 years old. Because of his age and the fact that the last chapter occurs on Easter Sunday, some readers may see Benjy as a Christ-figure. (For further information, see *Faulkner in the University,* pp. 17, 18, 84, 87, 95, 139; and *Faulkner at Nagano,* pp. 103–04.)

Compson, Candace (Caddy)   The second child and only daughter of Jason Richmond COMPSON and his wife, Caroline Bascomb COMPSON. Although she is an off-stage character in *The SOUND AND THE FURY,* she very much dominates the thoughts of her three brothers—Benjy, Quentin, and Jason COMPSON IV, who narrate the first three chapters of the novel, respectively. In one of Faulkner's explanations of the initial idea behind *The Sound and the Fury,* he states that the concept for the work began with a picture of Caddy climbing a tree to look through a window at her deceased grandmother laid out in the parlor and the image of the muddy bottoms of her drawers (*Faulkner in the University,* pp. 1, 17, and 31; for a slightly different account, see *Faulkner at Nagano,* pp. 103–04). He wrote the novel to "try to draw the picture of Caddy"; to him, "she was the beautiful one" and his "heart's darling" (*Faulkner in the University,* p. 6). For Faulkner, "the symbolism of the muddy bottom of the drawers became the lost Caddy, which caused one brother [Quentin] to commit suicide and the other brother [Jason] had misused her money that she'd send back to the child, the daughter" (p. 31–32).

Caddy is a lively, independent, and strong-willed person whose behavior is often at odds with her parents and in contradiction to what her brothers, Quentin and Jason, expect of her. Her sexual activity disarms Quentin's fragile mental state and leads him to incestuously covet her. Each brother perceives and responds to Caddy very differently. Benjy sees her partly as a maternal figure who loves and comforts him and partly as a considerate and compassionate older sister who plays and spends time with him. Quentin sees her as a romantic ideal and an image of Southern womanhood whose chastity must be preserved. Jason views Caddy as a means

to an end, to be exploited by his selfish tendencies. He forever disdains her when the bank position promised him by her fiancé, Sydney Herbert HEAD, falls through after Caddy's short-lived marriage ends in divorce. When Head realizes that the child to whom Caddy gives birth was fathered by another man before their marriage, he divorces her and never gives Jason the job.

Although her child is a girl, Caddy names her Quentin, after her brother who committed suicide. Caddy leaves her child with her parents to rear and leaves JEFFERSON, MISSISSIPPI. Throughout the years, she is diligent in sending her daughter money every month, but Jason intercepts this money and misuses it.

Caddy appears as a young inquisitive child in "THAT EVENING SUN" and very briefly in the short story "A JUSTICE"; she is referred to in *The MANSION.* For further information, see Faulkner's appendix to *The Sound and the Fury* and *Faulkner in the University,* pp. 1–2, 6, 74, 148, 247, 262–63, and 274.

Compson, Caroline Bascomb (Mrs. Compson)   In *The SOUND AND THE FURY,* the hypochondriacal wife of Jason Richmond COMPSON and mother of Quentin, Candace (Caddy), Jason and Benjamin (Benjy) COMPSON. Of her four children, she favors Jason, for in her mind he is more a Bascomb than a Compson; she leaves Benjy, whose name she changes once it is known that Benjy is severely retarded, to the care of others. (At birth, Benjy was named after Mrs. Compson's brother Maury.) A self-indulgent and self-pitying woman, she takes an unwarranted pride in her side of the family, which she believes is more genteel and sophisticated than her husband's. Mrs. Compson's negative effect on her immediate family is evident throughout *The Sound and the Fury,* especially in the second chapter, which Quentin narrates. In an insightful critical essay on the novel, Cleanth BROOKS discusses Mrs. Compson's devastating impact on her family and argues that she is a source of their spiritual sickness (see *William Faulkner: The Yoknapatawpha Country,* pp. 333–35).

Mrs. Compson also appears in Faulkner's appendix to *The Sound and the Fury* (see Appendix IV) and in the short story "THAT EVENING SUN"; she is referred to in *The MANSION.*

Compson, Charles Stuart   A British soldier during the Revolutionary War who was left for dead in a swamp in Georgia. He is the father of Jason Lycurgus COMPSON I; he appears in Faulkner's appendix to *The Sound and the Fury.* (See Appendix IV.)

Compson, Jason IV   The third child (and second son) of Jason Richmond COMPSON and his wife, Caroline Bascomb COMPSON, and brother of Quentin, Candace (Caddy), and Benjamin (Benjy) COMPSON. He is a major character in *The SOUND AND THE FURY* (he narrates chapter 3), and appears in *The MANSION,* "THAT EVENING SUN," and "A JUSTICE." He is also described by Faulkner in the appendix to *The Sound and the Fury* (see Appendix IV) and is referred to in *The TOWN.*

Jason is an insensitive and selfish person whose logic reflects a cold, calculating mind. In the short story "That Evening Sun," in which he is a young child, the person he will become begins to shine through in his comments and behavior. The cliché-ridden style of his section of *The Sound and the Fury* reflects from the very opening line—"Once a bitch always a bitch" (180)—an uncreative and shallow thought process tainted by common prejudices and stock phrases. As head of the Compson family in *The Sound and the Fury* (his father has died by the time he narrates chapter 3), he is accountable to virtually no one for his actions. Jason is a compassionless man whose relations with the world are seen in terms of business and what he can get out of them for himself. His dealings with his mistress, LORRAINE, for example, show an uncaring man, detached from any emotional or romantic life. His treatment of DILSEY, Benjy, his niece (Miss) Quentin COMPSON especially, and even his mother, who favors him and whose side of the family, according to her, he takes after, is at times cruel, usually intolerant, at best indifferent. Jason thinks of himself as rational, level-headed, and justified in his resentment and anger for having been cheated of opportunities. Jason reasons that the money his father got by selling the pasture adjacent to their home was wasted on sending his brother Quentin to Harvard, where he committed suicide, and on Caddy's wedding celebrating a marriage that lasted less than a year. Because Caddy was divorced by her husband, Sydney Herbert HEAD, for bearing another man's child, Jason was denied a bank position that Head had promised him. His lingering anger over having lost this job justifies in his own mind the way he treats his niece, Caddy's daughter, who is being reared by the self-pitying Mrs. Compson. He steals the monthly stipend Caddy sends him for her daughter.

According to Faulkner's appendix, Jason commits Benjy to an asylum when their mother dies in 1933. He moves out of the family house and lives above his store. A slightly different version is recounted in *The Mansion:* Jason brings Benjy home to assuage his whining mother, but within two years after his return, Benjy burns the house down with himself in it. Jason then buys a new home in town with his mother and later buys back the property his father sold. He sells it to Flem SNOPES and at first thinks he tricked Flem into buying land that was rumored to be, but not suitable for, a government airfield. When he realizes that Flem will make a hefty profit because the land will be used to build new housing for Jefferson's growing population, Jason unsuccessfully tries to find a flaw in the original deed to the property.

Compson, Jason Lycurgus I   Character referred to in *REQUIEM FOR A NUN* (Act One, "The Courthouse") and in Faulkner's appendix to *The SOUND AND THE FURY.* Jason is the son of Charles Stuart COMPSON, a British soldier during the Revolutionary War, and the father of General Jason Lycurgus COMPSON II. (According to Faulkner's appendix to *The Sound and the Fury,* Jason [I] was the grandfather of General Compson.) In 1779, Jason (I) is taken by his grandfather, Quentin MacLachan, from Carolina to Kentucky. In 1811, he becomes a clerk in the Chickasaw Agency at Okatoba in Mississippi, and later is the agent's partner. He trades his swift mare with IKKEMOTUBBE for a square mile of land where he builds his home, known as the Compson place. In *The MANSION,* however, in 1821 Quentin [MacLachan] Compson [II] was granted land from the Chickasaw matriarch MOHATAHA.) One of the founders of JEFFERSON, MISSISSIPPI, Jason's square mile "was to be the most valuable land in the future town of Jefferson" (*Requiem,* p. 12). (For Faulkner's descriptions of the Compsons, see Appendix IV).

Compson, Jason Lycurgus II (General)   The grandfather of Quentin COMPSON, who narrates the Sutpen story in *ABSALOM, ABSALOM!,* General Compson (he was a brigadier general in the Civil War) knew Thomas SUTPEN as a poor young man and loaned him seed cotton to help him make a start as a planter. The general transmits a version of the Sutpen saga to his son Jason Richmond COMPSON, who in turn passes it on to Quentin, who balances Rosa COLDFIELD's embittered narrative with his grandfather's more judicious account. General Compson died in 1900.

General Compson also appears in *The UNVANQUISHED, GO DOWN, MOSES, INTRUDER IN THE DUST, The REIVERS,* and in the short stories "BEAR HUNT" and "MY GRANDMOTHER MILLARD AND GENERAL BEDFORD FORREST AND THE BATTLE OF HARRYKIN CREEK." He is referred to in *REQUIEM FOR A NUN* and *The TOWN.*

Compson, Jason Richmond (Mr. Compson; Jason III)   The son of General Jason Lycurgus COMPSON II, and the father of Quentin, Candace (Caddy), Jason IV, and Benjamin (Benjy) COMPSON. He appears in *The SOUND AND THE FURY* and in the novel's appendix (see Appendix IV), *ABSALOM, ABSALOM!,* "THAT EVENING SUN," and "A JUSTICE"; he is referred to in *GO DOWN, MOSES* ("The Bear"). An attorney and a Southern gentleman, Mr. Compson is disillusioned and cynical. Quentin, on the day of his suicide, recalls his father once saying that "a man is the sum of his misfortunes." Mr. Compson is an individual more inclined to philosophize about life than to practice law. He is sensitive and attentive, especially to his son Quentin, whose thinking and judgement he has heavily influenced, and he is very much adversely affected by his daughter Caddy's sexual behavior and Quentin's death. Against his doctor's advice he drinks heavily, which eventually causes his death in 1912.

Compson, (Miss) Quentin In *The SOUND AND THE FURY,* the daughter of Candace (Caddy) COMPSON and probably Dalton AMES; she appears in Faulkner's appendix to the novel (see Appendix IV) and is referred to in *The MANSION.* Named after her deceased uncle, Quentin is a rebellious 17-year-old who lives with the Compsons. As an infant, she was left in the care of her self-pitying grandmother when Caddy departed from JEFFERSON, MISSISSIPPI. Throughout her young life, her uncle Jason COMPSON IV mistreats her and robs her of the money Caddy sends monthly for her welfare. Jason's behavior toward his niece stems in part from the anger he harbors against his sister, whose former husband had promised Jason a bank job that Jason never got because of Caddy's divorce. Before running off with a carnival worker, Quentin breaks into Jason's locked room through a window and takes almost $7,000, much of which really belongs to her. When Jason realizes what happened, he tries in vain to find her.

Compson, Mr. *See* COMPSON, JASON RICHMOND.

Compson, Mrs. (1) Character in *ABSALOM, ABSALOM!,* *The UNVANQUISHED,* and the short story "MY GRAND-MOTHER MILLARD AND GENERAL BEDFORD FORREST AND THE BATTLE OF HARRYKIN CREEK"; referred to in *The TOWN.* She is General Jason Lycurgus COMPSON's wife. In the short story when the Yankee scouts come into JEFFERSON, MISSISSIPPI, she sits fully dressed on a wicker basket of silver in the outhouse. In *The Town,* a reference is made to her having given old HET a purple toque 50 years earlier.

In *The Unvanquished,* she loans Rosa MILLARD a hat and a parasol as she sets out on her adventures in Yankee-occupied north Mississippi in 1863. Mrs. Compson's eccentric husband had been locked up long ago for shooting sweet potatoes off the heads of Black children with a rifle.

Compson, Mrs. (2) *See* COMPSON, CAROLINE BASCOMB.

Compson, Quentin Son and oldest child of Jason Richmond COMPSON and his wife, Caroline Bascomb COMPSON; he appears in *The SOUND AND THE FURY* (where he narrates chapter 2), Faulkner's appendix to the novel (see Appendix IV), *ABSALOM, ABSALOM!* (much of which he narrates), and he also narrates the short stories "THAT EVENING SUN," "A JUSTICE" and "LION." Quentin is referred to in *The MANSION.*

Quentin is a romantic idealist with chivalrous notions of womanhood. In *The Sound and the Fury,* he is obsessed with protecting and defending his sister Caddy's virginity and honor. In the appendix to the novel, Faulkner writes

that Quentin "loved not his sister's body but some concept of Compson honor." Yet, at the same time, Quentin has incestuous longings for Caddy, longings that he could never act on. In a conversation with his father, who heavily influences his thinking, Quentin says that he has committed incest with her, a lie he tells perhaps in hope that he and Caddy together will be forced into exile; in this way, he would achieve his goal of protecting her. Quentin is also a Hamlet-like figure for Caddy, who wants him either to act boldly (as when Quentin offers to kill her and then himself, but is unable to do so) or to leave her alone. His ineffectiveness comes out again in his confrontation with Dalton AMES, Caddy's lover. Ames contemptuously hands his pistol to Quentin and dares him to shoot, but Quentin cannot.

Faulkner develops Quentin with great consistency. In *ABSALOM, ABSALOM!,* the themes of sexuality, the brother-sister relationship, and death are major concerns seen through Quentin's eyes. When retelling the story of the Sutpens to his roommate Shreve MCCANNON, Quentin reflects especially on Henry SUTPEN's killing of his sister Judith's fiancé, Charles BON, who without her knowing, is her half brother. Quentin is aware that Henry is compelled to commit this act to defend the Southern notion of womanly honor and uphold Southern notions of racial correctness, for Charles also has a trace of black blood. However, it is not the incest that forces Henry's hand, but miscegenation. Even though Charles passes as a white man, he cannot be one. These themes resonate in Quentin's mind.

On June 2, 1910, at the end of his freshman year at Harvard, Quentin drowns himself in the Charles River in Cambridge, Massachusetts.

For further information, see *Faulkner in the University,* pp. 2–3, 5, 17–18, 32, 71, 75, 77, 84, 94–95, 121, 135, 141, 247, 262–63, 274–75.

Compson, Quentin MacLachan The orphaned son of a Glasgow printer. A Jacobite supporter of Bonnie Prince Charlie's failed attempt (1645–46) to regain the British throne for the deposed Stuarts, he fled Culloden Moor for Carolina. He appears in Faulkner's appendix to *The SOUND AND THE FURY.* (See Appendix IV.)

Compson Mile Fictional place in JEFFERSON, MISSISSIPPI, the original domain of the Compson family. Jason Lycurgus COMPSON I acquired the square mile of virgin land about 1811 from the Chickasaw chief IKKEMO-TUBBE in exchange for a race horse.

The Compson holdings were mortgaged after the Civil War and sold piecemeal. In *The SOUND AND THE FURY,* Jason Richard COMPSON sells the pasture to a golf club to pay for his daughter Caddy's wedding and his son Quentin's Harvard tuition. By then, all that remained of the Compson land, according to Faulkner in his appendix to *The Sound and the Fury,* was "the house and the kitchengarden and the collapsing stables and one servant's cabin."

Compson's Creek   Fictional name for Burney's Branch, a creek that flows less than a mile east of the courthouse in OXFORD, MISSISSIPPI. In *REQUIEM FOR A NUN*, CHICKASAW INDIANS bathe their legs in the stream before going to Compson's store.

Comyn   Character in *SARTORIS* and in the short story "AD ASTRA." In *Sartoris*, Comyn, known to his friends as "that big Irish devil," is involved in a wartime brawl in the Cloche-Clos café in Amiens. In "Ad Astra," he is constantly in search of a fight.

Confederate States of America   A league of 11 southern states, including Mississippi, that seceded from the United States in 1860–61 over issues of slavery and states' rights and that fought an unsuccessful four-year civil war for independence.

Faulkner used incidents and issues from the War Between the States, as many southerners call the Civil War, in a number of works, including *ABSALOM, ABSALOM!* and *The UNVANQUISHED*. His great-grandfather William Clark FALKNER briefly commanded the 2nd Mississippi Infantry in Virginia and later led a partisan cavalry unit in northern Mississippi.

The defeated South loomed large in Faulkner's tragic vision, yet he was no lost-cause sentimentalist. A reporter once asked him what part of the Southern tradition he hoped his grandson would continue, and what part he would reject. "I hope that his mother and father will try to raise him without bigotry as much as can be done," Faulkner answered. "He can have a Confederate battle-flag if he wants it, but he shouldn't take it too seriously" (Blotner, *Faulkner: A Biography,* volume 2).

Confrey, Mame   Character in *LIGHT IN AUGUST*. She is the blonde wife of Max CONFREY, proprietor of the restaurant and brothel where Bobbie ALLEN works.

Confrey, Max   Character in *LIGHT IN AUGUST*. He and his wife Mame CONFREY run a combination restaurant and brothel. Bobbie ALLEN works for the Confreys as a waitress and prostitute; the Confreys disapprove when she and Joe CHRISTMAS become lovers.

Conner, Buck   The city marshal of JEFFERSON, MISSISSIPPI, Conner is involved in the Joanna BURDEN murder investigation in *LIGHT IN AUGUST* and escorts Lucas BURCH to jail as the hunt for Joe CHRISTMAS, Joanna's killer, proceeds.

In the short story "CENTAUR IN BRASS," Conner investigates the missing brass fittings at Jefferson's power plant. Faulkner revised the short story for chapter 1 of *The TOWN*, where Buck's last name appears as Connors.

Connors, Buck   City marshal of JEFFERSON, MISSISSIPPI, in *The TOWN*. See also CONNER, BUCK.

Conventicle   Welsh flight sergeant in LEVINE's squadron in *A FABLE*. He apparently has taken Levine under his wing, and Levine feels a kind of kinship for him.

Convict, the   Character in *IF I FORGET THEE, JERUSALEM* ("The Old Man"). A young innocent from the Mississippi hill country, his reading of paperback crime novels inspires him to attempt a train robbery, more for the satisfaction of carrying out a well-conceived scheme than for the money. The robbery misfires, and he is arrested and sentenced to 15 years in prison.

The tall convict, as he is usually styled, resents not the police and courts but instead the crime-story writers who misled him. He is a model prisoner. As a result, he is taken from the prison during the Great Mississippi Flood of 1927, given a skiff, and asked to rescue a man on a cotton house and a pregnant WOMAN who has taken refuge in a tree.

He finds the woman but not the man. The flood carries them far downstream and he fights against impossible odds for their lives. The prison officials give him up for drowned, but he heroically pursues his goals to deliver the woman and her newborn baby to safety and return to his place of security in prison.

The prison warden has long since reported the tall convict dead; his eventual return is an embarrassment. To cover it, he adds 10 years to the convict's sentence for attempted escape. Relieved to be free of the woman and back in prison, the convict hardly cares.

The tall convict is physically adept but limited in intelligence. The critic Malcolm COWLEY once characterized him as "the ideal soldier for a fascist army." Others have found him more timid than alarming, so afraid of the world that he gratefully returns to his haven behind bars.

Cook, Celia   Character in *The UNVANQUISHED*. As a young girl, she watches the Confederate cavalry commander Nathan Bedford FORREST ride down South Street in OXFORD, MISSISSIPPI; she commemorates the event by etching her name into a windowpane with a diamond ring. (See also FARMER, CECILIA.)

Cooper   A minor character in *PYLON*. Cooper is sent by his editor HAGOOD to replace the unnamed REPORTER covering the air meet celebrating the opening of Feinman Airport in New Valois, Franciana.

Cooper, Miss Minnie   Character in "DRY SEPTEMBER" (in *Collected Stories*). A JEFFERSON, MISSISSIPPI, spinster of about 40, she is said to have been "attacked, insulted, frightened" by a young African American named Will MAYES, and a lynch mob forms to avenge her.

Corporal In *A FABLE,* the appellation used most often for STEFAN, the mystical leader of the 13 French soldiers whose pacifist beliefs incite the mutiny in the novel. In these entries, he is called Corporal Stefan for clarity, but this combined form is never used in *A Fable.*

Cotton, Ernest Main character in Faulkner's short story "THE HOUND." Cotton is not fully satisfied with the reward he receives for housing Jack HOUSTON's stray hog, over the winter. A fiercely proud and independent man who feels taken advantage of, Cotton later settles the matter by killing Houston. The story ends with his arrest.

Faulkner revised the story for Book Three of *The HAM-LET.* In the revision, the bachelor Cotton is married with two children and his name is changed to Mink SNOPES. Another significant change occurs in the way Faulkner presents the conflict between Houston and Cotton. In the story, it is Houston's hog that Cotton winters, but in the revision Houston winters Snopes's scrub yearling, and the court awards him a three-dollar pasturage.

Coughlan, Robert (unknown) Journalist and profiler of Faulkner. *Life* magazine assigned Coughlan to do a 6,000-word piece on Faulkner in spite of the novelist's notorious distaste for publicity. He interviewed Faulkner and others in OXFORD, MISSISSIPPI, in August 1951. The result, a two-part article that appeared in the September 28 and October 5 issues of 1953, was the first substantial biographical treatment of Faulkner.

Coughlan included a good deal of personal detail, including mention of Faulkner's heavy drinking. The novelist's mother, Maud Butler FALKNER, disliked the pieces so intensely that she canceled her *Life* subscription. The journalist offered the standard justification for the intrusion: "Because he has created [the books], he does not belong entirely to himself."

Coughlan expanded the material into a book, *The Private World of William Faulkner,* published in 1954.

"A Courtship" *(Collected Stories)* Short story relating a tall tale set in mid-19th-century YOKNAPATAWPHA COUNTY. The nameless narrator nostalgically recounts the comic saga of a competition for a beautiful woman, as told to him by his father. IKKEMOTUBBE, a CHICKASAW INDIAN, and David HOGGANBECK, a steamboat pilot, first try to attract Herman BASKET's sister with a series of displays, presents, and a horse race. When she remains indifferent, the contest escalates into feats of physical prowess, including drinking, dancing, eating, and culminating in an epic footrace through the wilderness.

As the action progresses, the two men develop a close bond of respect and affection that transcends their disappointment when the woman instead chooses as mate an indolent harmonica-playing Indian. This rejection causes Ikkemotubbe to leave for NEW ORLEANS, where he will be transformed into Doom, or the Man (in French, *de l'homme*), after being corrupted by the white man's values.

This tale first appeared in the *Sewanee Review* (autumn 1948), and in 1949 won the O. Henry Award for the best American short story. "A JUSTICE" follows Ikkemotubbe after his return from New Orleans.

Cowan, Mrs. Character in "HAIR" (in *Collected Stories*). She is the landlady of the JEFFERSON, MISSISSIPPI, barber Henry STRIBLING (Hawkshaw).

Cowley, Malcolm (1898–1989) Editor and literary critic, born in Belasco, Pennsylvania. His influential *Exile's Return* (1934; revised 1951) analyzed the American expatriate writers he had known in Paris in the 1920s—the "Lost Generation." Cowley served as associate editor of the *New Republic* from 1929 to 1944 and as literary advisor to the VIKING PRESS from 1948 to 1985.

Cowley edited the anthology *The Portable Faulkner,* published in 1946, which established Faulkner's reputation as a serious literary artist. In early 1944, at a time when nearly all of Faulkner's 17 books were out of print, Cowley had taken stock of Faulkner's standing.

The critic proposed a long essay on Faulkner to "redress the balance between his worth and his reputation." A portion of it appeared in the *New York Times Book Review* of October 29, 1944, as "William Faulkner's Human Comedy." Cowley continued his reclamation project with the anthology.

He worked closely with Faulkner to arrange and explicate the material and wrote the introduction and prefaces to the book's seven sections. Faulkner supplied character genealogies and a map of YOKNAPATAWPHA COUNTY. The final product pleased Faulkner with its clear exposition of his artistic aims.

Cowley's book and his private lobbying had the effect, too, of bringing Faulkner's work back into the marketplace. At his suggestion, RANDOM HOUSE published a Modern Library edition of *The SOUND AND THE FURY* and *AS I LAY DYING.*

Cowrie, Captain British RAF officer in *A FABLE.* He shares a hut with Major BRIDESMAN.

Crack First Sergeant in the Sartoris Rifles, a JEFFERSON, MISSISSIPPI, U.S. Army company organized in 1917 by Captain MCLENDON in honor of Colonel John SARTORIS. Crack is referred to in *The MANSION.*

Crain, Amos Character in "ARTIST AT HOME" (in *Collected Stories*). He farms the place across the creek from the Howeses. According to his wife, Crain is afraid to plow his lower field because the Howeses' bohemian houseguests have been known to bathe naked in the creek.

Crain, Mrs.   Character in "ARTIST AT HOME" (in *Collected Stories*). She is the wife of Amos, a farmer neighbor of the Howeses.

Cranston, Lily   Character in "DOCTOR MARTINO" (in *Collected Stories*). A neat, gray spinster, she is the proprietor of the resort at Cranston's Wells, Mississippi, where Louise KING and old Dr. MARTINO meet each summer.

Crawfishford (Craw-ford)   Character in "A JUSTICE" (in *Collected Stories*). A boyhood friend of Doom and Herman BASKET, he is the Chickasaw Indian father of Sam FATHERS by a slave woman.

Crawford, Dr.   Character in GO DOWN, MOSES ("The Bear"). The camp physician at the HOKE'S STATION sawmill, he treats the dog Lion, Sam FATHERS, and Boon HOGGANBECK after the climactic battle with the bear, Old Ben.

Crenshaw, Jack   Revenue field agent in *The TOWN*. Crenshaw informs Sheriff HAMPTON of the whiskey found in the photography studio that Montgomery Ward SNOPES operates; the studio is actually a front for peep shows. The discovery leads to Montgomery Ward's arrest and imprisonment at the state penitentiary in PARCHMAN and serves the machinations of Flem SNOPES, who had planted the liquor in the first place.

"Crevasse" *(Collected Stories)*   Short story, originally an episode in the longer World War I story "VICTORY." On a spring day, a group of Scottish soldiers, including a wounded man carried by two stretcher bearers, carefully makes its way around a French battlefield under artillery and small arms fire. After crawling through shell craters, the soldiers come to a canal and refill their canteens, unaware that the water is contaminated. They eventually reach a desolate valley eerie in its silence and the absence of any bird or insect life. There they find a half-buried French rifle and many skulls. Suddenly the ground opens, plunging them into a cavern beneath. Twelve of the men are buried alive, but 14 survive to struggle out, passing the still uniformed skeletons of Senegalese troops, probably gassed as they hid there in May 1915. Finally reaching the surface, the men kneel in a circle to give thanks. The captain thinks of the longer days of the summer to come, and the wounded man wails meaninglessly.

This story first appeared in *These 13* (1931).

Crossman County   Faulkner's fictional Pontotoc County, Mississippi, east of LAFAYETTE COUNTY. The murdered timber buyer Jake MONTGOMERY in *INTRUDER IN THE DUST* is from Crossman County.

Crowe   Character in *IF I FORGET THEE, JERUSALEM* ("The Wild Palms"). He hosts the party in the NEW ORLEANS studio where Harry WILBOURNE and Charlotte RITTENMEYER first meet.

Crump, Lucas   Character in the short story "IDYLL IN THE DESERT" (in *Uncollected Stories*). A mail rider with a route in the Arizona desert, he befriends the tubercular Darrel HOWES and, later, Howes's lover, who arrives to care for him and then becomes infected herself.

Cunninghame, Sergeant   Character in "VICTORY" (in *Collected Stories*). A British soldier, he tries to save young Alec GRAY from punishment for failing to shave before parade by neglecting to take down his name. Cunninghame's officer threatens Gray with the penal battalion.

Dad   In *The MANSION*, the man who works for Brother J. C. GOODYHAY. He robs Mink SNOPES of all the money he has, $10.

Daingerfield, Miss   In *The SOUND AND THE FURY*, one of the two young women at Mrs. BLAND's picnic that Quentin COMPSON also attends before committing suicide on June 2, 1910. See also HOLMES, MISS.

Daisy   Character in *GO DOWN, MOSES* ("The Bear"). She is the wife of Uncle Ash WILEY (1), the Black cook at Major DE SPAIN's hunting camp in the BIG BOTTOM.

Damuddy   In *The SOUND AND THE FURY*, the maternal grandmother of the Compson children. "Damuddy" is the nickname they gave her. She died in 1898. Although they were not immediately informed of her death, the three-year-old Benjamin (Benjy) COMPSON, according to Quentin' COMPSON's reminiscences, knew of it and cried (p. 90). In *Faulkner at Nagano*, Faulkner explains that the idea for the novel started with the image of the children "being sent away from the house during the grandmother's funeral" because "[t]hey were too young to be told what was going on" (p. 103). Faulkner credits Candace (Caddy) COMPSON with being brave enough to climb a tree and peek through a window in order to find out what was happening (see *Faulkner in the University*, p. 31).

Dan   Character in *GO DOWN, MOSES* ("The Fire and the Hearth"). One of the African-American lotmen on the Edmonds plantation, he looks after the mules on the place. Dan helps Carothers EDMONDS search for the missing mule Alice Ben Bolt.

Dandridge, Maggie   Character in *INTRUDER IN THE DUST*, Miss Maggie is Chick (Charles, Jr.) MALLISON's grandmother. Lucas BEAUCHAMP confuses her with Crick's mother, Margaret Stevens MALLISON.

"A Dangerous Man" (*Uncollected Stories*)   A short story about Mr. BOWMAN, a slightly deaf but extremely aggressive man who defends himself and Southern womanhood unquestioningly. The story is told by an unnamed male observer who claims that women know more than do men. This narrator-observer seems attuned to the gossip of the village and to Mr. Bowman's hypervolatility. The title of the story itself is taken directly from the narrator's first description of Mr. Bowman, who, at the beginning of the story, unhesitatingly accompanies Zack STOWERS on his way to defend Mrs. Stowers's honor against two drummers (traveling salesmen). The drummers claim to be unjustly accused. Mr. Bowman, with a reputation for fierceness—he once disarmed and killed a robber in the railway express office he managed—is willing to fight both men at once, but Stowers keeps him from doing so. There is much ironic humor behind this scene, for Mr. Bowman's wife, a large, shrewish woman, secretly is carrying on an affair with WALL, an insurance salesman. For all the narrator's protestations of deference to women, he seems unaware that his tale mocks not only the highly strung Mr. Bowman but, by extension, the honor of Southern womanhood.

Written sometime around 1929, "A Dangerous Man" was published posthumously in *Uncollected Stories of William Faulkner.*

Davy   Character in "THE LEG" (in *Collected Stories*). An American, he is the friend and Oxford classmate of the Briton GEORGE (2), who is killed in World War I. Not long after, Davy has a leg amputated. In delirium, he pleads with George to confirm that the leg is dead.

Deacon   (1) *See* ROGERS, DEACON.

Deacon   (2) In *The SOUND AND THE FURY*, an elderly black man living near Harvard University who is fascinated with parades and would take part in any parade that came along. In the second chapter of the novel narrated by Quentin COMPSON, he is reported as never having missed an incoming train with students at the beginning of the school year in 40 years, and it is said that he could always detect Southerners and even identify their home state by their accents. Employing a white boy of about 15, Deacon has the students' luggage carried from the station to their rooms (p. 97). On the day of Quentin's suicide, Quentin gives Deacon a letter to deliver the next day to Shreve MACKENZIE, Quentin's Harvard roommate.

"Death Drag" (*Collected Stories*)   A short story telling of three barnstormers who come to a small Southern town to put on their aeronautical show of death-defying acts.

JOCK, the pilot, is a former World War I aviator. His two cohorts are GINSFARB, the wing walker, and JAKE (1), the driver. In the act, Ginsfarb hangs onto a rope ladder and leaps from the airplane into a moving car that Jake drives on the runway. The airplane circles close to the ground; Ginsfarb grabs the ladder and pulls himself back into the aircraft in a maneuver called the "death drag."

There is an undercurrent of distrust among the three men, who are tied together by their act. Ginsfarb, who takes most of the physical risks, feels he deserves more money. The other two are more interested in making whatever they can and then leaving town before the local authorities discover that the plane is not properly licensed.

The story is told mostly by Captain WARREN, who knew Jock at flight school in World War I. During the performance described in the story, the act ends in what appears to be tragedy, but which turns out to be almost slapstick humor. As Ginsfarb hangs from the ladder, he demands to know how much money he will get. Jake refuses to tell him. The plane circles again, and again the argument between the hanging acrobat and the driver takes place. As the plane climbs to circle around once more, Ginsfarb lets go of the ladder and falls to the ground. The onlookers are horrified, but, miraculously, Ginsfarb hits the rotted roof of an old barn, falls into a hayloft, and emerges with only a deep cut on his face and a ripped coat. The pilot lands and punches Ginsfarb. Captain Warren gives them money and sends them on their way, still arguing.

In response to a question, Faulkner explained that "Death Drag" is a story about "a human being in conflict with his environment and his time. This man who hated flying, but that was what he had to do, simply because he wanted to make a little money" (*Faulkner in the University*, p. 68). The story was first published in the January 1932 issue of *Scribner's Magazine* 91, pp. 34–42; it was reprinted with minor revisions as "Death Drag" in *Doctor Martino and Other Stories*, The PORTABLE FAULKNER, and COLLECTED STORIES OF WILLIAM FAULKNER. For more information, see *Selected Letters of William Faulkner*, pp. 205, 207, 278; *Faulkner in the University*, pp. 48, 68; and Diane Brown Jones, *A Reader's Guide to the Short Stories of William Faulkner*, pp. 204–20.

"Delta Autumn"   *See GO DOWN, MOSES.*

De Marchi   British Royal Air Force officer in *A FABLE*. He shares a hut with BURK and LEVINE.

Demont   Marthe DEMONT's husband in *A FABLE*. A Frenchman by birth, he had been in the garrison in Beirut when he and Marthe met and married. He acted as father to the young STEFAN (then approximately nine years old). He meets Marthe and her sister MARYA with a cart when they bring Stefan's body back to be buried on the family farm. His concern is for his wife, but even more for the farm, which he describes as ruined. He dies not long after Stefan is buried, after yet another artillery barrage destroys the land once again and causes Stefan's body to disappear.

Demont, Marthe (Magda)   Half sister to Corporal STEFAN in *A FABLE*. She brings her brother to France after she marries a Frenchman, DEMONT. She informs the OLD GENERAL that Stefan is his son, conceived out of wedlock in some unnamed Middle Eastern country. The result of that pregnancy, she tells the old general, was to destroy her family. Her mother left their village, taking the two girls with her, and they traveled until Christmas Eve, when Stefan was born. The mother died in childbirth, but before dying she revealed to Marthe (then called Magda) the name of Stefan's father. It was Marthe's desire to force some recognition out of the old general that induced her to go to France. Marthe buries Stefan on the farm.

de Montigny   Character in *IF I FORGET THEE, JERUSALEM* ("The Wild Palms"). He owns the tuxedo FLINT borrows so Flint can loan his own tuxedo to Harry WILBOURNE for the party at CROWE's.

De Montigny, Captain   Minor character in *A FABLE*. De Montigny interviews the relatives of Corporal STEFAN before the OLD GENERAL sees them.

de Montigny, Paul   Character in "ELLY" (in *Collected Stories*). A young man, part African American, he becomes the lover of the bored, restless JEFFERSON, MISSISSIPPI, girl ELLY, but refuses to marry her. She retaliates by causing the crash of de Montigny's car, which kills him and a second passenger, Elly's grandmother. Elly herself survives the crash.

Depre, Mrs. Virginia   *See DU PRE, VIRGINIA.*

de Spain, Major (Cassius) (1)   (sometimes De Spain) A retired major of the Confederate cavalry and, after the Civil War, a landowner and sheriff of YOKNAPATAWPHA COUNTY. In *ABSALOM, ABSALOM!*, de Spain leads a posse to Wash JONES's shack, the site of Thomas SUTPEN's murder, and in self-defense kills Wash when he lunges toward de Spain with a scythe. De Spain buys a portion of Sutpen's land (see BIG BOTTOM), which he converts into a hunting camp where he hosts annual hunting parties. In the short story "BARN BURNING" (and as retold in Book I of *The HAMLET*), de Spain charges his tenant farmer Ab SNOPES 20 bushels of corn for having ruined his wife's expensive French rug. A judge reduces the charge to 10 bushels when Ab sues, but that does not stop Ab from taking revenge by burning down de Spain's barn. (Details of the burning barn episode in the novel differ slightly from those in the short story.)

In *The TOWN*, Major de Spain's stock holdings—two of the three biggest blocks—in Jefferson's Sartoris Bank make it possible for his son Manfred DE SPAIN to become president of the bank. In *The MANSION* de Spain is mentioned several times, and in *INTRUDER IN THE DUST* he is identified as a cousin of Chick (Charles, Jr.) MALLISON's grandfather. In Faulkner's last novel, *The REIVERS*, de Spain, along with Isaac MCCASLIN and General Jason Lycurgus COMPSON II, is one of Boon HOGGANBECK's "proprietors" (p. 18). He also appears in "Lion," "The Old People," "The Bear," and "WASH," and is referred to in "Delta Autumn," "A BEAR HUNT," and "SHALL NOT PERISH."

de Spain, Major (2) The son of old Major (Cassius) DE SPAIN, he too is called Major, after his father. In the short story "SHALL NOT PERISH," this younger de Spain is married and is not to be confused with the bachelor Manfred DE SPAIN (a different character Faulkner may have loosely based on the younger Major de Spain). Like Manfred, however, he is a banker and political figure. This young Major de Spain becomes cynical and despondent after the death of his 23-year-old aviator son, killed by the Japanese during World War II. A visit from Mrs. GRIER, whose son Pete (GRIER) also died three months earlier in the war, seems to keep de Spain from committing suicide. De Spain also appears in the short story "A BEAR HUNT."

de Spain, Manfred (sometimes De Spain) One of the main characters in *The TOWN*. He is the mayor of JEFFERSON, MISSISSIPPI, the owner of a car agency, and the lover of Mrs. Eula Varner SNOPES. A graduate of West Point, de Spain served as a second lieutenant in Cuba during the Spanish-American War. In deference to his father, Major (Cassius) DE SPAIN (1), on occasion he is called Major. Because of his father's stock holdings in Jefferson's Sartoris Bank, Manfred becomes its president when Bayard SARTORIS (3) dies, and serves in this position until Flem SNOPES forces him out by divulging to Will VARNER, Eula's father, the adulterous relationship that Manfred and Eula have been carrying on for 18 years. During that time, Manfred had rewarded Flem, who supposedly was unaware of his wife's adultery, by creating for him the new position of superintendent of Jefferson's power plant; later on, Flem maneuvers to become the vice president of the bank. Throughout *The Town*, the sensitive and romantically idealistic attorney Gavin STEVENS opposes Manfred and Eula's relationship, but he is unsuccessful in ending it. Eventually, Varner forces Manfred to resign from the bank and sell his bank stock to Flem. Manfred expects to leave Jefferson with Eula, but Eula commits suicide. After Eula's funeral, de Spain, who, in the words of the narrator Charles MALLISON JR., "flouted the morality of

marriage" (*The Mansion*, p. 338), leaves Jefferson for good under the pretense of business and health (p. 339).

de Spain, Mrs. Wife of the young Major DE SPAIN (2), who has succeeded his father as the head of the hunting club. She is referred to in "A BEAR HUNT," the third in the collection of Faulkner's hunting stories, *BIG WOODS*.

de Spain, Mrs. (Lula) Wife of Major DE SPAIN (1). In "BARN BURNING," Ab SNOPES ruins her imported, expensive French rug when he intentionally treads across it in manure-covered boots. This episode is also found in Book I of the *The HAMLET*.

Despleins, Jules Minor character in *PYLON*. He is a French pilot who performs aerial acrobatics at the opening of Feinman Airport in New Valois, Franciana.

de Vitry, Soeur-Blonde Character in *GO DOWN, MOSES* ("The Old People") and other works. The New Orleans friend of the Chickasaw chief IKKEMOTUBBE, he gives the chief his sobriquet of *du homme*—Doom. The name is doubly apt because Doom attains power by using poison to frighten off the incumbent chief, MOKETUBBE.

De Vitry also appears in the short stories "RED LEAVES" and "A COURTSHIP."

Devries, Colonel In *The MANSION*, a decorated veteran of World War II. He is elected to Congress after his opponent, Clarence Eggleston SNOPES, withdraws from the race. Devries has had one leg amputated because of a war injury. He also appears in the short story "By the People," which Faulkner revised for the novel.

Dick, Nathaniel Character in *The UNVANQUISHED*. An Ohio officer in the Union army, he feigns not knowing that the fugitives Bayard SARTORIS (3) and Ringo STROTHER are hiding under Granny Rosa MILLARD's skirts when he comes to Sartoris to investigate an ambush attempt.

Later, Miss Rosa appeals to the benevolent Colonel Dick to restore her stolen silver and mules. He repays her many times over when he gets his general to sign an order turning captured livestock over to her. She exploits the order to rustle a small fortune in enemy horses and mules.

Dilazuck In *The MANSION*, Dilazuck is the owner of a livery stable.

Dilsey *See* GIBSON, DILSEY.

"Divorce in Naples" (Collected Stories) Short story that humorously relates a crisis in the homosexual "marriage" of two seamen: GEORGE, a dark Greek second cook, and CARL, a young blond mess boy. A group of shipmates, including the nameless narrator and three Italian women, are drinking the night away in a Naples cafe. They tease George and Carl about their relationship. All depart, leaving behind George, Carl, and one of the women. A flashback to Galveston, Texas, 34 days earlier describes George and Carl's arrival in Naples on board the cargo ship and reveals Carl's history.

The next day, neither of the two men returns to the ship. George has landed in jail, accused of insulting the king of Italy after he accidentally stepped on some coins bearing the monarch's portrait. He had been distraught to find that Carl and the woman, a prostitute, had slipped away from him; George blames the woman. Released from imprisonment, George returns to duty but repeatedly goes ashore to search for Carl. At last Carl comes back on his own, and for some days the two avoid each other on the ship, which is sailing back to Texas. Eventually they reconcile and return to their evening entertainment of dancing together on deck to music played on a Victrola phonograph.

This story first appeared in *These 13* (1931).

Doane's Mill, Alabama   Fictional place. It is the orphaned Lena GROVE's home village in *LIGHT IN AUGUST*. Lucas BURCH, her seducer, worked in the sawmill there, but left when Lena became pregnant. At the start of the novel, Lena Grove leaves Doane's Mill on foot for Mississippi to search for Burch, the father of the child she is carrying.

Doc (1)   In *SANCTUARY,* one of the three young men Gowan STEVENS picks up as he is driving into town after taking Temple Drake (STEVENS) back to her dorm from the dance. Though it is very late at night, Stevens is able to find bootleg liquor with their help.

Doc (2)   Character in *IF I FORGET THEE, JERUSALEM* ("The Wild Palms"). He is part owner, with MCCORD, of the Wisconsin lakeside cabin Harry WILBOURNE and Charlotte RITTENMEYER use as a refuge.

Doctor, the (Doctor Richardson)   Character in *IF I FORGET THEE, JERUSALEM* ("The Wild Palms"). He owns the Mississippi Gulf Coast cottage that Harry WILBOURNE and the dying Charlotte RITTENMEYER rent. Narrow-minded and moralistic, he suspects they are not married and deeply disapproves.

When the doctor responds to Harry's call for aid and learns Charlotte is dying of a botched abortion, his outrage overcomes his medical instincts and he seems more intent on having Harry arrested than on treating Charlotte.

"Doctor Martino" *(Collected Stories)*   Short story that recounts a struggle for the heart and soul of Louise KING by her mother, by the enigmatic Dr. Jules MAR-TINO, by her suitor Hubert JARROD, and by Louise herself. The domineering Mrs. Alvina KING sets out to loosen the mysterious hold that Dr. Martino, an invalid, exerts over Louise. Ambiguously, he is either a wise and nurturing mentor, or a parasite feeding off the life force of the young woman, or perhaps both.

The plot is revealed, for the most part, through the viewpoint of the somewhat obtuse Hubert, a wealthy Yale student. When he is attracted to Louise, her mother engineers their engagement. The main action takes place at the Mississippi spa of Cranston Wells. Louise is determined to ride a dangerous horse with the encouragement of Dr. Martino. Using trickery, Mrs. King breaks the bond between Dr. Martino and Louise. As Hubert and Louise drive off to elope, Dr. Martino quietly dies alone, seated on his accustomed bench back at the resort.

This story first appeared in *HARPER'S MAGAZINE* (November 1931) and was included in *Doctor Martino and Other Stories* (1934).

Doctor Martino and Other Stories   A collection of 14 short stories published by SMITH AND HAAS in April 1934. With the exception of "BLACK MUSIC" and "THE LEG," all of the stories had been previously published: "HONOR" (July 1930), "FOX HUNT" (September 1931), "DOCTOR MARTINO" (November 1931), "DEATH-DRAG" (January 1932), "TURN ABOUT" (March 5, 1932), "SMOKE" (April 1932), "MOUNTAIN VICTORY" (December 1932), "THERE WAS A QUEEN" (January 1933), "BEYOND" (September 1933), "ELLY" (February 1934), "PENNSYLVANIA STATION" (February 1934), and "WASH" (February 1934). (For further publication details, see Appendix I.)

Doctor Martino and Other Stories was Faulkner's second collection of stories to be published; the first was *THESE 13*. In his study of Faulkner's works, Michael MILLGATE comments that with the exception of "Wash" and "The Hound," the stories in this second collection do not show "Faulkner at his best" (*The Achievement of William Faulkner,* p. 265). As Joseph BLOTNER points out, "The reviews . . . tended to go to either extreme" (*Faulkner: A Biography,* pp. 330–31); in general, however, they were unfavorable. A few of the stories were incorporated into larger works.

Dodge, Granby   Character in *KNIGHT'S GAMBIT* ("Smoke"). A cousin of the Holland twins, he is the beneficiary of one of them, Virginius HOLLAND. In his quest to inherit the Holland property, Dodge murders old Anselm HOLLAND, the father of the twins, and hires a Memphis gangster to kill Judge DUKINFIELD. Gavin STEVENS eventually foils him.

Dollar   Character in *LIGHT IN AUGUST.* Eupheus (Doc) HINES sits in front of Dollar's store in MOTTSTOWN while his wife tries to see Joe CHRISTMAS in his jail cell.

Don Character in "MISTRAL" (*Collected Stories*) and its companion piece, "SNOW" (*Uncollected Stories*). A young American, he and the American friend who narrates the story become mixed up in a complicated situation involving a priest, a girl, and her lover in an Italian village during the season of the mistral. (The mistral is a cold, dry Mediterranean wind that sets people's nerves on edge.) In "Snow," Don is the one who first spies the funeral in the village through a powerful spyglass and later learns some of the story of the funeral from the village mayor.

"Don Giovanni" (*Uncollected Stories*)   A humorous short story about the self-deceptions of HERB, a vain middle-aged widower who, tired of celibacy and worried about his thinning hair, decides to go a-courting. He prides himself on what he thinks is thorough understanding of the psychology of women, mostly gained from years working as a buyer of women's clothing for a large department store. When visiting his friend MORRISON (who unsuccessfully tries to avoid him), Herb discusses his tactical plan for an evening out with Miss STEINBAUER. He tells Morrison that the ingredients of romantic success are boldness and indifference. Enamored of his own schemes, Herb is oblivious to Morrison's observations and cynicism. His bold plan to win over Miss Steinbauer by making her jealous fails miserably; he returns to Morrison's apartment to recount his moves and ask where he went wrong. Finally, at home, he decides that he has not been bold and cruel enough. He telephones Morrison to share this insight with him, and as he is explaining that he has to be cruel and brutal, a woman on Morrison's line sarcastically retorts: "'You tell 'em, big boy; treat 'em rough'" (*Uncollected Stories of William Faulkner*, p. 488).

Written sometime around 1925, "Don Giovanni" was posthumously published in *Uncollected Stories of William Faulkner*. Throughout the story, Faulkner incorporates obvious Freudian allusions to sexuality and suppressed emotions; he also subtly alludes to T. S. Eliot's poem "The Love Song of J. Alfred Prufrock" (references to Herb's thinning hair, for instance, echo Prufrock's self-descriptions). Faulkner often recycled elements from earlier works into later ones. His treatment of Dawson FAIRCHILD and Ernest TALLIAFERRO in *MOSQUITOES*, for example, are clearly drawn from Morrison and Herb respectively. For further information, see *Uncollected Stories of William Faulkner*, p. 705.

Doom   (1) *See* FATHERS, SAM.

Doom   (2) *See* IKKEMOTUBBE.

Doshey   In *The HAMLET*, the family name of Eustace GRIMM's first wife. She is one of the Calhoun County Dosheys. Doshey is an old family name in the area of FRENCHMAN'S BEND.

The Double Dealer   A literary magazine established in New Orleans in January 1921, it was an outlet for Faulkner's early work. The founders, Julius Weis Friend and Albert Goldstein, patterned their journal after H. L. Mencken's magazine *The Smart Set* and named it for a William Congreve play in which a character declares he can deceive people by speaking the truth. They subtitled *The Double Dealer* "A National Magazine from the South."

The editors admired the modernist revolt of James JOYCE, Ezra Pound, and others (see MODERNISM). They published the poetry of Hart Crane, John Crowe Ransome, Allen TATE, and Robert Penn WARREN and prose by Sherwood ANDERSON, Ernest HEMINGWAY, and Thornton Wilder. The magazine rarely could afford to pay contributors; Friend kept it going with money from his own pocket. *The Double Dealer* published Faulkner's poem "Portrait" in June 1922 and more of his poems, prose sketches, and critical articles over the following three years.

Dough, James   Mrs. WARDLE's nephew in *SOLDIERS' PAY*. In World War I, he flew for two years with the French air corps, sustaining wounds that crippled his arm and cost him a leg. He sits and watches the dancing at Mrs. WORTHINGTON's.

Downs, Mrs.   Character in *INTRUDER IN THE DUST*. Something of a sorceress, she tells fortunes, cures hexes, and finds missing objects.

Drake, Hubert   In *SANCTUARY*, the youngest of the four brothers of Temple Drake (STEVENS); she calls him Buddy. The four brothers are with their sister and father when Temple testifies at Lee GOODWIN's trial in JEFFERSON, MISSISSIPPI.

Drake, Judge   Temple Drake (STEVENS)'s father in *SANCTUARY*, a judge in Jackson. After Temple testifies (falsely) at Lee GOODWIN's trial in JEFFERSON, MISSISSIPPI, he takes her to Paris.

Drake, Temple   *See* STEVENS, TEMPLE DRAKE.

"Dry September" (*Collected Stories*)   Short story of how the rumor of a rape spurs a mob of Southern Whites to violence against a black man. Faulkner uses a technique that forces the readers, and characters, to try to construct what actually occurred from fragments of gossip, ambiguous hearsay, and things left unsaid.

On a stifling evening that follows 62 days of drought, the JEFFERSON, MISSISSIPPI, barber Hawkshaw (see STRIBLING, HENRY) tries to calm an agitated group by insisting that Will MAYES, the reported attacker, is a good man. This attempt proves futile and the mob, led by the war veteran Jackson MCLENDON, rushes off to take action;

Hawkshaw follows them. The viewpoint shifts to the White spinster Minnie COOPER, the apparent rape victim. Her life, empty and idle, has been one of romantic disappointments. The story implies that she has made up the story of the assault to gain attention for herself. The racists seize Mayes to drive him to an isolated spot. Hawkshaw manages to escape from the car, and walks back to town. He is passed by the returning car, this time without Mayes. That same evening, Miss Cooper walks with friends to the cinema. During the film she becomes hysterical and is taken home. John McLendon also returns home, where he treats his wife with brutality.

Many critics list this among Faulkner's finest short stories. Hans Skei calls it "classical in its tragic intensity." Joseph Reed commends the way "atmosphere, metaphor, theme, character, structure, merge in frustration, compulsion, entrapment, and isolation." John Vickery and others have linked it to an archetypal scapegoat ritual, as described by James Frazer in *The Golden Bough*.

This story first appeared in *SCRIBNER'S MAGAZINE* (January 1931) and was included in *These 13* (1931).

Dukinfield, Judge Character in *KNIGHT'S GAMBIT* ("Smoke") and *The TOWN;* also referred to in *The MANSION*. He is the executor of old Anselm HOLLAND's will. Granby DODGE has him killed to further his scheme of inheriting the Holland property. In *The Town,* Judge Dukinfield hands over to Judge STEVENS the hearing on the brass fittings that were stolen from JEFFERSON, MISSISSIPPI's, power plant. The attorney Gavin STEVENS, Judge Stevens's son, had planned to use the hearing as a legal basis to remove Mayor Manfred DE SPAIN from office.

"Dull Tale" (*Uncollected Stories*) A short story that essentially reworks the plot of the story "THE BIG SHOT." In this version, the story is told in the third-person omniscient point of view, concentrating on Dr. Gavin BLOUNT, a relatively minor character in "The Big Shot." As in the earlier story, the crux of "Dull Tale" is wangling an invitation to the annual debutante coming-out party for Miss Laverne MARTIN (referred to as Wrennie Martin in "The Big Shot"). Miss Martin's father is Dal MARTIN, a wealthy self-made contractor and political boss. He first attempts to get his daughter invited to the Nonconnah Guards ball (which is called the Chickasaw Guards ball in "The Big Shot") by offering a cash bribe to Dr. Blount, head of the Nonconnah Guards. After this ploy fails, Martin offers to build a new armory; this too is spurned. Finally Martin offers to build an art gallery for the city of Memphis and to name it in memory of Dr. Blount's grandfather, a hero of the Confederate army who was killed riding with Nathan Bedford FORREST. This enticement

garners the coveted invitation. In this short story Miss Laverne Martin attends the ball but is snubbed and treated shabbily. (In "The Big Shot," Miss Wrennie never gets to the ball; ironically, she is killed by POPEYE, a bootlegger, who runs her over while driving a carful of whiskey to Mr. Martin's house.) Dr. Blount, who had predicted this outcome, is filled with shame at the self-knowledge of "selling out." As in "The Big Shot," Dr. Blount cannot live with his guilt and kills himself.

Faulkner's reworking of the material in "Dull Tale" is a definite improvement on "The Big Shot." By using a third-person point of view and the central consciousness of Dr. Blount, Faulkner, as James Ferguson points out, "turned the work into a very characteristic study of an obsessed, solipsistic consciousness in the process of discovering some unpleasant truths about himself" (*Faulkner's Short Fiction*, p. 101). The story was written sometime around 1929 or 1930, but it was not published during Faulkner's lifetime; "Dull Tale" was published posthumously in *Uncollected Stories of William Faulkner.*

Du Pre, Virginia (Genevieve Du Pre; Virginia Sartoris) "Aunt Jenny" is the strong-minded sister of Colonel John SARTORIS in *SARTORIS, The UNVANQUISHED,* and other works. She is an admired type of traditional Southern woman, slender, with a weary expression.

Aunt Jenny had been married only two years when her South Carolinian husband was killed in a Civil War battle. She comes to her brother's home seven years a widow in 1869 and lives to see many of the male Sartorises die violently.

In *The Unvanquished,* Jenny fiercely approves of her nephew Bayard SARTORIS (2)'s decision not to take revenge on his father's killer, Ben REDMOND. She also appears as the 90-year-old wheelchair-bound Miss Jenny in the short story "THERE WAS A QUEEN" and in the novel *Sanctuary,* where she lives in her large family home with Narcissa Benbow SARTORIS, the widow of her great nephew. In *Sanctuary,* Miss Jenny does not hesitate to speak her mind or to criticize, but she can also be sympathetic and supportive, as in the case of Narcissa's brother Horace BENBOW's defense of the falsely accused Lee GOODWIN. She is referred to in *The Town* and *The MANSION,* and as Aunt Jenny Sartoris in the short story "ALL THE DEAD PILOTS," and as Mrs. Virginia Depre in *REQUIEM FOR A NUN.*

Durley Minor character in the short story "SPOTTED HORSES." When talking with Lon QUICK and WINTERBOTTOM, Durley suggests that ERNEST fetch Henry ARMSTID's wife to tell her that her husband was injured trying to catch the wild pony he supposedly bought at the auction.

Earl *See* TRIPLETT, EARL.

Ed (1) In *SOLDIERS' PAY,* a police officer. At a train station, Ed tries to arrest the returning ex-soldiers Joe GILLIGAN and Julian LOWE for being intoxicated and disorderly on the train, but Gilligan and Lowe outwit him and reboard the train.

Ed (2) Character in *MOSQUITOES.* He is the captain of Patricia MAURIER's yacht, *Nausikaa.*

Ed (3) One of two rival bootleggers in "ONCE ABOARD THE LUGGER" (II). He is apparently a drug user ("hophead") and dangerous.

Ed (4) Character in *The REIVERS.* He is the judge of the horse race between Lightning (Coppermine) and Acheron.

Edmonds, Alice Character in *GO DOWN, MOSES* ("The Bear"). She is the wife of McCaslin EDMONDS, who succeeds to ownership of the McCaslin plantation. She teaches Sophonsiba BEAUCHAMP (2), the daughter of the slaves Tomey's Turl and Tennie BEAUCHAMP, to read and to write a little.

Edmonds, Carothers (Roth) Character in *GO DOWN, MOSES* ("The Fire in the Hearth," "Pantaloon in Black," "Delta Autumn," "Go Down, Moses") and other works. The grandson of McCaslin EDMONDS and the son of Zack, he inherits the old McCaslin plantation and supports his cousin Isaac MCCASLIN, the true heir who long ago relinquished his claim to the place.

In "The Fire and the Hearth," Edmonds is the often exasperated landlord of Lucas BEAUCHAMP and George WILKINS. In "Delta Autumn," he fathers a child with his mistress, a young Northern schoolteacher, then leaves her. Unknown to him, she is part black and is the great-great-great granddaughter of old Carothers.

The harsh, cynical Edmonds's private code prohibits marriage, his mistress understands this. All the same, she goes with their infant son to the hunting camp in the Delta in search of him. Expecting her, he leaves the camp and asks his elderly kinsman Isaac McCaslin (Uncle Ike) to offer her a thick sheaf of banknotes and invite her to leave.

In "Go Down, Moses," he evicts Lucas and Molly (Mollie) BEAUCHAMP's grandson Samuel BEAUCHAMP for robbing the plantation commissary.

Edmonds is Lucas's landlord and an old friend of Gavin STEVENS in *INTRUDER IN THE DUST.* He is also an offstage character in *The TOWN,* where he signs a note to help Lucius HOGGANBECK buy a Model-T Ford.

Edmonds, Louisa (Cousin Louisa) Character in *The REIVERS.* She is the wife of Zachary EDMONDS, the incumbent on the old McCaslin plantation in 1905. Lucius PRIEST (Loosh) is supposed to stay with the Edmondses when his parents travel to Bay St. Louis for the funeral of Grandfather LESSEP. Instead, Lucius goes off to MEMPHIS with Boon HOGGANBECK and Ned MCCASLIN.

Edmonds, McCaslin (Cass) Character in *GO DOWN, MOSES.* As the nine-year-old narrator of "Was," the first story in the novel, set in the years before the Civil War, he accompanies his great uncle Theophilus MCCASLIN (Uncle Buck) to the Beauchamp place a half-day's ride distant and is fascinated by Miss Sophonsiba BEAUCHAMP's roan tooth.

In "The Old People," Cass is presented as the cousin of Uncle Buck's son Isaac MCCASLIN. Cass traces Sam FATHERS's complicated racial heritage for Ike, allows Sam to go off and live permanently in Major DE SPAIN's hunting camp, and takes Ike on his first hunting trip into the big woods.

In "The Fire and the Hearth," Cass, a descendant of the McCaslins in the female line, takes control of the McCaslin estate, seizing it from the true heir (Ike). Faulkner significantly revises this arrangement in "The Bear." In that story, Ike rejects his patrimony on his 21st birthday and forces the reluctant Cass to accept it. Ike struggles to explain his complex, sophisticated, and even mystical notions of responsibility to the land and his belief that it carries a curse.

McCaslin Edmonds also appears in *The TOWN, The REIVERS,* and the short story "A BEAR HUNT." In *The Reivers,* Faulkner retells the story of Ike McCaslin abdicating as owner of the McCaslin estate in favor of Edmonds.

Edmonds, Robb Character in "Race at Morning" (in *BIG WOODS*). A member of an old YOKNAPATAWPHA COUNTY family, he joins the November deer hunt.

Edmonds, Roth *See* EDMONDS, CAROTHERS.

Edmonds, Zachary (Zack; Cousin Zack) Character in *GO DOWN, MOSES* ("The Fire and the Hearth") and *The REIVERS*. In *Go Down, Moses,* he is the son of McCaslin EDMONDS and the landlord of Lucas BEAUCHAMP. Lucas's wife Molly nurses Edmonds's infant son along with her own boy, Henry BEAUCHAMP.

Molly stays on at the Edmonds place for nearly six months. Her husband becomes jealous, perhaps suspecting a sexual involvement with Zack. Lucas fetches Molly home, then confronts Zack in his bedroom at dawn, first with a knife, then with Zack's pistol. The pistol misfires.

In *The Reivers,* Lucius PRIEST (Loosh) is supposed to stay with Cousin Zack and his wife when his parents travel to Bay St. Louis in May 1905 for the funeral of Grandfather LESSEP.

Elly (Ailanthia) Character in "ELLY" (in *Collected Stories.*) Bored and restless, she drops her fiancé, an assistant bank cashier in JEFFERSON, MISSISSIPPI, for Paul DE MONTIGNY. When de Montigny refuses to marry her, she causes the car crash that kills him and her disapproving grandmother, whom she detests.

"Elly" (Collected Stories) Short story that tracks an obsession in the consciousness of a self-centered young woman to its violent conclusion. The daughter of a respectable family in JEFFERSON, MISSISSIPPI, ELLY fluctuates between boredom with the monotony of her small-town existence, despair over her future, and rebellion against the Southern way of life personified by her apparently malevolent grandmother.

After flirting with numerous beaus, Elly fixates on and pursues Paul DE MONTIGNY, a young man of black ancestry who insists he will never marry her. She uses Paul to taunt her grandmother. Eventually Elly becomes engaged to PHILIP, a suitable young man with a future in banking. When her mother asks Elly to go with Philip to bring back her grandmother for the wedding, Elly instead decides to make the trip with Paul, and Philip agrees to the substitution. Stopping on the drive to Mills City, Elly and Paul sexually consummate their relationship, but Paul still refuses to marry her. Over her grandmother's strong opposition, Paul spends the night in Elly's uncle's house before their return to Jefferson the next day. On the drive back, Elly grabs the steering wheel and sends the car over a precipice. She is thrown free, while Paul and her grandmother are killed.

The first version of "Elly," titled "Selvage" or "Salvage," was a revision of a story originally written by Faulkner's wife, (Lida) Estelle Oldham FAULKNER. Faulkner biographer Frederick Karl believes it is loosely based on the triangle between Faulkner, Estelle, and her first husband. Many scholars compare Elly's frustrated and willful char-

acter to such other Faulkner women as Emily GRIERSON, Candace (Caddy) COMPSON, Temple Drake STEVENS, and Minnie COOPER. Edmond Volpe considers the story a "brilliantly wrought" study of a woman "torn by irreconcilable forces unravelling into madness."

"Elly" first appeared in *Story* (February 1934) and was included in *Doctor Martino and Other Stories* (1934).

Elma, Miss In *The TOWN,* she is Sheriff HAMPTON's office deputy and the previous sheriff's widow.

Elmer The title of an unfinished novel Faulkner began to write while in Paris in 1925. A typescript was published posthumously in *Mississippi Quarterly* 36 (summer 1983), pp. 343–447, and later, in a limited edition, edited by Dianne L. Cox with a foreword by James B. Meriwether, by Seajay Press of Northport, Alabama, in 1983. Faulkner mentioned putting the novel aside in a September 1925 letter to his mother. Although Faulkner abandoned the work, he appropriated ideas from it in *MOSQUITOES, IF I FORGET THEE, JERUSALEM* ("The Wild Palms"), and *The HAMLET;* in 1935, this unfinished work provided the basis of the short story "A PORTRAIT OF ELMER" (posthumously published in *Uncollected Stories of William Faulkner,* pp. 610–41).

For more information, see *Selected Letters of William Faulkner,* pp. 13, 16, 17, 20, 31, 32, and 63; Thomas L. McHaney, "The Elmer Papers: Faulkner's Comic Portraits of the Artist" in *Mississippi Quarterly* 26 (summer 1973), pp. 281–311, or in *A Faulkner Miscellany,* edited by James B. Meriwether (Jackson: University Press of Mississippi, 1974), pp. 37–69; Cleanth Brooks, *William Faulkner: Toward Yoknapatawpha and Beyond* (Baton Rouge: Louisiana State University Press, 1990), pp. 100–28; and *Uncollected Stories of William Faulkner,* p. 710.

Elnora Character in *SARTORIS*. She is the African-American daughter of Simon STROTHER and a servant in the home of old Bayard SARTORIS. Faulkner sometimes styles her "Elnore." She also appears in the short stories "ALL THE DEAD PILOTS," in which she knits socks for Johnny SARTORIS, and "THERE WAS A QUEEN," in which she is presented as Colonel John SARTORIS's daughter by a slave.

Emmeline Character in "THAT WILL BE FINE" (in *Collected Stories*). She nurses Aunt LOUISA's baby, and complains of being asked to take on extra work at Christmas.

Emmy The servant at Rector MAHON's house in *SOLDIERS' PAY*. Emmy had been a childhood companion of the rector's son, Donald MAHON. Together, Emmy and Donald, when they were young, dammed up the creek to make a swimming hole, where they would innocently swim together on hot afternoons and then nap on an old blanket. When Emmy's drunken father discovers what they are doing, he forbids her from seeing Donald again. One night, however, when she is 16 and Donald is 19, Donald comes for her and they spend the night together swimming and making love. Although Donald is engaged to Cecily SAUNDERS at the time, Emmy believes that this night proves that he loves Emmy more. Soon after, Emmy leaves her home and lives with a seamstress, Mrs. MILLER. Rector Mahon finds her there and takes her into his home while Donald is overseas during World War I. When the wounded Donald returns, he does not recognize Emmy, who is heartbroken by his amnesia. Emmy is seduced by Januarius JONES after Donald dies in the last chapter of *Soldiers' Pay*.

Ephraim   Character in *INTRUDER IN THE DUST*. The father of PARALEE, the Mallisons' cook, he uses his extrasensory powers to find a ring belonging to Maggie MALLISON. Something of a philosopher, Ephraim tells Charles (Chick) MALLISON, Maggie's son, not to bother with men when he needs something done "outside the common run," but to apply to women and children instead.

Ephum   Character in *The REIVERS*. A black employee of Miss BALLENBAUGH, he accepts Boon HOGGANBECK's invitation for a ride in the Priest car. Because the Ballenbaugh inn is segregated, Ned MCCASLIN spends the night at Ephum's place.

Ernest   Minor character in the novel fragment *FATHER ABRAHAM* and in "SPOTTED HORSES," the short story Faulkner derived from it. Ernest fetches Mrs. ARMSTID when her husband injures himself trying to catch the wild pony he thought he bought at the auction in FRENCHMAN'S BEND.

Ernest, Mr.   Character in "RACE AT MORNING" (in *BIG WOODS*). A farmer, he is the adoptive father of the 12-year-old narrator, whose parents have abandoned him. During the November hunt, Ernest intentionally allows a prize buck to escape unharmed so the hunters can stalk it the next year.

Ernie   Character in "FOX HUNT" (in *Collected Stories*). Harrison BLAIR's valet and bodyguard, he helps Steve GAWTREY seduce Blair's neglected wife.

"An Error in Chemistry"   *See KNIGHT'S GAMBIT.*

Erskine, Albert (unknown)   A Tennessean, Erskine edited the *Southern Review* with Robert Penn WARREN and Cleanth BROOKS before moving on to RANDOM HOUSE in 1947.

Erskine helped Saxe COMMINS edit the novel *INTRUDER IN THE DUST*, and later worked with Commins to put together the hefty volume of short fiction published as *The Collected Stories of William Faulkner* (1950).

After Commins's death, Erskine handled the editing of *The MANSION*, the third novel in the SNOPES TRILOGY. He was troubled, as Commins had been, by the discrepancies among *The HAMLET, The TOWN*, and *The Mansion*.

Faulkner made no objection to Erskine's efforts to sort out the details, although he did offer this observation: "What I am trying to say is, the essential truth of these people and their doings is the thing; the facts are not too important." (*Selected Letters*, p. 422).

Essays, Speeches, and Public Lectures by William Faulkner
Collection of Faulkner's articles, speeches, forewords, book reviews, and public lectures, edited by James B. MERIWETHER. The collection was published by RANDOM HOUSE in 1966. In addition to several public letters on various topics, a few book reviews (including one of Ernest HEMINGWAY's *The Old Man and the Sea*), two forewords, and an introduction (including the introduction to The Modern Library edition of *SANCTUARY* and the foreword to *The FAULKNER READER*), the collection contains essays on various writers such as Sherwood ANDERSON and Albert CAMUS, on Faulkner's impressions of Japan (also published in *FAULKNER AT NAGANO*) and of New England, and on social issues such as race relations. The speeches include his eulogy for Caroline BARR and his NOBEL PRIZE acceptance speech. Not included in the collection are a few unpublished public letters, early reviews, and essays Faulkner wrote when he was a student at the UNIVERSITY OF MISSISSIPPI and when he was a fledgling poet.

Ethel   Character in "A PORTRAIT OF ELMER" in (*Uncollected Stories*). One of Elmer HODGE's Houston girlfriends, she has a baby by the 18-year-old Elmer but refuses to marry him.

Eula   *See SNOPES, EULA VARNER.*

Eunice   Character in *SARTORIS*. She is the Benbows' black cook.

"Evangeline" (*Uncollected Stories*)   Short story written in 1931. It introduced the doomed Sutpen family of YOKNAPATAWPHA COUNTY and formed the basis for Faulkner's novel *ABSALOM, ABSALOM!* (1936). Rejected by two magazines, "Evangeline" remained unpublished until 1979, when the editor and biographer Joseph BLOTNER included it in *Uncollected Stories of William Faulkner*.

Faulkner wrote "Evangeline" during the intense burst of creativity that produced *The SOUND AND THE FURY* (1929) and *AS I LAY DYING* (1930). He finished the story in late June or early July, just six weeks or so before he began work on another of his major novels, *LIGHT IN AUGUST* (1932). In quick succession, the *Saturday Evening Post* and *Women's Home Companion* turned it down.

As Faulkner's biographer Frederick Karl notes, the title alludes to Henry Wadsworth Longfellow's poem about two lovers separated by events beyond their control. In Faulkner's telling, miscegenation, bigamy, and murder keep Judith SUTPEN and her suitor Charles BON apart.

An unnamed narrator tells the story. Bon is the close friend of Henry SUTPEN, Judith's brother. When Henry accompanies Bon to his home in NEW ORLEANS just before the outbreak of the Civil War, he discovers secrets about his friend that make it impossible, in his view, for Bon to marry his sister. Henry returns home alone and orders Judith to break off the engagement, although he will not explain the reasons for his demand. Bon and Judith marry over his objection. When the war begins, Henry and Bon join the Confederate army and are away for four years. With the South's surrender, Henry returns home with Bon's corpse—he has been killed, Henry announces, by the "last shot of the war."

Old Colonel SUTPEN, Henry and Judith's father, dies in 1870. Judith dies about 1885, and her ghost is said to haunt the old house. The narrator goes out to the Sutpen place to try to unravel the mystery, and an old black servant named Raby takes him upstairs to a dark, sealed room. When Raby lights a candle, the narrator sees the dying Henry lying in a dirty bed. When they return downstairs, Raby tells the narrator that Bon had been married to another woman in New Orleans; she also announces that Henry is her brother. But she refuses to reveal the rest of the story.

The narrator discovers that Henry had killed Bon with "the last shot of the war." He learns this final detail, however, only after Raby burns down the house with herself and Henry inside. A photo of Bon's New Orleans wife survives inside a fire-blackened metal case. Inspecting it, the narrator sees "all the ineradicable and tragic stamp of negro blood"—to Henry Sutpen, something worse than bigamy, and so intolerable that he saw no choice but to kill Bon for marrying his sister.

Faulkner extensively reworked "Evangeline" for *Absalom, Absalom!* The novel replaces the flip, slangy tone of the nameless narrator and his friend Don with Quentin COMPSON and Shrevlin MCCANNON. Faulkner also adds the element of incest to the novel: Charles Bon is Thomas SUTPEN's son, and thus half brother to Judith and Henry.

Ewell, Bryan   Character in *KNIGHT'S GAMBIT* ("An Error in Chemistry"). One of Sheriff Hub HAMPTON's deputies, he is sent to watch Wesley PRITCHEL, Joel FLINT's father-in-law.

Ewell, Walter   Character in *GO DOWN, MOSES* ("The Old People," "The Bear," "Delta Autumn") and other works.

A member of the annual hunting parties that gather at Major DE SPAIN's camp in the TALLAHATCHIE RIVER valley, he is a crack shot—his rifle never misses.

Ewell also appears in *The MANSION, The REIVERS,* and the short stories "A BEAR HUNT" and "RACE AT MORNING."

In *The Reivers,* Ewell retells how Boon HOGGANBECK, a notoriously bad marksman, fired at a buck five times from 10 paces and missed each time.

Ewing, Ira, Jr.   Character in "GOLDEN LAND" (in *Collected Stories*). He runs away from his family's bleak Nebraska farm at 14, jumps a freight train that carries him to California, and becomes a successful real estate dealer in Beverly Hills. But he and his wife are at daggers drawn, his children are awful, and he drinks to escape the wreckage of his life.

Ewing has a mistress who seems to love him. He visits his widowed mother every day, but fails to keep the tragedy of his family life from her.

Ewing, Ira, Sr.   Character in "GOLDEN LAND" (in *Collected Stories*). A Nebraska pioneer, a wheat farmer and a part-time preacher, he tries to teach his son Ira EWING Jr., "something about fortitude." Ewing's widow comes to live with Ira Jr. in Beverly Hills.

Ewing, Mitch   Character in "HAIR" (in *Collected Stories*). He is the freight agent at the depot in JEFFERSON, MISSISSIPPI.

Ewing, Samantha   (1) Character in "GOLDEN LAND" (in *Collected Stories*). The widowed mother of Ira EWING Jr., the Beverly Hills real estate tycoon, she is alone and homesick for Nebraska, although she lives without material want in Glendale, California, in the former home of her son and his family.

Because Ira handles all her finances, Mrs. Ewing cannot put aside money for train fare back to Nebraska and realizes she is trapped in California, doomed to live there to the end of her days. Ira tries to keep his children's troubles from her, but she learns the sorry details from her gardener, KAZIMURA.

Ewing, Samantha   (2) Character in "GOLDEN LAND" (in *Collected Stories*). The daughter of Ira EWING Jr., she is a promiscuous would-be starlet who lands extra parts under the name of April Lalear. Samantha turns up in the newspapers as one of three people charged in a case involving sex orgies.

Ewing, Voyd   Character in "GOLDEN LAND" (in *Collected Stories*). The effeminate son of Ira EWING Jr., he favors women's underwear. Voyd and his father detest each other. Ira discovers the underwear when he puts the youth to bed drunk, and he beats him even though he is unconscious.

A Fable Faulkner's 16th novel, published on August 2, 1954, by RANDOM HOUSE. Faulkner, who considered it to be his most significant work, spent about nine years writing the novel and incorporated a revision of NOTES ON A HORSETHIEF, which was published by The Levee Press, Greenville, Mississippi, in 1951. During this time he also wrote and published other works including INTRUDER IN THE DUST and REQUIEM FOR A NUN. In 1955, *A Fable* received both the Pulitzer Prize for Fiction and the National Book Award.

The title of *A Fable* itself offers the key to its understanding and lends perspective to the reader. Although it contains many passages of powerful, and even horrifying, realism, the novel is an intended fable or parable with obvious tall-tale elements, but the blending of the fabulous and realistic, according to Cleanth BROOKS, is unsuccessful because it is not always "clear where the fabulous leaves off and the realistic begins" (*William Faulkner: Toward Yoknapatawpha and Beyond*, Baton Rouge: Louisiana State University Press, 1990, pp. 230–31).

The plot of the novel is fairly simple. Sometime in the latter half of 1918, in the fifth year of trench warfare in France during World War I, a French regiment, for reasons that are never made particularly clear, is ordered to attack a small hill held by the Germans. The commanding officer is certain the attack will fail. Instead, it never takes place: The regiment mutinies and simply, completely, adamantly refuses to leave its trenches to make any attack whatsoever. Major General Charles GRAGNON, the division commander who passed along the order to attack despite knowing it would be disastrous, orders the arrest of the entire regiment and demands that every man in it be shot for cowardice or disobedience to orders. He knows that his career is also over, and he is fearful that the war will be lost as well. For an anxious hour, while the mutinous regiment is placed under arrest, disarmed, and withdrawn, General Gragnon expects a massive German counterattack in this sector. But the Germans do not take advantage of the weakness in the French line. Indeed, peace, or rather peacefulness, breaks out along the whole front, and within hours of the troops' refusal to attack, all the French troops are disengaged. They do not pull back from their trenches anywhere, but they stop firing, stop probing, stop trying to kill the Germans. The British and American troops flanking the French line also

stand down, and the Germans, mysteriously, do not attack. They too become inactive, and an unintended armistice becomes general.

As the incident is investigated, it is discovered that the mutiny was incited or inspired by 13 soldiers in the French Army, although four of them, including their leader, Corporal STEFAN, whose last name is never given, are not French nationals. (Throughout the novel, Stefan is mostly referred to simply as "the Corporal.") These soldiers have advocated peace or a kind of military civil disobedience for four years up and down the lines and have traveled as a unit to visit with the Americans and British as well as the French and even, it would seem, with the Germans. The Corporal's message is simple: "Thou shalt not kill."

The French higher command imprisons the regiment and segregates the ringleaders. The Corporal is brought before the French commander-in-chief (called the OLD GENERAL) in a scene that Cleanth BROOKS compares to the meeting of the Grand Inquisitor and Christ in Dostoyevski's novel *The Brothers Karamazov* (see *William Faulkner: Toward Yoknapatawpha and Beyond*, pp. 231–32). The old marshal recognizes the Corporal as his own son, but he is unable to tempt him from his mission of peace. In the end, the old marshal is compelled to order the execution of the Corporal and of Major General Gragnon (for whose sake the killing is made to appear the result of an enemy bullet on the field of honorable battle).

This novel is complex and to some critics a masterpiece. In *Perspectives U. S. A.* (No. 10, 1955), Delmore Schwartz in his review of the novel called it "a unique fulfilment of Faulkner's genius" (p. 127). But other reviews were negative, and many critics thought that Faulkner's ambitions were too lofty. The novel uses techniques of religious allegory and employs numerous religious symbols. There are obvious parallels between the figure of the Corporal and Christ. For example, the reader immediately notes that the Corporal has 12 disciples. The Corporal is followed also by three women, one named Marthe (also called Magda), one Marya, and one unnamed prostitute from Marseilles—like the Martha, Mary, and Mary Magdalene of the Gospels. When the Corporal is brought before the old marshal, he is tempted, as Jesus was during his 40 days in the desert. Further, evidence is presented that the Corporal

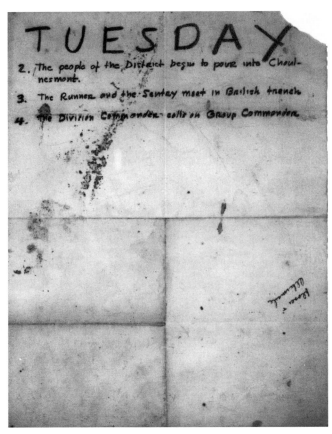

William Faulkner's draft of the "Tuesday" outline of the novel
A Fable, *c. 1952. Faulkner wrote these notes and others on his*
study wall in his home at Rowan Oak. (Brodsky Collection,
Center for Faulkner Studies, Southeast Missouri State University)

has died and been buried at least three times during
the war. POLCHEK, one of the Corporal's disciples and a
Judas figure, betrays him; another called Pierre BOUC,
like Peter, denies knowing him at all. In Corporal Stefan's death scene, Faulkner continues obvious Christ
parallels: the Corporal is 33 when he is shot to death;
he is executed—standing tied to a fence post—between
the two thieves, LAPIN and CASSE-TÊTE ("Horse"); when
he falls dead into a shallow trench, a coil of barbed wire
forms a crown (of thorns) about his head; his body is
given to his wife (a prostitute) and sisters who bury it in
a cavelike sepulcher on the family farm; and the body
mysteriously disappears from the grave during an
artillery barrage. All of this action takes place within a
week. The order to attack is given on Monday; by 3 in
the afternoon on Tuesday, the fighting has ceased; by
Wednesday, Corporal Stefan is caught (after Polchek
betrays him) and put in prison; and by Friday, the corporal is executed.

Faulkner, also, much like Mark Twain, uses elements
of the American tall tale in *A Fable*. A subplot of the
novel concerns a British soldier to whom all the other

men of his regiment are indebted. Before the war, this
soldier had been a groom for a trainer of a race horse.
Through various outrageously unbelievable events, the
soldier and a black stable worker (see SUTTERFIELD,
Rev. Toby) contrive to steal an injured race horse and
run it at small tracks throughout America. The horse is
supposedly a miracle horse, capable of winning races
while running on only three good legs, but it can also
be seen as a metaphor, which, according to Schwartz,
Faulkner adeptly incorporates into his overall concerns
of the novel: "The horse is . . . the cause of belief and
nobility in other human beings just as the illiterate corporal is, an identification which does not become
explicit until, after much mystery, the corporal's true
nature is made clear" ("Faulkner's 'A Fable,'" *Perspectives U. S. A.,* p. 130).

Another character whose story is rife with hyperbole is
the RUNNER, a British soldier who had risen from the
ranks to become an officer. Then after about seven
months, he tried unsuccessfully to resign his commission,
so while on leave the runner makes such a public spectacle of himself that he is broken back into the ranks. It is
the runner who notices a scheme that resembles a tall
tale. In order to arrange a secret parley between the
Allies and a German general, the Allies provide blank
ammunition for hundreds of antiaircraft guns and for a
flight of three SE5 fighter planes. The German general
flies to the meeting though this "safe" corridor to discuss
with his counterparts how to get the fighting to begin
again—how, in short, to undo the Corporal's work.

In a final scene entitled "Tomorrow" (a title with
apocalyptic overtones anticipating the future), one last
tall tale or fable is retold. After the end of the war, a
squad of 12 soldiers, commanded by LANDRY, a fussy
sergeant, is sent to a battered fortress in the lines
around Verdun. Their orders are to find and bring
back to Paris a body of a French soldier unidentified
and unidentifiable by name, regiment, or rank to be
buried with honor in the Tomb of the Unknown Soldier with a perpetual flame. The soldiers complete the
first part of their mission, but the body they find they
sell to a woman who claims that the soldier is her son.
Needing another body to fill the coffin they carry, the
soldiers, led by PICKLOCK, use the watch they stole from
a dead German officer to buy a replacement body
found by a farmer in the nearby village of Vienne-la-
pucelle. This replacement is the Corporal, unwittingly
or miraculously disinterred to become the honored
Unknown Soldier, underscoring the anonymity of war.

This scene demonstrates Faulkner's use of irony,
sometimes heavy-handed irony, in *A Fable*. Faulkner
began writing the novel in December 1944, during the
last winter of World War II, and completed it in November 1953, just after the end of the Korean conflict. In
1950 Faulkner was awarded the NOBEL PRIZE IN LITERA-
TURE, and in his acceptance speech expressed some of

his beliefs about humanity and the role of the novelist. *A Fable* reflects these beliefs and concerns, as Michael MILLGATE explains in his study of Faulkner: "the whole novel is in the nature of a gloss upon this most famous of Faulkner's public statements. It is thus a 'committed' novel, a book with a message. . . ." (*William Faulkner*, New York: Grove Press, 1961, p. 99). The novel shows the deep disgust Faulkner felt toward war as a solution to human struggles and as act of statecraft. It also shows his mistrust of political and military leaders and displays a type of pacifism reminiscent of Leo Tolstoy's.

In his review of *A Fable*, Malcolm COWLEY observed that the novel "is based on a contradiction between feeling and logic. The feeling of the novel is deeply pacifist. . . . Faulkner's logic, on the other hand, says that some wars are right, or at least necessary, and that the men who refuse to have any part in them are fools. If the corporal is a fool, he cannot be truly Christlike" ("Faulkner's Powerful New Novel: Biblical Overtones, Daring Symbols," *New York Herald Tribune Books*, August 1, 1954, p. 8).

For more information, see *Faulkner at Nagano*, pp. 7, 9, 23, 46–47, 50–51, 129–30, 159–60; *Faulkner in the University*, pp. 25–26, 27, 51–52, 62–63, 85–86; and *Selected Letters of William Faulkner*. Faulkner recorded a portion of the novel for Caedmon (TC–1035).

Fadiman, Clifton (1904–1999)   Literary critic and sometimes unfriendly reviewer of Faulkner's work. Fadiman had qualified praise for Faulkner's early fiction, and with the publication of *SANCTUARY* in 1931 he placed Faulkner in the front rank of younger American novelists.

In a famously scathing review in the *New Yorker* in 1936, he called *ABSALOM, ABSALOM!* "the most consistently boring novel by a reputable writer to come my way during the last decade."

Four years later, Fadiman's notice of *The HAMLET*, the first of the Snopes novels, was even nastier. "All in the line of duty," he wrote in the *New Yorker*, "I have spent part of this week weaving through 'The Hamlet.' From the intense murk of its sentences I emerge, somewhat shaken, to report that the author apparently continues to enjoy as lively a case of the 'orrors as you are apt to find outside a Keeley-cure hostelry."

Fadiman drew the assignment of presenting Faulkner with his second National Book Award, for *A FABLE*, in 1954.

Fairchild, Dawson   Character in *MOSQUITOES*. A novelist with a taste for mischief, Fairchild is the malicious guiding spirit of the yachting party aboard the *Nausikaa*. Though he resembles a "benevolent walrus," Ernest TALLIAFERRO for some reason regards him as an authority on love; Fairchild prankishly urges the inexperienced Talliaferro to be forceful with women. Talliaferro tries out the new attitude, but women are not impressed.

Falkner/Faulkner   Faulkner created an elaborate new biography for his enlistment in the Royal Air Force in June 1918. Among the fictional details he concocted for Canadian recruiters in New York City was a *u* added to the family name. From then on, the world knew him as William Faulkner. His brother Dean (who died in 1935) followed suit, also becoming a Faulkner. His other brothers retained the Falkner spelling.

Some scholars regard the name change, though slight, as not only an expression of independence on Faulkner's part but also as an act of hostility toward his family, a way of distancing himself from a family in decline.

Falkner, John Wesley Thompson (1848–1922)   Faulkner's paternal grandfather, a lawyer, banker, and politician. The son of William Clark FALKNER, he graduated from the UNIVERSITY OF MISSISSIPPI and gained admission to the state bar in 1869. He established what would soon become a successful law practice in RIPLEY, MISSISSIPPI, and married Sallie McAlpine Murry (FALKNER), the daughter of a leading Tippah County family. They raised three children, Murry Cuthbert FALKNER (born 1870), Mary Holland Falkner WILKINS (born 1872) and John Wesley Thompson FALKNER Jr. (born 1882).

Known as the Young Colonel, Falkner moved his family from Ripley to OXFORD, MISSISSIPPI, 40 miles to the southeast, in late 1885, and there went into practice with the prominent, politically connected lawyer Charles Bowen Howry. While he immersed himself in business and Democratic party politics, Sallie Murry devoted her considerable energies to Women's Christian Temperance Union activities and the Women's Book Club of Oxford. In 1886 Falkner won appointment as deputy U.S. attorney for the Northern District of Mississippi.

Friends talked him out of revenging himself on Richard THURMOND for the 1889 murder of his father. His legal and political affairs continued to prosper into the 1890s. In 1895 the voters of Lafayette County sent him to the state senate, and the governor appointed him to the University of Mississippi board of trustees. He sold the "family" railroad, the GULF & CHICAGO RAILROAD, in 1902 to concentrate his efforts on law and politics. In 1910, he founded the First National Bank of Oxford, the third of the town's three banks, and a profitable business almost from the start.

A legendary drinker, Falkner, at his wife's insistence, submitted to periodic cures at the KEELEY INSTITUTE of MEMPHIS—the foundation of a family tradition that would pass through his son to his novelist grandson. He took leave of his business affairs once or twice a year to join hunting expeditions for bear, deer, and lesser game in the near-wilderness of the MISSISSIPPI DELTA.

William Faulkner saw a lot of the Young Colonel, for his home after 1900, known as "The Big Place," was the center of family activity. The novelist used elements of his grandfather's experience to form the fictional character of Bayard SARTORIS (3), Colonel John SARTORIS's son. In *The UNVANQUISHED,* Bayard is an adolescent witness to episodes of the Civil War in north Mississippi; in *SARTORIS* and *FLAGS IN THE DUST,* he is an irascible, imposing old banker, much like the patriarchal figure young Billy Falkner had known.

Sallie Murry Falkner died in 1906. Her husband missed her terribly; his grandsons recalled seeing him seated in the Square, tracing her name in the air with his walking stick. The Young Colonel married Mary Kennedy, the widow of a ship's cabinetmaker, in San Jose, California, in 1912. They separated and she returned to California after less than a year of married life.

Younger stockholders forced the increasingly deaf, irascible, and forgetful Falkner out of the First National Bank early in 1920. He died of heart failure in March 1922, the last of Faulkner's grandparents to go.

Falkner, John Wesley Thompson, Jr. (1882–1962) Faulkner's uncle. The ambitious and capable youngest child of John Wesley Thompson and Sallie Murry FALKNER, he studied law at the UNIVERSITY OF MISSISSIPPI, became a partner in a grocery, managed the family-owned Opera House in OXFORD, MISSISSIPPI, and eventually joined the law, banking, and Democratic Party political enterprises of his father.

The family knew him as "John, honey." Faulkner spent considerable time with Judge Falkner in the 1920s, acting as his chauffeur in at least two of his unsuccessful campaigns for political office. The experience provided Faulkner with a fund of anecdotes, including material for the wild ponies episode in book 4 of *The HAMLET.*

Though unable to win political office for himself, John Falkner Jr. proved a talented political organizer and campaign manager. In business as in politics, he succeeded in most of what he attempted, in contrast to his feckless older brother, Murry Cuthbert FALKNER, the novelist's father.

Uncle John had scant regard for Faulkner as a young man, regarding him as the black sheep of the family.

Falkner, John Wesley Thompson III ("Johncy") (1901–1963) Faulkner's younger brother, the third of four Falkner children, known as Johncy. He studied engineering at the UNIVERSITY OF MISSISSIPPI and married his childhood sweetheart, Lucille (Dolly) Ramey. They had two children, James (Jimmy) Murry FAULKNER (born 1923), a favorite of his novelist uncle, and Murry Cuthbert II (born 1928), known as Chooky.

In the early 1930s, Johncy took flying lessons from an aviator and preacher whose airplane carried the legend "Jesus Saves" on the fuselage. He later worked as a manager at a MEMPHIS airport and oversaw a LAFAYETTE COUNTY, MISSISSIPPI, farm Faulkner owned.

Clever and imaginative, he was so good at telling stories to his children that he decided to write them down for sale to the magazines. Faulkner grudgingly supplied editorial introductions, but the SATURDAY EVENING POST rejected the first two stories Johncy sent in.

Johncy Falkner's *My Brother Bill: An Affectionate Memoir* was published in 1963. For the book, Johncy added a *u* to his last name.

Falkner, Maud Butler (1871–1906) Faulkner's proud, determined, iron-willed mother. The daughter of Charles and Lelia Swift BUTLER, she grew up in straitened circumstances in OXFORD, MISSISSIPPI. Her mother was a gifted amateur painter, and clever with her hands. Her father, the town marshal for a dozen years, vanished with town funds late in 1887, leaving a penniless family behind.

Maud Butler overcame poverty and distress to graduate from the Mississippi Women's College. She held a secretarial job to support herself and her mother. After a short courtship, she married Murry Cuthbert FALKNER, the son of the prominent Oxford lawyer John Wesley Thompson FALKNER and brother of her friend Mary Holland Falkner WILKINS, on November 7, 1896. The newlyweds settled in a plain one-story clapboard house at Cleveland and Jefferson streets in NEW ALBANY, MISSISSIPPI, where Murry worked for the family-owned GULF & CHICAGO RAILROAD. Their first child, William Cuthbert, was born in New Albany on September 25, 1897. Maud reported him as a colicky baby who kept her up nearly every night during the first year of his life.

With Murry Falkner's promotion to treasurer of the railroad, the family moved up the line to RIPLEY, MISSISSIPPI. The Falkners' second and third children, Murry C. FALKNER Jr. (born 1899; known as Jack), and John Wesley Thompson FALKNER III (born 1901; known as Johncy) were born there.

The Falkners moved to Oxford in 1902 when Maud's father-in-law, the Young Colonel, sold the railroad that had employed her husband. With the loss of his job, Murry wanted to strike out for Texas and become a rancher. Maud refused to consider the idea. They stayed on in "the old Johnny Brown place," a gift of the Young Colonel, on Second South Street, a few blocks from the Courthouse Square.

The marriage was difficult. Maud and Murry Falkner were temperamentally at odds—she interested in books and painting, he a bluff, liquorish outdoorsman. She hated his drinking, which sometimes took a serious turn: when that happened, she and the children escorted him to the KEELEY INSTITUTE near MEMPHIS for a several days' "cure."

The family moved into the Rowsey house on South Street, three blocks from the Square in 1905. Maud delivered the couple's fourth and last child, Dean Swift (FAULKNER), there in 1907.

Maud Falkner assumed full responsibility for the children's physical and spiritual welfare. When she saw firstborn Billy walking with a stoop, she laced him tight in a canvas vest every day for two years. That straightened his posture—and kept it straight for the rest of his life. She saw to the boys' religious training, raising them as Methodists (though she had grown up a Baptist) and taking them to revivalist camp meetings every summer. She also passed along her love of literature to them. She invited the ladies of the Twentieth Century Book Club to her house for discussion, and took part in the deliberations of the Oxford chapter of the Browning Society.

Billy was her clear favorite. She tolerated his youthful eccentricities (and they were almost without number), for she suspected him of being a "genius." She defended him when Oxford expressed outrage over the violence and perversion in some of his early work, particularly SANCTUARY.

She was small, barely five feet tall, with fine features and dark eyes. She could be stern and inflexible; she met hardship and disappointment with courage. The motto "Never Complain, Never Explain" hung over the stove in her kitchen, and she practiced it faithfully. She never completely accepted Faulkner's wife, (Lida) Estelle Oldham (FAULKNER), a divorcée who drank whiskey. To the end of her life, Faulkner visited her every day when he was in Oxford; he usually called alone, knowing how his mother felt about Estelle.

Her youngest son Dean's death in an airplane crash in 1935 nearly destroyed her; she talked of suicide for a time. Murry Falkner's passing three years earlier had left her strangely unmoved, however.

Maud Butler Falkner died on October 16, 1960. She kept up her interest in books to the end: a copy of Lawrence's *Lady Chatterley's Lover* lay on the stand next to her bed the night she suffered a cerebral hemorrhage and lapsed into a coma. She died in the Oxford hospital.

Falkner, Murry Charles, Jr. (1899–1975)   Faulkner's younger brother, nearest him in age, known as Jack. Only two years separated the brothers, and they were much together as children, with Billy, as the elder, usually taking the lead in amusements and mischief. Jack enlisted the U.S. Marines near the end of World War I, went to France with the 5th Marine Regiment, and saw action in the late summer of 1918 at Belleau Wood.

Wounded in the knee and head near the Argonne Forest on November 1, 1918, Jack returned home to OXFORD, MISSISSIPPI, after several months' convalescence and entered the UNIVERSITY OF MISSISSIPPI. He took a law degree from Ole Miss, worked in his uncle John Wesley Thompson FALKNER Jr.'s law office, obtained a position in the U.S. Treasury Department, and went on to become one of the first agents in the newly organized Federal Bureau of Investigation.

Like his brothers, Jack Falkner loved to fly. He bought his own airplane in the late 1930s, an 85-horsepower Aeronca that he loaned to Faulkner in 1940 when the FBI transferred him to Alaska.

Falkner served in U.S. Army counterintelligence during World War II and saw action in North Africa. He came home in 1945 with a French bride, Suzanne (he had married and divorced an Oxford woman, Cecile Hargis), and returned to the FBI. He was a godparent to Faulkner's only child, Jill FAULKNER.

A large, bluff man who greatly resembled his father, Jack got along well with his novelist brother, though there were constraints in their relationship and they were not intimate. His memoir *The Falkners of Mississippi* (1967) is a valuable source of Falkner (and Faulkner) lore.

Falkner, Murry Cuthbert (1870–1932)   Faulkner's hapless, inebriate father, the son of John Wesley Thompson and Sallie Murry FALKNER. Raised in his parents' prosperous households in RIPLEY and OXFORD, MISSISSIPPI, he was restless at school and dropped out of the UNIVERSITY OF MISSISSIPPI after two undistinguished years to go to work on the family railroad, a merger of three small lines rechristened the GULF & CHICAGO RAILROAD, where he did duty as fireman, engineer, and conductor.

Murry Falkner inherited the family propensity to violent encounters. A gambler and grocer named Elias Walker once approached him at a lunch counter after an argument over a girl and discharged a 12-gauge shotgun into his back at close range. He dropped to the floor and Walker shot him with a pistol, wounding Falkner in the mouth and shattering several teeth. Falkner survived to make a full recovery and returned to the Gulf & Chicago. (A jury acquitted Elias Walker.) A promotion to general passenger agent at the NEW ALBANY, MISSISSIPPI, depot in 1896 gave him the wherewithal to seek a wife. He married Maud Butler (FALKNER), the daughter of a one-time Lafayette County sheriff who had deserted his family, in November 1896 after a secretive courtship. She bore their first child on September 25, 1897: William Cuthbert, named for his great-grandfather, the Old Colonel, and his father. Three more boys followed: Murry Cuthbert FALKNER Jr., known as Jack, in 1899; John Wesley Thompson FALKNER III, called Johncy, in 1901; and Dean Swift FAULKNER, born in 1907.

Strains appeared early in the marriage. Murry Falkner read Western adventure novels, liked to hunt and fish, raised bird dogs, drank hard, lacked ambition and self-confidence, and resented his over-dependence on his powerful father. Maud knew something of literature and art, was energetic and determined, and detested her husband's drinking. Though William Faulkner never broke openly with his father, he plainly took his mother's side. He regarded his father as dull, uninteresting, a failure. In turn, Murry Falkner claimed never to have read anything his novelist son wrote.

Gravesite of Faulkner's parents and brothers, in Oxford, Mississippi. When enlisting in the Royal Air Force in 1918, Faulkner added the "u" to the spelling of Falkner. (Harriett and Gioia Fargnoli)

Falkner rose to become treasurer of the Gulf & Chicago and expected to succeed his father as president. It was not to be. The Young Colonel sold the Gulf & Chicago in 1902, turning Murry out of a job he loved. Circumstances forced him to move to Oxford and live in a house of his father's. Murry Falkner's long decline and defeat, compounded by alcoholism, had begun.

He ran a livery stable for a time, but business fell off rapidly with the coming of the automobile. A coal-oil agency was no more successful. In 1912 he bought a hardware store on the Square in Oxford. But Falkner proved a poor salesman—none of the Falkners could "sell a stove to an Eskimo or a camel to an Arab," he once said—and he chafed at a merchant's sedentary life. In 1917, through his father's influence, he obtained a position in the University of Mississippi's business office, rising to become business manager and secretary of the university. But he lost that job, his last, in a political shuffle.

Faulkner came to regard his great-grandfather, the legendary Old Colonel, as his true father. As critics have noted, key Faulkner characters are boys or men with absent or inadequate fathers: Quentin COMPSON in

The SOUND AND THE FURY, Charles BON in *ABSALOM, ABSALOM!* The theme of family decline runs through much of Faulkner's fiction. Yet not all of Murry Falkner's influence was negative. There were regular Sunday afternoon rides in the trap. Murry taught his sons to ride and shoot. Faulkner probably got along best with his father at the Club House, the Falkners' cabin in the woods along the TALLAHATCHIE RIVER, where Murry used to go to hunt, fish, and drink. Faulkner drew on these experiences for descriptions and events of "the big woods"—the Delta country of the novella "The Bear" (see *GO DOWN, MOSES*) and other works. Murry also formed the basis for an affectionate portrait of the livery stable owner Maury PRIEST in *The REIVERS.*

Murry Falkner died of a heart attack 10 days short of his 62nd birthday. His doctor had warned that heavy drinking would kill him; he ignored the warning. William Faulkner at once assumed the role of head of the family.

Falkner, Sallie McAlpine Murry (1850–1906)
Faulkner's paternal grandmother. The daughter of a Tippah County, Mississippi, doctor, she married John Wesley Thompson FALKNER in 1869. They reared three children: Murry Cuthbert FALKNER (Faulkner's father, born 1870); Mary Holland (Auntee) Falkner, (born 1872); and John Wesley Thompson FALKNER Jr. (born 1882).

She was capable, decisive and quick-thinking. When the doctors had all but given up on her son Murry, near death from a bullet wound to the mouth, she dosed him with the evil-smelling resin asafetida, causing him to vomit up the imbedded slug. He made a full recovery.

Sallie Murry Falkner may have formed a partial basis for the character of Granny Rosa MILLARD, the indomitable matriarch in *The UNVANQUISHED.* She died after a long, wasting illness on December 21, 1906. Billy Falkner, aged nine, attended her funeral.

Falkner, William Clark (1825–1889) Faulkner's paternal great-grandfather. He was a Confederate soldier, lawyer, railroad developer, and author. According to Faulkner's biographers, he was the violent, impulsive, and energetic model for the fictional Colonel John SARTORIS.

The son of Caroline and Joseph Falkner, he was born in Knox County, Tennessee, where his parents paused in their migrant journey from North Carolina to the Mississippi River town of St. Genevieve, Missouri. He moved to his aunt Justiana Word Thompson's home in RIPLEY, MISSISSIPPI, in 1841 or 1842; she and her husband, John Wesley Thompson, eventually adopted him. Falkner acquired a rudimentary education and read law. He served in the Mississippi militia during the Mexican War; in a mysterious incident, he was wounded in the hand and foot before he saw any actual fighting and returned home to convalesce. A brawler, he killed two men in separate incidents, claiming self-defense both times; in each case, the jury agreed. He married Holland Pearce in 1847; she delivered their son, John Wesley Thompson FALKNER, in September 1848. Holland Pearse Falkner died in 1849, and Falkner married Elizabeth Houston Vance in 1851. Four of their children lived to adulthood: William Henry, Willie Medora, Effie Dun, and Alabama Leroy. There is circumstantial evidence that he also produced a shadow family, the result of miscegenation with slaves he owned (see Joel Williamson, *Faulkner and Southern History*).

Falkner bought and sold slaves, farmed, and practiced law. With the coming of the Civil War, he raised a volunteer rifle company, the MAGNOLIA RIFLES, and won election in April 1861 as colonel of the 2nd Mississippi infantry. He fought at First Manassas (see BULL RUN, first battle of) in July 1861; two horses were shot from under him during the battle.

Denied reelection in April 1862, Falkner returned home to Mississippi, raised the irregular cavalry unit known as the 1st Mississippi Partisan Rangers, and carried on intermittent guerrilla warfare—horse-stealing, bridge-burning, tearing up railroad track, occasional skirmishing—in north Mississippi through the middle of 1863. The Partisans accomplished little militarily, though, and at the cost of a long list of dead and wounded. Falkner resigned in October 1863, citing poor health, and by family report passed the rest of the war

Colonel W. C. Falkner (c. 1889), William Faulkner's great-grandfather and model for the fictional John Sartoris. (Brodsky Collection, Center for Faulkner Studies, Southeast Missouri State University)

running cotton through the Yankee lines into MEMPHIS. Federal troops burned his home in Ripley in July 1864.

He rebuilt on the ruins of his law practice after the war and, as the fictional Colonel John Sartoris would do, participated in the postwar boom of railroad construction (and reconstruction) in the South. He became a principal in the Ripley Railroad Company, which built a 25-mile narrow gauge line from Ripley to Middleton, Tennessee, for a connection with the long-haul Charleston & Memphis. By 1886 he had gained full control of the railroad, now rather grandly named the GULF & SHIP ISLAND RAILROAD (the locals called it the "Doodlebug" line), from his partner Richard J. THURMOND. Exploiting Mississippi's notorious convict labor system (prisoners could be leased from the state for $50 per man per year), he extended the line 40 miles south of Ripley to NEW ALBANY and Pontotoc, Mississippi.

Falkner privately published his first literary effort in 1851, a long poem titled *The Siege of Monterrey*, based on his Mexico experiences. He enjoyed considerable success, or at least sales, with his postwar work: the melodramatic novel *The White Rose of Memphis* (1880) reportedly remained in print for 30 years and sold 160,000 copies. He followed with a novel called *The Little Brick Church* (1882) and the travel book *Rapid Ramblings in Europe* (1884).

Falkner won election to a seat in the Mississippi legislature on November 5, 1889. Late that afternoon his bitter rival, Thurmond, approached him in front of the courthouse on the square in Ripley and shot him once in the head with a .44-caliber pistol. He died of the wound late the following night. A jury acquitted Thurmond of manslaughter in February 1890.

Falls, Will   Character in *SARTORIS*. A 93-year-old tenant of the county poor farm, he is given to retailing the near-legendary exploits of Colonel John SARTORIS. He successfully treats old Bayard SARTORIS's wen (or cyst) with a home remedy.

Farinzale, Giulio   Character in "MISTRAL" (in *Collected Stories*). He returns from a tour in the army to reclaim his girlfriend, a wild young woman and a ward of the village priest. The priest had arranged for her betrothal to a rich young man of the parish.

Farmer   In *REQUIEM FOR A NUN*, the turnkey (jailor) in JEFFERSON, MISSISSIPPI, during the Civil War.

Farmer, Cecilia   In *REQUIEM FOR A NUN*, the daughter of FARMER. Out of boredom, she scratches her name and the date with a diamond ring on a windowpane of her father's jail. At the end of the war, she meets and marries a former Confederate soldier and moves with him to his farm in Alabama. See also COOK, CELIA.

Farmington Hunt Club An Albemarle County, Virginia, social and sporting organization, the Farmington Hunt Club followed the traditions of the British hunt: pink coats, white stocks, black topboots and derbies. Fox hunting over Albemarle's rolling hills with the Farmington club and the KESWICK HUNT CLUB became a passion of Faulkner's last years.

The novelist was nearly 60 when he sought jumping instruction from the Farmington's huntsman, Grover Vandevender. He first took to the field with the hunt in the autumn of 1958. The club killed a fox only four or five times a year; that suited Faulkner, who enjoyed the chase far more than the kill.

A daring but accident-prone rider, he suffered serious shoulder and back injuries in falls. But he never let a mishap slow him down. "He was all nerve," Vandevender said of Faulkner. "It could rain or snow, but he stayed out to the last hound bark."

Faulkner rode with both hunts, sometimes four or five times a week in season. He became a member of the Farmington club in the winter 1959.

Farr, Cecily Saunders *See* SAUNDERS, CECILY.

Farr, George A young man of Charlestown, Georgia, in *SOLDIERS' PAY*. He takes up with Cecily SAUNDERS after her fiancé, Donald MAHON, is presumed dead in France during World War I. When Mahon returns, Cecily drops Farr. Confused and upset, he persists in his attentions, and Cecily eventually begins to go for rides with him again. Finally, Cecily allows Farr to seduce her so that she can get out of her promise to marry Donald, who is crippled, horribly scarred, and going blind. Farr and Cecily elope, but they return to Charlestown before Donald's death.

Father Abraham An unfinished novel Faulkner started writing around 1926. A limited edition with an introduction and textual notes by James B. MERIWETHER was published posthumously by Red Ozier Press, New York, in 1983. In 1984 a facsimile edited by Meriwether, with wood engravings by John DePol, was published by RANDOM HOUSE.

This unfinished work forms the basis of *The HAMLET;* a portion of it was written as "SPOTTED HORSES," a short story that Faulkner again revised and enlarged for chapter 1 of book 4 of *The Hamlet.*

Fathers, Sam (Had-Two-Fathers) Character in *GO DOWN, MOSES* ("The Old People," "The Bear," "Delta Autumn") and other works. The son of the Chickasaw chief IKKEMOTUBBE ("Doom") and a quadroon slave, he is for many years the blacksmith on the McCaslin plantation, where he is treated with the deference due a skilled craftsman.

Also a skilled hunter, Fathers teaches woodcraft to Isaac MCCASLIN. In "The Old People," after 12-year-old Ike kills his first buck, Fathers smears the animal's warm blood on the boy's face as a coming-of-age ritual.

He teaches Ike humility, patience, and reverence and respect for the land. In "The Bear," Fathers has left the plantation and is living in a hut deep in the woods not far from Major DE SPAIN's hunting camp. For years he is the chief woodsman during the annual hunt for the wily, seemingly indestructible bear the hunters call Old Ben.

Finally Old Ben is brought down, slain by Boon HOGGANBECK with the assistance of Lion, the dog Fathers has trained for the purpose. Some of the party find Fathers lying facedown in the trampled mud. Dr. CRAWFORD, summoned from the sawmill at HOKE'S STATION, sews up the mortally wounded Lion and examines Sam.

The hunters break camp, and only Boon and Ike stay behind. With Old Ben dead, Fathers realizes that the wilderness that has been his life is no more. Following Fathers's instructions, Boon builds a Chickasaw grave platform of freshly cut saplings bound between four posts, kills him, and lifts his blanket-wrapped body onto the platform. In the end, McCaslin EDMONDS and Major de Spain return to the woods, drive Boon away, and bury Fathers.

Sam Fathers also appears in *INTRUDER IN THE DUST, THE REIVERS,* the short story "RED LEAVES" (as Had-Two-Fathers), and the short story "A JUSTICE," where the tale of his mixed-race parentage is told.

Faulkner Character in *MOSQUITOES*. A sunburned, shabbily dressed, self-confessed professional liar, he tells Genevieve (Jenny) STEINBAUER that if the straps of her dress were to break she'd "devastate the country".

Faulkner also appears as the hero of the tongue-in-cheek short story "AFTERNOON OF A COW." This Mr. Faulkner—also referred to as Mr. Bill—is a novel writer and Southern gentleman, but supposedly not William Faulkner himself.

Faulkner, Dean Swift (1907–1935) Faulkner's high-spirited, restless youngest brother. His father's favorite, Dean Faulkner (who adopted his novelist brother's spelling of the surname) was a star athlete at the UNIVERSITY OF MISSISSIPPI who evidently did not find grownup life to his taste. Wild and unstable, he seemed incapable of settling down. Faulkner became a sort of guardian to him. He loaned Dean money to pay for flying lessons, and flying paradoxically seemed to bring Dean back to earth. He turned out to be a skilled, responsible, and careful pilot.

Dean Swift Faulkner died in a crash at an air show in PONTOTOC, MISSISSIPPI, on November 10, 1935. Only 28 years old, he left his wife, Louise Hale, pregnant with their first child. (She delivered a daughter, Dean, the following March.) For an inscription on his gravestone, Faulkner borrowed the epitaph he had given

At Faulkner's funeral, Estelle Faulkner (standing) is assisted by her son, Malcolm Franklin. Seated at left are Faulkner's daughter, Jill, and her husband, Paul Summers. (AP/Wide World Photos)

John SARTORIS in *SARTORIS:* "I bare him on eagles' wings and brought him unto Me."

Faulkner, (Lida) Estelle Oldham (1896–1972)

Faulkner's wife, born in OXFORD, MISSISSIPPI, the daughter of Lemuel Early OLDHAM, a prominent lawyer, and Lida Allen OLDHAM. Billy Falkner and Estelle Oldham lived within a few blocks of each other as children.

Estelle had a conventional Southern girl's upbringing. She became an accomplished pianist, a good dancer, and an amusing light conversationalist. She attended Mary Baldwin College in Virginia for a year before returning, homesick, to enroll as a special student at the UNIVERSITY OF MISSISSIPPI.

She was a petite, popular girl, and she never suffered for lack of suitors. Estelle came to a sort of understanding with the unprepossessing Faulkner. Her parents strongly disapproved of him, however, and her mother maneuvered her into an engagement to the young Ole Miss law graduate Cornell FRANKLIN. Estelle offered to elope with Faulkner; he insisted that they seek her father's permission. Lemuel Oldham categorically refused to grant it, and Estelle and Franklin were married in April 1918. She accompanied her husband to Honolulu, where he had set up as a lawyer, and later went with him to China. Faulkner was devastated.

Estelle and Franklin produced two children, Melvina Victoria and Malcolm FRANKLIN, but the marriage foundered, partly as a consequence of Franklin's dissipations. Estelle spent long periods on furlough at home in Oxford, where she again took up with Faulkner.

She returned to Mississippi for good in 1928 and her divorce became final the following year. Desperate and unhappy, an anomaly as a divorcée in conservative Oxford, she evidently pressured Faulkner to provide her a way out of her troubles. He overcame his ambivalence and they decided to marry, Faulkner writing his publisher to ask for a $500 advance to meet the expenses of the ceremony and honeymoon.

Lem Oldham's daughter was 33 and alone with two children, but he still hesitated before agreeing to his daughter's second marriage. Faulkner, Estelle, and the children set off for a honeymoon in PASCAGOULA, MISSISSIPPI, after a brief ceremony in the parsonage of the College Hill Presbyterian Church on June 20, 1929. Faulkner corrected proofs of The SOUND AND THE FURY there. On edge, displeased with the editing of the novel, he became uncommunicative and withdrawn—an early taste for Estelle of what married life with the artist would be like.

The marriage seems to have been a failure from the start. Estelle was voluble, Faulkner silent; she was shallow, he was utterly committed to his art. Estelle liked to dance and party; her husband preferred solitude, time with the children, hunting, fishing or riding. They both were self-destructive drinkers, and their alcoholism caused incalculable grief. Estelle developed a habit of making public threats of suicide. Her extravagance—she had been used to luxury as Franklin's wife—infuriated her husband. Faulkner once threw out several pieces of expensive furniture she had imported into ROWAN OAK in his absence and then placed a personal notice in the Oxford and Memphis newspapers denying responsibility for any debts Mrs. William Faulkner or Mrs. Estelle Oldham Faulkner might incur.

The Faulkners' first child, a girl named Alabama, was born two months premature in January 1931 and lived only 10 days. The ordeal drew the two together briefly. But both resumed their drinking shortly thereafter. Estelle had bouts of ill health too. The birth of their only surviving child, Jill (FAULKNER), in June 1933 did little to heal the rifts.

From the mid-1930s on, Estelle had to deal with her husband's affairs with a succession of young women: Meta CARPENTER, Joan WILLIAMS, Jean STEIN. Faulkner once cruelly threw Estelle together with Carpenter at a harrowing Hollywood dinner party. In the early 1950s, in the midst of Faulkner's involvement with Williams, Estelle considered divorcing him. When Faulkner took up with Stein in the late 1950s, Estelle again offered him a divorce, this time more forcefully, but Faulkner turned her down. The affair with Jean Stein ended; it was his last. Estelle curbed her drinking and began attending Alcoholics Anonymous meetings. The Faulkners remained together.

Estelle Faulkner survived the novelist by 10 years.

Faulkner, James Murry (Jimmy) (1923–) Faulkner's nephew, the son of John and Dolly Falkner III, known as Jimmy. Faulkner liked to play with the toddler Jimmy and, as he grew older, would take him hunting or aloft in one of the Waco aircraft he used to fly. Jimmy called Faulkner "Brother Will," and became a surrogate son to him.

Jimmy Faulkner volunteered as a Marine aviation cadet in 1943 and carried his uncle's goggles and leather flying jacket into the service with him. He saw combat action in the Pacific during World War II, surviving a crash at sea off Okinawa. He returned to active duty during the Korean War and stayed on afterward in the Marine reserves, rising to the rank of lieutenant colonel.

They remained close to the end of Faulkner's life. "I think that Jim is the only person who likes me for what I am," Faulkner once said of him. A few months before his death, Faulkner told Jimmy of his premonition of the end and asked him to take care of some things after he had gone. In July 1962, Jimmy Faulkner drove the novelist to Wright's Sanitarium in BYHALIA, MISSISSIPPI, for the last of his visits there.

In the 1985 film version of the short story "BARN BURNING," produced by Learning in Focus, Inc. (an educational series on American short stories hosted by Henry Fonda), Jimmy Faulkner played the minor role of Major DE SPAIN; the film stars Tom Lee Jones, Diane Kagan, and Shawn Wittington.

Faulkner, Jill (Jill Faulkner Summers) (1933–) Faulkner's only child, his "heart's darling" (supplanting the fictional Candace (Caddy) COMPSON of The SOUND AND THE FURY), born in OXFORD, MISSISSIPPI, on June 25, 1933. Caroline BARR, "Mammy," took care of Jill in her infancy. With two troubled parents—a drunken mother and a drunken, often absent father—she had a difficult childhood.

Jill called him "Pappy." Father and daughter had a good relationship in the early years, at least when Faulkner was in residence at ROWAN OAK. He sang to her, read to her, and invented stories for her about the escapades of Virgil Jones, a guitar-strumming squirrel.

Faulkner brought Jill out to Hollywood in 1943, arranged horseback riding lessons for her, introduced her to his lover, Meta CARPENTER, and sent her back home to Mississippi in the autumn with a prized possession—a gentle mare named Lady Go-Lightly.

Jill probably saved Faulkner's marriage to (Lida) Estelle Oldham FAULKNER, such as it was; he dreaded the estrangement from his daughter a divorce would make inevitable. But she clearly suffered from her parents' troubles and often upbraided her father about his drunkenness.

Faulkner proved a stern father as Jill grew older. He seemed to encourage her tomboy tendencies, but once, when he saw her on the Courthouse Square wearing shorts, he passed her by without a word. He told her later that ladies did not dress that way in public. Nor, for a long time, would he allow her a radio, a phonograph, or, later, a television.

Jill accompanied the novelist to Stockholm in December 1949 to accept his Nobel Prize. Faulkner spoke at Jill's graduation from Oxford High School in May 1951 and at her graduation from Pine Manor Junior College in Wellesley, Massachusetts. He dedicated the novel A FABLE (1954) to Jill, explaining that it was his way of saying farewell to her childhood.

Faulkner gave her away to Paul D. SUMMERS Jr. at her wedding at Rowan Oak in August 1954. Jill and Summers became the parents of three sons. They named the middle boy, born in 1958, William Cuthbert Faulkner.

From the late 1950s onward, Faulkner spent as much time as possible in Charlottesville, Virginia, where Jill and her lawyer husband had settled. By then, he and Estelle had long since negotiated the armistice that ended their long-running marital war. Still, when all was said, being Faulkner's child had been a difficult business. "Given his independent personality," Jill said of him, "he shouldn't have burdened himself with a family" (Joel Williamson, *William Faulkner and Southern History*, p. 294).

Faulkner, William (1897–1962) Novelist, author of *The SOUND AND THE FURY, LIGHT IN AUGUST, ABSALOM, ABSALOM!, GO DOWN, MOSES, The HAMLET*, and other works, winner of the NOBEL PRIZE IN LITERATURE (awarded 1949), and by critical consensus a leading literary artist of the 20th century.

Born William Cuthbert Falkner in NEW ALBANY, MISSISSIPPI, on September 25, 1897, he was the first child of Murry Cuthbert and Maud Butler FALKNER and the great-grandson of the soldier, author, banker, and railroad builder William Clark FALKNER, known as the Old Colonel, a near-legendary figure and the prototype of Colonel John SARTORIS of Faulkner's fictional JEFFERSON, MISSISSIPPI, and YOKNAPATAWPHA COUNTY.

The novelist's mythic Yoknapatawpha has become a permanent feature of the world's literary geography. It is a suffering, defeated place, a haunt of grotesque and villainous Snopeses and Sutpens, with a troubled heritage of slavery and war. But it is an enduring and timeless place too, peopled with ordinary men and women such as Dilsey GIBSON, V. K. RATLIFF, and Isaac (Ike) MCCASLIN who rise to heroic stature and in whom hope has not died.

Faulkner's ancestry was mostly Scots or Scots-Irish. He evidently regarded the violent, impulsive, grasping, creative Old Colonel as his spiritual father. W. C. Falkner, born in 1825, migrated from North Carolina via Missouri to northern Mississippi, settling in RIPLEY, MISSISSIPPI, in the early 1840s. He read law, served in the Mississippi militia during the Mexican War, and established himself during the 1850s as a prosperous, slaveholding lawyer, businessman, and farmer.

With the coming of the Civil War, a calamity that would live in his great-grandson's imagination, Falkner raised a volunteer company, the MAGNOLIA RIFLES, and in May 1861 won election as colonel of the 2nd Mississippi Infantry. In July 1861 he fought at the First Manassas (see BULL RUN), where his rather ostentatious bravery (he had two horses shot from under him) caught the attention of his superior officers. Denied reelection to the regimental command in the spring of 1862, he returned to Mississippi, raised a regiment of irregular cavalry, and carried out intermittent raids on federal communications lines before leaving the army for good in October 1863. His early retirement did not, however, deter federal troops from burning his Ripley home in 1864.

After the war, the Old Colonel rebuilt his law practice and, like the fictional John Sartoris, gained influence, power, and prosperity as a banker and railroad developer. He also found time to write; his melodramatic novel *The White Rose of Memphis,* published in 1881, remained in print for 30 years and reportedly sold 160,000 copies. He followed up this publishing success with *The Little Brick Church,* another novel, in 1882, and *Rapid Ramblings in Europe,* an account of his travels, in 1884.

Ripley sent Falkner to the Mississippi legislature on November 5, 1889, but he did not live to take his seat. Late on the afternoon of election day, his business and political rival Richard J. THURMOND shot and fatally wounded him on the Courthouse Square, an assassination Faulkner would fictionalize in the novels *SARTORIS* (1929) and *The UNVANQUISHED* (1938).

The Old Colonel's son, John Wesley Thompson FALKNER (1848–1922), expanded the family's banking and railroad enterprises and made successful forays into Mississippi politics. He married Sallie McAlpine Murry (FALKNER) in 1869; she delivered their first child, Murry Cuthbert FALKNER, the following year. The Young Colonel moved his family from Ripley 40 miles southeast to the LAFAYETTE COUNTY town of OXFORD, MISSISSIPPI, in late 1885 and established a law practice there. His legal, business, and political affairs flourished into the early years of the new century, in spite of the near-legendary drinking bouts that sent him from time to time to the KEELEY INSTITUTE of Memphis for "the cure." The Young Colonel's alcoholism would pass from him through his son Murry to his novelist grandson. (See FAULKNER AND ALCOHOLISM.)

A good deal less is known of the background of Faulkner's mother's family. The Butlers were among the earliest settlers of Lafayette County. Maud Falkner, born in 1871, the daughter of Charles Edward and Lelia Swift BUTLER, claimed the Confederate general Felix Zollicoffer as a kinsman and boasted of several

Faulkner (middle row, second from left) and his schoolmates at Oxford Graded School in 1908. (Brodsky Collection, Center for Faulkner Studies, Southeast Missouri State University)

forebears who had fought in the Civil War. Charles Butler served for a dozen years as the Oxford town marshal. He abandoned his wife and two children in 1887, vanishing with as much as $3,000 in town funds and, so the gossip ran, with a beautiful young octoroon mistress. Faulkner never knew his maternal grandfather, and he remained always reticent about his Butler antecedents.

The infant Willie, as his parents called him at first, was a colicky newborn, and his mother recalled rocking him in a stiff-backed chair for many hours a night during the first year of his life. He survived early frailties to grow up tough and durable, if small. The Falkners moved from New Albany to Ripley, where Murry worked for the family-owned GULF & CHICAGO RAILROAD, in November 1898. Two more sons—Billy's brothers Murry Charles (known as Jack) and John Wes-

ley Thompson III (known as Johncy)—were born there before the family removed permanently to Oxford, the Young Colonel's seat, on September 24, 1902, a day before Billy Falkner reached his fifth birthday.

Murry Falkner's decline began in this period. His father's abrupt and unexpected sale of the Gulf & Chicago, for $75,000 in May 1902, robbed him of his vocation, and he mourned the loss. Though the Young Colonel backed Murry financially in a succession of small businesses, nothing could replace his beloved railroad. His wife vetoed his dream of resettling in Texas and raising cattle, and he slipped ever deeper into the shadow of his powerful and successful father.

Strains in the Falkners' marriage were only too evident. They were temperamentally incompatible. Maud Falkner was steely and determined, her husband feckless and alcoholic. Her interests lay in books and pictures; his in guns, dogs, and horses. Billy Falkner grew up in a tense, emotionally edgy household in which his mother held dominion. She ran the place on Second South Street with the assistance of a capable, ever-present lieutenant, Caroline (Callie) BARR, who had been born into slavery and who was known as Mammy. Murry seemed to fail at everything he attempted. Weak or absent fathers modeled on Murry Falkner would recur in Faulkner's fiction; the theme of family decline would run through much of his work.

The elder Falkner ran a livery stable and a cottonseed oil mill, sold coal oil, and operated a hardware store on Confederate Square in Oxford. The coming of factory-made automobiles doomed the livery stable. Murry sold the South Street house and moved the family into a more modest place on North Street to raise

William Faulkner in 1914. (Brodsky Collection, Center for Faulkner Studies, Southeast Missouri State University)

money to buy himself into the hardware business. But he chafed at the sedentary life of a merchant, and showed no aptitude for the work.

Yet aspects of Billy Falkner's boyhood were idyllic. Woods stretched out behind the Falkners' first Oxford home, a large one-story frame house with a barn and paddock; six blocks up the street lay the Oxford Square. With a population of 1,800, three times Ripley's, Oxford in the first decade of the 20th century had a four-faced clock in the courthouse tower, dry goods, confectioners and other stores on the square, a new 140-foot-high water tower, and the UNIVERSITY OF MISSISSIPPI.

There were the immemorial pastimes of small-town boyhood: pickup games of football and baseball, explorations of the nearby woods and fields with Mammy Callie, hit-and-run raids on enemy neighborhoods. Billy absorbed Civil War lore from cronies of his grandfather, a leader of the SONS OF CONFEDERATE VETERANS fraternal organization, and entertained his brothers with scraps of speeches picked up at soldier reunions. Their father took the boys for Sunday afternoon rides in the trap, and on summer and autumn weekends they would journey farther afield, to the Club House, the family's hunting and fishing lodge in the TALLAHATCHIE RIVER bottoms 15 miles north of Oxford.

The Big Place, the Old Colonel's home, served as the center of Falkner social life. It had wide porches and a finished attic, venues where the young Falkners gathered with the neighborhood children, among them Lida Estelle Oldham, who in due course became Billy's particular friend.

Billy's three brothers (Dean Swift [FAULKNER], the fourth Faulkner son, arrived in August 1907) looked up to him as the great organizer and improviser. One summer, he directed the boys and his cousin Sally Murry in assembling a virtually full scale airplane from plans in *American Boy* magazine, using his mother's bean poles for a frame and newspapers applied with flour paste as the skin. The boys and their cousin launched Billy from the edge of a 10-foot-deep ditch at the back of the Falkner's lot. The frail craft broke apart on takeoff.

Billy Falkner, age 8, entered the first grade in Oxford's all-White elementary school in September 1905. He did well in Miss Annie Chandler's class—well enough to be allowed to skip second grade. Maud Falkner was literate, conversant with books and the arts. She taught the Falkner boys to read and introduced them to James Fenimore Cooper, Charles Dickens, Mark Twain, Robert Louis Stevenson, and the Grimm brothers, and later to Shakespeare, Balzac, Poe, Kipling, and Conrad. For some reason, though, Billy turned against school. By the autumn of 1909, when he was in the sixth grade, he found himself in more or less constant trouble for skipping class, failing to turn in his homework, and general inattention to matters at hand.

But he was learning in other ways, observing, experiencing, storing up material his imagination would one day transform. Oxford taught him early the nuances of South's rigid system of racial subordination. The majority of Oxford's African Americans lived in Freedmantown, the black quarter north of the railroad tracks. Many, domestic servants for the most part, inhabited cabins in the yards behind the big houses of the white folks. The Falkners employed Callie Barr and other blacks as servants and the boys always had black playmates. There were black Falkner cousins too, circumstantial evidence suggests; the Old Colonel had fathered a "shadow family" with one of his former slaves, though these Falkners were never acknowledged.

Black-white relations were easy, often affectionate, so long as blacks made no bid to breach the racial barrier. Whites reacted fiercely to any attempt to cross the line. Race and racial identity would become major themes of Faulkner's mature fiction, most pervasively in the novels *Light in August, Absalom, Absalom!,* and *Go Down, Moses.* (See FAULKNER AND RACE.)

So he picked up his novelist's education outside the schoolroom. Helping out at his father's livery stable, he absorbed the lore of horses and horsetrading that would infuse the SNOPES TRILOGY, *The REIVERS,* and other works. Relations with his father grew steadily more difficult as Billy reached adolescence. Murry called him "Snake Lips," a dig at his Butler features; Billy had the Butler physical form, short and slight. Murry only too plainly favored the second son Jack, a Falkner in build: tall, bulky, florid.

Between them, Estelle Oldham and Billy's friend Philip Avery STONE, the son of a prominent lawyer and banker, taught him more than any Oxford school. To impress Estelle, a popular girl, Billy affected the dress and manners of a dandy. He learned to recognize the Beethoven sonatas she played on the piano in the Oldham parlor, and he tried to dance. There were many rivals for Estelle's attention, but even so, she and Billy seemed to have an understanding.

Falkner dropped out of high school after the 10th grade and went to work in his grandfather's bank. He had met Phil Stone in the summer of 1914 and had tentatively shown him his verse. Four years Falkner's senior, Stone was educated at the UNIVERSITY OF MISSISSIPPI and Yale. Cultured, cosmopolitan and fluent, he talked literature with Billy, loaned him books, introduced him to classic and modern writers; in fact, he shaped the young artist's viewpoint and style, or so he afterward claimed.

Stone's teaching encompassed the Lafayette County hill people and the MEMPHIS underworld as readily as the literary moderns. Falkner explored the MISSISSIPPI DELTA wilderness with Stone; his father's Delta hunting camp would form the model for the camp in the novella "The Bear" (in *Go Down, Moses*). The novelist would also exploit the entrée Stone provided into the world of gam-blers and prostitutes in a number of stories and novels, from *SANCTUARY* (1931) to *The Reivers* (1962).

War in Europe filled Billy Falkner's thoughts and imagination in 1915 and 1916. He had actually seen an airplane by then and he devoured newspaper and magazine accounts of the flying aces of the Western Front. (See FAULKNER AND FLYING.) America entered World War I in the spring of 1917, but by then Falkner's motives for action had become more personal than patriotic. Lemuel OLDHAM refused to accept Billy Falkner as a suitor for his daughter. Estelle's mother maneuvered her into an engagement with a young lawyer named Cornell FRANKLIN, and they were married in April 1918. Billy sought escape at a U.S. Army Air Corps recruiting office.

The air service turned him down, citing his short stature (he stood five feet, five inches tall), according to the biographer Joseph BLOTNER. He fled Oxford all the same, traveling to New Haven, Connecticut, where Phil Stone was studying law at Yale. Faulkner briefly worked in an arms factory there before managing to pass himself off as an expatriate Englishman named William Faulkner (adding a *u* to the family name) and enlisting as a cadet in the ROYAL AIR FORCE. Around the same time, Jack Falkner enlisted as a private soldier in the U.S. Marine Corps.

Faulkner—he would retain the *u,* part of the fictional biography he created for the RAF—reported to ground school in Toronto, Canada, in July 1918. Jack landed in France in August. For all his later elaboration of himself a wounded flying hero, Faulkner proved an indifferent flying cadet. As it happened, he never came near the cockpit of an airplane, let alone flew solo, crashed, or shot down German fighters over France, as he later suggested he had done. (He would, however, obtain a pilot's license in 1933.) Jack was badly wounded in the Argonne Forest in early November, shot in the head and leg during the Saint-Mihiel offensive. After the armistice of November 11, 1918, the RAF moved swiftly to cut its trainees loose. Faulkner arrived home in Oxford in December with $42.58 in severance pay and a promise of an eventual honorary second lieutenant's commission.

For weeks afterward, Faulkner roamed about Oxford in his British officer's uniform, playing the returned war hero and accepting the salutes of authentic veterans. It was the second of the many roles he would play, following that of Oxford dandy. The biographer Frederick Karl regards the RAF experience as crucial in Faulkner's artistic development. "The war turned Billy into a storyteller, a fictionalist, which may have been the decisive turnabout of his life," he wrote. The returned flyer retained the clipped, formal, buttoned-down pose of the English officer through the autumn of 1919, when he enrolled as a special student at Ole Miss and reprised the role of dandy.

He studied French, Spanish, English, taking only the classes that interested him, indifferent to much of the college life around him. Faulkner's earliest published works date from this time: two drawings in the Ole Miss yearbook. His revised poem "L'Apres-Midi d'un Faune" appeared in the student newspaper, *The MISSISSIPPIAN*, in October 1919; the paper accepted his short story "Landing in Luck" in November. Nine Faulkner poems appeared in *The Mississippian* during the spring semester of 1920.

His social life was hit or miss. He joined the Sigma Alpha Epsilon fraternity and a drama club known as the Marionettes, but ran afoul of many of the Ole Miss hearties, his mannerisms and airs earning him the unflattering sobriquet of "Count No-'Count." And his "decadent" poems inspired a set of parodies, including "Une Ballade d'une Vache Perdu," about the lost and wandering heifer Betsey.

Murry Falkner had been business manager at Ole Miss, a patronage appointment, since 1918. The job came with a house on campus, and Billy would keep a room at his parents' home for a full decade. This secure base gave him the freedom to wander and to perfect the latest of his poses, that of the hard-drinking bohemian poet.

He journeyed to New York in the fall of 1921 at the invitation of the author Stark YOUNG, an Oxford native. Faulkner worked briefly in a Lord & Taylor bookstore for Elizabeth PRALL, the future wife of Sherwood ANDERSON. Phil Stone worried that his friend would lose his artistic bearings in the great city and recalled him to Oxford after a few weeks. In the interval, Stone had arranged the job of University of Mississippi postmaster for him.

Faulkner converted the post office into a private club. He and his cronies read, played cards, drank, and sometimes shut down the office altogether to play the university's "golfing pasture." He mishandled the mail. He tossed magazines and journals into the trash. He ignored the requests of patrons. Amazingly, he held onto the job for three years. A postal inspector finally turned up to investigate the scandalous operation. Faulkner took his removal calmly.

Meantime, Phil Stone arranged and subsidized the publication of Faulkner's first book, *The MARBLE FAUN*, a collection of poems. The FOUR SEAS COMPANY of Boston released an edition of 1,000 copies on December 15, 1924. Stone wrote the preface; Faulkner dedicated the book to his mother. ("Phil Stone and Mother were the first ones to believe in Bill," Johncy Falkner would write.) He presented a signed copy to Estelle Oldham Franklin, by now the mother of two young children: a girl, Melvina Victoria FRANKLIN and a boy, Malcolm Argyle FRANKLIN. She and Franklin had settled first in Hawaii and then in Shanghai, but by the mid-1920s their marriage was in trouble and she was spending long furloughs at home in Oxford. When not attending to the Oxford boy scout troop he headed or going off to immerse himself in the bohemian world of NEW ORLEANS's Vieux Carré, eight hours from Oxford by train, Billy was as attentive to her as ever.

Through Elizabeth Prall, he met Sherwood Anderson in New Orleans, and he found an outlet for verse, essays of criticism, and prose sketches in the new little magazine, *The DOUBLE DEALER*, published there. He also placed a series of vignettes of local life in the *NEW ORLEANS TIMES-PICAYUNE* newspaper. He was writing constantly, drinking heavily, and playing the part of wounded war hero to the hilt. He walked with a limp, and let it be known that he had suffered a serious head wound.

All the while, Faulkner worked on his first novel, originally titled *MAYDAY*, eventually published as *SOLDIERS' PAY*. Anderson agreed to recommend the book, completed in May 1925, to his publisher, Horace LIVERIGHT. Liveright accepted it on behalf of the firm of BONI & LIVERIGHT. With publication assured and a $200 advance in hand, Faulkner sailed for Europe with a New Orleans acquaintance, William SPRATLING, in July.

He traveled in Italy, Switzerland, France, and England, working fitfully on a manuscript titled *ELMER*, which would grow to novel length but never be published during his lifetime. He spent time in Paris, but shied from making an approach to James JOYCE or lesser expatriate literary figures settled there. "I knew of Joyce," he said many years later, "and I would go to some effort to go to the café that he inhabited to look at him. But that was the only literary man that I remember seeing in Europe in those days." With money running short, he sailed for home from Cherbourg, France, on December 9.

Boni & Liveright published *Soldiers' Pay* on February 25, 1926. Faulkner spent part of the spring in New Orleans and the summer at the Stones' beachfront house in PASCAGOULA, MISSISSIPPI, where he worked on his second novel, *MOSQUITOES*, and ineffectually courted a Tennessee-born artist and sculptor named Helen BAIRD. He completed the manuscript on September 1, with a dedication "To Helen." Liveright published it on April 30, 1927. Helen Baird married the New Orleans lawyer Guy Lyman on May 4.

By then, Faulkner had put aside a manuscript he called *FATHER ABRAHAM*, in which the fateful Flem SNOPES made his first appearance, and turned to work on a novel originally titled *FLAGS IN THE DUST*, launching the Sartoris saga. The two works were the origin of Faulkner's legendary Yoknapatawpha County. He completed *Flags* in late September and sent it on to Liveright. Liveright's letter of rejection reached him late in November. The publisher judged the novel hopeless, and advised the author to withdraw it altogether. "It is diffuse and non-integral with neither very much plot development nor character development," Liveright wrote. "We think it lacks plot, dimension and projection."

Faulkner sank into depression and gloom, but he recovered quickly from this episode and set about scheming to free himself from Boni & Liveright and to find a publisher for the Sartoris novel. (HARCOURT, BRACE AND COMPANY would publish it as *Sartoris* in January 1929.) Early in 1928, he began a story called "Twilight," about a little girl named Candace (Caddy) COMPSON and her brothers Quentin, Jason, and Benjy, the genesis of *The Sound and the Fury*.

Faulkner claimed long afterward that Liveright's rejection had freed him to approach what would become his finest work, and the one nearest his heart. He forgot, he said, about commercial publishing, about making money, about recognition.

"Twilight" touched off a creative explosion. Faulkner would produce much of his best work between 1928 and 1936: *The Sound and the Fury,* published in October 1929; *AS I LAY DYING,* written in a short burst during his night-shift supervisory job at the Ole Miss power plant and published in October 1930; *Light in August,* published in October 1932; and *Absalom, Absalom!,* published in October 1936.

He achieved both money and literary fame against a backdrop of private agonies: alcoholism, financial troubles, and an impending marriage, one that would prove destructive for each partner, to Estelle Franklin. The impressionistic and technically difficult *The Sound and the Fury* was an immediate critical success. "A great book," Faulkner's friend Lyle Saxon called it in a New York *Herald Tribune* review, a judgment that has stood the test of time. Financial gain—and notoriety—came in 1931 with publication of *Sanctuary,* set in the Memphis underworld and peopled with gangsters and an ambiguous heroine, a blonde Ole Miss student named Temple Drake (see Temple Drake STEVENS). Faulkner set out to write an attention-grabber, and he succeeded.

Like some of his critics, Faulkner himself always seemed slightly queasy about *Sanctuary,* which includes a rape with a corncob. His first view of the galleys in December 1930 sent him into a panic, and he began furiously to rewrite it. For better or worse, it remained the book most closely associated with his name during his lifetime.

Work provided Faulkner an escape from his torments. With pen in hand, he could forget his miseries—or at least transform them into fictions. Estelle's divorce had come through finally in the spring of 1929. A single woman with children, she had been intensely uncomfortable in conservative Oxford, and her family brought pressure to bear on her longest-running beau, Bill Faulkner. They were married in the parsonage of the College Hill Presbyterian Church in Oxford on June 20, 1929.

They went off to Pascagoula for their honeymoon. Faulkner corrected the galley proofs of *The Sound and*

the Fury there, a project that left him nervy and out of sorts. He became withdrawn and silent, and he drank heavily. He and Estelle returned to Oxford in the autumn of 1929. They lived in an apartment for a time before Faulkner, on the strength of several short-story sales, bought the "old Shegog place," a dilapidated antebellum house on the outskirts of Oxford, for $6,000, payable in monthly installments of $75 each. The Faulkners took possession in June 1930. Rather grandly, Faulkner renamed it ROWAN OAK, after a tree that represents good fortune in Scottish folklore.

At first, Rowan Oak represented anything but peace and security: Estelle did not like the house, and there were rumors that it was haunted; Faulkner went into debt buying and fixing it up. Their first child, Alabama, named for a favorite Faulkner aunt, was born prematurely on January 11, 1931, and lived only nine days.

But Faulkner loved the place. To him, Rowan Oak represented shelter from a hostile world. Even Oxford was changing. The Square had been paved over, the horse troughs removed, the elm trees felled. Faulkner's grandfather, the Young Colonel, had died in 1922, and the Big Place, once a proud landmark, afterward knew indignity and abuse, a metaphor for Falkner family decline: The mansion was cut up into apartments, and the corner lot sold off for a gasoline station.

Faulkner could *work* at Rowan Oak. He began what would become *Light in August,* the novel some critics judge his most satisfying work artistically, there in August 1931; the novel's genesis was in a short story whose central character, Gail HIGHTOWER, is obsessed with his grandfather, a Civil War soldier. He set the novel aside briefly in the autumn of 1931 for trips to a writers conference in Charlottesville, Virginia, and to New York City, where he became the darling of the literary set. He finished *Light in August* at Rowan Oak in the late winter of 1932, sending the manuscript off to his publisher, CAPE & SMITH, in mid-March. But the house, Estelle's extravagances, and his own profligacy (he would lay out several thousand dollars for a powerful airplane in 1933) left him in low water financially. Then Cape & Smith went into bankruptcy, another victim of America's Great Depression. The firm failed, owing Faulkner $4,000 in royalties.

Relief came in the spring of 1932 in the form of Faulkner's first offer from Hollywood, a $500-a-week screenwriting contract with METRO-GOLDWYN-MAYER. The novelist set off for the first of what would be a series of involvements, some of them unredeemably miserable, with "the industry." Faulkner had scant aptitude for the job, and still less liking for California.

Word of his father's death on August 7, 1932, reached him in Hollywood. Murry had lost his university job in a political shuffle in the late 1920s and afterward had failed rapidly. Heavy drinking accelerated the decline; he died of a heart attack a few days short of his 62nd birthday.

For the novelist, his father's passing meant added financial burdens. So did an increase to his own immediate family, which already included Estelle's children, various Oldhams, Callie Barr and other servants, and his youngest brother Dean. His and Estelle's only surviving child, Jill FAULKNER, was born on June 24, 1933. Jill was his "heart's darling," but life at Rowan Oak with a drunken, emotionally unstable mother and a drunken, often absent father would be the reverse of idyllic for her.

Faulkner's money troubles mounted, and by the summer of 1935 he was approaching the edge of bankruptcy. Meantime, he was furiously at work on a new novel, with a title he would borrow from the biblical story of the son of King David who rose against his father. *Absalom, Absalom!* began as the short story "EVANGELINE" in 1931. In the story, a young man named Henry SUTPEN kills his sister's suitor, Charles BON, after he discovers that Bon has a trace of black blood. Faulkner took up the Sutpen saga again with the short story "WASH" of 1933. He began converting the stories and characters into a novel, called "Dark House" at first, early in 1934, using Quentin COMPSON as the narrator.

Faulkner worked on the last stages of the novel in an abyss of debt and grief. The director Howard HAWKS came to his financial rescue late in 1935 with a screenwriting offer of $1,000 a week. But nothing could assuage the pain of the death of his youngest brother, Dean Swift Faulkner, who at age 28 was killed in an airplane crash during an airshow near PONTOTOC, MISSISSIPPI, on November 10, 1935. Faulkner had introduced Dean to aviation; he blamed himself for his brother's death, and said he saw Dean's shattered form in nightmares long afterward.

He completed *Absalom, Absalom!* on the last day of January 1936. Faulkner had been drinking heavily for some weeks, and he finally suffered a total collapse. The bout ended with his first visit to the sanitarium at BYHALIA, MISSISSIPPI, where, for a few days, Dr. Leonard Wright enforced a regimen of vitamins, drugs, and rest.

Faulkner's recuperative powers were astonishing. He was in Hollywood by the end of February 1936, working on a movie called *Banjo on My Knee* and single-mindedly pursuing Hawks's Mississippi-born aide and "script girl," Meta CARPENTER. She was wary: Faulkner was married, older, pretty obviously a hard drinker. He persisted; she finally consented to go out to dinner with him, the beginning of a tortured, on-again, off-again 15-year affair.

The Hollywood tour inaugurated a bleak decade for Faulkner. It began with the promise of his first real love, Meta. He had just completed one of his masterworks, and he had settled in with his fifth—and last—major publisher, RANDOM HOUSE, which brought out *Absalom* in October 1936.

But the coming years would bring debt, heartache, despair. One by one, his books would go out of print and he would lapse into obscurity. He bought GREENFIELD FARM, a run-down Lafayette County hill farm, in 1938; in playing the role of farmer, yet another Faulkner persona, he would know stretches of something like peace. He produced the last of his greatest works—*The Hamlet* (1940) and "The Bear," part of *Go Down, Moses* (1942). There were other works, too: short stories, the linked Civil War stories collectively titled *The Unvanquished* (1938) and the novel *The Wild Palms* (1939; see IF I FORGET THEE, JERUSALEM), which sold well for a time. But he also wasted long stretches buried in Hollywood film studios.

Estelle refused to agree to a divorce—or rather, threatened to ruin him in exchange for one. So the Faulkners remained together, locked in conflict. Meta Carpenter married an Austrian emigré pianist later in 1936, but she and Faulkner would rekindle their affair during the novelist's Hollywood periods.

Yet Faulkner had not only a family but also an ever-lengthening list of relations and servants to whom he assumed some financial responsibility. Faulkner's portrait appeared on the cover of *Time* magazine in January 1939, but by January 1941 he couldn't raise $15 to pay the Rowan Oak light bill. He owed $600 to an Oxford grocer. He wrote reams of what he called "trash" in an effort to remain solvent. He revised "The Bear" from memory for the high-paying SATURDAY EVENING POST so that he could make a quick sale.

Faulkner was disappointed, too, at failing to find a niche in the war effort. He had begun casting around for a role after the fall of France in 1940. When the United States entered World War II after the Japanese attack on Pearl Harbor in December 1941, he tried to join the Navy and then the Army Air Corps. None of the services had need of an alcoholic middle-aged novelist. Desperate, he agreed in the summer of 1942 to a contract at $300 a week—far less than he had commanded in the mid-1930s—with the WARNER BROTHERS studio. He neglected to read the fine print. The agreement contained seven years of options, essentially an indenture to Jack Warner.

As it happened, Faulkner contributed to a couple of good films that both starred Humphrey BOGART: *To Have and Have Not,* loosely adapted from an Ernest HEMINGWAY novel, and *The Big Sleep,* based on the detective novel of the same title by Ramond Chandler. While Faulkner's royalties from Random House for 1942 did not exceed $300, Warner at least paid the bills.

Faulkner fled Hollywood for the last time in September 1945, determined to free himself from Warner Brothers no matter what the cost. Around this time too, the critic Malcolm COWLEY undertook the literary reclamation project that would vault the novelist into his rightful place in the front rank of literary artists.

"In publishing circles your name is mud," Cowley wrote him in 1944. "They are all convinced your books won't sell. Now when you talk to writers, it's quite a different story; there you hear almost nothing but admiration, and the better the writer the greater the admiration is likely to be." (*The Faulkner-Cowley File*, pp. 9–10)

Of his 17 books, only the equivocal *Sanctuary* remained in print in 1945. On the other hand, Faulkner's reputation stood high in France. The translator Maurice COINDREAU had been interested in his work since the early 1930s, and recommended it to the Paris publisher Gaston Gallimard (see GALLIMARD EDITIONS) in 1931 after reading *The Sound and the Fury* and *As I Lay Dying*. Gallimard had taken Faulkner, and the French had responded.

"For the young people of France, Faulkner is a god," the philosopher and novelist Jean-Paul Sartre told Cowley (Williamson, p. 268). The critic launched the Faulkner boom with an appreciative essay, "William Faulkner's Human Comedy," in the *New York Times Book Review* of October 29, 1944. To further "redress the balance between his worth and his reputation," Cowley proposed an anthology of Faulkner's work to the Viking Press.

The PORTABLE FAULKNER (1946) contained selections from the novelist's major works. Cowley wrote the introduction and prefaces to the book's seven sections. Faulkner himself supplied character genealogies and a map of Yoknapatawpha County. The only point of contention was Cowley's biographical sketch. Here Faulkner's fantasies about his RAF experience returned to haunt him. In the end, Cowley simply noted that the novelist had been in the RAF. Faulkner pronounced himself thoroughly satisfied with the "spoonrivering" (i.e., anthologizing) of his major works.

Cowley's lobbying helped persuade Random House to bring out Modern Library editions of *The Sound and the Fury* and *As I Lay Dying*. But it was a lesser work, *INTRUDER IN THE DUST* (1948), a thinly plotted murder mystery with an underlying racial theme, that saved Faulkner financially. MGM paid $50,000 for the films rights and shot much of the movie in Oxford in early 1949. The film had its premiere in Oxford's Lyric Theater in October.

Reprints of *Light in August*, *The Wild Palms*, *Go Down, Moses* and *The Hamlet* were issued in 1949. Faulkner arranged the scheme of the *Collected Stories*, the third (and last) anthology of his short fiction, which Random House would publish in 1950. The Swedish Academy considered Faulkner for the NOBEL PRIZE IN LITERATURE.

Three members of the Nobel committee dissented, however, and the academy withheld the award for 1949. In November 1950, Faulkner learned that he would be given the prize after all, "for his powerful and independent artistic contribution in America's new literature of the novel." It carried a cash gift of $30,000.

Having shunned publicity for most of his career, in his later years Faulkner began to use his fame to influence causes in which he believed. (Library of Congress, Prints and Photographs Division, Carl Van Vechten Collection, [LC-USZ62-424851])

Faulkner declined at first to travel to Sweden to claim the prize. Pressures were brought to bear, and in December, he and Jill flew to Stockholm. There he met Eise Jonsson, the widow of the Swedish translator of his works, with whom he would have an intermittent affair. The Nobel presentation speech judged him "the unrivaled master of all living British and American novelists as a deep psychologist" and "the greatest experimentalist among twentieth-century novelists."

Pale, nervous, quaking with stage fright, Faulkner raced through his acceptance speech. No one sitting more than a few feet from the dais could interpret his rapid murmurings. But the printed version remains indelible, one of the best known of all Nobel acceptances.

"I believe that man will not merely endure: he will prevail," Faulkner said. "He is immortal, not because he alone among creatures has an inexhaustible voice, but because he has a soul, a spirit capable of compassion and sacrifice and endurance."

Faulkner's literary reputation was secure. True, there had been quibbles in America with the Nobel decision. A fair number of critics and reviewers in his own country had always been ambivalent about his work (see FAULKNER AND CRITICISM). "Nothing would justify an open quarrel with regard to the Prize," the *New York Herald* wrote, "even though one would have preferred the choice of a laureate more smiling in a world which is gradually getting darker." Faulkner could afford to ignore this sort of dissent now.

But as his fame approached its peak, his private life remained a shambles. Joan WILLIAMS came into his life in the summer of 1949. A star-struck 19-year-old Bard College student from Memphis with an ambition to write, she ignored the "PRIVATE—KEEP OUT" sign Faulkner had painted himself and posted at the entrance of the Rowan Oak drive and knocked on his door, commencing a strange and pathetic love affair. He pursued her relentlessly. She tried to fend him off. Estelle learned of the entanglement and intervened; there were drunken scenes, talk of divorce, almost unbearable tension.

Faulkner sailed on Sardis Reservoir, played at being a farmer, and worked on the manuscript of what would become *A FABLE*, an allegorical fiction set in France during World War I—the only one of his novels not located in the South.

He had begun the allegory, which revolved around a Christlike figure and a mutiny in a French army regiment, as early as 1943. He found it slow going, perhaps because he had come to regard it, wrongly, as his masterwork. He would put it aside for long stretches, then take it up again. He finished it finally on November 1953.

With the Nobel award, the Howells Medal from the American Academy of Arts and Letters, and National Book Awards for the *Collected Stories* and *A Fable*, Faulkner became a public figure. He continued, though, to resist publicity. Robert COUGHLAN's 1954 profile for *Life*, filled with details about his private life, enraged and mortified him.

"What a commentary," he complained in a letter to Phil Mullen, the editor of the hometown OXFORD *EAGLE*. "Sweden gave me the Nobel Prize. France gave me the Legion d'Honneur. All my native land did for me was to invade my privacy over my protest and my plea." (*Selected Letters*, p. 354).

Yet Faulkner was prepared to use his fame and influence to further causes in which he felt an interest. He undertook cultural goodwill trips for the U.S. State Department to South America in 1954 and to Japan, the Philippines, and Europe in 1955. In 1956, he chaired the writers' group of President Eisenhower's "People to People" program, which aimed to transmit American culture into Communist Eastern Europe. And he became notorious for his brief, unhappy involvement in the Civil Rights movement in the South, in which he pulled off the difficult feat of

alienating partisans on all sides of the issue (see FAULKNER AND RACE).

His cautious endorsement of integration infuriated the Oxford Falkners and brought him hate mail and threatening phone calls. The writer and educator W. E. B. Du Bois, a founder of the National Association for the Advancement of Colored People (NAACP), challenged him to a debate on the steps of a Mississippi courthouse on his gradualist approach to desegregation, a challenge he wisely declined.

Faulkner dropped out of the great racial controversy and turned back to his work. He took up the Snopes saga again, finishing *The TOWN*, the second book in the trilogy, following *The Hamlet*, in August 1956. On the home front, he and Estelle negotiated an armistice in their long and bitter war. Estelle entered Alcoholics Anonymous in 1955. She took his latest (and last) affair with a younger woman gently, worrying mainly that Jill, who had married in 1954, would learn of his involvement with Jean STEIN. Jean herself brought things to an abrupt close in February 1957, touching off a drinking binge that landed Faulkner in the hospital yet again.

But his last years brought a measure of stability, if not serenity. In 1957 and 1958 Faulkner was writer-in-residence at the UNIVERSITY OF VIRGINIA, where a group of English Department admirers that included his future biographer Joseph Blotner attended him faithfully. Jill and her husband, Paul D. SUMMERS, had settled in Charlottesville, and the Faulkners decided to move there permanently to be near Jill and the grandchildren. Faulkner attended University of Virginia football games (the play-by-play announcer, in a halftime interview, introduced the famous fan to his radio audience as the winner of the "Mobile Prize for Literature") and took up fox hunting in the rolling

The Faulkner gravesite in Oxford, Mississippi, where he and his wife, Estelle Oldham Faulkner, are buried. (Harriett and Gioia Fargnoli)

This historical marker was placed near Faulkner's gravesite by the Oxford Rotary in 1990. (Harriett and Gioia Fargnoli)

hills of Albemarle County, proudly wearing the pink coat of the FARMINGTON HUNT CLUB.

Faulkner closed out the Snopes chronicle with *The MANSION*, published in November 1959. Maud Falkner, 88 years old, died in Oxford in October 1960. Faulkner finished his last novel, *The Reivers,* comic but elegiac too in its casting back to his Oxford boyhood, in August 1961.

He took two hard falls from horses in Virginia early in 1962, aggravating old back injuries. In June, his horse threw him violently as he rode along the Old Taylor Road near Rowan Oak. He reached for his usual remedy: prescription painkillers and whiskey. Soon he was deep into another alcoholic episode, incoherent, undernourished, virtually comatose.

On July 4, Estelle and his nephew James (Jimmy) FAULKNER decided to take him to Wright's Sanitarium in Byhalia. To their surprise, he offered no protest. Dr. Wright himself admitted him at 6 P.M. on July 5. William Faulkner died of a heart attack there at 1:30 on the morning of July 6, 1962. He is buried in Oxford.

Faulkner and alcoholism   The affliction of alcoholism came to Faulkner through his father and grandfather. John Wesley Thompson FALKNER, the novelist's paternal grandfather, periodically drank himself into a stay at the KEELEY INSTITUTE in Memphis. His father, Murry Cuthbert FALKNER, continued the family pattern of heavy drinking. He too checked into Keeley's at intervals to purge himself of alcohol.

Doctors and biographers have offered physiological and psychological explanations for Faulkner's regular, often predictable, and always prodigious bouts of drinking. In 1953, a New York psychiatrist, Dr. S. Bernard Wortis, concluded after examining Faulkner that increased worry, strain, or misery lessened his naturally low tolerance for alcohol. Wortis theorized that

Faulkner drank in an attempt to narcoticize intense and ever-present emotional pain.

Alcohol troubles were familiar—though evidently not especially terrifying—to Faulkner from his early childhood in OXFORD, MISSISSIPPI. He knew about the Young Colonel's trips to the Keeley Institute, where Dr. Leslie E. Keeley treated his patients with injections of double chloride of gold, a potion said to leave an extreme distaste for liquor in an alcoholic's mouth. In his 1896 study *The Non-Heredity of Inebriety,* Keeley classified alcoholism as a disease susceptible to treatment, not a fault of character, and argued that every alcoholic has within himself the power to recover.

Murry Falkner's appearances at the clinic must have shaken the doctor's faith in his theories about heredity, alcoholism, and the primacy of the will. Falkner's teetotalling wife, Maud Butler FALKNER, used to pack him off to the Keeley Institute when his drinking became unbearable. She hated liquor, and to emphasize her point she sometimes brought the boys along on the trip to Memphis. In the boys' recollections, though, the trips do not sound unpleasant. While their father submitted to the cure, Billy and his brothers amused themselves with streetcar excursions into the city. On one such journey, they caught their first glimpse of the Mississippi River.

Faulkner seems to have taken up drinking in the first instance out of boredom. In 1915 the family, concerned about his apparent aimlessness, put him to work at the Young Colonel's bank, an apprenticeship he found intolerable. To pass the time, he dipped into his grandfather's brand whiskey.

"Learned the medicinal value of his liquor," Faulkner remarked later. "Grandfather thought it was the janitor. Hard on the janitor."

As time went on, Faulkner's drinking became a cause for alarm. His friend Stark YOUNG, who saw a good deal of the aspiring novelist in New York City in 1921, expressed astonishment at the amount of alcohol—whiskey and sometimes cheap gin—he could put away. Faulkner was, after all, a small man, and slightly built. In the autumn of 1928, after he finished correcting proofs of *The SOUND AND THE FURY,* he locked himself in his room on Macdougal Street in New York and drank himself into unconsciousness.

Faulkner called alcoholism "the chemistry of craving." The drinking bouts became a recurring pattern in the last stages of his creative work: Tired, emotionally spent, prone to feelings of depression and emptiness, Faulkner would enscript a date neatly on the last page of a manuscript, or finish correcting the last page of proofs, and then begin to drink.

The publication of *SANCTUARY* in 1931 brought him a degree of celebrity, and he made the rounds of literary parties during a seven-week interval in New York that autumn. But what he really enjoyed were evenings drinking with Dashiell Hammett, a master of the detective novel and a formidable alcoholic himself. The good times with Hammett ended in Faulkner's disappearance for several days on a lonely binge in his hotel room.

The completion of ABSALOM, ABSALOM! in 1936, coupled with Faulkner's all but chronic money troubles and his enduring grief over his youngest brother's death in an airplane crash, touched off another bout of self-destructive drinking. His mother and his stepson Malcolm FRANKLIN took turns sitting by his "drunk bed," but the episode grew so prolonged that they decided to send Faulkner off for the first of what would be several stays at Wright's Sanatorium, a small private hospital in BYHALIA, MISSISSIPPI.

Faulkner's love affairs, especially his long-running association with Meta CARPENTER, would sometimes trigger a binge. Carpenter's marriage to another man sent him into a spin in the autumn of 1937. In a drunken stupor, he fell against a steampipe in the bathroom of his room at the ALGONQUIN HOTEL in New York and seared his back. A doctor treated him for severe burns and dosed him with paraldehyde to kill his craving for alcohol.

Faulkner's work for WARNER BROTHERS in Hollywood in the 1940s drove him to a despair that often ended in a drinking episode. His studio friends would intervene, making excuses for him, warning him against drinking on the job, finally cutting off his supply of liquor. At such times Faulkner would try to negotiate. The novelist was famously sparing with his signature. But on one occasion he signed a stack of his books piled on the coffee table of his movie friend A. I. (Buzz) BEZZERIDES, with whom he happened to be living, and then pleaded for a drink.

The approaching end of his strange affair with Joan WILLIAMS, coupled with recurring back pain (the result of falls from a horse), landed Faulkner in the Gartley-Ramsay Hospital, a private psychiatric institute in Memphis, in the fall 1952. He resumed drinking, mixing whiskey and beer with the sedative Seconal, when he returned home to ROWAN OAK, and narrowly missed serious injury when he fell down the stairs there. His wife, (Lida) Estelle Oldham FAULKNER, desperate, phoned Faulkner's friend and editor, Saxe COMMINS, who traveled down to Oxford from New York at her summons. Commins found the novelist semiconscious on a couch, battered, incontinent, and near delirium; he wrote to his wife that he was witnessing "the complete disintegration of a man."

Commins saw Faulkner back into the Gartley-Ramsay Hospital. He returned two weeks later to find Estelle launched on a prolonged drinking spell of her own, having discovered Joan Williams's letters to Faulkner.

The critic and biographer Federick Karl regards Faulkner's drinking as suicidal. The episodes were "virtu-

ally acts of self-destruction," Karl wrote, "since he needed to be saved by others"—his mother, Estelle, friends such as Commins. "With alcohol, he had found the middle ground or perfect balance between life and death," Karl continued. "Suicide by direct means was out, but suicide through drinking was a way of dealing with life."

Karl speculates, too, that Faulkner may have prized alcohol as the fuel for his artistic flame, much as had the romantic and symbolist poets he admired as a young man.

Faulkner himself used to make light of what was patently an unalloyed private horror, as though offering a handout for public consumption. It is true that he actually liked whiskey, preferring Jack Daniel's when he could afford it.

In a PARIS REVIEW interview with Jean STEIN in 1956, Faulkner observed that all a writer needed for his work were paper, tobacco, a little food, and whiskey.

"Bourbon, you mean?" she asked.

"No, I ain't that particular," Faulkner answered. Then, parodying himself and satirizing his own tortured emotional life, he went on, "Between scotch and nothing I'll take scotch."

Critics have noted that alcoholics in Faulkner's fiction are rarely aggressive or dangerously violent. Some are quiet, almost gentle, and defeated, like the elder Jason COMPSON in *The Sound and the Fury*. Boon HOGGANBECK in "The Bear," (see GO DOWN, MOSES) *The Reivers*, and other works is a rare example of an exuberant drinker in Faulkner's fiction. RIDER, a character in the short story "Pantaloon in Black" (in *Go Down, Moses*), consumes vast quantities of moonshine in cold, furious despair, hoping to dull the pain of his wife's death.

Faulkner's last binge began with bourbon, taken along with doses of prescription painkillers for his back. His nephew James Murry (Jimmy) Faulkner raised the subject of the cure, even though the novelist had gone through only about a fifth and a half of whiskey and it was early yet in the drinking cycle. To Jimmy's surprise, Faulkner agreed to go to Wright's Sanatorium, where he died early in the morning of July 6, 1962.

Faulkner and criticism Faulkner's general status as a skillful and important writer began to emerge shortly after World War II and more or less coincided with the publication in 1946 of *The PORTABLE FAULKNER*, edited with an introduction by Malcolm COWLEY. Robert Penn WARREN considered this publication "the great watershed for Faulkner's reputation in the United States" ("Introduction: Faulkner: Past and Present," in *Faulkner: A Collection of Critical Essays*, edited by Robert Penn Warren, p. 10), published at a time when all of Faulkner's works except SANCTUARY (1931) were out of print. Faulkner's status was significantly bolstered in 1950 when he was awarded the 1949 NOBEL PRIZE IN LITERATURE. From this period on, serious Faulkner criticism began in the United States. (It should be noted that outside of this country, and especially in France as early as the 1930s, Faulkner was highly regarded by such writers as Jean-Paul Sartre; André Malraux; Maurice Coindreau, one of Faulkner's first French translators; and Valery Larbaud. For further information about Faulkner's international status, see the fine collection of essays in *Faulkner: International Perspectives,* edited by Doreen Fowler and Anne J. Abadie.)

Prior to Faulkner's award of the Nobel Prize and the publication of *The Portable Faulkner,* most critics in one way or another attacked Faulkner and his perplexing style. One commentator, Henry Seidel Canby, clearly showed his disgust of Faulkner in the very title of his review of *Sanctuary,* "The School of Cruelty," which appeared in the *Saturday Review of Literature* in May 1931. Other critics, however—Robert Penn Warren, Conrad AIKEN, George Marion O'Donnell, and Warren Beck—voiced favorable responses to Faulkner's writings. As close readers attempting to see beyond the disparaging assessment of Faulkner's style and charges that he exploited violence and sex, these critics began to judge Faulkner on his own terms and virtually laid a foundation for later commentators. Cowley, for example, in his introduction to *The Portable Faulkner,* expands upon an interpretation regarding the overall unity in Faulkner's works first touched upon by O'Donnell in his essay "Faulkner's Mythology," published in the summer 1939 issue of the *Kenyon Review.* Others, too, had picked up on the thematic integrity of Faulkner's work and the value of his achievement in relation to the whole of his writings, as Kay Boyle pointed out in her March 1938 review of *The UNVANQUISHED* that appeared in the *New Republic.*

By the late 1940s and early 1950s, Faulkner criticism began to come into its own. Studies of individual novels started to appear. The summer 1949 and autumn 1950 issues of *Perspective,* both of which were devoted to Faulkner, included Summer Powell's discussion of *The SOUND AND THE FURY* and Olga W. VICKERY's study of *As I Lay Dying,* among others. Although Evelyn Scott published a study of *The Sound and the Fury* in 1929 when the novel first came out, a study Frederick J. Hoffman called "a landmark in Faulkner criticism" for its thorough discussion of form and point of view ("An Introduction," in *William Faulkner: Three Decades of Criticism,* edited by Frederick J. Hoffman and Olga W. Vickery, p. 17), it was really not until the late 1940s and after that critics began in earnest to concentrate on specific works, including the short stories, and on such varied topics as the coherence of the works, individually and collectively; rhetorical and stylistic devices; Faulkner's profound sense of place and time; biographical and historical interests; textual concerns; and specialized issues like gender, race, popular culture, religion, and

films. With his published interviews, FAULKNER AT NAGANO (1956) and *Faulkner in the University* (1959), both following the published version (1951) of his Nobel Prize acceptance speech in December 1950, Faulkner himself added his own voice to Faulkner criticism. A few noteworthy studies chosen at random include Irving Howe's *William Faulkner: A Critical Study* (1951); Vickery's *The Novels of William Faulkner: A Critical Interpretation* (1959, 3rd edition 1995); Cleanth Brooks's *William Faulkner: The Yoknapatawpha Country* (1963); Melvin Backman's *Faulkner: The Major Years* (1966); Michael Millgate's *The Achievement of William Faulkner* (1966); Brooks's *William Faulkner: Toward Yoknapatawpha and Beyond* (1978), a companion piece on Faulkner's works Brooks did not cover in his earlier volume; John T. Matthews's *The Play of Faulkner's Language* (1982); *New Essays on "Light in August"* (1987), edited by Michael Millgate; André Bleikasten's *The Ink of Melancholy: Faulkner's Novels from "The Sound and the Fury" to "Light in August"* (1990); and *New Essays on "Go Down, Moses"* (1996), edited by Linda Wagner-Martin. An invaluable source of Faulkner information and short critical pieces is *Teaching Faulkner,* published twice annually by the Center for Faulkner Studies, Southeast

Faulkner at home in Mississippi in 1950, shortly before he won the Nobel Prize in literature. (AP/Wide World Photos)

William Faulkner (left) with an unidentified woman and his editor, Saxe Commins, at the National Book Award presentation in New York on January 25, 1955. (Brodsky Collection, Center for Faulkner Studies, Southeast Missouri State University)

Missouri State University, edited by Robert W. HAMBLIN with Charles A. Peek as associate editor.

Character studies, general introductions to Faulkner, and guides and indexes to his characters also started appearing in the late fifties and early sixties: John Lewis Longley Jr.'s *The Tragic Mask: A Study of Faulkner's Heroes* (1957); Lawrence Thompson's *William Faulkner: An Introduction and Interpretation* (1963; 2nd edition 1967); Robert W. Kirk's *Faulkner's People: A Complete Guide and Index to the Characters in the Fiction of William Faulkner* (with Marvin Klotz, 1963); Edmond L. Volpe's *A Reader's Guide to William Faulkner* (1964); and Thomas E. Connolly's *Faulkner's World: A Directory of His People and Synopses of Actions in His Published Works* (1988). In 1999, *A William Faulkner Encyclopedia,* the first encyclo-

pedia of Faulkner's life and work, edited by Robert W. Hamblin and Charles A. Peek was published.

Although a few biographical resources were available relatively early on—for example, the anecdotal account of Faulkner, *My Brother Bill: An Affectionate Reminiscence* (1963), by Faulkner's brother John; *The Falkners of Mississippi* (1967), by Faulkner's brother Murry (known as Jack); and Millgate's extensive introduction to *The Achievement of William Faulkner* (1966)—the first full-scale biography of Faulkner was published in 1974 by Joseph BLOTNER, *Faulkner: A Biography* (2 vols.; revised one-volume edition, 1984). Other lengthy biographies followed, such as Joel Williamson's *William Faulkner and Southern History* (1993) and Richard Gray's *The Life of William Faulkner: A Critical Biography* (1994).

The important area of textual studies, including concordances, glossaries, and commentaries, started to appear in the early 1980s and is virtually synonymous with the Faulkner scholar Noel POLK. Under the editorship of Polk and Blotner, the Library of America has published corrected texts of Faulkner's novels: *William Faulkner: Novels 1930–1935; William Faulkner: Novels 1936–1940; William Faulkner: Novels 1942–1954;* and *William Faulkner: Novels 1957–1962.*

For a list of Faulkner's works, see Appendix I; for a secondary bibliography, see Appendix II.

Faulkner and film   On a recommendation from Leland Hayward, Ben WASSON's superior at the American Play Company, Faulkner was invited by Sam Marx at METRO-GOLDWYN-MAYER Studios to Hollywood. Faulkner arrived in Hollywood in May 1932 to work as a screenwriter for MGM. In that same year his father died and *LIGHT IN AUGUST* was published. Faulkner continued to work on and off in Hollywood for MGM, Twentieth Century–Fox, and WARNER BROTHERS for the next 22 years, an opportunity that provided him with a much-needed income to supplement his sparse earnings as a fiction writer. In late 1935, Faulkner met Meta CARPENTER, also a native of Mississippi, who was working as a secretary for the director-producer Howard HAWKS. The two developed an intimate relationship over the next 15 years.

Although Faulkner's reputation as a novelist was not universally acclaimed in 1932, he was known and respected. Hawks, with whom Faulkner became friends, had been favorably impressed with *SOLDIERS' PAY* (1926), Faulkner's first novel. Hawks also purchased the rights to Faulkner's "Turn About" (see "TURNABOUT"), a short story dealing with air and sea combat in World War I, and requested that Faulkner write the screenplay. He did so with Edith Fitzgerald and Dwight Taylor. The story was the basis for Hawks's 1933 film *Today We Live.*

Though Faulkner was not enamored with Hollywood, his personal biases never interfered with his professional responsibilities. As Joseph BLOTNER comments in his biography of Faulkner, the short story "GOLDEN LAND" clearly reveals Faulkner's attitude toward Hollywood: "Set in Beverly Hills, its every page seemed imbued with the distaste and unhappiness he had felt. The terrain, the climate, the architecture, the people, their behavior, their dress—all displeased him" (p. 342). During his association with Hollywood, Faulkner worked or collaborated on well over 40 films, including the following six, which he coauthored and for which he received screen credit: *Today We Live* (1933), *The Road to Glory* (1936), *Slave Ship* (1937), *To Have and Have Not* (1944), *The Big Sleep* (1946), and *Land of the Pharaohs* (1955). *To Have and Have Not,* loosely based on Ernest HEMINGWAY's novel of the same title, is, as Gene D. Phillips observes in *Fiction, Film, and Faulkner: The*

Art of Adaptation, the only film in history "to be the creative product of two Nobel Prize winners" (p. 43).

Faulkner invested much time, energy, and creative talent on other scripts, none of which ever made it to the big screen. These screenplays included, for example, *Manservant* (1932), *The College Widow* (1932), and those dealing particularly with the war effort, such as *The Life and Death of a Bomber/Liberator Story* (1942/1943), *The De Gaulle Story* (1942), and *Battle Cry* (1943).

In addition to "Turn About," many other Faulkner works have been adapted to film. One critic, Bruce F. Kawin, observes that Faulkner is "the most cinematic of novelists. Such techniques as montage, freeze-frame, slow motion and visual metaphor abound in his fiction" (*Faulkner and Film,* p. 5). Faulkner's works adapted by other screenwriters include *INTRUDER IN THE DUST* (film by same title, 1949), *PYLON* (film titled *Tarnished Angels,* 1957), *The HAMLET* (film titled *The Long Hot Summer,* 1958), *The SOUND AND THE FURY* (film by same name, 1959), *SANCTUARY* and *REQUIEM FOR A NUN* (film titled *Sanctuary,* 1961), and *The REIVERS* (film by same name, 1969).

For more information, see *Selected Letters of William Faulkner;* Louis Daniel Brodsky and Robert W. Hamblin, eds., *Faulkner: A Comprehensive Guide to the Brodsky Collection,* vols. 3 (*The De Gaulle Story*) and 4 (*Battle Cry*); Bruce F. Kawin, ed., *Faulkner's MGM Screenplays;* Louis Daniel Brodsky and Robert W. Hamblin, *Faulkner and Hollywood: A Retrospective from the Brodsky Collection;* and Joseph Blotner, "Faulkner in Hollywood," in *Man and the Movies,* edited by W. R. Robinson, pp. 261–303.

Faulkner and flying   The notion of flight long fascinated Faulkner. His simple boyhood curiosity grew into a complex involvement when he chose the persona of aviator-hero as one of the many fronts he presented to the world. Later, flying itself provided opportunities for a brush with the ultimate that Faulkner seemed to crave.

As a boy, Billy Falkner led his brothers and their cousin Sally Murry in building an airplane from a pattern in *American Boy* magazine. Setting up shop in a barn on the Falkner place, the boys used their mother's bean poles for the frame and old newspapers stuck on with flour paste for the skin.

The final product was close to full scale. Billy took the first test flight, launched from the lip of a 10-foot-deep sand ditch in the Falkners' back lot. The plane came apart in midair.

The air war over France in 1914–18 caught Faulkner's imagination; in early 1918, at age 20, he tried to join the U.S. Army Flying Corps. The army judged him too short and too light of weight. In the spring, Faulkner and his friend Philip STONE plotted a scheme to infiltrate him into the ROYAL AIR FORCE as a flying cadet. Faulkner invented an English background (he claimed his birthplace as Finchley in Middlesex) and added the *u* to his last name. He and Stone even forged reliable-looking references from England. Faulkner successfully enlisted in the RAF in New York City on June 18, 1918.

Faulkner's hometown newspaper, the Oxford EAGLE reported on June 27: "Mr. William Falkner who has been spending a few months in New York is visiting his parents Mr. and Mrs. Murry Falkner. He has joined the English Royal Flying Corps and leaves the eighth of July for Toronto, Canada, where he will train."

Faulkner later invented an immodestly eventful flying career, essentially creating a fictional character for himself: British flying officer and wounded war hero. As late as 1932, a UNIVERSITY OF MISSISSIPPI professor writing about Faulkner remarked approvingly of the novelist's modesty about his war career, even though he had "two enemy planes to his credit and several times barely escaped death." In NEW ORLEANS in the 1920s, Faulkner walked with a manufactured limp, claimed he wore a silver plate in his head, and explained that he drank immoderately to dull the pain of his war injuries.

"During the war he was with the British Air Force and made a brilliant record," the New Orleans little magazine DOUBLE DEALER wrote in introducing the aspiring poet and critic in the mid-1920s. "He was severely wounded."

Faulkner was somewhat more truthful with his family; after all, his brother Jack, a Marine, actually had been seriously wounded, and in the head too, fighting on the Argonne front in northern France in November 1918. Faulkner claimed he had flown solo, and had cracked up a couple of aircraft in the service of the Crown.

In fact, Faulkner never got out of ground school. He turned up at the RAF recruits' depot in Toronto in July 1918 carrying a suitcase labeled "William Faulkner, Oxford, Mississippi," and gained an indoctrination into military life. By November, he claimed to have been flying for three months, and to have logged four hours' solo time aloft.

There is no evidence that Faulkner flew at all, let alone banged up any aircraft. And his ground school marks were mediocre—around 70 percent, according to his service record. With the armistice of November 11, 1918, the British government moved rapidly to discharge surplus air cadets. Faulkner was home in Oxford by late December, with $42.58 in demobilization pay and a promise that he eventually would be made an honorary second lieutenant.

Faulkner anticipated the honorary designation, posing at home in his British officer's uniform, with second lieutenant's pips affixed to the shoulder straps, unearned pilot's wings on the tunic, a swagger stick under his arm. Frederick Karl, a Faulkner biographer, suggests that the elegant uniform and the imposture gave him an edge over the authentically wounded Jack and over their shambling and most unmilitary father. Karl regards the brief RAF experience, and Faulkner's

use of it, as crucial in the artist's development because it turned him into a storyteller.

The military experience, real and imagined, informed Faulkner's novels SOLDIERS' PAY (1926), SARTORIS (1929) and A FABLE (1954), as well as several short stories, including "AD ASTRA" and "ALL THE DEAD PILOTS."

Faulkner finally earned a pilot's license in 1933 under the instruction of the veteran aviator Vernon OMLIE. He told Omlie that he had become afraid after crashing as an RAF pilot and wanted to recover his courage as well as his skills. Though Omlie reported him as a slow learner and dangerously clumsy on landings, Faulkner lifted off for his first solo flight on April 20, 1933.

Omlie introduced Faulkner to the world of aerial circuses, with their stunt flyers, wingwalkers, and parachutists. These performers caught Faulkner's imagination. He saw them as the gypsies of the industrial age, misfits driven by an urge to escape the earthbound world. Much of the barnstormer material made its way into the novel PYLON (1935), whose main characters, Roger and Laverne Shumann, were partly modeled on Vernon Omlie and his wife, Phoebe.

Faulkner used money from the sale of the film rights for his novel SANCTUARY to buy his own airplane, a Waco cabin cruiser, in the autumn of 1933. He eventually turned the machine over to his younger brother Dean FAULKNER, who had learned to fly—and had developed a career out of it—at Faulkner's suggestion. Dean Swift Faulkner died in a crash during an airshow at PONTOTOC, MISSISSIPPI, in November 1935. Faulkner blamed himself for the tragedy and had nightmares about it long afterward.

Horses eventually supplanted airplanes as one of Faulkner's means (drinking was another) of risking himself. Reckless riding over rough country aboard powerful mounts supplied some of the danger that doubtless formed a necessary part of flying's appeal—no exaggerated danger, so it happened, for Faulkner suffered painful back injuries in a series of falls from horses.

Faulkner biographer Joel Williamson argues that horses were an explicit extension of the novelist's earlier role as a wounded flyer, that there was an essential similarity between the man and his airplane and the man and his horse: "Both attempted to assert mastery over awesome power that gave amplitude to themselves," Williamson wrote. "More important, that power was dangerous, capricious, and liable to go out of control for no discernable reason—with hardly a second's warning and with devastating and often fatal results."

By the 1940s, fame forced the novelist to correct his heavily fictionalized military biography, or anyway attempt to erase it from the record. Malcolm COWLEY planned to use the 1920s war hero story, including the fiction of his having been in combat over France, as part of his biographical sketch for The PORTABLE FAULKNER (1946). He dropped it on Faulkner's strong protest.

Johncy Falkner either believed his brother's fictions about his RAF service or decided to repeat them out of family loyalty. In his memoir *My Brother Bill,* published in 1963, a year after Faulkner's death, he noted that Billy was the first of the Falkner boys to learn to ride a bicycle. "I think it was his sense of balance that helped him live through flying Camels in the First War, for there was never a more tricky airplane built than a Sopwith Camel," Johncy wrote.

Faulkner and history   Past and present clash eternally in Faulkner's fiction. In his use of the past he is, in the words of the critic and biographer Frederick Karl, "the most historical of our important writers: one who broke away from the past in his techniques even while the past meant so much to him." As a child, he absorbed a living history in the tales of aging Civil War veterans; he witnessed as a young man the final destruction of the wilderness of the Mississippi CHICKASAW INDIANS; he died only a few weeks before a young African American defied race, class, and the legacy of Southern history and enrolled in the UNIVERSITY OF MISSISSIPPI.

For Faulkner, the past was a palpable presence. "He was steeped in the legends of the Highlanders, reports by old hunters of the original wilderness, the primitive isolation of Mississippi before 'the Wawh,' [the Civil War] the violent separation of the races ordained by God," the critic Alfred KAZIN wrote in *An American Procession* (1984). "Faulkner lived with sacred history like a character in the Bible." Biblical, too, is a powerful sense in all of Faulkner's work of the South's, and of America's, sins. For him, slavery and despoliation of the natural world are facets of original sin.

Faulkner exploited the past in some of his most important fiction, most notably in ABSALOM, ABSALOM! (1936), but also in *The SOUND AND THE FURY* (1929), *GO DOWN, MOSES* (1942), and the SNOPES TRILOGY—*The HAMLET* (1940), *The TOWN* (1957) and *The MANSION* (1959).

Faulkner's fictional reach extends back to the 1790s, when a few thousand Native Americans and Black slaves peopled his YOKNAPATAWPHA COUNTY region. By the 1830s, the new world encroaches and the elements are assembled for the great conflict that echoes through all of Faulkner's work: the conflict of man in nature and in society. Settlers arrive from east of the Appalachians with their slaves and their notions of ownership. Thomas Sutpen buys a hundred square miles of land from an old Chickasaw chief who has no right to sell and implements his grand design, creating "a country all divided and fixed and neat with a people living on it all divided and fixed and neat because of what color their slaves happened to be and what they happened to own" (*Absalom, Absalom!*, p. 221). The Civil War destroys Sutpen and brings his design to nothing. The sins live on, though: the legacy of slavery, the destruction of the Big Woods. Sutpen, near ruin,

sells off tracts of wilderness to the planter and businessman Major DE SPAIN, who first opens the Delta bottoms to the logging companies.

The old, proud South found itself reduced to the status of an economic dependent of the North after the war, exporting low-cost raw materials—cotton, forest products—in return for expensive manufactured goods. The North imposed high tariffs and railroad freight charges. Money was scarce, the cost of borrowing high. Those who adapted to modern, Northern ways stood the best chance of survival: Jason COMPSON, the cotton speculator in *The Sound and the Fury;* Flem SNOPES in *The Hamlet, The Town* and *The Mansion.* Descending from the Civil War–era bushwhacker class of landless Whites, Snopes displaces the crumbling planter aristocracy, ruthlessly trampling their antique codes and values in the process.

Jason Compson pays out $10 a month to a New York advisory firm for daily information on the cotton market. The Compsons, once powerful planters and masters of all they surveyed, are reduced in three generations to a state of dependency on an anonymous Northern cotton tipster. And it doesn't even work: Compson's $10 a month of inside information proves worthless.

In *Go Down, Moses* and other works, Faulkner linked the destruction of the wilderness to the loss of values that bring on decline and ultimate fall. Isaac MCCASLIN, the hunter of the "The Bear" (in *Go Down, Moses*) turns 21 and renounces his plantation inheritance, claiming that man had "cursed and tainted" what God created. Ike learns early that the bear, the quarry of the annual autumn hunting parties into the vanishing woods, may seem indestructible but in truth is too big for the country it inhabits. The hunters finally bring down the old two-toed bear. Within a few years, as Major de Spain sells off timber rights, the industrialists—the modernizers—effect an astonishing change.

Faulkner's fictional history closely paralleled his family's history. The Civil War ended 32 years before Faulkner's birth, but it lived on still in turn-of-the-century OXFORD, MISSISSIPPI.

"Lying behind nearly everything he wrote was the great American divide, the Civil War," Frederick Karl observed. "Little can be understood in Faulkner without an awareness of that great hovering presence, the shadow of courage and debacle."

Faulkner's paternal great-grandfather, William Clark FALKNER, commanded the 2nd Mississippi Volunteers at BULL RUN in 1861. Returning home a year later, he raised a unit of irregular cavalry for operations in North Mississippi. In 1864, Federal troops burned Falkner's home in RIPLEY, MISSISSIPPI, and the Oxford hotel of Burlina Butler, the future novelist's maternal great-grandmother. Burlina's son Henry died in a Georgia hospital of wounds received in the fighting around Atlanta in 1864.

The stories and novels mirror this. The husband of Aunt Virginia (Jenny) DU PRE (in *SARTORIS* and *The*

UNVANQUISHED) is killed in Charleston at the beginning of the war. Her brother Bayard SARTORIS (1) dies in a raid on a Yankee headquarters in Virginia. Henry SUTPEN (in *Absalom, Absalom!*) is wounded at SHILOH. Quentin Compson's grandfather loses his right arm there.

Like the fictional Snopeses, the Falkners adapted to postwar conditions. W. C. Falkner, the Old Colonel, built railroads using methods as ruthless as those of any Flem Snopes. His son, John Wesley Thompson FALKNER, the Young Colonel, maintained the family position for another generation through banking and the law. Younger rivals eventually drove him out of his bank. Circumstances forced him to break up the family mansion, the Big Place, into apartments and sell off the corner lot to a gasoline retailer. The Falkners were slipping. The novelist's hapless father, the Old Colonel's grandson, lacked the wherewithal to arrest the decline.

As an artist, Faulkner stood somewhat outside this pattern of failure and disintegration. Even so, it is suggestive that he chose for a dwelling place a deteriorated antebellum mansion, a Compson sort of place, built on land purchased from a Chickasaw chief. When he could afford it, he bought a rundown LAFAYETTE COUNTY hill farm of the type the marginal people, White and Black, of this Yoknapatawpha fiction worked on shares.

Faulkner remarked in a 1933 letter that Southern writers tended either "to draw a savage indictment of the contemporary scene" or to create, as an escape, "a make-believe region of swords and magnolias and mockingbirds." His *Absalom, Absalom!* appeared the same year as Margaret Mitchell's Civil War fantasy *Gone with the Wind,* the apotheosis of make-believe. Faulkner's issues were race and history, not gallantry in battle; his South was not noble—it was morally corrupt.

Still, Faulkner himself approached the "hoop skirts and plug hat" (his phrase) school of historical fiction in a series of stories originally written for magazine publication. In 1938, he linked them to form the novel *The Unvanquished,* in which young Bayard SARTORIS (3) and his Black friend Ringo STROTHER experience a series of adventures in north Mississippi during the Civil War and early Reconstruction. The South may have been losing the war, but the boys consistently outwit the invading Yankees.

For all its picturesqueness, *The Unvanquished* takes up serious themes too. In a moving passage, Faulkner shows the impact of the promise of freedom on north Mississippi slaves. In their thousands, they put themselves in motion toward the Yankees and tell the narrator Bayard that they are "Going to cross the Jordan."

In the violent aftermath of the war, Bayard's father, John SARTORIS, the ruthless, intolerant and homicidal fictional counterpart of W. C. Falkner, attempts to restore the antebellum order, challenging the carpetbagging Burdens. Sartoris shoots down two of the Burdens at the voting hall and carries away the ballot box.

There is no nostalgia for the past in Faulkner. The modern world overwhelms a society that deserves to collapse. "The Old Order, he clearly indicates, did *not* satisfy human needs, did *not* afford justice, and therefore was 'accurst' and held the seeds of its own ruin," the novelist and critic Robert Penn WARREN wrote in *New and Selected Essays.* Faulkner's fiction is a critique of what has gone before and what is; it is also, as Warren suggests, a parable. "From the land itself, from its rich soil yearning to produce, and from history, from an error or sin committed long ago and compounded a thousand times, the doom comes," Warren remarked. "That is, the present is to be understood, and fully felt, only in terms of the past."

Modernity chews up the landscape as it chews up the past. In "DELTA AUTUMN," the process is nearly complete. The axes and plows have gnawed away till barely a patch of the Big Woods survives. The hunters used to make their way slowly into the nearby wilderness in mule-drawn wagons; now they must drive hundreds of miles to find a wilderness in which to hunt.

With the Civil Rights movement of the 1950s, the past caught up to the South, and to America. Faulkner played an equivocal part in the struggle. All the same, the crisis fulfilled the prophecy and the historical vision of his fiction. In the end, the issues he addressed are common to all, "a general plight and problem," as Warren observed. His concerns were not ultimately with the South, but with the general philosophical question of the interrelationship of man and nature.

Faulkner and race   Faulkner's attitudes on white and black relations in a South cursed with the legacy of slavery were complex and profoundly ambiguous. A Mississippian, a traditionalist, and a literary artist of the first rank, Faulkner created a powerfully liberal body of fiction, yet his public pronouncements on race were confused, contradictory, and ill-judged. More than any white writer of his time, he invented fully realized and sympathetic black characters. Yet an unconscious racism pervaded Faulkner's thought, his actions, and his literary works.

The Falkners of OXFORD, MISSISSIPPI, employed blacks as servants and had blacks as near neighbors. The Falkner boys had black playmates. Circumstantial evidence suggests that William Clark FALKNER, the Old Colonel, Faulkner's great-grandfather, produced a "shadow family" of at least two children with one of his former slaves. The future novelist would weave miscegenation themes into his fiction: a number of memorable characters, among them Clytemnestra SUTPEN, Joe CHRISTMAS, Sam FATHERS and Lucas BEAUCHAMP, are of mixed parentage. Blacks lived in every section of Oxford in the early 1900s, even if the largest concentration lay in the black quarter known as Freedmantown.

For all this familiarity, hysteria about racial matters convulsed the Mississippi of Faulkner's childhood. Demagogic politicians and popular fiction such as Thomas Dixon's *The Clansman* (1908) portrayed blacks, especially black men, as retrogressing into savagery since the end of slavery in 1865. Lynching became a terrible symptom of white hysteria. More than 200 blacks died at the hands of white mobs in Mississippi between 1889 and 1909—more than in any other state.

Billy Falkner absorbed this atmosphere as a boy. In October 1908, a 2,000-strong mob lynched a black bootlegger named Nelse Patton on the Square in Oxford within earshot of the Falkner home. He had been accused of assaulting a white woman; the mob broke into the jail, dragged Patton to the square and strung him up naked on a telephone pole, fired a fusillade at him, and left him hanging through the night. Faulkner may have used the memory of the Patton murder in "DRY SEPTEMBER," a 1931 short story in which a middle-aged white woman's accusation touches off the lynching of an innocent black man. In the novel INTRUDER IN THE DUST (1948), a mob forms outside the jail where Lucas Beauchamp awaits trial on a murder charge.

Billy's first teacher owned a copy of *The Clansman*, and somehow the book eventually passed into his library. The stage version of the novel played in the Opera House in Oxford only a few weeks after Patton's murder. John Wesley Thompson FALKNER, Billy's grandfather, owned the theater.

Strict subordination, white over black, governed racial relations in the Oxford of Faulkner's childhood. Billy and his brothers attended the all-white grade school. Their black playmates made do with dramatically inadequate schools. Faulkner's family—his parents, his brothers, his wife—accepted segregation as though it were the natural order of things. In this as in so much else Faulkner stood apart. He came to be deeply troubled over the South's racial past and present.

His attitudes toward individual African Americans were a blend of paternalism, generosity, gratitude, and real affection, even love. He regarded the longtime Falkner servant Caroline BARR, known to the family as Mammie Callie, as a second mother. She lived for nearly a century, long enough to help rear Faulkner's own daughter, Jill FAULKNER, born in 1933. He maintained close and affectionate relations, too, with the elderly retainer Ned BARNETT.

Faulkner purchased GREENFIELD FARM, a run-down 320-acre farm in LAFAYETTE COUNTY in 1938 and, in the face of advice to convert it into a modern cattle operation with minimal labor requirements, peopled the place with black tenants. He probably lost money on the farm, and he liked to complain of having to support the tenants he had settled there. All the same, the farm filled a need in Faulkner. He could play the role of farmer there—and of seigneur, too, patron of the black families who worked the place under his benign supervision. He could draw satisfaction from doing his best for individual blacks.

Callie Barr, Ned Barnett, and the Greenfield farmers were, of course, in a familiar and accepted social position: They were servants and tenants, clearly subordinate to whites. Faulkner's attitudes toward such people may reflect what the biographer Frederick Karl diagnoses as his unconscious racism. In the early 1940s, a time when racial questions had begun to claim Faulkner's attention, he consistently used the epithet "nigger" in correspondence with his friend and editor Robert HAAS, a Northerner and a Jew who, as Karl notes, almost certainly would not have used it himself.

"For a man so alert to language and to nuance . . . it is inconceivable he did not know what he was doing or thought he was using the word neutrally," Karl wrote. "At its deepest levels, his continued use of the word indicates a racism so unconsciously insistent it becomes a force in his personal assessment of racial issues and racial justice."

But Faulkner was no bigot, even if he did lapse into the use of racial slurs. That sort of crudeness did not seep into his art. As Karl observed, "Faulkner's views on race *in his fiction* were highly sophisticated."

Faulkner characters learn their racial lessons early. In "The Fire and the Hearth," one of the linked stories in GO DOWN, MOSES, Henry BEAUCHAMP's White McCaslin "foster brother" shows a sudden, unexpected change in their relationship. They will no longer sleep in the same bed, eat at the same table. Henry's mother understands. She lays a single plate at the table for the McCaslin boy. "So he entered his heritage," the narrator comments. "He ate its bitter fruit" (*Go Down, Moses*, p. 110).

Caroline Barr is commonly regarded as a model for one of Faulkner's best-known characters, white or black, Dilsey GIBSON of *The SOUND AND THE FURY* (1929). Struggling heroically to keep the disintegrating Compson family together, she represents essential qualities of loyalty, fidelity, sacrifice and endurance. She is, said the novelist and critic Robert Penn WARREN, "the very ethical center of the book, the vessel of virtue and compassion." Yet Dilsey retains the traditional role of service to white folks and dependence on them. So do Clytie Sutpen in ABSALOM, ABSALOM! (1936) and Molly BEAUCHAMP in *Go Down, Moses* (1942) and *Intruder in the Dust*.

Faulkner does not, however, restrict himself altogether to this pattern. Joe Christmas in LIGHT IN AUGUST (1932) is anything but subservient, though he is deeply wounded. Wrote Warren, "With his mixed blood, he is the lost, suffering, enduring creature, and even the murder he commits at the end is a fumbling attempt to define his manhood, an attempt to break out of the iron ring of mechanism." There is no actual proof that Christmas has black blood, but he thinks he does, and so do others. He is a marginal figure, uncertain of his identity: a paradigm, so it seems, for the *human* dilemma.

Lucas Beauchamp is fiercely proud both of his descent from the white McCaslins and of his blackness. In the character of Beauchamp, Faulkner seems to suggest the South is a single race, white and black. Like Sam Fathers, the sage of the forest in *Go Down, Moses* and elsewhere, Beauchamp is a stoical hero, "a focus of dignity and integrity," in Warren's words, a man prepared to stand on his principles no matter what the cost. "*We got to make him be a nigger first,*" outraged whites say of him. "*He's got to admit he's a nigger. Then maybe we'll accept him as he seems to intend to be accepted*" (*Intruder*, p. 18; italics Faulkner's) But Beauchamp refuses to be intimidated. He defiantly refuses to follow white strictures on how blacks should behave.

World War II focused Faulkner's attention on race as never before. In a letter to his stepson Malcolm FRANKLIN in 1943, he remarked on the irony of an all-black fighter squadron flying combat missions in North Africa on the same day 20 blacks were killed in a race riot in Detroit. He predicted that the war would bring necessary changes.

Intruder in the Dust, a call for Southern whites to do justice to blacks, grew out of this pattern of thinking. More tract than novel, with a creaky murder-mystery plot, it is a powerful expression nevertheless of Faulkner's concern. Gavin STEVENS, the White lawyer who defends Lucas Beauchamp on a charge of murder, exhorts white Southerners to do justice to blacks without Northern prodding (or, for that matter, Northern interference).

Faulkner's views sound wholly inadequate today, but in 1948 they set Faulkner apart from all but a few white Southerners. In protest of tentative federal government moves toward integration, white Southern Democrats bolted from the national party to form the segregationist "Dixiecrats." Their presidential candidate, Strom Thurmond of South Carolina, polled more than 1.1 million votes in the 1948 election. Faulkner's family utterly rejected his comparative liberalism on race. Someone once suggested to his uncle John Wesley Thompson FALKNER Jr., an Oxford lawyer, that he had served as the model for the Stevens character. His response summarizes the Falkners' attitude on the matter, and on their famous kinsman's work as well: "Me, that nigger-lovin' Stevens? Naw, I don't read Billy's books much. But he can write them if he wants to. I guess he makes money at it—writing those dirty books for Yankees."

Intruder is a faithful reflection of Faulkner's confusion about racial questions. He seems to have drawn back from the implications of his beliefs, perhaps partly because he was a man of his time and place after all, and partly too because he dreaded changes in the pattern of Southern life. For Faulkner, change all too often meant destruction—as in the lumber companies' clear-cutting of the Big Woods of the MISSISSIPPI DELTA, the last wilderness of the novelist's home country.

Confused or not, Faulkner became increasingly drawn into racial politics, usually in response to white atrocities against blacks. In a letter to the Memphis *Commercial Appeal* in 1950, he protested a Mississippi court's decision to sentence a white man to life in prison for the killing of three black children. The killer surely would have been put to death had the children been white, Faulkner argued. In 1951, he challenged the conviction and execution of a black man, Willie McGee, accused of raping a white woman. The local prosecutor suggested Faulkner had "aligned himself with the communists" in speaking out for McGee.

The conflict escalated with the U.S. Supreme Court's May 1954 ruling in *Brown v. Board of Education* that segregated schools were unconstitutional. A year later, the high court instructed federal district courts to require a start toward desegregation; the court eventually extended the ruling to apply to public gathering places, transportation, and state-supported colleges and universities.

In the spring of 1955, Faulkner sent a series of letters to the *Commercial Appeal* attacking Mississippi's segregated schools, saying that they were not good enough for whites or blacks. Such comments earned Faulkner the epithet of "Weeping Willie" in Oxford. Nor could he turn to his family for support. With the *Brown* ruling, his brother Johncy announced he would stand at the schoolhouse door with a gun to block the integration of Oxford's schools.

With Faulkner's celebrity (he had won the 1949 NOBEL PRIZE IN LITERATURE), journalists eagerly sought out his views on controversial issues. Faulkner himself initiated the contact in Rome in the summer of 1955 with a statement on the Emmett TILL lynching in Mississippi. Whites accused the 14-year-old Till, a Chicagoan visiting relatives in Greenwood, Mississippi, of whistling at a white woman and making an obscene remark to her. The boy disappeared and was later found dead; two of the woman's relatives were charged with his murder. The killing revolted Faulkner. "Perhaps the purpose of this sorry and tragic error committed in my native Mississippi by two white adults on an afflicted Negro child is to prove to us whether or not we deserve to survive," he said in a broadside released through the U.S. Information Service. "Because if we in America have reached that point in our desperate culture when we must murder children, no matter for what reason or what color, we don't deserve to survive, and probably won't."

Mississippi juries acquitted the two white men accused of the abduction and murder of Emmett Till. Faulkner's comments on these and other racial matters brought him hate mail and threatening phone calls in the night. Possibly the threats frightened him; more probably, they made clear to him the full fury of Southern resistance. For whatever reason, the Autherine Lucy case threw him off his balance. In early 1956, a federal judge ordered the University of Alabama to admit this young black woman. Though Faulkner remained broadly sympathetic to her aims, he urged her to abandon the attempt to enroll. He thought enraged whites would murder her, and that the incident would touch off a race war in the South.

In a "Letter to the North" published in the mass-circulation *Life* magazine on March 5, 1956, Faulkner argued for a gradual approach to integration and for the South to be allowed to work out the problem undisturbed. Elaborating on the Gavin Stevens argument in *Intruder in the Dust,* he asserted that only the South alone could find a way out of the dilemma. The issues were spiritual and moral; the solution was understanding and conversion, not legislation.

Unfortunately, Faulkner had more to say on the subject of Autherine Lucy. The Lucy case worried him deeply. In an attempt to amplify his warnings, he offered an interview to a British journalist, Russell Howe, for publication in the public affairs periodical the *Reporter.* He had been drinking steadily before the interview, perhaps a partial explanation for the noxious remarks Howe attributed to him. The piece appeared on March 22, 1956. "If that girl goes back to Tuscaloosa she will die," Faulkner said. "Then the top will blow off. The government will send its troops and we'll be back at 1860. They must stop pushing these people. The trouble is the North doesn't know that country. They don't know the South will go to war." "But," Faulkner continued, "if it came to fighting I'd fight for Mississippi against the United States even if it meant going out into the streets and shooting Negroes. I will go on saying that the Southerners are wrong and that their position is untenable, but if I have to make the same choice Robert E. Lee made then I'll make it."

Faulkner tried afterward to repudiate the comments about shooting down blacks, saying they were "foolish and dangerous." He also claimed he had been misquoted. Howe responded that he had transcribed the interview verbatim from shorthand notes.

Autherine Lucy ignored Faulkner's advice and entered the University of Alabama, igniting three days of white rioting. When she accused university officials of conspiring with the rioters, the trustees expelled her. The Lucy matter seemed to mark a turning point in Faulkner's attitudes about race, or perhaps a reversion to earlier views. From then onward he aligned himself with the forces of gradualism. His later utterances had a lecturing, patronizing tone, sometimes offensive and always in sad contrast to the subtlety and empathy of much of his literary output.

In his last public effort on the race question, Faulkner invited his adopted state of Virginia to lead the way to racial justice. Once again, though, his comments sounded unworthy of an important writer.

Whites, he said, "must teach the negro the responsibility of personal morality and rectitude—either by taking him into our own white schools or giving him white teachers in his own schools until we have taught the teachers of his own race to teach and train him in these hard and unpleasant habits."

Faulkner had little to say about race during his last years. In any event, a temporary lull had fallen on the racial battlefield. Segregation remained largely intact in the South when Faulkner died in July 1962. Some weeks later, when a black student named James Meredith enrolled at the UNIVERSITY OF MISSISSIPPI, the battle flared again in all its ferocity.

Faulkner and time   One of the first impressions readers may have when encountering Faulkner is wonderment at his intricate use of time in the lives of his characters and in the stylistic devices of his narrative, especially the INTERIOR MONOLOGUE. Time is not a static dimension disassociated from the world of Faulkner's fiction. It plays a significant role in the depiction of characters seen within a context larger than that of individual experience, a context that often includes the effects of the past and of historical reminiscences. Faulkner's notion of time is also a part of the dynamic of his storytelling. It integrates different time periods in his narrative, a stylistic device indentifiably Faulknerian. Time in Faulkner is not merely chronological; it is more akin to the Greek notion of *kairos* (time as memorable event) than *chronos* (time that can be measured). History and the remembrance of the past, both immediate and distant, can be a formidable force in the present. If Faulkner's sense of time poses difficulties for the reader by demanding special attentiveness, it also engages the reader in the dynamics of storytelling.

On a few occasions, Faulkner commented on his understanding of time. In one interview, he stated, "I agree pretty much with [the French philosopher Henri] Bergson's theory of the fluidity of time. There is only the present moment, in which I include both the past and the future, and that is eternity. In my opinion time can be shaped quite a bit by the artist; after all, man is never time's slave" (*Lion in the Garden: Interviews with William Faulkner, 1926–1962,* edited by James B. Meriwether and Michael Millgate, p. 70). In another interview recorded by Meriwether and Millgate, Faulkner said that "time is a fluid condition which has no existence except in the momentary avatars of individual people. There is no such thing as *was*—only *is*" (p. 255). In his chapter titled "Faulkner on Time and History" in *William Faulkner: Toward Yoknapatawpha and Beyond,* Cleanth BROOKS examines these passages and Bergson's possible influence on Faulkner and concludes that for the novelist "time does not exist apart from the consciousness of some human being. Apart from that stream of living

Faulkner and John Dos Passos attended a reception at the University of Virginia, where Faulkner was writer-in-residence during 1957–58.
(William Faulkner Collection, Special Collections Department, Manuscripts Division, University of Virginia Library. Photo by Ralph Thompson.)

consciousness, time is merely an abstraction. Thus, *as actually experienced,* time has little to do with the time that is measured off with the ticking of the chronometer. . . . Though clock time, as an abstraction, might be deemed to be in some sense unreal, Faulkner, like Bergson himself, conceded that clock-and-calendar time had its uses and that no human life of the slightest complexity could get along without constant reference to it" (p. 254). If time in Faulkner's narratives jumps from one tense to another, it does so to underline an aesthetic or artistic claim. The integrity or wholeness of art is not constrained by the dimension of time. In this respect, in the act of reading itself time is momentarily suspended and subordinate to art.

The French philosopher and writer Jean-Paul Sartre also discusses Faulkner's concept of time. When in *Lit-erary and Philosophical Essays* Sartre observes that it becomes "immediately obvious that Faulkner's metaphysics is a metaphysics of time" and that humanity's misfortune lies in "being time-bound" (p. 85), he quotes a statement that Quentin COMPSON, on the day of his suicide in *The SOUND AND THE FURY,* remembers his father saying "a man is the sum of his misfortunes. One day you'd think misfortune would get tired, but then time is your misfortune" (p. 104). Sartre considers time the real subject of the novel. In fact, time is the key to understanding many of Faulkner's characters and themes. The thoughts of Quentin's idiot brother Benjy (see COMPSON, BENJAMIN) while apparently free from the rational burden of time, are bound to sensations and perceptions of the present. The fluidity of time runs through one's consciousness; thus, as in the case of Benjy the past (or the future) can become the present. This sentiment is not dissimilar to what Gavin STEVENS says in *REQUIEM FOR A NUN:* "The past is never dead. It's not even past" (p. 80).

The Bundrens in *AS I LAY DYING* take a different tack. Hearkening back to a promise he made to his wife, Addie, Anse BUNDREN is determined to take her body to JEFFERSON, MISSISSIPPI, for interment with her family. Through their actions in delaying Addie's burial for 10 hot summer days after her death, the Bundrens are, in effect, denying the effects of the passage of time. Dewey Dell's progressing pregnancy and Addie's putrefaction, of course, counter the stoppage of time. Anse's unseemly remarriage on the same day as Addie's burial again is a denial of time, as he leapfrogs the traditional mourning period.

Clock time, however, also has its place in Faulkner's works and in the lives of his characters. He carefully crafted the time schemes of his fiction, though not in a way as apparent as in the works of someone like James JOYCE. References to particular days, years, and seasons are found throughout Faulkner's works and give the reader the necessary time-markers to understand a work's chronology. For characters such as Henry SUTPEN in *ABSALOM, ABSALOM!,* Mink SNOPES in *The MANSION,* and even for Dal MARTIN in the short story "The BIG SHOT," chronological time is very much a part of their consciousnesses as something to be endured in order to execute their designs. In this respect, the characters transcend the limits of time through sheer determination.

Finally, Faulkner puts historical time to work in his novels. In the introduction to his study of the uses of the past in Faulkner's novels, Carl Rollyson comments, "Faulkner's novels are historical in the sense that their concern is frequently with characters who are obsessed with a personal, family, or regional past" (*Uses of the Past in the Novels of William Faulkner,* p. 1). The Yoknapatawpha novels especially create an informal history of this fictional region of northern Mississippi, weaving actual events and people into the lives of Faulkner's characters. In *Requiem for a Nun,* however, Faulkner employs history as a symbolic underpinning to events in the present. He uses what has happened over the passage of years in social and political spheres to illuminate what is happening in the moral realm of the novel. In several ways, then, this novel brings together Faulkner's stylistic experimentation with his philosophical understanding of time to pin his characters into their fates. To Faulkner, "no man is himself, he is the sum of his past. There is no such thing really as was because the past is. It is a part of every man, every woman, and every moment" (*Faulkner in the University,* p. 84).

Faulkner and Yoknapatawpha Conference   *See* ANNUAL FAULKNER AND YOKNAPATAWPHA CONFERENCE.

Faulkner at Nagano   A collection of interviews, colloquies, short written statements, and the Nobel Prize address. Edited with a preface by Robert A. Jelliffe, the volume was published by Kenyusha, Ltd., Tokyo, in July 1956. On an invitation of the Exchange of Persons Branch of the United States Department of State as part of a round-the-world trip, Faulkner went to Japan in August 1955 to participate in the Summer Seminars in American Literature at Nagano. Over a period of 10 days, Faulkner met and spoke with seminar members— about 50 Japanese teachers of American literature— and freely answered their many questions and inquiries recorded in the book. Like any collection of interviews and statements by Faulkner, this volume contains valuable bits of information regarding Faulkner's own writings and comments he voiced on other authors and their works. Many of the interviews were re-edited and rearranged for publication in *Esquire* 50 (December 1958), 139, 141–42.

Faulkner in the University   A comprehensive collection of the conferences Faulkner held at the University Of Virginia when he was writer in residence there for the spring terms (February to June) of 1957 and 1958. First published by the University Press of Virginia in 1959, these transcripts of 36 recorded sessions were edited by Frederick L. Gwynn and Joseph L. BLOTNER; a new edition with an introduction by Douglas Day was published in 1995. During these sessions, Faulkner freely responded to hundreds of questions on a variety of topics relating to his writings and his views on literature and art, race and society, and other writers. Faulkner's responses provide readers with an invaluable, although not always trustworthy, resource for scholarship. (For further information, see UNIVERSITY OF VIRGINIA.)

The Faulkner Reader   A selection from Faulkner's works published by Random House in 1954. With a foreword by Faulkner, the selection contains his Nobel Prize address; one complete novel, *The SOUND AND THE FURY;* several important short stories, including "A ROSE FOR EMILY," "BARN BURNING," "THAT EVENING SUN," and "DRY SEPTEMBER"; and selections from *GO DOWN, MOSES* ("The Bear"), "The Wild Palms" ("The Old Man"), *The HAMLET* ("Spotted Horses"), and other works. Faulkner's editor at Random House, Saxe COMMINS, was responsible for the edition. In the foreword, Faulkner reflects on the notion of the artist as uplifting the human heart, an idea that he said came from the foreword of a book written by the Polish Nobel laureate Henryk Sienkiewicz (1846–1916) that was in his grandfather's library. This was the first foreword, Faulkner wrote, that he "ever took time to read" (p. vii). The notion of uplifting the human heart and that of the role of the writer Faulkner had incorporated in his 1950 Nobel Prize acceptance speech.

Feinman, Colonel H. I.   In *PYLON*, the man who builds the airport named after him in New Valois, Franciana. He is an attorney and chairman of the Sewage Board. Wanting to make sure the paying public get their money's worth of air events, Feinman gives permission to Roger SHUMANN to fly Matt ORD's unsafe plane, which causes Shumann's death.

Fentry, G. A.   Character in *KNIGHT'S GAMBIT* ("Tomorrow"). A YOKNAPATAWPHA COUNTY hill farmer, he is the father of the stubborn juryman Stonewall Jackson FENTRY.

Fentry, Jackson Longstreet   Character in *KNIGHT'S GAMBIT* ("Tomorrow"). A waif, he is taken in and raised by Stonewall Jackson FENTRY. His Thorpe uncles eventually claim him.

Fentry, Stonewall Jackson   Character in *KNIGHT'S GAMBIT* ("Tomorrow"). A "little, worn, dried-out hill man," he refuses as a juror to acquit BOOKWRIGHT for the killing of Buck THORPE. Fentry had raised the orphaned Thorpe.

Ffollansbye   Character in "ALL THE DEAD PILOTS" (in *Collected Stories*). A British flyer in France in 1917–18, he is a friend of the American John (Johnny) SARTORIS (1). Ffollansbye also appears in the short story "THRIFT." He tells part of the history of MACWYRGLINCHBEATH, a Scotsman who becomes famous for his parsimony, which causes MacWyrglinchbeath to refuse a commission as a second lieutenant because he has figured out that he will make more money as a warrant officer.

"The Fire and the Hearth"   *See GO DOWN, MOSES.*

Fittie, Aunt   Character in *The REIVERS*. An Arkansas brothel operator, she raised Everbe Corinthia (HOGGANBECK) after her mother's death and introduced her to the business when she came of age.

Flags in the Dust   An early Faulkner novel, unpublished in its original form until 1973, it was substantially revised and released in 1929 as *SARTORIS*. Together with the unpublished *FATHER ABRAHAM*, which dates from roughly the same period, it is Faulkner's first important excursion into his fictional YOKNAPATAWPHA COUNTY.

Begun in the autumn of 1926, *Flags in the Dust* is the story of generations of the Sartoris clan, loosely based on the Falkners of LAFAYETTE COUNTY, MISSISSIPPI, with a diverse collection of secondary characters that reappeared in later novels and stories. Faulkner here called his fictional county Yocona and the county town JEFFERSON. With *Father Abraham*, which introduced the hill-country Snopes clan, and

Flags, which involved the planter-class Sartorises, Faulkner established the fictional opposites of his mythical Yoknapatawpha.

The novel is set just after World War I, with flashbacks to the Civil War and the antebellum northern Mississippi of virgin land and slaves. Slow-paced and discursive, it contrasts the generations, old Sartorises and young, and the times: buggies and fast roadsters, Civil War cavalry charges and Great War airplane duels.

"*Flags in the Dust* powerfully conveys the difference between the older members of a traditionalist society, still sure of itself and possessing a clearly defined code of manners and conduct, and its younger members who have been jarred loose by the new ideas, events and experiences," the critic Cleanth BROOKS wrote.

Faulkner worked on the manuscript through the spring and summer of 1927, first in OXFORD, MISSISSIPPI, later in the Gulf Coast resort of PASCAGOULA, MISSISSIPPI. He finished on September 29 with high hopes for the novel.

His publisher, Horace LIVERIGHT, rejected the 583-page manuscript, comparing *Flags* unfavorably even to *MOSQUITOES* (1927), which he had not much liked. "We think it lacks plot, dimension and projection," he wrote Faulkner (*Selected Letters*). "If the book had plot and structure, we might suggest shortening and revisions but it is so diffuse that I don't think this would be any use."

Liveright granted Faulkner permission to approach other publishers, and HARCOURT, BRACE AND COMPANY agreed to take the book. Rewritten and heavily edited, *Flags in the Dust* resurfaced as *Sartoris* in January 1929.

Flem   *See SNOPES, FLEM.* "Flem" is also the title of book 1 of *The HAMLET.*

Flint   Character in *IF I FORGET THEE, JERUSALEM* ("The Wild Palms"). An intern with Harry WILBOURNE, he talks a reluctant Wilbourne into celebrating Wilbourne's birthday by accompanying him to a party at an artist's studio in the Vieux Carré of NEW ORLEANS.

Wilbourne meets Charlotte RITTENMEYER at the party.

Flint, Ellie Pritchel   Character in *KNIGHT'S GAMBIT* ("An Error in Chemistry"). The "half wit" spinster daughter of the misanthropic Wesley PRITCHEL, she marries Joel FLINT in order to escape her father. Flint later murders Ellie and her father and tries to collect the proceeds from the sale of Pritchel's farm.

Flint, Joel   Character in *KNIGHT'S GAMBIT* ("An Error in Chemistry"). A Yankee, an outlander who operates a "pitch" in a street carnival and sometimes goes by the name of Signor CANOVA, master of illusion, he marries the spinster daughter of the irascible old hill farmer Wesley PRITCHEL.

Flint later murders his wife and father-in-law, then impersonates the old man in a bid to collect on the illegal sale of his farm.

Fonck, Rene (1894–1953)   Historical aviator referred to in *A FABLE*. See BALL, ALBERT.

Fonzo   *See* WINBUSH, FONZO.

"Fool About a Horse" (*Uncollected Stories*)   A humorous short story about the harmless trickery involved in horse trading. Told from the perspective of a 12-year-old boy, the story recounts a day in the life of the boy's father, PAP (2), who is intent on vindicating the honor of YOKNAPATAWPHA COUNTY by outwitting the horse-and-mule trader Pat STAMPER and beating him at his own game. Pap, however, loses and even ends up trading his wife Vynie's cream separator for the very same horse he had traded Pat earlier that day. Vynie does get the separator back, but at the cost of Pap's horse and mule.

The critic James Ferguson rightly points out that "Fool About a Horse" is an example of the "exuberant delight in oral storytelling that is so basic an aspect of Faulkner's art" and that the pleasure this work and others such as "SPOTTED HORSES" and "SHINGLES FOR THE LORD" give the reader "surely derives as much from the telling as from what is told, from the sense they convey of not just the fun in but the joy of storytelling" (*Faulkner's Short Fiction*, p. 116). Oral tradition was very much a part of Faulkner's youth and it significantly contributed to his skillful use of comic language and the tall tale. "Fool About a Horse" owes much of its success to Faulkner's manipulation of point of view, comic dialect, and tone.

"Fool About a Horse" was first published in August 1936 in *SCRIBNER'S MAGAZINE* 100, pp. 80–86. A revision was included in book 1 of *The HAMLET*; the original version was reprinted in *Uncollected Stories of William Faulkner*. For more information, see *Selected Letters of William Faulkner*, pp. 90, 92, 115, and *Uncollected Stories of William Faulkner*, pp. 684–85.

Foote, Mr.   In "TWO SOLDIERS" (in *Collected Stories*), a police officer in JEFFERSON, MISSISSIPPI. While trying to get to Memphis to enlist in the army in order to be with his older brother, Pete GRIER, the nine-year-old narrator of the story, meets Mr. Foote, whom he refers to as the Law. After leaving the narrator in the custody of the ticket agent at the bus depot, Mr. Foote seeks the assistance of two Jefferson women who question the young boy about his brother and decide to send him on to Memphis in search of him.

Foote, Shelby (1916–   )   Novelist and historian, born in Greenville, Mississippi. He wrote five well-received novels before turning to the work for which he is best known, his three-volume history *The Civil War: A Narrative* (1958–1974), the work of 20 years.

Faulkner's friend Ben WASSON introduced the admiring Foote to the novelist in June 1941. Foote later sent him signed copies of his own novels. Like Foote, Faulkner had a deep interest in the Civil War. In April 1952, on the 90th anniversary of the battle of SHILOH in southwestern Tennessee, Foote escorted Faulkner around the battlefield. They talked about writing that day, and Foote recalled later that Faulkner there had delivered the only piece of writerly advice he ever offered him: Don't work when you're tired.

Forrest, Nathan Bedford (1821–1877)   Confederate soldier, born in Bedford, Tennessee. A prewar livestock dealer and slave trader with scant formal education, Forrest became the most feared Confederate cavalry commander of the Civil War. After the war, he was a leader of the Ku Klux Klan terror organization.

Forrest operated extensively from 1862 to 1865 in northern Mississippi and western Tennessee—the home country of Faulkner's great-grandfather, Colonel William C. FALKNER, and his 1st Mississippi Partisan Rangers. Family legend held that the Old Colonel rode with Forrest, though that was almost certainly a fiction.

Union troops passed through RIPLEY, MISSISSIPPI, Falkner's hometown, early in June 1864 in pursuit of Forrest's command. Faulkner's great-grandmother allegedly supplied false information to a Yankee officer who sought information on Confederate movements. Forrest inflicted a sharp defeat on the Union forces at Brice's Cross Roads, Mississippi, on June 10. On General William Tecumseh SHERMAN's order, Union troops set fire to public buildings in Ripley later in the summer. The blaze spread and destroyed several homes, including Colonel Falkner's.

Faulkner reworked the family tale of the encounter between the Yankee officer and his great-grandmother into a scene featuring Granny Rosa MILLARD in his Civil War novel, *The UNVANQUISHED*. He retold the story, possibly apocryphal, of Forrest's brother's riding into the lobby of the GAYOSO HOTEL in Yankee-occupied MEMPHIS in *The REIVERS*, sending the fictional Theophilus MCCASLIN along as one of Forrest's escorts.

Fortinbride, Brother   Character in *The UNVANQUISHED*. Wounded serving as a private in the first battle of Colonel John SARTORIS's regiment during the Civil War, he comes home to die but recovers miraculously to preach at the colonel's church, even though he is not a minister.

Brother Fortinbride helps Rosa MILLARD distribute money and stolen Yankee mules to the YOKNAPATAWPHA COUNTY hill folk, and he officiates at Miss Rosa's funeral.

Four Seas Company This small Boston publishing house, specializing in young unknown poets (including William Carlos Williams in 1922), was Faulkner's first book publisher. Faulkner approached the firm in June 1923 to offer a collection of his verse, which was rejected.

In May 1924, Faulkner's friend Philip STONE proposed to pay publication costs if Four Seas would publish Faulkner's poem cycle the *The* MARBLE FAUN. The house offered to do a first edition of 1,000 copies for $400.

Stone and Faulkner raised the money. Four Seas duly published *The Marble Faun,* a 51-page volume between green covers dedicated to Faulkner's mother and with an introduction by Stone, on December 15, 1924.

"Fox Hunt" *(Uncollected Stories)* A short story relating a melodramatic tale of manipulation, entrapment, betrayal, and possibly mistaken assumptions. The lives of the protagonists and the events that occur during a fox hunt are witnessed from afar or passed on as gossip, and are interpreted through the shifting viewpoints of minor characters with more and less apparent prejudices.

The beautiful red-haired Mrs. BLAIR, wealthy from Oklahoma oil, and the corrosive and alcoholic Harrison BLAIR, the scion of a New York banking family, were manipulated into marriage by Mrs. Blair's mother at a time when Mrs. Blair still was attached to a childhood sweetheart. The shady Steve GAWTREY is attracted to Mrs. Blair and plots with Mr. Blair's valet to insinuate himself into the Blair circle. Mrs. Blair detests Gawtrey, but admits him once as a visitor on the day she learns of her Oklahoma sweetheart's marriage. After that she adamantly refuses to see him again.

The Blairs spend the hunt season at the old Carolina family farm that Mr. Blair gave to his wife as a wedding present. On the day of the hunt Gawtrey, who has finagled an invitation from Mr. Blair, rides next to Mrs. Blair. Mr. Blair's obsessively ruthless pursuit of the fox ends in his vicious and unorthodox killing of the animal. The repeated identification of Mrs. Blair with the fox suggests that her husband is acting out of a jealous rage motivated by what he perceives as her adultery with Gawtrey.

The events of the hunt are reported by an old and young man, both poor sharecroppers, who freely voice their contempt for northerners, rich folk, and Blair's reputed hunting methods. The couple's personal history is passed on by Mr. Blair's valet, who seems to harbor feelings of hostility and vengefulness toward his employer. In a key statement at the beginning, the old man warns the youth, "Don't believe anything you hear, and not more than half you see." This raises the probability that Mrs. Blair is no adulteress but, rather, a respectable woman trapped in a difficult marriage who continues to fight off the unwelcome advances of her unpleasant pursuer. In the end, the truth remains cloaked in ambiguity.

This story first appeared in HARPER'S MAGAZINE (September 1931) and was included in *Doctor Martino and Other Stories* (1934).

Fox, Matt Character in "HAIR" (in *Collected Stories*). A coarse, fat, gossiping barber, he works in MAXEY's shop in JEFFERSON, MISSISSIPPI.

Frank (1) In "FRANKIE AND JOHNNY," the prizefighter father of FRANKIE (1), the protagonist of the short story. He dies trying to save a woman bather at Ocean Grove Park.

Frank (2) In SANCTUARY, Ruby LAMAR's undaunted, but unwise, lover who was shot to death by her angry father. He is an offstage character referred to by Ruby when she is talking with Temple Drake (STEVENS) in the kitchen at OLD FRENCHMAN PLACE.

Frankie (1) The protagonist in the short story "FRANKIE AND JOHNNY" who falls in love with JOHNNY, a minor gangster-type character. At the conclusion of the story, Frankie is carrying Johnny's child but swears she needs no man to keep her.

Frankie (2) Character in SARTORIS. A guest at Belle Mitchell (BENBOW)'s, she plays tennis with Horace BENBOW.

"Frankie and Johnny" (*Uncollected Stories*) A short story traces the brief love affair of a small-time gangster, JOHNNY, and a poor young woman he picks up on the street, FRANKIE (1), the protagonist of the story. Frankie is usually adept at giving men like Johnny the brush-off, but he catches her at a moment of particular vulnerability and they become sweethearts. Frankie's mother, a widow (and an apparent prostitute), warns Frankie away from Johnny. When Frankie becomes pregnant with Johnny's child, Johnny leaves, but this circumstance seems to liberate rather than entrap Frankie. Through her pregnancy, she comes into her own. When her mother frets about Frankie's condition, Frankie calls her a fool and bluntly retorts by saying that she was not trying to force Johnny to marry her by getting pregnant. In a moment of insight, Frankie affirms that she does not need a man to keep her and challenges her mother to do the same.

The Faulkner critic James Ferguson sees "Frankie and Johnny" as one of several examples—in this case an early example—showing Faulkner's "compassionate characterizations of women in difficult or impossible situations" (*Faulkner's Short Fiction,* p. 74). Written sometime around 1925, the short story was first published in the *Mississippi Quarterly* 31 (summer 1978), 454–64; it is included in UNCOLLECTED STORIES OF WILLIAM FAULKNER, edited by Joseph BLOTNER (New York: Vintage International, 1997), pp. 338–47. For more information, see *Uncollected Stories of William Faulkner,* p. 698.

Franklin, Cornell Sidney (unknown–1959) The first husband of (Lida) Estelle Oldham FAULKNER. A UNIVERSITY OF MISSISSIPPI graduate and a lawyer, Franklin settled in Hawaii and did well there, becoming assistant district attorney in Honolulu. After a long, curious courtship, much promoted by the Franklin and Oldham families, he and Estelle Oldham were married on April 18, 1918.

Before the ceremony, Estelle had offered to elope with Billy Falkner. He insisted on obtaining their families' permission. When the Oldhams and the Falkners strongly disapproved, Estelle went ahead with the Franklin wedding.

She moved to Hawaii with her husband and later to Shanghai. They had two children, Melvina Victoria and Malcolm Argyle FRANKLIN but increasingly became estranged, Franklin pursuing his business interests and his private pastime of gambling and Estelle spending increasing amounts of time back home in Oxford, where she saw much of Faulkner.

Cornell Franklin and Estelle Oldham were divorced in April 1929. Franklin died in 1959.

Franklin, Malcolm Argyle (1923–1977) Son of Cornell Sidney FRANKLIN and Lida Estelle Oldham Franklin (later FAULKNER). Faulkner assumed a parent's role with young Malcolm (known as Mac), whom he came to know well before he married Estelle in 1929.

As children, Mac and his older sister, Melvina Victoria FRANKLIN, viewed their mother's friend as a glamorous figure—a free spirit and an airman. Faulkner used to tell them elaborate stories and supply them with candy. They looked forward to his visits during his long courtship of their mother.

Faulkner took his stepson hunting and for walks in the woods, encouraged his interests in natural history and archeology, and taught him to play chess. When he grew older, Malcolm helped his mother manage the novelist during his alcoholic illnesses.

Mac Franklin served as an army medic in Europe during World War II, and after the war took a biology degree from the UNIVERSITY OF MISSISSIPPI. As an adult, he generously attributed his good qualities to his stepfather's influence. Still, their relationship was sometimes difficult. Mac admired his stepfather, but Faulkner often neglected him for his work as he neglected other family relationships.

Mac Franklin's marriage ended in divorce, and his ex-wife remarried in 1957 without informing him. He began to drink heavily and threaten violence. An unsigned letter advising Mac to "act like a man" in the situation touched off a family crisis. Mac thought Faulkner had written it; in fact it came from his aunt Dorothy OLDHAM, who simply had neglected to sign it.

Mac's friends blamed the Faulkners—particularly the novelist—for his troubles. Mac realized finally that Faulkner had not sent the offending letter, although he resented him still for endorsing its contents.

Malcolm Franklin published a memoir, *Bitterweeds: Life with William Faulkner at Rowan Oak*, in 1977, the year he died.

Franklin, Melvina Victoria de Graffenreid (1919–) Daughter of Cornell Sidney FRANKLIN and (Lida) Estelle Oldham Franklin (later FAULKNER). Faulkner met her for the first time when her mother brought her to OXFORD, MISSISSIPPI, from Hawaii as an infant. Victoria's Chinese nurse bestowed the nickname Cho-Cho—butterfly—on her.

Faulkner actively parented Cho-Cho and her younger brother Malcolm. When her husband, Claude Selby, left not long after their marriage in 1936 and the birth of their daughter, Faulkner gave her typing work to keep her occupied and was solicitous in other ways.

Victoria Franklin had a successful second marriage. She and William Fielden, an executive with the British-American Tobacco Company in China, were married at her father's home in Shanghai in 1940. They returned to Mississippi for the duration of the war, went back to China after 1945, and later settled in Manila, the Philippines.

Franz Character in "AD ASTRA" (in *Collected Stories*). A German army officer, the titled brother of the prisoner MONAGHAN takes under his wing, he is shot off his horse by a sniper in a Berlin street.

Fraser (1) Character in "A BEAR HUNT" (in *Collected Stories*). He is a member of young Major DE SPAIN's hunting club.

Fraser (2) Character in KNIGHT'S GAMBIT ("Monk"). He is a childless widower, an old moonshiner whose whiskey is highly regarded. Stonewall Jackson (Monk) ODLETHROP lives with him after the death of his grandmother, Mrs. OLDETHROP.

Fraser, Doyle Character in INTRUDER IN THE DUST. He is the son of storekeeper Squire Adam FRASER. Vinson GOWRIE is murdered near the Fraser store and Lucas BEAUCHAMP is falsely accused of the crime.

Fraser, Squire Adam Character in INTRUDER IN THE DUST. He owns the store near where Vinson GOWRIE is shot to death. Lucas BEAUCHAMP is falsely accused of the murder.

Fraser's store Fictional place in BEAT FOUR, YOKNAPATAWPHA COUNTY, where Lucas BEAUCHAMP, who is black, is alleged to have shot and killed Vinson GOWRIE, a White man, in INTRUDER IN THE DUST.

Frazier, Judge Character in KNIGHT'S GAMBIT ("Tomorrow"). He is the judge who tries BOOKWRIGHT for the murder of Buck THORPE. The trial ends in a hung jury.

Fred, Cousin Character in "THAT WILL BE FINE" (in *Collected Stories*). He is the cousin of GEORGIE, the seven-year-old narrator of the story.

Fred, Uncle Character in "THAT WILL BE FINE" (in *Collected Stories*). He is the husband of the narrator GEORGIE's Aunt LOUISA.

Freeman In book 4 of *The HAMLET,* one of the men lounging about on the gallery of VARNER'S STORE. He is the first to recognize Flem SNOPES as he returns from Texas with the wild ponies. Freeman buys one of them at the auction. It is his suggestion to catch one wild horse at a time. He also appears in "SPOTTED HORSES," the short story Faulkner revised for this section of *The Hamlet.*

Freeman, Mrs. FREEMAN's wife. In *The HAMLET,* she sees Eckrum (Eck) SNOPES's wild pony break its neck when it runs into the rope Eck and his son tie across the end of a lane on her property.

Frenchman's Bend Fictional place, a settlement on the Yoknapatawpha River in southeastern YOKNAPATAWPHA COUNTY, peopled mostly by poor White farmers who raise cotton and corn and live precariously in broken-backed "dogtrot" houses.

In AS I LAY DYING, a washed-out bridge at Frenchman's Bend prevents Anse BUNDREN from crossing the flooded Yoknapatawpha to carry his wife's body to JEFFERSON, MISSISSIPPI, for burial. The settlement figures prominently in *The HAMLET* and is mentioned in SARTORIS, *The UNVANQUISHED,* and REQUIEM FOR A NUN.

A description of Frenchman's Bend opens *The Hamlet,* the first novel in the SNOPES TRILOGY. At this time (1907), Will VARNER owns most of the original plantation granted to the French settler Grenier, having systematically bought up the small farms parcelled out of the abandoned OLD FRENCHMAN PLACE. His son Jody VARNER runs VARNER'S STORE, the chief enterprise and gathering place in Frenchman's Bend.

Frony (Gibson) Dilsey and Roskus GIBSON's daughter and sister of T. P. GIBSON and Versh GIBSON. She appears in *The SOUND AND THE FURY* and in the novel's appendix (see Appendix IV) and is referred to in the short story "THAT EVENING SUN." Frony is the mother of the 14-year-old LUSTER (1), who watches Benjamin (Benjy) COMPSON during the present time of the novel (April 1928). She attends Easter services with her mother, Luster and Benjy. Because both white and black people gossip, Frony does not like that Dilsey, a black woman, takes the idiot Benjy to her church, but that does not faze Dilsey a bit.

Frost, Mark Character in MOSQUITOES. Frost is an indolent poet who spends most of his time smoking cigarettes. He calls on Miss Dorothy JAMESON after the yacht trip and misses an amorous opportunity when, not long after she has retired to her bedroom to change into something more comfortable, he dashes out of her house to catch a streetcar.

G

Gabe Character in *The REIVERS*. A short, powerfully built African American with a badly twisted leg from an on-the-job injury, he is Maury Priest Sr.'s blacksmith.

Gallimard Editions Faulkner's French publisher. The firm's head, Gaston Gallimard, moved to acquire the French rights to Faulkner's fiction in April 1931 on the recommendation of the translator Maurice COINDREAU. Coindreau first translated *AS I LAY DYING* and continued with other Faulkner works. Faulkner's novels sold well in France, and he enjoyed a high literary reputation there even as his stock slumped in the United States.

Gambrell, C. L. Character in *KNIGHT'S GAMBIT* ("Monk"). He is warden of the prison in which the wrongly convicted Stonewall Jackson (Monk) ODLETHROP is an inmate. At fellow prisoner Bill Terrel's instigation, Monk kills the warden.

Gant, Jim Horse and livestock trader in the short story "MISS ZILPHIA GANT." Gant leaves his wife (Mrs. GANT) and baby daughter (Zilphia GANT) to run off with Mrs. VINSON, the woman at the tavern. He intends never to return; his vindictive wife tracks down Gant and Mrs. Vinson in Memphis and kills them both.

Gant, Miss Zilphia (Zilphy) Daughter of Jim GANT and Mrs. GANT in the short story "MISS ZILPHIA GANT." Her mother murders her father for an infidelity and displays a lifelong hatred and distrust of men. Zilphia unsuccessfully attempts to break away from her mother. Even after Zilphia marries a painter, her own neuroses force her to return to her mother, who drives off the husband and imprisons Zilphia once more. After the mother dies, Zilphia waits for her husband's return. She eventually hires a detective and discovers that her husband has gone to Memphis and has remarried. When Zilphia finds out that her husband's wife died during childbirth and that the husband was killed by a car, she leaves town and returns three years later with a three-year-old daughter.

Gant, Mrs. The domineering mother in the short story "MISS ZILPHIA GANT," whose rage at having been left by her husband, Jim GANT, leads her to find him and his mistress, Mrs. VINSON, in Memphis, where she murders them

both. She rears her daughter almost as a prisoner, attempting to keep her away from the opposite sex.

Gargne, Madame Wife of Monsieur GARGNE, *patronne* of the RUNNER's apartment.

Gargne, Monsieur The French *patronne* (landlord) of the apartment house in *A FABLE* where the RUNNER lived while studying architecture in Paris.

Garraway, Mr. Minor character in *The TOWN*. He is the owner of a store at SEMINARY HILL and an "inflexible unreconstructible Puritan" (p. 312). In protest over Mayor Manfred DE SPAIN's affair with Eula Varner SNOPES, he is the first to transfer his account from Colonel John SARTORIS's bank, when de Spain is appointed president, to the Bank of Jefferson.

Gary, Dr. A physician who examines Donald MAHON in *SOLDIERS' PAY*. He is insensitive in his manner of telling Donald's father, Rector MAHON, that his son will lose his sight. He is romantically interested in Cecily SAUNDERS.

Gatewood, Jabbo Minor African-American character in *The TOWN*. Uncle Noon GATEWOOD's son Jabbo is the best auto mechanic in the county. When he is arrested for drunkenness, he never spends more than a night in jail because he is in such demand as a mechanic.

Gatewood, Uncle Noon Minor African-American character in *The TOWN*. Uncle Noon runs a blacksmith shop where Gavin STEVENS, with the help of Little Top SANDER, goes to sharpen a rake used to puncture the tires of Manfred DE SPAIN's car. Uncle Noon helps V. K. RATLIFF turn his Model T into a pickup truck.

Gawtrey, Steve Character in "FOX HUNT" (in *Collected Stories*). He cadges an invitation to Harrison BLAIR's country place by allowing Blair to think he has a fine horse for sale. With the valet ERNIE's assistance, Gawtrey manages to make love to Blair's wife (Mrs. BLAIR).

Gayoso Hotel A Civil War–era MEMPHIS hostelry named for an 18th-century Spanish governor. The hotel is famous in Southern lore for cavalry commander Nathan Bedford FORREST's surprise raid in August 1864. Forrest's brother and his escorts allegedly rode into the Gayoso and terrorized the Yankee officers gathered there. When Forrest retreated from the Union-held city, he left behind 62 men dead or wounded.

Faulkner's narrator in *The REIVERS* muses about the Gayoso as a "family shrine" because Theophilus MCCASLIN was one of Forrest's horsemen.

Once the city's leading hotel, the Gayoso fell into dilapidation and closed around 1960.

Gene   A Memphis bootlegger in *SANCTUARY*. At RED's funeral—held at the Grotto, a nightclub—Gene supplies the liquor for the punch free of charge for all who attend.

General (the German General)   Character in *A FABLE*. He arrives in a two-seater plane at the British airfield in France to meet with his enemy counterparts so together they can resume World War I. The fighting has temporarily halted on both sides because of the mutiny caused by Corporal STEFAN and his disciples.

George   (1) Character in "DIVORCE IN NAPLES" (in *Collected Stories*). The Greek cook aboard a merchant ship, he is jealous when his 18-year-old-friend CARL has a sexual encounter with a woman in Naples. George's attachment has obvious homosexual overtones.

George   (2) Character in "THE LEG" (in *Collected Stories*). A student at Oxford, he and his American friend DAVY meet Everbe Corinthia RUST, a lockkeeper's daughter, on the Thames. George develops a crush on her. Later he is killed while serving in the British Army during World War I.

George   (3) Character in "THAT WILL BE FINE" (in *Collected Stories*). He is the father of GEORGIE, the seven-year-old narrator of the story. George manages the family's livery stable in JEFFERSON, MISSISSIPPI. Married to Uncle RODNEY's sister, George has a cynical attitude toward his brother-in-law, who he says will use any means to raise money except working.

George   (4) In *The HAMLET*, one of Sheriff Hub HAMPTON's deputies. Mink SNOPES is handcuffed to him when being taken to jail for murdering Jack HOUSTON.

Georgie   Character in "THAT WILL BE FINE" (in *Collected Stories*). He is the seven-year-old narrator of the story who abets his thieving, adulterous Uncle RODNEY. Georgie is too young to understand his uncle's actions, but old enough to attempt to extract a fee of

20 quarters for his services. Georgie's greed and unwitting complicity lead to Uncle Rodney's death.

Gianotti, Father   An older priest referred to by the unnamed seminarian in the short story "THE PRIEST."

Gibson, Dilsey   The Compsons' black cook in *The SOUND AND THE FURY* and in the short story "THAT EVENING SUN." Kindhearted, considerate, compassionate, and loving, Dilsey is one of Faulkner's most significant and humane characters, and the one who holds the Compson family together. She shows special kindness to Benjamin (Benjy) COMPSON whose 33d birthday she celebrates with a cake purchased with her own money. She defends Miss Quentin COMPSON against the mean-spirited Jason COMPSON and at one time suggests that he hit her instead of Quentin. Although not narrated by her, a major portion of the last chapter of *The Sound and the Fury* is seen through her eyes. As the preacher nears the end of his sermon on Easter Sunday (the setting of the last chapter), tears come to her eyes, when she leaves the church with FRONY, LUSTER (1), and Benjy, Dilsey says, "I seed de beginnin, en now I sees de endin" (p. 297). The excerpt from *The Sound and the Fury* reprinted in *The Portable Faulkner* is titled "Dilsey."

For further information, see *Faulkner in the University*, pp. 5, 85, 119; *Faulkner at Nagano*, p. 69; and Appendix IV.

Gibson, Roskus (Rocius)   DILSEY's husband in *The SOUND AND THE FURY*, and the father of T. P. GIBSON, Versh GIBSON, and FRONY. Roskus suffers from rheumatism, which prevents him from driving the carriage and milking. He is convinced that the Compsons, for whom he works, are bad luck. His presence in the chapter Benjy narrates in *The Sound and the Fury* indicates past time, for he died sometime before 1928. Roskus also appears in the short story "A JUSTICE."

Gibson, T. P.   Dilsey and Roskus GIBSON's son, brother of Versh GIBSON and FRONY in *The SOUND AND THE FURY*; he also appears in Faulkner's appendix to the novel and in the short story "THAT EVENING SUN." T. P. is Benjamin (Benjy) COMPSON's caretaker before LUSTER (1); his presence therefore in the first chapter of the novel, the chapter Benjy narrates (April 7th, 1928), indicates past time. At Caddy COMPSON's wedding, which was celebrated on April 25, 1910, T. P. and Benjy get drunk. When his father is laid up with rheumatism, T. P. helps with the milking and other chores for the Compsons. For further information, see *Faulkner in the University*, pp. 261–62.

Gibson, Versh   Dilsey and Roskus GIBSON's oldest child, brother of T. P. GIBSON and FRONY in *The SOUND AND THE FURY*; he also appears in the short story "THAT

EVENING SUN." When Benjy COMPSON is a child, Versh takes care of him. His presence in the first chapter of *The Sound and the Fury* indicates past time in Benjy's mind. For further information, see *Faulkner in the University,* pp. 262–62.

Gihon In *The MANSION,* a federal agent. He meets with Gavin STEVENS and informs him that Linda Snopes KOHL carries a Communist Party card. He expects Stevens, who is Linda's friend, to convince her to give up her party membership and to give Gihon the names of other members in exchange for immunity.

Gihon, Danny Character in "PENNSYLVANIA STATION" (in *Collected Stories*). A young criminal, he forges a note and steals $130 his mother has paid down on her coffin. Although Danny cannot attend her funeral, he sends a $200 wreath.

Gihon, Margaret Noonan Character in "PENNSYLVANIA STATION" (in *Collected Stories*). An elderly charwoman, the mother of the young punk Danny GIHON, she puts down 50¢ a week for her coffin. The knowledge that her son has forged her signature and stolen the coffin money, which totals $130, brings on the fever that leads to her death.

Gihon County, Alabama Fictional place. In *The UNVANQUISHED,* Granny Rosa MILLARD, Bayard SARTORIS (3), and Ringo STROTHER travel during the Civil War to HAWKHURST in Gihon County, home of Miz Millard's sister, the war widow Louisa HAWK.

Gillespie (1) A farmer in *AS I LAY DYING.* Gillespie shows compassion to Anse BUNDREN and his family and allows them to stay overnight, storing the coffin containing Addie BUNDREN's remains in his barn. During the night, a fire breaks out in the barn. Gillespie and his son rush into the flames to rescue their horses and cow. Darl and Jewel BUNDREN also help with the rescue of the livestock, and Jewel returns again when the fire is even more intense to save his mother's coffin. Later it is discovered that Darl set the fire. Gillespie insists that Darl be held accountable; by the end of the novel, Darl is sent to the asylum in Jackson.

Gillespie (2) Character in *IF I FORGET THEE, JERUSALEM* ("The Wild Palms"). Along with MCCORD and DOC (2), he is an owner of the lakeside cottage McCord loans to Harry WILBOURNE and Charlotte RITTENMEYER.

Gillespie, Mack In *AS I LAY DYING,* the son of the farmer—GILLESPIE (1)—with whom the Bundrens stay on their 10-day journey to bury Addie BUNDREN. Mack

helps his father and Darl and Jewel BUNDREN save the Gillespie livestock when a fire breaks out in the barn.

Gilligan, Joseph Character sometimes called Yaphank (World War I slang for a soldier). At the start of *SOLDIERS' PAY,* Gilligan is a drunken soldier on the train with Julian LOWE, Captain BLEYTH, and Donald MAHON. Gilligan takes on the task of bringing the severely wounded Donald home to Charlestown, Georgia, although he knows that Donald is doomed to die soon. He allies himself with Mrs. Margaret POWERS, and together they remain in Charlestown to take care of Donald. A realist, Gilligan tells Mrs. Powers that Donald's fiancée, Cecily SAUNDERS, will abandon him—and she does. Gilligan, the strongest male character in the novel, shows compassion for Donald, Donald's father (Rector MAHON), and even for Cecily Saunders. He has no illusions about life, yet no lasting bitterness, either. A "downhome" intellectual, Gilligan reads Gibbon, and Rousseau to Mahon. He also has a strong moral sense and is protective of Lowe, Mrs. Powers, EMMY, Donald, and others whom he respects. Gilligan disapproves of Januarius JONES and George FARR and is contemptuous of Cecily Saunders. He and Mrs. Powers are Faulkner's moral agents in the novel. At the end of *Soldiers' Pay,* he proposes to Margaret Powers, now twice-married and twice-widowed (she marries Donald Mahon shortly before he dies); but she, also a realist, turns him down. In a moment of unobtainable longing, Gilligan runs after Margaret's train, thinking in vain that she has changed her mind.

Gillman Character in *LIGHT IN AUGUST.* He owned the sawmill in which Eupheus (Doc) HINES once worked as foreman.

Ginotta Character in *MOSQUITOES.* The father of Joe and Pete GINOTTA, he regrets his sons' Americanization of his New Orleans Italian restaurant.

Ginotta, Joe Character in *MOSQUITOES.* The son of an old restaurateur, GINOTTA, he refurbishes the family restaurant in New Orleans and converts it into a nightclub. Joe also runs a profitable bootlegging business on the side.

Ginotta, Mrs. Character in *MOSQUITOES.* The deaf and silent wife of GINOTTA, she is reduced after his death to pottering about the modernized kitchen of the family restaurant, preparing Italian dishes for her Americanized sons.

Ginotta, Pete Character in *MOSQUITOES.* He delivers liquor for his bootlegger brother, Joe GINOTTA. With his girlfriend, Jenny STEINBAUER, he goes aboard the

Nausikaa at Patricia ROBYN's invitation, though he dislikes the yachting party.

Ginsfarb The wing walker in the short story "DEATH DRAG." He is called Demon Duncan in the printed advertisements for the air show that he, JOCK, and JAKE (1) put on in small Southern towns. As explained by Jock to his former Royal Flying Corps mate, Captain WARREN, Ginsfarb throws himself from the wing of the aircraft (a trick called the death drop), hangs from beneath the aircraft at the end of a rope ladder, jumps to the roof of a car, and then once more grabs the rope ladder and pulls himself back up to the airplane (called the death drag). Ginsfarb feels that he is underpaid for the risks he takes, and the story revolves around his insistence on being paid more money. At the end of the story he goes on strike, more or less, and accidentally falls from the airplane at the wrong time. Miraculously, Ginsfarb crashes through the rotted roof of an old barn and lands safely in a hayloft; he sustains only a cut on the face and a ripped coat.

Glasgow Fictional town in CROSSMAN COUNTY, an eastern neighbor of YOKNAPATAWPHA COUNTY. In *INTRUDER IN THE DUST*, Jake MONTGOMERY steals sawed lumber from his partner, Vinson GOWRIE, and hauls it away to Glasgow or HOLLYMOUNT at night. Montgomery's father farms just outside Glasgow.

"Go Down, Moses" *See* GO DOWN, MOSES.

Go Down, Moses Novel published in 1942. It began life as a series of short stories, some of which had appeared previously in print. Desperate for money, Faulkner in the spring of 1941 conceived the notion of welding the stories into a larger work. He shaped the novella "The Fire and the Hearth" and the short stories "Was," "Pantaloon in Black," "The Old People," "The Bear," "Delta Autumn" and "Go Down, Moses" into a novel that related the story of the McCaslin family, white and black. As it evolved, the improvisational *Go Down, Moses* became Faulkner's most important exploration of black-white relations.

As it happened, Faulkner found the task of building the novel rather more difficult than the cut-and-paste job that produced *The UNVANQUISHED* out of a set of previously published short stories in 1938. For one thing, this project involved more rewriting. "The Fire and the Hearth," which Faulkner had originally intended to lead off *Go Down, Moses,* required the extensive reworking of source material in four existing short stories.

The short story "A Point of Law," published in *Collier's* in June 1940, formed the basis for the first section of chapter 1 of "The Fire and the Hearth." The story turned on the comic circumstance of the Black tenant farmer

Lucas BEAUCHAMP's daughter Nathalie Beauchamp WILKINS and her husband George WILKINS establishing a still on Lucas's place. Faulkner opened with a new introductory passage detailing Lucas's troubles with Wilkins and the relationship between the entwined white and black families of the McCaslin plantation. The plantation owner, the elder Carothers (Roth) EDMONDS, is a collateral descendant of Lucius Quintus Carothers MCCASLIN, the founder of the estate and of the two family lines. Faulkner added most of the second section, a long flashback that develops Lucas's troubled relationship with Zachary EDMONDS, Carothers's father.

Chapter 2 of the novella is a revised version of the short story "Gold Is Not Always," published in The *ATLANTIC MONTHLY* in November 1940, which details Lucas Beauchamp's growing obsession with finding treasure allegedly buried on the McCaslin plantation. Faulkner based the concluding chapter 3 on an unsold story called "An Absolution," later retitled "Apotheosis." The narrative relates Lucas's wife Molly's bid to divorce him because of his treasure-hunting mania. The novelist added significant new material, including a brief history of the black family line of old Lucas Quintus Carothers McCaslin.

Faulkner reworked the short story "Almost," written in 1940 but unsold, into "Was," the piece that he eventually would select to lead off the novel. In "Almost," the boy narrator Bayard relates the story of Theophilus (Uncle Buck) MCCASLIN's chase of the slave Tomey's Turl BEAUCHAMP to a neighboring plantation where his lover lives. In the revised version, the narrator is nine-year-old McCaslin (Cass) EDMONDS, the older cousin of Isaac (Ike) MCCASLIN, who will become the novel's central figure. Ike has not been born in 1859, the year the story takes place; he will hear about events secondhand. Jason Prim of "Almost" becomes Hubert BEAUCHAMP, the owner of the plantation to which Tomey's Turl continually runs.

Faulkner made few alterations to the manuscript of "Pantaloon in Black," published in *HARPER'S MAGAZINE* in October 1940. Substantial changes were required for "The Old People," written in 1939 and originally published in *Harper's* in September 1940. The young narrator of the story is given a name, Ike McCaslin, the orphaned son of Buck McCaslin.

In the revision of the hunting story "Delta Autumn," written in December 1940 and published in *Story* magazine in May 1942, a character named Dan Boyd becomes the younger Roth Edmonds, a tormented figure who repudiates his black mistress. Here Faulkner changed his original plan, deciding he needed a hunting piece to precede "Delta Autumn," which he set near the end of Ike McCaslin's long life. The result was the incomparable novella "The Bear." It opens with Ike at 16 and flashes back to a younger Ike. Section 2 of "The Bear" incorporates material from the short story

"Lion," published in *Harper's* in December 1935. Section 3 details the killing of the larger-than-life bear, Old Ben. In section 4, Ike repudiates the land and his heritage in expiation of his family's guilt: his grandfather's incest and miscegenation. In the novella's conclusion, Ike returns to the vanishing woods for the last time and muses upon his patrimony.

The short story "Go Down, Moses" narrates Molly BEAUCHAMP's quest to bring her son, executed for a murder in Illinois, back to JEFFERSON, MISSISSIPPI, for burial. The title story brings the novel to a close. Faulkner wrote that he conceived the idea for it in July 1940 when he saw a coffin unloaded from a train. Faulkner initially called the young man Henry Coldfield Sutpen and identified him as the grandson of one of Thomas SUTPEN's slaves. He eventually settled on the name Samuel Worsham BEAUCHAMP. The *Post* rejected the story. *Collier's* accepted it for publication on January 25, 1941.

With the final lineup of "Was," "The Fire and the Hearth," "Pantaloon in Black," "The Old People," "The Bear," "Delta Autumn" and "Go, Down, Moses," Faulkner had conjured up a powerful work of art. With revisions and additions, he transformed the separate elements into a searching exploration of YOKNAPATAWPHA COUNTY blacks and whites together and apart, comic and tragic by turns.

Looking ahead to "The Bear," "Was" opens with old Ike McCaslin, "a widower now and uncle to half a county and father to no one" (p. 3). The story proper begins in section 2, with Uncle Buck and his twin Uncle Buddy, sons of old Carothers McCaslin; the slave Tomey's Turl; his girlfriend Tennie BEAUCHAMP; the spinster Miss Sophonsiba BEAUCHAMP (1); and a poker game. After the cards are dealt, Tennie returns to the McCaslin place and Buck marries Sophonsiba. Ike hears the story of his parents' courtship and marriage from his cousin and surrogate father, Cass Edmonds, born in 1850 and 17 years Ike's senior.

The plot is comic, with Buck McCaslin summoning all his poker-playing skills in an attempt to get his brother out of trouble with Sophonsiba, although Buddy does marry her in the end. But there is an underlying seriousness in the story. Buck and Buddy McCaslin are inarticulate abolitionists. They refuse to live in their father's mansion and they prod their slaves into working their way to emancipation.

"The Fire and the Hearth," set in 1940, is a comic exploration of Lucas Beauchamp's money obsession, with a long dramatic flashback detailing Lucas's confrontation with his white landlord, Zack EDMONDS. Lucas's wife Molly, called to Edmonds's home when his wife dies in childbirth, nurses the Edmonds son and stays on at the big house for six months. A jealous and resentful Lucas breaks into Edmonds's bedchamber and, in a violent confrontation at daybreak,

demands Molly's return. He imagines himself the first McCaslin's rightful heir, and feels it is his duty to reclaim his wife.

In the concluding section of the story, Molly, exasperated by Lucas's continuing search for buried treasure on the Edmonds place, files for a divorce. With the intervention of Roth Edmonds (the son of Zack), Lucas agrees to drop his quest and Molly withdraws her suit.

Faulkner develops Lucas Beauchamp and Isaac McCaslin, black and white descendants of the original McCaslin, as the central figures of *Go Down, Moses*. The character of Lucas is more than a racial contrast, and far more than a comic figure. Lucas regards Ike as weak. In his view, Ike allowed his cousin Cass Edmonds (Zack's father) to seize the McCaslin lands from him. By novel's end, Lucas has emerged as a powerful figure, with the pride, strength, and independence of old Lucius Quintus Carothers McCaslin himself.

In "Pantaloon in Black," which the critic Cleanth BROOKS likened to a story by Ernest HEMINGWAY, the tough, inarticulate hero, RIDER, suffers deeply over the death of his young wife, MANNIE. As Brooks notes, he expresses his grief in violence: shoving others aside and filling in his wife's grave himself, manhandling logs at the sawmill where he works, drinking himself into a stupor, and finally slashing the throat of the white night watchman who has long been cheating the Black millhands at craps.

"Pantaloon" has only a passing connection with the other stories in *Go Down, Moses*. Rider, as it happens, is another of Roth Edmonds's tenants. Just as Lucas Beauchamp had done, he builds a permanent fire in the hearth on the night of his wedding. Brooks speculates that Faulkner decided to include the story in *Go Down, Moses* "simply because it reveals one more aspect of the world in which 'The Bear' takes place."

"The Old People," the fourth story in the novel, is more intimately related to the others. The boy in the story is Ike McCaslin. The piece is essentially a character sketch of the woodland genius Sam FATHERS, part black, part CHICKASAW INDIAN. In an act of self-emancipation, Fathers quits the plantation, where he is a skilled and highly independent blacksmith, for a life in the big woods. When Ike kills his first buck, Fathers cuts the animal's throat, dips his hands in the warm blood, and wipes them on the boy's face. Priestlike, he officiates at this initiatory rite as Ike's mentor and spiritual father. He teaches the boy pride, humility, and reverence for the land.

In a discussion with University of Virginia students in the 1950s, Faulkner addressed the question of Ike's education in the school of Fathers, Boon HOGGANBECK, and the other hunters: "They didn't give him success but they . . . gave him what would pass for wisdom—I mean wisdom as contradistinct from the schoolman's wisdom. . . . They gave him that," he said

(*Faulkner in the University,* p. 54). In the end, Ike passes on what he learns from Fathers to following generations.

The novelist pressed on with "The Bear" through the summer of 1941, completing section 1 of the novella in July. The opening introduces the annual ritual, the quest for the near-mythical bear, Old Ben. (p. 194). In the short story "The Lion," the genesis of section 2, the narrator, Quentin COMPSON, is a boy of 16, and Ike McCaslin an old man. In the recast version, told by an omniscient narrator, Ike is the 13-year-old student in woodcraft of Sam Fathers. Section 3 opens with a comic interlude in which Ike, now 16, accompanies Boon Hogganbeck on a mission to Memphis to restock the hunting camp's whiskey supply. On their return, they join in the climactic last hunt for Old Ben, Ike observing from muleback. Old Ben is brought to bay; the dog Lion springs upon the bear; Boon Hogganbeck throws himself onto the creature's back and drives his knife into its heart. With the destruction of the bear—the symbolic destruction of the wilderness—Sam Fathers collapses. Boon carries the dog, nearly disemboweled in his encounter with Old Ben, back to camp. The section ends with the deaths of Sam and Lion.

In need of cash, Faulkner in November recast the first three sections of "The Bear," simplified the story-line for a mass audience, and offered it to The *Saturday Evening Post.* The magazine responded with a request for Faulkner to alter the ending. The novelist proved accommodating. The *Post* bought the revision, with symbolic elements removed in favor of an uncomplicated story of a boy's rite of initiation, for $1,000 for publication in May 1942.

With the cash infusion, Faulkner returned to the larger work. He had promised the final manuscript for December 1, 1941, but needed extra time to work on Section 4, the philosophical center of the novella. Here Ike at 21 decides to renounce the land and heritage of his fathers, turning over his inheritance to his second cousin (and surrogate father) Cass Edmonds. "Freed" by the mystic woodsman Sam Fathers, Ike can no longer accept the sins of the family's founder nor carry the burden of the larger guilt of slavery. Entries in the old plantation ledgers bring the full extent of old Carothers's outrageous behavior home to Ike: the old man's seduction—in effect, the rape—of his own daughter, whom he had fathered by his slave Eunice.

Ike argues—as Abraham Lincoln had done in his second inaugural address—that God brought on the Civil War to destroy slavery and expiate the sin of it. Ike thus regards the Confederacy's defeat as providential. In long discussions with Cass, he speaks of basing his hopes for the future of the descendants of slaves on their capacity to endure. Ike and Cass argue over the "curse" of the South. Cass believes the land is cursed; Ike responds that the curse lies on "us."

In section 5, the renunciation of the land wrecks Ike's marriage and leaves him a sort of recluse, cut off from the life of the town. Ike revisits the scene of the hunt and finds lumbermen slashing away at the woods. An epoch has ended with the killing of Old Ben. The novella closes on a comic and ironic note. Passing Sam Fathers's grave and the place where Lion is buried, Ike encounters Boon Hogganbeck. The forest canopy is alive with the scurrying of squirrels, a suggestion of the vanishing woods' old abundance. Frustrated and clumsy as ever, Boon fumbles with his jammed gun while the squirrels caper mockingly overhead. Boon tells Ike not to touch the squirrels: "They're mine!"

The relationship of the first three sections of the novella to the fourth "philosophical" section has long engaged Faulkner critics. In *William Faulkner,* Irving Howe argues that the story would be more satisfying in some ways with Section 4 omitted. "The narrative would flow more evenly toward its climax; there would be a more pleasing unity of tone; and the meaning, never reduced to the brittle terms of Isaac's political and moral speculations, would be allowed to rest in a fine implication," he suggests. Nonetheless, Howe concedes that the fourth section makes the story richer and more challenging for the reader.

In "Delta Autumn," the sixth of the seven stories in *Go Down, Moses,* Faulkner emphasizes the historical wrong done to blacks and the parallel wrong of man's destruction of his natural heritage. The story is set in 1940 in what remains of the big woods—it is a long car ride now to reach the hunting grounds. Ike, here an old man, witnesses the younger Roth (Carothers) Edmonds repeat the sin of Carothers McCaslin: miscegenation and a form, perhaps, of incest. Edmonds has repudiated his mistress, a young black woman who, unknown to him, is a granddaughter of James BEAUCHAMP (Tennie's Jim), Lucas's brother, who had migrated north in the 1890s.

Ike meets the young woman and advises her to return north and marry into her own race. Some critics have seen in Ike's attitude a compromise with segregation. Faulkner himself regarded Ike both as a man of his time and a passive figure. Passivity, according to the novelist, explains Ike's bleak comment that racial harmony and justice may be a thousand years in the future (*Faulkner in the University,* p. 246).

The story "Go Down, Moses" brings the novel to a close. Samuel Worsham Beauchamp, the grandson of Lucas and Molly Beauchamp, flees Yoknapatawpha for a life of petty crime in Chicago. He kills a policeman, is convicted and executed. Molly blames Roth Edmonds for his death, because Roth ran him off the plantation for breaking into the commissary.

Members of the white community recognize their complicity in young Beauchamp's end. Gavin STEVENS, the editor of the local newspaper, and a number of Jefferson merchants take up a collection to bring his body home to Jefferson for burial. They recognize the symbolic importance of the journey for Molly.

Faulkner sent off the last of *Go Down, Moses* to New York to his editors at RANDOM HOUSE, in mid-December. On January 21, 1942, Faulkner dedicated *Go Down, Moses* to the long-time family retainer Caroline BARR, whom Faulkner knew as Mammy. A traditional figure, Callie Barr is in sharp contrast to the independent Lucas Beauchamp of the novel—a contrast that suggests Faulkner's own ambiguous response to race and caste.

The book was published on May 11, 1942. In typical fashion, the early reviewers expressed annoyance at the hard labor to which Faulkner's difficult prose sentenced them. The anonymous reviewer of the *Times Literary Supplement* found Faulkner "an exasperating writer" with his "prodigious, mountainous, dizzily soaring wordiness." Writing in *The Nation*, the critic Lionel Trilling agreed: "Mr. Faulkner's new book is worth effort but not, I think, the kind of effort which I found necessary: I had to read it twice to get clear not only the finer shades of meaning but simple primary intentions, and I had to construct an elaborate genealogical table to understand the family connections," he wrote. Trilling wondered, too, why Faulkner had included "Pantaloon in Black," which he regarded as misplaced and inferior in conception and execution. That said, he nonetheless judged the novel important and enduring: "The six McCaslin stories are temperate and passionate, and they suggest more convincingly than anything I have read the complex tragedy of the South's racial dilemma."

Random House initially published the book as *Go Down, Moses and Other Stories*. Faulkner objected, insisting on the work's coherence as a novel. In subsequent editions beginning in 1949, the title became simply *Go Down, Moses*. Later critics generally do not quibble over the form of *Go Down, Moses,* and most rank its most powerful component, "The Bear," with *The SOUND AND THE FURY, LIGHT IN AUGUST* and *ABSALOM, ABSALOM!* as one of the peaks of Faulkner's achievement.

Go Down, Moses and Other Stories   *See GO DOWN, MOSES.*

"Golden Land" *(Collected Stories)*   Short story portraying southern California as a pseudoparadise undermined by moral decay. The uneventful action follows the real estate entrepreneur Ira EWING Jr. through one day: He awakens with his usual hangover, fights with his wife and son over breakfast, visits his mother, stops for a business errand, and goes with his mistress to the beach.

Ewing may live in luxury, but he is an alcoholic, his marriage is in tatters, and his children are an embar-

rassing disappointment. His son is effeminate, with transvestite tendencies; his daughter, a movie extra, is embroiled in a lurid scandal. His widowed mother, for whom he provides a house and everything else she needs, still yearns for the one thing he will not allow her—to return to her Nebraska home. Nebraska's bleak prairies and its staunch pioneer values contrast with the sunny gardens and ephemeral culture of expediency in Los Angeles. Ewing does not hesitate to exploit his daughter's notoriety for his own commercial gain, and even his mother exploits her grandchildren for money after their relationship breaks down. She finally accepts that California is to be her home until the end of her days.

This story first appeared in *American Mercury* (May 1935).

Goldie   The serious-minded nurse in the short story "MR. ACARIUS."

Gombault   Character in "THE TALL MEN" (in *Collected Stories*) as well as in *The TOWN* and *REQUIEM FOR A NUN*. In "The Tall Men," he is the marshal who escorts the draft board investigator to the McCallum place and tactfully handles the matter of the boys' failure to register for the draft. In *The Town*, he is the U.S. marshal called in to JEFFERSON, MISSISSIPPI, to investigate Montgomery Ward SNOPES and his photography shop. In *Requiem*, he is referred to as "'Uncle Pete' Gombault, a lean clean tobacco-chewing old man, incumbent of a political sinecure under the designation of United States marshal" (p. 313).

Goodwin, Lee   In *SANCTUARY*, a bootlegger at OLD FRENCHMAN PLACE accused of murdering the dimwitted TOMMY and raping Temple Drake (STEVENS) with a corncob. Though sexually stirred, as are the other men, by Temple's presence at Old Frenchman place, Goodwin is innocent of the rape and murder, but he does nothing to defend himself against the charges or to incriminate POPEYE, the actual rapist and murderer, because he fears Popeye's revenge. He is opposed to having his common-law wife, Ruby LAMAR, testify at the trial, but his lawyer, Horace BENBOW, puts her on the witness stand. The night of his conviction, an angry mob pulls him from his jail cell and burns him to death.

Some readers question the consistency of Goodwin's character, because his cowardice and fear of Popeye while in jail do not seem to square with his past deeds that occurred prior to the time frame of the novel. Goodwin is an ex-convict: when serving in the Philippines, he had killed a fellow soldier over a woman. Sent to Leavenworth prison, Goodwin was released to fight in World War I and was awarded two medals. After the war he returned to prison, but was later pardoned. In the novel, his behavior toward VAN at Old Frenchman place also seems to demonstrate that Goodwin is not one who is easily intimidated.

Goodyhay, Brother J. C. In *The MANSION,* he is a former Marine sergeant turned preacher. During World War II, he saved a soldier from dying during an enemy attack in the Pacific. When Mink SNOPES (who worked on Goodyhay's chapel for a few days after his release from prison) was robbed of $10, Goodyhay started a collection for Mink to make up the loss.

Gordon Character in *MOSQUITOES.* An artist and sculptor, he accepts an invitation to join the *Nausikaa* yachting party out of an interest in Patricia ROBYN. After the yachting trip, Gordon makes a bust of Patricia MAURIER so artistically accurate that his friends regard it with astonishment.

Gordon, Charles Character in "A RETURN" (in *Uncollected Stories*). A Confederate officer, gallant but doomed, he marries the planter's daughter Lewis RANDOLPH at the outset of the Civil War and leaves her a widowed mother.

Gordon, Randolph Character in "A RETURN" (in *Uncollected Stories*). He is the son of the indomitable but unsentimental Civil War widow Lewis RANDOLPH.

Govelli A bootlegger who supplies whiskey to Dal MARTIN in the short story "THE BIG SHOT." In this story, POPEYE works for Govelli.

Gowan, Judge Character in *Go Down, Moses* ("The Fire and the Hearth"). He tries Lucas BEAUCHAMP and his son-in-law George WILKINS for making illegal whiskey and lets them off when they promise to pour out their supply of liquor and destroy the stills.

Gower Character in *IF I FORGET THEE, JERUSALEM* ("The Wild Palms"). He is the district attorney who prosecutes Harry WILBOURNE after the death of Charlotte RITTENMEYER. Gower wants to convict Wilbourne of murder; the judge reminds him he is charged with manslaughter.

Gowrie In *INTRUDER IN THE DUST* and *The TOWN,* an old family name in YOKNAPATAWPHA COUNTY.

Gowrie, Amanda Workitt Character in *INTRUDER IN THE DUST.* The late wife of N. B. Forrest GOWRIE, the eldest of old Nub GOWRIE's six sons, she is buried in the Gowrie family plot in the pinewoods.

Gowrie, Bilbo Character in *INTRUDER IN THE DUST.* One of six sons of the widower Nub GOWRIE, he is the twin of Vardaman GOWRIE. The boys, the next to

youngest of Nub's sons, are named for powerful populist Mississippi politicians Theodore G. BILBO and James K. VARDAMAN.

Gowrie, Bryan Character in *INTRUDER IN THE DUST.* The third son of Nub GOWRIE, he runs the Gowrie family farm.

Gowrie, Crawford Character in *INTRUDER IN THE DUST.* The second of Nub GOWRIE's six sons, he deals in lumber in partnership with his brother Vinson GOWRIE and Uncle Sudley WORKITT. Lucas BEAUCHAMP witnesses him stealing lumber from his partners and threatens him with exposure. Crawford kills Vinson, and tries to frame Lucas for the crime.

When Crawford observes a third man, the blackmailer Jake MONTGOMERY, removing Vinson's body from its grave, he kills Montgomery too, buries him in Vinson's grave, and dumps Vinson's body into a bed of quicksand.

Through the investigations of Chick Mallison (Charles MALLISON Jr.), Aleck SANDER, and Eunice HABERSHAM, Crawford's crimes are ultimately discovered. He kills himself before the sheriff arrives to arrest him.

Gowrie, Mr. Minor character in *The TOWN.* A bootlegger who provides liquor for JEFFERSON, MISSISSIPPI's, drinkers.

Gowrie, N. B. Forrest Character in *INTRUDER IN THE DUST.* Nub GOWRIE's oldest son, he manages a cotton plantation in the MISSISSIPPI DELTA above Vicksburg.

Gowrie, Nub Character in *INTRUDER IN THE DUST.* A fierce, ill-tempered widower, a short, lean, weathered old man with one arm, he is a YOKNAPATAWPHA COUNTY hill farmer and the father of six grown sons.

Nub refuses at first to allow the authorities to open his son Vinson (GOWRIE)'s grave. He only relents when he is told that Vinson's body has been removed.

Nub Gowrie is mentioned in *The MANSION,* first in reference to Mink SNOPES (Mink alleges that he sold his cow to Gowrie) and then as the Beat Nine farmer from whom Flem SNOPES might have bought the whiskey which Flem used to frame his cousin Montgomery Ward SNOPES.

Gowrie, Vardaman Character in *INTRUDER IN THE DUST.* One of six sons of old Nub GOWRIE, he is the twin of Bilbo GOWRIE. With the sheriff looking on, the Vardaman and Bilbo open their brother Vinson (GOWRIE)'s grave and find Jake MONTGOMERY's body there.

Gowrie, Vinson Character in *INTRUDER IN THE DUST.* The youngest son of old Nub GOWRIE, he is involved in a number of business enterprises, among them a lumber partnership with his brother Crawford (GOWRIE), who has been stealing from him. When Lucas BEAUCHAMP discovers the theft and threatens to reveal it, Crawford kills Vinson and tries to pin the crime on Beauchamp.

Grady   Minor character in *PYLON*. He is one of several reporters present when Roger Shumann's plane comes apart and crashes. Grady tries to put an end to the other reporters' gossip about Shumann's unconventional *ménage à trois* marriage.

Gragnon, Charles (Major General)   In *A FABLE*, commander of the division of the French army chosen to make an attack. The regiment he designates to make the doomed attack mutinies and refuses to leave the trenches. When Gragnon realizes what has happened, he orders the arrest of the entire 3,000-man unit and demands that they be shot for cowardice. Gragnon himself is executed by a trio of American soldiers who are instructed to shoot him with a German pistol to imply that he was killed while leading his troops in the attack, thereby enabling the French high command to cover up the mutiny. Gragnon's own pride demands that the world know what happened to him, and he refuses to face his killers. Even while Philip Manigault BEAUCHAMP is holding Gragnon and BUCHWALD is aiming the gun, Gragnon manages to twist his head so that he is shot in the back. Buchwald tells Beauchamp, a would-be undertaker, to fill in the bullet hole with wax; they shoot Gragnon again, this time in front.

Graham, Eustace   Character in *SARTORIS* and *SANCTUARY*. A lawyer, he is described as a cripple. In *Sartoris*, Graham tries to introduce young Bayard SARTORIS to Mr. GRATTON, a World War I veteran, in DEACON's café. The attempt nearly touches off a brawl.

In *Sanctuary*, Graham is the ambitious, manipulative district attorney with a clubfoot who prosecutes Lee GOODWIN for a murder and rape of which he is falsely accused. During the trial, Graham intentionally tries to incite the jury's anger against the accused Goodwin.

Grammaw (Bunden)   Juliet BUNDEN's grandmother in the short story "ADOLESCENCE" with whom Juliet lives after her father, a widower, marries a woman Juliet hates. When she discovers Juliet and Lee HOLLOWELL innocently lying naked together in a horse blanket, the enraged Grammaw calls Juliet a slut and prohibits her from ever seeing Lee again. She informs Juliet's father of the apparent wrongdoing so he can arrange to get her married.

Grant, Joe   Minor character in *PYLON*. Grant is one of the pilots in the air meets celebrating the opening of Feinman Airport in New Valois, Franciana.

Grant, Ulysses S. (1822–1885)   Soldier and 18th president of the United States, born in Point Pleasant, Ohio. As commander of the Union Army of the Tennessee and later as senior Union commander in the West, Grant defeated Confederate forces at SHILOH in 1862 and captured the strategic fortress of Vicksburg on the Mississippi River in 1863 (see VICKSBURG CAMPAIGN).

Grant's troops campaigned in northern Mississippi, including RIPLEY and OXFORD, MISSISSIPPI, both of which were Falkner hometowns, in 1862–63. The general was alleged to have looked down South Street in Oxford and declared it one of the prettiest streets in America.

In 1864–65, he was commander in chief of all Union forces, with headquarters in the field in Virginia. Grant accepted Confederate General Robert E. Lee's surrender of the Army of Northern Virginia at Appomattox Courthouse on April 9, 1865. The surrender effectively brought the Civil War to a close.

Gratton, Mr.   Character in *SARTORIS*. He is a veteran of the western front in World War I. Young Bayard SARTORIS brushes off Eustace GRAHAM's attempt to introduce him to Gratton in Deacon's café, nearly touching off a fight.

Gray, Alec (young)   Character in "VICTORY" (in *Collected Stories*). A young Scotsman from a family of shipwrights, he enlists in the British army and is sent into combat in France.

Gray murders his martinet sergeant major during an attack, wins a citation for bravery in the action, and is sent to officer training school. He returns to the front and distinguishes himself in battle. After the war, Gray finds it impossible to return to the Clydeside shipyard. Though he slips slowly into penury, he never loses his crisp officer's mien.

Gray, Alec (old)   Character in "VICTORY" (in *Collected Stories*). Young Alec GRAY's grandfather, he approves of the boy's decision to enlist in the British army during World War I.

Gray, Annie   Character in "VICTORY" (in *Collected Stories*). She is wife of Matthew GRAY Sr. and the mother of the young soldier Alec GRAY. Mrs. Gray does not wish to see her son wearing his regimentals because she opposed his joining the army.

Gray, Elizabeth   Character in "VICTORY" (in *Collected Stories*). The infant sister of young Alec GRAY, she is born after he joins the British army and goes into combat in France.

Gray, Jessie   Character in "VICTORY" (in *Collected Stories*). The soldier Alec GRAY's younger sister, she marries after he returns from France and finds work in London.

Gray, John Wesley   Character in "VICTORY" (in *Collected Stories*). He is a younger brother of the British soldier Alec GRAY.

Gray, Matthew, Jr.   Character in "VICTORY" (in *Collected Stories*). He is the youngest brother of Alec GRAY, a British soldier in World War I.

Gray, Matthew, Sr.   Character in "VICTORY" (in *Collected Stories*). The son of old Alec GRAY, he is the father of the soldier young Alec GRAY and four other children. Gray wants his oldest son, bedazzled by his wartime officer status, to return to the family trade of Clyde River shipwright.

Gray, Simon   Character in "VICTORY" (in *Collected Stories*). The brother of old Alec GRAY, he is a former soldier and the winner of Britain's Victoria Cross for valor.

A Green Bough   A collection of poems with illustrations by Lynd Ward, published in April 1933 by Harrison Smith and Robert Haas. Of the 44 poems, 13 were previously published (see Appendix I for specific titles and dates), and most were composed during the first half of the 1920s; earlier versions of a few of the poems are found elsewhere in Faulkner, for example, in *MISSISSIPPI POEMS* and in his novels *MOSQUITOES* and *SOLDIERS' PAY*. Several of the poems in *A Green Bough* were reprinted in *Mississippi Verse*, a collection edited by Alice James and published in 1934 by the University of North Carolina Press, Chapel Hill. *A Green Bough* was reproduced photographically from its original edition (along with *The MARBLE FAUN*) and published in 1965 by RANDOM HOUSE.

The poems in *A Green Bough*, like most of Faulkner's poetry, reflect the influence of such writers as T. S. Eliot, A. E. Housman (in particular, the poems of *A Shropshire Lad*), Algernon Charles Swinburne, John Keats, and others. Although in general the poems in this collection are more convincing as poems than the poetry in *The Marble Faun*, they, like the earlier volume, tend to be overly "literary," an observation made by Cleanth BROOKS in his discussion of Faulkner's poetry in *William Faulkner: Toward Yoknapatawpha and Beyond*, p. 17. However, *A Green Bough*, as Michel Gresset discusses in *Fascination: Faulkner's Fiction, 1919–1936*, is an important step in Faulkner's apprenticeship and in his artistic development as a prose writer. Also see Judith Sensibar, *Faulkner's Poetry: A Bibliographic Guide to Texts and Criticism*. (For more information, see *Selected Letters of William Faulkner*, pp. 37, 55, 59–60, 67, and 138; and *Faulkner in the University*, p. 4.)

Green, Captain   In *Soldiers' Pay*, a local community leader who recruited the company of soldiers from the Charlestown, Georgia, area, which included Dewey BURNEY and Rufus MADDEN. Both Green and Madden are killed in France.

Greenfield Farm   Faulkner bought a run-down 320-acre hill farm in LAFAYETTE COUNTY, MISSISSIPPI, 17 miles northeast of OXFORD, MISSISSIPPI, in February 1938, borrowing $2,000 from the New Orleans Land Bank for the purpose. He named it Greenfield Farm, and his brother John Wesley Thompson FALKNER III ("Johncy") managed it for him for the first few years.

Under Faulkner's supervision, Johncy refurbished the farmhouse and bought a used tractor to clear the Puskus Creek bottomlands, though he and Faulkner's four black tenant families used mules for the actual cultivation of the crops. The brothers raised corn and cotton and hogs at Greenfield Farm, and kept a stable of brood mares with a stud horse named Big John. The farm had a commissary that sold flour, meal, sugar, lard, soap, corn, tobacco, clothing, and farm gear. Faulkner himself presided over an annual Fourth of July barbecue there. The novelist fancied himself a farmer, and a sort of seigneur too. He loved the place, though it arguably represented a financial drain for him, and he poured his farming experiences directly into his fiction, particularly when he wrote about the small farmer class, white and black, as in *AS I LAY DYING*, *LIGHT IN AUGUST*, *GO DOWN, MOSES*, and the SNOPES TRILOGY.

Faulkner used to take his daughter, Jill, out to Greenfield Farm for a few days at hog-killing time in late autumn. They stayed in The Lodge, a large cabin on the place, while he checked the commissary accounts, supervised the slaughter, and saw to the mending of the fences.

Faulkner deeded Greenfield Farm (along with ROWAN OAK, his Oxford house) to Jill on her 21st birthday in 1954.

Greenleaf   Family name in *INTRUDER IN THE DUST*. The Greenleafs were early settlers in YOKNAPATAWPHA COUNTY.

Grenier, Louis   In *REQUIEM FOR A NUN*, one of the first settlers of YOKNAPATAWPHA COUNTY and owner of a vast plantation which becomes FRENCHMAN'S BEND. The ruined mansion on the original property is the OLD FRENCHMAN PLACE, once owned by Will VARNER in *The HAMLET* and later the bootlegger Lee GOODWIN's hideout in *SANCTUARY*. Grenier is the first settler to bring slaves to the county and the county's first cotton planter.

Grenier, a Huguenot, is referred to in *INTRUDER IN THE DUST* as a Paris-trained architect and something of a dilettante. He is also referred to in *KNIGHT'S GAMBIT*

("Hand Upon the Waters"), *The TOWN,* and *The REIVERS; The Hamlet* mentions a Grenier County. Grenier's last descendant is the dull-witted squatter Lonnie GRINNUP.

Grenier County   Fictional place, sharing a southern border with YOKNAPATAWPHA COUNTY. In *THE HAMLET,* Ab SNOPES burns the barn of a GRENIER COUNTY farmer named HARRIS (4).

Grier, Mrs.   Character in "TWO SOLDIERS" and "SHALL NOT PERISH" (in *Collected Stories*). She is the mother of Pete GRIER, a young soldier killed in World War II, and of the young unnamed narrator of these two stories and "SHINGLES FOR THE LORD." In "Shall Not Perish," she is the main character, grieving for her son killed in the early months of America's involvement in the war. She makes a sympathy call on Major DE SPAIN, who is in deep despair over the death of his own son, also killed in the war. Her courage, sympathy, and directness help the grieving de Spain to draw back from the brink of suicide. (In her speech to Major de Spain, Mrs. Grier appears to be speaking in Faulkner's own voice, prefiguring some of the sentiments in his Nobel Prize speech in 1950 (see comments on "Shall Not Perish").

Grier, Pete   Character in the short story "TWO SOLDIERS" whose death is later reported in the short story "SHALL NOT PERISH" (in *Collected Stories*). Pete is the 18-year-old brother of the young unnamed narrator of both stories. (In "Two Soldiers" [p. 98], the narrator tells Colonel MCK-ELLOGG's wife that he is almost nine.) The two brothers listen to the news each night over Old Man KILLEGREW's radio and hear of the Japanese attack on Pearl Harbor. Resolved to fight for his country, Pete leaves home in FRENCHMAN'S BEND for MEMPHIS to enlist in the army. The next morning, Pete's younger brother sneaks off to Memphis, where he tries to enlist too, but he is sent back. Pete is killed the following April when his transport ship is sunk in the Pacific Ocean.

Grier, Res (Pap)   Character and unnamed narrator in "SHINGLES FOR THE LORD," "TWO SOLDIERS" and "SHALL NOT PERISH" (in *Collected Stories*). He is the father of Pete GRIER, a young soldier killed in World War II, and one of the volunteer roofers at the Reverend WHIT-FIELD's church. Unintentionally, Grier burns the church down. He is referred to in *The MANSION.*

Grierson, Miss Emily   Character in "A ROSE FOR EMILY" (in *Collected Stories*). A JEFFERSON, MISSISSIPPI, spinister, she takes the Yankee Homer BARRON for a lover and then poisons him when he attempts to break off the affair. Miss Emily keeps his body in a locked upstairs room, as though he were living and they were married. At the end of the story, the townspeople find

a strand of her gray hair on a pillow next to Homer's skeletal remains, which indicate that the body was once in the position of an embrace. Thus, in her mind, some readers may argue, she preserves her honor by killing the lover who was about to desert her. However, Faulkner commented that Miss Emily knew that it is wrong to murder someone and that she was expected to marry and never take a lover. According to Faulkner, "she knew she was doing wrong, and that's why her life was wrecked. . . . [S]he was expiating her crime" (*Faulkner in the University,* p. 58). For more information, see *Faulkner in the University,* pp. 26, 47–48, 87–88, 184–85.

Grimm, Eustace   A young tenant farmer living about 10 or 12 miles from FRENCHMAN'S BEND. In *The HAMLET,* Eustace helps his cousin Flem SNOPES trick V. K. RATLIFF, Odum BOOKWRIGHT, and Henry ARMSTID into buying OLD FRENCHMAN PLACE, a worthless piece of property said to contain buried treasure. Worried that Eustace might buy the property before they have the chance, the three partners quickly purchase the land after they dig up the three bags of coins Flem has buried as bait. Only after the sale does Ratliff realize the role Eustace played in Flem's scheme. Eustace also appears in "LIZARDS IN JAMSHYD'S COURTYARD," the short story Faulkner revised for this section of *The Hamlet.*

In *AS I LAY DYING,* Eustace works a farm belonging to one of his cousins, a Snopes. He delivers to Armstid's a pair of mules that Anse BUNDREN traded for Jewel BUN-DREN's horse. Eustace also informs Anse that Jewel did deliver the animal, despite his family's fears that he would ride off to Texas rather than give up his beloved horse.

Grimm, Percy   Character in *LIGHT IN AUGUST.* A 25-year-old captain in the Mississippi National Guard, he compensates for having been too young to fight in World War I by carrying out his duties as a part-time soldier with fanaticism.

Grimm tracks down and captures Joe CHRISTMAS after Joanna BURDEN's murder, shoots him, then castrates him with a butcher's knife. Faulkner once said that in Grimm he had created a Nazi before he ever knew Nazis existed.

Grinnup, Lonnie   Character in *INTRUDER IN THE DUST* and *KNIGHT'S GAMBIT.* He is the last descendant of Louis GRENIER, architect, lawyer, and one of the founders and the first great landowner of YOKNAPATAWPHA COUNTY. Grinnup squats in a riverside shack on the last scrap of land still owned by his family.

In *Knight's Gambit,* Lonnie Grinnup is a murder victim, killed for his insurance.

Grinnup, Old Dan   Character in *The REIVERS.* An employee of the Priest livery stable, he is the drunken, debased descendant of Louis GRENIER, one of the three original YOKNAPATAWPHA COUNTY settlers. Grinnup's daughter was the wife of the stable foreman BALLOTT, and Maury PRIEST Sr. hunted with his father as a boy.

Grove, Lena   Character in *LIGHT IN AUGUST*. A country girl from the Alabama hamlet of DOANE'S MILL, she sets out on foot for Mississippi in search of her lover, Lucas BURCH, by whom she is pregnant, because he has not yet carried out his promise to send for her.

Lena Grove frames the tragic story of Joe CHRISTMAS, supplying the novel's beginning and end. Critics see her as one of Faulkner's several embodiments of the female: some portray her as an earth goddess, others as a near saint. She is a carrier of life, a symbol of hope and endurance requiring—and deserving of—protection. Lena is serene, simple, trusting, and not overly intelligent.

When Lena decides to seek out Burch after months of waiting, she reaches JEFFERSON, MISSISSIPPI, and, through a similarity in names, comes under the watchful eye of the sawmill hand Byron BUNCH.

Though he falls in love with her, Byron eventually brings Lena and Burch (who is living in Jefferson under the alias of Joe Brown) together. When Burch flees, Byron takes Lena and the newborn on the road again in what he thinks is a renewed search for the child's father.

Lena's last odyssey is comic in effect, making *Light in August,* in the words of the critic Irving Howe, "a comedy that underscores the tragic incommensurability between the fates of Joe Christmas and herself."

Grove, McKinley   Character in *LIGHT IN AUGUST*. The brother of Lena GROVE, 20 years her senior, he takes her into his DOANE'S MILL, ALABAMA, home after their father dies. He has no sympathy for her when she becomes pregnant, however, and calls her a whore.

Grumby, Major   Character in "Riposte in Tertio" and "Vendée" in *The UNVANQUISHED*. He is the vicious, cowardly leader of a band of bushwhackers who terrorize north Mississippi civilians. When Miss Rosa MILLARD, Colonel John SARTORIS's mother-in-law, confronts Grumby about some stolen horses he has hidden away at an abandoned cotton compress, Grumby shoots and kills her. Bayard SARTORIS (3) and his friend Ringo STROTHER track Grumby down and exact their revenge, nailing his body to the door of the compress and attaching his severed hand to Miss Rosa's wooden gravemarker.

In *The HAMLET,* V. K. RATLIFF refers to this episode when he is recounting Ab SNOPES's horse dealings during the Civil War.

Grummet   In *AS I LAY DYING,* the owner of the hardware store in Mottson (MOTTSTOWN) where Anse BUNDREN buys 10 cents' worth of cement to fashion a makeshift cast for Cash BUNDREN's broken leg.

Gualdres, Captain   Character in *KNIGHT'S GAMBIT* ("Knight's Gambit"). An Argentine army officer, he is a house guest of the Harrisses and the fiance of Miss HARRISS, whose brother, Max HARRISS, suspects he really wants to marry their mother for her money.

Gualdres eventually marries Miss Harriss and volunteers for a U.S. Army cavalry regiment.

Gulf & Chicago Railroad   William C. FALKNER, Faulkner's great-grandfather, formed this grandly named branch railroad line in 1888. The Gulf & Chicago offered service from Middleton, Tennessee, to PONTOTOC, MISSISSIPPI—a distance of 63 miles. By the autumn of 1888 the line was carrying enough traffic to persuade the Old Colonel to operate two trains a day.

Faulkner's father, Murry C. FALKNER, worked for the Gulf & Chicago as a young man, first as a mail agent, later as a general passenger agent, and finally as treasurer and auditor.

Faulkner's grandfather, John Wesley Thompson FALKNER, decided to sell the line to the Mobile, Jackson and Kansas City Railroad Company in 1902, putting the future novelist's father out of a job.

Gulf & Ship Island Railroad   In his second railroad venture, William C. FALKNER, Faulkner's great-grandfather, and a partner obtained a legislative charter in February 1882 for a line to extend southward for an eventual link with a line building to the north from Hattiesburg, Mississippi.

Falkner pushed the railroad from RIPLEY, MISSISSIPPI, the terminus of his SHIP ISLAND, RIPLEY & KENTUCKY RAILROAD, 37 miles south to PONTOTOC, MISSISSIPPI, over the next four years. He also bought out his partner Richard J. THURMOND's share of the Ship Island, Ripley & Kentucky.

In 1888, he merged the Gulf & Ship Island into new, larger company, the GULF & CHICAGO RAILROAD, which eventually absorbed the Ship Island, Ripley & Kentucky.

Guynemer, Georges (1894–1917)   Historical aviator referred to in *A FABLE*. See BALL, ALBERT.

H

Haas, Robert K. Faulkner's editor and publisher. He graduated from Yale and fought in France during World War I before going into publishing. A founder of the Book-of-the Month Club, he came out of retirement in 1932 to join Harrison SMITH in the firm of SMITH & HAAS.

Haas joined RANDOM HOUSE as a partner when the larger firm absorbed Smith & Haas early in 1936. Haas worked with Faulkner there for more than two decades—long enough to see him mature and then pass his peak as an artist.

Faulkner first proposed the idea that grew into *The REIVERS* (1962) to Haas as far back as 1940, calling it a "sort of Huck Finn" story.

Habersham Character in *The UNVANQUISHED*. He is the JEFFERSON, MISSISSIPPI, bank clerk who signs Colonel John SARTORIS's peace bond after he shoots and kills the carpetbagger Burdens in a dispute over Black voting rights.

Habersham's wife, Martha HABERSHAM, helps arrange the marriage of Sartoris and Drusilla Hawk (SARTORIS).

Habersham, Doctor Samuel In *REQUIEM FOR A NUN,* a pioneer doctor and, with Louis GRENIER and Alexander HOLSTON, one of the original settlers and founders of JEFFERSON, MISSISSIPPI. Until he resigned in protest, Habersham was the first Chickasaw agent of the settlement, which at one time was known by his name: "as Doctor Habersham's, then Habersham's, then simply Habersham" (p. 7). His motherless son married one of ISSETIBBEHA's granddaughters and in the 1830s emigrated to Oklahoma with her "dispossessed people" (p. 7). Doctor Habersham is referred to in *INTRUDER IN THE DUST* and *The TOWN.*

Habersham, Emily *See* HABERSHAM, EUNICE.

Habersham, Eunice Character in *INTRUDER IN THE DUST* and *The TOWN.* An elderly spinster who lives in an unpainted columned house on the edge of JEFFERSON, MISSISSIPPI, and the descendant of one of the founders of YOKNAPATAWPHA COUNTY, she earns a subsistence by selling chickens and vegetables from the back of an old pickup truck.

In *Intruder in the Dust,* Miss Eunice takes an interest in the Lucas BEAUCHAMP murder case because her parents once owned Molly BEAUCHAMP's parents as slaves. Eunice accompanies Charles (Chick) MALLISON Jr. and Aleck SANDER to the Gowrie burial plot and helps the boys persuade the sheriff to reopen his investigation into Vinson GOWRIE's murder.

In *The Town,* she uses her homemade truck to deliver orchids for the florist Mrs. ROUNCEWELL. When Byron SNOPES's wild children are sent back to their father in Mexico, she calls the Travelers' Aid in New Orleans to put them on the train to El Paso and then calls the El Paso Aid to get them to the Mexican police, who will return them to their father. (In editions of *The Town* prior to the 1961 Vintage edition, Eunice Habersham's first name is Emily.)

Habersham, Martha Character in *The UNVANQUISHED*. The meddlesome wife of a JEFFERSON, MISSISSIPPI, bank clerk, she acts as a surrogate for Aunt Louisa HAWK, whose daughter Drusilla, an ex-Confederate soldier, is living platonically at Sartoris with her former regimental commander, Colonel John SARTORIS.

With other Jefferson ladies, Mrs. Habersham pressures the couple into marrying.

Habersham, Mrs. An elderly woman and social worker in JEFFERSON, MISSISSIPPI, in the short story "TWO SOLDIERS" (in *Collected Stories*). She and a younger colleague are called on by the police officer, Mr. FOOTE, to deal with the nine-year-old narrator of the story, who is trying to reach MEMPHIS to join his older brother, Pete GRIER. After questioning the boy, Mrs. Habersham agrees to let him travel on to Memphis in search of his brother.

Had-Two-Fathers *See* FATHERS, SAM.

Hagood In *PYLON,* the city editor of the newspaper that the unnamed REPORTER writes for. Angry with the reporter's obsession with the private sex lives of the pilot Roger SHUMANN, his wife Laverne, and the parachuter Jack HOLMES, Hagood fires the reporter for not reporting the news of the air show celebrating the opening of Feinman Airport at New Valois, Franciana. In the end, however, Hagood rehires the reporter and even loans him money.

"Hair" *(Collected Stories)* Short story that reveals the private life of Henry STRIBLING, known as Hawkshaw, to be vastly different from how he is perceived by the public, most of whom regard him as pathetic or perhaps even perverted. Set in JEFFERSON, MISSISSIPPI, the story is narrated by an unnamed traveling salesman who also hears of and witnesses Hawkshaw's activities elsewhere.

After Hawkshaw arrives to work as a barber, the townspeople gossip about his attentions to the orphan girl Susan REED, even after she matures into an apparently promiscuous young woman. Speculation about the two continues while the narrator learns and conceals the truth. In fact a man of exceptional integrity and devotion, Hawkshaw once was engaged to a young woman who died. He paid for her burial and later those of her parents, paid off her father's mortgage debt, and now takes his annual April vacation on the anniversary of her death in order to tend to the house and yard. In the end everybody, including the narrator, is astounded to hear that Hawkshaw has married Susan, whose yellow-brown hair is the same color as that of his dead fiancée.

This story first was published in *American Mercury* (May 1931), and was included in *These 13* (1931).

Hait, Lonzo Character referred to in *The* TOWN, *The* MANSION, and the short story "MULE IN THE YARD," which Faulkner extensively revised for *The Town*. With I. O. SNOPES, Hait participates in a scheme to have mules killed on train tracks in order to collect damages from the railroad companies. In *The Town*, Hait has been dead for three years. He was killed by a train as he tied five mules to the tracks.

Hait, Mrs. Mannie Character in *The* TOWN and in the short story "MULE IN THE YARD," revised by Faulkner for the novel. In *The Town*, she is the widow of Lonzo HAIT who chops her own firewood, plows her own field, and works her own vegetable garden (p. 232). When her husband is hit and killed by a train as he is tying mules to the track, she collects $8,000 in damages from the railroad company and outwits I. O. SNOPES, who thinks he is entitled to some of the money because the mules were his. Because of the continuing dispute between the two, Snopes is eventually forced by his kinsman, Flem SNOPES, to leave JEFFERSON, MISSISSIPPI.

Halliday Character in *LIGHT IN AUGUST*. He recognizes the fugitive Joe CHRISTMAS on the street in MOTTSTOWN.

Halliday, Jim Character in *INTRUDER IN THE DUST*. He is the district attorney, with an office in Harrisburg.

Hamblett, Jim Character in *ABSALOM, ABSALOM!* A magistrate, he tries Charles Etienne BON for fighting with blacks. When Hamblett begins to lecture Bon about his duties as a white man, General (Jason Lycurgus II) COMPSON, aware of Bon's mixed racial background, intervenes, quashes the indictment, and pays Bon's fine.

Hamblin, Robert W. (1938–) Director of the Center for Faulkner Studies at Southeast Missouri State University, where he is professor of English and editor of the newsletter *Teaching Faulkner*. With the collector and scholar Louis Daniel BRODSKY, Hamblin edited the five-volume work *Faulkner: A Comprehensive Guide to the Brodsky Collection* (Jackson: University Press of Mississippi, 1982–88), the most complete collection of Faulkner books, letters, holograph and typescript manuscripts, galley proofs, art work, movie scripts, photographs, and biographical material. Hamblin's scholarship is characterized by close reading and perceptive textual analysis.

The Hamlet The first novel of the SNOPES TRILOGY, which also includes *The* TOWN and *The* MANSION; it is considered one of Faulkner's most humorous works. It is dedicated to Faulkner's close friend Phil STONE, as are the other two in the trilogy. In Faulkner's original plan for the three novels, *The Hamlet* was tentatively called *The Peasants*, the title he later gave to book 4 of the novel (see *Selected Letters of William Faulkner*, p. 107).

Although published on April 1, 1940, *The Hamlet*, as Faulkner remarked, began as short stories written in the late 1920s (see *Faulkner in the University*, p. 14). Thus the novel contains versions of several previously published and one unpublished story: "SPOTTED HORSES" (*Scribner's*, June 1931 [in chapter 1, book 4]), "THE HOUND" (*Harper's*, August 1931 [in chapter 2, book 3]), "FOOL ABOUT A HORSE" (*Scribner's*, August 1936 [in chapter 2, book 1]), "LIZARDS IN JAMSHYD'S COURTYARD" (The *Saturday Evening Post*, February 27, 1932 [in chapter 3, book 1, and chapter 2, book 4]), a portion of "BARN BURNING" (*Harper's*, June 1939 [in chapter 1, book 1]), and "AFTERNOON OF A COW" (written in 1937 but not published until after *The Hamlet* in a French translation in 1943 [in the second section of chapter 1, book 3]). Faulkner explains the compositional history of the work in an August 1945 letter to Malcolm COWLEY, in which he notes that he conceived *The Hamlet* as a novel from the outset (see *Selected Letters of William Faulkner*, p. 197). Several short stories Faulkner produced when writing the novel found their way into it as well. Another source for *The Hamlet* is the fragment of the novel *FATHER ABRAHAM*, which Faulkner abandoned sometime around 1927 when he began *FLAGS IN THE DUST*.

Taking place around 1907, *The Hamlet* begins the Snopes saga with the arrival of the sharecropper Ab SNOPES and his son Flem SNOPES in YOKNAPATAWPHA COUNTY's rural village of FRENCHMAN'S BEND. It describes how this unsuspecting hamlet, accustomed to the autocratic dealings of Will VARNER, Frenchman's Bend's principal landowner, is forced to adapt to the rise to power of the Snopes clan, whose varied activities dominate most of the action of the novel and some of which produce grotesquely humorous episodes, such as Isaac SNOPES's romantic obsession with a cow and Mink SNOPES's ludicrous attempt to remove the murdered body he stuffed into the empty hollow of a tree trunk. The Snopeses alter the social and economic conditions of a village whose denizens, ironically, become inadvertent participants in their own exploitation and demise.

The novel opens with the image of the decayed ruins of the OLD FRENCHMAN PLACE, a pre–Civil War plantation with overgrown gardens and neglected fields. The rumor of buried money on the premises reinforces an image of unrealistic hopefulness on the part of anyone foolish enough to dig for it. By the end of the novel Flem, the most successful Snopes, dupes even the shrewdest of observers, V. K. RATLIFF. Snopes sells Ratliff and two others the worthless plantation, and with prospects for even greater success—the subject matter of the second and third novels in the trilogy— departs from Frenchman's Bend for JEFFERSON, MISSISSIPPI. "'Couldn't no other man have done it,'" an unidentified character says at the close of the novel. "'Anybody might have fooled Henry Armstid. But couldn't nobody but Flem Snopes have fooled Ratliff'" (*The Hamlet*, p. 405).

The Hamlet is a comic novel that mingles irony and satire with deep human pathos. The effectiveness of the ironic and humorous tone Faulkner achieves is partly the consequence of having Ratliff narrate much of the novel. An astute and detached observer of events, Ratliff is at times also an active participant in them, reinforcing the novel's ironic and satiric elements. The novel consists of four major divisions, each contributing to the delineation of the Snopes takeover and Flem's ultimate successes: book 1, "Flem"; book 2, "Eula"; book 3, "The Long Summer"; and book 4, "The Peasants."

Book 1 opens with a brief account of the history of Frenchman's Bend and an amusing description of Will Varner pictured leisurely sitting on a chair his blacksmith made from an empty flour barrel, a substitute (and mock) throne from which he surveys his holdings. Against this tranquility and the security of a landowner contemplating his next foreclosure, Jody, Varner's son, rents a farm to Ab Snopes, a tenant farmer and reputed barn burner, a fact Jody discovers only after the deal. To protect his property (a form of fire insurance, as Ratliff wryly remarks to Will Varner [p. 25]), Jody hires Flem as a clerk in his store. Flem uses this opportunity to advance his interests and business schemes. Among his successful ventures, he builds and furnishes a new blacksmith shop that forces Varner's to close. In addition to introducing the Snopes family and detailing Flem's entrepreneurial

maneuvers, this first book also includes the memorable account of Ab Snopes's horse dealings, a story Faulkner first used in "Fool About a Horse." It contains an episode that captivates readers: the air-bloated horse Ab Snopes unwittingly gets as a trade from Pat STAMPER.

In book 2, "Eula," the title character (Eula Varner SNOPES) is portrayed in heightened language evocative of Greek mythology and her presence associated with the revelry and ripeness of a Dionysic era. At the age of eight when she starts school at her brother Jody's insistence, Eula, as seen through the eyes of her schoolteacher LABOVE (2), is likened to an earth goddess of fecundity. When Labove one morning turns from the blackboard, he beholds before him "a face eight years old and a body of fourteen with the female shape of twenty, which on the instant of crossing the threshold brought into the bleak, ill-lighted, poorly-heated room . . . a moist blast of spring's liquorish corruption, a pagan triumphal prostration before the supreme primal uterus" (p. 126). In juxtaposition to the mock heroic description of this modern-day Helen is Jody's satiric and coarse comment: "'She's like a dog! Soon as she passes anything in long pants she begins to give off something. You can smell it! You can smell it ten feet away!'" (p. 99).

Of the four books, book 2 is the shortest but also the most concentrated in its account of a single character (Eula) and the most dramatic in its delineation of the *immediate* (and at times *frenzied*) effect she has on others. Although serene and inert in herself, Eula causes strong emotions and strange behavior in those around her. Labove's mad passion for her is likened to "a man with a gangrened hand or foot [who] thirsts after the axe-stroke which will leave him comparatively whole again" (p. 131). Eula discovers his after-school ritual of kneeling and placing his face on the still-warm bench where she sat during the day, and wards off Labove's bungled attempt to ravish her with a blow to the face that knocks him and the bench over. That night Labove leaves Frenchman's Bend for good, but others faithfully take his place. By the time Eula is 15, a half dozen young men engage in a savage Sunday night rite of beating up on one another. A year after that, Hoake MCCARRON, an outsider living 12 miles from Frenchman's Bend, begins to court Eula. Three months later he learns that she is pregnant with his child—and he vanishes. Jody wants revenge and Varner a practical solution, which the latter finds in his clerk Flem Snopes. Flem marries Eula out of greed and, on their wedding day, gets money and the deed to the Old Frenchman place from Varner. Eula and Flem honeymoon in Texas until after her baby, Linda, is born. Book 2 ends with Ratliff's imaginative description of Flem outwitting the Prince of Evil and ultimately possessing hell itself.

The passions and obsessions of love and greed dominate book 2. In book 3, variations on these passions ironically play off one another through the characters of Ike Snopes, Jack HOUSTON, and Mink Snopes. Though the language in some passages of book 3 is as heightened as that in the previous book, there is a marked change in the narrative tone, particularly in the section relating Ike Snopes's infatuation for Houston's cow. However the reader may judge (and react to) Ike's sexual behavior, a tone of tenderness and compassion nonetheless comes through the episode.

Book 3, "The Long Summer," opens with Ratliff meeting Will Varner on his way to preside over the trial that will take place in the makeshift courtroom of VARNER'S STORE. As justice of the peace, Varner hears the suit Mink brings against Houston for taking possession of the scrub-yearling Mink claims is his. When Ratliff, the normally impartial observer, hears that the ruling favors Mink, he provides a commentary in mock imitation of the proverb-prone I. O. SNOPES: "'Snopes can come and Snopes can go, but Will Varner looks like he is fixing to snopes forever. Or Varner will Snopes forever—take your pick'" (p. 179).

In the next section, the lyrical description of Ike's devotion to Houston's cow elevates his passions to the level of unselfish love, which Ike is able to mimic but is incapable of ever knowing. The sentiments and emotions as well as the sexual overtones and pastoral imagery in this episode are a powerful and ironic evocation of the Song of Solomon with its themes of the tenderness of love and of the union, separation, and reunion of lovers. If Ike's ingenuous love provides a sharp contrast to the love stories of Houston and Mink that immediately follow as flashbacks in the narrative, it also provides a contrast to the scheming devices others in the novel employ in their daily dealings. Houston and Mink, however, may be as much the victims of fate as the simpleminded Ike is. Houston has failed in his attempt to flee "not from his past, but to escape his future" and learned that one "cannot escape either of them" (p. 234). He abruptly ends a seven-year common-law marriage to a woman he had taken from a brothel and returns to Frenchman's Bend to marry his former schoolmate, Lucy Pate (HOUSTON). Within six months, she is killed by the stallion he bought as a wedding present. Houston "grieved for her for four years in black, savage, indomitable fidelity" (p. 227). Later, he becomes the victim of Mink Snopes's revenge for having taken possession of his scrub-yearling. Houston is murdered by a man whose own life reflects the forces of a fate that make escape improbable.

In trying as a young man to escape a sharecropper's life of poverty and degradation, Mink tries to run off to sea but ends up instead on a logging camp in southern Mississippi. When it goes out of business, he marries the owner's nymphomaniac daughter and returns to "his native country" to become a sharecropper. His murder of Jack Houston is as much an act of defiance and reclamation of honor as it is revenge. After shoot-

ing him, Mink has to repress the desire to leave a signed note on the body: "*This is what happens to the men who impound Mink Snopes's cattle . . .* But he could not, and here again, for the third time since he had pulled the trigger, was that conspiracy to frustrate and outrage his rights as a man and his feelings as a sentient creature" (p. 242). When Mink arrives home at dusk, his wife knows what has happened, confronts him, and leaves after he strikes her several times.

When he hears the baying of Houston's hound during the night, Mink returns to the dead body, drags it through slime, and hides it in the hollow shell of a pin oak, in which he himself almost gets stuck. He later meets with his wife and, although he has no money with which to run away, refuses to accept the $10 she has for him because he realizes she got it by selling herself either to Will or to Jody Varner. His cousin Lump tries several times to con Mink into taking him to the body in order to steal the money he believes is still in Houston's purse. Mink, however, refuses. At two different times, he knocks Lump unconscious so he will not interfere with his plans to retrieve the body from the tree hollow. Mink had seen buzzards circling over the tree during the day, revealing the location of Houston's corpse. As Mink hurls the decaying body from the river bank, he notices that one of its limbs is missing, and while searching for the missing arm, he is arrested. Book 3 ends with Mink in jail in Jefferson and his wife and two children boarding at Ratliff's house. Eck SNOPES informs Ratliff that he paid the full amount ($20) for Ike's cow so it could be destroyed and replaced it with a wooden effigy worth two bits. A folk remedy for the cure of beastiality suggested by the village minister, WHITFIELD, required slaughtering the animal and having Ike eat of it.

In book 4, "The Peasants," Flem returns from Texas with Buck HIPPS, a Texan who auctions off the wild ponies they transported on the way. Hipps opens the auction by giving Eck a horse, which by the end of the day runs wild through Mrs. Littlejohn's yard, up the steps of her hotel, through the front door, and into Ratliff's room. Henry ARMSTID bids five dollars he takes from his wife on a horse he can neither afford nor catch. When he tries to capture it, he is injured as the wild ponies run through the lot toward an open gate before scattering throughout Frenchman's Bend. Armstid is carried into Mrs. Littlejohn's hotel with a broken leg. Eck's horse gallops into Vernon TULL's wagon as he and his family are crossing a bridge on their way home. Tull is knocked unconscious when his "frantic mules" (p. 336) pull him from the wagon. Although there are financial as well as physical casualties in this episode, the account of the auction, its bidding, and of the wild ponies breaking loose, is humorous, even though it is set against the backdrop of another of Flem's schemes to exploit those around him. Hipps assures Mrs. ARM-

STID that Flem will return the five dollars; Flem, however, pockets the money. The Armstids file suit against Flem Snopes and the Tulls against Eckrum Snopes, but both plaintiffs lose.

The last part of the novel reintroduces the legend of the buried pre–Civil War money at the Old Frenchman place. Armstid, Ratliff, and Bookwright watch Flem digging at night and assume he is looking for the treasure; in fact he is salting the worthless property to lure them into buying it. The next night the three arrive with Uncle Dick BOLIVAR, a diviner, to help them search for the money. They find the three bags of coins Flem buried to trick them and buy the place a few days later. But when Ratliff and Bookwright examine the dates of their coins (dates all much later than 1861), they realize that they have been duped. Armstid, however, mulishly continues to dig. On his way to Jefferson, where he is moving with his family and where he possesses Ratliff's share of a restaurant, Flem goes three miles out of his way to pass by the Old Frenchman place to have one more look at the foolish Armstid. The second novel of the Snopes trilogy, *The Town*, continues the story of Flem's pursuit of money.

In 1958, Twentieth Century–Fox released a film version of the novel titled *The LONG, HOT SUMMER*, directed by Martin Ritt and starring Paul Newman and Joanne Woodward.

For more on *The Hamlet, see Faulkner in the University* and *Selected Letters of William Faulkner.*

Hamp   Character in *IF I FORGET THEE, JERUSALEM* ("The Old Man"). He impersonates a judge at the warden's request and adds 10 years to the CONVICT's sentence for attempted escape.

Hampton (Hope or Hubert [Hub])   The steady, capable sheriff of YOKNAPATAWPHA COUNTY. In *The HAMLET*, he arrests Mink SNOPES for having killed Jack HOUSTON and takes him to the JEFFERSON, MISSISSIPPI, jail. In *INTRUDER IN THE DUST*, where his first name is Hope, he takes Lucas BEAUCHAMP into custody for the murder of Vinson GOWRIE and protects him from a Gowrie-led lynch mob. When Chick MALLISON and Aleck SANDER, with help from Miss Eunice HABERSHAM, present Hampton with evidence that Lucas is not the killer, he agrees to reopen the case. In the end, Crawford GOWRIE is revealed as his brother's murderer and Lucas goes free. Hampton also appears in *The TOWN*, where he figures out that Flem SNOPES has a hand in changing Montgomery Ward SNOPES's offense from running a pornographic picture shop to bootlegging, a less serious offense that has Montgomery sent to the state penitentiary at Parchman. In *The REIVERS*, Hampton briefly detains Boon HOGGANBECK after a shooting incident in 1905.

Faulkner was not consistent in giving Hampton a first name: he has none in *The Hamlet* or in *The Reivers*, but in *The Town*, it is Hub and in *The MANSION*, Hubert, although he is also referred to as old Hub Hampton.

Hampton, Hub (Little Hub)   Character in *The REIVERS*, HAMPTON's grandson and sheriff of JEFFERSON, MISSISSIPPI.

Hampton, Hubert, Jr. (Hub)   In *The MANSION*, Sheriff Hub Hampton's son, who, like his father, alternates a four-year term as sheriff with Ephriam Bishop.

Hampton, Mrs. (Hope)   Character in *INTRUDER IN THE DUST*. She is the wife of the YOKNAPATAWPHA COUNTY sheriff, Hope HAMPTON.

Hampton, Sally   *See* PARSONS, SALLY HAMPTON.

"Hand Upon the Waters"   *See KNIGHT'S GAMBIT.*

Handy, Professor   Minor African-American character in *The TOWN*. A musician from Beale Street in Memphis, Professor Handy (possibly named after W. C. HANDY) and his band come to JEFFERSON, MISSISSIPPI, to play for the Cotillion Ball at Christmas time.

Handy, W. C. (1873–1958)   Alabama-born musician and composer of such famous songs as "St. Louis Blues" and "Beale Street Blues." A trumpeter, Handy used to come down from Memphis to perform with his band at OXFORD, MISSISSIPPI, dances the teenage Billy Falkner attended. Estelle Oldham, Faulkner's future wife, danced to Handy's music when he played at UNIVERSITY OF MISSISSIPPI parties and balls. It is from the first line of "St. Louis Blues"—"I hates to see that evening sun go down"—that Faulkner got the title of his short story "THAT EVENING SUN."

Hank   The announcer of the air events and races in *PYLON*. He explains to the pilots that two and a half percent will be taken from the prize money to cover the cost of new programs.

Hanley   A Royal Air Force aviator and hut mate of LEVINE in *A FABLE*.

Harcourt, Brace and Company   New York City publisher, founded in 1920. Harcourt, Brace published Faulkner's third novel, *SARTORIS*, in January 1929 after BONI & LIVERIGHT had rejected the manuscript (then titled *FLAGS IN THE DUST*.)

Alfred Harcourt had grave doubts about Faulkner's next submission, *The SOUND AND THE FURY*. He allowed one of his editors, Harrison SMITH, to take the manuscript with him when Smith left to establish his own firm; CAPE & SMITH published *The Sound and the Fury* in October 1929.

Harcourt, Brace published *By Their Fruits,* a novel by Faulkner's brother Johncy (John Wesley Thompson FALKNER III), in 1941.

Harker, Mr.   Minor character in *The TOWN* and the short story "Centaur in Brass," which Faulkner revised for the novel. In *The Town,* Harker, a veteran sawmill engineer, runs the power plant in JEFFERSON, MISSISSIPPI.

Harker, Otis   Minor character in *The TOWN.* Otis is Mr. HARKER's relative who runs the sawmill, a job Mr. Harker gave up for the job at the power plant. On occasion, Otis comes in to the plant when Harker wants a night off. Otis succeeds Grover Cleveland WINBUSH as night marshal.

Harpe, Big (Wiley)   In *REQUIEM FOR A NUN,* one of the three or four highwaymen named in the legendary early history of YOKNAPATAWPHA COUNTY. He is also referred to as Wiley Harpe.

Harper   Character in "TURNABOUT" (in *Collected Stories*). He is Captain BOGARD's aerial gunner. Midshipman L. C. W. HOPE replaces him for one mission over France in 1918 and is deeply impressed by the steady nerves required for the job.

Harper's Magazine   Venerable literary periodical, founded as *Harper's Monthly Magazine* by the publisher Harper & Bros. in New York City in 1850. By Faulkner's time, *Harper's* had changed from a strictly literary format to a mix that included politics and social issues.

The magazine published a half-dozen or more Faulkner short stories in the 1930s, beginning with "THE HOUND" in August 1931. Payment usually ran $350 to $400 per story, not the top magazine rate, but important income nevertheless to the financially hard-pressed writer.

Faulkner's "On Fear: The South in Labor," an essay on race relations, appeared in *Harper's* in June 1956. Faulkner expressly directed his agent to place it there or in the *ATLANTIC* rather than in *Life* or another of the "slick" magazines, which he believed were biased against the South. *Harper's* paid $350 for "On Fear."

Harpes   In *REQUIEM FOR A NUN,* two of the three or four Natchez bandits who break out of jail.

Harris (Mr.)   The farmer in Grenier County who brings Ab SNOPES to trial and accuses him of barn burning. The trial opens the short story "BARN BURNING," in which the Justice demands that Snopes leave the country before dark. Although Snopes is obviously guilty, he cannot be convicted because of the lack of hard evidence. The incident is referred to in the first chapter of *The HAMLET.*

Harris   (2) Character in "HONOR" (in *Collected Stories*). The owner of a flying circus, he employs the stunt flyers Buck MONAGHAN and Howard ROGERS.

Harris   (3) Character in "DEATH DRAG" (in *Collected Stories*). He rents his car to the touring aviators for the "death drag" stunt.

Harris   (4) Character in *SANCTUARY.* He owns a livery stable in whose office Eustace GRAHAM (Lee GOODWIN's prosecutor) would play poker during his university days.

Harris, Elmer   Character in "BLACK MUSIC" (in *Collected Stories*). He is the police chief who heads up the VAN DYMING investigation of the strange case of the faun chasing Mrs. (Matilda) VAN DYMING through the woods of her Virginia estate.

Harris, Meloney   Character in *SARTORIS.* She leaves service with Belle MITCHELL to open a beauty parlor. One of her admirers, Simon STROTHER, an elderly servant of old Bayard SARTORIS (3), is found dead in her cabin, his head crushed.

Harris, Plurella   Character in *The UNVANQUISHED.* This is a nom de guerre for Rosa MILLARD, invented by Ringo STROTHER for Miss Rosa's use in her campaign to inveigle the Yankees out of horses and mules.

Harrison   Character in *The UNVANQUISHED.* A Union soldier, he searches Sartoris after Bayard SARTORIS (3) and Ringo STROTHER shoot one of his unit's horses from ambush.

Harriss   Character in *KNIGHT'S GAMBIT* ("Knight's Gambit"). A wealthy NEW ORLEANS bootlegger, he ostentatiously rebuilds his wife's deteriorated, once noble JEFFERSON, MISSISSIPPI, house.

Harriss eventually is the victim of a gangland-style killing. He is mentioned in *The MANSION.*

Harriss, Max   Character in *KNIGHT'S GAMBIT* ("Knight's Gambit"). The son of the bootlegger HARRISS, he resents the fact that Captain GUALDRES can outride him on his own horses and once outfenced him with a hearth-broom, and so tries to arrange for a wild horse to kill him.

Harriss, Melisandre Backus   *See* STEVENS, MELISANDRE BACKUS HARRISS.

Harriss, Miss   Character in *KNIGHT'S GAMBIT* ("Knight's Gambit"). The daughter of a wealthy bootlegger (HARRISS) and Melisandre Backus Harriss (STEVENS), she marries the Argentine fortune hunter Captain GUALDRES.

Harry, Mr. The name used by Toby SUTTERFIELD to refer to the English groom in *A FABLE*. Sutterfield pronounces the name "Mistairy." In the novel, Harry is more commonly called "the sentry." A private in the British army, the sentry is renowned among the troops for a sort of "bank" he runs. He lends each man enrolled in his informal organization 30 shillings. They, in turn, repay him at usurious rates, but the sentry is in essence betting the men that they will live until next payday. An angry and unpleasant man, he had been a groom employed at an English racing stable until he bonded with a spectacularly gifted race horse. When the horse is sold to an Argentine millionaire, he accompanies it. The horse is resold to an American, and the sentry goes to America, too. The train carrying the sentry, the horse, and Sutterfield (a groom at the American's horse farm) is derailed in a Mississippi swamp and the horse is badly hurt. The sentry and Sutterfield doctor the horse and steal it, racing it at small racetracks all across America. In a small valley in eastern Tennessee, the sentry becomes a Mason. The RUNNER convinces the sentry to lead his regiment into no-man's-land where they meet a like-minded unarmed German battalion. While the two units mingle in peace, a combined German and Allied barrage kills nearly all of them.

Harvard University The first North American institution of higher learning, founded in 1636 in Cambridge (then New Towne), Massachusetts, near Boston. It remains one of the two or three best-known and most prestigious American universities.

Faulkner's fictional Quentin COMPSON is a student at Harvard in 1909–10 in *The SOUND AND THE FURY* and *ABSALOM, ABSALOM!* At the end of his first year at Harvard Quentin commits suicide by drowning himself in the Charles River. Gavin STEVENS and his nephew Charles (Chick) MALLISON Jr., who appear in several of Faulkner's works, are educated at Harvard.

In the fall of 1948, Professor Carvel Collins taught a seminar at Harvard on Faulkner's work—the first such course anywhere. In 1959, Faulkner told the University of Texas scholar James MERIWETHER that he wanted to see his manuscripts go to Harvard because it was the nation's oldest university.

Hatcher, Louis A superstitious black man in *The SOUND AND THE FURY* with whom Quentin COMPSON and Versh GIBSON hunt possums in the woods.

Hatcher, Martha Louis HATCHER's wife in *The SOUND AND THE FURY*.

Hawk, Dennison Character in *The UNVANQUISHED*. The father of Drusilla Hawk (SARTORIS) and Dennison HAWK Jr., he is dead at the time of the novel's action and lies buried among cedars on a knoll overlooking his plantation, HAWKHURST.

Hawk, Dennison, Jr. (Cousin Denny) Character in *The UNVANQUISHED*. He is Drusilla Hawk's (SARTORIS) younger brother, only 10 years old during the war that engulfs his home, HAWKHURST.

Later, Cousin Denny studies law and establishes a practice in Montgomery, Alabama. Drusilla goes to live with him there after she leaves Sartoris.

Hawk, Drusilla *See* SARTORIS, DRUSILLA HAWK.

Hawk, Louisa Character in *The UNVANQUISHED*. The mother of Drusilla Hawk (SARTORIS) and Dennison HAWK Jr., she is Rosa MILLARD's sister. From her home in Alabama, she becomes convinced that Drusilla and Colonel John SARTORIS are living in sin, and she goes to JEFFERSON, MISSISSIPPI, to confront the situation. With assistance from Mrs. COMPSON and Martha HABERSHAM, she pressures the couple into marriage.

Hawkhurst Fictional place, the GIHON COUNTY, ALABAMA, home of Rosa MILLARD's widowed sister, Louisa HAWK, and Louisa's children Drusilla Hawk (SARTORIS) and Dennison HAWK Jr. In *The UNVANQUISHED*, the place is a ruin when Granny Millard, Bayard SARTORIS (3), and Ringo STROTHER arrive as refugees in 1863. Yankee raiders had burned it, just as they had burned Sartoris plantation.

Hawks, Howard (1896–1977) Movie director, born in Goshen, Indiana, educated at Phillips Exeter Academy and Cornell University. He served with the Army Air Corps during World War I. His *Dawn Patrol* (1930), a classic film of World War I air warfare, established Hawks as one of Hollywood's leading directors.

Hawks and Faulkner became friends in the early 1930s, during Faulkner's first scriptwriting sojourns in Hollywood. In the 1940s, they collaborated on the WARNER BROTHERS movies *To Have and Have Not* and *The Big Sleep*. Hawks brought Faulkner to Egypt in the early 1950s to work on the script of *Land of the Pharaohs*.

Hawks and Faulkner had flying and hunting in common and got along well together. Each had a high regard for the other's craftsmanship.

Hawkshaw *See* STRIBLING, HENRY.

Head, Sydney Herbert Caddy COMPSON's husband in *The SOUND AND THE FURY*; he is not, however, the father of the baby she gives birth to seven months after their wedding. A northerner from South Bend, Indiana, Head brings money to the nearly impoverished Compson family, giving Caddy a car, for example, as a wedding present. An unsavory character, Head was expelled from HARVARD UNIVERSITY for cheating on exams, and was blackballed also by his Cambridge, Massachusetts, club for cardsharping. He is arrogant and supercilious toward Quentin COMPSON, Caddy's brother, leading Quentin to beg Caddy not to marry. Jason COMPSON, however, is in favor of the match, primarily because Head has promised Jason a position in the bank the Head family owns. The position falls through (and Jason is forever resentful) when Head divorces Caddy after he realizes that her baby is another man's child.

Helen: A Courtship   Cycle consisting of an introductory poem and 15 sonnets, written between June and September 1925. In part, it is Faulkner's declaration of love to the sculptor Helen BAIRD. Critics see echoes of the English poet A. E. HOUSMAN.

Faulkner presented the hand-lettered, hand-bound poem cycle to Baird in 1926. She rejected him as a suitor, however, and married the New Orleans lawyer Guy Lyman. Together with *MISSISSIPPI POEMS, Helen: A Courtship* was published posthumously in 1981 by Tulane University and Yoknapatawpha Press.

Hell Creek   Fictional name for Spring Creek, which flows into the TALLAHATCHIE RIVER north of OXFORD, MISSISSIPPI. The road from Oxford to MEMPHIS crosses Spring Creek between the Tallahatchie and the town of Waterford.

In *The REIVERS*, Boon HOGGANBECK darkly warns Lucius PRIEST and Ned MCCASLIN of the difficulties he expects to encounter in taking Grandfather Priest's automobile through boggy Hell Creek bottom.

The car becomes hopelessly stuck in the mire. A farmer with two mules stationed at the bridge rapaciously charges Boon six dollars to free the car and tow it to high ground on the far side of the creek.

Hemingway, Ernest (1899–1961)   Writer and celebrity, a doctor's son, born in Oak Park, Illinois. After serving with a Red Cross ambulance unit in Italy (1917–18) during World War I, he worked as a journalist and as an expatriate in Paris in the 1920s established himself with *In Our Time* (1925), *The Sun Also Rises* (1926), and *A Farewell to Arms* (1929) as one of the leading American writers of his generation.

In this early work, Hemingway perfected his distinctive and much-imitated style, so different from Faulkner's: simple sentences, exact description, terse, highly suggestive dialogue. He returned to the United States in 1927 but never settled down, moving restlessly from Florida to Cuba to Europe and back again. He sought release (and material for his work) in hunting and fishing, bullfighting, and war. *Death in the Afternoon* (1932) grew out of his passion for the bullring; he

based *For Whom the Bell Tolls* (1940), regarded as one of his better novels, on his experience in Spain during the Spanish Civil War of 1936–39. He won critical and popular acclaim for *The Old Man and the Sea* in 1952, and was awarded the NOBEL PRIZE IN LITERATURE in 1954.

Faulkner and Hemingway were sometimes admiring but more often wary of each other. Hemingway praised Faulkner as the most talented writer of his time, admitting, according to the critic Malcolm COWLEY, that he ranked Faulkner above himself. But he also regarded Faulkner's work as uneven and undisciplined.

Faulkner did not hold Hemingway in such high esteem, though he did have one of his characters, Temple Drake (STEVENS) in *REQUIEM FOR A NUN* (1951), quote the character Maria in *For Whom the Bell Tolls*. Nor was Faulkner much impressed with Hemingway's image as a man of action. He once remarked dismissively that of all the ways of dying, "Hemingway would like most to be gored by a bull."

At a UNIVERSITY OF MISSISSIPPI seminar on the novel in 1947, Faulkner extemporaneously listed Hemingway fourth of the five major novelists of his generation, after Thomas Wolfe, himself, and John Dos Passos, and just ahead of John Steinbeck. Hemingway never overreached his talent, Faulkner said; he never tried anything he was not sure he could pull off. "He has no courage, has never climbed out on a limb," Faulkner famously said.

The comment got back to Hemingway in Cuba and deeply wounded him. Altogether missing the point, he started a letter to Faulkner listing his combat actions, then asked a soldier familiar with his war record to set Faulkner straight. The Mississippian tried to make it clear and he meant only to question Hemingway's courage as a writer, but the remark followed him for the rest of his life. Certainly Hemingway never forgot it.

Faulkner's main criticism of Hemingway was of the latter's values rather than his technique: In much of Hemingway's work, Faulkner believed, God, a Creator, was absent, except in *The Old Man and the Sea*.

Hemingway produced little of enduring value in his last years. Deeply depressed and apparently afraid he had written himself out, he took his own life in an Idaho hunting lodge in 1961. *A Moveable Feast*, a memoir of his Paris years, appeared three years after his death.

Henderson, Mrs.   The interfering and disapproving elderly woman on the train in the novel *SOLDIERS' PAY* who inquires about Donald MAHON's health.

Henri   A minor character in *A FABLE*. A French army commander whose troops include the mutinous regiment under Major General GRAGNON.

Henry   **(1)** An African-American porter on the Buffalo-bound train at the start of *SOLDIERS' PAY*.

Henry (2) One of Quentin COMPSON's classmates in *THE SOUND AND THE FURY*, referred to in Quentin's reminiscences as a boy who paid better attention in school than Quentin did. One time when Quentin is preoccupied in class, Henry answers a question for him.

Henry (3) Character in *GO DOWN, MOSES* ("The Fire and the Hearth"). He is the toothpick-chewing deputy marshal in the court of Judge GOWAN, who tries Lucas BEAUCHAMP and George WILKINS for making illegal whiskey. Henry also appears in "A Point of Law," a short story that Faulkner revised for the novel.

Henry (4) In *REQUIEM FOR A NUN*, the governor of mississippi, whom Temple Drake STEVENS and Gavin STEVENS visit during the middle of the night to ask for a stay in the execution of Nancy MANNIGOE. He denies their pleas.

Henry (5) In *The MANSION*, a black man who works on Jack HOUSTON's farm. He is present when Mink SNOPES tries unsuccessfully to get his cow back from Houston.

Henry, Uncle Character in *SARTORIS*. He supplies one of his dogs for young Bayard SARTORIS's possum hunt, which begins behind his house.

Herb (Herbie) The main character in the short story "DON GIOVANNI." Herb is a wholesale women's clothing buyer for a large department store and a lonely widower. Vain, worried about his thinning hair, and tired of celibacy, Herb decides to practice his psychology of women on the unsuspecting Miss STEINBAUER. He ignorantly assumes that a woman falls for a bold and indifferent man. Instead of feeling humiliated when his plans fail, he thinks he has learned from the fiasco and decides to try harder next time by adding cruelty to his boldness. (In depicting the character of Ernest TALLIAFERRO in *MOSQUITOES*, Faulkner draws on his treatment of Herb.)

Het (Old Het) Minor African-American character in *The TOWN* and the short story "MULE IN THE YARD," which Faulkner extensively revised for the novel. Het sleeps in the poorhouse during the night and travels from house to house for food scraps during the day. After the death of Mrs. HAIT's husband, old Het establishes "a kind of local headquarters or advanced foraging post in Mrs. Hait's kitchen" (*The Town*, p. 232).

Hightower, Gail (1) Character in *LIGHT IN AUGUST*. A self-taught lawyer and a Civil War cavalryman, he is the grandfather of Gail HIGHTOWER (2), the solitary and introspective failed minister who tries to save Joe CHRISTMAS. The younger Gail is obsessed with his grandfather's wartime exploits.

Hightower, Gail (2) Character in *LIGHT IN AUGUST*. The only child of an intimidating 50-year-old father and an invalid mother, he grows up regarding his parents as phantoms. As an adult he decides that he has "skipped a generation" and is the figurative son of his Civil War cavalryman grandfather, the first Gail HIGHTOWER.

Obsessed with his grandfather's legend, he decides at seminary that he must follow his pastor's vocation in JEFFERSON, MISSISSIPPI, the town where the first Gail was shot dead in a henhouse in an absurd ending to a wartime raid on a federal supply depot. His young wife helps him arrange the appointment. He takes up the post, and for several years he preaches hysterical sermons that weirdly blend Presbyterianism with his grandfather's soldierly exploits. The congregation is baffled at first. Eventually it comes to see the pastor as "a figure antic as a showman, a little wild: a charlatan preaching worse than heresy" (*Light in August*, p. 488).

His Presbyterians never accept him, and the rumors that swirl around his marriage prove his undoing. He is thought to be an "unnatural" husband and to lapse into homosexual practices. His wife makes several unexplained trips out of town—to meet a lover in Memphis, it turns out. When she is killed in a fall from a window of the Memphis hotel room where she and her lover had registered as husband and wife, the terrible truth comes out. The church turns against Hightower and forces him to resign.

Hightower stays on in Jefferson in a small, unpainted, obscure house. He fails at his second vocation, that of an art teacher and photographer, and withdraws, hermitlike, into his cottage. He is persecuted by the townspeople, but he refuses to leave.

Byron BUNCH, his only friend, rekindles his interest in life. Other people's troubles seem to restore his link to the world. He befriends Lena GROVE and delivers her baby. He hears out the story of Mrs. HINES and her mad husband. In the end, he does his best to save Joe CHRISTMAS from the lynch mob, swearing that he and Christmas had been together on the night of Joanna BURDEN's murder. But in this, as in so much else, he fails.

Faulkner, according to the critic Irving HOWE, developed Hightower as a "reflective consciousness" to register the conduct of Christmas, Bunch, Lena Grove, and other characters. But Howe and others find him inadequate in some ways.

Hightower is "too vague, too drooping, too formless, in a word too much a creature of defeat and obsession, to compel our interest or our belief," wrote the critic Alfred KAZIN.

Hightower, Hiram Character in *The REIVERS*. A Baptist parson, a giant of a man and a Civil War veteran of Nathan Bedford FORREST's cavalry, in 1886 he uses his fists and his Bible to subdue and convert the uproarious riverside settlement of the younger BALLENBAUGH (2).

Hill, Dr. The physician in charge of the clinic in "MR. ACARIUS."

Hiller, Emil A mountain guide in the short story "SNOW." Hiller works for BRIX, guiding the amateur German mountain climber VON PLOECKNER. Hiller survives the accident that kills Brix.

Hilliard Character in *The UNVANQUISHED*. A livery stable operative in OXFORD, MISSISSIPPI, he supplies Ringo STROTHER with a horse when he comes to the university to tell Bayard SARTORIS (2) of his father's death.

Hines, Eupheus (Doc) Character in *LIGHT IN AUGUST*. A deranged religious fanatic who delivers harangues on white supremacy in African-American churches, he is the killer of his daughter Milly HINES's lover, alleged to be part black, and the de facto killer of Milly herself, for whom he refuses to call a doctor when she goes into labor; she eventually dies in childbirth. Hines places the surviving child on the steps of the white orphanage where he works as a janitor.

After his grandson, called Joe CHRISTMAS, is given up for adoption at age five, old Hines does not see him again until he is taken captive in MOTTSTOWN and accused of murder. The old man urges the townspeople to lynch him.

Hines, Milly Character in *LIGHT IN AUGUST*. The daughter of Eupheus HINES, she runs off with a circus employee said to be a Mexican but rumored to be part black. She dies in childbirth. Their child, dubbed Joe CHRISTMAS, spends the first five years of his life in an orphanage.

Hines, Mrs. Character in *LIGHT IN AUGUST*. She is the wife of Eupheus HINES and the mother of Milly HINES. For 30 years she does not know whether Milly's child is dead or alive. When she learns her grandson is the murderer Joe CHRISTMAS, she begs Gail HIGHTOWER (2) to save him from the lynch mob.

Hipps, Buck Character in *The HAMLET*. In book 4 ("The Peasants," part 1 of chapter 1), he is the Texan who accompanies Flem SNOPES to FRENCHMAN'S BEND with wild ponies to be auctioned off. Although in partnership with the unscrupulous Flem, Hipps shows a genuine sensitivity toward Mrs. ARMSTID, whose impetuous husband Henry (ARMSTID) takes her hard-earned money to buy a horse. Hipps refuses to sell him one and returns the five dollars to his wife. When Henry forces the money from her again to give to Flem, Hipps tells her she can get it back the next day, but the greedy Flem keeps it. An earlier version of this episode appears in *FATHER ABRAHAM*, where Hipps is identified by his first name. He asks people to call him Buck in *The Hamlet*, but the narrator refers to him exclusively as the Texan. In the short story "SPOTTED HORSES," another version of the episode, Buck is referred to as "the Texas man" by the narrator and by his first name by Flem.

Hoake Character in *The HAMLET*. The father of Alison Hoake MCCARRON, and a well-to-do landowner, he leaves his property to his grandson, Hoake MCCARRON. When his only daughter elopes with McCarron, he sits with a loaded shotgun across his knees and waits 10 days for their return.

Hodge, Elmer Character in "A PORTRAIT OF ELMER" (*Uncollected Stories*). A would-be artist from Texas, he has lived an adventurous life for one so young. He is a father at 18; a tramp; a wounded convalescent in an army hospital in England; and finally a painter in Paris in love (or so he thinks) with a wealthy young Texas woman.

Elmer's courtship of Myrtle MONSON ends in farce in his Paris room when he is forced to use one of his paintings to wipe himself.

Hodge, Jo Character in "A PORTRAIT OF ELMER" (*Uncollected Stories*). Elmer HODGE's sister, she sends him a box of paints in recognition of his artistic potential.

Hodge, Mr. Character in "A PORTRAIT OF ELMER" (*Uncollected Stories*). He is Elmer HODGE's father. Oil is discovered in the yard of his Houston, Texas, home.

Hodge, Mrs. Character in "A PORTRAIT OF ELMER" (*Uncollected Stories*). Elmer HODGE's mother, she dies while Elmer is convalescing from a training camp wound in England. Her husband seems happier after her death.

"Hog Pawn" (*Uncollected Stories*) Short story about the eccentric behavior of a cantankerous, vindictive, and penny-pinching old man, Otis MEADOWFILL, who, among other threatening things, shoots at his neighbor's hog as it strays onto Meadowfill's property. When an oil company approaches Meadowfill to buy a portion of his land, he refuses to sell. Since the legal ownership of the land is in dispute—it either belongs to Meadowfill's neighbor SNOPES (2) or to Meadowfill's daughter, Essie Meadowfill (SMITH), to whom Meadowfill transferred the property when he applied for relief under the Roosevelt administration—the oil company needs both parties to agree to sell. Eventually the town attorney (and sometime private eye) Gavin STEVENS gets involved. After finding the booby trap that Snopes attached to the window Meadowfill shoots from, Stevens settles the dispute between the two neighbors. Confronted with the evidence, the usurious Snopes must sell his lot to Essie. The story ends on a happy note: Essie will marry the World War II veteran McKinley SMITH, sell the land to the oil company, and, together with her husband, buy a farm.

Several disparate themes—a father's opposition to the marriage of his daughter, a defiant older man in conflict with his neighbor, and perennial struggles with SNOPESISM and its defeat—merge in "Hog Pawn," but, as James Ferguson comments, "the triumph of 'good guys' and the defeat of the Snopeses through various machinations in 'By the People' and 'Hog Pawn' seem unconvincing because the stories are turgid, listless, dull—and unfunny" (*Faulkner's Short Fiction*, p. 76).

"Hog Pawn" is narrated by Gavin Stevens's nephew Chick MALLISON. The story was written around October 1954 and published posthumously in *The Uncollected Stories of William Faulkner*. A revised version was included in chapter 14 of book 3, "Flem," of *The Mansion*. For more information, see *Uncollected Stories of William Faulkner*, p. 697.

Hogben   Character in *IF I FORGET THEE, JERUSALEM* ("The Wild Palms"). The engineer who operates the ore train at the Utah mine, he explains to Henry WILBOURNE that he must make a trip every 30 days in order to keep the franchise.

Hogganbeck, Boon   Character in *GO DOWN, MOSES* ("The Old People," "The Bear," "Delta Autumn"), *The REIVERS*, and other works. In *Go Down, Moses*, he is the large, rough, uneducated, hard-drinking grandson of a Chickasaw woman and works as a handyman at Major DE SPAIN's hunting camp. He is a comic central figure in Faulkner's last novel, *The Reivers*.

In "The Bear," he is as devoted to the old dog Lion as he is to de Spain. In the climactic scene, the bear Old Ben swipes at Lion, mortally wounding him. Boon, a notoriously bad shot, leaps on the bear and stabs him to death. When Sam FATHERS, equating the slain bear to the vanishing wilderness, loses the will to live, he instructs Boon to kill him and place his blanket-wrapped body on a Chickasaw grave platform.

In *The Reivers*, Hogganbeck is the 41-year-old night assistant to Mr. BALLOTT at the Priest livery stable. He takes loving responsibility for Boss (Lucius) PRIEST's Winton Flyer, one of JEFFERSON, MISSISSIPPI's, first cars, keeping it gleaming and driving it whenever he can. Along with young Lucius PRIEST, he develops a plan to "borrow" the Flyer for a trip to MEMPHIS when the senior Priests leave town for Grandfather LESSEP's funeral.

The two, with Ned MCCASLIN as a stowaway in the boot of the Flyer, embark on a series of adventures involving a Memphis brothel, the prostitutes who work there, a racing horse, and an obnoxious deputy sheriff named Butch LOVEMAIDEN. In the end, the travelers return safely to Jefferson. Boon marries one of the prostitutes and names their first-born after Lucius Priest.

Boon Hogganbeck is referred to in *INTRUDER IN THE DUST*, *The TOWN*, and the short story "A BEAR HUNT."

Hogganbeck, David   Character in "A COURTSHIP" (in *Uncollected Stories*). The pilot of Captain STUDENMARE's steamboat, he challenges the powerful Chickasaw leader IKKEMOTUBBE (Doom) for the affections of Herman BASKET's beautiful sister.

Hogganbeck, Everbe Corinthia (Miss Corrie)   Character in *The REIVERS*. She is one of the girls in Miss Reba RIVERS's brothel, and a particular favorite of Boon HOGGANBECK.

A small-town Arkansas madam named Aunt FITTIE takes in Everbe after her mother dies and introduces her to the business at age 11 or 12. A big girl, personable, appealing and gentle, she advances to work in the better-paying MEMPHIS house of Miss Reba and begins to call herself Miss Corrie, figuring that the name Everbe Corinthia is "too countrified" for her sophisticated patrons. When her adolescent nephew OTIS, a budding criminal, comes from Arkansas on a visit, she gives him five cents a day to keep quiet about her full name.

When Boon visits the CATALPA STREET house, jealously overwhelms him and he demands to have Miss Corrie all to himself, much to Reba's disgust.

Miss Corrie and the innocent young Lucius PRIEST are drawn to each other from the start. When Otis coarsely details her background to Lucius and explains "pugnuckling," some sort of sexual act, Lucius flies into a rage and attacks him. His action so touches Corrie that she tearfully promises him that she will quit the oldest profession for good. She even refuses Boon.

With Boon and Lucius, Miss Corrie becomes caught up in Ned MCCASLIN's horseracing scheme. She persuades Sam CALDWELL, another of her admirers, to arrange railroad transportation from Memphis to PARSHAM, TENNESSEE, for Ned and the horse Lightning (Coppermine), and she breaks her vow and entertains Deputy Sheriff Butch LOVEMAIDEN so he will release Ned and Lightning from custody. Lucius is devastated by her fall from grace.

After the race, Miss Corrie renews her pledge and declines to go back to Memphis with Miss Reba. She and Boon eventually marry, set up in a little house in JEFFERSON, MISSISSIPPI, and produce a son whom they name for Lucius Priest.

Hogganbeck, Lucius Priest (Luke)   Character in *The REIVERS* and other works. He is the son of Boon HOGGANBECK and his bride, Everbe Corinthia HOGGANBECK, named for Lucius PRIEST, a companion on the MEMPHIS adventure that leads to the Hogganbecks' marriage.

In *The Town*, Luke is the owner of JEFFERSON, MISSISSIPPI's, first Model-T Ford; Roth (Carothers) EDMONDS and other townsmen sign the note that finances the car's purchase. In *The MANSION*, he operates an automobile jitney.

In the short story "A BEAR HUNT," Luke visits an Indian camp at V. K. RATLIFF's suggestion for relief from hiccups. The cure gives him such a fright that he thrashes Ratliff for suggesting the treatment.

Hogganbeck, Melissa   Character in KNIGHT'S GAMBIT ("Knight's Gambit"). She is Chick MALLISON's history teacher. Miss Hogganbeck changes the name of the course to "World Affairs."

In *The TOWN,* she teaches history at the Academy in JEFFERSON, MISSISSIPPI, where Linda Snopes (KOHL) is a student for a year and a half, until Flem SNOPES allows Linda to enter the state university 50 miles away. A die-hard confederate in whose courses history does not reach Christmas Day, 1865, Miss Melissa Hogganbeck is unwilling to admit that the South was ever defeated.

Hogganbeck, Mrs.   Character in "A BEAR HUNT" (in *Collected Stories*). She is the wife of the improvident Lucius Priest HOGGANBECK, the son of Boon HOGGANBECK. Mrs. Hogganbeck takes in sewing to support the family.

Hoke's Station   Fictional place, a "tiny log-line junction" with sidetracks, a loading platform and a commissary store in Major DE SPAIN's hunting preserve in the MISSISSIPPI DELTA wilderness. In GO DOWN, MOSES, Isaac (Ike) MCCASLIN returns after a long absence to find the little wilderness outpost transformed.

Holcomb, Ashley   Minor character in *The TOWN*. He is one of Chick MALLISON's boyhood friends. In exchange for the dollar he owes Aleck SANDER, Ashley jumps from a tree.

Holcomb, (Sister) Beth   In *The MANSION,* a member of Brother J. C. GOODYHAY's religious congregation. Right after his release from prison, Mink SNOPES does yard work for her because he needs money to travel to MEMPHIS and JEFFERSON, MISSISSIPPI. After she feeds Mink dinner, she sends him on to Brother Goodyhay's, four miles down the road.

Holiday   Glossy travel and leisure magazine. The editors approached Faulkner in 1952 with an offer of $2,000 for a piece on his native country; his 10,500-word fictional memoir "Mississippi" appeared in *Holiday* in April 1954.

The magazine in 1954 asked Faulkner for an article on Vicksburg, Mississippi. He declined on account of unfamiliarity with the place.

Holland, Anselm, Jr. (Young Anse)   Character in "Smoke" in KNIGHT'S GAMBIT. The son of Anselm (old Anse) HOLLAND Sr., with whom he constantly feuds, and the twin of Virginius HOLLAND, he runs away from home in his teens and returns a decade later to demand his share of the family property. Old Anse and Virginius refuse him.

Holland, Anselm, Sr. (Old Anse)   Character in *The HAMLET* and other works. He is referred to as Old Man Anse Holland in *The Hamlet,* where he rents farms to V. K. RATLIFF's father and Ab SNOPES. Without Anse's knowledge, Snopes trades Anse's worn-out sorghum mill and straight plow stock to Beasley KEMP for a horse. (In an earlier version of the episode in the short story "A FOOL ABOUT A HORSE," Holland's bob-wire and busted tools are traded.)

In "Smoke" in KNIGHT'S GAMBIT, he is the "crazed, hate-ridden" father of the twins Anselm and (Young Anse) Virginius HOLLAND. Granby DODGE murders him in a bid to get possession of the Holland property.

Holland, Cornelia Mardis   Character in "Smoke" in KNIGHT'S GAMBIT. She is the deceased wife of Anselm (Old Anse) HOLLAND and the mother of the twins, Young Anse and Virginius HOLLAND.

Holland, Mr. (1)   Character in "Tomorrow" in KNIGHT'S GAMBIT. He is the jury foreman in the murder trial of BOOKWRIGHT, accused of killing Buck THORPE.

Holland, Mr. (2)   In *The MANSION,* the president of the Bank of Jefferson. As a gesture of kindness, Holland has a needed bathroom installed in Otis Meadowfill's home despite Meadowfill's outrage and gives Meadowfill's daughter, Essie Meadowfill SMITH, a job for life in the bank.

Holland, Virginius (Virge)   Character in "Smoke" in KNIGHT'S GAMBIT. He is the son of Anselm (Old Anse) HOLLAND and the twin of Anselm HOLLAND Jr. (Young Anse). A good farmer, he longs to take over the mistreated land from his father and restore it to productivity. But the old man eventually drives him away and he sets to farming his cousin Granby DODGE's land.

Hollowell, Lafe   Father of Lee HOLLOWELL in the short story "ADOLESCENCE." Lafe and Joe BUNDEN are killed by Revenue agents who raid the moonshine whiskey still.

Hollowell, Lee   Friend of Juliet BUNDEN in the story "ADOLESCENCE." Lee has a somewhat Adam-like role in the Edenic childhood innocence with Juliet as they swim together naked, hunt, and fish. Lee's father, Lafe HOLLOWELL, is killed by Revenue agents, along with Juliet's father, Joe BUNDEN.

Holly Springs   A market town and railroad junction in a cotton-growing region of northern Mississippi.

Faulkners bound from OXFORD, MISSISSIPPI, to MEMPHIS used to change trains in Holly Springs.

The Confederate general Earl Van Dorn raided the Union supply depot at Holly Springs on December 20, 1862. Faulkner used the operation as a model for the engagement that cost Charley Gordon his life in the posthumously published short story "Rose of Lebanon" (see "A RETURN"). In the story, Gordon is killed not in the attack on Grant's warehouses but ingloriously in a raid on a henhouse.

Faulkner reworked the material, changing the location and other particulars, for the novel LIGHT IN AUGUST, in which Gail HIGHTOWER (2) broods on his grandfather's death in an operation much like the Holly Springs raid.

In the early 1950s, Faulkner occasionally arranged to rendezvous in Holly Springs with the young Memphis writer Joan WILLIAMS, with whom he had a rather tortured affair.

Hollymount   Fictional town in CROSSMAN COUNTY, east of YOKNAPATAWPHA COUNTY. Jake MONTGOMERY runs stolen timber into Hollymount and neighboring GLASGOW in INTRUDER IN THE DUST.

Holmes, Jack   The parachuter or jumper who accompanies the pilot Roger SHUMANN in PYLON. In a ménage à trois relationship, Holmes openly lives with Shumann and his wife Laverne. After Laverne's son is born, Holmes and Shumann roll dice to decide who will marry her and be the child's legal guardian. Shumann wins, but the boy is named Jack, after Holmes. When Shumann crashes his plane in the lake and dies, Holmes asks the REPORTER to send the body to Shumann's father in Ohio, but the body is never found. At the end of the novel, Laverne and Holmes go to Ohio to leave little Jack to live with Shumann's father. Laverne is also pregnant at this time with (she believes) Holmes's child.

Holmes, Miss   With Miss DAINGERFIELD, one of the two young women at Mrs. BLAND's picnic in The SOUND AND THE FURY. Quentin COMPSON also attends; it is the same day Quentin commits suicide (June 2, 1910).

Holston, Alexander (Alec Holston)   In REQUIEM FOR A NUN, identified with Doctor Samuel HABERSHAM and Louis GRENIER as one of the three original settlers of YOKNAPATAWPHA COUNTY. He arrives "as half groom and half bodyguard to Doctor Habersham, and half nurse and half tutor to the doctor's eight-year-old motherless son" (pp. 6–7). Holston is the owner of the lock whose humorous role in the early history of the settlement is narrated in the prose prologue to act 1, "The Courthouse (A Name for the City)," of Requiem. He is also the first publican in the county, owner of the tavern known

during the time period of Requiem and the SNOPES TRILOGY as the Holston House. In ABSALOM, ABSALOM!, Thomas SUTPEN rooms at the Holston House when he first comes to JEFFERSON, MISSISSIPPI. Holston is also mentioned in INTRUDER IN THE DUST, KNIGHT'S GAMBIT ("Hand Upon the Waters"), The TOWN, and The MANSION. In Requiem, Holston, who dies a generation before the Civil War, is said to be a childless bachelor, but in the later time frame of "Skirmish at Sartoris" (a short story revised with same title as chapter 6 of The UNVANQUISHED), there appears a Mrs. HOLSTON, and in The Mansion, the Holston House is "owned and run by two maiden sisters . . . who were the last descendants of Alexander Holston" (p. 383).

Holston, Dr.   Character in "MY GRANDMOTHER MILLARD AND GENERAL BEDFORD FORREST AND THE BATTLE OF HARRYKIN CREEK" (in Collected Stories). A JEFFERSON, MISSISSIPPI, physician, during the Civil War he warns the Compsons that Yankee troops are approaching their place in northern Mississippi.

Holston, Mrs.   Character in The UNVANQUISHED. She is the elderly lady whose Black porter witnesses Colonel John SARTORIS's killing of the carpetbagging Burdens at a polling station in JEFFERSON, MISSISSIPPI.

Holston House   Fictional place, the leading hotel in JEFFERSON, MISSISSIPPI, dating from the days when Jefferson was a mere village of a few stores, a blacksmith and livery stable, and a saloon. It is named for YOKNAPATAWPHA COUNTY's first tavernkeeper, Alexander Holston.

The Holston House figures in ABSALOM, ABSALOM!, The UNVANQUISHED, and other works. In The REIVERS, Lucius PRIEST describes it as well-appointed, with carpets, leather chairs, brass cuspidors, and linen tablecloths in the dining room.

"Honor" *(Collected Stories)*   Short story relating an episode in the rootless life of one-time World War I aviator Buck MONAGHAN. Ready to quit his current job after only three weeks, he recalls his days as a test pilot and the reckless death of White, a fellow pilot. During his next job as a wing walker, he started a romance with a married woman, Mildred ROGERS. Learning of the affair, her selfless husband, Howard ROGERS, decided to let her go.

The next morning Monaghan was reluctant to perform his wing walking feat with Rogers as pilot. Once they were up in the air, Monaghan got into a dangerous situation and Rogers risked his own life to save him. He quit the job and Rogers reconciled with his wife. This reminds Monaghan of the comradeship of his war days, and he thinks backs to armistice night in 1918 (see "AD ASTRA"), when he was condemned to an existence as one of the walking dead. The story ends as Monaghan walks away once more, this time from his auto salesman job.

This story first appeared in *American Mercury* (July 1930) and was included in *Doctor Martino and Other Stories* (1934).

Hood, Uncle Parsham   Character in *The REIVERS*. A lean old African American, he involves himself in the doings, sometimes sordid, occasionally dangerous (as when Deputy Butch LOVEMAIDEN is present), of the horse racing partnership of Boon HOGGANBECK, Lucius PRIEST, and Ned MCCASLIN.

Hood's grandson, Lycurgus BRIGGINS, is a key ally of Ned's. Hood himself provides crucial information that allows Lightning (Coppermine) to win a decisive race—he notices that the horse runs well until he sees nothing but empty track ahead, then slows. Ned contrives to lure him on to greater efforts by rewarding him at the finish line with a pungent and aromatic "sourdeen" (sardine).

Eleven-year-old Lucius, homesick and confused, turns to "Uncle Possum" for safety, security, and authority in a hostile adult world. In the face of disapproval from PARSHAM, TENNESSEE's, white community, he insists on staying in Hood's home. He confides in him, seeks comfort from him, and always calls him "sir."

Hood finally orders Ned to tell the bewildered Lucius all that has happened. Ned explains that Everbe (HOGGANBECK) reluctantly submitted to Butch and "entertained" him; and that a jealous and enraged Boon had beaten them both and landed himself in jail.

Things all come right in the end, thanks in no small part to Hood, who gains a much-deserved $20 in gambling winnings for his church.

Hooper   Character in *MOSQUITOES*. A businessman and Rotarian, he arranges to have lunch with the novelist Dawson FAIRCHILD to satisfy his curiosity about NEW ORLEANS bohemian life.

Hope, L. C. W. (Claude)   Character in "TURNABOUT" (in *Collected Stories*). A young officer in the Royal Navy, he is the second-in-command of a torpedo boat based in France during World War I. Homeless (he sleeps in the street), drunken, and infantile, he is deeply impressed with the dangers of flying when he accompanies Captain BOGARD on a bombing mission. Bogard is later equally impressed with the dangers of Hope's raids into German waters. The young midshipman dies in action at sea, along with the other three men in his crew.

Hopkins   A cotton speculator in *The SOUND AND THE FURY* who frequents the telegraph office to learn how the stock market is doing. He is especially interested in what Jason COMPSON IV is buying and selling.

Horn   British soldier in *A FABLE* who is knocked out by the RUNNER when he frees the sentry (Mr. HARRY).

Hotel Peabody   A stately house on Main Street in MEMPHIS. Faulkner and his wife, (Lida) Estelle Oldham FAULKNER, usually took a room at the Peabody for overnight and occasional weekend visits in Memphis.

In *The REIVERS*, Lucius PRIEST, looking back on a long-ago trip to Memphis, mentions passing the Peabody ("they have moved it since") with Boon HOGGANBECK and Ned MCCASLIN in Grandfather's car, though he notes that his family always patronized the GAYOSO.

"The Hound" *(Collected Stories)*   Short story first published in August 1931 in *HARPER'S MAGAZINE* 163, 266–74, and reprinted in *Doctor Martino and Other Stories* (1934) and in *A Rose for Emily and Other Stories by William Faulkner* (1945). Faulkner revised the story for book 3 of *The HAMLET;* the original version is reprinted in *Uncollected Storie of William Faulkner.*

The story recounts Ernest COTTON's murder of Jack HOUSTON and Cotton's abortive attempt at disposing of the body. Cotton shoots Houston in revenge for what he sees as an injustice: He is not content with the meager one dollar fee that the court awards him for wintering Houston's stray hog. Cotton first forces the corpse into the rotten shell of a cypress tree, but a few days later he notices vultures flying above it. He returns during the night to disentangle the decaying body from the tree trunk and toss it into a river. He notices that one of the body's limbs is missing, and when he returns to retrieve it he is caught by the sheriff and his deputies.

"The Hound" is a story of the internal psychological processes of a man obsessed with his own code of honor and self-worth in conflict with the norms of societal justice. The critic James Ferguson comments that "the anguish and terror the protagonist has gone through have been so intense that our reactions at the end of the story are not those of relief or triumph but of exhaustion—and of compassion for Cotton" (*Faulkner's Short Fiction*, p. 76).

In the revision, Faulkner changed the name of the main character from Ernest Cotton to Mink SNOPES. Unlike Cotton, a bachelor, Snopes is a married man with two children. Faulkner also changed the conflict that occurs between Houston and Mink. In the story, it is Houston's hog that Cotton winters, but in the revision Houston winters Snopes's scrub yearling and the court awards Houston three dollars for pasturage. The revised story is also referred to in *The TOWN* and *The MANSION*. For more information, see *Selected Letters of William Faulkner*, pp. 115, 197, 202, and 430, and *UNCOLLECTED STORIES OF WILLIAM FAULKNER*, pp. 688–89.

Housman, A. E. (1859–1936)   English poet and classical scholar, professor of Latin at Cambridge University. Housman published three volumes of lyric verse: *A Shropshire Lad* (1896), *Last Poems* (1922), and *More Poems* (1936).

As a young man Billy Falkner deeply admired *A Shropshire Lad* and patterned some of his own early verse on Housman's melancholy, sometimes cynical ballads.

Houston (1) Character in *SARTORIS (FLAGS IN THE DUST)*. He is the Black waiter in Deacon's café, where Bayard SARTORIS (4) and Rafe MCCALLUM have drinks.

Houston (2) In *AS I LAY DYING,* a neighbor who attends the funeral of Addie BUNDREN.

Houston, Doris One of the main characters in the short story "TWO DOLLAR WIFE." An 18-year-old, Doris, like her beau, Maxwell JOHNS, is careless and self-indulgent. On a whim, she agrees to marry Maxwell, but she regrets the notion immediately and reneges. On a drunken New Year's Eve, however, she and Maxwell bribe a justice of the peace to marry them. Doris's mother sends Maxwell off when he tries to tell her of the marriage after the couple arrives at Doris's home.

Houston, Jack Character in *The HAMLET,* a childless widower and farmer in the vicinity of FRENCHMAN'S BEND. At 16, Houston leaves home to avoid a romantic involvement with his country school friend Lucy Pate (HOUSTON), whom he returns to marry 13 years later. While away, he works at different jobs, one of which is a locomotive fireman, and lives with a woman for seven years after taking her from a brothel in Galveston. Before he returns to Mississippi to marry Lucy Pate, he shares his money with his common-law wife. Six months after Houston's wedding to Lucy, she is killed by the stallion he gave her as a wedding present. He becomes embittered and isolated.

The idiot Ike SNOPES is in love with Houston's cow and steals it; after tracking Ike down, Houston gives him the cow in disgust.

At 33, Houston is killed by Mink SNOPES, the result of a dispute over Mink's stray yearling that Houston penned up.

References to Houston appear in *THE TOWN*—in one place his first name appears as Zack (36) and in another Jack (78); in *The MANSION;* and in an earlier published short story, "THE HOUND," where he is referred to as a "prosperous and overbearing man" (*Uncollected Stories of William Faulkner,* p. 157).

Houston, Lucy Pate Character in *The HAMLET.* Jack HOUSTON's schoolmate, she later becomes his wife. Six months after marrying Houston, she is fatally kicked by the stallion he gave her as a wedding present. (In editions prior to the 1961 Vintage paperback edition of *The TOWN,* the second novel of the SNOPES TRILOGY, her name is Letty Bookwright, and she is the youngest daughter of Cal BOOKWRIGHT.)

Houston, Mrs. Doris HOUSTON's mother in the short story "TWO DOLLAR WIFE." On New Year's Eve, Doris and her beau, Maxwell JOHNS, stay out far later than Mrs. Houston had indicated was allowed; they have, in fact, gotten married. But Mrs. Houston is more concerned with the fate of her son, who swallowed a needle that Maxwell carelessly left in a chair, than with the marriage. She sends Maxwell away when he tries to assert that the marriage is valid.

Hovis, Mr. Minor character in *The TOWN*. The cashier at Sartoris's bank where Manfred DE SPAIN is president.

Hovis, Mrs. Character in "UNCLE WILLY" (in *Collected Stories*). She is one of the JEFFERSON, MISSISSIPPI, ladies who tries to break Uncle Willy CHRISTIAN of his drug habit. She alternates with Mrs. MERRIDEW in standing watch over him until his sister arrives from Texas.

Howe, Irving (1920–1993) Writer, literary and social critic, born in New York City. Influential in the left-leaning New York literary world of the 1950s, he cofounded the journal *Dissent* and contributed frequently to *Partisan Review* and the *New Republic*.

Howe published *William Faulkner: A Critical Study,* an important survey of major Faulkner novels and short works, in 1952. A revised and expanded edition appeared in 1975. Other Howe works include *Politics and the Novel* (1957) and *World of Our Fathers* (1976).

Howes, Anne Character in "ARTIST AT HOME" (in *Collected Stories*). The wife of novelist Roger HOWES, she thinks briefly that she is in love with the poet John BLAIR, a houseguest, then changes her mind.

Howes, Darrel Character in "IDYLL IN THE DESERT" (in *Uncollected Stories*). A tuberculosis patient, he comes to the Arizona desert to recover and is looked after by the mail rider Lucas CRUMP and, later, by his lover who abandons her family in New York to come to him.

Howes eventually recovers and leaves. His lover, however, has become infected and must stay behind. When Howes, traveling with his new wife, accidentally encounters the woman years later, he fails to recognize her.

Howes, Roger Character in "ARTIST AT HOME" (in *Collected Stories*). A successful novelist, he has run dry at the time the poet John BLAIR visits as his houseguest. Blair's visit jolts Howes out of his complacency. Inspired by the poet's hopeless love for Howes's wife, Anne HOWES, he writes a successful novel on the theme. The brief, painful episode draws Roger and Anne together again.

Hoxey, Major The mayor of JEFFERSON, MISSISSIPPI, in the short story "CENTAUR IN BRASS." A Yale graduate and wealthy bachelor, Major Hoxey appoints Flem SNOPES superintendent of the municipal power plant after starting an adulterous affair with Flem's beautiful wife, Eula. The mayor is also referred to as Colonel Hoxey. (See also DE SPAIN, MANFRED.)

Hub Character in *SARTORIS*. With young Bayard SAR-TORIS (4), he and his friend Mitch serenade Narcissa Benbow (SARTORIS) at the close of a long night's drinking.

Hughes, Manny Character in "IDYLL IN THE DESERT" (in *Uncollected Stories*). The postmaster in Blizzard, Arizona, he helps Lucas CRUMP deceive Darrel HOWES's consumptive ex-lover about the source of the support payments she receives in the mail.

Hule Character in "MOUNTAIN VICTORY" (in *Collected Stories*). The younger brother of VATCH, a bushwhacker, he tries to save the life of Major Saucier WEDDEL, a Confederate soldier returning home after the war. Vatch kills Hule accidentally.

Hulett Character in *GO DOWN, MOSES* ("The Fire and the Hearth"). He is the court clerk in the interrupted divorce proceeding between Lucas and Molly BEAUCHAMP.

Hume Character in "AD ASTRA" (in *Collected Stories*). Hume speculates that young Bayard SARTORIS (4) has revenged himself on the German aviator who shot down his twin brother Johnny's airplane. Johnny SAR-TORIS was killed in the crash.

Hurtz, Mr. An offstage character referred to in *PYLON*. He marries the REPORTER's mother and honeymoons in Santa Monica.

I

"Idyll in the Desert" *(Uncollected Stories)* Short story of devotion and self-sacrifice in the face of ingratitude, set in Arizona. The nameless narrator engages in conversation with a mail rider, Lucas CRUMP, who relates a rambling tale laced with sardonic wit. Ten years earlier, Crump took Darrel HOWES, a tuberculosis patient, by wagon to the isolated cabin where Howes hoped to recover his health. On his weekly route Crump delivered food and mail to him and, when his condition worsened, prepared meals and cut firewood for him.

A telegram to New York brought his lover, who abandoned her two children and husband in order to care for Howes. Howes recovered and left; the woman, who had become infected herself, stayed on. Over the next eight years Crump faithfully watched over her, with the assistance of her husband. The two men let her believe that the envelopes of cash paying for her stay came from Howes. Near the end, Crump took her by stretcher to the train. Coincidentally getting off the train were Howes and his new bride; Howes did not recognize his former lover. When she arrived dead at her destination, her husband did not recognize her either, as she had aged so much from her ordeal.

This story first was issued as a limited signed edition of 400 copies on December 31, 1931, by RANDOM HOUSE.

If I Forget Thee, Jerusalem A novel in the form of two alternating stories titled "The Wild Palms" and "The Old Man," this work was published by RANDOM HOUSE in 1939 as *The Wild Palms*. A later authoritative edition restored Faulkner's original title. Most critics regard *If I Forget Thee, Jerusalem* as a minor work; some judge it a failure for its pairing of two essentially separate tales.

The critic Michael MILLGATE describes the book as "a double novel with two plots." It begins with the first of five sections of "The Wild Palms," the story of Harry WILBOURNE and Charlotte RITTENMEYER, who sacrifice everything for love. The five sections of "Old Man," in which an unnamed prison convict is caught up in a great Mississippi River flood, are a counterpoint to the tale of Harry and Charlotte.

The only direct connection between the two stories is the Mississippi state prison at Parchman. "Old Man" takes place in 1927; "The Wild Palms" is set a decade later. Though Harry will eventually serve hard time at

the convict's prison, none of the characters in the two stories meet or cross paths.

Some critics argue that the situations and themes of the paired stories unify *If I Forget Thee, Jerusalem.* The theme of flight and refuge is an obvious link. Harry and Charlotte sacrifice all in their bid for freedom and love; the tall convict, offered his freedom and a sort of love as well, wants only to return to the safe haven of prison. Each story details an escape from confinement to a provisional freedom and then to an ultimate, still more circumscribed confinement. Harry, in aborting Charlotte's pregnancy, takes life; the convict, in delivering the flood refugee's baby, gives it.

Faulkner started work on the book in the fall of 1937. Distracted by personal troubles and in chronic pain from a back injury, he initially reported slow progress to Robert HAAS, his editor at Random House. By year's end, however, he found himself well along with the parallel stories.

The novel opens in present time with Charlotte Rittenmeyer hemorrhaging in the bedroom of a rented beach cottage in a town modeled upon the Gulf Coast resort of PASCAGOULA, MISSISSIPPI. She is near death from complications of a botched abortion. Faulkner introduces the tall CONVICT, Harry Wilbourne's foil, in the second section. He is serving a 15-year prison sentence for a train robbery, the plans for which he took from a pulp detective magazine. Rain falls incessantly, and news of a flood seeps into the prison. Finally a levee breaks nearby, and the inmates are evacuated.

Section three is a flashback. Close to the end of an internship in a NEW ORLEANS hospital, Harry meets Charlotte, a sculptor married to the humdrum businessman Francis RITTENMEYER and the mother of two little girls, at a Vieux Carré party. They fall in love at once. Even more improbably, the impecunious Harry finds $1,278 in a lost wallet to fund their flight on what Charlotte fiercely insists will be a perpetual honeymoon. The lovers—Charlotte driven, insistent and uncompromising, Harry pliant—set off for Chicago, leaving Francis Rittenmeyer, the girls, and Harry's medical career behind.

In the fourth section, the convict is turned loose during the flood with instructions to search for a WOMAN trapped in a tree and a man stranded on the roof of a cottonhouse. The prison authorities later report the convict drowned, but in fact he and the woman, also unnamed, are adrift on the surging waters.

In section five, Harry and Charlotte find shelter in Chicago. He gets work as an intern but loses the job; she lands a temporary job dressing windows in a department store. Gradually their money runs out. A sympathetic newspaper friend, MCCORD, offers them a haven in a cottage on a Wisconsin lake. With the approach of winter, the idyll ends and they return to Chicago. Harry senses a descent into domesticity and realizes they must take flight again. He accepts the offer of a job as doctor in a Utah mining camp, and they strike out for the mountains.

Section six finds the convict and the rescued woman, who is pregnant, swept along with the flood. It carries them up the Yazoo River and into the Mississippi—the "Old Man" river of the story's title. They pass Vicksburg, then Baton Rouge. The woman goes into labor. The convict grounds the skiff on a snake-infested Indian mound and delivers her baby, cutting the umbilical cord with the jagged edge of a tin-can lid.

In section seven, set in the frozen waste of the Utah mining camp, Faulkner introduces two new characters, the BUCKNERS, "Buck" and Billie BUCKNER. The four become friends and even share quarters and an inefficient gasoline heater as bitter cold clamps down on the mountains. Eventually Buck asks Harry to perform an abortion on Billie. He refuses, but Charlotte talks him into it and he carries out the procedure successfully. Not long afterward, Charlotte tells Harry that she, too, is pregnant.

In section eight, the convict finds haven in a Louisiana swamp. He goes into partnership with an alligator hunter known as the CAJAN and, for a time, experiences fulfillment in freedom. But the flood finally reaches the bayou and he and the woman, with her child, are forced to flee. The convict eventually returns to his starting point and reports back to the prison officials, delivering the skiff and its passenger.

Section nine returns to the present. Harry has sent for his landlord, who happens to be a physician; the doctor promptly sends for the authorities. An ambulance carries Charlotte to the hospital, and Harry is taken to jail. Charlotte dies in surgery; Harry is convicted of manslaughter and sentenced to 50 years in prison. Before her death, Charlotte had asked her husband to plead for Harry, and he obediently turns up to ask the court for mercy. Later, Rittenmeyer offers Harry bail bond money and the chance to escape to Mexico; when he refuses, Rittenmeyer presents him with a cyanide capsule. Harry turns this down too, opting for prison and the memory of his love for Charlotte: he decides, "*between grief and nothing I will take grief.*" (*Jerusalem,* p. 273).

Section 10 concludes the novel on an antiromantic and farcical note. The tall convict is back in Parchman prison with 10 years added to his sentence for attempted escape. His one-time girlfriend, the woman for whom he planned and attempted the low comedy train robbery, visits him in prison. Then the visits stop, and he learns she has married a prison guard. On her honeymoon, she sends him a postcard signed, "*Your friend (Mrs) Vernon Waldrip.*"

Faulkner wired Random House on June 17, 1938, that he had finished the novel except for revisions. He sent off the manuscript bearing the title *If I Forget Thee, Jerusalem* before month's end. Haas had strong objections to the title, drawn from Psalm 137 ("If I forget thee, O Jerusalem, let my right hand forget her cunning," an allusion to the ferocity with which Charlotte protects her notion of love) and to some of the language, especially the convict's vulgarities.

Perhaps insincerely, Faulkner offered to substitute ellipses for the offending words, then proposed allowing Haas to change the title if he would let the vocabulary stand. Haas agreed, and the book was published in January 1939 as *The Wild Palms.*

Early reviews were mixed. "William Faulkner has written another tortured, bitter novel, and again emerged the victor over his own sentence structure," Ralph Thompson wrote in the *New York Times.* Malcolm COWLEY wrote that neither story gained anything from the juxtaposition. The news magazine *Time* published a cover story on Faulkner on January 23 and, like most other commentators, the author Robert Cantwell found the grainy, deeply depressing story of Charlotte and Harry distasteful. "But not even careless writing can weaken the cumulative effect of Faulkner's imaginative fertility, the boldness and originality of his themes," he wrote. Perhaps because of the boost from mass-market *Time,* the book sold briskly at first, at a rate of 1,000 copies a week.

Later critics generally endorsed the initial judgements—that "Old Man" was greatly the superior of the two stories, and that the pairing of "The Wild Palms" and "Old Man" seemed whimsical at best. Faulkner offered at least two explanations for his decision to alternate the stories.

"When I reached the end of what is now the first section of *The Wild Palms,* I realized suddenly that something was missing, it needed emphasis, something to lift it like counterpoint in music," he said in the *PARIS REVIEW* interview of 1955. On another occasion, though, he seemed to suggest he joined the two tales simply because he needed to fill out a book: each story alone was too short.

The critic Irving HOWE gives Faulkner the benefit of the doubt, arguing that more than whim or the exigencies of the bookmaking trade led him to the pairing. "The correspondences and joined oppositions between the two stories are so numerous and suggestive that we are obliged to take them seriously, as elements of a literary design," he wrote. Noel Polk, who edited the definitive LIBRARY OF AMERICA edition of *I Forget Thee, Jerusalem,* concluded from typescript and manuscript analysis that Faulkner did not interleave existing stories, but wrote "The Wild Palms" and "Old Man" together.

Ike   Character in KNIGHT'S GAMBIT ("Hand Upon the Waters"). He is the head of the party that carries Lonnie GRINNUP away for burial.

Ikkemotubbe   Character in ABSALOM, ABSALOM! and other works. A CHICKASAW INDIAN chief, he sells Thomas SUTPEN 100 square miles of Yoknapatawpha bottomland, the future SUTPEN'S HUNDRED.

Known as "Doom"—*du homme,* the man, doom—in "The Old People" (in GO DOWN, MOSES), he threatens the reigning Chickasaw chief, his cousin MOKETUBBE, with poison, frightens him into abdicating, and assumes the tribal leadership himself. He performs a marriage ceremony joining a quadroon woman pregnant with his child to one of his slaves. She delivers a boy named Had-Two-Fathers, who will become the hunter Sam FATHERS of *Go Down, Moses,* INTRUDER IN THE DUST, *The REIVERS,* and the short story "A JUSTICE." Ikkemotubbe later sells bride, groom, and child to the white planter Carothers MCCASLIN.

Ikkemotubbe is mentioned in *REQUIEM FOR A NUN,* *The TOWN,* and the short stories "RED LEAVES" and "A COURTSHIP."

Immelmann, Max (1890–1916)   Historical aviator referred to in *A FABLE.* See BALL, ALBERT. (Faulkner spelled his name Immelman.)

Ingraham   Family name in INTRUDER IN THE DUST. The name of one of the early YOKNAPATAWPHA COUNTY farm clans, it has passed into common usage as Ingrum, just as Urquhart has evolved into Workitt.

Ingrum, Willy   Character in INTRUDER IN THE DUST. He is the talkative JEFFERSON, MISSISSIPPI, marshal. When the sheriff, Hope HAMPTON, wants to move Lucas BEAUCHAMP from the jail to a safer place, he gives Willy a false route and destination so that he will pass it along and throw the Gowrie lynch mob off the scent.

interior monologue   A narrative technique that presents to the reader the flow of a character's inner thought processes and impressions. First exploited by the French writer Edouard Dujardin (1861–1949) in his novel LES LAURIERS SONT COUPÉS (1887; English title, *We'll to the Woods No More*), this technique was used by James JOYCE, Virginia Woolf, and others, including William Faulkner. It is similar to the stream-of-consciousness technique in that it represents the fluency and disconnectedness of ideas, memories, and sensations that comprise one's conscious thoughts. It is different in that the interior monologue tends to disregard basic grammatical and syntactical rules. Although it sometimes causes interpretative obstacles for the reader, the interior monologue can give a much richer and a much more penetrating portrait of a character's intimate thoughts than traditional narrative techniques.

Joyce's use of the interior monologue in *Ulysses* was an influence on Faulkner, particularly on *The SOUND AND THE FURY* and *AS I LAY DYING.* The Joyce scholar Michael Groden has observed that with the interior monologue technique Faulkner was able to resolve serious characterization problems that he confronted when writing the earlier novels SOLDIERS' PAY and *MOSQUITOES* (see "Criticism in New Composition: *Ulysses* and *The Sound and the Fury,*" *Twentieth Century Literature* 21 [October, 1975], 266).

According to James Joyce, the first to use the term *interior monologue* was the French novelist and translator Valery Larbaud, in reference to *Ulysses;* see *Letters of James Joyce,* vol. 3, edited by Richard Ellmann, New York, Viking Press, p. 83.

Intruder in the Dust   A novel, published in 1948, that explores the South's racial predicament delivered through the medium of a murder mystery. *Intruder in the Dust* attracted considerable attention when it first appeared. The subject was timely—an antilynching measure was then before Congress, and the 1948 Democratic Party platform called for civil rights for blacks, which led to the Dixiecrat revolt of southern Democrats—so *Intruder* found an eager if somewhat divided audience. Few critics today rank it with Faulkner's best work.

According to the biographer Joseph BLOTNER, Faulkner based the plot on an actual event in OXFORD, MISSISSIPPI, in the late 1930s in which the authorities accused a black man of killing a white. While the jury deliberated, a mob of 75 whites broke into the Oxford jail, seized the prisoner, carried him away, and hanged him along a country road.

For the central character, he reclaimed Lucas BEAUCHAMP from GO DOWN, MOSES (1942). Now in his late 60s, a descendant of the YOKNAPATAWPHA COUNTY planter and slaveholder Lucius Quintus Carothers MCCASLIN, Beauchamp is fiercely independent and stubbornly proud of his mixed racial heritage. Contemptuous, too, of Mississippi's strict racial conventions, he refuses to adopt an attitude of submissiveness. His defiant bearing, coupled with some sketchy circumstantial evidence, makes him an automatic suspect when Vinson GOWRIE, a member of a large clan of hill country white farmers, is found murdered.

David Brian as John Stevens, Juan Hernandez as Beauchamp, and Claude Jarman, Jr., as Chick Mallison in the film version of Faulkner's Intruder in the Dust. (Museum of Modern Art/Film Stills Archive)

Faulkner turned to the story in early 1948 when he found himself in trouble with the intractable manuscript, a work of many years, that would become *A FABLE* (1954). He wrote to his agent, Harold OBER, that he envisioned the new project as a short novel. As he thought it through, however, the manuscript would grow to more than twice the originally projected size, and carry a heavy freight of social implication.

Faulkner uses a familiar device to develop the story, one he had used before. Lucas Beauchamp attempts to unravel the mystery of Vinson Gowrie's killing with the assistance of two juvenile inseparables, Charles (Chick) MALLISON, the nephew of attorney Gavin STEVENS, and Chick's Black friend Aleck SANDER, the son of the Mallisons' cook, PARALEE. The novelist enlists the elderly spinster Eunice HABERSHAM to provide timely assistance to Chick and Aleck. The two boys' partnership recalls that of Bayard SARTORIS (3) and Ringo STROTHER, who with Granny Rosa MILLARD foil the Yankee invaders and homegrown bushwhackers in Civil War–era northern Mississippi in *The UNVANQUISHED* (1938).

The novel opens with a favorite Faulkner device, an extended flashback. Out hunting near the Beauchamp place, Chick falls into an icy creek; Lucas Beauchamp pulls him out of the water, dries him off, takes him home and feeds him. Chick offers money for the hospitality. Lucas angrily rejects it, flinging the coins to the floor. Chick broods on his blunder for a long time afterward, wondering how he can make up for it. He gives the Beauchamps a Christmas present: cigars for Lucas, snuff for his wife, Molly BEAUCHAMP. Later, he sends Molly a dress. Lucas responds with a gift of a gallon of sorghum molasses.

Chick's opportunity for repayment comes when Lucas is accused of the Gowrie killing. Lucas had tumbled onto Crawford GOWRIE's steady theft of lumber from his brother Vinson and his business partner, Sudley WORKITT. Anticipating exposure, Crawford kills Vinson and manages to make it appear that Lucas, who is seen standing over the corpse with a recently discharged pistol in his pocket, is the culprit.

Lucas is arrested and jailed. Gowrie friends and kin talk of forming a lynch mob. Attorney Stevens visits Lucas in his cell and advises him to plead guilty when he goes before the judge the next day and be sent to the penitentiary for his own protection.

When Chick visits him in jail, Lucas asks him to dig up the Gowrie grave at CALEDONIA CHAPEL out in BEAT FOUR, a lonely country district peopled by clannish and violent white hill farmers. He enlists Aleck's assistance, and Miss Habersham agrees to help out. The body, it turns out, is not Vinson's but that of a CROSSMAN COUNTY timber buyer named Jake MONTGOMERY. They return later with the sheriff and the Gowries to exhume the body; this time the casket is empty. The boys eventually find Montgomery's body in a shallow grave and Vinson's in quicksand under the highway bridge. Crawford Gowrie is exposed as the killer, and Lucas goes free.

Faulkner completed a rewrite of the draft in late April 1948 and mailed it off to his editor, Robert HAAS, at RANDOM HOUSE. As Chick becomes a man in the course of the novel, he shows a growing comprehension of the white community's attitudes on race. Whites resented Lucas Beauchamp because he acted more like his white McCaslin ancestors than a descendant of slaves. Gradually Chick comes to understand the brutal, dehumanizing reality of white-black relations in Yoknapatawpha County.

Faulkner has Gavin Stevens ponder the larger problem. Stevens takes a gradualist view not unlike Faulkner's own: Justice must prevail, blacks must be permitted the advantages of full citizenship someday soon, but the problem is the South's to solve, free of northern interference. In a series of long, murky passages, Stevens articulates his views on the South and on southern resistance to the federal government's halting but increasingly forceful support of the Civil Rights movement.

Random House published the novel on September 27, 1948. With its timely content, it drew an immediate response from reviewers. "*Intruder in the Dust* does not come to us merely as a novel: it also involves a tract," the critic Edmund Wilson wrote in *The New Yorker.* "The book contains a kind of counterblast to the anti-lynching bill and to the civil rights plank in the Democratic platform." Wilson reads Gavin Stevens's speeches "as something in the nature of a public message delivered by the author himself," one that reserves the racial question to the white South itself, free of outside intervention. That said, Wilson found the novel impressive,

particularly in its delineation of the character of Lucas Beauchamp, certainly one of Faulkner's stronger creations, white or black.

Writing in the *Hudson Review,* the novelist Eudora Welty called *Intruder* "a double and delightful feat, because the mystery of the detective-story plot is being raveled out while the mystery of Faulkner's prose is being spun and woven before our eyes."

Like Wilson, the critic Malcolm COWLEY focused on the novel's political message. "The tragedy of intelligent Southerners like Faulkner is that their two fundamental beliefs, in human equality and in Southern independence, are now in violent conflict," Cowley wrote in the *New Republic.*

The book sold well, and Random House attracted a lucrative screen rights offer from Hollywood: METRO-GOLDWYN-MAYER paid $50,000 for a movie version of *Intruder.* Filmed on location in Oxford in the spring of 1949, the movie generated much local controversy: residents objected to the making of a movie in their town that portrayed the South negatively. There were also difficulties with housing the biracial cast in segregated Oxford. Juan Hernandez, a Puerto Rican actor who played Lucas Beauchamp, ended up staying in the home of G. W. Bankhead, Oxford's black undertaker.

Faulkner read the script and approved most of the scenes. He liked the film, which he saw in preview in Memphis in September. A crowd of 800—tickets cost $2.60—filled Oxford's Lyric Theatre for the formal opening of *Intruder in the Dust* on October 11, 1949.

Irey The jailer in the American horse racing section of the novel *A FABLE.* He is holding the Reverend Toby SUTTERFIELD and Sutterfield's grandson for the theft of the horse. An ineffectual man, he is unable to stop a mob from entering the courthouse, but he is able to help the two prisoners escape. Irey also appears in the novella *NOTES ON A HORSETHIEF,* the earliest version of which was published in a limited edition in 1950. This story was later revised and used in *A Fable;* this section of the novel appeared as a short story in *Vogue* in 1954.

Iron Bridge Fictional place, carrying the highway from YOKNAPATAWPHA COUNTY to MEMPHIS over the TALLAHATCHIE RIVER. In *The REIVERS,* Faulkner places it at Wyott's Crossing, an old ferry site.

Isham Character in GO DOWN, MOSES ("Delta Autumn"). He is an elderly African-American servant at the MISSISSIPPI DELTA hunting camp.

Isom Character in SARTORIS and SANCTUARY. A black servant of the Sartorises, he is the son of ELNORA and the grandson of Simon STROTHER. In *Sanctuary,* he is Narcissa Benbow SARTORIS's driver.

Issetibbeha Character in *GO DOWN, MOSES* ("The Old People," "The Bear") and other works. A CHICKASAW INDIAN chief, he is the uncle of the ambitious IKKEMO-TUBBE (called Doom). After his death, his son MOKE-TUBBE succeeds him, but Ikkemotubbe forces him to abdicate.

Issetibbeha also is mentioned in *REQUIEM FOR A NUN*, *The TOWN*, *The REIVERS*, and the short stories "RED LEAVES" (in which Issetibbeha is Ikkemotubbe's son) and "A COURTSHIP."

J

Jabbo, Captain In *The* MANSION, a prison guard at the Mississippi state penitentiary at PARCHMAN, where Mink SNOPES serves time for the murder of Jack HOUSTON. Captain Jabbo kills Jake BARRON when Barron tries to escape.

Jack Character in "HONOR" (in *Collected Stories*). An acquaintance of Buck MONAGHAN, he recommends Buck to Howard ROGERS, a stunt pilot who is looking to hire a wing walker.

Jackie Character in *The REIVERS*. She is one of the girls in Miss Reba's (see RIVERS, REBA) CATALPA STREET brothel.

Jackson, Al Character in *MOSQUITOES*. He is a character in one of Dawson FAIRCHILD's fabulous tales, a web-footed descendant of Andrew Jackson who with his father runs the largest fish ranch in the world.

Jackson, Art Minor character in *PYLON*. Jackson is the pilot whom JIGGS pairs up with after Roger SHUMANN's crash and death. At the end of the novel, Jiggs becomes Jackson's parachute jumper.

Jackson, Claude Character in *MOSQUITOES*. He is the brother of fish rancher Al JACKSON. He turns into a shark while herding amphibious sheep and becomes notorious for chasing blonde women swimmers off Gulf Coast beaches.

Jackson, Old Man Character in *MOSQUITOES*. A character in a Dawson FAIRCHILD tale, he is a descendant of Andrew Jackson and is the father of Al and Claude JACKSON. A one-time bookkeeper, he becomes a fish rancher when the sheep on his swampy Louisiana estate turn gradually into fish.

Jake (1) Third member of the barnstorming troupe in the short story "DEATH DRAG" (in *Collected Stories*). Jake is the man who drives the car that GINSFARB leaps to from a rope ladder suspended beneath the airplane.

Jake (2) Character in "BEYOND" (in *Collected Stories*). He is the delusive Judge ALLISON's African-American gardener.

James, Lieutenant Colonel Commander of the battalion that the RUNNER joins after having been demoted from officer to common soldier in *A FABLE*.

Jameson, Dorothy Character in *MOSQUITOES*. A member of the *Nausikaa* yachting party, she is a portrait painter, a reckless driver, and a virgin who has scant success with men.

Jarrod, Hubert Character in "DOCTOR MARTINO" (in *Collected Stories*). A well-to-do student at Yale, he is engaged to Louise KING, the young girl who is caught under Dr. MARTINO's spell. Hubert allies with Louise's mother to break the doctor's hold on Louise.

Jason *See* COMPSON, JASON, IV.

Jean One of the 12 disciples of Corporal STEFAN in *A FABLE*. He sat on the corporal's left when the prisoners ate on Thursday night (a parallel to Christ's Last Supper, also on a Thursday evening), and he commented on POLCHEK's lack of appetite.

Jefferson, Mississippi Fictional place, seat of Faulkner's imaginary YOKNAPATAWPHA COUNTY, Mississippi. It is based on the actual OXFORD, MISSISSIPPI, and in part on RIPLEY, MISSISSIPPI, but with significant changes. In his fiction, Faulkner kept the UNIVERSITY OF MISSISSIPPI in "Oxford," which he sited 50 miles (and on occasion 40) from Jefferson. Many of the houses described in the fictional Jefferson have no exact counterpart in the real Oxford.

Many Oxford landmarks are, however, used in Jefferson: the Courthouse Square, the center of community life and the Saturday afternoon destination of Yoknapatawpha country people; the courthouse, with its four-faced clock; the jail; and the railroad depot down the hill and to the west of the square.

Faulkner describes the Jefferson square in *REQUIEM FOR A NUN*. The centerpiece is the courthouse in a grove in the square "quadrangular around it." The novelist moved the cemetery, which lies northeast of the square in Oxford, to a point northwest of the Jefferson square so the statue of the fictional "Colonel John Sartoris, CSA," could overlook the railroad Sartoris built. A statue of John SARTORIS's model, William C. FALKNER, the novelist's great-grandfather, gazes out at the Falkner railroad from the cemetery in Ripley.

Oxford's history and Jefferson's correspond roughly, as well. The first settlers arrive about 1815. The prosperous town of the 1850s withers during the Civil War; Sherman's forces burn the square in 1864. The Sartorises and the Compsons and the de Spains rebuild on the ruins, but by the turn of the new century the Snopeses are encroaching, threatening the continued social and economic leadership of Jefferson's leading families. The elms and the horse troughs and the hitching posts will disappear with the arrival of automobiles and paved roads; Flem Snopes and his kin will become Jefferson's new dominant clan.

By the end of the Yoknapatawpha saga, Jefferson's big old wooden houses with their shaggy lawns and great trees are decayed, and characterless new neighborhoods, "neat small new one-storey houses designed in Florida or California set with matching garages," proliferate (*Intruder*, p. 118).

Faulkner's sketch map in *ABSALOM, ABSALOM!* shows some of Jefferson's landmarks: a statue of John Sartoris, from *SARTORIS*; the cemetery where Addie BUNDREN is buried in *AS I LAY DYING*; the Courthouse from *SANCTUARY* and *The SOUND AND THE FURY*; the Burden place from *LIGHT IN AUGUST*; and the bank from *Sartoris* and *The TOWN*.

The jail where Lucas BEAUCHAMP is held in *INTRUDER IN THE DUST* is shown too, as are the dwelling places of Miss Rosa COLDFIELD (*Absalom*), Gail HIGHTOWER (*Light in August*), the Compsons (*The Sound and the Fury*), and Horace and Narcissa Benbow (*Sartoris*).

Jerry Character in "TURNABOUT" (in *Collected Stories*). An American flyer in France, he is dismissive of Midshipman HOPE because of Hope's immature way of expressing himself. Captain BOGARD takes Jerry aside and tells him to leave the young Englishman alone.

Jesus Character in "THAT EVENING SUN" (in *Collected Stories*). A short black man with a scar on his face, Jesus is the husband of the drunken, promiscuous Nancy (MANNIGOE), who cooks for the Compsons when DILSEY is indisposed. Nancy is afraid that Jesus will kill her with his razor during the night, but he does not.

For more information, see *Faulkner in the University*, pp. 21 and 79.

Jiggs Roger SHUMANN's drunken airplane mechanic in *PYLON*. Hung over the morning of Shumann's second air race, Jiggs does not properly maintain the plane's engine, causing Shumann to crash. Although the plane is destroyed, the pilot survives to race again in what will prove to be his last flight. After Shumann, Jiggs becomes a parachute jumper for the pilot Art JACKSON. At the end of the novel, Jiggs pawns his new boots to buy gifts for Shumann's widow, Laverne, and son Jack SHUMANN.

Jim (1) In *The HAMLET*, one of Sheriff HAMPTON's deputies. When Mink SNOPES is arrested for having killed Jack HOUSTON, Jim drives the wagon that takes Snopes to jail.

Jim (2) The horsetrader Pat STAMPER's black assistant in "FOOL ABOUT A HORSE" and *The HAMLET*. Jim is an artist at disguising mules and horses that Stamper trades.

Jim (3) Captain Joe THOMS's black tenant farmer in the short story "Mississippi."

Jingus Character in *The UNVANQUISHED*. He is an African-American servant of the Hawks, who move into his cabin after federal troops burn HAWKHURST.

Job Minor African-American character in *The SOUND AND THE FURY*. An easy-going person, Job is one of Earl TRIPLETT's employees at the supply store in JEFFERSON, MISSISSIPPI; Earl calls him Uncle Job. Jason COMPSON IV, who also works for Earl, is often sarcastic to him and treats him derisively.

Job, Uncle Character in *KNIGHT'S GAMBIT* ("Smoke") and *The TOWN*. Judged DUKINFIELD's black doorkeeper in "Smoke," he sees and hears nothing when the judge is murdered. In *The Town*, where he is referred to as old man Job, he has been the judge's janitor for longer than anyone in JEFFERSON, MISSISSIPPI, remembers.

Jobaker (Joe Baker) Character in *GO DOWN, MOSES* ("The Old People," "The Bear"). A CHICKASAW INDIAN, he is a market hunter and fisherman who lives as a hermit in a foul little shack on the Edmonds place. When he dies, Sam FATHERS buries him in a secret place and sets fire to his hut.

Joby (1) Character in *The UNVANQUISHED*. A slave of the Sartoris family, he is Ringo Strother's grandfather. Though he complains about his work load, he remains loyal to the family when the Yankees arrive.

He also appears in the short story "MY GRANDMOTHER MILLARD AND GENERAL BEDFORD FORREST AND THE BATTLE OF HARRYKIN CREEK."

Joby (2) Character in "THERE WAS A QUEEN" (in *Collected Stories*). The son of ELNORA, the Sartoris cook, he has migrated to Beale Street in MEMPHIS.

Jock Character in "DEATH DRAG" (in *Collected Stories*). A veteran World War I aviator with shaky nerves, he is the pilot of GINSFARB's stunt plane. Jock is a near-do-well barnstormer, badly dressed in dirty overalls, travelling the small towns of the south, staging air shows with his friends Ginsfarb and JAKE (1). At one of the towns where Jock lands, he is greeted by Captain WARREN, another World War I veteran, whom Jock had known in flight training school.

Jody (1) The boy who works in the drugstore in JEFFERSON, MISSISSIPPI, in the last section of AS I LAY DYING. Jody acts as a lookout for Skeet MACGOWAN while MacGowan discovers that Dewey Dell BUNDREN is seeking a drug to abort her baby. Jody also acts as a voice of conscience, which MacGowan ignores.

Jody (2) *See* VARNER, JODY.

Joe (1) Character in SARTORIS. He is a tennis player at Belle Mitchell's (see BENBOW, BELLE MITCHELL).

Joe (2) In SANCTUARY, the proprietor of the Grotto, where RED's funeral is held. He wants the orchestra to play American songs only, but not jazz.

Joe (3) Older brother of PETE (1) in the short story "ONCE ABOARD THE LUGGER" (I). Joe sends Pete on the bootlegging trip that ultimately results in Pete's death in "ONCE ABOARD THE LUGGER" (II).

Joe (4) Character in INTRUDER IN THE DUST. He is a young African-American employee of Carothers EDMONDS.

Joe (5) Character in KNIGHT'S GAMBIT ("Hand upon the Waters"). A deaf and mute orphan, he is a ward of Lonnie GRINNUP. Joe kills Lonnie's murderer, Boyd BALLENBAUGH.

John Character in "HONOR" (in *Collected Stories*). He is the husband of a woman who is shopping for a car at the lot where Buck MONAGHAN has landed a job.

John Henry Character in SARTORIS. With the help of his reluctant father, he pries young Bayard SARTORIS (4) from the wreck of his car where it comes to rest in the creek and drives Sartoris to JEFFERSON, MISSISSIPPI, in a farm wagon, using his straw hat to screen the injured man's face from the sun.

John Paul Character in "THAT WILL BE FINE" (in *Collected Stories*). An African-American servant of the narrator GEORGIE's family, he tells Georgie his father would like to make the trouble-prone Uncle RODNEY a Christmas present without waiting for Christmas, namely, a job (p.270).

Johnny The young gangster type in the short story "FRANKIE AND JOHNNY." He is able to penetrate through Frankie's hard, defensive shell, but abandons her when he finds out that she is pregnant with his child.

Johns, Maxwell One of the major characters in the short story "TWO DOLLAR WIFE." Suspended from Sewanee, Maxwell is careless and self-indulgent. The title refers to the cost of a marriage license, which Maxwell and Doris HOUSTON obtain on a dare by their friend Walter MITCHELL. Doris refuses to elope, however, and Maxwell carries the license with him as a kind of talisman. On New Year's Eve, the pair use the license to get married before a justice of the peace. When they return to Doris's home, the pair discover that her baby brother has almost died from swallowing a needle and thread that Maxwell stuck in a chair at the beginning of the evening.

Jonas Character in GO DOWN, MOSES ("Was") He is one of the slaves on the plantation of the MCCASLIN twins, Amodeus and Theophilus.

Jones (1) Character in SARTORIS, known as Doctor. He is the African-American janitor in the Sartoris' bank.

Jones (2) Character in "DEATH DRAG" (in *Collected Stories*). He is the secretary of the Fair Association in JEFFERSON, MISSISSIPPI. One of the stuntmen seeks him out to arrange details of the air show.

Jones, Herschell An offstage character referred to in SANCTUARY, he is the widowed Narcissa Benbow SARTORIS's gentleman caller prior to Gowan STEVENS.

Jones, Januarius A highly charged character in SOLDIERS' PAY. Jones is a literal bastard who views life as a series of contests between men and women. To Jones, sexual conquest means domination. He meets Rector MAHON early on the day that the rector's wounded son, Donald MAHON, is brought home by Joe GILLIGAN and Mrs. Margaret POWERS at the end of World War I. The overweight and pompous Jones is described as a goat-like satyr. He has taught Latin at a small college and has some intellectual pretensions. The narrator presents Jones as one of the careless civilians of the era right after World War I. Jones hangs around Cecily SAUNDERS and EMMY, attempting to seduce one or both of them. Seeing through him, Gilligan warns him away from Mrs. Powers. At the end of SOLDIERS' PAY, Jones takes advantage of the empty house (and of Emmy's even emptier broken heart) to seduce Emmy during Donald's funeral.

Jones, Melicent Character in ABSALOM, ABSALOM! The daughter of Wash JONES and the mother of Milly JONES, she is rumored to have died in a MEMPHIS brothel. She is mentioned by name in the novel's appendix.

Jones, Milly   Character in *ABSALOM, ABSALOM!* The 16-year-old granddaughter of Thomas SUTPEN's factotum, Wash JONES, she bears Sutpen, then 60, a daughter. Disappointed because he wants a son, Sutpen insults her.

Thinking he is protecting the girl from a future of pain and degradation, Wash cuts her throat with a butcher's knife.

Jones, Wash   Character in *ABSALOM, ABSALOM!* A squatter in an abandoned fishing shack at SUTPEN'S HUNDRED, he is the admirer and sometime drinking companion of Thomas SUTPEN.

When Miss Rosa COLDFIELD first sees him in 1865, he is "a gaunt gangling man" of indeterminate age. It is Wash who bears the first report that Henry SUTPEN has killed his sister's suitor, Charles BON.

Jones builds the coffin in which Bon is buried, and he later reluctantly turns to and helps his hero Sutpen rebuild the ruined plantation. He offers consolation to Sutpen, who after two or three drinks and reflections on the Civil War would lapse into defeat, call for his horse and pistols, and threaten to ride to Washington and shoot Lincoln and Sherman.

Wash abets Sutpen's seduction of his granddaughter Milly JONES, supplying the ribbons and beads and candy Sutpen offers the girl. He has misgivings, but in the end he persuades himself that Sutpen is an honorable man.

Sutpen repudiates Milly when she delivers a daughter instead of the son he wanted to replace the vanished Henry and carry out his grand design. Thus betrayed, Wash attacks and kills Sutpen with a rusted scythe. A little later he slits Milly's throat, thinking he is sparing her from suffering. When the scythe-wielding Wash rushes at Sheriff de Spain, the sheriff shoots and kills him.

Jonsson, Else   The widow of a Swedish translator of Faulkner's works, she met the novelist in Stockholm in December 1950 when he turned up to claim his 1949 NOBEL PRIZE IN LITERATURE. Faulkner and Else Jonsson managed several secret rendezvous in Europe in the early 1950s.

Jordon, Mrs.   Character in "THAT WILL BE FINE" (in *Collected Stories*). She takes in GEORGIE, the narrator, for the night after his Uncle RODNEY is killed.

Jornstadt   The Princeton man who wins large sums of money from the local boys in the unnamed southern town in the short story "TWO DOLLAR WIFE."

Joyce, James (1882–1941)   Self-exiled Irish novelist and poet whose influence on 20th-century literature is immeasurable. Having shaped both the modernist and postmodernist canon with his publications of *A Portrait of the Artist as a Young Man* (1916), *Ulysses* (1922), and *Finnegans Wake* (1939), Joyce has had one of the most enduring influences not only in English but also on the whole of 20th-century literature. With T. S. Eliot and Virginia Woolf, he is considered one of the principal modernist writers. (See MODERNISM and POSTMODERNISM.)

The eldest child of John Stanislaus and Mary Jane (May) Murray Joyce, James Joyce was born in Rathgar, a fashionable suburb of Dublin, on February 2, 1882. In 1888 he entered Clongowes Wood College, one of the best Jesuit schools in Ireland, located in Sallins, County Kildare, and remained a student there until June 1891, when he withdrew because of his family's financial difficulties. After a brief interruption in his formal education, Joyce resumed his studies in 1893 at Belvedere College, a Jesuit school in Dublin, and graduated five years later. He attended University College, Dublin, founded as Catholic University by John Henry Cardinal Newman in 1853, and graduated with a degree in modern languages in 1902. In June 1904, Joyce met for the first time Nora Barnacle. By October they left Ireland and eventually settled in Trieste, where he taught at the Berlitz School and where his two children, Giorgio and Lucia, were born. While in Trieste, Joyce published *Chamber Music* (1907), *Dubliners* (1914), and *A Portrait of the Artist as a Young Man;* he also wrote his only play, *Exiles* (1918), and began *Ulysses.* With the outbreak of World War I, Joyce and his family moved to Zurich, where he continued writing *Ulysses.* After the war they returned to Trieste for a brief time before moving to Paris in 1920. With the outbreak of World War II, a few months after the publication of *Finnegans Wake* in May 1939, the Joyces moved from Paris to Saint-Gérand-le-Puy, a small village near Vichy, where they stayed for a year before departing for Zurich, where Joyce died on January 13, 1941, two days after what appeared to be successful abdominal surgery. Two days later he was buried in Fluntern cemetery.

Joyce's works reflect the 20th-century's major movements in literature from symbolism and realism to modernism and postmodernism. His use of the INTERIOR MONOLOGUE and the STREAM OF CONSCIOUSNESS techniques, along with other innovative narrative strategies, have influenced generations of writers including William Faulkner, who on several occasions mentioned his debt to Joyce. In a 1958 interview with Richard Ellmann, Joyce's biographer, Faulkner said he thought of himself as Joyce's heir when writing *The SOUND AND THE FURY* (see *James Joyce* [New York: Oxford University Press, 1982], p. 297, asterisked note). Although Faulkner, according to Ellmann, did not read *Ulysses* in its published form as a book until 1930, he did read portions of the novel as they were serialized in the *Little Review* between 1918 and 1920 and discussed the work at length with his close friend Phil STONE. There is evidence, however, that Faulkner in fact read *Ulysses* as early as 1924 when he received a copy of the novel from Stone (see *William Faulkner: The Carl Petersen Collection*, Berkeley,

William Faulkner in Paris in 1925. (Brodsky Collection, Center for Faulkner Studies, Southeast Missouri State University)

Calif.: Serendipity Books, 1991, p. 70.), and in *Faulkner at Nagano,* edited by Robert A. Jelliffe (Tokyo: Kenkyusha Ltd., 1962), Faulkner, in response to a question of whether he read *Ulysses* before or after he began to write, said, "No, I began to write before I read *Ulysses.* I read *Ulysses* in the middle 20's and I had been scribbling for several years" (*Faulkner at Nagano,* p. 203). He had never met Joyce but knew of him and, when in Paris in 1925, "would go to some effort to go to the café that [Joyce] inhabited to look at him" (*Faulkner in the University,* p. 58). Joyce was "the only literary man" Faulkner remembered seeing while in Europe.

Critics have readily recognized the influence of *Ulysses* on Faulkner's *The Sound and the Fury* and *AS I LAY DYING,* two novels that very skillfully incorporate the narrative technique of the interior monologue that Joyce pioneered, and to a lesser degree employed in *SOLDIERS' PAY* and *MOSQUITOES.* "With this technique," as Michael Groden observes in "Criticism in New Composition: *Ulysses* and *The Sound and the Fury*" published in *Twentieth Century Literature* 21 (October, 1975), "Faulkner discovered a solution to crucial problems in

characterization that had plagued him in his first three novels [*Soldier's Pay, Mosquitoes,* and *SARTORIS*]" (p. 266). Faulkner was familiar with other works by Joyce, including his poetry. For instance, one of the poems that Faulkner would recite from memory was "Watching the Needleboats at San Sabba," first published by Joyce in 1913 in the *Saturday Review* and later reprinted in *Pomes Penyeach* (1927). In "Faulkner's 'Portrait of the Artist'" published in *The Mississippi Quarterly* 19 (summer 1966), 121–31, Joyce W. Warren closely examines the parallels between Faulkner's second novel, *Mosquitoes* and Joyce's *A Portrait of the Artist as a Young Man.* Richard P. Adams also touches upon Faulkner's reading of Joyce in "The Apprenticeship of William Faulkner," *Tulane Studies in English* 12 (1962), 138–40.

Two comments that Faulkner made about James Joyce on two separate occasions recorded in *Faulkner in the University* may be misleading to readers who have not studied Joyce's compositional methods. The first, that Joyce was "a genius who was electrocuted by the divine fire" (p. 53)—or "touched by the divine [afflatus]," as he phrased it in an interview recorded in *Faulkner at Nagano* (p. 44)—and the second, that he "had more talent than he could control" (p. 280), can give the impression that Joyce himself wrote under the spell of the stream of consciousness or under a wild dadaist inspiration. Nothing can be further from the truth. Joyce was one of the most meticulous writers of his age; he carefully controlled and shaped his works word by word and would revise even up to the last moments before publication. (For a few examples of Joyce's influence on Faulkner, see Cleanth BROOKS's brief comments in *William Faulkner: Toward Yoknapatawpha and Beyond* [Baton Rouge: Louisiana State University Press, 1990, pp. 370–72].)

Jubal   Character in "MOUNTAIN VICTORY" (in *Collected Stories*). He is Major Saucier WEDDEL's Black servant and companion. Weddel refuses to abandon him in the mountains.

Jug   A newspaper photographer in *PYLON.*

Juliet   *See* BUNDEN, JULIET.

Julio   In *The SOUND AND THE FURY,* an Italian immigrant whose little sister meets Quentin COMPSON in a Cambridge, Massachusetts, bakery and starts following him. Although Quentin attempts to take the little girl to her home, Julio thinks he is kidnapping her. He springs upon Quentin, knocks him to the ground, and has him arrested.

Junkin, Professor   In *The SOUND AND THE FURY,* Miss Quentin COMPSON's high school principal (or teacher). He calls Jason COMPSON (IV) to say that if Quentin is absent once more, she will have to leave school.

"A Justice" *(Collected Stories)* Short story that recounts the return home of IKKEMOTUBBE, now named Doom and corrupted by the white man's ways, and his rise to power through murder, intimidation, and ruthless exploitation of even his closest friends. The tale is framed by an adult Quentin COMPSON looking back to his boyhood, when he heard the story from his grandfather's carpenter Sam FATHERS.

Using a laconic, comic tone, Sam tells how, long ago, Doom gave him the name Had-Two-Fathers. With what may be an Indian storytelling strategy of deception, he relates an elliptic and ambiguous tale that implies rather than spells out key events. After Doom gains power, probably by poisoning the old CHICKASAW INDIAN chief and his son, he forces his men and his slaves to transport, by means of heroic exertions, a stranded steamboat through the wilderness. At the same time he renders justice to a black slave whose wife is pursued obsessively by Crawford, Sam's "pappy." Doom gives the man his best fighting cock in order to defeat Craw-ford's bird. When the black man's wife bears a light-skinned baby, Doom names him Had-Two-Fathers. According to this story, Craw-ford appears to be the biological father, but Faulkner has stated elsewhere that Doom actually is the father (*Selected Letters,* p. 208). Doom forces Craw-ford and Herman BASKET to erect a palisade fence around the black man's cabin. Once it is complete, the man shows them a new baby, this time seemingly completely black. Quentin Compson, innocent at age 12, does not quite grasp the role of violence and sex in this saga; its meaning only becomes clearer to him when he is older.

This story first appeared in *These 13* (1931). The steamboat episode was revised for BIG WOODS (1955). Events in "A COURTSHIP" precede this story.

Jupe Character in *LIGHT IN AUGUST.* He briefly encounters Joe CHRISTMAS during Joe's distracted walk through the black section of JEFFERSON, MISSISSIPPI.

K

Kauffman, Julius (1) Character in *MOSQUITOES*. He is the "Semitic man," the brother of the poet Eva WISE-MAN. Kauffman and the novelist Dawson FAIRCHILD are close friends; Kauffman pokes fun of Fairchild's circle of self-conscious artists.

Kauffman, Julius (2) Character in *MOSQUITOES*. The grandfather of Julius KAUFFMAN (1), he helped old MAURIER, the defunct husband of the owner of the yacht *Nausikaa*, make a series of dubious but lucrative land deals under the Yankee occupation of NEW ORLEANS during the Civil War.

Kaye, Major C. Character in "ALL THE DEAD PILOTS" (in *Collected Stories*). A British officer, he notifies Aunt Jenny DU PRE of young Johnny SARTORIS's death in action in France on July 4, 1918.

Kazimura Character in "GOLDEN LAND" (in *Collected Stories*). Samantha EWING's gardener, he shows her a newspaper that recounts the equivocal doings of her granddaughter, a would-be starlet who seeks to advance her Hollywood career by taking part in sex orgies.

Kazin, Alfred (1915–1998) Literary critic and teacher, born in New York City. His *On Native Grounds* (1942) is a classic study of modern American prose fiction, and in the 1940s and 1950s he was an influential and widely read book reviewer.

Kazin did not greatly admire Faulkner's later work. In a review of *The UNVANQUISHED* (1938) in the New York *Herald Tribune*, Kazin charged that Faulkner wrote "like a wilful sullen child in some gaseous world of his own, pouting in polysyllabics, stringing truncated paragraphs together like dirty wash, howling, stumbling, losing himself in verbal murk." But along with Cleanth BROOKS and others, he wrote a critical appreciation of the novelist for a Faulkner issue of the *Harvard Advocate* in 1951.

The critic found *The TOWN* (1957), the second of the three Snopes novels, deeply disappointing: "The truth is not merely that *The Town* is a bad novel by a great writer, but also that Faulkner has less and less interest in writing what are called 'novels' at all."

In a more considered judgment in *An American Procession* (1982), Kazin linked Faulkner to Hawthorne and Melville and elaborately praised *The SOUND AND THE*

FURY (1929), setting it above the seminal work that may have influenced its experimental technique, James JOYCE's *Ulysses* (1922).

"*The Sound and the Fury* is a greater *novel*" than *Ulysses,* Kazin wrote, "more dramatic, more universally representative through the interior life of everyone in it."

Keeley Institute A treatment center for alcoholics located 15 miles from MEMPHIS, the Keeley Institute was much frequented by Faulkner's paternal grandfather, J. W. T. FALKNER, and his father, Murry C. FALKNER. The institute's founder, Dr. Leslie E. Keeley, claimed in *The Non-Heredity of Inebriety* (1896) that alcoholism was a disease, not a vice.

The Keeley cure involved injections of double chloride of gold, said to give a patient an extreme distaste for whiskey. Dr. Keeley reported a relapse rate of only 5 percent; Falkner father and son were among that small minority of returnees.

Maud FALKNER, the future novelist's mother, used to deliver her husband to the Keeley Institute when his drinking became unbearable. Sometimes she brought the children along. While their father took the cure, Billy and his brothers amused themselves by exploring the institute grounds and riding the streetcar to Memphis and back.

Kemp, Beasley A minor character in the short story "FOOL ABOUT A HORSE," which was later revised and used in *The HAMLET*. Beasley trades a horse with PAP (2) in the short story, and with Ab SNOPES in the novel.

Kennedy, Watt Character in *LIGHT IN AUGUST*. He is the heavyset sheriff who leads the hunt for Joe CHRISTMAS.

Kenny In *The SOUND AND THE FURY*, one of the three fellows who are fishing that Quentin COMPSON sees as he crosses a bridge on the morning of the day he commits suicide (June 2, 1910).

Keswick Hunt Club Faulkner rode as a guest with this hunt club, established in the late 19th century and the oldest in Albemarle County, Virginia, beginning in late 1958.

The Keswick, better known locally than its younger rival, the FARMINGTON HUNT CLUB, had a reputation as rough-riding, hard-drinking band more interested in hunting than show. By Faulkner's time, though, the differences between the two clubs had blurred. Faulkner rode with one or the other as often as four or five times a week in season.

Ketcham Character in *GO DOWN, MOSES* ("Pantaloon in Black"). He is the jailer to whom RIDER is delivered after Rider slashes BIRDSONG's throat.

Killegrew, Hampton Character in *KNIGHT'S GAMBIT* ("Knight's Gambit"). The night marshal in Jefferson, MISSISSIPPI, he passes the time in the pool hall or the Allnite Inn.

Killegrew, Hunter In *The MANSION*, the deputy who escorts Montgomery Ward SNOPES to PARCHMAN (Mississippi's state penitentiary).

Killegrew, Miss Minor character in *The TOWN*. She is the teller at the Sartoris's Bank in JEFFERSON, MISSISSIPPI.

Killegrew, Old Man Character in "SHINGLES FOR THE LORD," "TWO SOLDIERS," and "SHALL NOT PERISH" (in *Collected Stories*). An old farmer, he loans his tools (a froe and maul) to Pap GRIER, one of the volunteer roofers in "Shingles for the Lord."

In "Two Soldiers," Pete GRIER and his little brother after supper stand outside Killegrew's house to listen to the war news coming over Killegrew's radio, which he turns up for his deaf wife to hear.

King, Alvina Character in "DOCTOR MARTINO" (in *Collected Stories*). The devious, scheming mother of Louise KING, she tricks Dr. MARTINO into releasing his hold on Louise, who has been under his spell since she was a little girl. Mrs. King fears that the doctor will drive away Louise's wealthy suitor, Hubert JARROD.

King, Louise Character in "DOCTOR MARTINO" (in *Collected Stories*). As a young girl, she falls under the spell of Dr. MARTINO, an elderly man with a failing heart who, in his capacity to endure, teaches her valuable lessons about courage during their encounters at Lily CRANSTON's summer resort.

Her mother begins to fear that Louise's connection with Dr. Martino threatens her engagement with the wealthy Hubert JARROD, so she tricks the doctor into writing the note that releases his hold on the girl.

Louise and her fiance speed away from the resort, presumably on their way to be married.

Kitchener (Kit) Character in "ALL THE DEAD PILOTS" (in *Collected Stories*). She is the London girlfriend of Johnny SARTORIS, so nicknamed because she is involved

with many soldiers—including SPOOMER, Sartoris's superior officer.

Klopfer, Donald Publisher. He cofounded RANDOM HOUSE, Faulkner's publisher, with Bennett CERF in 1927. Along with Cerf, he was a strong supporter of Faulkner's work, and he sometimes acted as an informal financial adviser to the novelist.

Klopfer and his wife, Pat, entertained Faulkner at their Lebanon, New Jersey, country house and in their New York City apartment. Faulkner hand-delivered the 175,000-word manuscript of *A FABLE* to Klopfer at Random House in November 1953.

Kneeland, Mr. Offstage character in *The TOWN*. He owns the tailor shop in JEFFERSON, MISSISSIPPI, where the men who are going to the annual Cotillion Ball at Christmas rent their dress suits.

"Knight's Gambit" *See KNIGHT'S GAMBIT.*

Knight's Gambit Collection of five previously published short stories and an eponymous novella. Published in 1949, *Knight's Gambit* is one of Faulkner's slighter works.

The stories are "who-done-its" (Faulkner's phrase), detective pieces with the lawyer and sometime County Attorney Gavin STEVENS as chief investigator and central character. Along with the YOKNAPATAWPHA COUNTY setting and a gallery of the plain people of Mississippi, Stevens, who appears at the end of *GO DOWN, MOSES* (1942) and as a major player in *INTRUDER IN THE DUST* (1948), gives the collection of six pieces written from 1931 to 1948 such unity as it possesses.

The early version of the title story seems to have been the genesis of the book. Faulkner wrote it in 1941 as a 20-page short story narrated by Charles Weddel, Stevens's adolescent nephew. The plot involves a teenage boy's conspiracy to murder his sister's suitor. *HARPER'S MAGAZINE* rejected "Knight's Gambit" in 1942 and Faulkner took it up again, revising and adding to it. Again, there were no takers. The story lay on the shelf until 1948, when Faulkner decided to expand it to novella length.

As 1948 ended, Faulkner worked away at "Knight's Gambit." He had seemed for some time to regard it as a novel in short-story clothing, and the expansion proceeded rapidly and smoothly. To conform with other Gavin Stevens stories, the narrator, Weddel, becomes the lawyer's nephew Chick MALLISON of *Intruder in the Dust*.

After mulling the thematic links of the stories he intended to join with "Knight's Gambit," Faulkner settled on a final order: "Smoke," first published in *Harper's* in April 1942; "Monk," published in *SCRIBNER'S MAGAZINE* in May 1937; "Hand Upon the Waters," published in the *SATURDAY EVENING POST* in November 1939;

"Tomorrow," published in the *Post* in November 1940; "An Error in Chemistry," written in 1940 but not published until June 1946 in the magazine *Story;* and the unpublished title piece.

Meantime, he pushed on with "Knight's Gambit," the long last entry in the volume. To the original plot, Faulkner added Stevens's reunion with the long-lost love of his youth, Melisandre Backus STEVENS, the wealthy widow of a bootlegger. The plot remained the same: Melisandre's son, Max HARRISS, tries to scare away his sister's suitor, the Argentine cavalry officer Sebastian GUALDRES. Like a knight on a chessboard, Gualdres appears capable of moving in two directions: either toward Max's sister or toward his monied mother. When Gualdres refuses to be scared off, Max decides to kill him, using an unbroken stallion as the murder weapon.

In "Smoke," crabbed, violent Anselm HOLLAND Sr. (Old Anse) is found dead with his foot in his horse's stirrup, an obvious attempt to make the killing look like an accident. Suspicion immediately falls upon one of his twin sons, Anselm HOLLAND Jr. (Young Anse). The real murderer, who kills because he covets the Holland farm, is a cousin of the twins, Granby DODGE. Under suspicion by Judge DUKINFIELD, Dodge hires a Memphis gangster to kill the judge. Stevens ultimately unravels the mystery by tracing the "city cigarette" the hitman smokes.

The plot of "Monk," the second story in the collection, turns on a false murder accusation that sends the feeble-minded Stonewall Jackson ODLETHROP, known as Monk, to prison for life. There he kills the prison warden at the instigation of another convict. In sorting out the details of Monk's star-crossed career, Stevens shows compassion for Monk, doubly a victim, and a reformer's contempt for Mississippi's corrupt prison system.

In "Hand Upon the Waters," Stevens, now county attorney, identifies the murderer of Lonnie GRINNUP, a degraded descendant of one of the first of the Yoknapatawpha County settlers. A fisherman, he is found drowned on his own trotline. As Stevens discovers, Boyd BALLENBAUGH has killed the cheerful, childlike Lonnie to collect on his insurance policy.

"Tomorrow" turns on the murder of a young bravo called Buck THORPE. A FRENCHMAN'S BEND farmer named BOOKWRIGHT is accused of killing him for running off with Bookwright's 17-year-old daughter. The jury is prepared to find the homicide justifiable, for Thorpe seems born for the hangman. But one juror holds out. As Stevens discovers, juryman Stonewall Jackson Fentry had taken the orphan Thorpe into his home as a boy.

In "An Error in Chemistry," a man named Joel FLINT murders his wife and father-in-law; he is arrested, but escapes from jail and vanishes. Flint hid the old man's body, which was never found; this allows him to impersonate his wife's grieving father, sell the man's farm and

go off with the proceeds. Stevens discovers the ruse and brings Flint, a conjuror by trade, to justice.

In "Knight's Gambit," the boy narrator Chick Mallison watches his Uncle Gavin play a potentially deadly chess game involving the vicious young Max Harris, Captain Gualdres, and the two unwitting women, mother and daughter. In the end, Stevens prevents the murder; Gualdres marries the girl, and the middle-aged sleuth wins the hand of his middle-aged sweetheart.

Faulkner read and corrected the galleys in mid-July and RANDOM HOUSE brought out *Knight's Gambit* on November 27, 1949. Reviewers were not greatly impressed. *Commonweal* called the book a "rather miserable and mawkish performance." In a left-handed compliment, the *Saturday Review of Literature* judged *Knight's Gambit* just the thing for readers put off by the novelist's more difficult works. Writing in *The New Yorker,* the critic Edmund Wilson could hear faint echoes of Faulkner at his best: "In spite of all one can say against the book, certainly very inferior Faulkner, none of these stories, however farfetched, fails to awaken that anxious suspense as to what is going to be revealed, to summon that troubled emotion in the presence of human anomaly, which make the strength of his finer fiction."

Knopf, Alfred A. (1892–1984) Publisher. He established his own firm in 1915 and, with his wife, made it one of the leading literary houses in America. Among Knopf's authors were 16 Nobel laureates and 26 Pulitzer Prize winners.

In the early 1930s, Knopf showed interest in publishing Faulkner. They met at a party at Knopf's New York City apartment in late 1931. Faulkner, in company with the writer Dashiell Hammett, fell to the floor drunk.

Knopf and Faulkner met again at a gathering at Bennett CERF's not long afterward. As the biographer Joseph BLOTNER tells the anecdote, Knopf approached Faulkner with a request for his signature on several first editions of his works. Faulkner was reluctant, explaining that special signed editions were a source of income, but at Bennett Cerf's prompting he agreed to sign one, because "Mrs. Knopf has been very kind to me."

Knopf headed the firm, which eventually became a division of RANDOM HOUSE, until his death.

Kohl, Barton Linda SNOPES's husband in *The MANSION.* Kohl is a sculptor, a communist, and a Jew. Before marrying, Barton and Linda live together for several years in Greenwich Village. In 1936, right after they marry, they leave for Spain and fight for the Loyalists during the Spanish Civil War. He is killed when his air plane is shot down by the Germans.

Kohl, Linda Snopes Character in *The TOWN* and *The MANSION,* also mentioned as an infant in *The HAMLET.* She is the daughter of Eula Varner SNOPES and Hoake

MCCARRON. Conceived out of wedlock and born after Eula marries Flem SNOPES, Linda grows up in JEFFERSON, MISSISSIPPI, assuming until her late teens that Flem is her father. During her high school days, the romantic Gavin STEVENS, in an ostensibly avuncular manner, treats Linda to ice-cream sodas after school and takes a strong interest in her education and reading, especially in the area of poetry. At first Flem forbids her to go away to college, allowing her only to attend the Academy in Jefferson. When he later permits her to attend the university 40 miles away, she is so grateful that she cries in his arms and calls him "Daddy" for the first time, and signs over her inheritance to him. Soon after Eula commits suicide in 1927, Linda moves to Greenwich Village, where she meets and lives with Barton KOHL, an avowed communist. They marry and together go to Spain to fight with the Loyalists in the Spanish Civil War. Her husband is killed when his airplane is shot down, and she is wounded when a shell explodes near the ambulance she is driving, leaving her completely deaf. She returns to Jefferson in August 1937 and lives with Flem, although she has virtually nothing to do with him. She clearly sees Flem for what he is, an enemy, a rapacious and exploitative person largely responsible for her mother's suicide. For a time during World War II, she works for the war effort in Pascagoula. When Linda returns to Jefferson, she spends her time drinking bootlegged whiskey and walking around aimlessly until she finds another cause to work for: namely, to have Mink SNOPES pardoned of his crime in killing Jack Houston. She plays a key role in his release from prison in 1946, knowing all along that he will avenge his treatment by Flem. Linda is in the house when Mink sneaks in to kill Flem, and she helps him find his way out. Later, through Gavin Stevens, she gives him money to run away with and plans to regularly send him more to live on. Before leaving Jefferson for good, Linda gives the mansion, which once belonged to Manfred DE SPAIN's family, back to Manfred's only living relatives as a final act of justice.

Kyerling, R.   Character in "ALL THE DEAD PILOTS" (in *Collected Stories*). A British flyer, he witnesses Johnny SARTORIS's death in action over France on July 4, 1918.

L

Labove (1) Father of the schoolteacher LABOVE (2) in *The* HAMLET. On a business trip in an adjacent county, Will VARNER happens to meet Labove at dusk and is invited to spend the night in Labove's cabin. Varner also happens to be on the lookout for a schoolteacher, and when he finds out that Labove's son is a university student who at one time wanted to be a teacher, Varner suggests to Labove that his son come over to FRENCHMAN'S BEND to see him about the job.

Labove (2) In *The* HAMLET, a student at the university who takes a teaching job in FRENCHMAN'S BEND before graduating from the university. Although he does not care for football, he plays to pay for his education, and during the summer he works in sawmills. Labove sends football cleats to his family so they will have shoes to wear outdoors. Will VARNER provides him with a horse to ride the 40 miles from the university in OXFORD, MISSISSIPPI, to Frenchman's Bend so Labove can keep up with his schooling and continue to play football. Labove is stricken by the sensuous beauty of Varner's 13-year-old daughter, Eula Varner (SNOPES), and decides to stay on as a teacher after he graduates and is admitted to the bar. He is so enamored of Eula that he kneels at her bench to feel her body warmth after his students leave for the day. When Eula discovers him one afternoon, he attempts to ravage her but fails. Eula knocks him down. Labove abruptly leaves town for good, knowing that Eula was so unimpressed that she would not even bother to tell her brother of the attempted rape.

Lafayette County, Mississippi A 679-square-mile county in north-central Mississippi, formed in 1836, it was the model for Faulkner's fictional YOKNAPATAWPHA COUNTY.

The TALLAHATCHIE RIVER, with its rich bottomlands, forms part of the county's northern boundary; the YOCONA RIVER (given on old maps as Yocanapatafa, the origin of the name of Faulkner chose for his fictional Lafayette) drains the southern portion. OXFORD, MISSISSIPPI, at the county's center is the seat, with a courthouse and the UNIVERSITY OF MISSISSIPPI; other towns include College Hill to the northwest, Taylor to the southwest, and Lafayette Springs to the east. CHICKASAW INDIAN burial mounds are found at scattered sites.

Faulkner's grandfather, J. W. T. FALKNER, won election as state senator from Lafayette County in 1895. In the novelist's childhood, the county had a population of around 22,000. Nearly half the inhabitants were black. White or black, most were small farmers dependent on cotton. Decades of reliance on a single crop marked the landscape of the novelist's youth: Cotton depleted the soil and overcultivation left the county nearly treeless, its hills and ravines scored by erosion.

Lafe The farmhand in *AS I LAY DYING* who impregnates Dewey Dell BUNDREN. Lafe never actually appears in the novel, but Dewey Dell relates the story of their lovemaking in the woods by the Bundrens' field. He gives Dewey Dell $10 to buy a drug that would abort her pregnancy.

Lallemont In *A FABLE,* commander of the French army corps that includes Major General GRAGNON's division. He orders Gragnon to make the attack that results in the mutiny led by Corporal STEFAN. A friend of Gragnon's, Lallemont had been a fellow subaltern in the same division at the start of their careers.

Lamar, Ruby In *SANCTUARY,* the bootlegger Lee GOODWIN's common-law wife who cooks for him and the other men at their hideout, the OLD FRENCHMAN PLACE. She is the mother of a sickly baby less than a year old. When the frightened Temple Drake (STEVENS) arrives at Old Frenchman Place, Ruby is both protective and scornful of her. Prior to the time frame of the novel, she paid Goodwin's legal fees by sexually giving herself to the lawyer who unsuccessfully tried to get him out of Leavenworth prison. When Horace BENBOW decides to defend Goodwin against the false charges of murder and rape, Ruby tells him that she cannot afford to pay and assumes that he will accept sexual favors instead. Benbow takes on the case but does not sexually exploit her. She is also referred to as Mrs. Goodwin.

Landry, Sergeant In *A FABLE,* he commands a squad of 12 French soldiers who are sent to a fortress in the Verdun region with orders to bring back an unidentified and unidentifiable body of a French soldier to be buried in the Tomb of the Unknown Soldier. A fussy man who neither smokes nor drinks, Landry has served far behind the actual fighting line during World War I.

Lapin Thief and murderer in *A FABLE* who is executed next to Corporal STEFAN. He is the friend and protector of CASSE-TÊTE.

Laura, Miss In *The SOUND AND THE FURY,* one of Quentin COMPSON's teachers in school at JEFFERSON, MISSISSIPPI.

Laverne *See* SHUMANN, LAVERNE.

Lawington, Miss According to Cora TULL in *AS I LAY DYING,* Miss Lawington gave her advice to buy a good breed of chickens and told her of a woman in JEFFERSON, MISSISSIPPI, who needs special cakes for a party. (Cora bakes the cakes but is disappointed to find out that the unnamed buyer has changed her mind.)

Leblanc A minor character in *PYLON.* A police officer at Feinman Airport during the celebration of its opening, Leblanc is persuaded by the REPORTER not to arrest Roger SHUMANN's mechanic, JIGGS, who is drunk.

Ledbetter, Mrs. Minor character in *The TOWN* and *The MANSION.* She lives in Rockyford and buys a sewing machine from V. K. RATLIFF.

"The Leg" *(Collected Stories)* Short story, a supernatural tale of the World War I era. As students at Oxford University in June 1914, the Englishman GEORGE (2) and the American DAVY, the narrator, enjoy a day boating on the river Thames. George falls overboard and is rescued by the lockkeeper Simon RUST and his son Jotham RUST, who are, respectively, the father and brother of Everbe Corinthia RUST, with whom George is carrying on a flirtation.

A year later, George and Davy are soldiers in France. George is killed and Davy's leg is amputated. In a series of hallucinations and dreams, Davy speaks with George's apparition, begging him to find the leg and to make sure that it is dead. Jotham Rust, also a soldier, returns home on leave and finds his sister Corinthia mysteriously sneaking away at night. When he follows her, he hears a weird laugh and finds her lying beside the river; she screams all day and dies at dusk. Their father Simon dies from grief soon after. Jotham deserts his unit to track down the owner of the terrifying laugh. He finally finds Davy, whom he tries to stab, but trips over the wooden leg propped up by the bed. After Jotham is executed for desertion, the army chaplain brings Davy a photograph found among Jotham's effects. Davy is amazed to see that it is a portrait of himself, but with a vicious face unlike his own. The dedication to Corinthia in childlike handwriting is followed by

an unprintable phrase. The tale ends with the refrain, "I told him to find and kill it. . . . I told him to. I told him."

This story first appeared as "Leg" in *Doctor Martino and Other Stories* (1934).

Legate, Bob Character in *The REIVERS.* He is one of the regulars at Major DE SPAIN's hunting camp in the big woods.

Legate, Will Character in *GO DOWN, MOSES* and other works. A member of the MISSISSIPPI DELTA hunting party, he is the grandson of Bob LEGATE, one of the hunters who used to gather each autumn at Major DE SPAIN's camp in the BIG BOTTOM 60 years back. He teases Roth (Carothers) EDMONDS about his interest in "does," an allusion to the young woman who seeks him out at the camp.

In *INTRUDER IN THE DUST,* Legate, an excellent shot, stands guard outside the JEFFERSON, MISSISSIPPI, jail to protect Lucas BEAUCHAMP from a lynch mob. He later escorts Beauchamp from the besieged jail to the sheriff's house.

Legate also appears in the short story "RACE AT MORNING."

Lena, Missy Character in *The UNVANQUISHED.* She is a black servant of the Hawks. Ringo STROTHER sleeps in her cabin when Rosa MILLARD and her grandson Bayard SARTORIS (3) come to visit Hawkhurst.

Lessep, Alexander Character in *The REIVERS.* He is the great uncle of the narrator, Lucius (Loosh) PRIEST.

Lessep, Grandfather Character in *The REIVERS.* He is the maternal grandfather of Lucius (Loosh) PRIEST. Lucius makes the excursion to MEMPHIS with Boon HOGGANBECK and Ned MCCASLIN when the adult Priests attend his grandfather's funeral in Bay St. Louis 300 miles from JEFFERSON, MISSISSIPPI.

Lessep, Grandmother Character in *The REIVERS.* She is Lucius (Loosh) PRIEST's maternal grandmother.

Lester, Miss Judy The girlfriend of WATKINS in the short story "MR. ACARIUS." She smuggles half-pint bottles of whiskey into the clinic for alcoholics by hiding them in her brassiere.

Levine, Gerald David An 18-year-old inexperienced fighter pilot in *A FABLE* who, nonetheless, notices that the bullets he is firing at the German GENERAL's aircraft are blanks. He asks Major BRIDESMAN, his commander, for the truth about this, but is rebuffed. Although he has dreamed of glory flying and fighting for England, Levine, a Jew, feels estranged from his fellows. He considers himself and his honor betrayed by the subterfuge and commits suicide.

Levitt, Matt Minor character in *The TOWN*. He is a boxer from Ohio, where he won the Golden Gloves. After coming to JEFFERSON, MISSISSIPPI, he takes a job as a mechanic and dates the 16-year-old Linda Snopes (KOHL). Jealous of any rivalry, he interprets Gavin STEVENS's avuncular affections toward Linda as a threat and beats him up. After fighting Anse MCCALLUM, (2) whom he also beats up, he loses his job and is told by Sheriff HAMPTOM to leave town for good, which he does.

Lewis, Matt Character in "IDYLL IN THE DESERT" (in *Uncollected Stories*). A livery stable owner, he helps Lucas CRUMP look after the tuberculosis patients at Sivgut in the Arizona desert.

Library of America A book imprint, the Library of America was established in 1979 with a self-proclaimed mission to publish the country's most significant writing in authoritative, durable editions. The first volumes appeared in 1982.

Four volumes of Faulkner's novels had been published as of 1999. All were edited by the leading Faulkner scholars Joseph BLOTNER and Noel POLK.

Faulkner: Novels 1930–1935 (1985) contains *AS I LAY DYING, SANCTUARY, LIGHT IN AUGUST,* and *PYLON.*

Faulkner: Novels 1936–1940 (1990) contains *ABSALOM, ABSALOM!, The UNVANQUISHED, IF I FORGET THEE, JERUSALEM,* and *The HAMLET.*

Faulkner: Novels 1942–1954 (1994) contains *GO DOWN, MOSES, INTRUDER IN THE DUST, REQUIEM FOR A NUN,* and *A FABLE.*

Faulkner: Novels 1957–1962 (1999) contains *The TOWN, The MANSION,* and *The REIVERS.*

Liddy The black cook in the short story "SEPULTURE SOUTH: GASLIGHT" who, with her husband, ARTHUR, leaves the family she is working for shortly after the death of the family's grandfather. Her quitting is seen as a rite of passage or superstition, which she follows regretfully but faithfully. Liddy's predecessor had left seven years before, upon the death of the grandmother.

Light in August One of Faulkner's masterpieces, published in 1932, the novel tells the contrasting stories, one broadly comic, the other tragic, of Lena GROVE and Joe CHRISTMAS. *Light in August* is peopled with a gallery of compelling secondary characters who move about in a succession of richly imagined YOKNAPATAWPHA COUNTY scenes.

"Few American novels are so lavish in dramatic incident, so infused with images of sensation, so precisely fixed in place and weather," the critic Irving HOWE wrote in *Willam Faulkner; A Critical Study.* Most commentators

rank it among Faulkner's greater fiction, along with *The SOUND AND THE FURY* (1929), "The Bear" (1942) *ABSALOM ABSALOM!* (1936), and *The HAMLET* (1940).

Conventional in structure, *Light in August* is told chronologically over nine days of present time, with long flashbacks. Lena Grove frames the story. The novel opens with Lena sitting beside the road on the way to JEFFERSON, MISSISSIPPI, in search of the father of her unborn child. As she approaches, smoke is visible on the horizon: she arrives on the day of Joanna BURDEN's murder and the burning of her house. The core of the book is the story of Miss Burden's murderer, Joe Christmas, in a flashback that takes up seven central chapters. The book returns to the present with the aftermath of the Burden killing and closes with Lena on the move once again, heading north from Jefferson on a futile search for the newborn's father.

In a succession of vividly narrated episodes, Faulkner introduces the themes of man in tension with nature, alienation from the community, and man's inability to fulfill himself outside the community. Present, too, is the American South's peculiar obsession with race and with the regions' heroic and tortured past.

Faulkner began the novel in OXFORD, MISSISSIPPI, on August 17, 1931. He originally called it "Dark House," a title he would later briefly consider for *Absalom, Absalom!* According to the biographer Joseph BLOTNER, the novelist's wife suggested the change when she observed the unique qualities of light on an August evening. Another story persists that Faulkner borrowed the title from a Mississippi folk idiom for giving birth: a pregnant woman would be "light in August," or in whatever month her child appeared. Faulkner himself said it had to do with "a peculiar quality to light" in northern Mississippi in August.

Faulkner, not always reliable on such matters, claimed he launched the novel without a plan, only the image of a young pregnant woman walking on a road. By January 1932, the orphan Joe Christmas had taken over the novel. Faulkner found himself absorbed in his story of a man doomed and alone, caught up in a violent, intensely painful search for a sense of his own self and a place in society.

The external events of the story are succinctly told. Lena Grove, a simple, trusting country girl from Alabama, comes to Jefferson in search of her lover, Lucas BURCH, who abandons her after he learns of her pregnancy. Through a similarity of surnames she meets Byron BUNCH, a meek and withdrawn bachelor who works as a sawmill hand and is also a choirmaster in a country church. Byron falls in love with her and looks after her until her child is born.

Lena arrives toward evening of the day of the murder of Joanna Burden, a descendant of New England abolitionists and, though long a resident of Jefferson, an outcast there. Her killer is her lover, the bootlegger

Joe Christmas. Joe has long passed as white; after the killing, Burch (alias Joe Brown), his junior partner in the whiskey-running enterprise, denounces him to the sheriff as black, a claim that at once persuades the sheriff of his guilt. Christmas is caught and jailed; he escapes and flees to the house of the Reverend Gail HIGHTOWER (2), like Miss Burden a pariah. A self-appointed guardian of the community, the aptly named Percy GRIMM, pursues Christmas into Hightower's kitchen, fires five shots into him, and castrates him with a butcher's knife as he dies.

Meantime, the reclusive Hightower, drawn back into the life of the community through his involvement with Byron Bunch, Lena Grove, and Christmas, is midwife to the birth of Lena's child. The unspeakable Lucas Burch vanishes again. The novel closes with Lena and her baby moving placidly off in search of him, with the faithful Bunch trailing along as escort and protector.

The extended flashback develops the story of Joe Christmas. Faulkner introduces him as a foundling left on the steps of a Memphis orphanage on Christmas night. His mad grandfather, Eupheus (Doc) HINES, believing Joe's father is Black, has placed him there. In a memorable scene, a young girl named ALICE (1), who has befriended the child Joe, wakes him up to say goodbye when she is released from the orphanage. Joe is introduced to sex in another brilliant scene. He innocently eavesdrops on the dietician Miss ATKINS's lovemaking with an intern. Dreading exposure, she tells the matron that Joe is black, figuring he will then be sent away to the "nigger orphanage."

The matron instead arranges for Joe to live with a poor white farmer, Simon MCEACHERN, and his wife. A strict and fanatic Calvinist, McEachern literally tries to beat his religion into the boy. Joe hates McEachern, but he stoically accepts the thrashings. He despises his foster mother and rejects her efforts to make life easier to him. Joe acknowledges a bleak rightness in Calvinistic patterns of crime and punishment, and resents Mrs. McEachern for trying to alter the pattern through pity or sentimentality.

Joe escapes the McEacherns and takes up with the prostitute Bobbie ALLEN. She turns on him when he tells her he is part black. This is part of a recurrent pattern: Joe seems to seek out trouble wherever he finds himself, flaunting his black blood, telling whites he is black, telling blacks he is white. Faulkner deliberately leaves the question vague. Doc Hines rejects his daughter Milly HINES's claim that the father is Mexican, but has no proof that he is black; when Joanna Burden quizzes Joe about his parents, he admits he doesn't really know.

Joe Christmas is in torment about his background, which causes most of his adult troubles. "He is perpetually made aware of society's inflexible requirement that a man be *either* black *or* white and act accordingly," the critic Michael MILLGATE wrote.

Joe leaves home at age 17, a flight touched off when McEachern follows him to a dance hall and confronts him with Bobbie Allen there. Joe breaks a chair over his foster father's head and leaves him unconscious, perhaps dying, on the dance floor. Bobbie abruptly abandons him and returns to Memphis. He wanders for the next 15 years. Recurrent, usually deliberate, acts of violence mark his progress. Eventually he turns up in Jefferson, finds work in a sawmill, and becomes the lover of the spinster outcast Joanna Burden.

Their lovemaking is savage. Her frigidity dissolves into nymphomania and finally into religious mania. With her sudden religious conversion, or perhaps relapse, Joanna comes to believe that because Joe is part black she has sinned against the stern Calvinist God of her forebears in her sexual encounters with him. A fatalistic calm settles on Joe as he makes his way to the Burden house for the final scene. Joanna demands that Joe kneel with her and pray for forgiveness. When he refuses, she threatens him with an old Civil War pistol. The weapon misfires. He slashes at her throat with a razor, nearly taking her head off.

Joe sets the house afire and takes flight. After a week on the run he approaches MOTTSTOWN, only 20 miles from Jefferson, and prepares to give himself up. Here Faulkner uses the striking image of a circle for the sum of Joe's life (p.339).

Joe surrenders and is taken to the Mottstown jail. His lunatic grandfather, full of racial hatred and religious fervor, tries to whip up the townspeople into a lynch mob. He is escorted to Jefferson, where he briefly breaks free of his captors. The avenger Percy Grimm tracks him down for the final chilling scene in Hightower's kitchen.

Faulkner clearly is sympathetic to Joe Christmas, subject as he is to the oppressions of Miss Atkins, mad Doc Hines, Simon McEachern, and others. Race and heredity are not really his problem; he is a victim of his upbringing and of society at large.

"The pressures that mold him into an Ishmael have, as Faulkner knows, nothing to do with biology as such," the critic Cleanth BROOKS observed. "The decisive factor is the attitude that the world takes toward Joe and the attitude that he takes—toward other men and toward himself."

The link between Lena Grove and Christmas is plain enough, even though they never actually meet. They have much in common: both are in flight, both have been deceived and abandoned, both end up in Jefferson. But their fates are painfully different.

Light in August ends as it began, with Lena Grove on the track of Lucas Burch. The final scene is played for humor; Brooks and other critics argue that in spite of everything the closing sequence makes the predominant mode of the novel comedy. But Faulkner's humor has a deeper purpose than occasional relief from the pressures of the story. According to Brooks, "Its function is to maintain sanity and human perspective in a scene of brutality and horror."

Faulkner finished *Light in August* in Oxford on February 19, 1932. Extensive revisions occupied him until mid-March, when he sent off the 165,000-word, 507-page manuscript to his publishers, Harrison SMITH and Robert HAAS. He reportedly experienced a kind of revulsion when the first copies reached ROWAN OAK in the early autumn, not at all how he felt at his first sight of *The Sound and the Fury* printed and bound. He also had no interest in reading the reviews, the first of which appeared in the *Saturday Review*, the *New York Times*, the *New York Tribune* and the *Nation*. Most reviewers treated Faulkner as a major novelist, but most also had reservations about his latest work.

Writing in the *New York Sun* in October 1932, the novelist James T. Farrell remarked that Faulkner draws readers in with his sensationalism, his obsession with psychopathology; this becomes troubling only on reflection. "When one strives to reconstruct or to tell a Faulkner plot in retrospect one sees this melodrama clearly, but when one is reading, one is swept along by the man's driving pen," Farrell wrote. He predicted that Faulkner would limit himself as a novelist through his preoccupation with insanity and violence.

A British reviewer, the poet Richard Aldington, discerned a deeper purpose in Faulkner's choice of material, in his stern Calvinist characters with their obsessions about the past and about race. "In spite of the hard-boiled style in which Mr. Faulkner writes, there cannot be the slightest doubt of his meaning and sympathies," Aldington wrote in the London *Evening Standard* in February 1933. "He is engaged in the not very popular task of criticising the fundamental assumptions of his own people." F. R. Leavis, in the June 1933 number of the journal *Scrutiny*, faulted Faulkner for falling short of "an intimate and subtle rendering" of Joe Christmas's consciousness. Because Christmas is seen from the outside, the furies that drive him, and the necessity of his killing Joanna Burden, are not entirely clear.

Leavis's views on Joe Christmas anticipate later criticism, as do the poet and novelist Conrad AIKEN's strictures on the novel's lack of unity. Powerful as they are individually, do the episodes show a coherent pattern of meaning? Generally admiring of Faulkner's work, Aiken judged *Light in August* a failure on this ground.

As Cleanth Brooks wrote, "What possible relation is there between the two main characters, Lena and Joe Christmas, who go their separate ways, the one placidly, the other violently?" Brooks went on to argue that the notion of community unifies the novel. Most of the characters in *Light in August* bear a special relationship to the community. They are strangers or outcasts. The community protects Lena, as when Mrs. ARMSTID gives

her a few coins out of her small hoard. It persecutes Gail Hightower and destroys Christmas.

Faulkner biographer Joseph Blotner observed that Faulkner integrates Lena into the Christmas plot through her relationship with Lucas Burch, the father of her child; under the alias Joe Brown, he joins Christmas in the bootlegger trade. She is, as virtually every commentator has noted, the life-bearing counterpoint to the doomed Christmas.

Irving Howe regarded the issue of unity as a phantom. In novels, he wrote, "the actual relation between form and content is almost always unfinished and improvisatory, rarely as neat as critics like to suppose." Howe argued that Faulkner's moral vision, his power, overcome the book's structural flaws: "In *Light in August* a new voice is heard, partly Faulkner's own and partly, as it were, an over-voice speaking for the memories and conscience of a people. . . . [T]his voice records the entire Yoknapatawpha story."

Lilley   Character in *Intruder in the Dust*. He owns a small store with business chiefly from JEFFERSON, MISSISSIPPI, black community. All the same, he offers to join the mob that forms to lynch Lucas BEAUCHAMP. As Gavin STEVENS notes, there are no hard feelings on Lilley's part; he is simply acting like a white man, "implicitly observing the rules" of the racial relationship.

Linscomb, Colonel   Character in *The REIVERS*. A lawyer, he owns Acheron, the horse that races Lightning (Coppermine); the half-mile track on which the races are run; and a considerable plantation near the little town of PARSHAM.

Colonel Linscomb is host to Grandfather Lucius PRIEST when he comes up to Parsham to recover his automobile, his grandson, and his retainers Boon HOGGANBECK and Ned MCCASLIN. Ned narrates the tangled story of the horseracing scheme in the colonel's fine office, and details of the fourth—and final—race between Acheron and Lightning are worked out there.

A hospitable man, he invites Miss Reba BINFORD (see RIVERS, REBA) into his home for supper. She politely declines.

Littlejohn   In *The HAMLET* and *INTRUDER IN THE DUST*, a family name of early farmers in YOKNAPATAWPHA COUNTY. In *AS I LAY DYING*, a Littlejohn is one of Addie BUNDREN's neighbors present at her funeral; he is gathered on the porch with other men. A Littlejohn also appears in *The MANSION* as the owner of a half-Airedale terrier. See also LITTLEJOHN, MRS.

Littlejohn, Mrs.   In *The HAMLET*, the owner and sole manager of LITTLEJOHN'S HOTEL in FRENCHMAN'S BEND. A hard-working and kindhearted woman, she provides a place in her barn for the idiot Ike SNOPES, who does various chores for her, and she helps Henry ARMSTID when he breaks his leg trying to catch the wild pony he thinks he bought from the Texan Buck HIPPS. When one of the wild horses that escape comes running toward her, she dauntlessly breaks a washboard over its face. This episode is found in the earlier FATHER ABRAHAM and "SPOTTED HORSES," which Faulkner incorporated into *The Hamlet*, and is again referred to in *The TOWN*. Mrs. Littlejohn also appears in "LIZARDS IN JAMSHYD'S COURTYARD" (revised for *The HAMLET*) and in FLAGS IN THE DUST. (For more information, see *Faulkner in the University*, p. 66.)

Littlejohn's Hotel In *The HAMLET*, the boardinghouse in FRENCHMAN'S BEND owned and run by Mrs. LITTLEJOHN. It is one of only two multistory houses (Will VARNER's being the other) in the hamlet. The sewing machine salesman V. K. RATLIFF stays here when he is travelling in the area, and in the lot next to the hotel the Texan Buck HIPPS auctions off the wild ponies. The hotel also is mentioned in *The TOWN*. During Faulkner's time, there was an actual Littlejohn's Store on the New Albany Road (now Mississippi Route 30) northeast of OXFORD, MISSISSIPPI.

Liveright, Horace Publisher. A one-time toilet paper manufacturer, he and his newspaperman partner, Albert Boni, founded the Modern Library in 1917; their firm, BONI & LIVERIGHT, published works by Ezra Pound, T. S. Eliot, Eugene O'Neill, Ernest HEMINGWAY, and Theodore Dreiser.

Liveright accepted Faulkner's first novel, SOLDIERS' PAY, on Sherwood ANDERSON's recommendation in 1925 and published it the following year. He published Faulkner's second novel, MOSQUITOES, in 1927. To the novelist's chagrin, Liveright in November 1927 turned down FLAGS IN THE DUST (published as SARTORIS in 1929), saying the novel was so poorly put together that Faulkner should withdraw it altogether.

Faulkner resolved to offer the book to another publisher, and he plotted to sever his contractual tie to Boni & Liveright. It seemed a risky move at the time, but in the end, Liveright let Faulkner go without penalty. Harcourt, Brace published *Sartoris* in January 1929 and brought out *The SOUND AND THE FURY* in October of that year, paying its author a $200 advance against royalties.

"Lizards in Jamshyd's Courtyard" *(Uncollected Stories)* A humorously told short story about the craftiness of Flem SNOPES and his unscrupulous business practices. The setting is the bucolic hamlet of FRENCHMAN'S BEND, where the sewing machine agent and itinerant salesman, SURATT, stays about every six weeks when travelling through the countryside. On one of his stopovers, Flem overhears Suratt's plans to buy and sell goats and intervenes by purchasing them before Suratt has the chance. Although he buys from Suratt the contract to

sell the goats, Flem makes a much greater profit than the one dollar Suratt gains from the deal. Three years later, Flem pulls off yet another scheme that involves Suratt and two residents of Frenchman's Bend, Henry ARMSTID and Vernon TULL. Taking full advantage of the rumor that there is buried treasure on OLD FRENCHMAN PLACE, a worthless piece of property, Flem purchases it from Will VARNER and salts it with a few small canvas sacks of silver dollars. He knows that Suratt and the others will spy on him, so he pretends that he is digging for the money that was buried during the Civil War. The night after Suratt, Armstid, and Tull watch Flem, they arrive with the diviner Uncle Dick (see BOLIVAR, UNCLE DICK) to help them locate the coins, which they eventually do. Convinced that there is a trove of coins to be dug up, they unhesitatingly buy the property from Flem, but once Suratt and BOOKWRIGHT examine the dates on their coins, they realize that they have been duped. Armstid, however, the one who has the most to lose, refuses to stop digging and becomes obsessed with finding what is not there. Every evening his wife brings him cold food in a pail as onlookers from all around gaze in rapt attention at his folly.

In discussing Faulkner's sense of the literary marketplace, John T. Matthews argues that "Lizards in Jamshyd's Courtyard" reflects "on its own status as a work of art in the age of commodification." Armstid's "spectators themselves become a part of the spectacle" the readers of the story perceive ("Shortened Stories: Faulkner and the Market," in *Faulkner and the Short Story*, edited by Evans Harrington and Ann J. Abadie, p. 21). But Faulkner's aesthetic goals are not compromised by his awareness of mass literary consumption.

"Lizards in Jamshyd's Courtyard" was first published on February 27, 1932, in the SATURDAY EVENING POST 204, 12–13, 52, 57; it was revised and included in book 4 of *The Hamlet*. The original version was reprinted in UNCOLLECTED STORIES OF WILLIAM FAULKNER. For more information, see *Uncollected Stories of William Faulkner*, pp. 686–88.

Lizzie Character in "BARN BURNING" (in *Collected Stories*). The aunt of Colonel Sartoris SNOPES, she urges Sarty's mother to let him leave the house and try to prevent his father from setting the de Spain barn on fire.

"Lo!" *(Collected Stories)* Short story, a satirical tale of how a CHICKASAW INDIAN chief, a master strategist and trickster, outplays the reputedly omnipotent American president in the great colonialist games of power, justice, and real estate dealings. During a snowy February the nameless president, based on Andrew Jackson, has been held hostage for three weeks in the White House by a large number of Indians camped in the grounds and squatting in the hallways. Chief Francis WEDDEL has come from Mississippi to Washington to seek justice. His nephew is suspected of murdering the white man who purchased from them a small but vital plot of land on which he then erected a tollgate.

Though the Indians act in a manner both dignified and respectful, their attire, activities, and omnipresence increasingly become a source of inconvenience and embarrassment to the president as the negotiations stretch out. The occupation finally ends when, surrendering to expediency, the president feigns a cursory investigation of the affair and pens a document acquitting the nephew. Weddel deems the occasion insufficiently impressive and forces the president to take over the large hall of Congress to enact a formal ceremony featuring the president reading in Latin, followed by a salvo of cannon fire. The Indians depart and all is calm until a letter from Weddel reports a recurrence of the tollgate affair and his intention to come back for more justice. Spurred to immediate action, the president draws up a document assigning the land in perpetuity to the Indians, provided they do not leave it. Just in case, he mobilizes the army to defend against Weddel should he still be inclined to return.

This tale first appeared in *Story* (November 1934) and was selected for *Best American Short Stories 1935 and the Yearbook of the American Short Story* (1935). The episode is briefly retold in "MOUNTAIN VICTORY."

Log-in-the-Creek   Character in "THE COURTSHIP" (in *Collected Stories*). A lazy and unambitious young CHICKASAW INDIAN, he eventually wins the hand of Herman BASKET's beautiful sister, besting two powerful rivals, the chief-to-be, Doom (see IKKEMOTUBBE), and David HOGGANBECK, the steamboat pilot.

The Long, Hot Summer   In 1958, a film version of *The HAMLET*, directed by Martin Ritt and starring Paul Newman, Joanne Woodward, Anthony Franciosa, Orson Wells, Lee Remick, Angela Lansbury, and Richard Anderson, was released by Twentieth Century–Fox. The screenplay was written by Irving Ravetch and Harriet Frank, Jr., and based on book 3 ("The Long Summer") of the novel and on the short stories "BARN BURNING" and "SPOTTED HORSES."

Long, Judge   Minor character in *The TOWN* and *The MANSION*. Judge Long is the federal judge of the district that includes JEFFERSON, MISSISSIPPI. He sent the bootlegger Wilbur PROVINE of FRENCHMAN'S BEND to prison not for making whiskey but instead for letting his wife carry water over a mile from a spring to their home. In *The Mansion*, Judge Long sentences Montgomery Ward SNOPES to two years in the state penitentiary for possessing a gallon of moonshine whiskey, which was planted in his photography store by Montgomery's kinsman, Flem SNOPES.

Loos, Anita (1893–1981)   Novelist, playwright, and screenwriter. Her novel *Gentlemen Prefer Blondes* (1925),

subtitled *The Illuminating Diary of a Professional Lady*, satirized naive, gold-digging women of the Jazz Age and became a great success. Loos later wrote satires of Hollywood and a series of autobiographical works, including *This Brunette Prefers Work* (1956).

Faulkner met Loos in the Vieux Carré in NEW ORLEANS in the mid-1920s through Sherwood ANDERSON, an Ohio friend of Loos's husband, John Emerson. Faulkner was impersonating a wounded war hero at the time, and was said to have a metal plate in his head.

Faulkner liked *Gentlemen Prefer Blondes* and wrote to Loos in admiration of the main character, Lorelei Lee's friend Dorothy.

After a long lapse, Faulkner and Loos became reacquainted in Hollywood in the 1950s.

Loosh (Lucius)   Character in *The UNVANQUISHED*. A slave of the Sartorises, he shows federal troops the hiding place of the family silver. Drawn by the lure of freedom, Loosh follows the Yankees for a time, but returns eventually to Sartoris.

Lorraine   Minor (offstage) character in *The SOUND AND THE FURY* and referred to by Faulkner in his appendix to the novel (see Appendix IV). A prostitute in MEMPHIS, she is the younger Jason COMPSON's mistress who, after the death of his mother, visits him in JEFFERSON, MISSISSIPPI.

Lorraine, Miss   With Miss MYRTLE, she visits and drinks with Miss Reba RIVERS on the day of RED's funeral in *SANCTUARY*.

Louisa   Character in *IF I FORGET THEE, JERUSALEM* ("The Wild Palms"). She is a maid in the San Antonio brothel where Harry WILBOURNE asks for medicine that will cause Charlotte RITTENMEYER to abort.

Louisa, Aunt   Character in "THAT WILL BE FINE" (in *Collected Stories*). Uncle RODNEY's sister and the aunt of the narrator, seven-year-old GEORGIE, Louisa is protective of her ne'er-do-well brother. In trying to protect Rodney from being arrested, she does so less out of affection for him than out of concern for her father and for the reputation of the family.

Louisa, Cousin   Character in "THAT WILL BE FINE" (in *Collected Stories*). She is a cousin of GEORGIE, the narrator of the story.

Louvinia   *See* STROTHER, LOUVINIA.

Lovelady, Mr.   Character in "THAT EVENING SUN" (in *Collected Stories*). He collects on insurance policies in JEFFERSON, MISSISSIPPI's, black neighborhoods.

Lovemaiden, Butch Character in *The REIVERS*. A coarse, bullying, race-baiting deputy from Hardwick, the county seat 13 miles from PARSHAM, he turns up in the little town when he hears of a horse race about to be run there.

Lovemaiden launches an aggressive pursuit of Miss Corrie (Everbe HOGGANBECK) and touches off a violent conflict with Boon HOGGANBECK. He uses his authority to goad Boon into attacking him; this lands Boon and Ned MCCASLIN in jail. He then suggests to Miss Corrie that they will go free if she submits to his gross attentions.

Boon is duly freed, but when he learns the details he assaults Lovemaiden and beats him badly; Mr. POLEY-MUS, the Parsham constable, asserts his authority. Both Boon and Lovemaiden are arrested and taken to the Hardwick jail.

When they are released, Boon attacks him again, this time for calling Corrie a whore.

Lowe, (Cadet) Julian A 19-year-old would-be fighter pilot in *SOLDIERS' PAY*, who at first assists Joe GILLIGAN and Mrs. Margaret POWERS with the badly wounded Donald MAHON on the train. Lowe feels that the war ended too soon; he had been in his final weeks of training when the armistice was signed. He falls in love with the widow Mrs. Powers and asks her to marry him. Lowe believes her reluctance has something to do with Mahon's wound, a wound which Lowe interprets as a sign of heroism. When Mrs. Powers realizes that Lowe will be a hindrance, she gently but firmly sends him home to San Francisco so that she and Gilligan might bring Mahon home to die in his father's house in Charlestown, Georgia. Lowe continues to write to Mrs. Powers throughout the novel.

"Lucas Beauchamp" A short story written in 1948, it is an earlier version of the long flashback that opens the novel *INTRUDER IN THE DUST* (1948) in which a young white boy incurs an obligation to a proud old black man and tastes the first bitter fruits of the South's heritage of racial subordination.

Faulkner sent the story to his agent, Harold OBER, in May 1948 for possible magazine publication. The *Atlantic Monthly* and *HARPER'S MAGAZINE* turned it down. A copy from Ober's files came into the possession of the Faulkner scholar Patrick Samway in 1975, and Samway saw to its publication in the *Virginia Quarterly Review* in 1999. With minor differences, the story is the first 25 pages or so of *Intruder*. But as Samway notes, it can stand on its own. "Not only is it a Faulkner story—and that alone merits its publication—but it has the requisite literary qualities one expects of a story by one of America's greatest creative writers," Samway wrote.

On an icy morning, the unnamed 12-year-old protagonist falls into Nine Mile Branch and Lucas BEAUCHAMP escorts him home to his cabin to recover. The story narrates Lucas's antecedents—his descent from the enslaved son of the white great-grandfather of his present landlord, Carothers EDMONDS. Lucas is proud of his heritage and refuses to conform to white YOKNAPATAWPHA COUNTY's notions of black behavior.

The boy learns this too late. After Lucas and his wife, Molly BEAUCHAMP, have dried his clothes and fed him, the boy offers Lucas money—a half-dollar, a dime and two nickels. Lucas coolly ignores the offer. Shamed and embarrassed, the boy allows the coins to drop to the floor. Lucas orders the boy's two black companions to pick them up and return them.

For a long time, the boy is haunted by his terrible misjudgment. To make amends, he sends cigars and snuff to the Beauchamps for Christmas, and later sends a dress to Molly. Lucas responds with the gift to him of a gallon of sorghum molasses, and they are back where they started.

The boy believes he would be absolved if only Lucas would behave within the confines of Mississippi's racial code.

As the boy grows older, the shame gradually fades and he feels the need simply for "reequalization, reaffirmation of his masculinity and his white blood." In *Intruder in the Dust,* that comes when the boy, now called Chick MALLISON, helps Lucas prove his innocence of the murder of a white man.

Lucille Minor character in the short story "TWO DOLLAR WIFE" who accompanies Walter MITCHELL to the New Year's Eve party at the club. She is a witness to the impromptu wedding of Doris HOUSTON and Maxwell JOHNS.

Lucius Character in "MY GRANDMOTHER MILLARD AND GENERAL BEDFORD FORREST AND THE BATTLE OF HAR-RYKIN CREEK" (in *Collected Stories*). A slave on Sartoris plantation, he thinks only of his freedom and looks to the Yankees to deliver it.

Ludus (1) In *The MANSION,* the jailed husband of Miss Reba RIVERS's black maid, MINNIE. After he quit his job, Ludus loafed around, ate from Miss Reba's kitchen, and stole money from his wife which he gave to other women. When Minnie confronted him, Ludus hit her with a flatiron.

Ludus (2) Character in *The REIVERS.* One of Maury PRIEST's black drivers, he borrows a company wagon overnight, setting off a chain of events that ends when Boon HOGGANBECK shoots at him in broad daylight on the JEFFERSON, MISSISSIPPI, square. Boon goes after Ludus because, instead of buying Calvin BOOKWRIGHT's fine whiskey as he had been instructed to do, he delivered inferior "rot gut" liquor.

Lufbery A soldier referred to by Cadet Julian LOWE in the novel *SOLDIERS' PAY*. Lufbery is an offstage character.

Luis Character in "CARCASSONNE" (in *Collected Stories*). He operates the cantina in which a pauper (probably Wilfred MIDGLESTON of the short story "BLACK MUSIC") has an attic room.

Luke In *SANCTUARY*, an OXFORD, MISSISSIPPI, bootlegger. Gowan STEVENS gets liquor from him.

Luluque One of Corporal STEFAN's followers in *A FABLE*. A Midian, Luluque asks for grace to be said at their meal in prison.

Luster (1) The 14-year-old black youth who watches Benjamin (Benjy) COMPSON in *The SOUND AND THE FURY*. Luster is FRONY's son and DILSEY's grandchild. His presence in the novel's first chapter, narrated by Benjy, is April 1928. As the novel opens, Luster is looking for a lost quarter, which he needs to go to a show later that night. Not the most patient caretaker, Luster is at times mean and threatening to Benjy. Luster also appears in Faulkner's appendix to *The Sound and the Fury* (see Appendix IV)*;* this character would be too young to be the Luster who appears in *ABSALOM, ABSALOM!* See LUSTER (2).

Luster (2) In *ABSALOM, ABSALOM!*, one of the Compsons' black servants. Luster is with Quentin COMPSON and his father when they hunt quail, and as Shreve MCCANNON, Quentin's HARVARD UNIVERSITY roommate, notes, Luster leads Quentin's and his father's horses around the flooded ditch.

Luster (3) Character in *The REIVERS*. A black employee of the Priest livery stable, he helps carry a girl who is slightly wounded in Boon HOGGANBECK's shooting spree to the doctor's office.

Lytle, Horace Character in *The REIVERS*. A specialist in fine bird dogs, he comes to PARSHAM once a year for the Grand National trials.

Mac (1) In *The SOUND AND THE FURY,* a fellow in JEFFER-SON, MISSISSIPPI, who chats about baseball—in particular, the pennant race, the Yankees, and Babe Ruth—with a disagreeable Jason COMPSON.

Mac (2) In *PYLON,* the desk clerk in the Bayou Street police station where the drunken airplane mechanic, JIGGS, is being held for vagrancy. The REPORTER, who borrowed money from his editor, HAGOOD, pays Mac a $10 fine to have Jiggs released.

McAndrews Character in *GO DOWN, MOSES* ("Pantaloon in Black"). He is the foreman of the JEFFERSON, MISSISSIPPI, sawmill where RIDER works. McAndrews expects Rider to take the day off for his wife's burial, but he shows up for work anyway.

McCallum, Anse (1) (old) Character in *SARTORIS* (where his name appears as Virginius MacCallum), *The HAMLET* and the short story "THE TALL MEN." He is a self-reliant yeoman farmer in northeast YOKNAPATAWPHA COUNTY.

In *Sartoris,* he is the father of six grown sons: Jackson, Henry, Raphael (Rafe), Stuart, Lee, and Buddy. (In "The Tall Men," with Henry not mentioned, Anse has five sons.) A shaggy, silver-haired, twice-widowed veteran of Lee's army, he oversees the running of the family place in semiretirement. Young Bayard SARTORIS (4) stays with the MacCallums for a period just after the accidental death of old Bayard.

In *The Hamlet,* old Anse trades 14 rifle cartridges for two wild horses, which he brings back home from Texas and turns into a good team. In "The Tall Men," Anse has been dead for 15 years, and is remembered for having walked all the way from Mississippi to Virginia to enlist in Stonewall Jackson's army. Anse was 16 when the Civil War broke out.

McCallum, Anse (2) (young) Minor character in *The TOWN* and the short story "THE TALL MEN." He is Buddy MCCALLUM's son. In *The Town,* he twice fights Matt LEVITT, a Golden Glove boxer, and loses both times. In the first fight, Anse resorts to using a fence rail but the bystanders hold them apart until Sheriff HAMPTON comes and puts them in jail for the night. The next day, at the insistence of his father, Anse faces Matt in a fair fight and again

loses. In "The Tall Men," Anse and his brother Lucius MCCALLUM are sought after by a U.S. marshal (Mr. PEARSON) from Jackson for failing to register for the draft during World War II. In the presence of the marshal, their father tells them to pack, go to Memphis, and enlist.

McCallum, Buddy Character in *SARTORIS, INTRUDER IN THE DUST, The TOWN,* and the short story "THE TALL MEN." He is the father of young Anse and Lucius MCCALLUM. (In *Sartoris,* his last name appears as MacCallum and his real first name is Virginius.) A World War I veteran, he trades a "war trophy," a German Luger automatic pistol, with Crawford GOWRIE for a pair of foxhounds in the summer of 1919.

In "The Tall Men," Buddy, the youngest of old Anse MCCALLUM's sons, catches his leg in a hammer mill and has to have it amputated. He mortifies his father, who still has sentiment for the Confederacy, by serving in the "Yankee" army during World War I.

In *The Town,* he becomes angry with his son Anse for using a fence rail to fight Matt LEVITT and threatens to beat him up if he does not fight fairly. When Anse gets the worst of it, Buddy ends the fight and tells Matt to leave town.

McCallum, Henry Character in *SARTORIS,* the second of six sons of (old) Anse MCCALLUM (Virginius MacCallum Sr.), a self-reliant farmer. Henry runs the family still and is in charge of the kitchen.

McCallum, Jackson Character in *SARTORIS,* the eldest of farmer (old) Anse MCCALLUM's (Virginius MacCallum Sr.'s) six sons. Like his brothers Lee and Stuart, he is named for a Confederate general. Jackson's ambition is to raise a superior breed of hunting dogs.

McCallum, Lafe Minor character in *AS I LAY DYING,* where he is the twin brother of Rafe MCCALLUM. In *SARTORIS,* Rafe's twin is Stuart MCCALLUM. (Faulkner is not always consistent with the names of his characters.)

McCallum, Lee Character in *SARTORIS,* one of six sons of the farmer (old) Anse MCCALLUM (Virginius MacCallum Sr.). Moody and withdrawn, he has a good tenor voice and is much in demand for Sunday services. He also appears in "THE TALL MEN."

McCallum, Lucius Buddy MCCALLUM's son in "THE TALL MEN." When Mr. PEARSON, a U.S. marshal, appears to arrest him and his brother young Anse MCCALLUM for avoiding the draft during World War II, their father orders them to go to Memphis and enlist.

McCallum, Old Man Hundred-and-One In *The HAMLET*, a name V. K. RATLIFF uses when talking about Flem SNOPES and his wife, Eula Varner SNOPES, who have been married for 29 days. Although the exact identity of the person is not certain, it appears that Ratliff is speaking metaphorically. McCallum is a family name in YOKNAPATAWPHA COUNTY, dating back to the Civil War.

McCallum, Raphael Semmes (Rafe) Character in *SARTORIS*, a son of (old) Anse MCCALLUM (Virginius MacCallum Sr.) and Stuart's twin. Named for a Confederate sea raider, he is known as Rafe. He and young Bayard SARTORIS (4) get drunk together in DEACON's café the day Bayard is thrown from the wild stallion.

Rafe also appears in *KNIGHT'S GAMBIT* ("Knight's Gambit") and the short story "THE TALL MEN." A farmer and expert horse breeder and trader, he sells Max HARRISS the wild stallion that Harriss means to use to kill Captain GUALDRES in *Knight's Gambit*. McCallum, Gavin STEVENS, and Chick MALLISON arrive just in time to save Gualdres.

In "The Tall Men," Rafe greets the marshal, GOMBAULT, and the draft investigator, PEARSON, when they arrive to arrest his two nephews for failing to register for the draft. He is referred to in *AS I LAY DYING* and *The MANSION*.

McCallum, Stuart Character in *SARTORIS*, a son of (old) Anse MCCALLUM (Virginius MacCallum Sr.) and Rafe MCCALLUM's twin. He is a farmer. Stuart also appears in "THE TALL MEN."

MacCallum, Virginius, Jr. *See* MCCALLUM, BUDDY.

MacCallum, Virginius, Sr. *See* MCCALLUM, ANSE (OLD).

MacCannon, Shrevlin (Shreve) *See* MACKENZIE, SHREVLIN.

McCarron Character in *The HAMLET*, the father of Hoake MCCARRON. Before eloping with Alison Hoake (MCCARRON), he made his living by playing poker, but after his marriage he became a decent husband who successfully ran his father-in-law's farm. He apparently died in a gambling house 10 years after he was married.

McCarron, Alison Hoake In *The HAMLET*, the mother of Hoake MCCARRON. A determined and independent woman, she climbed out of a second-story window to elope with her husband. She is also referred to in *The TOWN*.

McCarron, Hoake In *The HAMLET*, one of Eula Varner (SNOPES)'s suitors. At 23, he looks older. Following a scandal involving the wife of an instructor at the agricultural college he was attending, Hoake withdrew. By chance one day he happens to ride through FRENCHMAN'S BEND and sees Eula, whom he begins to visit to the ire of her other admirers. When he is abused by his rivals, he fights them off with Eula's help but suffers a broken arm, which Will VARNER sets. After Varner goes to bed, Hoake—with his splinted arm supported by Eula—takes her virginity. When he finds out three months later that she is pregnant, he leaves for Texas, as do the other suitors. In *The TOWN* (where he is an offstage character), Hoake is known to be Linda SNOPES's natural father, and in *The MANSION*, with the encouragement of Gavin STEVENS, he attends her wedding in New York. Although he introduces himself to her as an old friend of the family, Linda knows who he really is.

McCaslin, Amodeus (Uncle Buddy) Character in *The UNVANQUISHED* and *GO DOWN, MOSES*. The twin brother of Theophilus MCCASLIN (Uncle Buck), he wins a card game to decide which of the brothers will go off to war, and serves in Tennant's brigade in the Army of Northern Virginia.

Uncle Buddy and his twin hold advanced ideas about social relationships and about the relationship of people to the land. The brothers also launch a plan to free their father's slaves; the slaves could earn their freedom not by paying the McCaslins for it but, instead, through work on the plantation.

In "Was" (*Go Down, Moses*), Uncle Buddy wins a hand at poker that frees his brother from a forced betrothal with Miss Sophonsiba BEAUCHAMP (1) and unites the slave girl Tennie (BEAUCHAMP) with her lover, a slave on the McCaslin place. Buddy also appears in "The Fire and the Hearth," "The Old People," "The Bear," and "Delta Autumn," all in *Go Down, Moses*.

McCaslin, Cousin Character in *The REIVERS*. The uncle of Zachary EDMONDS, he owns the mare that Ned MCCASLIN surreptitiously bred to a farm jack. The offspring, addicted to the sardines Ned offers him as an inducement to run, proves to be the fastest mule in YOKNAPATAWPHA COUNTY. When he dies, unbeaten, at 22, he is buried on the McCaslin plantation.

McCaslin, Delphine Character in *The REIVERS*. She is Sarah PRIEST's African-American cook, and the fourth wife of Ned MCCASLIN. Lucius PRIEST covers his escape to MEMPHIS with Boon HOGGANBECK (and with Ned as a stowaway) by telling his relatives he is staying with Ned and Delphine while his parents are away at Grandfather LESSEP's funeral.

McCaslin, Eunice   Character in *GO DOWN, MOSES* ("The Bear"). The wife of Thucydus MCCASLIN, a slave on the McCaslin plantation, she drowns herself in a creek on Christmas Day 1832 after she learns that her daughter Tomasina (Aunt TOMEY) is pregnant with the child of her own father, the white master.

McCaslin, Isaac (Cousin Ike, Uncle Ike)   Character in *GO DOWN, MOSES* ("Was," "Fire and the Hearth," "The Old People," "The Bear," "Delta Autumn") and other works. The son of Theophilus (Buck) MCCASLIN, born in 1867, he is a complex figure who repudiates his patrimony, the family plantation, because he believes that no man can own the land and that, in any case, slavery has laid a curse upon the YOKNAPATAWPHA COUNTY holdings.

Ike appears in "The Fire and the Hearth" as an old man living in a cheap frame house in JEFFERSON, MISSISSIPPI, surviving on whatever his kinsman Roth (Carothers) EDMONDS, now owner of the McCaslin place, chooses to give him. He is the boy narrator of "The Old People." At age 12, he slays his first buck, has its warm blood smeared on his face, and thus completes the rite of passage into manhood.

In "The Bear," Ike at age 10 is permitted to join Major DE SPAIN's hunting camp for the first time. From his part-Chickasaw mentor Sam FATHERS he learns woodcraft and gains a deep understanding of the relationship between man and the natural world. The years-long quest for Old Ben, the bear, is the symbol of that relationship. Ike finally catches a glimpse of the bear when he lays aside his gun, watch and compass, the instruments of civilization, and strikes deep into the woods.

The hunters abandon the camp after the killing of Old Ben and the death of Sam Fathers, and Major de Spain sells the timber rights to his holdings to a Memphis lumber company. When Ike returns after a long interval he finds the wilderness transformed: a large planing mill at HOKE'S STATION, long stacks of steel rails, piles of crossties, and a logging line into the woods.

Ike discovers the interrelationships of master and slave and the painful details of the "curse and taint" of slavery when he studies the plantation ledgers his father and uncle had kept: his grandfather's incest; the old man's slave daughter's suicide when she learns her daughter is pregnant with her father's child; his father's fumbling efforts to free his slaves. He finds in the ledgers an account of his grandfather's legacy to his black son Terrel (Tomey's Turl BEAUCHAMP) and his three children, and attempts to find them and deliver it.

Ike relinquishes the McCaslin estate, all but forcing it on his older cousin (and father figure) McCaslin EDMONDS, and supports himself by working as a carpenter. Though he marries, he remains childless, and never attempts to reclaim his patrimony.

In "Delta Autumn," Ike, now an old man, draws the unpleasant task of sending away Roth Edmonds's mistress, who is part black—the granddaughter, it turns out, of Jim BEAUCHAMP (Tennie's Jim), the son of Tomey's Turl and once a servant at the hunting camp. The encounter deeply disturbs him.

Faulkner presents Ike as a passive figure, a man overwhelmed, a pessimist. He is powerless to protect his beloved wilderness; he is helpless in the face of injustice. In "Delta Autumn," he tells Roth's bereft mistress that maybe in a thousand years whites and blacks will get along, but not now.

Ike stands for a sort of static decency that he hoped to pass on to future generations, an attitude the conservative in Faulkner understood and admired. "He was trying to teach what he knew of respect for whatever your lot in life is," the novelist remarked, "that if your lot is to be a hunter, you slay the animals with the nearest approach you can to dignity and decency." (*Faulkner in the University,* p. 54).

Isaac McCaslin is mentioned in *The HAMLET, INTRUDER IN THE DUST, The TOWN, The MANSION, The REIVERS,* and the short stories "A Bear Hunt" and "RACE AT MORNING." In *The Hamlet,* he allowed Ab SNOPES and his family to live in his storehouse when Ab worked for him. In *The Mansion,* where he runs a hardware store in Jefferson (the McCaslin Hardware Company), the narrator explains that he refused to sell Mink SNOPES buckshot shells that Mink wanted to use to kill Jack HOUSTON.

McCaslin, Lancaster   Character in *The REIVERS.* He is the grandfather of Ned MCCASLIN, whose parents are Lucius Quintus Carothers MCCASLIN and a slave.

McCaslin, Lucius Quintus Carothers   Character in *GO DOWN, MOSES.* The first McCaslin in YOKNAPATAWPHA COUNTY, he obtained the large grant of CHICKASAW INDIAN land that became the McCaslin plantation. Old Carothers is responsible for the tangled McCaslin racial history. He fathers Tomey's Turl (BEAUCHAMP) by a slave girl who is his own daughter, and so is Lucas BEAUCHAMP's grandfather.

He is mentioned in "The Fire and the Hearth," "The Old People" and "The Bear" in *Go Down, Moses* and in *INTRUDER IN THE DUST* and *The REIVERS.*

McCaslin, Ned William   Character in *The REIVERS.* He is Grandfather Lucius PRIEST's coachman, the natural son of old Lucius Quintus Carothers MCCASLIN and a slave, born in the McCaslin backyard in 1860. Proud of his mixed heritage, he is independent, shrewd, and resourceful enough to survive, even prosper, in a White man's world on his own terms.

When he hears of Boon HOGGANBECK's and young Lucius PRIEST's plans for a weekend trip to MEMPHIS in May 1905, he manages to stow himself away in the back of Grandfather Priest's Winton Flyer. He is soon discovered and accepted, grudgingly on Boon's part, into the party. In Memphis, he runs across his cousin Bobo BEAUCHAMP, who tells him he is $128 in debt to a white man, and that the debt comes due on Monday. Ned concocts an elaborate scheme to bail out Bobo that involves the Winton Flyer and a racehorse named Coppermine (later Lightning).

Without Boon's knowledge, Ned trades the car for the horse. He then enlists Boon, Lucius, the girls in Miss Reba's (see RIVERS, REBA) brothel, and others in his plan. With the help of a railroad flagman admirer of Miss Corrie's (Everbe Corinthia HOGGANBECK), he arranges for Coppermine to be transported to the little Tennessee town of PARSHAM, where it will run against the local champion, Colonel LINSCOMB's Acheron. With the proceeds, Ned expects to pay down Bobo's debt and recover the Winton Flyer.

The intervention of a bullying deputy named Butch LOVEMAIDEN complicates matters. Butch aggressively pursues Everbe, driving Boon to fits of jealous rage. For a time, Ned, Boon, and the horse are held in jail. With the help of Uncle Parsham HOOD and his grandson Lycurgus BRIGGINS, and an act of sacrifice on Everbe's part, Butch is confounded and the races finally come off.

Using the secret of the "sour dean" (sardine) to spur on Lightning, Ned wins enough to free Bobo from debt. But the intervention of Colonel Linscomb and Grandfather Priest force major last-minute alterations. A final race is run; Ned does not appear with the sardine; Acheron wins. But Ned has slyly bet on the colonel's horse, and he wins big for himself, with $20 to spare for Uncle Parsham's church. Coppermine/Lightning reverts to Mr. VAN TOSCH, and Grandfather Priest gets his car back—at a cost of $496.

Ned keeps his winnings for, as he confesses to young Lucius, it is too late for him to give up his ill-gotten gains. But he is proud of Lucius for refusing his share.

Faulkner once described *The Reivers* as "a sort of Huck Finn" (David L. Minter, *Faulkner: His Life and Work*, p. 246). If that is so, Ned McCaslin would be Faulkner's Jim, the runaway slave in Mark Twain's great novel who teaches Huck imperishable lessons about their common humanity. In a similar way, Ned helps young Lucius to adulthood and to his estate as a good man.

McCaslin, Theophilus (Filus, Uncle Buck) Character in *ABSALOM, ABSALOM!, GO DOWN, MOSES,* and other works. The twin brother of Amodeus (Uncle Buddy) MCCASLIN and father of Issac MCCASLIN, he and his brother are the inheritors of old Lucius Quintus Carothers McCaslin's vast YOKNAPATAWPHA COUNTY plantation holdings.

In *Absalom,* he assists at Charles BON's funeral, giving the rebel yell (Confederate battle cry) in lieu of the Catholic ceremonial, the words of which none of the funeral party know.

In *The UNVANQUISHED,* he helps Bayard SARTORIS (3) and Ringo STROTHER track down the bushwhackers that killed Bayard's grandmother. The story is retold in *The TOWN.*

Uncle Buck is an important character in "Was," "The Fire and the Hearth" and "The Bear" in *Go Down, Moses.* In "Was," he finds himself engaged to Miss Sophonsiba BEAUCHAMP (1) after he accidentally creeps into her bed by mistake one night. Though his brother frees him from the unwanted commitment by winning a hand at poker, he marries her anyway. Uncle Buck is a comic character, but he and his brother also represent Faulkner's notion of good men. In "The Fire and the Hearth," for instance, in the 1850s he and Uncle Buddy begin carrying out their scheme to free their father's slaves.

Faulkner reintroduces Uncle Buck in *The HAMLET* in connection with the horse thief Ab SNOPES, whose crippled leg, according to Uncle Buck, was a result of a gunshot wound Colonel John SARTORIS gave him for trying to steal the colonel's horse.

McCaslin, Thucydus Character in *GO DOWN, MOSES* ("The Bear"). A McCaslin slave, he is the husband of Eunice MCCASLIN. He evidently managed to negotiate his freedom, possibly through a work arrangement, and set up a blacksmith shop in JEFFERSON, MISSISSIPPI, in 1841.

McCord (Mac) Character in *IF I FORGET THEE, JERUSALEM* ("The Wild Palms"). A Chicago newspaperman, he befriends Harry WILBOURNE and Charlotte RITTENMEYER even though he is skeptical of their notions of love and commitment. McCord lends Harry and Charlotte the lake cabin he co-owns. He helps Charlotte find a job in Chicago. Later, McCord tries to talk Harry out of taking a job in a Utah mine that turns out to be a sham.

McCudden, James (1895–1918) Historical aviator referred to in *A FABLE.* See also BALL, ALBERT.

MacCullum Faulkner's early spelling of McCallum, a fictional family name in YOKNAPATAWPHA COUNTY. The name appears as MacCallum in Faulkner's third novel, *SARTORIS* (1929), and in *AS I LAY DYING* (1930), but the spelling changed; some characters have both spellings. In these entries, all members of this family are found under "McCallum," with appropriate notes about variant spellings.

McDiarmid Character in *The REIVERS.* He manages the eating room at the railroad depot in PARSHAM and is one of the judges of the race between the horses Coppermine (Lightning) and Acheron.

McEachern, Joe *See* CHRISTMAS, JOE.

McEachern, Mrs. Character in *LIGHT IN AUGUST*. The wife of Simon MCEACHERN, she tries to protect her foster son, Joe CHRISTMAS, from her hard, brutal husband. Joe rejects her kindnesses and steals from her little store of carefully hoarded money.

McEachern, Simon Character in *LIGHT IN AUGUST*. The rugged, vigorous, and Calvinistic foster father of Joe CHRISTMAS, he tries to beat his version of morality into the boy, without success.

Joe fails to learn his catechism. He sells a heifer without permission. He becomes interested in girls and otherwise violates Simon's stern code. One night Simon observes Joe slipping out of the house and follows him on horseback to a dance hall. There he confronts Joe and the waitress Bobbie ALLEN. When Simon calls Bobbie a harlot, Joe strikes him with a chair, leaving him unconscious on the dance floor.

McGinnis, Darrell (Mac) Character in "TURNABOUT" (in *Collected Stories*). An American flyer in France during World War I, he misinterprets Midshipman HOPE's infantile chatter and openly questions his courage.

McGowan, Skeets Minor character in AS I LAY DYING (where his name appears as Skeet MacGowan; he narrates chapter 15), INTRUDER IN THE DUST, *The TOWN*, and *The MANSION*. He is a clerk and soda jerker in Uncle Willy CHRISTIAN's drugstore in JEFFERSON. In *As I Lay Dying*, he takes sexual advantage of Dewey Dell BUNDREN when she comes into the drugstore to buy an abortifacient by convincing her that it is the treatment that will cause an abortion. In *The Mansion*, Skeets's bantering with Tug NIGHTINGALE so angers Tug that he gives Skeets a beating. By the time Tug is subdued, Skeets is in an ambulance on his way to the hospital.

MacGowan, Skeets *See* MCGOWAN, SKEETS.

McKellogg, Colonel Minor character in "TWO SOLDIERS" (in *Collected Stories*). An army officer in MEMPHIS, he arranges for a car and driver to take the little brother of enlistee Pete GRIER home to FRENCHMAN'S BEND.

McKellogg, Mrs. Minor character in the short story "TWO SOLDIERS" (in *Collected Stories*). The wife of Colonel MCKELLOGG, she takes in the enlistee Pete GRIER's little brother (the unnamed narrator of the story) and arranges for his safe return from MEMPHIS to his family in FRENCHMAN'S BEND. Before sending the boy back home, however, she feeds him lunch.

MacKenzie, Shrevlin (Shreve) Quentin COMPSON's HARVARD UNIVERSITY roommate from Canada in *The SOUND AND THE FURY* and *ABSALOM, ABSALOM!* (Though referred to only as Shreve in the latter novel, his last name appears as MacCannon in the novel's genealogy.) With an inquisitive mind probing the nuances of Southern history and with a lively imagination, Shreve actively contributes to Quentin's reconstruction of the Sutpen saga and at times becomes as much a part of the story as Quentin does. In *The Sound and the Fury*, he accompanies Quentin to court on false charges of kidnapping and is later one of the guests at Mrs. BLAND's picnic for her son. When at the picnic Quentin gets into a fight with Gerald BLAND and is beaten up, Shreve ministers to him.

McKie Character in "CREVASSE" (in *Collected Stories*). A British army junior officer in France during World War I, he is killed with 11 others in a cave-in on the front line. Fourteen other members of the unit manage to escape.

McLan Character in "VICTORY" (in *Collected Stories*). He is a soldier in young Alec GRAY's company. Captain Gray punishes him for turning up at an inspection with a dirty rifle.

McLean, Alabama Leroy Falkner (1874–1968) Faulkner's imposing, imperious great-aunt, the youngest child of William C. FALKNER, the Old Colonel, and his second wife Lizzie Vance, known to the family as Aunt 'Bama.

The Old Colonel called her Baby Roy, and she was his favorite. She used to fascinate her young nephew with stories of her near-legendary father: Confederate soldier, railroad builder, novelist. Faulkner corresponded regularly with her throughout his life, and she responded with interest and intense pride in his literary career. She was frugal, but she made Faulkner a gift of $20 just before he set off for Europe in 1925.

Faulkner named his first child, a daughter, after Aunt 'Bama. The baby lived only a few days. Aunt 'Bama herself survived her novelist grandnephew by six years.

McLendon, Captain (Jackson) Character in *LIGHT IN AUGUST* and other works. In a barbershop, he overhears the boasts of the drunken Joe Brown (Lucas BURCH) and discusses Joe CHRISTMAS's bootlegging activities with a man named MAXEY.

McLendon is referred to in *The TOWN* (as Jackson McLendon), *The MANSION*, and the short story "DRY SEPTEMBER." In the last work, he leads a lynch party. In *The Town* and *The Mansion*, he is a cotton buyer who organizes a JEFFERSON, MISSISSIPPI, company of soldiers known as Sartoris Rifles during World War I.

McWilliams Character in *KNIGHT'S GAMBIT* ("Knight's Gambit"). He is the conductor of the railroad that serves JEFFERSON, MISSISSIPPI.

McWillie   Character in *The REIVERS*. The son of Colonel LINSCOMB's chauffeur, he rides the horse Acheron in the races against Coppermine (Lightning).

MacWyrglinchbeath   Central character in the short story "THRIFT." He is a Scotsman whose main motivation is the amassing of wealth. Because he learns that the flyers in the Royal Flying Corps are better paid than infantrymen, he transfers into the RFC and later becomes a pilot. MacWyrglinchbeath becomes famous for his parsimony, which extends to his refusing a commission as a second lieutenant because, after figuring out that with the expenses associated with being an officer, he reckons he will make more money as a sergeant.

Madden, Rufus   One of the soldiers in the company raised in Charleston, Georgia, by Captain GREEN in the novel *SOLDIERS' PAY*. Madden witnesses the killing of Captain Dick POWERS by Dewey BURNEY, but he keeps the information to himself. Madden survives World War I and returns to Georgia, where he meets Mrs. POWERS.

Magda   *See* DEMONT, MARTHE (MAGDA).

Maggie, Miss   *See* VARNER, MRS. (MAGGIE).

Magnolia Rifles   William Clark FALKNER, Faulkner's great-grandfather, raised this volunteer infantry company in Ripley County, Mississippi, at the beginning of the Civil War in 1861.

The company became part of the 2nd Mississippi infantry regiment; Falkner won election as colonel of the regiment in May 1861. The 2nd Mississippi saw action at the first battle of BULL RUN (Manassas) in July 1861.

Mahon, Donald   The wounded and doomed soldier at the center of Faulkner's first novel, *SOLDIERS' PAY*. Lieutenant Mahon, a fighter pilot, was shot down and very badly wounded toward the end of World War I. He is the son of Rector MAHON of Charlestown, Georgia. In addition to having lost much of his memory, Donald has physical injuries that include a withered right arm, damage to his sight, and horrible scarring. Cadet Julian LOWE, the widowed Mrs. Margaret POWERS, and Joe GILLIGAN meet Mahon on a train, and the latter two bring him home to his father.

A man who had little time for society and the social graces, Donald Mahon is one of Faulkner's "natural men," whose relationship to the physical world, women, sex, and other aspects of the human condition is unforced and unself-conscious. In several places, the narrator even describes him as a faun. Before the war, Mahon and EMMY, a Charlestown girl of lower socioeconomic status than Mahon, had had a longstanding friendship, but Emmy's love for Mahon is unrequited after his engagement to Cecily SAUNDERS. Upon Mahon's return, however, Cecily Saunders is unable to bear the thought of marrying him; she marries George FARR instead. When a doctor called in to examine Mahon's eyes tells Mrs. Powers that he will go blind and soon die, Mrs. Powers marries Mahon. She has grown to love him, and instinctively knows that Mahon survived his injuries to come home to marry: once this task is completed he dies in peace.

Mahon, Margaret Powers   *See* POWERS, MRS. MARGARET.

Mahon, Rector (Uncle Joe)   The father of Donald MAHON in SOLDIERS' PAY. An Episcopal minister, Rector Mahon is a big, genial man who refuses to admit to himself that his beloved son will in fact die of his war wounds.

Mallison, Charles Jr. (Chick)   Character in *INTRUDER IN THE DUST*, *KNIGHT'S GAMBIT*, *The TOWN*, *The MANSION*, and the short story "HOG PAWN" (revised by Faulkner for chapter 14 of *The Mansion*). The young nephew of Gavin STEVENS, he is the precocious investigator of Vinson GOWRIE's murder in *Intruder*; Stevens's aide and the narrator of several tales in *Knight's Gambit* (namely, "Monk," "Tomorrow," "An Error in Chemistry"; although not narrated by him, the tale "Knight's Gambit" is told from Mallison's point of view); and an emerging opponent of SNOPESISM in *The Town* (in this novel, the young Mallison narrates nine chapters: 1, 3, 7, 10, 12, 14, 16, 19, 24). In *The Mansion*, Chick returns from a World War II prisoner of war camp to resume the struggle against the Snopes clan.

In *Intruder*, Lucas BEAUCHAMP, who is black, pulls him out of an icy creek and takes him home to his cabin to recuperate. Chick, supposing he is following the rules of Mississippi racial relationships, offers him money. Beauchamp refuses payment and resists Chick's subsequent attempts to pay off what he continues to regard as a debt.

With his young black friend Aleck SANDER, Chick finally settles accounts by undertaking to prove Beauchamp's innocence of the Gowrie murder. Along the way, he gains an awareness of the perversities of Mississippi's law-flouting racial code.

In *The Mansion*, Chick studies law at HARVARD UNIVERSITY and the UNIVERSITY OF MISSISSIPPI, tours Europe at his uncle's insistence, and considers becoming the lover of the radical Linda Snopes KOHL, who has just returned to JEFFERSON, MISSISSIPPI, from Spain. After war breaks out, he joins the Air Force and is shot down over Germany. He arrives home in time to witness the shrewd V. K. RATLIFF engineer the election defeat of the rabble-rousing, race-baiting Senator Clarence Eggleston SNOPES.

In the short story "A NAME FOR THE CITY," which Faulkner revised for *REQUIEM FOR A NUN*, Mallison, as Michael MILLGATE has pointed out, is the unnamed narrator whose source of information is his uncle Gavin (see *The Achievement of William Faulkner* [Lincoln: University of Nebraska Press, 1978], p. 224). For more information, see *Faulkner in the University*, p. 116.

Mallison, Charles Sr. Character in INTRUDER IN THE DUST, *The* TOWN, and *The* MANSION. He is the father of Charles (Chick) MALLISON Jr., one of the boy heroes of *Intruder*. In *The Town*, Charley, as his wife Margaret calls him, is often amused by his brother-in-law Gavin STEVENS's romantic interests and by the way Gavin defends his ideals.

Mallison, Margaret Stevens (Maggie) Character in *INTRUDER IN THE DUST*, *KNIGHT'S GAMBIT*, *The* TOWN, and *The* MANSION. She is Charles MALLISON Sr.'s wife, the mother of Chick MALLISON, and the twin sister of Gavin STEVENS. In *Knight's Gambit*, Maggie is the childhood friend of Gavin's future fiancée, Melisandre Backus Harriss (STEVENS). She is mentioned in *REQUIEM FOR A NUN*.

Mammy *See* SNOPES, VYNIE.

Mandy (1) Character in *SARTORIS*. She cooks for Virginius MacCallum Sr. (see MCCALLUM, ANSE [old]) and his six grown sons.

Mandy (2) Character in "THAT WILL BE FINE" (in *Collected Stories*). She is a cook for the grandfather of the narrator, GEORGIE. Trying to evade the authorities and an irate husband, Uncle RODNEY hides in her cabin for a time.

Mannie Character in GO DOWN, MOSES ("Pantaloon in Black"). RIDER's wife, she dies only six months after their wedding. Rider's grief knows no bounds.

Mannigoe, Nancy A character crucial to the story in "THAT EVENING SUN" and *REQUIEM FOR A NUN*. In "That Evening Sun," in which only her first name is used, Nancy takes in white people's laundry and is sometime kitchen help for the Compsons when their maid DILSEY is sick. A drug addict and occasional prostitute, she is pregnant, probably by the bank cashier and deacon in the Baptist church, Mr. STOVALL, who one day knocks her down in the street and kicks several of her teeth out when she publicly asks him for payment. She is taken to jail, where the next morning she tries to hang herself but is cut down and revived by the jailer. The short story revolves around the Compson children's witnessing Nancy's delusional fear of the dark and absent husband JESUS, who, she believes, will come back at night to kill her because of her marital infidelity and pregnancy.

In *Requiem for a Nun*, Nancy is nanny to Temple Drake STEVENS's two children. In scene 1 of act 1 of the novel, Nancy, described as a tramp, drunkard, and casual prostitute, is found guilty of the murder of Temple's six-month-old daughter and is to be hanged for the crime, a result of her desperate attempt to prevent Temple from leaving her husband and home for Pete (3), the younger brother of her late lover, RED, in SANCTUARY. In choosing a dope fiend as a servant, Temple shows a persistent attraction to evil and sees in Nancy a person with whom she is comfortable conversing. However, in a discussion prior to the murder (in scene 2 of act 2 of the novel), Nancy angers Temple by bluntly confronting her with the possible fate of the child if Temple leaves her husband: ". . . maybe taking her with you will be just as easy, at least until the first time you write Mr Gowan or your pa for money and they dont send it as quick as your new man thinks they ought to, and he throws you and the baby both out" (p. 161).

To Nancy's anguished thinking, Temple's daughter is as good as dead, and by smothering the baby in her cradle Nancy believes she is merely stopping a cycle of evil that began in *Sanctuary*. Through Nancy, Temple, who is well aware of the consequences of her past deeds, is forced to face her own responsibility and guilt, but Temple's direct appeal to the governor for a stay in Nancy's execution is unsuccessful.

In response to a question at the University of Virginia, Faulkner identified Nancy as the nun in the novel's title (*Faulkner in the University*, p. 196).

Mannock, Edward (1887–1918) Historical aviator referred to in *A FABLE*. See BALL, ALBERT.

The Mansion The third novel of the SNOPES TRILOGY, published by RANDOM HOUSE on November 13, 1959, two and a half years after the second volume, *The* TOWN (May 1957), and 19 years after the first volume, *The* HAMLET (April 1940). Like the first two volumes of the trilogy, *The Mansion* is dedicated to Phil STONE, Faulkner's close friend. Chapter 13 of *The Mansion* is a revision of "By the People," a short story first published in *Mademoiselle* 41 (October 1955). When writing *The Mansion*, Faulkner refashioned "HOG PAWN," a short story posthumously published in *UNCOLLECTED STORIES OF WILLIAM FAULKNER*, and included it in chapter 14 of the novel.

To this third volume, Faulkner added a prefatory note in which he informs the reader that discrepancies and contradictions in the novel are the result of the author's growth over three decades. He explains that he now knows his characters better and knows "more about the human heart and its dilemma" than he did when he first began the trilogy. Several months before its publication, Albert ERSKINE of Random House and the Faulkner textual critic James B. MERIWETHER went through *The Mansion* to reconcile discrepancies between this volume and the first two novels of the trilogy. In a February 10, 1959, letter to Erskine, Faulkner expresses his gratitude to him and offers a few general guidelines governing the correction of inconsistencies (see *Selected Letters of William Faulkner,* pp. 423–24).

The Mansion is divided into three major parts, with 18 chapters. The first section, "Mink" (chapters 1–5), covers the period in the life of Mink SNOPES from 1907, the year of his troubles with Jack HOUSTON, until his release from prison in September 1946. In 1908, Mink was convicted of killing Houston and sent to the Mississippi State Penitentiary at PARCHMAN. There are three narrators in this first section: omniscient (chapters 1, 2, and 5); V. K. RATLIFF, the sewing machine salesman, (chapter 3); and Montgomery Ward SNOPES, Mink's cousin, (chapter 4).

The second section of the novel, "Linda" (chapters 6–11), focuses on Linda Snopes KOHL and her life in JEFFERSON, MISSISSIPPI, after her return from Spain, where her husband, Barton KOHL, fighting for the Loyalists in the Spanish Civil War, died when his aircraft was shot down. In 1927, the year her mother, Eula Varner SNOPES, committed suicide, Linda left Jefferson for New York City, where she met and lived with Kohl for several years before marrying him. In August 1937, she returned to Jefferson from Spain as a widow whose eardrums were shattered by the sound of a shell that exploded while she was driving an ambulance; the accident left her deaf. This section also touches upon the complex relationship between Linda and Gavin STEVENS, and upon her life with Flem. There are three narrators (the same three as in *The Town*) in the second section of the novel: Ratliff (chapters 6, 7); Charles (Chick) MALLISON Jr., Gavin Stevens's nephew and a former prisoner of war during World War II (chapters 8, 9, 11); and Gavin Stevens, the county attorney (chapter 10).

The third part, "Flem" (chapters 12–18), returns to Mink and covers the days immediately following his pardon from prison on September 26, 1946. During this time Mink purchases a $10 pistol in Memphis and returns to Jefferson to kill his cousin Flem SNOPES.

The basic story line of *The Mansion* revolves around Mink and his resolve to kill Flem for not having come to his assistance when on trial for the murder of Houston. The single thought of avenging Flem's betrayal of blood kinship and clan loyalty sustains Mink throughout his 38 years at the state penitentiary; nothing will deter him from accomplishing that end, even the prospect of being hanged for the crime.

Whether Flem could have intervened to help or not does not matter to Mink, who simply sees Flem's failure to help as disloyalty. While serving time at Parchman for bootlegging, Montgomery Ward SNOPES, bribed by Flem, persuades Mink to escape in a woman's dress and sunbonnet and tries to convince him that Flem is looking out for his welfare. The abortive attempt is a ludicrous failure, and Flem in fact intended it to add time to Mink's sentence. Mink holds no bitterness against Montgomery Ward, and in the warden's office drily remarks that Flem "hadn't ought to used that dress" (p. 86).

Mink is certain that the day will come to avenge the wrong committed against him. It is a matter of patience and waiting, and in stoical anticipation of that day, he views the present moment as an extraneous reality that no longer matters; it is something to be endured. In his response to the warden's remark that he has been in prison for three years—"'Have I? . . . I aint kept count'" (p. 51)—Mink reveals an attitude of extreme indifference. When, 33 years later, the day nears, Mink is absolutely convinced as though by divine decree that the rusted and virtually dysfunctional pistol he bought to shoot his cousin will fire. When the day finally comes, the gun does not fire at first, but Mink's faith is undiminished. His second attempt is successful.

Linda Snopes plays a major role in Flem's death: She is responsible for getting Mink pardoned. She knows that once he leaves Parchman he will return to Jefferson to avenge the wrong Flem committed and therefore also avenge the wrong Flem has done Linda, her mother, and the many others whom he exploited throughout his rapacious life. Immediately after shooting Flem, Mink is startled to hear that Linda is behind him, and in a panic throws his pistol at her, which she catches and gives back to him as she helps him escape. It is not until the last chapter (chapter 18) that Gavin Stevens, the romantic idealist and county prosecutor whose duty it is to protect even a citizen as despicable as Flem, realizes what Linda has done. Stevens is forced to confront and accept his own moral vulnerability and weakness when he and V. K. Ratliff find Mink—not to arrest him, but to give him the money that Linda wants him to have.

In the novel, Faulkner portrays Mink as a man of honor and pride and as a character who elicits the reader's sympathies. The narrator in the opening pages of the novel explains that Mink is a victim of bad luck. In the last chapter of the first section, chapter 5, the narration ends with Mink's reaffirming thought: "*Not justice; I never asked that; jest fairness, that's all*" (p. 106). Even though Mink is first seen in the novel as a convicted murderer who contemplates a second murder, Faulkner presents him as the hero of the novel. Mink does not kill Houston, any more than he will Flem, for the sake of personal profit or gain, but instead for honor and from a deep sense of wounded pride. What causes his anger against Houston is not having to pay Houston for feeding his cow through the winter but instead the one-dollar fee that the court added to the cost. It is the insult that sparks Mink's deed.

In the confrontation between Mink and Houston, some critics see Faulkner touching upon the universal conditions of human life and upon the forces that cause struggle and the need for endurance. If Mink evokes sympathy in the reader, he does so because he is willing to defend his integrity and to stand against the forces of life that give one an accidental advantage over another. Mink, in his own way, clearly and powerfully understands the insult against the dignity of his person. But in presenting him as a man of honor, Faulkner does not attempt to hide serious flaws in his character. Mink is mean to his family, and while in prison he completely dismisses them from his life. His lawyer sees him as a snake. But the more the reader understands Mink's attitude and his deep sense of pride, the more the reader can sympathize with him and understand the motive behind his killing Flem, a man who represents nothing but greed.

In a review of *The Mansion* titled "The Last of the Snopeses," in the November 14, 1959, issue of the *Saturday Review,* the critic Granville Hicks remarked, "one feels [in Faulkner's novels after 1948] strength of will and mastery of technique rather than the irresistible creative power that surged forth so miraculously in the earlier work" (p. 21). Many other readers share this view and find the novel lacking in structural unity and thematically diffuse.

For further information, see *Selected Letters of William Faulkner.*

Manuel Street   Fictional street in the red-light district of MEMPHIS. Miss Reba RIVERS's brothel is on Manuel Street in *SANCTUARY.* (Faulkner moves Reba's place to CATALPA STREET in *The REIVERS.*) Manuel Street also figures as the tenderloin district in *REQUIEM FOR A NUN.*

The Marble Faun   Faulkner's first published book, a pastoral poem of 19 eclogues, with a prologue and epilogue, and with a preface by Faulkner's lifelong friend and onetime mentor, Phil STONE. It was published by the FOUR SEAS COMPANY, Boston, in December 1924. One early reviewer, John McClure, writing in the *New Orleans Times-Picayune Magazine* (January 25, 1925, p. 16), commented that the best a young poet can achieve is failure with honor. In his opinion, this is the case with Faulkner, but the book is "rich in promise" and "successful in part." He is "a born poet, with remarkable ability," McClure observes, and, although the poem is not a complete success, it "contains scores of excellent passages." Years later, the critic Cleanth BROOKS, although a bit harsher in his assessment, commented that the poem in several ways is "awkward and stumbling" but "there are occasional few passages of authentic poetry." The major shortcoming of *The Marble Faun,* Brooks argues, is that "the young poet is hag-ridden by the necessity of finding rhymes, and sometimes is forced into quasi-nonsense in his effort to come up with a rhyme. The meter fares not much better: often a line is metrically broken-backed" (*William Faulkner: Toward Yoknapatawpha and Beyond,* p. 6). Faulkner even judged himself a "failed poet." At the University of Virginia in 1957, for instance, he remarked: "I've often thought that I wrote the novels because I found I could-

n't write the poetry, that maybe I wanted to be a poet, maybe I think of myself as a poet, and I failed at that, I couldn't write poetry, so I did the next best thing" (*Faulkner in the University,* p. 4; also see *Lion in the Garden,* edited by James B. MERIWETHER and Michael MILLGATE, p. 217). In a technical sense, Faulkner may have been a failed poet—that is, not a craftsman of verse—but he more than compensated in his prose for any failure, a prose extraordinarily poetic and suffused with a commanding cadence and rhythm.

Though Faulkner wrote most of the verses in *The Marble Faun* in 1919, a few years before they were published, he arranged them into a seasonal pattern and cycle of days and nights for their publication. The plaintive voice in the poems is that of the marble faun, mourning his imprisonment to dreams and sighs for things he knows, "yet cannot know" (prologue, line 32). The faun's reflections on beauty, art, nature, and youth within a pastoral setting unmistakably reveal Faulkner's indebtedness especially to romantic and symbolist poets of the late 19th century. Indebtedness to Keats's "Ode on a Grecian Urn" is also apparent, but unlike that ode, which elevates art above nature, *The Marble Faun,* as Brooks has pointed out, places life above art: "it is the inferiority of art to life that is stressed—'wild ecstasy' that has become frozen into a 'cold pastoral,' the unaging faun who has been turned into inanimate marble" (p. 5). *The Marble Faun* has been reexamined by various critics and particularly by Judith L. Sensibar in *The Origins of Faulkner's Art.*

Marchand   Minor character in *PYLON.* A Cajun, Marchand works for Matt ORD's aircraft company. In Ord's absence, Marchand sells Ord's unsafe airplane to Roger SHUMANN and the REPORTER.

Marders, Mrs.   Character in *SARTORIS.* She is a friend of Belle MITCHELL and a regular visitor to her house.

Marengo   *See* STROTHER, RINGO.

Markey, Robert   Character in *KNIGHT'S GAMBIT* ("Knight's Gambit"). A MEMPHIS lawyer and politician, he studied at Heidelberg with Gavin STEVENS. At Stevens's request, Markey has Max HARRISS shadowed while Harriss is in Memphis.

The Marionettes   A play Faulkner wrote in the fall of 1920 for a UNIVERSITY OF MISSISSIPPI drama group called the Marionettes. A one-act verse drama showing the influence of the Symbolist movement of the late 19th century, it draws on elements of commedia dell'arte, or masked comedy, to relate a story of seduction and abandonment.

Faulkner produced six or eight hand-lettered copies of the play and illustrated it with 10 drawings by his own hand. Four copies survive. The biographer Frederick Karl judges *The Marionettes* not playable, and regards it as "a stillborn poem with strong visual effects." Faulkner withdrew from the university not long after completing the play.

Edited with an introduction by Noel POLK, *The Marionettes: A Play in One Act* was published by the University Press of Virginia in 1977. (For more information, see *Selected Letters of William Faulkner,* p. 89, and Lothar Hönnighausen's essay "Faulkner's Graphic Work in Historical Context" in *Faulkner: International Perspectives,* pp. 139–73.)

Marsh, Uncle   Character in "TWO SOLDIERS" (in *Collected Stories*). The brother of Pete GRIER's mother, he was wounded in France during World War I.

Martel, General   A former commander of the OLD GENERAL in *A FABLE*. Martel does not appear in the novel in person, but is referred to in a conversation as one whose signature was required on a citation for the old general when he was a younger officer. Seemingly supernatural occurrences twice prevent this action.

Martha   Character in *IF I FORGET THEE, JERUSALEM* ("The Wild Palms"). The wife of the doctor whose Gulf Coast beach house Harry WILBOURNE and Charlotte RITTENMEYER rent, she is more interested in her tenants' ability to pay the rent than in whether they are married. While her husband rages at Harry for what he regards as his immorality, Martha matter-of-factly brews and offers him a cup of coffee.

Marthe   *See* DEMONT, MARTHE (MAGDA).

Martin, Dal   The main character in the short story "THE BIG SHOT" and a major character in the story's revision, "DULL TALE." Illiterate and uneducated, Martin rises from poverty as a sharecropper's son to a wealthy political boss and crooked contractor in MEMPHIS. His rise in status has its origins in the disdainful treatment he received as a child from a wealthy landowner. In his dealings, Martin employs and protects the bootleggers POPEYE and GOVELLI. One of his obsessions is to seek a better, more sophisticated and respectable life than his own for his daughter Wrennie. (Martin's character foreshadows that of Thomas SUTPEN in *ABSALOM, ABSALOM!* and of Flem SNOPES in the SNOPES TRILOGY.)

Martin, Miss Laverne (Miss Wrennie)   The spoiled daughter of Dal MARTIN, she is a character in the short stories "THE BIG SHOT" (where she is referred to as Miss Wrennie) and "DULL TALE." She foreshadows the character of Temple Drake (STEVENS) in *SANCTUARY* and *REQUIEM FOR A NUN*. Like Temple, she has a reckless personality. In "The Big Shot," Miss Wrennie is run over and killed by POPEYE before she can go to the Chickasaw Guards Ball, which her father had arranged for her to attend by bribing Dr. BLOUNT. In Faulkner's retelling of the story in "Dull Tale," she goes to the Chickasaw Guards Ball but does not enjoy the experience, as predicted by Dr. Blount.

Martin, Wrennie   *See* MARTIN, MISS LAVERNE.

Martino, Dr. Jules   Character in "DOCTOR MARTINO" (in *Collected Stories*). An old man from St. Louis with a defective heart that could fail at any time, his annual summertime friendship with Louise KING, whom he has known since she was a girl, gives him the courage to live.

In turn, Louise admires his fortitude and falls under his spell. Her mother, fearing a threat to Louise's engagement with the wealthy Mississippian Hubert JARROD, hoodwinks Dr. Martino into writing a note that frees the girl from his hold. Not long afterward, the doctor is found dead on his favorite bench at Lily CRANSTON's resort.

Marya   Older sister of Marthe (DEMONT) and half sister of Corporal STEFAN in *A FABLE*. Marya is described as looking younger than her sister because she is to a degree mentally deficient, but she has good instincts about the actions of others and is a true support to her family.

Mason   In *REQUIEM FOR A NUN,* one of the legendary gang leaders referred to as part of the early history of YOKNAPATAWPHA COUNTY.

Massey, Linton R. (unknown)   A Virginian of the country squire class, he admired Faulkner and began collecting his work in 1930. Massey, his wife, Mary, and the Faulkners became close friends during Faulkner's UNIVERSITY OF VIRGINIA years in the 1950s.

In 1959, Massey organized a comprehensive exhibit in Charlottesville, Virginia, of Faulkner's works over a period of 40 years. Faulkner himself gave the exhibit its title: "Man Working."

Matthew   Character in *KNIGHT'S GAMBIT* ("Hand upon the Waters"). With IKE, POSE, and Jim Blake, he helps carry away Lonnie GRINNUP's body for burial.

Maurier   Character in *MOSQUITOES*. A one-time plantation overseer, he makes or steals a fortune during the Civil War, enabling him to win the hand of Patricia MAURIER. She dutifully gives up the boy she loves to marry him.

Maurier, Harrison   One of Cecily SAUNDERS's beaux referred to in passing in *SOLDIERS' PAY*. He is from Atlanta.

Maurier, Patricia   Character in *MOSQUITOES*. The wealthy widow of the Civil War profiteer MAURIER, she gathers together a party of artists for a cruise aboard her yacht, the *Nausikaa*. Mrs. Maurier seeks out the company of artists without really understanding what they are about. She ultimately discloses the tragedy of her life: She gave up the boy she loved to marry Maurier's fortune.

Maxey   Character in *LIGHT IN AUGUST*. In the barbershop, Captain MCLENDON and Maxey overhear Joe Brown's (Lucas BURCH) drunken boasts about his hijacking of a liquor truck with bootlegger Joe Christmas.

In the short story "HAIR," Maxey owns the barbershop where Henry STRIBLING (Hawkshaw) works.

Maycox, Judge   Character in *INTRUDER IN THE DUST*. Gavin STEVENS hopes to persuade the judge to issue an order for the opening of Vinson GOWRIE's grave.

Mayday   A hand-lettered book that Faulkner wrote, illustrated, bound, and dedicated to Helen BAIRD, with whom Faulkner was in love, and whom he wanted to marry, although she did not have the same feelings toward him. Faulkner dated the book "27 January, 1926." Edited with an introduction by Carvel COLLINS, *Mayday* was published in 1976. Collins comments that Faulkner gave Baird "the only known copy" (p. 3).

A fable of a young knight, Sir Galwyn of Arthgyl, *Mayday* is a story about a young man's search for the woman he is to love. After dismissing the three princesses he meets on his journey—Yseult, Elys, Aelia—the disillusioned Sir Galwyn finally encounters the woman he desires: Death. In his perceptive introduction, Collins discusses the historical and literary context behind the composition of *Mayday* and its place within Faulkner's writings. Collins also convincingly shows parallels between Sir Galwyn in this work and Quentin COMPSON in *The SOUND AND THE FURY*. One obvious parallel is their suicides by drowning.

Maydew   Character in *GO DOWN, MOSES* ("Pantaloon in Black"). He is the sheriff who arrests RIDER for the murder of the sawmill night watchman BIRDSONG.

Mayes, Will   Character in "DRY SEPTEMBER" (in *Collected Stories*). A JEFFERSON, MISSISSIPPI, mob lynches him over Hawkshaw's (Henry STRIBLING's) protest when Mayes, who is Black, is wrongly accused of assaulting a white spinster, Minnie COOPER.

Meadowfill, Essie   *See* SMITH, ESSIE MEADOWFILL.

Meadowfill, Mrs.   Otis MEADOWFILL's wife, and the mother of Essie Meadowfill (SMITH), in Faulkner's novel *The MANSION*. She is described as a "gray drudge of a wife" (p. 328).

Meadowfill, Otis   In *The MANSION*, an unfriendly, cantankerous, and nasty man in JEFFERSON, MISSISSIPPI. Until his one child, Essie Meadowfill (SMITH), helps support the household, Meadowfill does his own grocery shopping at side-street stores where he looks for leftovers at bargain prices. When a paralytic old lady neighbor dies, he immediately buys her wheelchair to sit in to guard his property against any trespassers, including his neighbor Orestes SNOPES's hogs, which he shoots at daily with tiny shot cartridges. When an oil company wants to buy his plot of land and the adjacent lot legally belonging to Flem SNOPES, Meadowfill refuses to sell, thus preventing the company from building a gas station. Eventually the town's attorney, Gavin STEVENS, intervenes, settling the dispute in favor of the Meadowfills.

Meeks, Doc   In *The MANSION*, a salesman of patent medicine.

Melisandre, Cousin (Melisandre Backus)   Character in "MY GRANDMOTHER MILLARD AND GENERAL BEDFORD FORREST AND THE BATTLE OF HARRYKIN CREEK" (in *Collected Stories*). A young girl living on Sartoris plantation during the Civil War, she retires into the privy with the family silver when the Yankees arrive. The Federals knock over the privy, or backhouse, but the dashing Lieutenant Philip S. BACKHOUSE arrives to chase them off. Melisandre cannot see her way clear to marrying him, however, until his name is converted to Backus.

Memphis   City in southwestern Tennessee, the state's largest. It is an important river port, and a leading cotton, livestock, manufacturing and transportation center of the mid-South. Andrew Jackson and others founded the settlement on a bluff overlooking the Mississippi River in 1819, and it was an important commercial center by the time of the Civil War. Union forces occupied Memphis in June 1862.

Corrupt Yankees and Southerners traded in contraband cotton during the Civil War; Faulkner's great-grandfather, William C. FALKNER, was alleged to have sought his fortune by running cotton through the Union lines. Memphis served as a base for federal offensives into northern Mississippi. The Confederate General Nathan Bedford FORREST carried out a famous raid into Memphis in August 1864.

Faulkner's grandfather and father were treated for alcoholism at the KEELEY INSTITUTE near the city. As a boy, Billy Falkner had his first glimpse of the Mississippi River from a Memphis streetcar.

Mississippians regarded Memphis, only 70 miles northwest of OXFORD, MISSISSIPPI, as a center of sophistication. Faulkner went there as a young man to gamble, drink, and to visit blues clubs along Beale Street. His friend Philip STONE introduced him to the city's bordellos and its colorful gangster underworld, material he exploited later in SANCTUARY and *The* REIVERS.

Memphis became notorious in the 1920s as "the Murder Capital of the U.S.A." Parts of *Sanctuary* are set in the city's violent and colorful tenderloin. The fictional POPEYE Vitelli is modeled partly on John Revinsky, who went to prison for the murder of a Memphis brothel madam, and partly on Popeye Pumphrey, a well-known Memphis gambler and bootlegger of the Prohibition era. In *The Reivers,* Lucius (Loosh) PRIEST describes his first view of a section the city's red light district, which ran along Gayoso and Mulberry Streets (p. 97).

Faulkner took flying lessons at the Memphis airport beginning in 1933. Later in the 1930s, he regularly took his wife, Estelle, and daughter, Jill, to Memphis, where they would stay in a suite at the Peabody Hotel after an exhilarating day of flying in the novelist's Waco cabin cruiser.

Memphis Commercial Appeal   Leading daily newspaper of southwestern Tennessee and northern Mississippi. The Falkners read the *Commercial Appeal* regularly in OXFORD, MISSISSIPPI; Faulkner could read and thoroughly understand the paper's sports page before he went to school.

The newspaper covered the novelist's rise in the 1930s and chronicled his doings thereafter. Faulkner published a series of letters to the editor—actually, short essays—on racial issues in the *Commercial Appeal* in the 1950s.

In a letter dated March 26, 1950, he protested a Mississippi court's decision to sentence a white man to life in prison for the murder of three black children, arguing that the killer would have been put to death had the children been white.

Faulkner's essay "On Fear: The South in Labor" first appeared as a letter to the editor of the Memphis paper on April 3, 1955. Another important topical essay, "To Claim Freedom is Not Enough," saw print first in the *Commercial Appeal* on November 11, 1955.

The letters, with their liberal (for the South) views on racial issues, brought widespread condemnation of "Weeping Willie Faulkner" in his home region.

Meriwether, James B.   Teacher. As a professor at the University of Texas in the 1950s, he established himself as a leading Faulkner bibliographer and textual scholar. Meriwether assisted RANDOM HOUSE editors in reconciling discrepancies between *The* HAMLET and *The* TOWN, the first two novels in the SNOPES TRILOGY, in 1957. He performed the same service for the third Snopes novel, *The* MANSION, in 1959.

Meriwether built up the University of Texas library's holdings in Faulkner manuscripts and other material. He negotiated the purchase of typescripts and other material from the novelist's longtime friend Philip STONE, a transaction that left Faulkner angry and embittered. Meriwether published the first book-length biography of Faulkner, *The Literary Career of William Faulkner,* in 1972.

Merridew, Mrs.   Character in "UNCLE WILLY" (in *Collected Stories*). She is the leader of the group of JEFFERSON, MISSISSIPPI, townspeople that tries to cure Uncle Willy CHRISTIAN of his dependence on drugs. Mrs. Merridew's lemonade, fried chicken, and ice cream fail to cure the addicted druggist.

Metcalf   Character in *LIGHT IN AUGUST.* He is the jailer in MOTTSTOWN. Mrs. HINES appeals to him to allow her to see Joe CHRISTMAS, who is being held there.

Metro-Goldwyn-Mayer   Hollywood movie studio. Samuel Goldwyn (1882–1974) and Louis B. Mayer (1885–1957) merged their independent production companies in 1925 to form MGM. Faulkner went to work as a scriptwriter at the Culver City studio in May 1932 on a six-week contract paying $500 a week. Faulkner had great difficulty adapting his talents to writing for the screen, nor did he care for California.

The director Howard HAWKS tutored Faulkner in the film arts, and on his recommendation MGM renewed the novelist's initial contract.

The studio bought the film rights to Faulkner's novel *The* UNVANQUISHED in 1938 for $25,000, with $19,000 going to Faulkner. In July 1948, MGM paid $50,000 for the rights to INTRUDER IN THE DUST. Faulkner's share came to $40,000—sufficient to free him from his detested association with the WARNER BROTHERS studio.

MGM came to Oxford in the winter of 1949 to film *Intruder.* The movie had its premiere in the Lyric Theater in Oxford in October of that year.

In 1957, Harold OBER, Faulkner's agent, learned that MGM had decided to exercise its option on *The Unvanquished.* Ober told Faulkner he could probably get him $50,000 to $75,000 for writing the screenplay. Now financially secure, Faulkner declined to pursue the matter.

Middleton, Captain   American officer in *A* FABLE who is confronted with Corporal STEFAN. He states that a man identical to Stefan was in his command but died and was buried at sea in 1917.

Midgleston, Martha   Character in "BLACK MUSIC" (in *Collected Stories*). She is the wife of an architectural draftsman who fancies himself a faun. When her husband is presumed dead, she collects his insurance money, remarries, and moves to Park Avenue in New York City.

Midgleston, Wilfred   Character in "BLACK MUSIC" (in *Collected Stories*). A middle-aged architectural draftsman assigned to help design a group of buildings in the Grecian style for a wealthy financier named Carleton VAN DYMING, he has a strange experience in which he imagines himself a faun. Naked and carrying a tin whistle, he chases Van Dyming's wife through the woods of their Virginia estate.

Midgleston disappears and is presumed dead. In fact, he turns up alive and in dire poverty in Latin America, living in an attic above a cantina with a roll of tar paper for a bed.

Mike An offstage character in *The SOUND AND THE FURY*. Gerald BLAND, who beats up Quentin COMPSON, is learning to box at Mike's gym in town (Cambridge).

Milhaud, Madame Proprietor of a bistro where the British aviators used to eat and drink near the aerodrome in *A FABLE*.

Millard, Grandfather Character in "MY GRANDMOTHER MILLARD AND GENERAL BEDFORD FORREST AND THE BATTLE OF HARRYKIN CREEK" (in *Collected Stories*). He is the late husband of Granny Rosa MILLARD.

Millard, Miss Rosa (Granny) Character in *The UNVANQUISHED* and other works (some of which were revised for the novel). The canny and indomitable mother-in-law of Colonel John SARTORIS and the grandmother of young Bayard SARTORIS (3), she manages the Sartoris plantation during the Civil War, when the master is away with the Confederate army.

As the fighting engulfs north Mississippi, Miss Rosa is forced to bend her notions of right and wrong, though never merely for her own benefit. With Ab SNOPES, she tricks the Federals into supplying her with a small fortune in horses and mules, then effaces the U.S. brands and sells them back to the enemy. With the proceeds, she aids the poor hill folk of YOKNAPATAWPHA COUNTY.

The bushwhacker GRUMBY kills her in a dispute over stolen horses. Young Bayard avenges her by tracking down and killing Grumby and nailing his severed hand to his grandmother's wooden grave marker.

Miss Rosa appears in the short stories "MY GRANDMOTHER MILLARD AND GENERAL BEDFORD FORREST AND THE BATTLE OF HARRYKIN CREEK" and "SHALL NOT PERISH." Her "horse-and-mule partnership" with Ab Snopes is also referred to in *The HAMLET*.

Miller Alcoholic patient of Dr. HILL in the short story "MR. ACARIUS." He arranges for liquor to be smuggled into the clinic in the brassiere of Miss Judy LESTER, a visitor.

Miller, Brother Character in "UNCLE WILLY" (in *Collected Stories*). He teaches the adult Bible classes the drug-addicted Uncle Willy CHRISTIAN is forced to attend.

Miller, Mrs. In *SOLDIERS' PAY*, Mrs. Miller is a seamstress in Charlestown, Georgia. EMMY lives with her for a short time after leaving her father's house. Rector MAHON takes Emmy in as a servant.

Millgate, Michael (unknown) Scholar. He is the author of the critical studies *William Faulkner* (1961), *The Achievement of William Faulkner* (1966), and *Faulkner's Place* (1997). In other works, he has painstakingly detailed Faulkner's seriocomic military career as a Royal Air Force cadet in Canada in 1918.

Millgate also is an authority on the life and works of the English novelist Thomas Hardy. His *Thomas Hardy: A Biography* appeared in 1982, and he edited with others a multivolume collection of Hardy's letters published between 1978 and 1988.

Mink In *The SOUND AND THE FURY*, the driver from the livery stable in JEFFERSON, MISSISSIPPI, whom Jason COMPSON IV gets to drive a hack that he rides in with Caudace (Caddy) COMPSON's infant child, Quentin. Although Jason's sister pays him $100 to show her the child, Jason orders Mink to speed up as he holds his infant niece to the window and Caddy leaps forward to see her. For his service, Jason buys Mink a couple of cigars.

Minnie Character in *The REIVERS*. Miss Reba's (see RIVERS, Reba) black maid, she has a stunning removable gold tooth, a bauble she saved for three years to acquire. It has a mesmerizing effect on men. OTIS, the visiting nephew of Miss Corrie (Everbe Corinthia HOGGANBECK), one of Miss Reba's girls, manages to steal the tooth; young Lycurgus BRIGGINS ultimately recovers it for Minnie. She appears in *The MANSION*, where her lazy husband, LUDUS (1), steals money from her, and when he is confronted he injures her ear with a flatiron. Minnie also appears in *SANCTUARY*.

Minnie Maude The 22-year-old ticket seller at the Rex Theater across the street from the express office in the short story "A DANGEROUS MAN." In her conversation with the unnamed narrator of the story, she divulges that Mrs. BOWMAN is having an illicit affair with a traveling insurance salesman named WALL.

"Mississippi" Essay presenting a fictionalized memoir of the Falkner family's native place, published in *Holiday* magazine in 1954. The editors of the glossy travel and leisure magazine approached Faulkner about writing the essay in 1952, offering $2,000 for a 7,500-word piece.

As critics have noted, Faulkner used the dramatic method of *REQUIEM FOR A NUN* (1951) in the essay, opening with a prologue that recounts the history of Mississippi up to the time of the author's childhood. From there, "Mississippi" becomes autobiographical, with Faulkner appearing as "the boy." His African-American servants Ned BARNETT and Caroline BARR (Mammy Callie) assume important roles in the narrative. Faulkner freely conceded that he introduced fictional details when he thought they would improve the story.

The concluding sections of "Mississippi" deal with Mammy Callie's decline and death and foreshadow Faulkner's own passing—nine years remained to him when he finished the essay in March 1953. Although he emphasized that he hated the racial intolerance, injustice, and inequality that mar so much of Mississippi's history, he ended with an expression of love for his home country. In a passage that recalls Quentin COMPSON in THE SOUND AND THE FURY (1929), Faulkner wrote that he loved Mississippi not for its virtues but in spite of its faults.

Holiday published "Mississippi," which came in 3,000 words longer than the contract had stipulated, in April 1954.

Mississippian, The   Student newspaper at the UNIVERSITY OF MISSISSIPPI, an early outlet for Faulkner's poetry, prose fiction, and criticism. His revised poem "L'Apres-Midi d'un Faune" appeared in the student paper October 1919. Faulkner published his first piece of fiction, the short story "Landing in Luck," in *The Mississippian* on November 26, 1919.

Nine Faulkner poems appeared in the paper during the spring semester of 1920. The poems provoked student rivals to produce a series of parodies of Faulkner's literary style and personal manner, among them "Une Ballade d'une Vache Perdue," describing the lost and wandering heifer Betsey.

The ballad inspired Faulkner's delayed-reaction joke short story "AFTERNOON OF A COW," attributed to the fictional author-critic Ernest V. TRUEBLOOD. Written in 1937, it was published a decade later.

Mississippi Delta   A flat, alluvial plain between the Mississippi and Yazoo Rivers and the most distinctive geographical region of Mississippi. Big cotton planters in the Delta counties dominated the state's political life until the early 20th century, which saw the rise of the hill country small farmer class. Faulkner's paternal grandfather, J. W. T. FALKNER, aligned himself politically with these populist challengers of Delta power.

During Faulkner's youth, patches of Delta wilderness still survived within 30 miles of OXFORD, MISSISSIPPI: flat, low-lying, densely forested country that sustained populations of deer, bear, and other game. His friend Philip STONE introduced him to the Delta wilderness. For a number of years Faulkner took part in the regular November deer hunt from Stone's father's hunting camp near Batesville on the edge of the wilderness.

By the late 1930s the elder Stone had sold off his several-thousand-acre hunting reserve to the timber companies, which had clear-cut the land and sold it off to farmers. The annual deer hunt moved 120 miles southwest to the Big Sunflower River in the Delta, near Anguilla, Mississippi.

Faulkner translated his experiences in the Delta wilderness into fiction in a series of hunting stories. In "The Bear" (see GO DOWN, MOSES) Faulkner records Ike MCCASLIN's memory of his first experience of the BIG BOTTOM, the wilderness area along the TALLAHATCHIE RIVER, at the age of 10. Later in the story, Major DE SPAIN sells off the timber rights to his wilderness kingdom to a Memphis lumber company. On that year's hunt, an older Ike sees "with shocked and grieved amazement" the first consequences of the sale: a nearly finished planing mill, vast stacks of steel rails and crossties, a complex of corrals for mules, and a tent city for the crews that would clear the woods.

In *The REIVERS*, the site of de Spain's camp is described as a drainage district, a one-time wilderness now "tame with corn and cotton."

"The Old People," "A BEAR HUNT," "RACE AT MORNING," and a revised version of "The Bear" were repackaged and published as *BIG WOODS* in 1954.

Mississippi Poems   A minor collection of poems Faulkner presented in typescript to his friend Myrtle Ramey in December 1924. Faulkner revised eight of the 12 poems to include in *A Green Bough*, published in 1933. With an introduction by Joseph BLOTNER and an afterword by Louis Daniel BRODSKY, *Mississippi Poems* was published posthumously in 1979 by Yoknapatawpha Press, Oxford, Mississippi, and reissued in 1981 by Tulane University, New Orleans.

"Miss Zilphia Gant" *(Uncollected Stories)*   A short story centering on the development of the title character, Miss Zilphia GANT, whose mother (Mrs. GANT) raises her as a virtual prisoner. In reality, the main character is Zilphia's mother, who passes on to her daughter her growing hatred of men and distrust of almost everyone. The genesis of this misanthropy is Mrs. Gant's horse-trader husband, Jim GANT, who leaves her with their baby, Zilphia, for another woman. Jim sends his hulking halfwit assistant to tell his wife that he is never coming back. When Mrs. Gant tracks down her unfaithful husband and his mistress in Memphis, she kills them with a borrowed pistol.

She purchases a dress shop and lives in a small room behind it, never letting Zilphia out until it is time for the girl to attend school. Even then she is reluctant to allow Zilphia any freedom. When Mrs. Gant finds Zilphia, now a teenager, lying with a boy in the woods, she takes her out of school and confines her once more to the dress shop. Zilphia becomes a seemingly docile young woman, while her mother grows less and less womanlike with each day. When the dress shop is painted, Zilphia falls in love with the painter. They elope and are married before a justice of the peace. The itinerant painter urges Zilphia to go away with him and never see her awful mother again, but Zilphia cannot. Hand in hand, the newlyweds go back to the house where Mrs. Gant asserts her fierce power, driving off her son-in-law and imprisoning her daughter. Mrs. Gant dies two days later, and Zilphia starts running her mother's business. Expecting to hear from her husband, Zilphia waits six months, but receives no word. She hires a detective to find him and discovers that he remarried; she also learns that her husband and his new wife had a baby, that the wife died in childbirth, and that the husband was hit and killed by a car. Zilphia goes away for three years and returns with a wedding band and a three-year-old child, whom she calls Zilphia. She rears the girl in the same room with barred windows in the back of the dress shop that once belonged to her mother.

Many critics see a connection between this early story and two later ones, "A ROSE FOR EMILY" and "DRY SEPTEMBER"; all three contain themes of repressed sexuality, revenge, violence, and isolation. In "Miss Zilphia Gant," Faulkner introduces themes that recur in other works. First published as *Miss Zilphia Gant,* a separate piece, in June 1932 by the Book Club of Texas (Dallas), with a preface by Henry Nash Smith, the short story is reprinted in the UNCOLLECTED STORIES OF WILLIAM FAULKNER; for more information, see *Uncollected Stories of William Faulkner,* p. 700.

"Mistral" *(Collected Stories)* Short story that follows two young American hikers as they attempt to solve the mystery of what has taken place in a northern Italian village. In an atmosphere rife with gothic gloom, tolling bells, and the piercing cold mistral wind, the two catch glimpses of the drama's protagonists: a beautiful girl, her soldier sweetheart, and her dead fiancé in his coffin. They meet only briefly with the main figure, the girl's guardian and village priest, who is in a state of agony. The revelation of the ambiguous events through fragments of gossip and the hikers' own questionable conjectures is hindered by the prejudices and dissimulations of their informants, a shifting language barrier, and probably by their own ever-increasing inebriation.

What emerges is the possibility that the priest tried to sever the attachment between the girl and her sweetheart by arranging to have the young man drafted into the army. He then manipulated a rich man into becoming engaged to the girl, although she was able to delay the wedding for three years. When the soldier finally was due to return, the priest forced the marriage to take place, but on its eve the fiancé died, perhaps of poison. The perpetrator of this deed may have been the soldier's aunt, who left the church when her nephew was drafted. Some villagers attribute the priest's spiritual torment to his lustful passion for his ward, but it may be due instead to his recognition that his unethical machinations have led to a man's death, have cost him the respect and loyalty of his parishioners, and have compromised his mission as a man of God. In the end, the truth remains obscure as the two travelers move on, fortified by yet another swig of brandy.

This story first appeared in *These 13* (1931).

Mitch Character in SARTORIS. A freight agent in JEFFERSON, MISSISSIPPI, Mitch, his friend Hub, and young Bayard SARTORIS (3) serenade Narcissa Benbow (SARTORIS) at the close of a riotous evening, drawing the attention of the Jefferson town marshal.

Mitchell Character in KNIGHT'S GAMBIT ("Hand upon the Waters"). A storekeeper, he is the banker to which Lonnie GRINNUP entrusted his burial money.

Mitchell, Belle *See* BENBOW, BELLE MITCHELL.

Mitchell, Harry Character in SARTORIS. The affluent, likeable husband of Belle Mitchell (BENBOW), he is a successful cotton speculator.

His wife is contemptuous of him, and she eventually leaves him for Horace BENBOW. Young Bayard SARTORIS (3) catches sight of Mitchell in a Chicago bar after the breakup. The woman he is with is trying to steal his diamond stickpin.

Mitchell is also referred to in SANCTUARY.

Mitchell, Hugh Character in *The HAMLET;* one of the men lounging on the gallery of Whiteleaf's store when Ab SNOPES comes by with a horse he says came from Kentucky. Knowing that is not true, Mitchell identifies the horse as once belonging to Herman SHORT, Pat STAMPER, and Beasley KEMP, and mockingly asks whether Snopes gave Beasley 50 cents for it.

Mitchell, Little Belle Daughter of Belle Mitchell BENBOW and her first husband, Harry MITCHELL, in SARTORIS and SANCTUARY. She is Horace BENBOW's stepdaughter, although there is no indication in either novel that she has taken his last name. Disingenuous toward Benbow, Little Belle, a teenager very much interested in boys, treats him as an annoyance rather than the father figure he would like to be in her life.

Mitchell, Mrs. One of the townspeople in SOLDIERS' PAY.

Mitchell, Unc Few Character in *The UNVANQUISHED.* He is a local figure, "born loony," according to Louvinia STROTHER, who mentions him in describing Colonel John SARTORIS's feigned deafness when federal troops are in the neighborhood.

Mitchell, Walter Minor character in the short story "TWO DOLLAR WIFE" who originally dares Maxwell JOHNS and Doris HOUSTON to get married. The couple eventually do so on a New Year's Eve.

modernism   A term that identifies the general characteristics of a movement in the arts that began in the late 19th century as a reaction against traditional art forms and became prominent in the first part of the 20th century. In literature, modernism is identified with a sense of historical discontinuity, cultural relativism, and continuing experimentation that includes the STREAM-OF-CONSCIOUSNESS technique, the device of the INTERIOR MONOLOGUE, and narrational uncertainty. Influenced by discoveries in the social sciences—psychology in particular—modernism questions the role of social institutions such as religion and the family to effect norms of behavior. Modernist writers include Ezra Pound, James JOYCE, T. S. Eliot, Virginia Woolf, and D. H. Lawrence. Many critics consider Faulkner's *The SOUND AND THE FURY*, with its unusual narrative strategies and unreliable multiple narrators, the classic American modernist work.

Mohataha   Character referred to in *REQUIEM FOR A NUN* and *The MANSION*. In *The Mansion*, she is the CHICKASAW INDIAN matriarch who, in 1821, grants Quentin (MacLachan) Compson (see COMPSON, JASON LYCURGUS IV) land that becomes very valuable in JEFFERSON, MISSISSIPPI. Mohataha is ISSETIBBEHA's sister and IKKEMOTUBBE's mother. In *Requiem*, she leaves Mississippi with her people for Oklahoma.

Moketubbe   Character in *GO DOWN, MOSES* ("The Old People") and other works. He is the fat, indolent son of the CHICKASAW INDIAN chief ISSETIBBEHA. He succeeds as chieftain when his father dies, but soon abdicates in favor of his cousin IKKEMOTUBBE, who uses the threat of poison to encourage him to stand down.

Moketubbe is also mentioned in *The REIVERS* and in the short stories "RED LEAVES" and "A COURTSHIP."

Monaghan (Buck, Captain)   Character in *SARTORIS*. He and young Bayard SARTORIS (4) were aviators together in France during World War I. They meet again in Chicago, where Monaghan refuses to test-fly an experimental aircraft. In *A FABLE*, he appears as Captain Monaghan, an American aviator flying in the RAF. He witnesses the murder of the German pilot by the German general and attacks the killer. He is dragged away by BRIDESMAN and THORPE.

He also appears in the short story "AD ASTRA" as host (in a French café) to a captured German flyer, outraging the French patrons of the place.

In the short story "HONOR," where he is given the first name Buck, Monaghan works as a wing walker in a flying circus and has an affair with the wife of his pilot. When the pilot risks his life to save Monaghan's, the latter leaves the circus, alone.

Monckton   Character in "DIVORCE IN NAPLES" (in *Collected Stories*). A merchant seaman, he joins CARL, GEORGE, and other crewmen for drinks at a sailor bar and brothel in Naples.

Monk   *See* ODLETHROP, STONEWALL JACKSON.

"Monk"   *See KNIGHT'S GAMBIT*.

Monk   A minor character in *PYLON*. He is a crew member of one of the pilots. JIGGS puts a bill in Monk's hand to give to Art JACKSON for flying the parachute jump.

Monson, Mrs.   Character in "A PORTRAIT OF ELMER" (in *Uncollected Stories*). She escorts her daughter Myrtle MONSON on a post–World War I tour of Europe, where they meet the American would-be artist Elmer HODGE.

Monson, Myrtle   Character in "A PORTRAIT OF ELMER" (in *Uncollected Stories*). A wealthy young woman from Houston, Texas, she is the object of the American artist Elmer HODGE's affection. They meet first in Texas and, later, in Europe where Myrtle is traveling with her mother.

Montgomery, Jake   Character in *INTRUDER IN THE DUST*. A timber dealer with other business interests, most of them of doubtful honesty, he buys lumber that he knows Crawford GOWRIE has stolen from his brother Vinson GOWRIE and Vinson's partner, Sudley WORKITT.

Jake also knows that Crawford killed Vinson and framed Lucas BEAUCHAMP for the crime. He digs up Vinson's body, evidently with the idea of showing the sheriff that Crawford is the murderer. Crawford discovers Jake in the act and kills him, dumping his body into Vinson's grave.

When Chick MALLISON and company find the corpse and rebury it, Crawford exhumes it and deposits it in a shallow grave. Sheriff HAMPTON finds Montgomery's body there.

Mooney   Character in *LIGHT IN AUGUST*. He is a foreman in the JEFFERSON, MISSISSIPPI, sawmill where Byron BUNCH, Joe Brown (Lucas BURCH), and Joe CHRISTMAS all work.

"Moonlight" *(Uncollected Stories)*   A moody, poetic short story about young love. Displaying a carefree and humorous depiction of youthful uncertainty, "Moonlight" is about an attempted seduction of a 16-year-old girl, Susan, by the unnamed protagonist, also 16. The protagonist, smarting from the humiliation of being literally kicked off Susan's premises by her uncle and guardian, Mr. BURCHETT, wants both to seduce Susan—although he does not seem too sure what seduction actually entails—and to take revenge against her uncle.

Susan sends the protagonist a note saying that she will meet him surreptitiously and be his for the night. He sends his best friend SKEET to fetch Susan. After some kissing, the protagonist realizes that all Susan wants to do is go to a show. She does not drink the moonshine whiskey he has brought and resists his clumsy seduction attempt.

Though never published in Faulkner's lifetime, this posthumously published version of "Moonlight" in the UNCOLLECTED STORIES OF WILLIAM FAULKNER is, nevertheless, a fully realized story, not an unfinished sketch like several of his other posthumously published pieces. According to Faulkner, the first and earlier version of "Moonlight" (a 16-page typescript) was written sometime between 1919 and 1921 and is perhaps the first short story Faulkner ever wrote (see James B. MERIWETHER, *The Literary Career of William Faulkner,* p. 87). Joseph BLOTNER points out that the version published in *Uncollected Stories,* a 14-page typescript, is "much closer to the mature style of Faulkner than the 16-page version which may represent its earliest form after the manuscript" (*Uncollected Stories,* p. 706). For more information, see *Uncollected Stories of William Faulkner,* p. 706, and Diane Brown Jones, *A Reader's Guide to the Short Stories of William Faulkner,* pp. 142–43, 144, 178.

Moore, Brother   Character in *SARTORIS*. He is part of the delegation that asks Simon STROTHER for an accounting of church funds for which Strother is responsible.

Morache   One of a detail of 12 soldiers in *A FABLE* who is sent to collect a body to be buried in the Tomb of the Unknown Soldier. The body the soldiers first obtain is sold to a peasant woman for money to buy liquor. To obtain a second body, PICKLOCK uses a watch Morache stole from a dead German officer to buy a substitute body, which is, apparently, that of Corporal STEFAN.

Morrison   Character in the short story "DON GIOVANNI." He is a friend and sounding board of HERB, the story's main character, who displays a remarkable insensitivity to women. Although he tries to give advice to Herb, Morrison reluctantly tolerates his friend's fantasies about how to seduce women. In the end, Herb, although confronted with his own folly, is unaware of his misunderstanding of women.

Mosby, Uncle Hogeye   Character in *INTRUDER IN THE DUST*. He is an epileptic inmate of the YOKNAPATAWPHA COUNTY poorhouse.

Mose, Unc   Character in "FOX HUNT" (in *Collected Stories*). He helps look after Harrison BLAIR's horses.

Moseley   In *AS I LAY DYING,* a pharmacist in Mottson (MOTTSTOWN). He refuses to help Dewey Dell BUNDREN when she asks him for a drug to abort her pregnancy, but tells her instead to marry LAFE, the father of the child, and raise babies. What she wants to do, he explains, is illegal. Moseley narrates chapter 45 of the novel.

Mosquitoes   Faulkner's second novel, published in 1927, is a work of apprenticeship, derivative, uneven, and tedious in places, though critics agree that it foreshadows the powerfully original fiction that followed.

"*Mosquitoes* is Faulkner's least respected novel and it is very easy to see why," wrote the critic Cleanth BROOKS. "There is almost no story line; nothing of real consequence happens to any of its characters." Brooks adds, however, that the novel does show Faulkner's "zest for language and his power to handle it."

Faulkner wrote most of the book in the summer of 1926 in the Gulf Coast resort of PASCAGOULA, MISSISSIPPI. Living and working conditions were pleasant. The novelist's room in the Stone family's large seafront cottage came equipped with a daybed, a chair, and a table for his portable typewriter. But he often worked outdoors, on one of the wooden benches that curved around the big live oaks in front of the place. Faulkner wrote a first draft on plain white paper, in a tiny script, striking off a fair copy on the typewriter when he reached the end of a section. He worked for several hours early in the morning, took a long break in the heat of the day, and went back to the manuscript for a stretch in the afternoon.

Mosquitoes is self-consciously a novel of ideas, according to Faulkner biographer Joseph BLOTNER. It is full of talk, most of it circling around two inexhaustible topics, literature and sex. One of the characters even complains of the incessant chatter. Blotner, Brooks, and others identify T. S. Eliot, James JOYCE, Aldous Huxley (*Chrome Yellow,* 1921) and D. H. Lawrence (*Women in Love,* 1920) as Faulkner's chief literary influences. Some of the content is daring for its time. Faulkner mentions masturbation, conception, constipation, evacuation, lesbianism, syphilis, and perversion in the course of the novel's 349 pages. He also indulges in artistic name-dropping: Byron, Shelley, Swinburne, Ibsen, Chopin, Grieg, Sibelius.

Faulkner uses a commonplace device, of the sort familiar to readers of English country house murder mysteries, to gather his characters: he brings a mixed group together for a cruise on *Nausikaa,* the yacht of a wealthy New Orleans matron with artistic interests, Patricia MAURIER. The characters are thus conveniently captive in one place for as long as the novelist requires them.

The protagonist, Ernest TALLIAFERRO, a wholesale buyer of women's clothing, is a widower whose clumsy attempts at ingratiating himself with women invariably fail. Blotner sees echoes of Eliot's Prufrock from the poem "The Love Song of J. Alfred Prufrock"; Brooks calls him "a kind of cultural flunky and go-between" for the dilettantish Mrs. Maurier. Dawson FAIRCHILD, an Indiana novelist, is patently modeled on Sherwood ANDERSON. GORDON (no surname given) is a sculptor with little to say. He might be a fictionalized version of Faulkner's New Orleans friend Bill SPRATLING. Mark FROST is a poet who talks a lot and produces very little. Patricia ROBYN, Mrs. Maurier's epicene niece, is an early Faulkner type, suggesting Faulkner's love interest of about this time, Helen BAIRD. Patricia boards with her twin brother, Theodore ROBYN, known as Josh, and with a working-class couple she has picked up in the French Quarter, the lush Jenny STEINBAUER and her boyfriend Pete GINOTTA, whose brother is a bootlegger. Dorothy JAMESON, a painter, prefers still lifes to portraits and is rather desperate for a man. Eva WISEMAN is a poet; Faulkner takes her work seriously. Her brother Julius, whose last name is hinted at as KAUFFMAN, is called "the Semitic man" more often than not, and is an articulate if obsessive literary theorist. Major AYERS, a stage Englishman, promotes a remedy for constipation. David WEST is the somewhat miscast yacht's steward.

The structure of *Mosquitoes* is simple. A prologue introduces the characters. Sections titled "The First Day" through "The Fourth Day" follow. The time of day captions the subsections. An epilogue in which the characters scatter closes the novel.

Mosquitoes opens on an evening in August with Talliaferro delivering an invitation to join the yachting party to the studio of the sculptor Gordon. The characters assemble. *Nausikaa* floats gently out into Lake Ponchartrain in a cloud of mosquitoes whose constant buzzing suggests the conversation on board. The yacht runs aground. Patricia and the steward West slip away in a small boat, but thirst, heat, and mosquitoes drive them back to the mother vessel. Brooks speculates on the significance of the title insect in his study of Faulkner's early work, *Toward Yoknapatawpha and Beyond* (1978): "My guess is that they stand for the unpredictable and annoying aspects of reality that human beings have to reckon with."

The *Nausikaa* returns to New Orleans. The party disperses, and Gordon, Fairchild, and Kauffman enter the city's red light district, a scene strongly suggestive of the Circe episode in Joyce's *Ulysses* (1922). *Mosquitoes* ends as it began, with Talliaferro alone.

What will become a Faulknerian habit of borrowing and recycling from his earlier works, published and unpublished, is much in evidence here. He lifts an image of New Orleans as "an aging and yet still beautiful courtesan" from one of his "New Orleans" sketches in *The DOUBLE DEALER* (see *NEW ORLEANS SKETCHES*). He shanghais the characters of Talliaferro, Fairchild, and Jenny Steinbauer from the unpublished short story "DON GIOVANNI."

Most significantly, Faulkner begins to develop the means by which he will telescope the universal into the local in the greater works of YOKNAPATAWPHA COUNTY, his "little postage stamp of native soil." Julius Kauffman states the aesthetic briefly by remarking that life essentially is the same everywhere.

Faulkner finished *Mosquitoes* in Pascagoula on September 1, 1926, except for revisions. In OXFORD, MISSISSIPPI, Phil STONE's law office provided typing services, and Faulkner mailed the completed manuscript to Horace LIVERIGHT in New York before the end of the month. Editors there deleted four substantial passages, including a two-page stretch of Fairchild conversation that equated writing with perversion, and a cabin-bunk scene involving Patricia Robyn and Jenny Steinbauer. They corrected his punctuation, too.

The publication date was April 30, 1927. The first reviews appeared in mid-June. Conrad AIKEN wrote the first major one, for the New York *Evening Post,* which praised the characters and dialogue. In the New York *World,* Ruth Suckow reported that the writing was occasionally good, "when it isn't Joyce," but the "all too recognizable mixture of suavity, brilliance, cynicism, tragedy, philosophy, obscenity, pure nature and thoughts on art" did not greatly impress her.

Maud Butler FALKNER once said *Mosquitoes* earned her novelist son about $400. It was true that the book did not sell especially well. By the end of 1930, combined sales of *Mosquitoes* and Faulkner's first novel, *SOLDIERS' PAY,* were a little short of 4,000 copies.

Mothershed   Character in "BEYOND" (in *Collected Stories*). He is Judge ALLISON's ill-tempered contact in The Beyond.

Mott County   Fictional place, corresponding to Calhoun County, Mississippi, south of LAFAYETTE COUNTY, and lying south of Faulkner's YOKNAPATAWPHA COUNTY.

Mottstown   Fictional town. The seat of Faulkner's Okatoba County, Mottstown is 45 minutes by train from JEFFERSON, MISSISSIPPI, and corresponds to Water Valley, Mississippi, 20 miles southwest of OXFORD, MISSISSIPPI. It is called Mottson in *The SOUND AND THE FURY* and *AS I LAY DYING*.

In *LIGHT IN AUGUST,* the fugitive Joe CHRISTMAS accepts a ride with a black wagoner bound for Mottstown. Christmas is later captured and held briefly in the jail there. Jason COMPSON IV in *The Sound and the Fury* loses the trail of his niece (Miss) Quentin COMPSON in Mottson. In *As I Lay Dying,* floods force the Bundrens to detour through Mottson on their way to Jefferson.

"Mountain Victory" *(Collected Stories)*   Short story set in wilderness Tennessee. It describes an encounter between an aristocratic Southern officer and an impoverished mountain family that ends, with mounting tension and inevitability, in tragedy. On the way from Virginia to Mississippi following the South's defeat in the Civil War, Major Saucier WEDDEL and his Negro slave, now servant, Jubal, seek shelter for the night.

For VATCH, the family's oldest son, who fought on the Union side, the war is not over yet; he obsessively taunts Weddel with growing hostility. Witnessing the officer's compassionate treatment of Jubal and hearing of his plantation, the younger son, HULE, and his sister dream of escape from a brutal family situation. The father, fearing the worst from Vatch, repeatedly urges Weddel to leave immediately. Weddel refuses, saying that the unconscious Jubal first must sleep off his intoxication.

In this clash of cultures, the two factions represent through shifting points of view the paradoxes of victory, defeat, peace, and home, as well as attitudes toward race. The desperate Hule unsuccessfully begs Weddel to take him and his sister away. In the violent climax, Weddel and Jubal ride off, aided and perhaps betrayed by Hule, into an ambush that leaves Weddel and Hule dead and Jubal about to be killed, facing the rifle Vatch has aimed at him.

For its complexity and power, as well as for its exploration of the Southern myth, many readers place this among Faulkner's best short stories. Irving HOWE rates it as his finest Civil War work. Scholars link Weddel to Faulkner's demoralized World War I soldiers who find that danger stimulates their sense of feeling alive. More problematic is the racism theme: the critic Erskine Peters judges Jubal's portrayal as offensively stereotypical. Others find racial conflict, reflected in Weddel's own ambiguous ancestry, to be the key dynamic.

This story first appeared in the SATURDAY EVENING POST (December 3, 1932) and was revised for Doctor Martino and Other Stories (1934).

Mount Vernon Fictional place. Described as 18 miles from JEFFERSON, MISSISSIPPI, in AS I LAY DYING, Mount Vernon is possibly Faulkner's name for Abbeville, a village north of OXFORD, MISSISSIPPI. The road to Mount Vernon is offered as an alternate route for the flood-harassed Bundrens in As I Lay Dying.

"Mr. Acarius" A short story about an idealist, Mr. ACARIUS, who has the odd notion that to experience humanity or the human condition at its grittiest, he needs to be committed to a hospital ward for alcoholics. He asks his old friend and doctor, Ab COCHRANE, for advice in this pursuit, and they arrange for him to be admitted to an expensive private clinic. To get there, he goes on a binge reminiscent of his college days. Though an idealist, Mr. Acarius is also a wealthy collector and a snob. He speaks of his Picassos and drinks only the finest scotch. Once in the ward, however, Mr. Acarius finds himself not in touch with reality or the human condition as he imagined it to be,

but instead cooped up with self-destructive liars and manipulators who are escaping from life and incapable of dealing with its complications and vicissitudes. Unable to bear the situation he had created for himself, Mr. Acarius escapes from the hospital. Once outside, he is stopped by the police. In the nick of time, his doctor intercedes and helps his patient to his apartment in an upper-class neighborhood, where the first thing Mr. Acarius does is to pour his supply of liquor down the drain.

A humorous story that reflects, perhaps, Faulkner's own bouts with alcoholism, "Mr. Acarius" has been described by James Ferguson as having "some psychological and biographical interest, but it is unpleasantly frenetic and uncontrolled, certainly one of the strangest stories he ever wrote" (Faulkner's Short Fiction, p. 46). Originally entitled "Weekend Revisited" (a title evocative of F. Scott Fitzgerald's short story "Babylon Revisited" [1931]), "Mr. Acarius" was written in early 1953 but published posthumously, first in the SATURDAY EVENING POST 238 (October 9, 1965), and later in UNCOLLECTED STORIES OF WILLIAM FAULKNER.

Mulberry In REQUIEM FOR A NUN, the metonymic name given to a black man who sold illegal whiskey that he concealed under a mulberry tree. A U.S. marshal during Reconstruction days, he was still known as Mulberry in 1925. For several lawyers, medical doctors, and even a bank, he worked various jobs, such as janitor and furnace-attendant.

"Mule in the Yard" Short story in which Mrs. Mannie HAIT outwits the scheming mule trader I. O. SNOPES, with whom her late husband had worked before losing his life in one of Snopes's scams. When Snopes's mules get loose in Mrs. Hait's yard, one kicks over a bucket of smoldering ashes that Mrs. Hait has left by the open cellar door when she goes to run after the animals. The bucket falls down the stairs and the house burns down. Instead of suing Snopes, Mrs. Hait offers to buy the offending mule for $10, an amount $50 less than what the railroad paid Snopes for each mule that was killed on the tracks 10 years before in a swindle. Mrs. Hait is evening the score, for her husband died tying Snopes's mules to the tracks. When Snopes argues that the mule is worth $150, Mrs. Hait calmly tells him that he can claim the mule up the road a piece where she hid it. After he leaves, Mrs. Hait's friend old HET asks what she did with it and learns that she shot it. Het happily remarks that that is justice.

"Mule in the Yard," according to Michael MILLGATE, is "one of Faulkner's greatest comic tours de force, has its furious crescendoes of farcical activity (The Achievement of William Faulkner, p. 236). The ironic pattern of Mannie Hait's victory over a Snopes significantly adds to the humor, for she uses tactics not unlike those used by

Snopes, one of which is deception. This short story can also be seen, as John T. Matthews argues, as an example of the empowerment of woman in the male market (see "Shortened Stories: Faulkner and the Market," in Evans Harrington and Ann J. Abadie, eds., *Faulkner and the Short Story,* pp. 29–35).

The short story was first published in SCRIBNER'S MAGAZINE, 96 (August 1934), pp. 65–70 and later in COLLECTED STORIES OF WILLIAM FAULKNER. The story was significantly revised and incorporated in chapter 16 of the second volume of the SNOPES TRILOGY, *The TOWN.*

For more information, see *Selected Letters of William Faulkner* and Diane Brown Jones, *A Reader's Guide to the Short Stories of William Faulkner,* pp. 248–59.

Murrel, John   One of the robbers named in the legendary early history of YOKNAPATAWPHA COUNTY referred to in *REQUIEM FOR A NUN.* Murrel was the head of the band.

Myers, Al   In *PYLON,* one of the pilots competing in the air meet celebrating the opening of Feinman Airport in New Valois, Franciana.

"My Grandmother Millard and General Bedford Forrest and the Battle of Harrykin Creek" (Collected Stories)   Short story of the Civil War era; it recounts a legendary Sartoris family episode. Granny Rosa MILLARD, an accomplished strategist, saves the family treasures from the Yankees, outwits the wily horse thief Ab SNOPES, and manipulates the Confederate General Nathan Bedford FORREST, into allowing a besotted young couple to wed.

The narrator, Bayard SARTORIS (3), recalls the events he witnessed as a boy, beginning with Granny's repeated rehearsals of burying their silver. This plan is thwarted when the Yankees arrive suddenly; Cousin MELISANDRE

instead is sent to hide with the trunk in the outhouse. The marauders shatter the privy with a battering ram, but are chased off singlehandedly by a Confederate officer, Philip BACKHOUSE. He is smitten with the young woman, who is unhurt, and comically preens himself for their formal introduction. She finds him attractive, but when she hears his name, a coarse reminder of her recent fright, she renounces any future between them. With the complicity of General Forrest, the recklessly courageous Backhouse is declared dead in the made-up Harrykin Creek battle and is replaced by one Lieutenant Philip Backus. Thus the marriage can take place. The tale's sole serious note is an ironic consideration of the word "freedom" and of its differing meanings for the family slaves and for the white Southerners who fight for the Confederacy.

This tale first appeared in *Story* (March–April 1943). It is closely related to the Sartoris family chronicles in *The UNVANQUISHED.*

Myrtle   **(1)** Character in *SARTORIS.* She is Dr. ALFORD's receptionist.

Myrtle   **(2)** In *The SOUND AND THE FURY,* the married daughter of the sheriff in JEFFERSON, MISSISSIPPI. She and her husband, VERNON (1), are present when Jason (see COMPSON, JASON IV) comes to the sheriff's house to report that (Miss) Quentin COMPSON and her boyfriend have stolen his money and taken off together.

Myrtle, Miss   Character in *SANCTUARY.* Miss Myrtle visits Miss Reba RIVERS after RED's funeral. Miss Myrtle is accompanied by Miss Lorraine and Uncle BUD, a child. At Miss Reba's brothel, the three women, who all attended the funeral, drink and pour out their feelings to one another.

"A Name for the City"   Short story first published in *Harper's Magazine* 201 (October 1950), 200–14 and later revised and included by Faulkner in the first section of the prologue to act 1 of *REQUIEM FOR A NUN*.

Nancy   *See MANNIGOE, NANCY.*

Natalie   In *The SOUND AND THE FURY,* a girl whom Quentin COMPSON hugs and kisses in the barn when they are children. Caddy COMPSON catches them and teases Quentin.

Nate   Character in *KNIGHT'S GAMBIT* ("Hand upon the Waters"). He is a black neighbor of Lonnie GRINNUP. Gavin STEVENS stops at Nate's cabin in the night and asks Nate to report him missing if he has not returned from Grinnup's camp by daylight.

Nelson, Callie (Aunt Callie)   An elderly black woman who was formerly a nanny for the young Donald MAHON in *SOLDIERS' PAY.* After the wounded Mahon is brought back to Charlestown, Georgia, Aunt Callie helps to nurse him.

Nelson, Loosh   Aunt Callie NELSON's grandson in *SOLDIERS' PAY.* He is a veteran of World War I and wears his uniform while visiting the wounded Donald MAHON.

New Albany, Mississippi   Town in Union County, Mississippi, on the TALLAHATCHIE RIVER northeast of OXFORD, MISSISSIPPI and a trading center for a cotton, corn, and dairy region. In the 1890s, New Albany had a population of about 600 and was the midpoint station on Colonel William C. FALKNER's GULF & CHICAGO RAILROAD.

Murry FALKNER, Faulkner's father, moved to New Albany in September 1896 to take up his duties as general passenger agent of the Gulf & Chicago. William Cuthbert Falkner was born in a plain one-story clapboard house at Cleveland and Jefferson Streets there on September 25, 1897.

Newberry, Colonel   Character in *The UNVANQUISHED.* A Union soldier from Illinois, he authorizes the last handover of mules to Rosa MILLARD before the Yankees catch on to her trickery.

New Hope Church   Fictional place in *AS I LAY DYING.* It is an intermediate destination in the Bundren odyssey in the novel. In Faulkner's time, there were four churches of that name in the vicinity of OXFORD, MISSISSIPPI.

New Orleans, Louisiana   Situated in southeastern Louisiana on a great bend of the Mississippi River 107 miles from the river's mouth, New Orleans is a cultural and economic center of the South, one of its largest cities, and a leading port of entry.

Developed by the French, at times under Spanish rule, New Orleans became part of the United States with the Louisiana Purchase of 1803. The cosmopolitan city's great age ended during the Civil War with the arrival of Union occupation forces in 1862. Long afterward, artists, writers, and musicians were attracted to the picturesque French Quarter, also known as the Vieux Carré, the historic district bounded by Canal Street, the Esplanade, North Rampart Street, and the river. Jazz had its origin among the black musicians of late 19th-century New Orleans.

Eight hours from OXFORD, MISSISSIPPI, by train, New Orleans provided an escape and an opportunity for young Faulkner in the early 1920s. He and Philip STONE ventured there for uproarious weekends and for discussions of art and artists. Young writers flourished in the Vieux Carré and found an outlet for their work in the little magazine *DOUBLE DEALER,* founded in New Orleans in 1921. The magazine published poetry by Hart Crane, Allen TATE, and Robert Penn WARREN, stories by Sherwood ANDERSON, and sketches and short literary essays by Faulkner.

Faulkner met Anderson, whose early work he admired, in New Orleans in 1924. The older writer tirelessly promoted the city as a haven for writers. Faulkner stayed in Anderson's apartment in St. Peter Street for several weeks in 1925 before moving on to William SPRATLING's attic in Orleans Alley in the Vieux Carré. He and Spratling sailed together from New Orleans to Europe in July 1925.

Faulkner published sketches of the city and its denizens for the *Double Dealer* and the *NEW ORLEANS TIMES-PICAYUNE* daily newspaper. He exploited his New Orleans experiences in his second novel, *MOSQUITOES* (1927), likening the city to "an aging yet still beautiful courtesan." He set the novel's early scenes in the Vieux Carré, the main action in a yacht adrift on Lake Ponchartrain, and the concluding sequences in the red light district.

In *PYLON* (1935), Faulkner opens with a fictional version of the dedication of Shushan Airport, built on land reclaimed from Lake Ponchartrain. Faulkner renames it Feinman Airport of the city of New Valois, built on filled land taken from Lake Rambaud.

In *ABSALOM, ABSALOM!* (1936), Thomas SUTPEN travels from JEFFERSON, MISSISSIPPI, to New Orleans to seek out the mistress and child of Charles BON, his daughter Judith's suitor. The unsophisticated Henry SUTPEN, Judith's brother, makes the same journey a little later to investigate Bon's background.

New Orleans Sketches   Collection of 11 short pieces and 16 prose sketches that Faulkner wrote for the *NEW ORLEANS TIMES-PICAYUNE* and the *DOUBLE DEALER* while he was living in New Orleans in 1925. Edited with an introduction by Carvel COLLINS, the collection was published by Rutgers University Press in 1958; an expanded and revised edition was published by RANDOM HOUSE in 1968. Prior to Collins's collection, 11 of the 16 prose sketches, titled "Mirrors of Chartres Street," with an introduction by William Van O'Connor, were published in *Faulkner Studies* in 1953. In 1954, two other sketches appeared in *Faulkner Studies*. In 1955, these 13 sketches, edited by Ichiro Nishizaki, were published as *New Orleans Sketches by William Faulkner.*

As Collins more or less demonstrates in his introduction, these sketches provide readers with an opportunity to view in Faulkner's early writings anticipatory themes, techniques, and character traits found in his later works. Collins also situates Faulkner in his New Orleans setting. In his review of Collins's edition, Joseph V. Ridgely concludes with a comment worth repeating: "Essentially . . . these early Faulkner pieces are amateur, derivative and overblown; and their chief interest may well lie in raising the question as to how their author, only four years later, could produce *The Sound and the Fury*" (*Modern Language Notes* 74 [February 1959], 176). (For information regarding titles, see Appendix I.)

New Orleans Times-Picayune   Leading daily newspaper of NEW ORLEANS, LOUISIANA, and an early paying outlet for Faulkner's work. He became friends with the newspaper's literary editor, John McClure, and other staffers and produced a series of New Orleans sketches for the *Times-Picayune* in 1925 (see *NEW ORLEANS SKETCHES*).

The first in the series, "Mirrors of Chartres Street," appeared on February 8, 1925. Others followed at intervals during the year. Faulkner also produced short stories, poems, and essays for the paper.

The *Times-Picayune* pieces helped finance Faulkner's sojourn in Italy, France, and England from August to November 1925.

Nightingale, Mr.   Father of Tug NIGHTINGALE in *The MANSION*. A widower, he is a staunch, inflexible Baptist who believes that the earth is flat and that General Lee's surrender at Appomattox was a betrayal of the South. When, in 1917, Tug, his only surviving child, joined the Sartoris Rifles organized by Captain MCLENDON, Nightingale disinherited him because he believed his son became a traitor by joining the Yankee army.

Nightingale, Tug   In *The MANSION*, a member of the JEFFERSON, MISSISSIPPI, military company known as the Sartoris Rifles, organized by Captain MCLENDON in 1917. When his widowed father (an unrelenting Confederate) found out that his only surviving child joined the Yankee army, Tug was disinherited. After the company trained in Texas, it was sent overseas, where Tug became a cook. In 1919, Tug returns to Jefferson and once again becomes a barn- and fence painter.

Nine-Mile Branch   Fictional stream running through willow and cypress bottoms in YOKNAPATAWPHA COUNTY. In *INTRUDER IN THE DUST*, it leads to the Gowrie clan's burial ground at CALEDONIA CHAPEL.

Nobel Prize in literature   Prestigious international award, established by the bequest of the Norwegian explosives manufacturer Alfred B. Nobel (1833–96). Sinclair Lewis (1930), Eugene O'Neill (1936), and Pearl S. Buck (1938) were the first American recipients.

The Swedish Academy failed to agree on a winner for 1949 and withheld the prize; the committee decided later to award two literature Nobels in 1950. In early November 1950, the wire services reported Faulkner and the British philosopher Bertrand RUSSELL as the leading candidates.

The academy selected Faulkner for the 1949 award on November 10, 1950, citing his "powerful and independent artistic contribution in America's new literature of the novel." Fifteen of the 18 members voted to award him the prize, which carried a cash grant of around $30,000.

Faulkner at first refused to travel to Sweden to accept. Nor did the honor seem to impress him, anyway at first. "They gave it to Sinclair Lewis and Old China Hand Buck," he told an OXFORD, MISSISSIPPI, journalist, "and they passed over Sherwood Anderson and Theodore Dreiser."

Political pressures were brought to bear; friends talked Faulkner around. He and his daughter, Jill FAULKNER, left for Stockholm in early December. The Nobel presentation speech graded Faulkner as "the unrivaled master of all living British and American nov-

Faulkner and his 17-year-old daughter, Jill, prepare to board a plane from New York to Stockholm, Sweden, where Faulkner would receive the Nobel Prize in literature in December 1950. (AP/Wide World Photos)

elists as a deep psychologist" and as "the greatest experimentalist among 20th-century novelists."

Faulkner then gave a memorable "Address upon Receiving the Nobel Prize in Literature"—a good deal more memorable in the printed version, actually, for Faulkner, nervous and deeply ill at ease, raced through a barely audible delivery (see Appendix IV).

The novelist ended the address with a moving affirmation of faith: "I believe that man will not merely endure: he will prevail. He is immortal, not because he alone among creatures has an inexhaustible voice, but because he has a soul, a spirit capable of compassion and sacrifice and endurance."

Faulkner ended up giving away the Nobel cash award in scholarships and other bequests. "I haven't earned it and I don't feel like it's mine," he explained.

Notes on a Horsethief   Novella, with decorations by Elizabeth Calvert, published in February 1951 (though dated 1950) by the Levee Press, Greenville, Mississippi; revised and incorporated into *A FABLE* (1954). The revised version was also published in the July 1954 issue of *Vogue* and in *Perspectives U. S. A.* 9 (autumn 1954), 24–59. In August 1947 when Faulkner was working on *A Fable*, he described the novella in a letter to his editor Robert K. HAAS as being a tall tale that begins a few years before World War I with one of the British soldiers in the novel, who at the time (1912) is a groom. He goes to the United States with an exceptional race horse and meets a black stable worker. Together they steal the horse after it breaks its leg, in order to prevent it from being retired as a stud. These men know that the horse is a champion and wants only to race. They run the horse, but not for their own financial gain, at small tracks throughout the South before they are caught by the police. (See *Selected Letters of William Faulkner*, pp. 253–54.)

Although *Notes on a Horsethief* contains obvious elements of the tall tale, Faulkner nonetheless skillfully integrates the story into the larger framework of the novel. For further information, see *Selected Letters of William Faulkner*, pp. 123–24, 256, 257, 258, 260–62, 264, 266.

Nunnery, Cedric   Minor character in *The TOWN*. He is a five-year-old child who gets lost. With a lighted lantern, Eck SNOPES foolishly looks for him in an empty oil tank. Though the child is not there, Eck kills himself when the tank containing gaseous fumes blows up.

Nunnery, Mrs.   Minor character in *The Town*. She is Cedric NUNNERY's mother.

"Nympholepsy"   Short story in which a farm hand becomes momentarily and dimly aware of greater possibilities than he is living when he sees, in the distance, a woman walking across a field. Enraptured by her presence, he moves to overtake her, but he slips into a stream and imagines that he feels a woman's thigh and the point of a breast. He drags himself out of the water, his clothes wet and heavy, and sees a woman—or the apparition of a woman, a nymph—running away through a wheat field. Unsure of the feelings welling up inside of him, he becomes confused and frightened of some unknown but "troubling Presence," now gone but still mocking him. Feeling again the exhaustion and emptiness of his long working day, he heads back to his rooming house in town, continuing with the monotonous cycle of his life.

The dream world and reality play off each other in "Nympholepsy," and, as David Minter points out, the story, like Faulkner's early poetry, abounds in echoes of Swinburne, Shelley, Keats, and others; Minter also observes that "though the deficiencies and inadequacies of reality provide the need and occasion of the dream, reality has the first and last word, and it remains unaltered" ("Carcassonne," "Wash," and "Voices of Faulkner's Fiction" in *Faulkner and the Short Story*, edited by Evans Harrington and Ann J. Abadie, p. 88). In his assessment of the story, James Ferguson comments that "one has no real sense that Faulkner knows where he is going or what he is trying to achieve in 'Nympholepsy'" (*Faulkner's Short Fiction*, p. 21). "Nympholepsy," like many of Faulkner's early short works published in *Uncollected Stories of William Faulkner,* is clearly an apprentice piece.

James B. MERIWETHER dates the composition of the story in early 1925. It was first published in the *Mississippi Quarterly* 26 (summer 1973), 403–09, and again in *A Faulkner Miscellany,* edited by Meriwether (Jackson: University Press of Mississippi, 1974), pp. 149–55; it is also published in UNCOLLECTED STORIES OF WILLIAM FAULKNER, edited by Joseph BLOTNER (New York: Vintage International, 1997), pp. 331–37. For more information, see *Uncollected Stories of William Faulkner,* p. 698.

Ober, Harold (1881–1959) Faulkner's literary agent. A native of Nashua, New Hampshire, he graduated from Harvard University in 1905 with ambitions to write, but decided he lacked the talent and went into the business of representing writers instead.

Ober founded his own agency in 1929. His client list included Paul Gallico, Catherine Drinker Bowen, and Agatha Christie; he loaned $20,000 to the chronically troubled F. Scott Fitzgerald and took Fitzgerald's daughter into his family for a time.

Faulkner and Ober met through Robert HAAS, Faulkner's editor and publisher and a Scarsdale neighbor of Ober's. In Ober's first effort for Faulkner, he sold the short story "BARN BURNING" to HARPER'S MAGAZINE in March 1938. He later negotiated lucrative film rights deals for Faulkner.

Both men were reserved and formal—so much so that they began calling each other Bill and Harold only after working together for four years.

Odlethrop, Mrs. Character in KNIGHT'S GAMBIT ("Monk"). Stonewall Jackson (Monk) ODLETHROP's presumed grandmother, she dies when Monk is six or seven years old.

Odlethrop, Stonewall Jackson (Monk) Character in KNIGHT'S GAMBIT ("Monk"). Mentally deficient, he is falsely accused of murder and sentenced to life in prison. When the real killer confesses five years later, Monk is pardoned; he refuses to leave the prison. At another convict's instigation, he murders the prison warden, GAMBRELL, and is executed for the crime.

"An Odor of Verbena" *See* THE UNVANQUISHED.

Odum, Cliff A minor character in *The* HAMLET. He is a farmer in FRENCHMAN'S BEND who helps Ab SNOPES's wife get her milk separator back from Pat STAMPER in exchange for a cow.

Okatoba County Fictional name for Yalobusha County, Mississippi, lying southwest of LAFAYETTE COUNTY. Miss HABERSHAM's fantasy car trip in INTRUDER IN THE DUST takes her into Okatoba County before she turns northward to return to YOKNAPATAWPHA COUNTY. Okatoba is also mentioned in KNIGHT'S GAMBIT.

Faulkner and several associates established the OKATOBA HUNTING AND FISHING CLUB in 1937.

Okatoba Hunting and Fishing Club With R. L. Sullivan and Whitson Cook, Faulkner founded this sporting club in 1937. General James Stone, the father of Faulkner's friend Philip STONE, gave the club hunting rights on his several thousand acres of MISSISSIPPI DELTA wilderness near Batesville. Faulkner wrote a state game warden that the club intended to protect the game from extermination.

Faulkner used these circumstances in "The Bear" (GO DOWN, MOSES). After selling off the timber rights to his share of the big woods, Major DE SPAIN offers Ike MCCASLIN and his hunting companions use of the house and hunting lands anytime. De Spain himself never goes there again, and loggers carry out a swift destruction of the wilderness.

Old Frenchman Place (sometimes referred to as Old Frenchman's Place) Fictional place near FRENCHMAN'S BEND in YOKNAPATAWPHA COUNTY. Flem SNOPES "unloads" the ruined plantation, rumored to be the site of buried treasure, on Henry ARMSTID, Odum BOOKWRIGHT, and the usually level-headed V. K. RATLIFF in *The* HAMLET, the first novel in the SNOPES TRILOGY. (This episode of the novel is a revision of the short story "LIZARDS IN JAMSHYD'S COURTYARD.")

Faulkner introduced the Old Frenchman Place in SANCTUARY. The gangster POPEYE murders TOMMY there and brutally rapes Temple Drake (STEVENS).

According to REQUIEM FOR A NUN, Old Frenchman Place was built by the wealthy Frenchman Louis GRENIER. In grandeur and size, it rivaled Thomas SUTPEN's mansion in ABSALOM, ABSALOM!

the old general (the Generalissimo, the marshal, the old marshal) The unnamed supreme commander of the allied American, British, and French forces in World War I in *A* FABLE. Through an illicit affair in a Middle Eastern country, he is the father of Corporal STEFAN, who leads the mutiny at the center of the novel. He meets with Stefan on two occasions and offers Stefan not only his freedom but great wealth and worldly power if he will renounce his twelve disciples and embrace the war. The old general is said to be from an ancient French family. Throughout his life, he is seen by many as the "hope of France." But the old general has consistently gone his own way, volunteering for harsh outposts and unglamorous assignments. He refuses to use his family connections to make his way to the pinnacle of the French military. Nevertheless, his brilliance and talent bring him the highest rank and honors. The old general tempts Stefan in a sort of parallel to Satan's temptation of Christ in the wilderness. When the corporal refuses to follow in his father's bloody footsteps, the old general orders his execution, along with the execution of Major General GRAGNON, who commanded the division that included the mutinous regiment (although Gragnon's death is made to appear as if it occurred during battle). The old general is committed to carrying on the war until the very last soldier has died. He arranges for the mutiny to be covered up as a failed attack. In the final scene of the novel the old general is buried with great pomp while the mauled and maimed RUNNER attempts to disrupt the funeral.

Oldham, Dorothy (Dot) (1905–1968)   Younger sister of Faulkner's wife, (Lida) Estelle Oldham FAULKNER. Dot Oldham and Billy Falkner spent much time together in OXFORD, MISSISSIPPI, in 1919, when Estelle was married to Cornell FRANKLIN and living in Honolulu. They used to play golf together.

She earned a master's degree in history from the UNIVERSITY OF MISSISSIPPI, ran soft drink and beer wholesaling businesses, and eventually became a librarian at Ole Miss, where she was curator of the Mississippi Collection.

Oldham, Lemuel Earl (1870–1945)   Faulkner's father-in-law. He graduated from the UNIVERSITY OF MISSISSIPPI and practiced law in Bonham, Texas, where his first daughter, Lida Estelle Oldham (FAULKNER), was born. He moved his family to OXFORD, MISSISSIPPI, in 1905 to take up the post of clerk of the U.S. District Court.

A Republican, a rarity in Mississippi in those days, Oldham surmounted this political liability to become a successful businessman and lawyer in Oxford, where he became known by the honorific "the major." He pursued banking and other interests, was general counsel for a railroad, and in 1921 won a patronage appointment as U.S. attorney for the Northern District of Mississippi.

The Oldhams and the Falkners were neighbors in Oxford, and Billy Falkner grew up with Oldhams as friends and playmates—Estelle, her sisters Victoria (Tochie) and Dorothy OLDHAM, and Estelle's brother Edward (who died in 1916).

In 1918, Lem Oldham refused his consent when Falkner sought to marry Estelle. He was hardly more encouraging in June 1929 when the novelist and Estelle prepared at last to marry.

Oldham's business ventures declined and he fell on hard times in the 1930s; for a time, Faulkner contributed $100 a month to the support of the major and his wife, Lida.

Oldham formed the basis for the character of the judge in the short story "Beyond the Gate." He died in May 1945.

Oldham, Lida Allen (1896–1956)   Faulkner's mother-in-law. She claimed Sam Houston and the Confederate general Felix Zollicoffer as ancestors; one grandfather was killed at the battle of SHILOH in 1862, and another died in a federal prisoner-of-war camp in Ohio.

The stepdaughter of a prominent federal judge in Mississippi, Miss Lida studied piano at the Cincinnati Conservatory of Music before settling into marriage with a young lawyer, Lemuel E. OLDHAM. They had four children: (Lida) Estelle (FAULKNER; born 1896), Victoria (Tochie), Dorothy (OLDHAM), and Edward (died 1916).

She taught her daughters (and later her granddaughter, Jill FAULKNER) to play the piano, and saw to it that all three girls attended college. Young Billy Falkner was deeply fond of Miss Lida. All the same, she opposed his efforts to marry Estelle as forcibly as did her husband.

"The Old Man"   See IF I FORGET THEE, JERUSALEM.

"The Old People"   See GO DOWN, MOSES.

Oliver   A minor character in the short story "AFTERNOON OF A COW." He helps the character named FAULKNER rescue a cow during a fire.

Omlie, Vernon C. (unknown–1936)   Faulkner's flying instructor. A North Dakotan, he took up flying in 1916 and served as a flight instructor during World War I. He and his aeronaut wife, Phoebe, alit with their flying circus in MEMPHIS in 1922 and established thriving aviation businesses there.

Omlie taught Faulkner to fly in the winter and spring of 1933 from a landing ground south of OXFORD, MISSISSIPPI. Faulkner took Omlie's Waco F biplane up on a solo flight on April 20—the first time he had ever gone aloft alone, in spite of his stories about flying for the ROYAL AIR FORCE. He evidently related some of his fictitious flying adventures to his instructor and asked him to keep quiet about the lessons.

Faulkner and Omlie collaborated in barnstorming and air circuses in Oxford and vicinity, with stunt flying and parachute jumps. Omlie and Faulkner's brother Dean FAULKNER were business partners before Dean's death in an airplane crash in November 1935.

Much of the aviation experience and lore Faulkner picked up from Omlie made its way into the novel PYLON (1935). The characters of Roger and Laverne SHUMANN were modeled in part on Vernon and Phoebe Omlie.

Omlie died as a passenger in a crash near St. Louis of a Chicago-bound airliner in August 1936.

"Once Aboard the Lugger" (I and II) Two short stories set among bootleggers out of NEW ORLEANS sometime during Prohibition in the mid-1920s. In "Once Upon the Lugger" (I), a young man serving as the boat's engineer recalls a voyage into the Gulf of Mexico, where the three crew members and the boat's captain uncover a buried cache of alcohol, probably from Cuba, and prepare to smuggle it back into Louisiana. In "Once Aboard the Lugger" (II), the second short story involving the fateful bootlegging run of a crew out of New Orleans, something happens to stop the progress of the smugglers' boat, now loaded with bootleg alcohol. The pumps must be used to bail out the boat, and the engine has been shut down. As the lugger drifts, another boat comes alongside and rival bootleggers hijack the cargo at gunpoint. PETE (1), the ineffectual younger brother of JOE (3), is taken unawares and unarmed. The hijackers kill Pete and another crew member, pistol-whip the captain, and then make their escape.

James Ferguson considers the second of these two stories, in particular, a story of initiation; "the narrator," Ferguson writes, "learns a great deal from the sudden intrusion of irrationality, of raw evil into the world of the mundane" (*Faulkner's Short Fiction*, pp. 61–62). "Once Aboard the Lugger" (I) was first published in *Contempo* I, 1, 4, and reprinted in UNCOLLECTED STORIES OF WILLIAM FAULKNER. "Once Aboard the Lugger" (II) was first published posthumously in *Uncollected Stories of William Faulkner*. For more information, see *Selected Letters of William Faulkner*, pp. 41–2, 56, and *Uncollected Stories of William Faulkner*, pp. 699–70.

Ord, Matt Famous (retired) pilot in PYLON and with ATKINSON owner of the Ord-Atkinson Aircraft Corporation. Behind Ord's back, Roger SHUMANN and the REPORTER buy an unsafe plane from an authorized agent of the Ord-Atkinson corporation to fly in one of the air races celebrating the opening of Feinman Airport in New Valois, Franciana. Although Ord tries his best to ground the plane (its engine is too powerful for its frame), Colonel H. I. FEINMAN permits Shumann to fly it. The plane breaks apart and Shumann dies in the crash.

Ord, Mrs. Matt ORD's wife in PYLON.

Oscar Character in GO DOWN, MOSES ("The Fire and the Hearth"). On the Edmonds place he helps DAN look after the mules.

Osgood, Captain A pilot in Lieutenant LEVINE's RAF squadron in *A FABLE*.

Otis Character in *The REIVERS*. He is the Arkansan nephew of Miss Corrie (Everbe Corinthia HOGGANBECK), an ill-mannered, perverse, greedy and thieving 15-year-old who passes for 10 and who seems to have a future of petty crime in front of him.

Miss Corrie takes Otis in to save him from his family's hardscrabble farm. All the same, he extorts whatever he can from everyone he meets. He looks through a peephole into Aunt FITTIE's Arkansas whorehouse, where Miss Corrie used to work; he charges Miss Corrie five cents a day to keep mum about her real name; he sells out the MEMPHIS brothel landlord Mr. BINFORD, whose only weakness is horses, for 85 cents; he steals MINNIE's prized removable gold tooth.

Ott, Jimmy One of the competing pilots mentioned in PYLON.

Owl-by-Night Character in "A COURTSHIP" (in *Collected Stories*). A Young CHICKASAW INDIAN, he drops out of the contest for Herman BASKET's sister after he learns that IKKEMOTUBBE is interested in her.

Oxford, Mississippi City in north-central Mississippi. The seat of LAFAYETTE COUNTY, Oxford was a farming, manufacturing, and tourist center, site of the UNIVERSITY OF MISSISSIPPI (Ole Miss), lifelong home of Faulkner, and the model for his fictional JEFFERSON, MISSISSIPPI. Oxford was settled in 1840s on patent lands of the Chickasaw Ho-Kah. In 1962 the city became briefly notorious when whites violently opposed the admission of an African-American student, James Meredith, to the university.

Federal forces under General Ulysses S. Grant occupied Oxford briefly in December 1862. The Union commander A. J. SMITH returned in the summer of 1864 in pursuit of Nathan Bedford FORREST's cavalry and set fire to the center of the town on August 22, 1864. Where "once stood a handsome little country town, now only remained the blackened skeletons of the houses and smoldering ruins," a *Chicago Times* correspondent wrote in the aftermath of Smith's visit.

Oxford still showed traces of Civil War damage when Faulkner's grandfather John Wesley Thompson FALKNER moved there from RIPLEY, MISSISSIPPI, in late 1885. The Young Colonel pursued banking, railroad, and legal business from his law office on the northeast corner of the Courthouse Square and became active in Democratic politics.

Murry FALKNER moved his family from Ripley to Oxford in September 1902, when his father sold the railroad that had employed him. In contrast with Ripley, the place struck the Falkner boys, Billy and Jack, as a metropolis.

Oxford in 1902 had a population of around 1,800, making it three times the size of Ripley. The town boasted a courthouse with a four-faced clock; Ole Miss, a mile west of the city center; a nearly new water tower,

140 feet high; a newspaper (the *OXFORD EAGLE*); and hardware, dry goods, confectioners, and other stores clustered on the square.

The Murry Falkners settled into "the old Johnny Brown place" on Second South Street. Billy Falkner entered the Oxford school in September 1905. He later attended high school there, took classes sporadically at the university, painted houses in Oxford, worked in the university post office and power plant.

In April 1931, Faulkner and his wife, (Lida) Estelle Oldham FAULKNER, bought the old Shegog place on the Old Taylor Road, built in the mid-1840s. Renamed ROWAN OAK, it was Faulkner's permanent residence for the rest of his life.

Oxford had altered considerably by the 1930s. The first automobile arrived in 1908, a red Winton Six touring car. Soon the roads were paved, inviting more cars.

This statue of William Faulkner (by sculptor William N. Beck-with) in Courthouse Square, Oxford, Mississippi, was dedicated on the centennial of Faulkner's birth, September 25, 1997. (Harriett and Gioia Fargnoli)

The Confederate Monument, a tribute to the county's Confederate heroes, in Courthouse Square, Oxford, Mississippi. Erected on the south side of the County Courthouse in 1907 by the Patriotic Daughters of Lafayette County, the monument's soldier faces the south, with his back to the north. (Harriett and Gioia Fargnoli)

The sidewalks and the Square were paved, too, the downtown storefronts "renovated." The Big Place, J. W. T. Falkner's home and the center of Falkner life in the early years of the century, was divided into apartments; a gas station went up on the corner lot. Faulkner and his family mourned the lost Oxford of their youth.

Oxford today is best known to the world as Faulkner's home. Rowan Oak is a museum. The University of Mississippi is a center of Faulkner scholarship.

Oxford is also a fictional place about 40 miles from Jefferson and FRENCHMAN'S BEND. In Faulkner's fiction, it serves as the location of the University of Mississippi, where in *ABSALOM, ABSALOM!* Henry SUTPEN meets his half brother Charles BON and where in *The HAMLET* the schoolteacher LABOVE (2) is a student and football player.

Oxford Eagle   Weekly newspaper. Established in OXFORD, MISSISSIPPI, in 1877, it recorded the business, social, and literary doings of the Falkners and Faulkners beginning in the 1880s.

The newspaper reported William Faulkner's marriage to (Lida) Estelle Oldham (FAULKNER) in 1929 and thereafter made note of his works as they appeared, usually with local reaction and a synopsis of outland critical opinion.

FAULKNER WRITES ANOTHER NOVEL ran the *Eagle*'s headline on the appearance of SANCTUARY in 1931. "It is said that in this novel Faulkner looses all the fury of his pen and this is one of the most stirring of the many books written by him," the paper reported, before going on to call the book "disgusting."

Phillip E. Mullen, a son of the *Eagle*'s proprietor, covered Faulkner sympathetically for many years, presenting this strange, exotic, and sometimes infuriating author to local people who knew him only by reputation rather than through his works. "Few Oxford people realize the distinction of having as a native son, William Faulkner," Mullen wrote.

Mullen also defended Oxford's most famous citizen from unfriendly outside criticism. *Time* magazine's 1934 characterization of *Doctor Martino and Other Stories* as "merely potboilers" moved Mullen to remark, "As the Greek philosophers have so aptly put it, a guy's gotta eat."

Faulkner gave his only extended interview after winning the NOBEL PRIZE to Phil Mullen. Faulkner's daughter, Jill FAULKNER, worked as an editor at the *Eagle* for a brief period in 1954.

P

Painter Character in "IDYLL IN THE DESERT" (in *Uncollected Stories*). A grocer, he extends credit to Lucas CRUMP so Crump can supply groceries to the consumptive Darrel HOWES.

"Pantaloon in Black" *See GO DOWN, MOSES.*

Paoli Character in *KNIGHT'S GAMBIT* ("Knight's Gambit"). He is Max HARRISS's fencing master.

Pap (1) A blind and deaf old man in *SANCTUARY*. Pap is being taken care of by Lee GOODWIN and others at OLD FRENCHMAN PLACE.

Pap (2) Main character in the humorous tale "FOOL ABOUT A HORSE." Pap tries to outwit the horse- and mule trader Pat STAMPER, but always loses. When Pap trades his wife Vynie's cream separator for a horse, he unwittingly gets the same horse he had earlier in the day traded with Pat. To get the separator back, Vynie trades their mule and horse with Stamper.

Pap (3) *See GRIER (PAP).* This character is most probably the Pap in "SHINGLES FOR THE LORD."

Paralee Character in *INTRUDER IN THE DUST*. The Mallisons' cook, she is the mother of Chick MALLISON's friend and fellow detective, Aleck SANDER.

Parchman Mississippi state penitentiary and penal farm. Faulkner uses Parchman as a locale in the short story "Monk" and sets the opening scene of "Old Man" there. The "tall convict" of the latter story is assigned to a Parchman chain gang. Faulkner later wove the two stories together to create "The Wild Palms" (1939; see IF I FORGET THEE, JERUSALEM).

In *The Hamlet*, the first volume of the SNOPES trilogy, V. K. RATLIFF speculates that Mink SNOPES is Parchman-bound for the killing of Jack HOUSTON. The time Mink spends at Parchman is covered in the first section of *The Mansion*, the third novel of the trilogy.

Paris Review Quarterly journal of poetry, prose fiction, and art and literary criticism, founded in 1953. With George Plimpton as editor, the *Paris Review* has published a notable series of interviews with authors, including Jean STEIN's interview with Faulkner in May 1956.

The biographer Joseph BLOTNER regards Stein's piece as the best and most comprehensive Faulkner interview ever published. In it, Faulkner explained how he came to develop the YOKNAPATAWPHA COUNTY cycle. "I like to think of the world I created as being a kind of keystone in the universe; that, as small as that keystone is, the universe itself would collapse. My last book will be the Doomsday Book, the Golden Book, of Yoknapatawpha County. Then I shall break the pencil and I'll have to stop."

Parker's In *The SOUND AND THE FURY*, Quentin COMPSON eats breakfast at Parker's restaurant on the morning of his suicide, June 2, 1910.

Parsham, Tennessee Faulkner's name for Grand Junction, Tennessee, a railroad town 65 miles northwest of OXFORD, MISSISSIPPI. The National Field trials for bird dogs have been conducted there since 1900. Oxford rail passengers bound for Memphis changed trains at Grand Junction.

The horse race in *The REIVERS* takes place in Parsham.

Parsons, Maurice Minor character in *The TOWN*. He gives both his wife, Sally Hampton PARSONS, and Grenier WEDDEL a black eye because of the corsage Grenier sent to Sally for the Cotillion Ball at Christmas time.

Parsons, Sally Hampton Minor character in *The TOWN*. She is Maurice PARSONS's wife; Maurice gives her a black eye after she accepts a corsage from Grenier WEDDEL for JEFFERSON, MISSISSIPPI's, Cotillion Ball at Christmas.

Pascagoula, Mississippi City in southeastern Mississippi, a resort, fishing and shipbuilding center, and port of entry on the Gulf of Mexico.

Faulkner spent parts of the summers of 1925, 1926, and 1927 in Pascagoula. He wrote, swam, wandered about, and conducted an unsuccessful courtship of Helen BAIRD. Faulkner worked on his first novel, *SOLDIERS' PAY*, in Pascagoula in June 1925; started his second novel, *MOSQUITOES*, there in June 1926; and finished *FLAGS IN THE DUST* (published as *SARTORIS*) in the Gulf city in late September 1927.

Faulkner and his wife, (Lida) Estelle Oldham FAULKNER, spent their honeymoon in Pascagoula in June 1929. The novelist returned to Pascagoula with Jean STEIN in November 1955. Among other sights, he showed her the circular bench where he had worked on *Mosquitoes*. They encountered only one other figure on the cold, windswept beach—Helen Baird.

Pascagoula also figures as a location in Faulkner's writing. For example, in *The MANSION*, Linda Snopes KOHL works for the war effort in Pascagoula for a time during World War II.

Pate, Lucy *See* HOUSTON, LUCY PATE.

Patterson In *The SOUND AND THE FURY*, the husband of the woman with whom Maury BASCOMB is having an affair and to whom he sends love letters delivered by Caddy and Benjy COMPSON. When Patterson comes upon one of these letters, he confronts Maury and beats him up. (The episode occurs in the first chapter of the novel, narrated by Benjy, and indicates a time period around 1902 or 1903.)

Patterson, Mrs. In *The SOUND AND THE FURY*, the woman with whom Uncle Maury (BASCOMB) is having an affair. He sends her love letters delivered by Caddy and Benjy COMPSON. When her husband finds out, he gives Maury a black eye and bloody mouth. (This episode occurs sometime around 1902 or 1903 and is part of Benjy's memory as he narrates his chapter of the novel, "April Seventh, 1928.")

the Patterson boy In *The SOUND AND THE FURY*, one of Jason COMPSON's childhood friends. Together they make kites which they sell for a nickel apiece; Jason is treasurer. (Presumably this boy is PATTERSON's son.)

Paul One of the 12 disciples of Corporal STEFAN in *A FABLE*. He is considered second in command to Stefan and is designated to be in charge in Stefan's absence.

Peabody, Doctor Doctor Samuel HABERSHAM's successor in *REQUIEM FOR A NUN*. In the early history of YOKNAPATAWPHA COUNTY, Doctor Peabody is one of the men who agree on the naming of their new city, JEFFERSON, MISSISSIPPI. See also COMPSON, JASON LYCURGUS I.

Peabody, Doctor Lucius Quintus Character in *SARTORIS* and other works. Eighty-seven years old and 310 pounds, he is a long-standing friend of the Sartoris family and had been Colonel John SARTORIS's regimental surgeon during the Civil War. Dr. Peabody has long since stopped keeping accounts and charging fees, and

cheerfully accepts a meal or a measure of corn or fruit for his services.

He and Dr. ALFORD consult about old Bayard SARTORIS's wen, disagreeing on the diagnosis. A home remedy eventually causes the wen to fall off.

In *The SOUND AND THE FURY*, Doc Peabody lets the Compson children hang onto his buckboard for a ride. He attends the deathbed of Addie BUNDREN and saves the broken and festering leg of Cash BUNDREN in *AS I LAY DYING*. (Peabody narrates chapters 11 and 54 of the novel.) In *The HAMLET*, V. K. RATLIFF buys a bottle of whiskey from Doc Peabody and gives it to Ab SNOPES when Pat STAMPER outwits Snopes on a horse trade. Doc Peabody also appears in *The TOWN* and *The REIVERS*, and in the short story "BEYOND."

Peabody, Lucius Character in *SARTORIS*. The surgeon son of Dr. Lucius Quintus PEABODY, he is known as young Loosh. He lives in New York and visits his father and other JEFFERSON, MISSISSIPPI, connections once or twice a year.

Pearson, Mr. Character in "THE TALL MEN" (in *Collected Stories*). A government draft board investigator, he serves warrants on Amodeus (Buddy) MCCALLUM's sons, Anse and Lucius MCCALLUM, for failing to register for the draft.

Peebles, E. E. Character in *LIGHT IN AUGUST*. He is Joanna BURDEN's lawyer, with an office on Beale Street in MEMPHIS.

Pemberton, John C. (1814–1881) Pennsylvania-born Confederate soldier. Commanding Confederate forces in Mississippi in 1862–63, he retreated into the river fortress of Vicksburg under pressure from the Union Gen. Ulysses S. Grant, and after a long siege surrendered Vicksburg to Grant on July 4, 1863 (see VICKSBURG CAMPAIGN).

Vicksburg was one of the decisive Union victories of the war, and the South never forgave Pemberton for his ineptitude in defending the place. In Faulkner's novel *The UNVANQUISHED* (1938), young BAYARD SARTORIS (3) and his enslaved friend Ringo STROTHER made a "living map" behind the smokehouse in the summer of 1863 and fought Pemberton's Vicksburg battles to a favorable conclusion.

"Pennsylvania Station" (*Collected Stories*) Short story set in New York City on a cold winter night. As they wait to be evicted from the warmth of the railroad station, two homeless men pass the time by talking. Through their dialogue, the older man reveals a central event of his life. His widowed sister Margaret GIHON, who cleaned houses, had been paying an undertaker for her coffin in installments. Her son, Danny GIHON, a young criminal, landed in jail in Florida and asked his uncle, the older man, who lived nearby, to help get him out. This led to the discovery that Danny already had extracted his mother's coffin money, by means of a forged note, from the undertaker. To protect her son from the law Mrs. Gihon, an illiterate woman, insisted that she had signed the note.

Her recognition, at last, of her son's evil nature so demoralized her that she died that night. Both his uncle and mother had tried to protect Danny since his troubled youth. The story implies that these efforts bankrupted the old man and resulted in his present dire situation. Despite his companion's sarcastic interjections and the facts of the narrative, the old man repeatedly insists on Danny's goodness. Though such loyalty in the face of ingratitude may seem naive, it serves an essential purpose. Throughout, the old man emphasizes his own remarkable ability to survive against all odds. His illusions are the foundation of his powerful optimism; ironically, this is what enables him to endure. The two men finally are ousted from the station and move on to spend the rest of the night in Grand Central Terminal.

This story first appeared in *American Mercury* (February 1934).

Pete   (1) A 19-year old in the short stories "ONCE ABOARD THE LUGGER" (I) and (II). Apparently this is his first bootlegging trip out into the Gulf of Mexico, and he becomes violently seasick. His seasickness in essence causes a delay when the crew, short one man because of Pete's incapacity, digs up the buried alcohol on an unnamed island. The delay is significant because in "Once Aboard the Lugger" (II), another bootlegger overtakes Pete's boat and hijacks the alcohol, killing Pete and a black crew member in the process.

Pete   (2) Character in *IF I FORGET THEE, JERUSALEM* ("The Wild Palms"). He works in the San Antonio brothel where Harry WILBOURNE goes in search of a drug that will cause Charlotte RITTENMEYER to have an abortion. Pete advises the brothel bouncer to "sock" (punch) Wilbourne.

Pete   (3) In *Requiem for a Nun*, the younger brother of Temple Drake's STEVENS's deceased lover, RED. Pete has letters Temple wrote to his brother and intends to blackmail her, but a romantic interest develops between them. Their plans to run off with each other are foiled when Temple's six-month-old daughter is murdered by her nanny, Nancy MANNIGOE.

"Peter" *(Uncollected Stories)* Short piece set in a NEW ORLEANS brothel. The nameless narrator (probably Faulkner himself) has accompanied his artist friend SPRATLING on a sketching expedition into the Negro district. As customers enter and leave, the young mulatto boy PETER, on watch for his mother and the other prostitutes, speaks with the two men about his own life, his mother's affairs, and of his more innocent longing to learn to spin a top. Peter asks the artist to draw him, but is too restless to hold his pose. Their conversation is punctuated by ragtime music from the Victrola and by sexually explicit exclamations from within the rooms. Finally Peter's mother comes down and ends the sketching session, to the boy's dismay.

Concurrent with the pieces in *NEW ORLEANS SKETCHES* (1958), this probably was originally intended for newspaper publication in 1925, but was not issued until its inclusion in *Uncollected Stories* (1979). William M. SPRATLING was Faulkner's close friend and New Orleans neighbor who accompanied him on his European trip.

Peter   Character in the short story "PETER" (in *Uncollected Stories*). A young mulatto whose mother works in a brothel, he asks the artist SPRATLING to do a sketch of him as part of Spratling's tour of the Black quarter. Peter has trouble holding a pose, though, and finally his mother comes down and puts an end to the sitting.

Pettibone   Character in *ABSALOM, ABSALOM!* A Virginia planter, he inspires both awe and resentment in young Thomas SUTPEN. The boy vows to someday acquire wealth and power equivalent to Pettibone's.

Pettigrew   Character in "BEYOND" (in *Collected Stories*). A JEFFERSON, MISSISSIPPI, lawyer, he draws up Judge ALLISON's will.

Pettigrew, Thomas Jefferson   The small and seemingly insignificant mail rider in REQUIEM FOR A NUN after whom the town of JEFFERSON, MISSISSIPPI, is named. Pettigrew shows a remarkable durability riding between the original settlement in northern Mississippi, which later became the town of Jefferson, and Nashville to deliver the mail every three weeks. He rides unarmed through bandit and Indian territories, showing almost casual bravery, using only a hunting horn to mark his coming and going. Pettigrew's physical courage is matched by his moral rectitude, which forces him to object to Jason Lycurgus COMPSON I's plan to pay Alec HOLSTON $15 for a lost lock out of funds provided by the federal government for the CHICKASAW INDIAN removal. Pettigrew's acquiescence is bought when the settlers offer to name the town Jefferson in his honor.

Peyton, George   Character in *The REIVERS*. A famous bird dog specialist, he comes to PARSHAM, TENNESSEE, once a year for the Grand National trials.

Philadelphia (Philadelphy)   Character in *The UNVANQUISHED*. One of the Sartoris slaves, she reluctantly goes off with her husband, LOOSH, who during the Civil War follows the Yankees in search of freedom.

Philadelphy also appears in the short story "MY GRANDMOTHER MILLARD AND GENERAL BEDFORD FORREST AND THE BATTLE OF HARRYKIN CREEK."

Philip Character in "ELLY" (in *Collected Stories*). He is an assistant bank cashier in JEFFERSON, MISSISSIPPI, engaged to ELLY. She is in love with Paul DE MONTIGNY, who refuses to marry her.

Phoebe (Fibby) Character in *GO DOWN, MOSES* ("The Bear"). A McCaslin slave, she is the wife of ROSCIUS (Roskus).

Pickett, George C. (1825–1875) Confederate soldier. On Gen. Robert E. Lee's orders, at a little after two o'clock in the afternoon of July 3, 1863, he led the doomed assault at Gettysburg known ever after—and known more familiarly to Southerners of Faulkner's generation than ever Lexington and Concord were—as Pickett's charge. Faulkner refers to Pickett's charge in *The UNVANQUISHED*.

OXFORD, MISSISSIPPI, claimed later that a locally raised infantry company, the UNIVERSITY GREYS of the UNIVERSITY OF MISSISSIPPI, "reached the highest point of the Confederacy" during Pickett's charge, "forty-seven yards beyond the farthest" advance of any other of General Pickett's troops.

Picklock A French private in *A FABLE*. Picklock, whose name comes from his civilian profession, leads a 12-man detail assigned to the task of getting a body to bury in the Tomb of the Unknown Soldier. After the detail obtains a body from a fortress in Verdun, Picklock steals brandy from Sergeant LANDRY's briefcase. In a drunken stupor the men sell the body to a bereaved old woman, who is convinced that it is her dead son. Still in need of a body, Picklock and MORACHE trade a stolen German officer's watch with a farmer for a replacement. This second body is that of Corporal STEFAN, who is thus resurrected and buried with honor as the Unknown Soldier.

Pinckski Character in "PENNSYLVANIA STATION" (in *Collected Stories*). He sells Margaret GIHON a coffin on the installment plan, with payments set at 50 cents a week.

Pinkie Character in "ARTIST AT HOME" (in *Collected Stories*). She cooks for Roger and Anne HOWES.

Pittsburgh Landing Tennessee town. See SHILOH, BATTLE OF.

Ploeckner Character in *SARTORIS*. A protégé of the German aviator RICHTOFEN, he shot down Johnny SARTORIS, the twin brother of young Bayard SARTORIS (4), in combat over France during World War I.

Polchek One of the 12 followers of Corporal STEFAN in *A FABLE*. Polchek corresponds to Judas in Christ's passion story. He betrays the corporal, telling the OLD GENERAL about the planned mutiny. In return, he is freed from the prison during the last meal they share. He later repents his action, and after the war's end he seeks out Marthe and MARYA at their farm. He offers them 29 coins, and adds the symbolic 30th from his pocket. When they refuse his money and his expiation, Polchek leaves in despair. On his way through their doorway he appears "as if he actually were hanging on a cord against the vacant shape of the spring darkness" (p. 366).

Poleymus Character in *The REIVERS*. He is the honest, capable constable of PARSHAM, TENNESSEE. When he learns that the deputy Butch LOVEMAIDEN is abusing his authority in his bid to sleep with the reformed prostitute Everbe Corinthia (HOGGANBECK), Poleymus strips Butch of his badge and jails him.

After the races, he hires Everbe as nurse and companion to his invalid wife.

Polk, Noel (1943–) Noted Faulkner textual scholar, critic, and professor of English at the University of Southern Mississippi. Among his critical writings, Polk has published *Faulkner's "Requiem for a Nun": A Critical Study* (1981); *An Editorial Handbook for William Faulkner's "The Sound and the Fury"* (1985); and *Children of the Dark House: Text and Context in Faulkner* (1996). For the Library of America editions of Faulkner's works, Polk has edited *William Faulkner: Novels 1930–1935* (with Joseph BLOTNER); *William Faulkner: Novels 1936–1940* (with Blotner); *William Faulkner: Novels 1942–1954* (with Blotner); and *William Faulkner: Novels 1957–1962* (notes by Blotner). Polk is also a founding member of the Mississippi Institute of Arts and Letters.

Pomp Character in *LIGHT IN AUGUST*. He is the husband of CINTHY and the servant of the Civil War cavalryman Gail HIGHTOWER (1). Refusing to believe his master has been killed, he goes off in search of him and is killed in his turn when he attacks a Yankee officer with a shovel.

Pontotoc, Mississippi Northern Mississippi town, 30 miles southeast of OXFORD, MISSISSIPPI, the native place of Colonel William C. FALKNER's first wife, Elizabeth Vance, and the southern terminus of the Old Colonel's GULF & SHIP ISLAND RAILROAD—"the Doodlebug Line." Several fine antebellum houses still stand.

Murry FALKNER, Faulkner's father, lived there in 1891 as an employee of the railroad and was shot and badly injured in a dispute with a local man. Faulkner's brother Dean Swift FAULKNER, flying in an air show, died in the crash of his airplane near Pontotoc in November 1935.

Popeye   In SANCTUARY, a gangster and bootlegger who kills the half-wit TOMMY and rapes Temple Drake (STEVENS) with a corncob; he is sexually impotent, and although he is a bootlegger he himself cannot consume alcohol, for it would kill him. On the same day he rapes Temple at OLD FRENCHMAN PLACE, Popeye drives her to a Memphis brothel. When Popeye brings his friend RED to her room, he watches Red and Temple have sex, but when they become lovers and plan to run away together, Popeye kills him. On his yearly visit to his mother in Pensacola, Popeye is arrested in Birmingham and convicted and hanged for the murder of a police officer in a small Alabama town that occurred on the same night Popeye killed Red.

Though Faulkner said in an interview at the University of Virginia that Popeye was not intended to be a symbol of evil but became one "in modern society only by coincidence" (*Faulkner in the University,* p. 74), many readers see in this character not merely a manifestation of moral indifference but of evil itself. The description of Popeye in the opening pages of the novel presages a sinister being: "His face had a queer, bloodless color as though seen by electric light; against the sunny silence, . . . he had that vicious depthless quality of stamped tin" (p. 4). But the reader's interpretation of Popeye may be slightly altered by the last chapter, which Faulkner added when revising the galleys of the novel in late 1930. The physical, psychological, and medical information on Popeye that the narrator provides may add, for some readers, a sympathetic perspective to the character.

Popeye is also referred to in *REQUIEM FOR A NUN,* where his last name is given as Vitelli. He first appeared in the short story "THE BIG SHOT," written around 1929 but not published in Faulkner's lifetime. In that story, Popeye, a bootlegger who works for GOVELLI, accidentally runs over and kills Wrennie MARTIN, the only child of the powerful political boss, Dal MARTIN.

The Portable Faulkner   Anthology of Faulkner's works, published in 1946 and revised in 1974. The writer and critic Malcolm COWLEY assembled the anthology, which includes shorter works—notably, "The Bear"—and excerpts from the novels *The SOUND AND THE FURY* (1929), *SANCTUARY* (1931), *ABSALOM, ABSALOM!* (1936), *The UNVANQUISHED* (1938), "The Wild Palms" (1939), and *The HAMLET* (1940).

Cowley conceived the project at a time when Faulkner's 17 books were effectively out of print. Cowley asked, "How could one speak of Faulkner's value on the literary stock exchange? In 1944 his name wasn't even listed there."

An essay on Faulkner in the *New York Times Book Review* represented Cowley's initial effort to "redress the balance between his worth and his reputation." *The Portable Faulkner* followed. Cowley and Faulkner collab-

orated on the selections and arrangement; Faulkner provided a set of character genealogies titled "The Compsons" and a map of YOKNAPATAWPHA COUNTY.

Cowley recounted their literary relationship, which continued until Faulkner's death, in *The Faulkner-Cowley File: Letters and Memories* (Viking, 1966). (Also see FAULKNER AND CRITICISM.)

"A Portrait of Elmer" *(Uncollected Stories)*   Short story derived from *ELMER,* the unfinished experimental novel Faulkner wrote in Paris in 1925. The story opens with an American, Elmer HODGE, sitting at a Parisian sidewalk cafe with his Italian friend ANGELO. In an interior monologue, Elmer meditates on his present surroundings, his impatience with Angelo, his plans to establish himself as an artist, and his hope of again meeting Myrtle MONSON, a Texan to whom he is attracted and who now is in Paris with her mother. He then recalls their first meeting in Houston.

In a series of flashbacks of Elmer's earlier life, Elmer first recalls the house fire that occurred when he was five and that introduces his disintegrating family. Only his sister, Jo HODGE, is heroic. She senses his artistic potential, sending him a box of paints after she leaves home. At age 14 Elmer is attracted to a cruel, beautiful boy and is devoted to the middle-aged teacher who encourages his aspirations; he flees when she makes a physical overture. At age 15, his sexual initiation takes place with VELMA, a neighbor girl. In another flashback, Elmer returns to Houston wounded from World War I, longing for Myrtle, to find his mother dead and his father cheerful.

The point of view shifts briefly to Angelo, who thinks of his own war days, delights in the women passing by, and considers Elmer with contempt.

Elmer next thinks back to his liaison at age 18 with ETHEL, who refused to marry him yet bore his son. This rejection sent him on the road as a menial laborer and hobo. He ended up in a Michigan lumber camp, where the cook encouraged him to join the Canadian army. During training he was injured by a grenade and shipped back from England. While in New York, he thought he saw his sister Jo at a war rally.

A second meditation by Angelo gives way to an account of Elmer's parents' marriage and of the discovery of the oil in his father's yard that funded his European trip. Elmer paints a watercolor landscape that is to be his introduction to the Paris art world. In the farcical conclusion, he is forced to use this painting to wipe himself when Myrtle and her mother unexpectedly visit his room.

This satirical portrait of the artist as a young man is notable for its play with chronology, INTERIOR MONOLOGUE, and point of view, and its echoes of T. S. Eliot and James JOYCE. It first was published in *Uncollected Stories* (1979).

Pose Character in *KNIGHT'S GAMBIT* ("Hand upon the Waters"). With IKE, Jim BLAKE, and MATTHEW, he helps carry Lonnie GRINNUP's body from the coroner's office to the burial ground.

postmodernism A movement in the arts stemming directly from (and in reaction to) MODERNISM. Although sharing certain characteristics with modernism (such as textual strategies and the questioning of the authority of social institutions), postmodernist fiction interrogates the legitimacy of the ontology of the text itself (or the ontology of the world which a text projects), but it does not, like modernism, substitute the moral authority of social institutions with that of the individual. Literary postmodernism also encourages extensive experimentation in narrative presentation and rhetorical and stylistic devices. An observation by Conrad AIKEN on the extraordinary effectiveness of Faulkner's style when seen as a whole, first published in the *ATLANTIC MONTHLY* in November 1939, is apropos of a discussion of Faulkner and postmodernism. If one views Faulkner's "sentences not simply by themselves . . . but in their relation to the book as a whole, one sees a functional reason and necessity for their being as they are. They parallel in a curious and perhaps inevitable way, and not without aesthetic justification, the whole elaborate method of *deliberately withheld meaning*, of progressive and partial and delayed disclosure, which so often gives the characteristic shape to the novels themselves. It is a persistent offering of obstacles, a calculated system of screens and obtrusions, of confusions and ambiguous interpolations and delays, with one express purpose; and that purpose is simply to keep the form—and the idea—fluid and unfinished, still in motion, as it were, and unknown, until the dropping into place of the very last syllable" ("William Faulkner: The Novel as Form" in *William Faulkner: Three Decades of Criticism*, pp. 137–38).

Faulkner, along with James JOYCE and Samuel Beckett, has long been seen as one of the precursors to the postmodernist movement. In *Postmodernist Fiction* (New York: Methuen, 1987), Brian McHale points to chapter 8 of *ABSALOM, ABSALOM!*, in which Quentin COMPSON and Shreve MCCANNON reconstruct the Sutpen murder mystery, as the precise moment when postmodernism took its bow. This chapter, according to McHale, "dramatizes the shift of dominant from problems of *knowing* to problems of *modes of being*—from an epistemological dominant to an *ontological one*. At this point Faulkner's novel touches and perhaps crosses the boundary between modernist and postmodernist writing" (p. 10). Both modernism and postmodernism share the common characteristic of textual positioning and the role of the text for both narrator and reader.

Powell, John Character in *The REIVERS*. The head hostler of the Priest livery stable in JEFFERSON, MISSISSIPPI, he is the proud owner of a pistol that he bought from his father the day he turned 21. Strictly against the rules, Powell brings the weapon to work with him, a fact known to all but never acknowledged, even by Maury PRIEST, whose gentlemanly code bars him from taking notice.

An enraged Boon HOGGANBECK takes the pistol from its resting place in Powell's jumper pocket and fires several times at the stable hand LUDUS (2), who has cheated him out of a jug of fine whiskey.

Powers, Mrs. Margaret A wise, compassionate woman in *SOLDIERS' PAY*. Mrs. Powers inspires confidence and love in those who meet her. A war widow (probably in her early to mid-20s), she meets the drunken Joe GILLIGAN, Cadet Julian LOWE, and Donald MAHON on a train. With Gilligan's help, she takes charge of getting Mahon back home to his father in Charlestown, Georgia. Mrs. Powers remains in Charlestown helping Gilligan and Aunt Callie NELSON take care of the dying lieutenant Mahon. When Mahon's fiancée, Cecily SAUNDERS, refuses to go through with marrying him, Mrs. Powers weds Mahon, who, as she expects, dies soon after. When Joe Gilligan asks Margaret to marry him, she refuses, saying that twice a widow was enough. Throughout the novel, Mrs. Powers receives letters from Cadet Lowe, who at the beginning of the novel had also asked her to marry him.

Powers, Richard (Dick) An officer in *SOLDIERS' PAY*. He is killed by one of his own men, Dewey BURNEY. Powers was very briefly married to Margaret POWERS, with whom he spent three days before going overseas in World War I.

Prall, Elizabeth (Elizabeth Prall Anderson) (unknown) Faulkner met this former teacher of Greek in New York City in the autumn of 1924, when she gave him a job clerking in the bookstore she managed at 38th Street and Fifth Avenue.

Prall married the writer Sherwood ANDERSON and settled with him in NEW ORLEANS. Faulkner renewed his acquaintance with her and met her husband there. At Prall's invitation, he stayed in the couple's Vieux Carré apartment for several weeks in early 1925.

The Andersons moved to Marion, Virginia, in 1927 and were separated two years later. By then Faulkner's initial friendship with Anderson had cooled to the point of rancor.

Price A store owner referred to in *SOLDIERS' PAY*.

"The Priest" A short story that contains almost no action other than a short walk taken by the protagonist, an unnamed seminarian, on the eve of his ordination. Although he seems completely sincere in his beliefs and is prepared to make the church his profession, he finds himself racked with guilt over physical desires and sexual curiosities that he has long suppressed. He notices girls everywhere and wonders about their simple daily chores and pleasures. Troubled by his thoughts of youth and women, he momentarily questions his religious commitment and philosophy. Although he believes his ordination will give him enough grace to renounce earthly desires, the unnamed priest-to-be is not completely convinced. The story ends with his promise to purge his soul and a prayer to the Blessed Virgin.

This early short narrative portrays the protagonist with an indefinite future and as an outsider in the world around him, a theme that Faulkner skillfully exploited throughout his mature writings. "The Priest" was written in 1925 and first published posthumously in the *Mississippi Quarterly* 29 (summer 1976), 445–50, where it was edited with an introduction by James B. MERIWETHER. The story is reprinted in *UNCOLLECTED STORIES OF WILLIAM FAULKNER*.

Priest, Alexander   Character in *The REIVERS*. He is the infant brother of the narrator, Lucius (Loosh) PRIEST.

Priest, Alison Lessep   Character in *The REIVERS*. She is the wife of Maury PRIEST Sr. and the mother of young Lucius PRIEST and his brothers—Lessep, Maury Jr., and Alexander PRIEST. She and her husband are away in Bay St. Louis for her father's funeral when Boon HOGGANBECK, Lucius, and Ned MCCASLIN set out for MEMPHIS.

Priest, Lessep   Character in *The REIVERS*. He is one of young Lucius PRIEST's younger brothers.

Priest, Lucius (Boss Priest; Grandfather)   Character in *The REIVERS*. The father of Maury PRIEST Sr. and the grandfather of the narrator, young Lucius PRIEST, he is a leading citizen of JEFFERSON, MISSISSIPPI, president of the rival bank to Colonel John SARTORIS's Merchants and Farmers Bank.

He buys an early automobile, a Winton Flyer, simply to spite his business rival, who has forced through a municipal ordinance banning motor vehicles on Jefferson's streets. Soon, at Boon HOGGANBECK's instigation, rides in the Flyer become a family institution.

Boss Priest turns up in PARSHAM, TENNESSEE, to collect the runaways and the car. He treats the escapade as minor, and even bets—ill-advisedly—on Lightning (Coppermine) to win the fourth heat against Colonel LINSCOMB's Acheron.

When young Lucius practically begs for a punishment for his transgressions, Grandfather tells him that he will have to live with the tangle of lies and deceptions associated with the Memphis trip because "[a] gentleman accepts the responsibility of his actions."

When Boon returns to Jefferson with his bride, Everbe Corinthia (HOGGANBECK), Boss Priest sells them a small house for 50 cents a week, payable on Saturdays.

Priest, Lucius (Loosh)   Character who is the narrator of *The REIVERS*. He is a member of a prominent, privileged JEFFERSON, MISSISSIPPI, family. In 1961, he spins out for his grandson the tale of his four-day adventure in MEMPHIS in May 1905, when he was a boy of 11.

With his parents away attending Grandfather LESSEP's funeral in Bay St. Louis, 300 miles distant, Lucius acquiesces in, and even helps advance, Boon HOGGANBECK's plan to borrow the family car, a Winton Flyer, for a trip to Memphis and the CATALPA STREET brothel of Reba RIVERS.

As the trip unfolds, Lucius gradually loses his innocence. Events force his early entry into grown-up life, and he becomes a willing and faithful servant of "nonvirtue." He learns about commercial sex, racing, and gambling, and picks up fresh lessons in duplicity, loyalty, betrayal, and racial bigotry.

Loosh enjoys an early triumph. He is immediately taken with Miss Corrie (Everbe Corinthia [HOGGANBECK]), Boon's particular interest at Miss Reba's, and she with him. When 15-year-old OTIS, Everbe's odious nephew, explains his aunt's role at Miss Reba's, Lucius attacks him. When Everbe learns that Lucius has risen to her defense, she is so touched that she vows to give up her work.

Nevertheless, he is drawn deeper into the grown people's schemes. Even though he is guilt-racked and homesick, Loosh does not ask Boon and Ned MCCASLIN to give up their racing scheme and carry him home. On the contrary, he agrees to replace the unreliable Otis as jockey aboard Lightning (Coppermine).

Lucius is fully engaged now, both as the defender of Everbe's virtue against the assaults of Boon and the corrupt deputy Butch LOVEMAIDEN, and as Lightning's rider. There is no turning back. He has entered the adult world.

At Uncle Parsham HOOD's insistence, Ned tells Lucius that Everbe has "entertained" Butch and that Boon has beaten them both. Inconsolable, the boy turns to Hood for solace. The next day, when Lucius wins the decisive third heat, he refuses to accept the money Miss Reba has made for him.

Lucius returns to Jefferson changed forever, innocence and childhood lost beyond recall. But he sees with a shock that home has not changed at all. He seeks, even begs for, punishment for his crimes. His father's display of the razor strop seems inadequate to the moral dimension of the case. Finally, Grandfather Priest intervenes and tells him he must take responsibility for his actions.

Boon eventually returns to Jefferson with Everbe Corinthia as his bride. As the tale closes, Lucius meets their newborn son, his namesake, Lucius Priest HOGGANBECK.

Priest, Maurice   *See* PARSONS, MAURICE.

Priest, Maury, Jr.   Character in *The* REIVERS. He is a younger brother of the narrator, Lucius (Loosh) PRIEST.

Priest, Maury, Sr.   Character in *The* REIVERS. He is the ineffectual father of the narrator, Lucius (Loosh) PRIEST, and the owner of the Priest livery stable in JEFFERSON, MISSISSIPPI.

After Lucius's MEMPHIS adventure, Maury takes his son to the cellar for a whipping, a wholly inappropriate punishment for his crimes.

Priest, Sarah Edmonds   Character in *The* REIVERS. She is the wife of the elder Lucius PRIEST and grandmother of the narrator, young Lucius PRIEST.

Pritchel, Wesley   Character in KNIGHT'S GAMBIT ("An Error in Chemistry"). He is the foul-tempered father-in-law of Joel FLINT and the owner of a back country YOKNAPATAWPHA COUNTY farm with valuable deposits of clay. Flint murders him in a bid to obtain possession of the farm.

Provine, Lucius   Character in "A BEAR HUNT" (in *Collected Stories*). He and his brother once led a wild gang of youths in which Luke HOGGANBECK figured prominently.

Provine, Wilbur   Minor character in *The* TOWN. Not able to prove that Provine makes whiskey illegally, Judge LONG instead sends him to prison for making his wife walk a mile and a half for water.

Pruitt   Character in "THAT WILL BE FINE" (in *Collected Stories*). The president of the Compress Association in MOTTSTOWN, he gives Uncle RODNEY a job to please his duplicitous wife, who is carrying on an affair with Rodney. When Rodney steals the association's bonds, Pruitt generously offers not to prosecute until after Christmas.

Pruitt, Mrs.   **(1)** Character in KNIGHT'S GAMBIT ("Tomorrow"). A white-haired old lady in a clean gingham sunbonnet and dress, she helps her son Rufus PRUITT narrate the story of the Fentrys to Gavin STEVENS, breaking in frequently to correct him or to add details.

Pruitt, Mrs.   **(2)** Character in "THAT WILL BE FINE" (in *Collected Stories*). The wife of the president of the Compress Association in MOTTSTOWN, she takes Uncle RODNEY as her lover, setting in motion events that end in Rodney's shooting death.

Pruitt, Rufus   Character in KNIGHT'S GAMBIT ("Tomorrow"). A hill country neighbor of G. A. FENTRY's, he tells Gavin Stevens the story of Fentry and his infant son. Pruitt's loquacious mother interrupts to correct him or supply details.

Pylon   One of Faulkner's non-YOKNAPATAWPHA COUNTY novels. Its setting is New Valois, Franciana, a thinly disguised New Orleans, Louisiana, during a three-day air show celebrating the opening of Feinman Airport at Mardi Gras time. The title refers to one of the posts marking a designated flight course for aircraft competing in events. The plot concerns a strange *ménage à trois* arrangement between Jack HOLMES, a parachuter; Roger SHUMANN, a racing pilot; and Laverne SHUMANN, mother of the young boy Jack SHUMANN. After the child was born (and not knowing whether Holmes or Shumann was the child's father), Laverne married Shumann when the two men cast dice to determine who would marry her and act as the legal father of the child. She gave the boy the first name of the man she did not marry.

Shumann manages to outfly pilots in more powerful, more modern aircraft to win second place in the first race. In covering the air show, the unnamed REPORTER becomes intrigued with the relationship among Roger, Laverne, and Jack, and tries to convince the editor, HAGOOD, to run a piece about them. Hagood tells him to write only about the news of the air show or risk being fired. The reporter does not care, however, about his editor's threat and continues to investigate and enter into the private lives of the other characters. Knowing that Shumann must wait a couple of days to collect the second-place winnings, the reporter allows this unconventional family and the team's mechanic, JIGGS, to stay in his flat. In the second race, Shumann crashes his plane because Jiggs, who was hung over, failed to maintain its engine properly. The reporter continues to assist Shumann in his pursuit of winning the last race with the largest purse in the competition, $2,000. He helps get a new airplane from the famous but retired pilot, Matt Ord. Knowing that the plane is unsafe because its engine is too powerful for its frame, Ord will not sell the plane and wants it grounded. However, Shumann and the reporter go behind Ord's back and sign a promissory note for the plane, which is accepted by an authorized agent of Ord's corporation. At first, Schumann flies well in the new airplane, but when he is about to take the lead, his aircraft begins to break up. Courageously maneuvering away from the crowds, Shumann takes his plane over the lake, where he crashes and dies. His body is lost forever.

As the novel closes, Jiggs joins the pilot Art JACKSON to become a parachuter. He gives gifts to Holmes, Laverne, and little Jack before they travel to Ohio, where Roger's father, Dr. Carl SHUMANN, lives. Holmes and Laverne (who is now pregnant, she believes, with

Holmes's child) leave her son with Dr. Shumann and his wife, Roger's mother, to rear. Although angry over not knowing the true paternity of the child, Dr. Shumann, nonetheless, takes the boy with the condition that Laverne never see him again. She leaves at night while little Jack is asleep. When Dr. Shumann discovers the $175 that the reporter hid as a gift in the boy's toy airplane, he talks about it with his wife, who convinces him that Laverne was hiding the money from Roger. Assuming that Laverne made the money illegally by prostituting herself, Dr. Shumann burns it. Back in New Valois, the reporter writes the story of Roger Shumann's death, after which he goes out to get drunk.

In addition to Shakespearean references (for example, Macbeth's "tomorrow and tomorrow and tomorrow"), throughout *Pylon,* Faulkner shows his indebtedness to James JOYCE and T. S. Eliot in particular. For instance, in the second chapter of the novel, "An Evening in New Valois," there are a few journalistic captions characteristic of the Aeolis episode in Joyce's *Ulysses,* and portmanteau words abound in the novel. The penultimate chapter of *Pylon* is entitled "Lovesong of J. Alfred Prufrock," after Eliot's well-known poem "The Love Song of J. Alfred Prufrock." Eliot's wasteland (*The Waste Land*) is also evoked through the treatment of the novel's central characters as they face an indefinite future. (The very description of the airport itself in the opening chapter of the novel states that it has been "raised up" and "created out" of a wasteland). The novel ends with the reporter's obituary of Shumann and on a literal note of despair that the reporter "savagely" pencils in beneath the obituary for his editor to read.

Pylon may be Faulkner's most self-consciously "modernistic" work. As Daniel J. Singal points out in *William Faulkner: The Making of a Modernist,* "the aviators in *Pylon* are viewed through a Modernist lens that preserves their standing as heroes but strips away virtually all the glamour. Distinctly ordinary men and women from nondescript midwestern backgrounds, they have chosen to risk their lives racing dangerous aircraft in order to escape the humdrum existence to which they would otherwise be consigned" (192–193).

In response to a question at the University of Virginia, Faulkner explained that he wrote *Pylon* to get away from writing *Absalom, Absalom!* (*Faulkner in the University,* p. 36). Because *Pylon* was written very quickly (according to Joseph Blotner, the last few months of 1934), it "must have given Faulkner a sense of freshness and even release," as Cleanth BROOKS comments in *William Faulkner: Toward Yoknapatawpha and Beyond* (p. 178).

Pylon was first published by Harrison SMITH and Robert HAAS in March 1935. A corrected text by Noel POLK was published in 1985 by the LIBRARY OF AMERICA (volume 1 of Faulkner's collected works: *Novels 1930–1935*), and again with illustrations by David Tamura in 1987 by Vintage. A film adaptation of the novel, titled *The Tarnished Angels,* was released by Universal-International in 1957, directed by Douglas Sirk and starring Rock Hudson as Burke Devlin (the unnamed reporter in the novel), Robert Stack as Roger Shumann, Dorothy Malone as Laverne Shumann, Jack Carson as Jiggs, and Chris Olsen as Jack Shumann.

Quentin (1) *See* COMPSON, QUENTIN.

Quentin (2) *See* COMPSON, (MISS) QUENTIN.

Quick (Lon, Isham) Character in *The HAMLET,* the short story "SPOTTED HORSES" (revised for the novel), *KNIGHT'S GAMBIT* ("Tomorrow"), and *AS I LAY DYING.* The son of Uncle Ben QUICK, Lon Quick operates the sawmill in FRENCHMAN'S BEND. In *The Hamlet,* he is the first to offer to buy one of the wild ponies Buck HIPPS is about to auction off. When the horses escape after the auction, Quick fails to capture the one he bought. In *Knight's Gambit* ("Tomorrow"), where his first name appears as Isham, his father runs the sawmill. Isham Quick finds the half-drawn pistol in the hand of Buck THORPE, whom the farmer BOOKWRIGHT has just killed for attempting to elope with his daughter. Later, after the Bookwright murder trial ends in a hung jury, Quick recalls the Fentry-Thorpe connection (Stonewall Jackson FENTRY raised the orphaned Thorpe) and explains it to Gavin STEVENS. In *As I Lay Dying,* Lon, a neighbor of Anse BUNDREN, trades Jewel BUNDREN a spotted horse in exchange for clearing a field. Anse later trades this horse for a new team of mules. (Faulkner was not always consistent with the names of certain characters.)

Quick, (Uncle) Ben Character in *The HAMLET,* where he is called Uncle Ben Quick. In this novel, he is an old man who raises goats and has a son, named Lon QUICK, who operates a sawmill in FRENCHMAN'S BEND. In *KNIGHT'S GAMBIT* ("Tomorrow"), Ben Quick owns the sawmill where Stonewall Jackson FENTRY works and has a son named Isham QUICK. (Faulkner was not always consistent with the names of certain characters.)

Quick, Lon (little) The son of old Lon QUICK in *AS I LAY DYING.* Quick finds Doc Peabody's team of horses, which Vardaman BUNDREN had chased off when he thought Peabody had caused his mother's death. Quick attends the funeral of Addie BUNDREN, where he reports that the river is rising rapidly. Later, as the Bundrens pass by SAMSON (1)'s farm on their way to JEFFERSON, MISSISSIPPI, Quick tells them the bridge is out.

Quick, Mrs. Character in "SHALL NOT PERISH" (in *Collected Stories*). She is the wife of Solon QUICK, builder and operator of the school bus that carries Mrs. GRIER and her son to JEFFERSON, MISSISSIPPI, for her visit to the grieving Major DE SPAIN.

Quick, Solon Character in "SHINGLES FOR THE LORD" and "SHALL NOT PERISH" (both in *Collected Stories*). The owner and operator of a school-bus truck he built himself, he is one of the volunteers on the roofing job at the Reverend WHITFIELD's church.

Quick draws Pap GRIER into the deal over a dog, a deal that ends up destroying the church.

In "Shall Not Perish," Quick drives Mrs. GRIER to JEFFERSON, MISSISSIPPI, for her visit to the grieving Major DE SPAIN. In *The MANSION,* Solon Quick appears as a constable in FRENCHMAN'S BEND when Jack HOUSTON has problems with Mink SNOPES's cow.

Quick, Theron A minor character in *The MANSION.* He is one of Eula Varner (SNOPES)'s suitors, who attack Hoake MCCARRON when he is riding with Eula in a wagon. Struck by Eula with the handle of a buggy whip, Theron is knocked unconscious. He and Herman BOOKWRIGHT leave FRENCHMAN'S BEND quickly when they find out that Eula is pregnant.

Quinn, Doctor In *SANCTUARY,* the physician for Miss Reba RIVERS's girls at the brothel. He is the one called to treat the bleeding Temple Drake (STEVENS) after POPEYE drops her off on the day he rapes her with a corncob. He is an offstage character.

Quistenbery, Dink A minor character in *The TOWN.* Drink married one of Flem SNOPES's sisters or relatives from FRENCHMAN'S BEND. When Flem sends I. O. SNOPES back to the country for his dealings with Mrs. HAIT, Dink and his wife take over the Jefferson Hotel, which was formerly called the Snopes Hotel. Dink puts Byron Snopes's wild children up at the hotel for a brief time.

R

"Race at Morning" Short story, narrated by a 12-year-old boy, about an annual deer hunt. Abandoned two years earlier by his tenant farmer parents, the boy was adopted informally by the widower, Mister ERNEST, who was their landlord and a farmer himself. The story opens on the eve of the hunt, when the boy spots the magnificent buck swimming in the river. After supper the hunters play poker and tease the boy, who obviously is quite intelligent, about his lack of schooling. Before dawn they begin the chase on horseback, following a pack of dogs through the Mississippi bayou country. With Mister Ernest and the boy in pursuit, the buck evades the other hunters and begins to circle back to its territory. Mister Ernest empties his rifle of ammunition before shooting at the buck when it presents a clear target. The two find their way back to camp in the dark by using a compass.

Mister Ernest later explains his deliberate refusal to kill the deer, saying that the joy of the hunt rather than the kill is what is important; the privilege of hunting is a reward for the hard work of cultivating the land during the rest of the year. He then dismays the boy by announcing that he now must start school, which will reinforce such lessons as an ethical attitude toward nature and responsibility toward other people.

This story first appeared in the SATURDAY EVENING POST (March 5, 1955) and was revised for BIG WOODS (1955).

Rachel Character in SARTORIS. Belle MITCHELL's African-American cook, she regards Belle as ruthless and self-centered, and takes the husband's part in the Mitchells' marital wars. Harry MITCHELL gives Rachel a glass of whiskey from time to time.

Rachel, Aunt Offstage character in "THAT EVENING SUN" (in *Collected Stories*). She is said to be the mother of Nancy's husband, JESUS, though she sometimes denies it. An old woman with white hair, Aunt Rachel lives in a cabin beyond Nancy's where she smokes a pipe all day. When Nancy, terrified that her absent husband will come during the night to kill her for being unfaithful, begins to panic, Mr. Jason Richmond COMPSON urges her to spend the night at Aunt Rachel's, but she refuses.

"Raid" *See* THE UNVANQUISHED.

Rainey, Paul (1) Character in *The REIVERS*. A hound expert, he acquires a large tract of Mississippi land as a hunting preserve. Rainey once took his pack of bear hounds to hunt lion in Africa.

Rainey, Paul (2) New York City millionaire sportsman, the squire of Cotton Plant, with a restored plantation house and the largest game preserve in Mississippi. Murry FALKNER, the novelist's father, advised Rainey on the stables at Cotton Plant.

Rainey lent something to the character of Harrison BLAIR in the short story "FOX HUNT." He appears in modified form as Sells Wells, "owner of a plantation measured not in acres but in miles," in Faulkner's fictionalized memoir "Mississippi" (1953) and under his own name in *The REIVERS*.

Ralph Character in *IF I FORGET THEE, JERUSALEM* ("The Wild Palms"). Charlotte RITTENMEYER's brother, he knew Charlotte's Chicago friend MCCORD slightly when both worked on a NEW ORLEANS newspaper.

Randolph, Lewis Character in "A RETURN" (in *Uncollected Stories*). A planter's daughter, she marries a gallant Confederate, Charles GORDON, at the outset of the Civil War and carries on with their son in great hardship after Charles is killed and the South is in ruins. Lewis views her long life and achievements in unsentimental terms.

Random House Leading American publisher, based in New York City. Bennett CERF and Donald KLOPFER founded the firm in 1927; Cerf served as its head for 40 years.

Cerf pursued Faulkner for the Random House lists for several years. In 1935, he invited Faulkner to name his terms, saying he would rather publish Faulkner than "any other fiction writer living in America."

Random House absorbed Faulkner's publishers, SMITH & HAAS, in 1936. On October 26, the firm published *ABSALOM, ABSALOM!* in an edition of 6,000 copies; Random House published every Faulkner work thereafter.

Random House never expected substantial sales of Faulkner's works, and during a period of the mid-1940s all his books were out of print. A postwar critical and popular resurgence culminated in Faulkner's NOBEL PRIZE IN LITERATURE for 1949, and sales soared. The firm reported in late 1950 that four Faulkner novels had sold a total of 140,000 copies in hardcover and that nearly 2.5 million copies of three novels were in print in paperback.

Ratcliffe, Nelly V. K. RATLIFF's great grandmother, referred to in *The MANSION*. Nelly, a farmer's daughter in Virginia, married Vladimir Kyrilytch, whom she found hiding out in a hayloft. Left to fend for himself after the defeat at Saratoga, this first V. K. had been a mercenary in General Burgoyne's army. He took Nelly's last name, which later became Ratliff.

Ratliff, V. K. (Vladimir Kyrilytch) One of the main characters and narrators in the SNOPES TRILOGY (*The HAMLET, The TOWN, The MANSION*) and *Big Woods* ("A BEAR HUNT"). Ratliff is an itinerant salesman with a "bland affable . . . face" and "a pleasant, lazy, equable voice" (*The Hamlet*, p. 14). Much of the action in the trilogy is recounted through his narrative voice, which is often dispassionate, ironic, and humorous. Ratliff is a shrewd observer of events and the major source of news throughout the counties in which he sells sewing machines and, later on, other items such as radios and televisions. In *The Hamlet*, the first novel of the trilogy, Ratliff discerns early on and before others the danger Flem SNOPES poses to the community. By the end of the novel he is nevertheless duped by Flem into buying the OLD FRENCHMAN PLACE, where he and his co-owners, Henry ARMSTID and Odum BOOKWRIGHT, foolishly expect to find treasure rumored to be buried on the property. To pay for his third of the Old Frenchman place, Ratliff sells his share of a sidestreet restaurant he owned in partnership with his cousin Aaron RIDEOUT. (In *The Town* and *The Mansion*, Aaron Rideout's name is changed to Grover Cleveland WINBUSH.)

Ratliff lives in JEFFERSON, MISSISSIPPI, with his widowed sister, who keeps house for him as he travels through several counties selling his sewing machines more often on promissory notes than for hard cash. On several occasions, Ratliff proves himself a humane and compassionate person. In *The Hamlet*, he opens his home to the displaced Mrs. Mink SNOPES and her children, for whom he buys new overcoats. He also leaves money with Mrs. LITTLEJOHN for the dimwitted boy Ike SNOPES and puts an end to the spectacle of watching Ike make love to a cow in Mrs. Littlejohn's barn.

In *The Town*, he narrates chapters 4, 6, 9, 11, 18, and 23, and along with the idealistic Gavin STEVENS opposes SNOPESISM, although neither he nor Stevens can do much to stop Flem Snopes's financial success at the expense of others and his rise to the presidency of the Sartoris Bank. The ever-perceptive Ratliff knows that the motive behind Flem's rapacity is, ironically, a desire to gain respectability.

In chapter 7 of *The Mansion* (Ratliff narrates chapters 3, 6, and 7), the reader learns that Ratliff is a descendent of a Russian mercenary, Vladimir Kyrilytch, who fought on the side of the British during the Revolutionary War and escaped when General Burgoyne surrendered at Saratoga. "[W]e didn't know his last name," Ratliff says to Gavin Stevens, "or maybe he didn't even have none until Nelly Ratliff, spelled Ratcliffe then, found him" hiding in a hayloft (*The Mansion*, p. 165). When Nelly became pregnant with his child, the first Vladimir married her, and a son in each succeeding generation was given his first two names; one moved to Tennessee, and the next one, to Mississippi.

In addition to the Snopes trilogy, Ratliff appears in the short story "A Bear Hunt." He also appears under the name V. K. SURATT in "LIZARDS IN JAMSHYD'S COURTYARD," "CENTAUR IN BRASS," *SARTORIS*, and *AS I LAY DYING*. In responding to a question on the characters in his novels who best adjust to progress, Faulkner exclusively identifies Ratliff as one who is able to accept without "anguish" or "grief" the inevitability of change in culture and environment. In Faulkner's words, Ratliff "possesses what you might call a moral, spiritual eupepsia" (*Faulkner in the University*, p. 253). In an August 1945 letter to Malcolm COWLEY, Faulkner mentioned that the short story "SPOTTED HORSES" produced a character he "fell in love with: the itinerant sewing-machine agent named Suratt," whose name Faulkner changed to Ratliff because "[l]ater a man with that name turned up at home" (*Selected Letters of William Faulkner*, p. 197).

Reba, Miss (1) *See* RIVERS, REBA.

Reba, Miss (2) The name of one of Reba RIVERS's two dogs in *The MANSION* (p. 72). Reba Rivers named one after herself and the other, Mr. BINFORD, after Lucius BINFORD, her late landlord for 11 years; he had also been her lover.

Red In *SANCTUARY*, Temple Drake (STEVENS)'s lover while she is at Miss Reba RIVERS's brothel in MEMPHIS. The gangster POPEYE first brings Red to Temple, but when Temple tries to run away with Red, Popeye kills him. At his funeral, which takes place at his hangout, the Grotto, a disturbance breaks out and his body falls out of the coffin, revealing the bullet wound to his forehead. He is referred to as Alabama Red in *REQUIEM FOR A NUN*.

Redlaw Character in *SARTORIS*. A former partner of Colonel John SARTORIS in a railroad building enterprise, he shoots and kills the colonel on September 4, 1876, on the square in JEFFERSON, MISSISSIPPI.

In *The UNVANQUISHED*, the character is presented more fully as the lawyer, railroad developer, and Sartoris rival Ben REDMOND, and the shooting incident is described in greater detail.

"Red Leaves" *(Collected Stories)* Short story of the ritual chase of Chickasaw chief ISSETIBBEHA's black servant so that the servant can be buried with his master. As they seek him in the slave quarters, two older Indians recall the death of the chief's father, Doom (see IKKEMOTUBBE), and how it took three days to catch his slave. Grumbling about the burden of slavery on the tribe, they go to the new chief to announce the slave's disappearance. Speculation over Issetibbeha's relationship with his son MOKE-TUBBE suggests the possibility of patricide.

An account follows of Doom's rise to power. Issetibbeha succeeds him and uses profits from slave breeding to travel to Paris, returning with a useless fancy bed and red-heeled shoes, which fascinate Moketubbe.

The point of view shifts to the hunted servant who, remembering his own journey from Africa, watches from hiding as Issetibbeha dies. He begins to run, but keeps circling back, chased by the Indians who drag the obese Moketubbe along on a litter. At night the chief's servant seeks out the other slaves; they give him food but already regard him as dead. A snake bites him, and he submits to capture on the seventh day. Accepting a last meal, he is unable to swallow. The story ends as he is about to be slain.

In the end, the vigorous black man seems superior, morally and culturally, to the corrupt Moketubbe. This story, rich in ironies, paradoxes, and ambiguities interwoven with poetic imagery and mythic symbolism, is one that many critics place among Faulkner's best.

First published in the *SATURDAY EVENING POST* (October 25, 1930), it was revised for *These 13* (1931), and its final sections were reworked as a prelude to "The Old People" in *BIG WOODS* (1955).

Redmond, Ben Character in *The UNVANQUISHED*. A lawyer, he is the railroad business partner and later the bitter business and political rival of Colonel John SARTORIS.

When their differences become irreconcilable, Redmond sells his share of the road to Sartoris. Escalating the feud, Sartoris challenges him in a legislative election and wins; this and Sartoris's incessant taunting ultimately drive Redmond to violence. Even Sartoris loyalists wish that Sartoris would leave Redmond alone.

Redmond shoots and kills the unarmed Sartoris on the square in JEFFERSON, MISSISSIPPI. When Sartoris's son Bayard SARTORIS (3), unarmed, confronts Redmond in his law office, he fires two shots at nothing, exits the office, walks down to the station, boards the just-arriving southbound train, and leaves Jefferson forever.

Faulkner narrated the story of the killing previously in *SARTORIS*, where Redmond appears under the name of REDLAW.

Reed, Susan Character in "HAIR" (in *Collected Stories*). An orphan, she lives with BURCHETT and his wife and is regarded as something of a loose woman by JEFFERSON, MISSISSIPPI, standards. She marries the barber Henry STRIBLING (Hawkshaw). With no last name, Susan also appears in the short story "MOONLIGHT," where she is the 16-year-old girlfriend of the unnamed protagonist. Told by her uncle and guardian, Mr. Burchett, not to see her boyfriend, Susan disobeys, writes a provocative note to her beau, and meets with him at an empty house one night. She rejects her boyfriend's amorous advances, however, and tells him she would rather go to a show.

Reed, W. M. (unknown) Proprietor of the Gathright-Reed drugstore on the Square in OXFORD, MISSISSIPPI, known as "Mac." In 1929, he helped Faulkner distribute campaign literature for his uncle John Wesley Thompson FALKNER Jr., which began a lifelong friendship.

Mac Reed sold Faulkner's novels in his store, even *SANCTUARY* (1931), which most of Oxford regarded as obscene. Faulkner in 1960 appointed his old friend a director of the William Faulkner Foundation.

Reeves Character in "TURNABOUT" (in *Collected Stories*). A crewman aboard the torpedoboat *X001*, he is killed in action when the boat is sunk in German-controlled waters.

Reeves, Don A newspaperman who tells the unnamed narrator the history of Dal MARTIN in the short story "THE BIG SHOOT."

Reichman Character in *MOSQUITOES*. Major AYERS approaches Reichman for financial backing for the laxative he hopes to launch in the American market. The narrative does not indicate whether Reichman invested in the product.

Reinhardt Character in "HONOR" (in *Collected Stories*). A car dealer, he hires Buck MONAGHAN as a salesman after Monaghan leaves the flying circus.

The Reivers Faulkner's last novel, published in 1962. *The Reivers* is a comic, reminiscent, and elegiac coming-of-age story with a plot involving automobiles, racehorses, and fallen women. Some critics have compared the novel favorably to Mark Twain's *Huckleberry Finn*. Unusually for Faulkner, it has a happy ending.

In *Faulkner: Essays* the critic Warren BECK contends that the book has been too readily dismissed as light and sentimental. "*The Reivers* merits recognition for a true virtuosity that combines exuberance, implicativeness, and commitment, as a narrative wherein humor and wit spring from judicious insight, a nice fusion of value judgments and hearty tolerant interest," he wrote. Intricately plotted, peopled with a rogue's gallery of sinful characters, it is, Beck adds, "a highly moral tale."

Set in 1905 in Faulkner's mythical JEFFERSON, MISSISSIPPI, and in the Tenderloin district of Memphis, *The Reivers* opens in present time—roughly 1960—with the words "GRANDFATHER SAID." With that announcement, Lucius (Loosh) PRIEST, 65 years old, relates to his grandson the crowning story of his own childhood. He looks back, sometimes fondly, sometimes censoriously, upon himself as an 11-year-old; his partners and corrupters Boon HOGGANBECK and Ned William MCCASLIN; the "borrowed" Winton Flyer automobile in which they all escape to MEMPHIS; Miss Reba's brothel; and the horse that ultimately wins a fixed race and thus frees them from the direst consequences of their wrongdoing. In the end, the scheming Ned commits a good deed, young Loosh learns the code of the gentleman, and the dim and loveable Boon happily weds his favorite whore, Miss Corrie (Everbe Corinthia HOGGANBECK).

Faulkner said that with *The MANSION*, the third novel in the SNOPES TRILOGY published in 1959, his serious writing life had come to an end. For some reason, though, he revived an old idea, one he had first proposed to Robert HAAS at RANDOM HOUSE some 20 years before.

The Reivers reintroduces familiar characters and situations. The Priests are the "cadet branch" of the McCaslin-Edmonds clan of *GO DOWN, MOSES*. Boon Hogganbeck is an antic figure out of "The Bear." Ned McCaslin is a cousin of Lucas BEAUCHAMP of *Go Down, Moses* and *INTRUDER IN THE DUST*. Faulkner lifted Miss Reba's brothel from *SANCTUARY*. There are coming-of-age parallels with Ike MCCASLIN of "The Bear" and Chick Mallison of *Intruder*.

Boon concocts the scheme; the circumstance that young Loosh's parents are away for the funeral of his maternal grandfather in Bay St. Louis provides the opportunity. Boon dearly loves his grandfather Lucius (Boss) PRIEST's Winton Flyer. He is infatuated, too, with one of Reba's girls, Miss Corrie. So Boon enlists young Loosh as collaborator in the odyssey from Jefferson to Memphis, 85 miles distant. Ned stows away in the trunk of the car and is discovered a few miles into the journey.

The travelers encounter and surmount two obstacles early on: Hurricane Creek and Hell Creek Bottom. They break for the night at Ballenbaugh's, a roadhouse with a violent and romantic past, and arrive at Miss Reba's house on CATALPA STREET the next day. A bit later, Ned turns up at the brothel with a racehorse in tow, which he acquired in exchange for the car.

Ned plans to take the racehorse—Coppermine, renamed Lightning—to the town of PARSHAM, TENNESSEE, to race against a local favorite, with the Winton Flyer as stakes. Ned's motives are pure: he hopes to free his cousin Bobo BEAUCHAMP from the snares of a $128 debt to a white man. With the assistance of Boon, Lucius, and the girls at Miss Reba's, he arranges for Coppermine (Lightning) to be shipped by railroad to Parsham for the race with Colonel LINSCOMB's champion, Acheron. If Coppermine wins, Ned will be able to pay off Bobo's debt *and* recover Boss Priest's car.

Meantime, a 15-year-old minor criminal named OTIS advances young Loosh's knowledge of the seamy side of life. He informs Loosh that Miss Corrie is a prostitute and that he, Otis, has made money by allowing men to observe her at work through a peephole. When Loosh attacks Otis with his fists, Otis slashes at him with a knife.

Touched by Loosh's devotion, Miss Corrie decides to reform and live a life of virtue. She even reverts to her given name, Everbe Corinthia, which she had discarded as frumpish. But Coppermine (Lightning) loses the first race, and a corrupt, bullying deputy sheriff named Butch LOVEMAIDEN inserts himself into the action. Pursuing Everbe, he provokes a clash with a jealous Boon, who with Ned lands briefly in jail. Everbe gives herself to the deputy as the price for freeing Boon. When Loosh learns of her fall, he is devastated.

There is urgency now, for the Priests are due home soon from Bay St. Louis. Coppermine (Lightning) wins the second race as Ned employs an artifice—in the form of a sardine (the horse likes sardines)—to make the creature run faster. A third heat, with Acheron's owner Colonel Linscomb and Grandfather Priest now present, is arranged to decide matters. When Ned fails to appear with the sardine, Acheron wins. As it turns out, Ned has bet on the colonel's horse. He wins big and bails out Bobo. And Grandfather Priest recovers his car with out-of-pocket expenses of nearly $500—a figure Ned regards as cheap at the price.

Lucius returns to Jefferson with his grandfather, chastened and miserable. His father's offer to whip him for his misdeeds strikes him as wholly inadequate as a punishment. Grandfather Priest tells him the only way he can atone for his crimes is to simply live with them.

Boon Hogganbeck eventually returns to Jefferson with his bride, Everbe Corinthia. They move into a tiny house that Boon buys from Grandfather Priest. In time, they produce an heir and name him Lucius Priest Hogganbeck.

Faulkner completed *The Reivers* on August 21, 1961. He originally titled the work *The Horse Stealers: A Reminiscence,* then shortened it to *The Stealers,* then hit on *The Reavers.* In the end, he settled on the archaic Scots of spelling the word, *reivers*—robbers or plunderers.

Most of the second-draft revisions were minor, name changes and such: for example, Mr. van Grafe, Coppermine's owner, became Mr. VAN TOSCH. Faulkner's agent, Harold OBER, arranged for excerpts to be published in the *SATURDAY EVENING POST* and *Esquire*. Bennett CERF wrote to say that the Book-of-the-Month Club had accepted *The Reivers* as a future selection.

Fittingly, Faulkner dedicated *The Reivers* to the five children of his daughter, Jill FAULKNER, stepdaughter Victoria (FRANKLIN) Fielden, and stepson Malcolm FRANKLIN. In the spring of 1962, he read from an advance copy to appreciative audiences at the U.S. Military Academy at West Point and the UNIVERSITY OF VIRGINIA. Random House published the novel on June 4, 1962.

George Plimpton wrote the first major review of Faulkner's last novel for the New York *Herald Tribune*. He listed other "boys' stories" it brought to mind: Stevenson's *Treasure Island*, Twain's *Huckleberry Finn*. Writing in the *New York Times Book Review*, Irving HOWE classified *The Reivers* as "a deliberately minor work," adding that it was to "The Bear" what *Tom Sawyer* was to *Huckleberry Finn*. The critic Leslie Fiedler, in a review in the Manchester (England) *Guardian*, found parts of the book unbearably sentimental, "as bad as anything he has ever done." In a rather severe and humorless appreciation in the *Christian Science Monitor*, Roderick Nordell called Faulkner's seriousness of purpose into question.

With the perspective of 15 years or so, Warren BECK in 1976 judged *The Reivers* "a substantial work, significant in the Faulkner canon." He saw sentimentality as one of its strengths, particularly the comic but also moving love story of Boon Hogganbeck and Miss Corrie. These were Faulkner's people, ones whose courage and strength he understood and admired. "Her reformation and marriage to Boon may be disparaged as facile sentimentality," Beck wrote, "but that implies denial of the way common vital people break through adverse circumstance into idealistic assertion, and thus 'endure.'"

Faulkner never paid much attention to reviewers or critics. At any rate, in the case of *The Reivers*, he could have seen only the earliest notices before his death on July 6, 1962, only a month after the book was published.

Renfrow   Minor character in *The TOWN*. After being fired from the restaurant by Flem, SNOPES, Eck SNOPES becomes the night watchman at Renfrow's oil tank at the depot.

Reno   Character in *SARTORIS*. A black clarinet player, he joins young Bayard SARTORIS (4) and his friends in the serenade of Narcissa Benbow (SARTORIS).

The reporter   In *PYLON*, the tall, emaciated, unnamed cadaver-like reporter sent by the city editor, HAGOOD, to cover the air shows celebrating the opening of Feinman Airport in New Valois, Franciana. The reporter resembles T. S. Eliot's J. Alfred Prufrock figure in his unrealized dreams and sexual desires. He is enamored with the obvious *ménage à tois* relationship between the racing pilot Roger SHUMANN, his attractive wife LAVERNE (with whom the reporter can only imagine a relationship), and Jack HOLMES, the parachute jumper. Although told by the city editor not to get involved in the trio's private sexual lives and to report only news of

the air show, the reporter does not heed this advice and is fired. During the course of the air meets, the reporter gives over his apartment to the three and their child, little Jack SHUMANN, and also strikes up a drinking relationship with their mechanic, JIGGS. When Shumann's plane crashes, the reporter helps the uninjured pilot acquire another plane, which proves to be fatal to Shumann. Holmes, Laverne, and their child depart for Ohio after Shumann's death, and the reporter, rehired by Hagood, writes Shumann's obituary before going to Amboise Street to get drunk.

In response to a question about the naming of his character, Faulkner commented that they name themselves and the few that do not he left nameless. "There was one in *Pylon*, for instance, he was the central character in the book, he never did tell me who he was" (*Faulkner at Nagano*, pp. 78–79).

The Reporter   Journal of social and political affairs. On March 22, 1956, it published a notorious interview with Faulkner on race.

Deeply worried about an explosion of racial violence in the segregated South, Faulkner himself pushed for the interview, which took place in Saxe COMMINS's office at RANDOM HOUSE in New York City. Faulkner had been drinking heavily, perhaps a partial explanation for the incendiary comments attributed to him.

Though broadly sympathetic to her aims, he urged a young black woman named Autherine Lucy to abandon her attempt to enter the University of Alabama, an NAACP-backed bid that had touched off white rioting in the university town of Tuscaloosa.

"If that girl goes back to Tuscaloosa she will die," Faulkner told the interviewer, Russell Howe. "Then the top will blow off. The government will send its troops and we'll be back at 1860. They must stop pushing these people. The trouble is the North doesn't know that country. They don't know the South will go to war."

Shockingly, Faulkner went on: "As long as there's a middle of the road, all right, I'll be on it. But if it came to fighting I'd fight for Mississippi against the United States even if it meant going out into the streets and shooting Negroes. I will go on saying that the Southerners are wrong and that their position is untenable, but if I have to make the same choice Robert E. Lee made then I'll make it."

Faulkner collapsed from the effects of alcohol shortly after the interview. By the time of publication he had recovered sufficiently to repudiate the statements about fighting for Mississippi and shooting down blacks, calling his words "foolish and dangerous." He also complained of having been misquoted.

"These are statements which no sober man would make, nor, it seems to me, any sane man believe."

Howe responded that he had transcribed the interview verbatim from shortland notes. "If the more Dixiecrat remarks misconstrue his thoughts, I, as an admirer of Mr. Faulkner, am glad to know it. But what I set down is what he said," Howe insisted.

Requiem for a Nun   One of William Faulkner's most experimental novels, told partly in play form, in three acts, and partly in prose. Each act is preceded by a prose passage that tells a portion of the history of YOKNAP- ATAWPHA COUNTY and the town of JEFFERSON, MISSISSIPPI. In the wide scheme of Faulkner's work, the prose sections of *Requiem* are the author's sole chronological history of Yoknapatawpha County, and they can be viewed as a summary of the history of Jefferson, from its founding in the early 1800s through a visionary look at the city in 1965. Although the history in each preface is not insignificant to Faulkner, the retelling, as Noel POLK points out, "is essentially just one more of the tools of his trade, which he used in much the same way that he used myth and literary allusion, as a device for the illumination of character. History, the past, is only one of many things that concern him and his people" (Noel Polk, *Faulkner's* "Requiem for a Nun": *A Critical Study,* Bloomington, Indiana University Press, 1981, p. 3).

Thematically within the novel, however, each prose section has a more symbolic meaning. The setting of the prose section is the stage-set for the drama that follows. The drama is in the here-and-now, but the three prose sections add the dimension of time, an almost geological overview of the meaning of three institutions with great societal significance: the courthouse, the statehouse, and the jailhouse.

Written in 1951, *Requiem for a Nun* is a sequel to Faulkner's 1931 novel SANCTUARY. As such, this 15th Faulkner novel follows up on the subsequent lives of Temple Drake, who has become Temple Drake STEVENS; her husband, Gowan STEVENS; Gowan's uncle, Gavin STEVENS; and Nancy MANNIGOE, whom Temple hires as a nanny for her two children. (It is Nancy to whom the word "nun" in the title of the novel refers; see *Faulkner in the University,* p. 196.) Temple and Gowan are central characters in *Sanctuary,* the action of which occurs some eight years prior to the opening of *Requiem.* In that earlier novel, Temple is a 17-year-old college freshman and Gowan a few years older. It is Gowan's heavy drinking that sets in motion the chain of events leading to the horrifying incidents of *Sanctuary.* Soon after the ending of that novel, Gowan does what he considers to be the honorable thing—he marries Temple.

Requiem for a Nun opens on the final day of Nancy's trial for having killed Temple's six-month-old daughter. Because the experiences of *Sanctuary* leave a mark upon Temple, she employs Nancy, a drug user and sometime prostitute, precisely because Nancy is someone Temple can talk to, someone who understands her. In scene one, Nancy, having already been found guilty of the murder, is sentenced to die by hanging. After the sentence is pro-

nounced, Temple, Gowan, and Stevens return to Gowan's house, where Gavin Stevens, Nancy's defense attorney, is made to feel unwelcome. He waits until his nephew goes out of the room before confronting Temple, demanding to know what really happened and why Nancy murdered the child. Although Temple refuses to answer, she indicates that there are reasons and that the murder was not the act of a madwoman or a vicious psychopath. Temple, however, cannot squarely face the questions, and flees with her son to California.

But Temple cannot stay away forever, and she returns to Jefferson the week before Nancy's scheduled execution. Giving her husband a sleeping pill one night so that she can be sure of not being overheard, Temple asks Gavin Stevens to come see her. She confesses that, in a very real sense, she had a hand in the death of her own daughter and wants to stop the execution, even though there is no doubt that Nancy did the actual killing. Although Stevens thinks that it may be too late, he suggests that they go to Jackson to appeal directly to the governor. At the close of act 1, Temple asks how much she will have to tell, a concern that echoes her experiences in *Sanctuary,* in which she gave perjured testimony against the innocent Lee GOODWIN. Wanting to make up for the mistakes of eight years ago and for the consequences of her actions in the immediate past, Temple agrees to speak frankly to the governor. In the very end of the act, the reader learns what Temple does not suspect: Her husband Gowan has overheard the entire conversation.

The second prose section of *Requiem* tells the story of the founding of the state capital, Jackson. In contrast to the almost comical founding of Jefferson, Jackson was carefully selected. Its site on a hill was chosen by three wise men, commissioners sent out by the state government, and it was deliberately named for the hero Andrew Jackson, a planter, a backwoods lawyer, a duelist, a slaveowner, and the architect of the Indian removals which, in essence, gave Mississippi, Alabama, northern Georgia, eastern Tennessee, and Florida to the white man. The power of the statehouse over the citizens of Mississippi crystallizes in this prose introduction.

In the dramatic act that follows, Temple confesses to the governor that she was ready to abandon her husband and son and run off with Pete (3), the younger brother of Alabama RED, Temple's lover in *Sanctuary.* (In the earlier novel, the bootlegger and gangster POPEYE first rapes Temple with a corncob, then virtually imprisons her in a Memphis brothel and watches while Red and Temple have sex; once he sees that Temple is falling in love with Red, Popeye murders him.) Before Red's murder, Temple wrote love letters to him sufficiently explicit that Pete uses them to blackmail her eight years later.

In an attempt to stop Temple from running off with Pete, Nancy smothers Temple's infant daughter, an act that also costs Nancy her own life, which she is willing to sacrifice. Many of Temple's decisions result in death: TOMMY's, Goodwin's, and Red's in *Sanctuary,* and in *Requiem,* her baby's and Nancy's. Temple now realizes that it is up to her to stop this cycle of evil, but it is too late: the governor has already refused to grant a stay of execution for Nancy.

In scene III of act II, when the governor is away from his office, Gowan silently takes his place behind the desk. Kneeling and with her face in her arms as she speaks, Temple, assuming that she is speaking to the governor, finishes her confessions, not to the man who has the power to stop the execution, but to her husband. In a scene of telling power, Temple acts as though her confession were the equal of a public execution. Gowan tells Temple that he, too, is sorry for all that has happened since their ill-fated trip to a baseball game in northern Mississippi; but the past is done, unchangeable. It is over. Temple lingers a bit with Gavin, and with him reflects on why the governor refused to grant clemency. She agrees with Gavin and, by extension, with Nancy, when Gavin says: "You came here to affirm the very thing which Nancy is going to die tomorrow morning to postulate: that the little children, so long as they are little children, shall be intact, unanguished, untorn, unterrified" (p. 181). Act 2 ends as Temple and Gavin are leaving the governor's office; her last words as they head home are: "To save my soul—if I have a soul. If there is a God to save it—a God who wants it—" (p. 182).

The third prose section of *Requiem* concerns the history of the Jefferson jail, which, as Faulkner points out, predates both the courthouse and the statehouse, and even the naming of Jefferson itself. Because the original log walls of the first impromptu jail are themselves walled in by the bricks of the current 20th-century jail, the reader can interpret the jail as a symbol not only of justice, law, and order, but also as the first social institution necessary to restrain the primitive rages of humanity before civilization can be built. Faulkner undercuts the jail's meaning, however, in two crucial ways. First, jails can be repositories of blind justice. For example, three persons lawfully convicted are innocent. Lee Goodwin was not the murderer of Tommy; Popeye, executed in Birmingham, Alabama, was the killer of both Tommy and Red, but not of the man for whose death he is hanged; and Nancy Mannigoe is innocent of murder, although not of homicide, because of her motives and the absence of malice aforethought. Second, true murderers, like Wiley Harpe (BIG HARPE) simply remove the wall of the jail and walk off. The ominous dread of the jail is also undercut by Faulkner's apparent digression about Cecilia FARMER, the daughter of the Jefferson town jailer in 1861. At that time, as in the time of *Requiem,* the jailer and his family lived in the jail. Described as lazy and weak, Cecilia cuts her name into the glass of a jailhouse window in early April 1861. Legend then has it

that during a retreat in 1864 a Confederate soldier sees Cecilia sitting at that same window and returns to marry her the next year. The jail, therefore, becomes a tourist attraction and the setting of sentimental stories instead of an emblem of society's implacable justice.

The events of act 3 are quickly told. With Gavin Stevens, Temple visits Nancy in her cell on the morning before her execution and explains that Nancy is not solely responsible for the death of the baby. Temple confesses that she wanted to go to the governor and to "tell him that it wasn't you who killed my baby, but I did it eight years ago that day when I slipped out the backdoor of that train . . ." (p. 235). Temple learns what Nancy already knows: such an act of confession would not, could not, also be an act of expiation. Somebody has to suffer for the death of Temple's infant. Nancy, who actually held the blanket over the struggling baby's nose and mouth, must die for that dreadful act, while Temple, whose actions and plans forced Nancy to commit the crime, must live with its consequences. Stevens and Nancy listen to Temple's reflections on her state of mind. Nancy advises Temple to trust in God, and adds that suffering is a way of staying out of "devilment" (p. 237).

Suffering is a major theme of *Requiem for a Nun.* The acceptance of all human suffering as the consequence of living is central to the novel. In *Sanctuary,* Faulkner shows the inevitability of evil, its pervasiveness and its potential presence within us all—even a seemingly innocent 17-year-old college student. In *Requiem,* Faulkner attempts to show that evil can, in fact, be resisted, but that suffering is the price we pay (or the reward we get) for succumbing to it. But through suffering and the recognition of one's guilt, there is spiritual redemption.

In 1951, with the help of Albert Marre, Ruth Ford, and Lemuel Ayers, Faulkner worked on an adaptation of *Requiem for a Nun* for the stage. On January 28, 1959, the play, directed by Tony Richardson, with Ruth Ford as Temple, Beatrice Reading as Nancy, and Zachary Scott as Stevens, premiered at the John Golden Theatre in New York City. (*Requiem for a Nun: a Play,* adapted to the stage by Ruth Ford, was published by Random House in 1959.) In his note to the play, Faulkner comments: "This play was written not to be a play, but as what seemed to me the best way to tell the story in a novel" (i). The world premiere of the play was in Paris on September 20, 1956. The stage adaptation was by Albert Camus.

For further information, see *Selected Letters of William Faulkner* and *Faulkner in the University,* pp. 79, 86, 96, 122, 196, and 266.

Res Character in *SARTORIS.* He is the cashier in old Bayard SARTORIS's bank.

"Retreat" *See The UNVANQUISHED.*

"A Return" *(Uncollected Stories)*   Short story, almost a novella, following the lives of Lewis RANDOLPH and her son Randolph GORDON from the Civil War to a 1930 Memphis dinner party. In 1861, Lewis, a plantation owner's daughter, elopes with the gallant and doomed Charles GORDON as he departs for the front. She returns home to give birth to her son. By then the full catastrophe of the war—starvation, destruction, wasted lives, and senseless slaughter—has befallen the South.

Lewis keeps things going by laboring alongside the blacks. Randolph goes to Memphis, where he works his way up to bank president. Obsessed with history, Dr. Gavin BLOUNT, a grandnephew of Charles Gordon's commander, seeks out Randolph. Blount romanticizes the Civil War and idealizes Lewis, whom he imagines as a flower of Southern womanhood. Finally when he finally meets the old woman, she rebuffs his fanciful recreation of the past by flinging a bowl of soup at him. Although Blount shifts his perspective, his future is in doubt. His skewed vision of the mythic South contrasts with Randolph's materialistic new South and with the indomitable Lewis, who survives by substituting for her original future of idleness and needlepoint a life of self-sufficiency and self-determination.

A revision of "Rose of Lebanon" (1930), a short story that was rejected by the SATURDAY EVENING POST, "A Return" was first published in *Uncollected Stories (1979).*

Rhys Davids, Arthur   Historical aviator, referred to as Rhys Davies in *A FABLE*. See BALL, ALBERT.

Rhys Davies   *See* RHYS DAVIDS, ARTHUR.

Rhodes, Miss   Character in *The REIVERS*. Young Lucius PRIEST's teacher, she allows him to make up schoolwork he missed during the jaunt to MEMPHIS.

Richard (Dick)   Character in *SARTORIS*. He is one of the MacCallums' black servants.

Richardson, Dr.   Character in *IF I FORGET THEE, JERUSALEM* ("The Wild Palms"). A skilled surgeon, he attends Charlotte RITTENMEYER in the hospital emergency room, where she dies.

Richthofen   Character in *SARTORIS*. A German military aviator, he is the instructor of PLOECKNER, the flyer who shoots down Johnny SARTORIS. Baron Manfred von Richthofen (1892–1918), known as the "Red Baron" from the color of his airplane, was Germany's top ace in World War I. He is also referred to in *A FABLE*. See also BALL, ALBERT.

Riddell   A family name referred to in *The TOWN*. The Riddell boy is an offstage character who catches polio, causing the school to be closed. His father is one of the engineers or contractors who help pave the streets in JEFFERSON, MISSISSIPPI.

Rideout   A minor character in *The HAMLET*. He is Aaron RIDEOUT's brother and V. K. RATLIFF's cousin.

Rideout, Aaron   A minor character in *The HAMLET*. Rideout is V. K. Ratliff's cousin and with him a half-owner of a sidestreet restaurant in JEFFERSON, MISSISSIPPI. Faulkner changes his name to Grover Cleveland WINBUSH in *The TOWN* and *The MANSION*.

Rideout, Dr.   Character in *GO DOWN, MOSES* ("The Fire and the Hearth"). Roth EDMONDS summons him to attend Molly BEAUCHAMP after she is found semiconscious in the creek bottom where her husband LUCAS has been treasure-hunting.

Rider   Character in *GO DOWN, MOSES* ("Pantaloon in Black"). An African-American sawmill hand, he lives quietly and industriously with his newlywed wife, MANNIE, in a cabin he rebuilds on Carothers EDMONDS's place. When Mannie dies only six months after the wedding, he is inconsolable, and refuses offers of succor from his friends and the old aunt who raised him.

Grieving and desperate, he becomes drunk on moonshine and joins a crooked dice game at the mill. When he accuses BIRDSONG of cheating (the night watchman has rigged the game and has been fleecing the hands for 15 years), Birdsong reaches for his pistol. Rider slashes his throat with a razor.

Rider is arrested and jailed for the murder. Birdsong's kinsmen take him from his cell and hang him from a bell rope in the black Schoolhouse two miles from the sawmill.

Ringo   *See* STROTHER, RINGO (MARENGO).

Ripley, Mississippi   Northern Mississippi town—the seat of Tippah County—35 miles northeast of OXFORD, MISSISSIPPI. William C. FALKNER, Faulkner's great-grandfather, migrated to Ripley from Missouri in 1839 and eventually established himself as a leading citizen of the place.

Falkner helped raise an infantry company, the Magnolia Rifles, in Ripley in 1861. In July 1864, Union forces under A. J. SMITH burned the courthouse and other buildings, including Falkner's house.

Falkner prospered in the law and railroad development in Ripley after the Civil War, building his GULF & SHIP ISLAND RAILROAD line south to Pontotoc 37 miles distant. Faulkner's father, Murry C. FALKNER, lived and worked in Ripley as a railroad official from 1898 to 1902. William Faulkner lived in Ripley from Age 1 to 5. The Falkners' second child, Jack, (John Wesley Thompson FALKNER III,) was born there in May 1899.

Ripley Railroad Company *See* GULF & SHIP ISLAND RAILROAD.

"Riposte in Tertio" *See The* UNVANQUISHED.

Rittenmeyer, Ann Character in *IF I FORGET THEE, JERUSALEM* ("The Wild Palms"). She is the younger daughter of Charlotte and Francis RITTENMEYER.

Rittenmeyer, Charlotte (1) Character in *IF I FORGET THEE, JERUSALEM* ("The Wild Palms"). A sculptor, fiercely independent, aggressive, and strong-willed, she meets Harry WILBOURNE, a poverty-stricken medical intern, at a party in the Vieux Carré in NEW ORLEANS and eventually leaves her well-to-do husband and two daughters for him.

With $1,278 in cash that Harry finds in a lost wallet, they set out for Chicago. The money begins to run low and they find jobs. Charlotte sells little sculpted figures, then works as a display designer in a department store.

She believes that marriage, children, and concern for comfort and security are the death of love. When money worries encroach, she and Harry move on—to a friend's lake cottage, back to Chicago, to a mine in the frozen Utah wilderness, to San Antonio, to a small town on the Mississippi Gulf Coast.

She has no use for Harry's anxieties and misgivings about their irregular life, but her pregnancy threatens her notion of love and she browbeats Harry into agreeing to perform an abortion on her. He is afraid; he wants her to carry the baby to term, even if it means applying to a charity ward. Charlotte refuses.

Something goes wrong with the procedure, and Charlotte fails to heal. She dies on the operating table of a Mississippi hospital.

Rittenmeyer, Charlotte (2) Character in *IF I FORGET THEE, JERUSALEM* ("The Wild Palms"). She is the older daughter of Charlotte and Francis RITTENMEYER.

Rittenmeyer, Francis (Rat) Character in *IF I FORGET THEE, JERUSALEM* ("The Wild Palms"). Charlotte RITTENMEYER's abandoned husband, rigid but devoted after his fashion, he is an observant Roman Catholic and refuses to grant his wife a divorce when she leaves him and their children for Harry WILBOURNE.

Rittenmeyer allows Charlotte to live without harassment so long as she gets in touch with him once a month, and he gives Wilbourne a check to cover her fare home in an emergency. At their last meeting, Charlotte tells him about her illness and makes him promise not to take action against Wilbourne if she dies.

After her death, Rittenmeyer fulfills his pledge. He offers to pay Wilbourne's bond and urges him to flee to Mexico. When Wilbourne refuses, he rises to make a plea for him in court. As a final effort, he brings cyanide to Wilbourne's cell; the convict refuses it.

Rivers, Lee In *SOLDIERS' PAY*, a young swain of Charlestown, Georgia, proud of his dancing ability and of his status as a former Princeton student. Lee is disliked by nearly everyone in the novel. He is especially enamored of Cecily SAUNDERS.

Rivers, Reba (Miss Reba) Madam of the brothel in MEMPHIS where POPEYE takes Temple Drake (STEVENS) in *SANCTUARY*. Known throughout Memphis, Miss Reba runs a tight establishment where some of the biggest men in town—lawyers, bankers, doctors, and police captains—go to drink and be with women. Miss Reba has two small, soiled white dogs that she names Miss Reba and Mr. Binford, one after herself and the other after Lucius BINFORD, her late landlord and lover. In *Sanctuary* and *The MANSION*, the naive Fonzo WINBUSH and Virgil SNOPES stay at her brothel, mistakenly thinking that it is a boardinghouse. In *The REIVERS*, Boon HOGGANBECK takes Lucius (Loosh) PRIEST to Miss Reba's. A kindhearted and compassionate woman, she insists, for example, in *The Reivers*, that her black maid MINNIE stay with her in her room at the hotel in PARSHAM, TENNESSEE. When signing in, she uses the name Mrs. BINFORD; during the time of the novel, her lover is alive.

Robert, Uncle Character in "UNCLE WILLY" (in *Collected Stories*). He is the uncle of the boy who narrates Uncle Willy CHRISTIAN's story.

Robinson The artilleryman who is assigned to MACWYRGLINCHBEATH's aircraft as observer in the short story "THRIFT." Robinson is killed during a dogfight.

Robyn, Henry Character in *MOSQUITOES*. He is the father of Patricia ROBYN and Theodore ROBYN.

Robyn, Patricia Character in *MOSQUITOES*. The thin, boyish, absent-mindedly provocative niece of Patricia MAURIER, she slips off to Mandeville with David WEST, the *Nausikaa*'s steward who has fallen in love with her, when the yacht runs aground. They are lost for a time and their adventure goes nowhere. When they return to the *Nauskikaa*, the lovelorn West quits his steward's job and disappears.

Robyn, Theodore (Gus; Josh) Character in *MOSQUITOES*. He is Patricia ROBYN's twin brother. Robyn detaches a piece of the *Nausikaa*'s machinery to make a tobacco pipe, an inadvertent sabotage of the steering gear that causes the yacht to run aground.

Rockyford Fictional village in YOKNAPATAWPHA COUNTY, east of JEFFERSON, MISSISSIPPI. In *The TOWN*,

V. K. RATLIFF sells a sewing machine to a Miz Ledbetter of Rockyford. The village is mentioned in *The MANSION*, the third novel of the SNOPES TRILOGY.

Rodney, Uncle The central character in the short story "THAT WILL BE FINE" (in *Collected Stories*). The uncle of the seven-year-old narrator GEORGIE, who abets his schemes, he is a thief and adulterer. Uncle Rodney is a ne'er-do-well who borrows money he does not intend to repay, carries on affairs with married women, and steals from his employer. After being caught embezzling and forging his father's name on a bad check, Uncle Rodney attempts to leave town with Mrs. TUCKER and her jewelry. Mr. TUCKER and five other men of MOTTSTOWN intercept Rodney and shoot him dead for one of the husbands he has cuckolded. (An Uncle Rodney also appears in the short story "SEPULTURE SOUTH: GASLIGHT"; his character prefigures that of Maury BASCOMB in *The SOUND AND THE FURY*.)

Roebuck, John Wesley Minor character in *The TOWN*. He is one of young Chick MALLISON's boyhood friends. For breaking in to Ab SNOPES's watermelon patch, John Wesley was shot in the back. As a game, dressed in two hunting coats and a sweater wrapped around his neck, John Wesley later tries to outrun the Number Six shot coming from Aleck SANDER's gun. John Wesley is not hurt, although Chick's hunting coat he was wearing is ruined.

Rogers, Deacon Character in *SARTORIS*. The proprietor of a grocery-café in JEFFERSON, MISSISSIPPI, he likes to drink the home-distilled whiskey young Bayard SARTORIS (3) and Rafe MACCALLUM bring to his place.

In *The SOUND AND THE FURY*, Earl TRIPLETT, the owner of the hardware store where Jason COMPSON IV works, eats at Rogers's.

Rogers, Howard Character in "HONOR" (in *Collected Stories*). A pilot in a flying circus, he risks his life to save that of his wing walker Buck MONAGHAN, even though he knows Monaghan is having an affair with his wife. When Monaghan leaves, Rogers and his wife reconcile. Monaghan becomes godfather to their newborn son.

Rogers, Mildred Character in "HONOR" (in *Collected Stories*). The wife of the stunt pilot Howard ROGERS, she falls in love with Howard's wing walker, Buck MONAGHAN. When the affair ends, she and her husband have a child and are happy together.

Roscius (Roskus) Character in *GO DOWN, MOSES* ("The Bear"). He is a McCaslin slave, the husband of PHOEBE.

"A Rose for Emily" *(Collected Stories)* Faulkner's first published short story in a nationally recognized magazine. It appeared in the April 1930 issue of the *Forum* (133, 233–38); a revision of the story was published in *These 13* (1931), *A Rose for Emily and Other Stories* (1945), *The PORTABLE FAULKNER* (1946), *COLLECTED STORIES OF WILLIAM FAULKNER* (1950), *THE FAULKNER READER* (1954), *A Rose for Emily* (1956), and *Selected Short Stories of William Faulkner* (1962).

"A Rose for Emily" is about Miss Emily GRIERSON, an elderly woman who lived the last 10 years of her life as a recluse. Told from the first person plural point of view (an indication that the narrator is speaking from the collective perspective of the town), the story opens with Miss Emily's funeral, which the whole town attends: "the men through a sort of respectful affection for a fallen monument, the women mostly out of curiosity to see the inside of her house" (p. 119), as though by seeing it they would bring to light a hidden secret of her personality. In fact, a secret is exposed at the end of the story when the narrator ties together various clues sprinkled throughout this gothic tale, or ghost story as Faulkner referred to it (*Faulkner in the University*, p. 26). Between the opening and closing paragraphs, the narrator tells just enough information about Miss Emily's personal life, the mental health of her family, her restrictive father, the stench that came from her house 40 years ago, and, in particular, about her romance with the Yankee construction foreman, Homer BARRON, who was last seen entering her kitchen door one evening. With the exception of a period of six or seven years, during which time Miss Emily gave lessons in china-painting, her life remained a mystery to the town until her death. Those who went to Miss Emily's house to look through it after the funeral knew that there was one upstairs room that "no one had seen in forty years" (p. 129) that would have to be broken into. The room was decked like a bridal chamber. In the bed were the skeletal remains of Homer Barron, and on one of the pillows a strand of Miss Emily's gray hair.

A highly anthologized work, "A Rose for Emily" has received a considerable amount of criticism. Cleanth BROOKS, for example, sees the short story "as an excellent example of Faulkner's skillful craftsmanship" (*William Faulkner: First Encounters*, p. 7). In his discussion of Miss Emily's character, Brooks focuses on her pride, strong will and independence; if one expects to learn a moral from the story, he concludes, it is "a warning against the sin of pride: heroic isolation pushed too far ends in homicidal madness" (*William Faulkner: First Encounters*, p. 14). For more information, see *Selected Letters of William Faulkner*, pp. 47, 63, 278; *Faulkner in the University*, pp. 47–48, 58–59, 87–88, 184–85, 199; and Diane Brown Jones, *A Reader's Guide to the Short Stories of William Faulkner*, pp. 87–141.

Rosie   Character in "THAT WILL BE FINE" (in *Collected Stories*). She is a black servant who looks after GEORGIE, the seven-year-old narrator of the story.

Ross, Frank   Character in "THE BROOCH" (in *Collected Stories*). He is the husband of Amy BOYD's friend Martha ROSS.

Ross, Martha   Character in "THE BROOCH" (in *Collected Stories*). A friend of Amy BOYD's, she calls Amy late at night to report she has found the brooch, an heirloom, in the car in which they had been riding earlier in the evening. Because Amy has not yet returned home, her husband answers the phone.

Rouncewell   (1) Character in *GO DOWN, MOSES* ("Go Down, Moses"). He owns the store in JEFFERSON, MISSISSIPPI, that Butch (Samuel Worsham) BEAUCHAMP breaks into.

Rouncewell   (2) Character in *The REIVERS*. A JEFFERSON, MISSISSIPPI, oil company agent, he supplies the fuel for Grandfather PRIEST's Winton Flyer.

Rouncewell, Mrs.   Character in *KNIGHT'S GAMBIT* ("Tomorrow") and other works. She owns the JEFFERSON, MISSISSIPPI, boardinghouse where the Bookwright jury deliberates.

In *The TOWN*, Mrs. Rouncewell is a florist; in *The MANSION*, she operates the Commercial Hotel for a time. In *The REIVERS*, she runs a boardinghouse in Jefferson in 1961.

Rouncewell, Whit   In *The TOWN*, the boy who saw two fellows robbing Uncle Willy CHRISTIAN's drugstore. Referred to as "the Rouncewell boy" in *The MANSION*, he may be Mrs. ROUNCEWELL's son.

Rowan Oak   Faulkner's home of 32 years, in OXFORD, MISSISSIPPI. An English architect designed and built the house, set in rugged grounds three-quarters of a mile south of the Oxford square on the Old Taylor Road, for Robert Shegog in 1844. A winding cedar-lined drive leads to the L-shaped, two-story house. In the front, four tall columns support a Grecian roof and a balcony projects over the Georgian front doors.

Mrs. Julia Bailey bought the house and most of the land from Shegog in 1872. The grounds, known thereafter as Bailey's Woods, were a favorite haunt of Oxford children; young Billy Falkner and his future wife, (Lida) Estelle Oldham (FAULKNER) both played there in the early years of the 20th century. By the late 1920s the old place had fallen into disrepair. Faulkner bought it from a Bailey descendant in April 1930.

When the novelist and Estelle and her children moved into the Shegog place in June 1930, they found rotted

Faulkner named his home Rowan Oak after the rowan tree, a symbol of strength and tranquility. Built in the late 1840s, the house needed major repairs when Faulkner purchased it in 1930. Faulkner restored and renovated the house over the next quarter-century. It is now maintained by the University of Mississippi. (Harriett and Gioia Fargnoli)

beams, a leaky roof, cracking plaster, and a mice- and squirrel infestation in the attic. The ghost of Judith Shegog, killed in a fall while trying to elope with one of the Yankee general A. J. SMITH's officers, haunted the house.

There was no electricity or plumbing. The Faulkners used oil lamps at first and carried water up from the wellhouse. Faulkner himself undertook much of the initial restoration, even the heaviest structural work, which involved jacking up the house to replace the rotted foundation sills. Within a few months, he had introduced wiring and running water, replaced the roof, and begun restoration of the lawn and gardens.

Faulkner renamed the property Rowan Oak, after a Scottish tree that signified peace and security. He wrote much of his best work there and loved the place, but outsiders sometimes found it disheartening. Saxe COM-

A partial view of Faulkner's study at Rowan Oak. (Harriett and Gioia Fargnoli)

MINS, who came to Oxford in 1952 to nurse Faulkner through an alcoholic episode, set down his reaction to Rowan Oak in a letter to his wife: "It is a rambling Southern mansion, deteriorated like its owner, built in 1838 and not much improved since. The rooms are bare and what they do contain is rickety, tasteless, ordinary. There is none of the charm and orderliness and comfort that you give to a home."

Faulkner prepared to leave Rowan Oak and move permanently to Virginia in the spring of 1962, but he lapsed into his final illness there in early July.

The house today is a Faulkner museum.

Roxanne, Aunt   Character in "MY GRANDMOTHER MILLARD AND GENERAL BEDFORD FORREST AND THE BATTLE OF HARRYKIN CREEK" (in *Collected Stories*). She is a black servant of Mrs. COMPSON (1).

Roy   Character in *MOSQUITOES*. He is a friend of Jenny STEINBAUER's friend THELMA (1).

Royal Air Force (RAF)   The air service of the British military, known as the Royal Flying Corps before April 1, 1918. William Cuthbert Falkner enlisted in the RAF, then in process of training squadrons in Canada, in New York City in June 1918, signing on as a cadet with a fictitious English background and using the name *Faulkner*.

He reported to the RAF depot in Toronto in July and trained for five months, until the armistice of November 11, 1918, brought his military career to a close. Though Faulkner never managed a training flight, he subsequently embroidered his record, first claiming to have graduated as a solo pilot and later promoting himself to wounded war hero with a steel plate in his head.

the runner   A British soldier in *A FABLE* who is promoted from a common enlisted man to officer's rank. After five months as an officer, he requests that he be made a common soldier again. His request is denied and he is forced to act in so outrageous manner while on leave that the British authorities have no recourse but to strip him of his rank. He becomes a regimental messenger. In this capacity, he travels the front lines and the rear areas extensively and is able to learn much about the Allied armies. An intelligent, sensitive man, the runner had been an architect before the war. He was among the first of the men of London to enlist in the army, but by 1918 he has become convinced of the stupidity and evil of war. When he learns of the mutiny led by Corporal STEFAN, he attempts to prolong the temporary cease-fire into an actual armistice. He convinces Mr. HARRY, the sentry, to use his influence to get another battalion to cross into no-man's land and make peace with the enemy. This action leads both armies to lay down a powerful barrage upon the peaceful mingled British and German soldiers, killing all but the runner, who is horribly maimed. The

runner later interrupts the funeral of the OLD GENERAL after the war. An outraged crowd beats him in spite of his injuries and leaves him bleeding in the gutter. One individual, also a veteran of World War I, comes to his aid. The runner says he is not going to die. The old soldier tells the runner that he is not laughing at him. "What you see," says the good samaritan in the final five words of the book, "are tears" (p. 370).

Russell   Character in *LIGHT IN AUGUST*. He is a sheriff's deputy in MOTTSTOWN, where the murderer Joe CHRISTMAS is briefly held in jail.

Russell, Ab   In *The SOUND AND THE FURY*, a farmer outside of JEFFERSON, MISSISSIPPI, from whom Jason COMPSON IV borrows an air pump. When searching for his niece Quentin and the carnival worker she ran off with, Jason stops near Russell's farm to look for them. Before they drive away, they let the air out of one of Jason's tires to prevent him from catching them.

Russell, Bertrand (1872–1970)   English mathematician and philosopher, the third earl Russell. Known particularly for his work in mathematical logic, he also wrote widely on education, economics, and politics. His major works include *The Analysis of Mind* (1921) and *Human Knowledge: Its Scope and Limits* (1948).

Russell and Faulkner briefly shared a publisher—BONI & LIVERIGHT, which brought out Faulkner's first novel. As the winner of the 1950 NOBEL PRIZE IN LITERATURE, Russell sat next to Faulkner at the ceremony in Stockholm honoring the American novelist as the winner of the 1949 prize. Russell later reported that Faulkner seemed reserved and shy.

Russell, Lee M. (1875–1943)   A Mississippi lawyer and politician, born in Dallas, LAFAYETTE COUNTY, into the poor farmer class, he obtained an education by dint of hard work and earned a law degree from the UNIVERSITY OF MISSISSIPPI, although his social status barred him from membership in a university fraternity.

J. W. T. FALKNER, Faulkner's grandfather, took Russell into his firm as a junior partner in 1903 and he prospered there. He also built connections among the small farmer class that helped him with election successively to the state legislature and state senate. In 1914, Mississippi voters elected him lieutenant governor. He became governor in 1920.

On the tide of the populist, small-farmer political surge known as the redneck revolt, Russell went on to win election as governor in 1919. One of his initiatives as governor involved the shutting down of fraternities and social clubs at Ole Miss.

Rust, Everbe Corinthia   Character in "THE LEG" (in *Collected Stories*). An English lockkeeper's daughter, she meets the young Oxford University students DAVY and GEORGE; George develops a crush on her. Later, George is killed in battle in France and Davy loses a leg. Not long after these events, Corinthia is drawn to the river by a weird laugh, and she dies of fright.

Rust, Jotham Character in "THE LEG" (in *Collected Stories*). The brother of Everbe Corinthia RUST, he suspects the amputee DAVY as the owner of the strange laugh that sends his sister into a fright that kills her. Leaving his regiment without permission, Rust attempts to kill Davy, but fails; he is tried and executed for desertion.

Rust, Simon Character in "THE LEG" (in *Collected Stories*). A Thames River lockkeeper, he is the father of Everbe Corinthia and Jotham RUST. Simon foresees his death, which comes not long after that of his daughter.

Saddie Character in "THERE WAS A QUEEN" (in *Collected Stories*). The daughter of ELNORA, the Sartoris cook, she looks after 90-year-old Aunt Virginia DU PRE.

Sales, Mac A minor character in *PYLON*. A federal agent, Sales inspects airplanes.

Salmagundi Five reprinted poems and three reprinted prose pieces published in April 1932 by Casanova Press in Milwaukee. The collection is edited with an introduction by Paul Romaine. A poem by Ernest HEMINGWAY, "Ultimately," appears on the back cover. (See Appendix I for titles.)

Salmon Character in *LIGHT IN AUGUST*. He has a "rent car" in MOTTSTOWN and offers to take Eupheus HINES and his wife to JEFFERSON, MISSISSIPPI, for the steep fare of three dollars. Mrs. Hines decides that Salmon is too expensive.

Sam A minor character in *The HAMLET*. Will VARNER's African-American manservant who carries Varner's daughter Eula (Varner SNOPES) when she is a child. When Flem SNOPES leaves FRENCHMAN's BEND for JEFFERSON, MISSISSIPPI, Sam helps Lump and Eck SNOPES load his wagon.

Samson (1) Character in *AS I LAY DYING* (narrator of chapter 29, "Samson"). A kindly neighbor of the Bundrens, Samson puts them up overnight at his farm when they are on their way to JEFFERSON, MISSISSIPPI, to bury Addie, the bridge was washed away. Confused by Anse BUNDREN's insistence on taking his wife's body to Jefferson even though two bridges have been washed away, Samson suggests that they bury her at New Hope, or, if they must go to Jefferson, that they go up by Mount Vernon, where a bridge is still standing. Samson also appears in *FLAGS IN THE DUST*.

Samson (2) Minor character in *The TOWN*. He is the hotel porter who carries the small valise (or "grip," as it is referred to in the novel) belonging to one of the bondsmen present at Gavin STEVENS's suit against Mayor DE SPAIN.

Samson, Rachel SAMSON (1)'s wife in *AS I LAY DYING*. She insists that the Bundrens stay at the Samson farm one night on their way to JEFFERSON, MISSISSIPPI, to bury Addie BUNDREN. She prepares them dinner and the next morning reprimands her husband for not insisting that the Bundrens stay for breakfast before leaving. Rachel says that it is "an outrage" for the family to drag the dead body of Addie "up and down the country" and she blames "all the men in the world" for what women must go through (pp. 117–18).

Samson's Bridge Fictional place, spanning a major river (either the TALLAHATCHIE or the YOCONA) in YOKNAPATAWPHA COUNTY.

In *LIGHT IN AUGUST*, someone at Samson's tells Lena GROVE that she will find Lucas BURCH at a planing mill in JEFFERSON, MISSISSIPPI. Floods have washed the bridge away in *AS I LAY DYING*. It is also referred to in the short story "SPOTTED HORSES."

Samuel Character in "The LEG" (in *Collected Stories*). He gives DAVY a hand when GEORGE falls out of the boat at the lock-gate.

Sanctuary Faulkner's sixth novel, first published by CAPE & SMITH on February 9, 1931; a corrected text of the novel by Joseph BLOTNER and Noel POLK was published in 1985 in *Novels 1930–1935*, volume 1 of Faulkner's collected works in the LIBRARY OF AMERICA series. *Sanctuary* is Faulkner's most shocking treatment of the indomitable power of evil, causing one reviewer, Henry Seidel Canby, to comment that with this novel sadism "has reached its American peak" ("The School of Cruelty," *Saturday Review of Literature* 7 [May 21, 1931], 674). Within weeks of its publication, however, the novel became a best-seller and attracted the attention of Hollywood. Though many readers reacted with outrage or horror and dismay, others saw literary value in the novel and praised its provocative powers. *Sanctuary* is more than the potboiler Faulkner made it out to be (see *Faulkner in the University*, pp. 90–1).

The title of the novel has ironic overtones. In addition to meaning holy or consecrated, the word *sanctuary,* derived from the Latin *sanctus,* means inviolable, that which is safe from profanation or violation. A sanctuary can also mean a safe haven. But virtually nothing—as the novel's idealistic attorney, Horace BENBOW, voices when speaking with Miss Jenny—is inviolable or safe form the pervasiveness of evil: "'. . . there's a corruption about even looking upon evil, even by accident; you cannot haggle, traffic, with putrefaction'" (p. 129). Horace is ultimately ineffectual against the power of evil, and once defeated by it his ideals of justice and southern womanhood fade into illusions. The same does not happen however, to the young woman Temple Drake (STEVENS), who significantly contributes to Benbow's defeat and despair and whose first name is a mock evocation of sanctity. Through the gangster POPEYE's brutal defilement, she responds to the presence of evil in her own nature, as Edmond L. Volpe suggests: "Her horrible corn-cob rape by Popeye does not initiate her moral collapse; it merely releases her from the restrictive convention which society has imposed upon her" (*A Reader's Guide to William Faulkner*, New York: Farrar, Straus & Giroux, 1965, p. 144). The realization of evil within human nature and the response of human beings to it thematically inform *Sanctuary*.

The novel opens with Popeye in a tight black suit watching Horace Benbow drinking from a spring near the OLD FRENCHMAN PLACE, a gutted plantation house. Horace, who is escaping from his marital problems, is travelling from his home in Kinston to JEFFERSON, MISSISSIPPI, where he used to live and where his widowed younger sister, Narcissa Benbow SARTORIS, still lives with her 10-year-old son, Benbow. Assuming that Horace is a revenue agent, the bootlegger Popeye, an undersized man with a dark pallor, bulging eyes and a chinless face, mistakenly thinks he has a gun in his pocket, but it is only a book. Popeye leads Horace to Old Frenchman Place, where he is given dinner. He meets Lee GOODWIN, another bootlegger, and others, including Goodwin's father, PAP (1) a blind and deaf man. Goodwin's common-law wife, Ruby LAMAR, cooks for the men. After dinner, some of the men sit on the porch, talking and drinking from a jug that they pass around. Popeye, however, is not one of them, for he has such a weak stomach alcohol would kill him. By the time Benbow gets a lift into Jefferson on Popeye's truck loaded with moonshine for Memphis, he is drunk.

The next afternoon, Horace is in Jefferson at his sister's house. There he meets Gowan STEVENS, a student at the University of Virginia, who boasts that he has learned how to drink like a gentleman. While Gowan and Narcissa walk in the garden after dinner, Horace mocks Steven's claim. Later, Gowan leaves for a date with Temple Drake, who attends the state university in nearby Oxford. After they go to the dance, he gets very drunk, retches, and passes out. When he wakes up the next morning in front of the railroad station, the special train leaving for a baseball game in Starkville, where he was to drive Temple, has already left, so he speeds on to Taylor, a town the train will pass through. Just as the train starts to pull out of the station, Temple sees his car and jumps off the train to be with him, but his appearance—a wild face, disheveled hair, ruined shirt—disgusts her. Instead of taking her back to Oxford as Temple requests, Stevens hurries on to Starkville to beat the train. On the way, he stops off at Goodwin's for a bottle of bootlegged whiskey, hits a tree lying across the dirt road leading up to Old Frenchman Place and wrecks his car, which turns on its side. Gowan and Temple are led to the house by the feeble-minded TOMMY, one of Goodwin's men. In the kitchen Temple meets Ruby, who tells her to wait in the dining room, where the men will be served dinner. Tommy attempts to seize Temple, but Goodwin stops him. When Temple runs out of the house, Tommy later follows with some food for her to eat. Temple's very presence arouses the sexual appetite of the men and fights start to break out because of her. In the meantime, Stevens, who is again drunk, is beaten unconscious and taken into the house. Temple ends up in one of the bedrooms, and when she is about to be ravished by VAN, another one of the bootleggers, Goodwin beats him down. Gowan, bloodied, is carried into the room and thrown onto the bed. Throughout the night, the men come in and out of the bedroom to look at Temple. At one point Popeye stands over the bed. Ruby sees what is going on, and after the men leave to transport their whiskey, she takes Temple to the barn.

By the next morning, Gowan, ashamed and still drunk, leaves Temple and searches for a car for hire. Because he cannot face her, Gowan pays and directs the driver to pick up Temple and take her back to the university. He then hitchhikes into town. When Temple finds out that Gowan has left, she seeks out Ruby and later hides in the barn. Frightened of Goodwin, Temple sees Tommy and asks him to protect her, but when the sexually impotent Popeye comes to the barn, he kills Tommy and violates the 17-year-old Temple with a corncob. Popeye later drives Temple to a Memphis brothel run by Reba RIVERS. Goodwin has Ruby go to their neighbor two miles away (the same neighbor Gowan visited) to telephone the sheriff. The sheriff, however, arrests Goodwin for Tommy's murder and takes him to jail in Jefferson.

Horace decides to defend Goodwin against the charges and provide a place for Ruby and her infant child to stay, even though he knows they have no money. Ruby mentions to Horace that she saw Popeye drive off with Temple. After going to the state university to find out what he can about Temple, Horace happens to meet Senator Clarence SNOPES on the train back to Jefferson. Snopes explains that a Jackson paper published a story saying that Temple was sent by her father, Judge DRAKE, to an aunt in Michigan. At a later date, Benbow meets Snopes again, and for a price, the senator informs Horace that Temple is at Reba Rivers's house of prostitution in Memphis. When he visits Temple there (where she has been for about three weeks) and hears her story, Horace knows that he needs her to testify at Goodwin's trial.

A few days after Horace leaves Memphis for Jefferson, Popeye brings RED to Temple and watches as they have sexual relations. Several days later, Temple bribes MINNIE, Miss Reba's Black servant, to let her sneak out to make a phone call. Later that evening, after several drinks during the day, she skips out again, but this time Popeye sees her as she is leaving. Refusing to go back in to Miss Reba's, she has Popeye drive her to the Grotto, a nightclub on the outskirts of Memphis, to meet Red. On the way, she ridicules Popeye's impotence and voyeurism. At the Grotto, Temple dances with her lover and continues to drink. When Red goes to a craps table, the inebriated Temple for a moment thinks that she is dancing again, but in fact two men are leading her out of the nightclub under Popeye's orders. As she is driven out of the parking lot, she sees Popeye sitting in a parked car. Popeye kills Red that night, and Red's funeral is held at the Grotto. With GENE, one of Red's bootlegger friends, supplying the drinks, a rowdy party breaks out and the coffin falls from its platform. The corpse slowly tumbles out; the center of Red's forehead reveals a bullet hole.

Popeye leaves Memphis with Temple the night of Red's murder. When Horace calls Miss Reba the day after the funeral (and the day before Goodwin's trial is to begin), he finds out that Temple is no longer there. Goodwin, innocent but also fearful of Popeye, does not want Ruby to testify, but she does. When Temple appears at the trial, she gives false testimony that it was Goodwin who violated her and killed Tommy. The jury takes eight minutes to convict Goodwin of the crime. Later that night, a vengeful mob rushes the jail and drags Goodwin out to burn him to death. Horace himself is almost overcome by the crowd. Stunned, the dejected and defeated Horace leaves Jefferson for Kinston to return to his wife, whom he had planned to leave at the beginning of the novel.

Popeye is arrested in Birmingham on his way to visit his mother in Pensacola and charged for the murder of a policeman in a small Alabama town. This murder occurred the same night that Red was killed. Refusing legal assistance and with no defense, Popeye is convicted, and ironically is hanged for a murder he did not commit. By this time, Temple is unhappily in Paris with her father.

Sanctuary is Faulkner's darkest novel, in that, with the discovery of evil, comes disillusionment and defeat. Though the motive (or motives) behind Temple's false statements at Goodwin's trial are not clear, the fact that she perjures herself is a form of corruption. Horace's idealism, especially as it relates to justice and the integrity and inviolability of southern womanhood, is shattered. Horace knows that Temple *was* brutally raped and violated, but he soon discovers that she perverts justice and violates truth by lying under oath, actions that lead to the

violent death of an innocent person. The image and sanctity of southern womanhood are at the center of the prosecutor's argument: "'You have just heard the testimony of the chemist and the gynecologist—who is, as you gentlemen know, an authority on the most sacred affairs of the most sacred thing in life: womanhood— who says that this is no longer a matter for the hangman, but for a bonfire of gasoline'" (pp. 283–84). Though stricken from the record, the provocative statement of his last 18 words foreshadows Goodwin's death. In effect, the innocent Goodwin is being tried not for murder but for sadistically violating a woman, the *idea* of which is so absolutely reprehensible to the town that death is a fitting punishment.

Some early critics charged Faulkner with sensationalism and with exploiting violence and sex, but the novel is rightly seen as an important work in Faulkner's canon with significant moral concerns. It is not merely a potboiler written to make money, for it contains, in spite of lurid passages—which in themselves actually help create part of the powerful effect of the novel— many of the major themes found throughout Faulkner's works: the discovery of the nature of reality and evil, disillusionment, the problem of corruption, and the quest for justice. The struggle of the human spirit in the face of defeat and despair is as much a part of *Sanctuary* as it is of any of Faulkner's major novels, including *The SOUND AND THE FURY. Sanctuary* was not "a cheap idea . . . deliberately conceived to make money" as Faulkner misled his readers to believe in the introduction to the 1932 Modern Library edition of the novel (See Appendix IV.)

In 1933, Paramount released a film based on the novel, *The Story of Temple Drake,* directed by Stephen Roberts and starring Miriam Hopkins as Temple Drake, Jack La Rue as Trigger (Popeye), William Gargan as Stephen Benbow (Horace Benbow), Sir Guy Standing as Judge Drake (Temple's father), Florence Eldridge as Ruby, Irving Pichel as Lee Goodwin, and Elizabeth Patterson as Aunt Jenny (Miss Jenny). Chapter 25 of the novel was published under the title "Uncle Bud and the Three Madams" in *The PORTABLE FAULKNER* (1946). In 1954, *Sanctuary* was issued together with *REQUIEM FOR A NUN* (a sequel to the novel) by the New American Library; a film adaptation based on the two works and titled *Sanctuary* was released in 1961 by Twentieth Century–Fox, directed by Tony Richardson and starring Lee Remick as Temple Drake Stevens, Yves Montand as Candy Man (Popeye), Harry Townes as Ira Stevens (Gavin STEVENS), Bradford Dillman as Gowan Stevens, and Odetta as Nancy (Nancy MANNIGOE). *Sanctuary: The Original Text,* edited, with an afterword and notes, by Noel Polk, was published in 1981 by Random House, New York; the corrected text with Faulkner's introduction in the editors' note was published by Vintage International, New York, in December 1993.

For further information, see *Faulkner in the University*, pp. 9, 49, 74, 85–86, 90–91, 96; *Selected Letters of William Faulkner*, pp. 18, 53, 54, 58, 61, 65, 68, 92, 106, 423; *Faulkner at Nagano*, pp. 9, 62–64, 76, 80, 125–26, 143, 190.

Sander, Aleck   Character in *INTRUDER IN THE DUST*. He is Chick MALLISON's friend and his collaborator, with Miss Eunice HABERSHAM, in the exhumation of Vinson GOWRIE, an attempt to prove Lucas BEAUCHAMP's innocence of a murder charge. Because Aleck is black, his involvement in Gowrie business is riskier than that of his white fellow detectives.

He reappears in *The TOWN* as the son of Big Top and Guster SANDER and the friend and sidekick of Chick Mallison.

Sander, Big Top   Minor African-American character in *The TOWN*. Married to Guster SANDER, Big Top is the father of Little Top SANDER and Aleck SANDER.

Sander, Guster   Minor African-American character in *The TOWN*. She is married to Big Top SANDERS and the mother of Little Top SANDER and Aleck SANDER. She cooks for Chick MALLISON's mother.

Sander, Little Top   Minor African-American character in *The TOWN*. Little Top is Aleck SANDER's older brother. Together with Gowan STEVENS, Little Top scatters tacks on the street to puncture Manfred DE SPAIN's tires, a ploy designed by Gowan's older cousin, Gavin STEVENS, who is annoyed by the noise that de Spain intentionally makes with his car as he races by the Stevens's home.

Sarah   Character in "THAT WILL BE FINE" (in *Collected Stories*). She is the mother of the seven-year-old narrator, GEORGIE, and the sister of the thieving, adulterous Uncle RODNEY.

Sardis Lake   Twenty-mile-long reservoir in Panola county and LAFAYETTE COUNTY in northern Mississippi, northwest of OXFORD, MISSISSIPPI, formed by the damming of the TALLAHATCHIE RIVER. Faulkner liked to camp, fish, and hunt along its shores.

In the late 1940s, he used to cruise the lake aboard the houseboat *Minmagary*, which he and several friends built. Through trial and error in his sloop-rigged dory *Ring Dove* during the summer of 1949, Faulkner became a skilled freshwater sailor.

Sartoris   Faulkner's third novel, published in 1929. *Sartoris* is the revised and sharply cut *FLAGS IN THE DUST*, the story of the Sartoris clan of fictional JEFFERSON, MISSISSIPPI. With *Sartoris*, Faulkner first enters a world of his own invention, the YOKNAPATAWPHA COUNTY of his best work. After a promising but uncertain start with *SOLDIERS'*

PAY (1926) and *MOSQUITOES* (1927), he had found his themes, his place, his characters, and his voice.

"Beginning with *Sartoris*," the novelist told Jean STEIN in a *PARIS REVIEW* interview in the 1950s, "I discovered that my own little postage stamp of native soil was worth writing about and that I would never live long enough to exhaust it. . . . so I created a cosmos of my own."

Sartoris is the story of two generations of planter class Mississippians. The older generation includes old Bayard SARTORIS (3) and Aunt Jenny DU PRE; the younger includes the Sartoris twins, Bayard's grandsons Johnny SARTORIS and young Bayard SARTORIS (4), and their contemporaries Horace BENBOW and his sister Narcissa Benbow (SARTORIS). The twins' and the Benbows' parents are absent and barely mentioned, allowing Faulkner to juxtapose the stable, traditional generation of the Civil War with the restless and alienated young men and women of the post–World War I wasteland.

Faulkner wrote *Flags in the Dust* in 1926–27. With rejection slips from several publishing houses, he turned in the late summer of 1928 to his friend and sometime agent Ben WASSON for help in placing the orphaned manuscript. HARCOURT, BRACE & COMPANY, agreed to take the book on, with the condition that Faulkner cut it substantially. According to Joseph BLOTNER, Faulkner's biographer, the novelist vehemently objected to cutting *Flags* and wanted no part of the job. But he authorized Wasson to rework the book, figuring it would remain unpublished otherwise.

"The trouble is that you had about six books in here," Wasson told him. "You were trying to write them all at once."

The contract with Harcourt called for the deletion of about 25,000 words, leaving a novel of about 110,000 words. An editor at Harcourt retitled the book. Wasson's editing reduced the role of the Horace Benbow character, which in *Flags* is a counterpoint to that of young Bayard Sartoris. Passages about Benbow's love affair and his incestuous feelings for Narcissa were deleted or shortened. Wasson dropped a long account of Narcissa Benbow's reflections on young Bayard's boyhood and cut or deleted several scenes involving Byron SNOPES, the author of a series of obscene letters to Narcissa.

The result is a tauter novel, but many Faulknerians were not impressed with Wasson's work. Cleanth BROOKS found more of Yoknapatawpha in *Flags*, more of Faulkner's "attempts to do justice within the confines of one novel to the landed gentry, the yeomen whites, black people, and even the Snopeses." Frederick Karl argued that Wasson had drained the book of characteristic Faulkner, turning a daring work of fiction into a safe one.

The book opens in 1919 with the furtive return from France of young Bayard Sartoris, a World War I aviator racked with guilt over the death in combat of his twin

John, who jumped out of his burning airplane without a parachute. There is no meaning to Bayard's life. He finds release in violence and in reckless behavior: riding a wild stallion through the streets of Jefferson, driving a powerful car fast over rough country roads, drinking himself into oblivion.

Bayard joylessly marries Narcissa Benbow but is unable to settle down with her. He kills old Bayard in a car accident and, ashamed to return home, takes refuge with the McCallums, stolid, self-sufficient country people from the hills north of Jefferson. He soon leaves the McCallums' farm, knowing they are bound soon to hear of the manner of his grandfather's death. He spends Christmas Eve in the cabin of a black sharecropper family. The next day his host drives him to the nearest railroad station, and he leaves Jefferson for good. A few months later he finally succeeds in killing himself, leaving Narcissa as she is about to give birth to another male Sartoris to carry on the line.

Horace Benbow, too, is a veteran of France, but a noncombatant: He had been a YMCA secretary and, as such, an object of derision to the fighting men. A dabbler in the arts, he is dreamy, aesthetic, ineffectual. Horace and young Bayard are opposed romantics, one a man of reflection, the other a man of action; both are equally out of place. Horace becomes involved with a married woman, Belle Mitchell BENBOW. She divorces, and much to Narcissa's disgust—she regards Belle as "dirty"—he marries her.

Bayard's obsessions are unconvincing. After all, he had little or nothing to do with his brother Johnny's death, beyond failing to talk him out of going aloft in his outgunned Sopwith Camel in the first place. Bayard watches helplessly as Johnny kicks himself free of the airplane and falls to his death. Why does Bayard blame himself?

"Young Bayard's story consists mainly of his repeated attempts to get himself killed," the critic Michael MILLGATE observed, "and it is one of the weaknesses of the novel that the pressures driving him are never made entirely clear."

Critic John W. Corrington provided one possible explanation, identifying Bayard's demons as fear and uncertainty of his own courage. These insecurities impelled him to prove through his foolhardy behavior that he can "as easily and gracefully fulfill the demands of the Sartoris myth as did Johnny."

Faulkner offers two partial answers. In Sartoris, Aunt Jenny explains it by reference to congenital Sartoris recklessness, something in the blood; early in the novel, she tells the story of her brother, the first Bayard SARTORIS (1), a Confederate cavalryman who lost his life in an antic raid of a Yankee headquarters in search of anchovies. In an interview many years later, Faulkner suggested the World War I experience as the cause of Bayard's dislocation.

The anxieties of the younger generation contrast with the stability of other characters in Sartoris. Old Bayard, the crotchety banker who refuses to own an automobile, and Aunt Jenny, sharp-tongued and shrewd, are survivors of the heroic age of the Civil War and its aftermath. (Faulkner developed their stories in The UNVANQUISHED and other works.) The McCallums, hill-country farmers, are rooted in the land. Another solid countryman is V. K. SURATT, the sewing machine salesman who will become the incomparable RATLIFF of later works. African-American characters, even when they are rather crude stereotypes, as in Simon STROTHER, the obsequious coachman, seem more animated than young Bayard and Horace Benbow.

Faulkner dedicated the revised and shortened novel to Sherwood ANDERSON; Harcourt published it on January 31, 1929, with an initial printing of about 2,000 copies. The first reviews appeared a few weeks later. Like Faulkner's first publisher, Horace LIVERIGHT, an anonymous critic in the New York Times found Sartoris seriously deficient, a "work of uneven texture, confused sentiment and loose articulation." Henry Nash Smith, writing in the Dallas Morning News, took a more generous view: "He learns his trade and broadens his thought almost vividly from chapter to chapter; and he is young."

Sartoris marks an important stage in Faulkner's development. There are fewer purple patches than in earlier work. As Michael Millgate observes, Faulkner's characteristic "obsession with time, death and the omnipresence of the past" is much in evidence.

The strength of the novel is the Yoknapatawpha world. It is a source for characters, scenes, and episodes that Faulkner would exploit in later work. Faulkner had carried over moods suggesting T. S. Eliot's The Waste Land from his earlier, more self-consciously literary work. After Sartoris, the influence of Eliot's poem would all but disappear.

"Bayard may be a lost soul, Horace an ineffectual dreamer," Cleanth Brooks wrote. "But the folk society that lies around them goes on in its immemorial ways."

Sartoris   Fictional place in YOKNAPATAWPHA COUNTY. Four miles north of JEFFERSON, MISSISSIPPI, Sartoris is the plantation home of John Sartoris. Yankee troops searching for Colonel Sartoris, a Confederate cavalry raider, burned the house in 1863. Sartoris's son Bayard SARTORIS (3) witnessed the episode with his grandmother, Rosa MILLARD. Colonel Sartoris rebuilt on the ruins of the old place after the war.

Sartoris, Bayard   **(1)** Character in SARTORIS, the infant son of young Bayard SARTORIS (4) and his first wife, Caroline White SARTORIS. Mother and child died on October 27, 1918, probably of influenza.

Sartoris, Bayard (2) Character in *SARTORIS* and *The UNVANQUISHED*, brother of Colonel John SARTORIS. General J. E. B. Stuart's aide-de-camp in 1862, he is killed just before the second battle of Manassas in a cavalry raid on the headquarters of the Yankee general Pope.

Sartoris, Bayard (3) (old) Character in *SARTORIS, The UNVANQUISHED*, and other works. The son of Colonel John SARTORIS, founder of the prominent JEFFERSON, MISSISSIPPI, family, he is the inheritor of his father's banking and related business interests. The character, according to Faulkner biographer Joseph BLOTNER and others, is modeled on Faulkner's paternal grandfather, John Wesley Thompson FALKNER.

In *Sartoris*, Bayard is old, irascible, hard of hearing, and resentful of the changes coming rapidly upon Jefferson. Even as the automobile, a symbol of modernity, becomes dominant, old Bayard insists that his old coachman Simon (STROTHER) drive him to and from his bank in the family carriage. When, in *The TOWN*, the first auto in Jefferson frightens Bayard's team of horses, he has Mayor ADAMS pass an edict against the use of all automobiles. Change triumphs over old Bayard, though, for he dies of a heart attack as he rides in his grandson's recklessly piloted car.

In *The UNVANQUISHED*, Bayard is the boy hero, with his black friend Ringo STROTHER, of a series of picaresque adventures set in Civil War and Reconstruction-era YOKNAPATAWPHA COUNTY. He and Ringo follow war events closely, and he glories in his father's violent exploits. He revenges himself on the bushwhacker who murders his grandmother, shooting him down and nailing his mutilated hand to her wooden grave marker.

As a young man, Bayard renounces his father's violent ways. Though he is expected to take revenge on the colonel's killer, Ben REDMOND (called REDLAW in *Sartoris*), he instead faces him down unarmed and forces him to leave Jefferson forever.

Bayard also appears in *The HAMLET*, where the story of his giving Ab SNOPES a beating for his role in the death of his grandmother is told, and in *GO DOWN, MOSES*, ("The Bear"), *REQUIEM FOR A NUN, The MANSION, The REIVERS*, and the short stories "A ROSE FOR EMILY" and "THERE WAS A QUEEN."

Sartoris, Bayard (4) (young) Character in *SARTORIS* and other works, grandson of old Bayard SARTORIS (3). A violent, noisy, impulsive, drunken, despairing American veteran of the ROYAL AIR FORCE, he mourns the death in aerial combat of his twin brother, Johnny SARTORIS.

Young Bayard illogically holds himself responsible for Johnny's death, but his own destructive behavior leads to the death of old Bayard, whose weak heart gives out when his grandson takes him on a fast car ride through the YOKNAPATAWPHA COUNTY countryside.

Young Bayard marries Narcissa Benbow (SARTORIS), a character scarcely less neurotic that he is himself. He dies violently in the crash of a faulty experimental aircraft on the day their son is born.

In the short story "AD ASTRA," a grieving Bayard takes off to search the skies of northern France for his brother's German killer. He also appears in the short story "THERE WAS A QUEEN" and in *The TOWN* and *The MANSION*.

Sartoris, Benbow (Bory) Character in *SARTORIS* and other works. The son of young Bayard SARTORIS (4) and Narcissa Benbow SARTORIS, he is born on the day his father is killed in an airplane crash.

In *The MANSION*, Benbow is presented at age 17 as one of the best bird shots in YOKNAPATAWPHA COUNTY. He also appears at various ages in *SANCTUARY, KNIGHT'S GAMBIT, The TOWN*, and the short story "THERE WAS A QUEEN."

Sartoris, Caroline White Character in *SARTORIS*, first wife of young Bayard SARTORIS (4). She and her infant son died on October 27, 1918, probably of influenza, while her husband was in France serving with the ROYAL AIR FORCE.

Sartoris, Colonel John Character in *SARTORIS, The UNVANQUISHED*, and other works, head of the founding family of Faulkner's YOKNAPATAWPHA COUNTY cycle. Faulkner modeled the character of the hard, violent, and imaginative John Sartoris on his great-grandfather, the soldier and railroad builder William Clark FALKNER.

Sartoris serves as an officer in Lee's army in the Civil War and later as the commander of a unit of partisan cavalry in northern Mississippi. After the war, he violently opposes Yankee "carpetbaggers," rebuilds his ruined plantation, develops a railroad, and defeats his bitter business rival to win election to the Mississippi legislature.

He tires of violence at the last, however. In *Sartoris*, he faces his rival REDLAW (called Ben REDMOND in *The Unvanquished*) alone and unarmed and is shot to death. His monument is a larger-than-life statue that gazes out across the valley toward the railroad he built.

The long-dead, by then legendary Sartoris is a hovering spirit in *Sartoris*. The novel opens with a spiritual communion between the colonel, the former soldier Will FALLS, and the colonel's son, old Bayard SARTORIS (3). Falls leaves, but the old colonel remains a palpable presence.

Later, old Bayard climbs to the attic to rummage among his father's preserved things: a blue forage cap of Mexican War vintage, a heavy cavalry saber and a pair of dueling pistols, a gray Confederate coat.

In *The Unvanquished*, set in northern Mississippi during the Civil War, Colonel Sartoris is presented as a soldier hero who causes so much grief for the Yankees that they put up a reward for his capture. His young son Bayard idolizes him. The colonel carries violence with him into postwar life, sallying forth on his wedding day in 1872 to shoot down two Yankees and so prevent a black candidate from winning election as JEFFERSON, MISSISSIPPI, marshal. In Faulkner's retelling of an episode from *Sartoris,* he later faces his rival Redmond unarmed and is killed.

Colonel Sartoris's legendary wartime exploits form part of the background of *The SOUND AND THE FURY.* Faulkner narrates his killing of the two Burdens, New England carpetbaggers by way of Missouri, in *LIGHT IN AUGUST.* In *ABSALOM, ABSALOM!,* Thomas SUTPEN rebuffs Sartoris in his effort to mobilize Yoknapatawpha planters against Reconstruction.

Sartoris is also mentioned in *The HAMLET,* where Uncle Buck MCCASLIN tells the story of his shooting Ab SNOPES in the foot for attempting to steal the colonel's horse during the Civil War; in *GO DOWN, MOSES* ("The Bear"), *REQUIEM FOR A NUN, The TOWN, The MANSION, The REIVERS,* and in the short stories "BARN BURNING," "SHALL NOT PERISH," "MY GRANDMOTHER MILLARD AND GENERAL BEDFORD FORREST AND THE BATTLE OF HARRYKIN CREEK," and "THERE WAS A QUEEN."

In the larger context of the Yoknapatawpha cycle, Colonel Sartoris stands at the head of an aristocratic family of the type that will pass from the scene with the rise of the Snopeses. Self-assured, with a firm code to live by, he is a standard by which neurasthenic younger generations of Sartorises are measured and found wanting.

Faulkner saw in his own family history a pattern of slow decline, and acknowledged similarities in character and experience between the founder of the Sartoris clan and his grandfather (*Faulkner in University,* p. 254).

Sartoris, Drusilla Hawk   Character in *The UNVANQUISHED.* The daughter of Dennison HAWK Sr. and Louisa HAWK, she cuts her hair, alters her mode of dress, and enlists in Colonel John SARTORIS's regiment after her fiancé, Gavin BRECKBRIDGE, is killed at the battle of SHILOH.

Drusilla survives the war and settles at SARTORIS plantation with the colonel and his family. Though she and Sartoris are not lovers, her mother and the elderly ladies of JEFFERSON, MISSISSIPPI, pressure the couple to marry. They acquiesce, even though they are probably not in love.

When his business rival REDMOND shoots and kills the colonel, Drusilla insists that Bayard SARTORIS (3) seek revenge. But Bayard no longer glorifies his father's violent ways and he does not respond to the hysterical Drusilla's goading.

Drusilla eventually accepts young Bayard's conduct in the Redmond matter. By the time she leaves Jefferson for good, they are reconciled.

Sartoris, John (1) (Johnny)   Character in *SARTORIS* and other works. He is the twin brother of young Bayard SARTORIS (4). An aviator, he is killed in combat while flying with the ROYAL AIR FORCE over France during World War I. His brother's grieving for him and self-reproach for failing to prevent his death is a motif of *SARTORIS.*

He is drawn as rash, reckless, and vengeful in the short story "ALL THE DEAD PILOTS," where he and his superior officer, SPOOMER, are rivals for the affections of two women. Johnny Sartoris also appears in "WITH CAUTION AND DISPATCH," where he is a supposedly skillful pilot but manages to crash three different Camel fighters on what should have been a simple short flight across the English Channel to France. He is referred to in *The TOWN, The MANSION,* and the short story "THERE WAS A QUEEN."

Sartoris, John (2)   Character in *SARTORIS.* He is the son of old Bayard SARTORIS (3), and the father of the twins young Bayard SARTORIS (4) and John (Johnny) SARTORIS (1). He dies of yellow fever in 1901.

John Sartoris also appears in the short story "THERE WAS A QUEEN."

Sartoris, Lucy Cranston   Character in *SARTORIS.* The wife of John SARTORIS (2) and mother of the twins Bayard SARTORIS (4) and John (Johnny), SARTORIS (1), she dies when the boys are young. The censorious Aunt Sally WYATT says she spoiled the twins.

Sartoris, Narcissa Benbow   Character in *SARTORIS* and other works. The sister of Horace BENBOW, and the second wife of young Bayard SARTORIS (4), she is obsessively interested in the emotional life of her ineffectual brother, but in other relationships she is a conventional young southern woman.

Rather joylessly in love with young Bayard from the start, she eventually marries him; she delivers their son on the day her husband is killed in the crash of an experimental airplane.

Narcissa Sartoris also appears in *SANCTUARY* and in the short story "THERE WAS A QUEEN." In *Sanctuary,* the widow Narcissa thwarts her brother Horace's attempts at defending the innocent Lee GOODWIN and at helping Goodwin's common-law wife, Ruby LAMAR. In *THE TOWN* and *The MANSION,* she is referred to by her maiden name, Narcissa Benbow.

Sartoris, Virginia   See DU PRE, VIRGINIA.

Sartoris Station   Fictional name of College Hill Station, a flag stop on the railroad four miles north of OXFORD, MISSISSIPPI. Lying two and a half miles from SEMINARY HILL (Faulkner's name for College Hill), Sartoris Station figures in *The TOWN,* the second novel in the SNOPES TRILOGY.

Sarty   See SNOPES, COLONEL SARTORIS.

Saturday Evening Post   Weekly magazine, established in 1821 to provide light weekend reading for Philadelphians. In 1897 a new owner converted the *Post* into a middlebrow national publication and eventually built circulation to three million. The old magazine failed in 1969 and reappeared two years later as a quarterly.

Faulkner began submitting work to the *Post* in the mid-1920s; the magazine routinely returned it. He made his first sale to the magazine in 1930 with the short story "THRIFT," published on September 6 of that year. The *Post* paid $750 for its second Faulkner story, "RED LEAVES," which appeared October 25, 1930. From then on Faulkner found the magazine a generally steady, always lucrative outlet for his short fiction. The *Post* offered $900 for "A BEAR HUNT" and published the story on February 10, 1934.

The magazine sometimes exasperated Faulkner, and he rather illogically resented it for tempting him to write lesser work for money. In negotiations over one set of stories, he wrote his sometime agent Morton Goldman that he didn't care who bought "trash" as long as he received the best possible price for it (*Selected Letters*, p. 84).

Faulkner sold several of the stories that became the novel *The UNVANQUISHED* to the *Post* in 1934 and 1936. The magazine published a version of the novella "The Bear" on May 9, 1942.

In 1957, Faulkner's agent Harold OBER sold the last chapter of *The TOWN,* the third novel in the SNOPES TRILOGY, to the *Post.* It appeared as "The Waifs" on May 4.

Saunders, Cecily (Cecily Saunders Farr)   A beautiful but cold young woman in *SOLDIERS' PAY.* Cecily Saunders is engaged to be married to Donald MAHON, but because Mahon has been missing in action during World War I and is presumed dead, Cecily begins to date George FARR, a local young businessman. When the wounded Mahon is brought back to Charlestown, Georgia, by Mrs. Margaret POWERS and Joe GILLIGAN, Cecily is torn between keeping her promise to marry Mahon and being repulsed by the hideous scar on Mahon's face. Farr, even while acknowledging that Cecily's suitor has returned from the war, nevertheless continues to pursue her. Cecily eventually allows George to seduce her, hoping that the status of a fallen woman would force Mahon's father, Rector MAHON, to absolve her of her engagement to Donald. She finally elopes with Farr.

Saunders, Minnie   Mother of Cecily SAUNDERS in *SOLDIERS' PAY.* After Cecily's badly wounded fiancé, Donald MAHON, returns to Charlestown, Georgia, from World War I, Mrs. Saunders seeks to end the engagement. In this matter, she is an overbearing wife who dominates her equivocating husband, Robert SAUNDERS Sr.

Saunders, Robert, Jr. (Bob)   Younger brother of Cecily SAUNDERS in *SOLDIERS' PAY.* Fascinated by the idea of Donald MAHON's horrible war injury, he begs to see it in person and later brings his friends to see it. Seen swimming naked by Mrs. Margaret POWERS and Joe GILLIGAN, he vows to get even by spying on them. After catching them kissing and eavesdropping on their conversation, he tells his sister that Mrs. Powers loves Donald and will take him away from her. Later, moved by Mahon's funeral procession, Bob runs home and cries in the arms of his family's servant, a black cook.

Saunders, Robert, Sr.   In *SOLDIERS' PAY,* the father of Cecily SAUNDERS and Robert SAUNDERS Jr. At first he feels that Cecily ought to keep her promise to marry Donald MAHON, despite his horrible wounds. For a time, Mr. Saunders is very stern with Cecily because of her objections to marrying Mahon, but his domineering wife eventually changes his opinion.

Schluss   In *SOLDIERS' PAY,* a traveling salesman of women's underclothes who meets the soldiers Joe GILLIGAN and Cadet Julian LOWE on the train. Asked by the conductor to look after the soldiers, who are inebriated, he himself gets drunk. When he leaves the train at Buffalo, the police arrest him instead of the soldiers for whom they were called.

Schofield, Dr.   Character in "THE TALL MEN" (in *Collected Stories*). A physician, he amputates Buddy MCCALLUM's leg, injured in an accident at the hammer mill.

Schultz, Reverend   Character in "UNCLE WILLY" (in *Collected Stories*). The preacher at Uncle Willy CHRISTIAN's church, he helps the JEFFERSON, MISSISSIPPI, ladies coerce Willy into leading a drug-free life. The Reverend and Mrs. MERRIDEW arrange for a clerk to takes over Willy's drug store.

Schultz, Sister   Character in "UNCLE WILLY" (in *Collected Stories*). She is the wife of Reverend Schultz, the preacher at Uncle Willy CHRISTIAN's church.

Scribner's Magazine   Distinguished American literary monthly magazine, a sometime publisher (after many rejections) of Faulkner's fiction. The younger Charles Scribner (1854–1930) established the magazine in 1887 after his father sold *Scribner's Monthly*. Contributors included Robert Louis Stevenson, Henry James, Rudyard Kipling, Edith Wharton, and Stephen Crane.

In the 1920s, *Scribner's* became the first literary magazine to publish the work of Ernest HEMINGWAY and Thomas Wolfe. The editors rejected several Faulkner stories in the late 1920s. On one rejection, editor Alfred Dashiell wrote that in "ONCE ABOARD THE LUGGER" Faulkner supplied too much atmosphere and not enough story. "It would seem that in the attempt to avoid the obvious you have manufactured the vague," Dashiell commented.

Faulkner continued to submit pieces to Dashiell, and the author's persistence paid off. *Scribner's* accepted "DRY SEPTEMBER" in May 1930, paying $200 for it; the short story appeared in January 1931. The magazine also published "SPOTTED HORSES" (1931), "MULE IN THE YARD" (1934), "SKIRMISH AT SARTORIS" (1935), and other stories.

Scribner's ceased publication in 1939.

Secretary Character in "UNCLE WILLY" (in *Collected Stories*). He is Uncle Willy CHRISTIAN's African-American driver. Secretary regularly chauffeurs Willy to MEMPHIS.

Seminary Hill Faulkner's name for the hamlet of College Hill, a once exclusively Presbyterian settlement five miles north of OXFORD, MISSISSIPPI. Faulkner peoples Seminary Hill with Baptists and Methodists.

In *The TOWN,* the second novel in the SNOPES TRILOGY, Gavin STEVENS drives out to Seminary Hill to Mr. Garraway's store to eat cheese and crackers and listen to old Garraway abuse Calvin Coolidge.

Semmes Character in *GO DOWN, MOSES* ("The Bear"). He is a MEMPHIS distiller. Major DE SPAIN sends Isaac MCCASLIN and Boon HOGGANBECK to Semmes to collect a supply of whiskey for the hunting camp.

the sentry *See* HARRY, MR.

"Sepulture South: Gaslight" *(Uncollected Stories)* A short story concerning an unnamed narrator's memories of the death and burial of his grandfather. The story indicates much more than mere sorrow: It shows the familial and social effects of death. In the society depicted, ties are dissolved when a death occurs; the black house servants, superstitiously—or through a kind of custom—leave the service of the house after a death. Death, in a sense, frees the servants, but not the family. The central conflict in "Sepulture South: Gaslight" is the narrator's inability to come to terms with death, which the narrator calls an ignominy that God should not allow. The horror of death has a hold on the narrator, who returns three or four times a year to the graveyard to consider death, not only of his own family, but also of all humans.

Told from the first person singular point of view, the story is a meditation on death in general and in particular. Believing that the domestic help are able to view death as a rite of passage, the narrator sees it instead as a horror and a burden, which, as he grows older, he later converts into a tie to his ancestry—and to all of humanity. At the end of the story, the narrator explains that he visits the cemetery several times a year and, while gazing upon the graves and monuments there— some undeniably associated with the Civil War—con-

templates how they shield the dead from the inhumanity of the living. The story, as James Ferguson explains, "conveys with warm nostalgia but without sentimentality the atmosphere and tonality of the distant past, of a childhood in the Deep South" (*Faulkner's Short Fiction,* p. 48). Because it contains both fictional and autobiographical elements, "Sepulture South: Gaslight" may be less of a short story than, as Ferguson remarks, "a personal essay" or "a kind of semifictional autobiographical reminiscence" that is at once lyrical, poetic, and evocative (p. 49).

"Sepulture South: Gaslight" was first published in December 1954 in *Harper's Bazaar* 138, 84–85, 140–41, and later reprinted in *UNCOLLECTED STORIES OF WILLIAM FAULKNER.* For more information, see *Selected Letters of William Faulkner,* p. 373, and *Uncollected Stories of William Faulkner,* pp. 703–04.

Sewanee Review Literary quarterly, the oldest journal of its kind in the United States. Founded in 1892 and published by the University of the South in Sewanee, Tennessee, the review's chief aim is to interpret the role of the South in American culture.

Part of the critic Malcolm COWLEY's important essay on Faulkner's fiction, "William Faulkner's Human Comedy," appeared in the *Sewanee Review* in the summer of 1945. The essay helped achieved Cowley's object, as he explained it, of righting "the balance between [Faulkner's] worth and his reputation."

Faulkner in 1948 sold the oft-rejected short story "A COURTSHIP," written in 1942, to the Tennessee quarterly for $200. He instructed the editors to change a character's name from Callicoat to Hogganbeck to be consistent with what Faulkner called his "Yoknapatawpha genealogy."

"A Courtship" won a 1949 O. Henry Memorial Award, given annually to the best short stories published in magazines.

Shack In *SANCTUARY,* one of the two university students traveling on the same train Horace BENBOW is on when going to OXFORD, MISSISSIPPI, to inquire about Temple Drake (STEVENS). Shack and his unnamed companion ride without paying; they convince the conductor that they have already given him their tickets.

"Shall Not Perish" *(Collected Stories)* A short story of mourning narrated by the same young Grier boy who narrates "TWO SOLDIERS." The story begins with the news of the death of Pete GRIER, the brother of the nine-year-old narrator, in World War I. The news arrives in April, the middle of the planting season, and although Pete's death devastates the family, the endless cycle of sowing and harvesting must continue. Three months later, in July, the unnamed son of Major DE SPAIN (2), another soldier from YOKNAPATAWPHA COUNTY, dies in the war, and Mrs. GRIER and her only surviving child, the young narrator, take the bus from FRENCHMAN'S BEND to JEFFERSON, MISSISSIPPI, to make a mourning call on the major. After their visit, Mrs. Grier and her son go to a small local museum that displays paintings of all parts of the United States. The narrator is reminded of his senile grandfather, who sometimes reacted violently to western movies, shouting out the names of long-dead Union and Confederate leaders in a vision of the Civil War. The museum, and its exhibit in particular, reinforces the notion that Frenchman's Bend, as the narrator explicitly indicates (*Collected Stories,* p. 111), is a microcosm of the United States. By implication, "Shall Not Perish" depicts the United States as omnipotent and a cause worth dying for. The story centers on a conversation between Mrs. Grier and Major de Spain; the major understandably voices despair and anger over the death of his only son in uncompromising tones. But Mrs. Grier, perhaps as the mouthpiece for Faulkner himself, responds in terms that anticipate the sentiments of love and honor and compassion and sacrifice Faulkner expressed in his Nobel Prize acceptance speech in December 1950. Mrs. Grier's timely visit prevents de Spain from committing suicide.

In several respects, however, "Shall Not Perish" is as unrealistic as its companion piece, "Two Soldiers," and both stories are regrettably jingoistic. Virtually nothing in Faulkner's earlier fiction, as James Ferguson writes, prepares us "for the saccharine inanities of 'Two Soldiers' and 'Shall Not Perish' (*Faulkner's Short Fiction,* p. 42). "Shall Not Perish" was first published in July–August 1943 issue of *Story* 23, 40–47; it is reprinted in COLLECTED STORIES OF WILLIAM FAULKNER and in *A Rose for Emily.*

For more information, see *Selected Letters of William Faulkner,* pp. 149, 150, 151, 274; and Diane Brown Jones, *A Reader's Guide to the Short Stories of William Faulkner,* pp. 73–83.

Shegog, Reverend In *The SOUND AND THE FURY,* the black preacher from St. Louis who gives the Easter Sunday sermon at the church DILSEY, FRONY, LUSTER, and Benjy COMPSON attend. He is a small man but a powerful preacher. His sermon, which begins almost dispassionately, becomes more and more emotionally charged as he proceeds, and by the time he finishes, Dilsey begins to cry and later utters: "I seed de beginnin, en now I sees de endin" (p. 297).

Sherman, William Tecumseh (1820–1891) Soldier. With Ulysses S. Grant, he was one of the leading Union commanders of the Civil War. He distinguished himself at the battle of SHILOH (1862) and in the VICKSBURG CAMPAIGN (1863) before succeeding Grant in command in the West. His campaigns in Georgia and the Carolinas in 1864–65 sealed the Confederacy's fate.

Sherman loomed large in Falkner family lore. Colonel William C. FALKNER's 2nd Mississippi Regiment captured four cannon from Sherman's command at the first battle of BULL RUN (Manassas) in 1861. In December 1862, Sherman, with 30,000 men, devastated the northern Mississippi countryside from a base at College Hill near OXFORD, burning gins, mills, barns, and houses, and confiscating or destroying livestock.

In 1864, General Andrew J. SMITH, with orders from Sherman to pursue the Confederate raider Nathan Bedford FORREST, burned public buildings and homes in RIPLEY and Oxford, including the Ripley residence of Colonel Falkner.

Shiloh, Battle of A two-day engagement, April 6 and 7, 1862, near Pittsburgh Landing in southwestern Tennessee, between the Union army of Ulysses S. Grant and Confederate forces under Albert Sidney Johnston and Pierre G. T. Beauregard.

Grant recovered from a surprise Confederate assault on the first day, regrouped overnight, and forced a Confederate withdrawal after hard fighting on the second day of the battle. One of the bloodiest of Civil War encounters, Shiloh claimed more than 23,000 total casualties, including 3,477 Union and Confederate dead.

Some 2,000 Confederate casualties were taken to hospitals in OXFORD, MISSISSIPPI, 80 miles to the southwest; more than a third of the wounded died there and were buried in a cemetery near the UNIVERSITY OF MISSISSIPPI campus.

Faulkner's character Gavin BRECKBRIDGE, Drusilla Hawk (SARTORIS)'s fiancé in *The UNVANQUISHED,* was killed at Shiloh; the battle is also mentioned in *ABSALOM, ABSALOM!* The novelist and historian Shelby FOOTE escorted Faulkner over the Shiloh battlefield on April 6, 1952, the 90th anniversary of the battle.

"Shingles for the Lord" (*Collected Stories*) Short story about Res GRIER, who accidentally burns down his church after his attempt at trickery backfires. When Grier and his son arrive late for their day of voluntary labor, the minister scolds him and the others tease him. Solon QUICK, a former Works Progress Administration (WPA) employee, jokingly calculates Grier's owed man-hour work units. Finally the men start splitting shingles—the others efficiently, the angry Grier violently and slowly.

When Solon offers to complete the rest of Grier's work in return for Grier's half-interest in a hunting dog, Grier figures out a way to outwit Solon. Grier and the boy secretly come back at night to strip the old shingles from the roof. When their lantern falls over and ignites the church, which burns down despite heroic efforts by all, the minister calls Grier an arsonist and bans him from joining the volunteers who will raise a new church. The boy recognizes the essential indestructibility of the church, the powerful faith of the rebuilders, and his father's fallibility. Back at home, Grier insists he will join the work crew the next morning.

First published in the SATURDAY EVENING POST (February 13, 1943), the tale was revised for *Collected Stories*.

Ship Island, Ripley & Kentucky Railroad In his first railroad venture, Faulkner's great-grandfather, William C. FALKNER, won a legislative charter for the Ripley Railroad Company, a narrow-gauge line connecting RIPLEY, MISSISSIPPI, with Middleton, Tennessee, on the Memphis & Charleston Railroad.

In January 1872, the legislature authorized a change of name to the Ship Island, Ripley & Kentucky. The first train on the Old Colonel's railroad ran in August 1872. The locals dubbed it "the Doodlebug line."

Short, Herman A minor character in the short story "FOOL ABOUT A HORSE," which was revised and used in *The Hamlet*. He swaps Pat STAMPER a mule and buggy for a horse which he then sells to Beasley KEMP for eight dollars.

Shreve *See* MACKENZIE, SHREVLIN.

Shumann, Dr. Carl The pilot Roger SHUMANN's father in *PYLON*. Although he wanted his son to be a physician, Dr. Shumann bought Roger his first plane. When Roger dies in a crash at an air meet, Roger's wife, Laverne, and their friend Jack HOLMES take their little boy Jack to live with Roger's parents in Ohio. Dr. Shumann agrees to take little Jack on the condition that Laverne never see him again.

Shumann, Jack Laverne SHUMANN's six-year-old son in *PYLON*. Born in a hangar in California, Jack's paternity is uncertain: his father is either Jack HOLMES, the parachute jumper, or Roger SHUMANN, the pilot. The three adults live openly in a *ménage à trois*. After the child is born, Laverne marries Shumann when the two men cast dice to determine who will act as the child's legal father; she gives the boy Jack Holmes's first name. When Roger dies in a crash, Laverne and Holmes take little Jack to live with Roger's father in Ohio.

Shumann, Laverne In *PYLON*, the young woman openly living in *ménage à trois* arrangement with Roger SHUMANN, a pilot, and Jack HOLMES, a parachute jumper. After giving birth to her son, whose paternity is uncertain, Laverne marries Roger when the two men roll dice to determine who the child's legal father will be. She gives the boy Holmes's first name. Flashbacks in the novel show Laverne to have been a sexually active and adventurous teenager. Infatuated with her way of life and sexually attracted to her, the REPORTER explains to Shumann that he would like to have sex with her. But she will have nothing to do with him. When Shu-

mann dies in the last air race at Feinman Airport, Laverne departs with Holmes and her son for Ohio, where she leaves little Jack with Shumann's parents. Pregnant with Holmes's child, Laverne travels on with Holmes, never to see her son again.

Shumann, Roger One of the racing pilots in *PYLON*. Although his father wanted him to be a physician, Shumann became a pilot instead, and with his father's money bought his first plane. He competes in the air meets that are part of the opening celebrations of Feinman Airport in New Valois, Franciana. Living openly in a *ménage à trois*, Shumann arrives with his wife, Laverne, Jack HOLMES, the parachute jumper, and their son little Jack. In the opening race of the meet, Shumann takes second place, beating out pilots with more powerful and more modern planes. In the second race, he crashes because the plane's engine was not properly maintained by Shumann's hungover mechanic, JIGGS. Desperate for money, Shumann is determined to fly in the last and biggest race of the meet with a purse of $2,000. Assisted by the REPORTER, Shumann buys a plane that proves to be fatally unsafe because its engine is too powerful for its frame. As he is about to take the lead in the last race, his aircraft breaks up and crashes in the lake. Shumann's body is not to be found.

Shumann epitomizes alienation in the mechanized world of speed and daring, and his life a commodity to be used. When Colonel H. I. FEINMAN permits the unworthy plane to compete in the last race, he is thinking more of entertaining the paying crowd than safeguarding Shumann's life.

Sibleigh Character in *SARTORIS*. He is a ROYAL AIR FORCE aviator in France, a comrade of young Bayard SARTORIS (4). This RAF flight commander is also mentioned in *A FABLE* and in the short story "WITH CAUTION AND DISPATCH."

Sickymo Character in *GO DOWN, MOSES* ("The Bear"). A former slave, he becomes a U.S. marshal in JEFFERSON, MISSISSIPPI, after the Civil War. He used to steal his master's grain alcohol, dilute it with water, and sell it from a cache in the roots of a big sycamore behind the drug store, an enterprise that gave him his name.

Simmons Referred to by Jason COMPSON IV as old man Simmons in *The SOUND AND THE FURY*. Simmons has a key to the old opera house in JEFFERSON, MISSISSIPPI, that stores papers of the failed Merchants' and Farmers' Bank. Jason finds a pad of blank checks there from a St. Louis bank, which he uses to fool his mother concerning the money that his sister, Caddy COMPSON, sends monthly to her daughter Quentin. He burns the phony check in front of his mother and keeps the real one for himself.

Simms Character in *LIGHT IN AUGUST*. The manager, or perhaps owner, of the JEFFERSON, MISSISSIPPI, planing mill, he hires Joe CHRISTMAS and Joe Brown (Lucas BURCH).

Simon (1) Character in "THERE WAS A QUEEN" (in *Collected Stories*). Probably the SIMON STROTHER of *SARTORIS* and *The UNVANQUISHED*, he is the late husband of the mother of ELNORA, the cook for the Sartoris family.

Simon (2) Character in "RACE AT MORNING" (in *BIG WOODS*). He is the African-American cook at the November deer hunting camp.

Skeet The 16-year-old friend of the unnamed protagonist in the short story "MOONLIGHT." The protagonist offers Skeet moonshine whiskey to help arrange a clandestine meeting with his girlfriend Susan.

Skipworth Character in *INTRUDER IN THE DUST*. The BEAT FOUR constable, he arrests Lucas BEAUCHAMP for the murder of Vinson GOWRIE, takes him to his home, and handcuffs him to a bedpost pending the arrival of the sheriff.

"Skirmish at Sartoris" *See The* UNVANQUISHED.

Smith, Andrew J. (1815–1897) Soldier. One of General William T. SHERMAN's subordinate commanders, he led several expeditions into northern Mississippi in 1864 in pursuit of the elusive Confederate cavalry commander Nathan Bedford FORREST.

On August 22, 1864, Smith's command burned the town center and several homes in OXFORD, MISSISSIPPI, including the 20-room mansion of Jacob Thompson, a high Confederate official who fomented sedition in the United States from his envoy's post in Canada.

According to legend, Judith Shegog of Oxford had fallen in love with one of Smith's young officers. She fell to her death from a second-floor balcony of the Shegog place in an attempt to elope with her Yankee. Faulkner acquired the Shegog place in 1930 and renamed it ROWAN OAK. Nearly 70 years after her death, Judith's ghost still haunted the place.

Smith, Essie Meadowfill In *The MANSION* and "HOG PAWN" (revised for the novel), Otis MEADOWFILL's daughter. When she graduates as valedictorian from high school in 1942, she makes the highest grades ever and is offered a $500 scholarship from Mr. HOLLAND (2), the president of the Bank of Jefferson, which she turns down. Instead, she borrows the same sum from him to have a bathroom installed in her home. Mr. Holland gives Essie a job for life, and soon after World War II she marries McKinley SMITH, an ex-marine. With the help of Gavin STEVENS, she gets Orestes SNOPES's deed to a strip of land that she sells to an oil company to buy a farm.

Smith, Harrison (Hal) (unknown) Publisher. They met after Faulkner's friend Ben WASSON delivered the manuscript of the rejected *FLAGS IN THE DUST* to Smith, an editor at HARCOURT, BRACE, in August 1928. Smith liked the novel and persuaded Alfred Harcourt to publish it as *SARTORIS* (1929).

Hal Smith left Harcourt in 1929 to start his own firm. With the English publisher Jonathan Cape, he formed CAPE & SMITH; he took the manuscript of *The SOUND AND THE FURY* along with him.

Cape & Smith thus became Faulkner's fourth publisher in four years. The firm soon ran into financial trouble, however, and Smith split with Cape in 1931. Robert HAAS joined him in 1932 to form SMITH & HAAS.

Partly on account of his own money troubles, Faulkner became disenchanted with Smith & Haas in 1935 and cast about for a new publisher. His opportunity came in January 1936, when RANDOM HOUSE bought Smith & Haas, hiring Smith for a one-year trial period. Smith continued to act as Faulkner's editor on *ABSALOM, ABSALOM!* Random House published the novel later in 1936.

Smith resigned from Random House, feeling he had been forced out, in January 1937. He remained friends with Faulkner long after his departure from Random House, and Faulkner sometimes joined him on his 38-foot ketch, *Cossack II*.

Smith, Lieutenant An officer in *A FABLE* subdued by the RUNNER when he frees the sentry (Mr. HARRY) from the guardhouse.

Smith, McKinley An ex-marine corporal who marries Essie Meadowfill (SMITH); he appears in "HOG PAWN" and *The MANSION*. (The short story was revised for the novel.) He is the son of a tenant farmer from east Texas. He marries Essie after he buys a small lot in Eula Acres, where he builds a home.

Smith, Miss Character in *KNIGHT'S GAMBIT* ("Tomorrow"). Stonewall Jackson FENTRY marries the pregnant Miss Smith, a "downstate" girl whose name actually is Thorpe, and rears her son after she dies in childbirth.

Smith, Mrs. Character in *SARTORIS*. She operates the switchboard for Dr. BRANDT, the Memphis specialist old Bayard SARTORIS (3) sees for treatment of his wen.

Smith, R. Boyce (Ronnie) Character in "TURNABOUT" (in *Collected Stories*). The commanding officer of torpedo boat X001, he is killed in action with the three men in his crew.

Smith & Haas Publishing firm, founded by Harrison SMITH and Robert HAAS in 1932. Smith spilt with Jonathan Cape, with whom (under the aegis of CAPE &

SMITH) he had published Faulkner's *The SOUND AND THE FURY* in 1929, to establish the partnership with Haas.

The new firm published the novel *LIGHT IN AUGUST* in October 1932, followed by *A GREEN BOUGH*, a collection of 44 of Faulkner's poems (13 of them previously published), in April 1933.

Smith and Haas brought out *Doctor Martino and Other Stories* in 1934 and the novel *PYLON* in 1935 before selling the firm to RANDOM HOUSE. Both the principals went on to Random House, with Smith, who remained only a short time, serving as editor of Faulkner's novel *ABSALOM, ABSALOM!* in 1936.

"Smoke"   *See KNIGHT'S GAMBIT.*

Snopes   **(1)** The name Faulkner gives to a rapacious group of kinsfolk who encroach upon the FRENCHMAN'S BEND area and the town of JEFFERSON, MISSISSIPPI, for personal gain. In chapter 2 of *The TOWN*, Gavin STEVENS momentarily reflects on their traits: "they none of them seemed to bear any specific kinship to one another; they were just Snopeses, like colonies of rats or termites are just rats and termites" (p. 40). See SNOPESISM.

Snopes   **(2)** In a few instances in Faulkner's works, there is a Snopes without a first name, for example, in *AS I LAY DYING*, "SHINGLES FOR THE LORD," and "HOG PAWN." In the novel, a Snopes is a "nephew" of Flem SNOPES living in the FRENCHMAN'S BEND area. This Snopes trades a team of mules to Anse BUNDREN in exchange for money and Jewel BUNDREN's horse. It is questionable whether this Snopes is Flem's actual nephew, since Flem's only brother, Colonel Sartoris SNOPES, according to the short story "BARN BURNING," ran away as a child and was never heard from again. In the short story "Shingles for the Lord," another Snopes with no given first name also is reported living near Frenchman's Bend, presumably the same person. In "Hog Pawn," a Snopes without a first name lives next to Otis MEADOWFILL and has a deed that covers part of Meadowfill's vacant lot. When Faulkner revised "Hog Pawn" for the third novel of the SNOPES TRILOGY, *THE MANSION*, he gave this Snopes a first name; see SNOPES, ORESTES (RES).

For specific Snopeses, see the separate entries that follow.

Snopes   **(3)** *See SNOPES, WESLEY.*

Snopes, Ab(ner)   A character in several of Faulkner's works: The novels *THE UNVANQUISHED, THE HAMLET, THE TOWN,* and *THE MANSION,* and the short stories "BARN BURNING" and "MY GRANDMOTHER MILLARD AND GENERAL BEDFORD FORREST AND THE BATTLE OF HARRYKIN CREEK." An unscrupulous scavenger, he is one of the first Snopeses in YOKNAPATAWPHA COUNTY. In response to a question Faulkner was asked while at the

University of Virginia, the author said that Ab Snopes was "a hanger-on" and "sort of a jackal" that stayed "around the outskirts of the kill to get what scraps might be left," and "nobody would have depended" on him because he "probably . . . wouldn't have held together when the pinch came" (*Faulkner in the University,* p. 250).

Ab Snopes was married twice. His first wife was a woman from JEFFERSON, MISSISSIPPI, name Vynie (SNOPES). In *The Hamlet,* he trades Vynie's milk separator to Pat STAMPER for a team of horses Snopes had lost to him. To get the separator back, Vynie gives Stamper the Snopeses' cow. With his second wife, Lennie, Ab has four children: Flem SNOPES, Colonel Sartoris (Sarty) SNOPES, and twin girls, one of whom is named Net SNOPES (in "Barn Burning"). Snopes does not join the Confederate Army during the Civil War but stays on at Colonel John SARTORIS's plantation. In collaboration with Sartoris's mother-in-law, Miss Rosa (Granny) MILLARD, he sells back to the federal troops the horses and mules Granny Millard steals from them. According to Uncle Buck MCCASLIN, Snopes was shot in the foot by Colonel John Sartoris for attempting to steal the Colonel's horse. Because of his connection with the death of Granny Millard, he was severely beaten by Bayard SARTORIS (3) and others.

But Snopes is especially known as a barn-burner. He is accused, but not convicted, of burning Mr. HARRIS's barn when he rents from him. When renting from Major DE SPAIN, Snopes ruins an expensive rug belonging to the de Spains. The major tries to have Snopes pay for the damage by charging him an extra 20 bushels of corn on top of Snopes's payment as a tenant farmer. Snopes, however, is not appeased by a judge's decision to reduce the charge to 10 bushels. He takes revenge by burning down de Spain's barn. Although there is no definite proof that Snopes committed the arson in either case, evidence clearly points to his guilt. (It is worth noting that slightly different versions of these incidents are found in the short story "Barn Burning" and the novel *The Hamlet.* For instance, in the short story, Snopes's son, Sarty, and not Flem, tries to prevent the fire and ends up running away from home.)

In *The Town,* Ab Snopes lives near Jefferson and tries to keep boys away from his watermelon patch. One night, Snopes shoots a boy named John Wesley ROEBUCK with squirrel shot. The next morning, Sheriff Hub HAMPTON tells Snopes he will go to jail if he ever uses the shotgun again.

Snopes, Admiral Dewey   Minor character in *The TOWN, The MANSION,* "SPOTTED HORSES," and *FATHER ABRAHAM.* He is Eck SNOPES's younger son and brother of Wallstreet Panic SNOPES. Because these three are atypical in that they are not rapacious Snopeses, Montgomery Ward SNOPES says in the chapter he narrates in *The*

Mansion that "they dont belong to us: they are only our shame" (p. 83).

Snopes, Bilbo Minor character in *The TOWN* and *The MANSION*. He is one of I. O. SNOPES's twin sons by his second wife. (Although not divorced from his first wife, I. O. married another woman.)

Snopes, Byron Minor character in *The TOWN* and *SARTORIS*. The brother of Virgil SNOPES, Byron is the son of a Snopes said to look like a schoolmaster or John Brown (*The Town*, p. 40). In *Sartoris*, he has Virgil BEARD write out anonymous love letters to Narcissa Benbow (SARTORIS). Byron attends a business college in Memphis and then gets a job as a clerk or bookkeeper in the Sartoris Bank. When Narcissa marries the younger Bayard SARTORIS (4), Byron steals the letters and later the same night robs the bank. He flees to Mexico and, after living there for several years, sends his four wild children—whose mother is a Jicarilla Apache—to Flem SNOPES. Flem takes them to FRENCHMAN'S BEND, where they stay for about a week with Dewitt BINFORD, whose wife is a Snopes. The children's wild behavior is so intolerable that they are sent back to Byron. This episode is mentioned in *The MANSION*. Although his name is not used, Byron's theft is referred to in "THERE WAS A QUEEN" when, years later, Narcissa is relating the story (p. 739).

Snopes, Clarence Eggleston Character in several of Faulkner's works: *SANCTUARY. The HAMLET, The TOWN, The MANSION, FLAGS IN THE DUST, FATHER ABRAHAM* (which Faulkner revised for *The Hamlet*) and the short story "By the People" (which Faulkner revised for *The Mansion*). Clarence is I. O. SNOPES's oldest son by his second wife (although he was not at the time divorced from his first wife). With the backing of Will VARNER, who previously had appointed Clarence constable of Beat Two, Clarence becomes state senator from YOKNAPATAWPHA COUNTY. V. K. RATLIFF singlehandedly eliminates Clarence's bid for the U.S. Congress by having two boys surreptitiously rub across the back of Clarence's trouser legs damp switches from a dog thicket, causing dogs to start sniffing and urinating on his trouser legs. This spectacle forces Varner to withdraw his support. In *Sanctuary,* the corrupt Clarence Snopes knows the whereabouts of Temple Drake (STEVENS), information which he readily sells to Horace BENBOW.

Snopes, Colonel Sartoris (Sarty) The 10-year-old son of the sharecropper Ab SNOPES in the short story "BARN BURNING" (*Collected Stories*). Confronted and disturbed by his embittered father's barn-burning, Sarty faces the choice between his father's unjustifiable actions and a moral sense of honesty. He chooses the latter and runs away from home for good.

Snopes, Doris The 17-year-old younger brother of Clarence Eggleston SNOPES. He lives in FRENCHMAN'S BEND. In *The TOWN*, he is described as almost exactly like Clarence in looks, but with a child's mentality and an animal's moral sense. When he takes in Byron SNOPES's four unruly children he intends to train them to hunt in a pack, but it does not work. They almost burn him to death when they tie him to a sapling and set ablaze a cord of wood stacked around him. He is rescued at the last minute when his mother runs for help after hearing his screams. The episode is also recounted in *The MANSION*. (In the edition of *The Town* prior to the 1961 Vintage edition, it is Clarence who is tied to the sapling and almost burned.)

Snopes, Eckrum (Eck) Character in *FATHER ABRAHAM, The HAMLET, The TOWN,* and "SPOTTED HORSES"; he is also referred to in *The MANSION*. Eck was married twice, the first time at 16. Within a year of his first marriage, he had a son, Wallstreet Panic SNOPES, whom he did not name until 10 years after the child was born. His second marriage produced three children, but only his son Admiral Dewey SNOPES is referred to by name. A cousin of Flem SNOPES, Eck is an honest, kindhearted, and considerate Snopes, such human qualities that make Montgomery Ward SNOPES comment that he does not consider Wallstreet, Admiral Dewey, or their father Eck real Snopes: "they are only our shame" (*The Mansion*, p. 83). According to Gavin STEVENS in *The Town*, without any doubt Eck is not a Snopes because he does not share their dishonesty and rapacious traits.

In *The Hamlet*, Eck, without any blacksmithing experience, works for his cousin (or uncle) I. O. SNOPES in the blacksmith's shop. When Minister WHITFIELD suggests that Eck and I. O. destroy the cow that the idiot Ike SNOPES is in love with, Eck ends up paying the full cost of the animal and then buys the boy a 25-cent toy cow substitute. At the auction of the wild ponies, Buck HIPPS starts off the bidding by giving Eck a horse that, after the auction, escapes with the others and severely injures Vernon TULL as he is crossing a bridge with his family. Although Eck offers to pay damages to Tull, the judge rules that Eck holds no liability because he never legally owned the horse.

In *The Town*, Eck arrives in JEFFERSON, MISSISSIPPI, wearing a neck brace because of an accident at Will VARNER's sawmill. (Eck prevented a cypress log from falling on a black man). He first takes Flem's place in the sidestreet restaurant Flem owns, and then, after he is fired for being honest, he works as the night watchman of an oil tank until he blows himself up looking for the five-year-old Cedric NUNNERY: he lowers a lighted lantern into an oil tank that he thinks is fully emptied of its gas. The only part of him that was ever found was the neck brace.

Snopes, Eula Varner   The 16th and youngest child of Will and Maggie VARNER; she is the wife of Flem SNOPES, and the mother of Linda Snopes (KOHL). In book 2 of *The HAMLET,* named for her, she is caricatured in vivid mythic terms redolent of the chaotic revelry of Dionysic times; like an earth goddess stirring the sexual appetite in men, she is enticing, aloof, and unattainable. Like her father, she is lazy. At age eight, Eula starts school at the insistence of her brother Jody VARNER, who is compelled to transport her on his horse because of her reluctance to walk any distance. By 10, she is taller than her mother. At 14 she is the indifferent and oblivious target of the amorous obsessions of her teacher, LABOVE, whose attempt to ravish her in the schoolhouse fails when she resists with a blow to his face that knocks him over. By 15, rivals for her affection fight over her on Sunday nights, and by 16, fully aware of her sexuality and seductiveness, Eula successfully helps Hoake MCCARRON fight off his attackers. When, three months later, Hoake realizes that Eula is pregnant with his child, he leaves FRENCHMAN'S BEND. Eula's father arranges her marriage to Flem Snopes, and while on an extended honeymoon in Texas, her daughter and only child, Linda, is born. After their return, they move to JEFFERSON, MISSISSIPPI, where, as narrated in *The TOWN,* the second novel of the SNOPES TRILOGY, Eula becomes the mistress of Manfred DE SPAIN, the town's mayor and later a bank president, with whom she and her daughter take an annual vacation together. Eula is faithful in her 18-year affair with de Spain, until, in an attempt to stop a city investigation of her husband's guilt in the theft of the missing brass fittings from Jefferson's power plant, she tries to bribe the city attorney, Gavin STEVENS, by giving herself to him. He rejects the advance. Eula may have been sent by her husband, but her motive for offering the bribe—and later, for her suicide—is to protect her daughter from shame. To spare Linda from the disgrace she would suffer if Eula were to run off with de Spain, Eula kills herself.

In *The Town,* Eula's relationship with Gavin Stevens is at once honest and complicated. Knowing that he is a gentleman, an intelligent cultured man of high principles and morals, she confides in him on several occasions, and at one point even asks him to promise to marry Linda. Gavin assures her that he will, if things do not work out for her daughter. In these conversations with Stevens, Eula also tells him about Flem's impotence and about his manipulative plans to fleece money from Linda's will.

Eula is a complex and beautiful woman, tragically confined by circumstances that overcome her will to live. In *The Town,* she is referred to as Helen, Semiramis, and Lilith, figures of immense attraction, sexual power, and beauty. She is "larger than life," Faulkner once commented, and no one place could hold her, neither Frenchman's Bend nor Jefferson (see *Faulkner in the University,* p. 31; for other details concerning Eula, see *ibid,* pp. 108, 115–16, and 118–19). Eula also appears in the fragment *FATHER ABRAHAM* and the short story "SPOTTED HORSES," which Faulkner revised for *The Hamlet.*

Snopes, Flem   Character in several of Faulkner's important works. The most rapacious and successful Snopes, an insensitive and acquisitive man, Flem appears in *FLAGS IN THE DUST, The HAMLET, The TOWN, The MANSION,* and in previously written works Faulkner revised for these novels: *FATHER ABRAHAM* (fragment of a novel revised and incorporated into *The Hamlet*), "SPOTTED HORSES" (revised from *Father Abraham* and recast in *The Hamlet*), "CENTAUR IN BRASS" (revised for *The Town*), "LIZARDS IN JAMSHYD'S COURTYARD" (revised for *The Hamlet*), and "By the People" (revised for *The Mansion*); Flem is also referred to in *AS I LAY DYING* and *The REIVERS.*

Flem is the son of Ab SNOPES by Ab's second wife. In *The Hamlet,* soon after Ab becomes Will VARNER's tenant farmer near FRENCHMAN'S BEND, Varner's son Jody hires Flem as a clerk in VARNER'S STORE. Jody sees Flem as fire insurance against Ab's tendencies to burn the barns of his employers. During his clerkship at the store, Flem stops giving credit to the customers and even charges Will Varner for his tobacco. The quiet but scheming Flem quickly rises from store clerk to Varner's assistant, helping him settle his business accounts and going along with him on Jody's roan to appraise cotton crops. In the meantime, Flem takes over Jody's role as superviser of the cotton gin, forcing Jody to return to clerking in the store; lends money at high interest rates to the townsfolk; deals in cattle; builds a new blacksmith shop that puts I. O. SNOPES out of business and that Flem sells to Varner for a profit; and, to advance his ambitions even further, marries Varner's daughter Eula Varner (SNOPES), who is pregnant with another man's child. As part of the dowry he gets the OLD FRENCHMAN PLACE, which he ends up tricking V. K. RATLIFF, Henry ARMSTID, and Odum BOOKWRIGHT into buying. To avoid Mink SNOPES's trial for having killed Jack HOUSTON, Flem does not return with his wife and daughter to Frenchman's Bend after his honeymoon in Texas. When he does come back, he is accompanied by the Texan Buck HIPPS and the wild ponies he has Hipps auction off, although Flem never admits that he is in partnership with Hipps. Flem's greed is especially acute when he refuses to refund Mrs. ARMSTID the five dollars her husband took from her to buy a horse, and even lies to her by saying that Hipps took all the money with him. *The Hamlet* ends with Flem and his family moving to Jefferson. In their wagon, they take one last look at Henry Armstid furiously digging for the treasure rumored to be buried at Old Frenchman Place.

In *The Town,* Flem goes from working in the side-street restaurant he owns in partnership with Grover Cleveland WINBUSH to the presidency of the Sartoris Bank. Along the way, he achieves his goals by exploiting his wife's 18-year love affair with Manfred DE SPAIN. First he becomes the superintendent of the town's power plant, a job created for him by de Spain, and stays in that position until auditors find that the brass safety valves for the boilers are missing. He ends up paying for them. Meanwhile, Flem is purchasing stock in the Sartoris bank, and when Colonel Bayard SARTORIS (3) dies, Flem becomes the bank's vice president. At this point, as Ratliff perceptively suspects, Flem is eyeing the president's job. In order to secure that position, and to take revenge on his wife and her lover, Flem reveals to Eula's father the affair she is having with Manfred. Linda Snopes (KOHL) too is not beyond the pale of Flem's rapacity. He succeeds in gaining her affections so she will sign over to him her inheritance. Outraged by his daughter's behavior, Varner, who holds much of the bank stock, agrees to force Manfred out as president and replace him with Flem. After Eula's suicide and funeral, Manfred leaves town for good. Flem chooses the following verse to be inscribed on her ornate tombstone:

A Virtuous Wife Is a Crown to Her Husband
Her Children Rise and Call Her Blessed.

In *The Mansion*, Flem, having reached financial success, lives in Manfred de Spain's ancestral home, which he redecorates to look like Mount Vernon. Portrayed as a man without family or friends, he lives alone until Linda, deaf from an accident, returns in August 1937 from the Spanish Civil War. Throughout the SNOPES TRILOGY, Flem has no qualms about his treatment toward anyone who stands in his way, whether relative or neighbor. When Montgomery Ward SNOPES becomes an embarrassment to him for running a photography shop as a front for peep shows, Flem devises a plan to have him arrested and sent to the state prison at PARCHMAN where Mink SNOPES is also serving time. Fearing that Mink will seek revenge for Flem's failure to show up at Mink's murder trial, Flem bribes Montgomery to entice Mink to escape. Mink, of course, is caught, and his prison term extended another 20 years. But when the 63-year-old Mink is finally pardoned in 1946, Flem seems indifferent and almost resigned to his inevitable death at Mink's hand.

Snopes, I. O.　Minor character in several of Faulkner's works, including the novels *The* SOUND AND THE FURY, *The* HAMLET, *The* TOWN, FATHER ABRAHAM (fragment of a novel incorporated into *The Hamlet*), FLAGS IN THE DUST, and the short stories "SPOTTED HORSES" (revised for *The Hamlet*) and "MULE IN THE YARD" (revised for *The Town*). He is also referred to in *The* MANSION.

In *The Hamlet*, this proverb-prone Snopes leases Will VARNER's blacksmith shop, even though he has no blacksmithing expertise, and later takes the teaching position that LABOVE vacates in FRENCHMAN'S BEND. He counsels Mink SNOPES, who is accused of Jack HOUSTON's murder, and cons his kinsman Eck SNOPES into paying most of the cost to destroy Ike SNOPES's cow. Although thought to be single, I. O. has two wives. The first shows up one day in Frenchman's Bend with a baby (Montgomery Ward SNOPES), causing I. O. to leave for JEFFERSON, MISSISSIPPI, where he replaces Flem SNOPES in the restaurant. In *The Town*, he is illegally married to another woman, the mother of his children Clarence SNOPES and the twins Vardaman and Bilbo SNOPES. His scheme to have mules killed on the railroad tracks to collect insurance money lasts until his partner Lonzo HAIT is also killed. Thinking he should be compensated by Hait's widow for lost money, I. O. expects to be paid, but she outwits him. Flem, to preserve his own respectability, gives I. O. some money under the condition that he leave Jefferson for good.

In *The Sound and the Fury*, I. O. appears as a cotton speculator. He is at the Western Union office when Jason COMPSON Jr., places his bids. In *Flags in the Dust*, I. O. runs a restaurant.

Snopes, Isaac (Ike)　Dim-witted character in *The* HAMLET, in love with Jack HOUSTON's cow. He is one of Flem SNOPES's cousins. After Ike runs away with it, Houston in disgust gives him the animal, which Ike keeps in Mrs. LITTLEJOHN's barn. Unaware that he is being watched, Ike has sex with the cow in view of the men lounging at VARNER'S STORE until V. K. RATLIFF puts a stop to it and has the cow destroyed. To replace the lost animal, the kindhearted Eck SNOPES buys the boy a toy cow. (For further information, see *Faulkner in the University*, pp. 131–32.)

Snopes, Launcelot (Lump)　A minor character in *The* HAMLET and in "THE HOUND" (a short story Faulkner revised for the novel), and referred to in *The MANSION*. Lump replaces his cousin Flem SNOPES as the clerk at VARNER'S STORE. A man without moral scruples, Lump takes a plank off Mrs. LITTLEJOHN's barn so he and others can spy on Ike SNOPES having sex with a cow. He also lies to protect his cousin Mink SNOPES, (accused of Jack HOUSTON's murderer); tries to get Mink to steal and share with him the money that the dead Houston has in his pocket; and perjures himself at the Armstid vs. Snopes trial when he says that he saw Flem give Armstid his money back. In fact, Flem did not.

Snopes, Linda　*See* KOHL, LINDA SNOPES.

Snopes, Mink (M. C.)　Character in *The* HAMLET, *The* TOWN, and *The* MANSION. In *The Hamlet* (and as retold in *The Mansion*), Mink is accused of killing Jack HOUSTON, who charged Mink a poundage fee in return for his yearling that strayed into Houston's pasture. It was the fee that incensed Mink enough to commit the murder. Fearing that the odor of Houston's body will be detectable a few days after he stuffs it into a hollow tree trunk, Mink retrieves the body and throws it into a nearby river. An arm is missing from the decayed corpse, and when Mink goes back to find it, he fights off Houston's dog, is arrested and taken to jail. He spends more than two months in a JEFFERSON, MISSISSIPPI, jail before being sent in 1908 to the state penitentiary at PARCHMAN.

All along, Mink expects his cousin Flem to rescue him. Flem, however, intentionally avoids his kinsman. During his prison term, which lasts until 1946, Mink, a believer in the power of absolute retributive justice, becomes resolute about killing Flem for not having shown up during the murder trial. In *The Mansion,* when Mink accepts his pardon (orchestrated by Linda Snopes KOHL), he is offered, but refuses, money from Gavin STEVENS to stay away forever from Jefferson. Five days after his release, Mink kills Flem in his home. On the following night, Stevens and V. K. RATLIFF find Mink hiding in the cellar of his abandoned cabin. This time Mink takes from Stevens the money Linda has set aside for him. Stevens asks Mink where he will be in three months to receive the next payment. (For Faulkner's remarks about on Mink, see *Faulkner in the University,* p. 262).

Snopes, Montgomery Ward   Character in *The TOWN* and *The MANSION* (he narrates chapter 4); referred to in *FLAGS IN THE DUST.* Montgomery Ward is I. O. SNOPES's eldest child by his first wife, whom I. O. does not divorce before marrying a second woman. With Gavin STEVENS, Montgomery Ward goes to France during World War I and runs a canteen for the YMCA. He turns part of it into a club and hires a young French girl for the entertainment of any soldier who wants more than chocolate bars. After he returns to JEFFERSON, MISSISSIPPI, he opens up an arty photography shop where he shows pornographic postcards from France. Flem SNOPES has Montgomery Ward arrested, not for pornography but instead for having moonshine liquor on his premises, which Flem himself planted there. Because of Flem's scheme, Montgomery Ward is sent to the penitentiary in PARCHMAN for the crime, a lesser offense than had he been convicted for pornography, which would have landed him time in a federal prison in Atlanta. In this way, Flem could use him to entice their kinsman Mink SNOPES to attempt an escape, knowing that Mink would certainly get caught. (Flem suspects that Mink, who is serving time at Parchman for the murder of Jack HOUSTON, wants to take revenge on Flem for not having come to his aid during the murder trial.) After Montgomery Ward is released from prison he travels to Los Angeles, where he gets a lucrative job working in the motion picture industry.

Snopes, Mrs. Eck   Minor character in *The TOWN.* She is Eck SNOPES's wife and the landlady of a boardinghouse in JEFFERSON, MISSISSIPPI.

Snopes, Mrs. Flem   *See* SNOPES, EULA VARNER.

Snopes, Mrs. I. O.   One of two of I. O. SNOPES's wives in *The HAMLET* and *The TOWN.* His first wife, the mother of Montgomery Ward SNOPES, arrives in FRENCHMAN'S BEND when I. O. is schoolmaster and while he is married to his second wife, the mother of Clarence SNOPES and the twins Bilbo and Vardaman SNOPES. His second wife, a Frenchman's Bend belle, is the niece of Mrs. Vernon TULL's sister. (A humorous account of the appearance of I. O.'s first wife while he is married to his second wife can be found in *The Town,* pp. 37–39.)

Snopes, Mrs. (Lennie)   Minor character in "BARN BURNING" and *The HAMLET.* Ab SNOPES's second wife and the mother of his children, she accompanies him as a sharecropper of one of Will VARNER's farms. In "Barn Burning," her first names appears as Lennie.

Snopes, Mrs. Mink (Yettie)   *See* SNOPES, YETTIE.

Snopes, Net   Character in "BARN BURNING" (in *Collected Stories*). Abner SNOPES's twin daughter, she tries to stop her 10-year-old brother, Colonel Sartoris SNOPES (Sarty), from running off to warn a victim of his father's barn-burning.

Snopes, Orestes (Res)   In *The MANSION* and "HOG PAWN" (revised for the novel), a bachelor relative of Flem SNOPES who in the early 1940s moves into the Compson carriage house, which Wat SNOPES has converted into a small two-story residence. Res buys and sells hogs and feuds with his neighbor, old man MEADOWFILL, whose orchard boundary—a few scattered fruit trees—was Res's hog-lot fence. Res gives a hog to Meadowfill's future son-in-law, McKinley SMITH, knowing that the old man dislikes him. The hog roams into Meadowfill's yard, and when the old man goes to shoot at it through an open window that has been booby-trapped, he himself is peppered with buckshot. Eventually JEFFERSON's attorney, Gavin STEVENS, settles the dispute: he returns the booby trap to Res in exchange for the deed to a small strip of land that an oil company wants to buy, along with Meadowfill's property, to build a gas station. The deed is made out to Meadowfill's daughter Essie. (In the short story, Snopes is not given a first name.)

Snopes, Saint Elmo   A minor character referred to in *The HAMLET.* I. O. SNOPES's son, he takes candy from VARNER'S STORE.

Snopes, Vardaman Minor character in *The TOWN* and *The MANSION*. The twin of Bilbo SNOPES, Vardaman is I. O. SNOPES's son by I. O.'s second wife. (I. O. is still married to his first wife at the time.)

Snopes, Virgil Minor character in *SANCTUARY* and *The MANSION;* referred to in *The TOWN*. He is the son of Wesley SNOPES. In *Sanctuary*, Virgil goes to barber college in MEMPHIS with Fonzo WINBUSH, and in one of the most amusing scenes in the novel the two take a room at Miss Reba RIVERS's brothel, mistaking it for a hotel (pp. 192–94). When they visit other brothels in the city, they worry whether Miss Reba will ever find out and evict them for their behavior. In *The Mansion*, Virgil's kinsman Clarence SNOPES happens upon Virgil in a brothel one night and learns of his "really exceptional talent" (p. 73) of sexually satisfying two girls in succession. He starts to brag about Virgil's powers in order to entice others into betting. Clarence would usually win the bets.

Snopes, Vynie Character in *The HAMLET*, Ab SNOPES's first wife. With Cliff ODUM's help, she gets her milk separator back from Pat STAMPER in exchange for a cow. In the short story "FOOL ABOUT A HORSE," which Faulkner revised for *The Hamlet*, Vynie appears with no last name; she is PAP's (2) wife. She is also referred to as Mammy by her son, the 12-year-old narrator of the short story.

Snopes, Wallstreet Panic (Wall) Character in *The HAMLET, The TOWN,* and *The MANSION*. Eck SNOPES's son by his first marriage, Wall was not given a first name until he was about 10 years old. Eck chose the name with the hope that his son would become as rich as those who ran the Wall Street panic. Like his father, Wall is not a typical Snopes. In *The Hamlet*, Wall helps his father in his futile attempt to catch the two wild ponies he gets at the auction. In *The Town*, he is studious and ambitious. With his wife, he becomes the owner of a very successful grocery store that he almost loses when he overbuys. However, he and his wife know enough not to borrow from the exploitative Flem SNOPES, and their business is saved. They then start a wholesale grocery business and move to MEMPHIS. In *The Mansion*, Wall has built a chain of wholesale stores throughout Mississippi, Arkansas, and Tennessee. When Flem dies, Wall attends the funeral.

Snopes, Watkins Products (Wat) In *The MANSION*, a carpenter whom Flem SNOPES hires to renovate his house and to convert the Compson carriage house into a two-story residence.

Snopes, Wesley Minor character in *The TOWN* and *The MANSION*. In *The Town*, where he is given no first name, Snopes is the father of Byron and Virgil SNOPES and described as possessing an uncanny ability for seducing others in serving his self-interests. He holds Sunday revival services in scattered country churches, but he does not stay in the area long: when he is caught with a 14-year-old girl, he is tarred, feathered, and chased out of the country. Some of the enraged fathers want to castrate him, but are dissuaded. This episode is also referred to in *The Mansion*.

Snopes, Yettie Mink SNOPES's wife in *The HAMLET* (where she is referred to as Mrs. Snopes) and *The MANSION* (referred to as Yettie). She has a letter written to her husband in the state penitentiary at PARCHMAN asking him when he wants her to visit and whether she should bring their daughters. When the warden reads the letter to Mink and asks for a reply, Mink says to tell her not to come because he will be out soon. In *The Hamlet*, she had unwittingly indicted her husband by telling everyone that Mink did not kill Houston.

Snopesism In reference to the SNOPES TRILOGY—*The HAMLET, The TOWN,* and *The MANSION*—a term designating the disruptive and invasive force embodied in the SNOPES (1) clan. Identified with the predatory activities of the Snopeses, and especially with those of the rapacious Flem SNOPES, the clan's ostensible leader, Snopesism is an encroachment upon the innocent and unsuspecting citizens of FRENCHMAN'S BEND and the town of JEFFERSON, MISSISSIPPI. Although the term does not apply to every Snopes (see, for example, Colonel Sartoris SNOPES and Eckrum SNOPES), the Snopeses tend to be scoundrels of one type or another. Snopesism, however, is not without its opponents. Gavin STEVENS, V. K. RATLIFF, and Linda Snopes KOHL, in particular, are very much its foes.

Snopes trilogy The name given, collectively, to three interrelated novels: *The HAMLET* (1940), *The TOWN* (1957), and *The MANSION* (1959). Two years after Faulkner's death on July 6, 1962, RANDOM HOUSE published a three-volume set under the title *Snopes*, as Faulkner had intended. The initial idea behind the trilogy goes back as far as the late 1920s, when Faulkner began *FATHER ABRAHAM*. Although he abandoned this work and turned his attention to writing about the Sartoris family, his interest in the Snopeses never waned. At first, Faulkner worked on related short stories and novel fragments that he would eventually incorporate into the trilogy. In a 1957 interview at the University of Virginia shortly before the publication of *The Town*, Faulkner explained that the story behind the trilogy came to him in a flash: "I thought of the whole story at once like a bolt of lightning lights up a landscape and you see everything but it takes time to write it" (*Faulkner in the University*, p. 90).

With a few flashbacks—for example, the story of Eula Varner (SNOPES)'s childhood and the account of Jack HOUSTON's life before his short-lived marriage to his childhood sweetheart, Lucy PETE—the Snopes trilogy covers a period of almost 50 years: Flem SNOPES's arrival in FRENCHMAN'S BEND in 1902; his manipulation of Will VARNER and marriage to Varner's daughter Eula, pregnant by another man; his departure for JEFFERSON, MISSISSIPPI, where he trades on his wife's adulterous relations with Manfred DE SPAIN to promote his ambition to become bank president; and Flem's murder by his kinsman Mink SNOPES in 1946. The trilogy's diversity of character, episodes, points of view, and themes are held together by its basic story or subject matter, the rise of SNOPESISM—an invasive and corrupting force in the life of a community. The central character behind the encroachment of the Snopes family is Flem, a quiet scheming man, ruthless and motivated by greed.

The novels contain episodes both humorous and tragic, sometimes both at once, as in the stories surrounding the innocent Ike SNOPES, a 21-year-old idiot. The multiple narrative perspective throughout the three novels adds to their vitality and enhances the individuality of storytelling. At times the fragmented, and perhaps even unreliable (see MODERNISM) points of view provide readers with a lively complexion of the society or world in which people live and struggle with one another. Because the novels were written over a 30-year period, discrepancies were bound to occur, and Faulkner himself acknowledged this in a brief comment in *The Mansion.* James B. MERIWETHER, a textual critic, assisted the publisher Random House in correcting some of these discrepancies. For further details, see *Selected Letters of William Faulkner,* pp. 107–08, 197, and James B. Meriwether, "Sartoris and Snopes: An Early Notice," *Library Chronicle of the University of Texas* 7 [summer 1962], 36–39.

"Snow" (Uncollected Stories)

A short story set in Switzerland, a setting somewhat unusual in Faulkner's fiction. The story is reminiscent of the more abrupt style of Ernest HEMINGWAY, as opposed to Faulkner's own more discursive and meandering voice. In the story, an American man remembers an incident from before World War II, when he and a friend from Alabama were climbing in the Swiss mountains. They witnessed a funeral and learned the details of a strange affair that had its beginnings the previous autumn. Two mountain guides had been asked to take a German amateur climber on what was reputedly an easy climb. One of the guides, BRIX, was engaged to be married and had, in fact, postponed his wedding day to take the client into the mountains. The German, VON PLOECKNER (also referred to as the Big Shot), insisted that the wedding take place, so the bride accompanied them on the climb. Brix and his bride were married in a mountaintop village, with the Big Shot paying all expenses and signing the marriage contract as a witness. On the way back, however, the four climbers met with an accident, and Brix fell to his death. The Americans, DON and the unnamed narrator, witnessed the retrieval of Brix's body, which had to wait

until the spring thaw, and were intrigued by the expensively dressed woman who mourned for Brix. She was, in fact, his bride, and had gone off with von Ploeckner after Brix's death. The story is framed by the narrator's seeing a newspaper article that reports the murder of a Nazi general, the same von Ploeckner, by his companion, whom the narrator recognizes as the Mrs. Brix he and Don had seen in the Swiss village years before.

Woven throughout many of Faulkner's works is the presence of a mystery or of a mysterious case that needs resolution, a device that certainly caught Faulkner's imagination. In *Faulkner's Short Fiction,* James Ferguson points out that "the basic narrative strategy of 'Mistral' and 'Snow'—the attempts by two young men to piece together elaborate and ominous mysteries—clearly fascinated Faulkner and was to receive its most elaborate embodiment in his masterpiece, *Absalom, Absalom!*" (p. 31)

Written sometimes around 1942, "Snow" was published posthumously in UNCOLLECTED STORIES OF WILLIAM FAULKNER. (See also "Mistral.") For more information, see *Selected Letters of William Faulkner,* pp. 149, 151, 161, 272; and UNCOLLECTED STORIES OF WILLIAM FAULKNER, pp. 711–12.

Sol

Character in *SARTORIS.* A black porter at the railroad station in JEFFERSON, MISSISSIPPI, he helps Horace BENBOW with his hand luggage.

Soldiers' Pay

Faulkner's first novel, originally titled *Mayday,* published by BONI & LIVERIGHT, New York, on February 25, 1926, on the recommendation of the American writer Sherwood ANDERSON, whom Faulkner met in NEW ORLEANS in 1924. *Soldiers' Pay* is the story of a doomed and severely wounded World War I flier, Donald MAHON; his homecoming to Charleston, Georgia; and the fiancée he left behind, Cecily SAUNDERS. Reviews of the novel were mixed, but *Soldiers' Pay* anticipates many of the themes and even the scenes of the far better novels to come.

Although Faulkner placed his story in the fictional town of Charleston, *Soldiers' Pay* is not a novel about the South. Instead, it is a story of post–World War I America, and its setting could be any small American town. The town itself is a kind of "first draft" of Faulkner's more famous JEFFERSON, MISSISSIPPI; like Jefferson, the YOKNAPATAWPHA COUNTY seat, Charleston is built around a courthouse square with its obligatory statue of a Confederate soldier. But the people about whom Faulkner writes in *Soldiers' Pay* are very different from the citizens of Yoknapatawpha County. If the characters in Faulkner's first piece of extended fiction have parents and children, their history and the history of their region go no further than that.

World War I just ended, *Soldiers' Pay* opens with two soldiers, Joe GILLIGAN and Julian LOWE, drinking on a train. The demobilized Gilligan is returning from the trenches in France, but the 19-year-old Lowe never reached the front lines; a cadet, his flight training was not yet complete when the armistice was signed. On the train, they meet Donald Mahon, a pilot who had been shot down and badly injured—his face is dreadfully scarred. Gilligan's experience tells him that Mahon, will not live long, and his pity leads him to take the wounded man under his care. Lowe, however, is both horrified by Mahon's injuries and intensely envious of the heroic status the wounds supposedly confer. Lowe wishes he could have those precious and awful accomplishments for his own; he considers his youth and inexperience as burdens and feels robbed of a chance for glory. In some ways, he is an innocent romantic. Also on the train is Mrs. Margaret POWERS, a young woman returning from service with the Red Cross. Unlike Lowe, Mrs. Powers sees no romance or glory in war. Her husband was killed in France, and although she did not love him, she is now a war widow who knows the pain of loss, an experience that may partly explain her motive in helping Mahon reach home.

Lowe falls in love with Mrs. Powers, and although he leaves the action of *Soldiers' Pay* by the end of the first chapter, his love letters to her punctuate the novel with a kind of longing that Mrs. Powers cannot reciprocate because, for her, the war changed everything. Her fate is to be with Mahon, trying to make his last days as comfortable and meaningful as possible. Mrs. Powers is the only civilian in the novel who is truly aware of the war and its effects. To the others, the war was "over there." Mrs. Powers and Gilligan form a pact to help the dying Mahon, who cannot help himself. His eyesight is failing and his memory fades almost completely. Gilligan and Mrs. Powers know where to take Mahon only from letters they find in his pockets.

Through the eyes of Januarius JONES, the novel turns from the soldiers and the war widow to the Mahon's family in Charleston. In Jones, Faulkner has created one of the stranger characters in all of his novels. A corpulent lazy sensualist, Jones comes with no more history than a brief reference to being "lately a fellow of Latin in a small college" (p. 52). His nature is that of a Pan or a satyr. When first meeting Donald Mahon's father, the Episcopalian rector Joseph Mahon, who thinks his son has been killed in the war, Jones is invited to have lunch with him. At lunch with Dr. Mahon (as Jones calls him), Jones meets EMMY, the rector's servant, and Cecily, Donald's fiancée. Both women also believe that Donald has been killed in the war. Emmy, who had once been intimate with Donald, grieves for him, and Cecily has begun to see George FARR, though out of consideration for RECTOR MAHON she has not announced her new affection.

In his goatish way, Jones is attracted to both women, but Cecily sees through him immediately. During the lunch, and afterward, he pursues her in an aimless, meaningless way, giving the reader the impression that for his generation sex is nothing more than a matter of conquest and surrender. As Jones and Cecily duel with words, Mrs. Powers comes to the house and informs the rector that his son has returned.

The remainder of *Soldiers' Pay* answers the questions that Donald's return brings. Reverend Mahon is overjoyed that his son has returned, but Cecily is horrified at the thought of marrying this ruined man, and Emmy is crushed that he does not remember her at all. Cecily's family is uncertain of how to take the news. Instead of envying Mahon's heroism as Lowe did, George Farr has only contempt for Mahon and a growing desire for Cecily. Mrs. Powers and Gilligan decide to stay on in Charleston to take care of Mahon, something no one else in the novel is truly capable of doing. When a specialist is brought in to see Mahon, he confirms what Gilligan has always maintained—Mahon is doomed. The doctor tells Mrs. Powers that he will surely die and "'should have been dead these three months were it not for the fact that he seems to be waiting for something'" (p. 150). The rector believes that his son will get well, although he accepts that Donald will be blind. He points out that Donald is to marry Cecily, and suggests that the wedding date be moved up. Knowing that Cecily does not want to keep her promise to Donald, Mrs. Powers disagrees with the rector, who ultimately defers to her. Cecily is moved by both pity and revulsion. At one point, she tearfully tells Donald she will marry him, but regrets her words soon after. When her parents try to stop the wedding, Cecily at first resists them and then loses her virginity to George Farr, which, she feels, makes her unworthy of Donald's love. She later elopes with Farr.

Mrs. Powers knows that what Mahon is waiting for is his own wedding. Marrying will complete Mahon's journey in life, and, as Mrs. Powers suspects, will free him to die. Knowing that Cecily will never marry Mahon, Mrs. Powers suggests to Emmy that she marry him. Emmy, whose passion for Mahon has never subsided but has basically turned to hatred, refuses, for she will not take Cecily's leavings. Mrs. Powers accepts this news calmly, probably already having made up her mind what to do next. When Revered Mahon tells Mrs. Powers what she already knows—namely, that Cecily had broken the engagement and that Donald will not be married—she tells him that she intends to marry Donald herself. Soon after the wedding, Mahon dies, reliving for one quick moment the day he was shot down over France. Whatever he was waiting for has passed.

In the final chapter of the novel, Mahon is buried. Jones, who has become obsessed with Emmy, uses the occasion of Donald's funeral to seduce her while she is alone in the house. Afterward, Margaret Powers refuses to marry Gilligan, who has loved her from the start.

Soldiers' Pay is not one of Faulkner's great novels, but it contains within it many of the elements that later went into his masterpieces. He shows his intimate knowledge of a small town, knowledge upon which he would build his fictional Jefferson in Yoknapatawpha County. He uses a single story (Donald Mahon's return home) as the center of many stories that spin out tangentially from it. He shows the dependence of men upon their women and the tangled skein of desire and love and of reticence and fear that will later be more fully developed in novels like *ABSALOM, ABSALOM!* and *The SOUND AND THE FURY.* The characters, too, prefigure later characters Faulkner will create. The helpless Donald Mahon, for example, anticipate someone like Benjy COMPSON, another desperately wounded character who seeks love.

For more information, see *Selected Letters of William Faulkner,* pp. 20, 27, 28, 31–2, 38, 40, 58, 141; *Faulkner in the University,* pp. 60–1; and *Faulkner at Nagano,* pp. 141–42.

Sometimes-Wakeup   Character in "A JUSTICE" (in *Collected Stories*). The brother of the poisoned Chickasaw chief, he prudently concludes he does not want to succeed as head of the tribe. The post goes instead to the poisoner, Doom (see IKKEMOTUBBE).

Sons of Confederate Veterans   A southern fraternal organization, with many chapters in the former Confederate states, established to keep memories of the Civil War fresh. John Wesley Thompson FALKNER, Faulkner's grandfather, helped organize and served as commander of the northern Mississippi Lamar Camp of the Sons of Confederate Veterans.

The Sound and the Fury   Faulkner's fourth novel. First published by CAPE & SMITH, New York, on October 7, 1929, the novel is widely considered his best work of fiction. Told from four different points of view, the novel concentrates on the breakdown of the Compson family over a period of three decades, from around 1898 to 1928. In response to questions about the novel, Faulkner explained that he started it with the image of a young girl, Caddy COMPSON, climbing a tree in order to look through the parlor window at her dead grandmother laid out in the house. The book had its inception, Faulkner said, "with the picture of the little girl's muddy drawers" and her brothers, who "didn't have the courage to climb the tree," waiting to hear "what she saw." Caddy is the central character in the novel, and the relationship her three brothers—Quentin, Jason, and Benjy COMPSON— have to her is the novel's integrative theme, which Faulkner tells from multiple points of view. The appendix to the novel, Faulkner explained in an interview at the University of Virginia, was written about 20 years later as another attempt at trying "to make that book . . . match the dream" (*Faulkner in the University,* p. 84; see Appendix

IV). On several occasions, Faulkner referred to *The Sound and the Fury* as his "best failure" and the one that he loved "the most" (*ibid,* pp. 61 and 77).

The novel's first chapter is literally a tale told by an idiot, Benjy Compson. Faulkner adapted the title from Shakespeare's *Macbeth* (5.5.26–8), where Macbeth describes life as "a tale/Told by an idiot, full of sound and fury,/Signifying nothing." Though the title comes from Benjy's section and applies particularly to him, the more Faulkner worked on the novel "the more elastic the title became, until it covered the whole family" (*Faulkner in the University,* p. 87). In this chapter, the reader receives direct and immediate impressions of the world as expressed in an INTERIOR MONOLOGUE of the longings and sensations of Benjy, the youngest son of Jason COMPSON Sr. and Caroline COMPSON. Emotionally, Benjy is very much a child who feels that he is loved only by his absent sister, Caddy. He is especially aware of odors and is often moved to remember his sister by the smell of trees and leaves. The novel opens on April 7, 1928, Benjy's 33d birthday. He and his 14-year-old black caretaker, LUSTER (1), are standing by the fence that separates the yard from the golf course that had once been the Compsons' pasture, where Benjy and his siblings spent much of their childhood. In 1909, the pasture had to be sold to supply the money for Caddy's wedding and Quentin's education at HARVARD UNIVERSITY. Benjy's reflections flutter back and forth between the present and the past and at times are permeated with unsettling flashbacks as when, for example, he recalls certain incidents relating to Caddy's wedding. The scenes with Luster take place during the present, while the scenes with T. P. GIBSON, Dilsey's youngest son, are set sometime between 1906 and 1912 and those with Versh GIBSON, between 1898 and 1900, when Benjy was a small child. To the careful reader, the presence of Benjy's attendants is thus a clue as to approximately when each scene takes place. (Faulkner also indicates time shifts with the use of Roman type and italics.)

Benjy's fragmented narrative begins with Luster searching along the fence for a lost quarter, which he needs to attend a traveling show in JEFFERSON, MISSISSIPPI, that night before it moves on to Mottston (MOTTSTOWN). As Luster searches, Benjy thinks back on the death of his grandmother, DAMUDDY, nearly 30 years before, when he and his brothers watched Caddy climb the tree to look into the parlor window and when Benjy saw his sister's muddy drawers. (Several important scenes that Benjy remembers from his family's past are revisited by Quentin and Jason in subsequent chapters.) Benjy recalls his name change from "Maury" to "Benjamin"; the loss of Caddy's virginity (he does not understand what this means, but he sensed the problem that occurred in the household); the sale of the pasture; Caddy's wedding; his brother Quentin's suicide and the day his body was brought home from Cambridge; his castration after he attacked a neighbor's daughter; and his father's death and funeral. In the present, Benjy and Luster come upon Miss Quentin COMPSON, Caddy's daughter, embracing the pitchman in the red tie. When Quentin sees Benjy and Luster, she reacts with annoyance.

The second chapter, titled "June Second, 1910," is narrated by Quentin, a romantic idealist and Hamlet-like figure, pensive and brooding. It is the day of his suicide in Cambridge. Like Benjy, Quentin's reminiscences mainly revolve around Caddy; he punctuates them with literary allusions, musings about time, and thoughts of death. In several respects, there is a parallel between the minds of Benjy and Quentin. Benjy is mentally deficient and Quentin, a Harvard student, is not. Yet Quentin has deeply neurotic thoughts and longings. He begins the last day of his life by skipping classes and by breaking the crystal and hands of his watch, a gift from his father. Quentin's act of destruction and the cut he receives when he breaks the watch are apt precursors to his plans and symbolic of the self-destruction to come.

Quentin waits until his roommate, Shreve MACKENZIE, leaves for class before carefully packing his trunk and writing a letter to his father and another to Shreve. Dressed in his best suit, Quentin leaves his room and goes to breakfast at PARKER'S, buys a cigar, and visits two different shops: a jeweler's, where he shows the jeweler his watch, and a hardware store, where he buys two six-pound flatirons that will weigh him down when he throws himself into the Charles River. (Quentin's suicide is not described in *The Sound and the Fury* but only referred to.) Feeling that he was never successful in protecting Caddy's honor, he recalls several humiliating incidents, including conversations with his father about having committed incest with Caddy, which he never did, and the time he tried to beat up Caddy's lover, Dalton AMES, but was easily overpowered. He thinks too of the library conversation he had with Caddy's husband, Sydney Herbert HEAD, on the day before her wedding and how irritated and annoyed he became with Herbert as he (Herbert) tried to ingratiate himself. He remembers, too, his father's words implying that Caddy did not want his protection. Quentin also remembers the time when he suggested to Caddy that they agree to a murder-suicide pact, but when she was willing to go through with it Quentin was unable to act. "In the end," the critic Cleanth BROOKS observes, "it is not the body of his sister but the river of death to which Quentin gives himself" (*William Faulkner: The Yoknapatawpha Country*, Baton Rouge: Louisiana State University Press, 1990, p. 332).

During his last day, Quentin stops at a bakery and meets up with a little Italian girl, whom he calls "sister." He assumes that she is lost and tries to escort her home. She refuses to tell or show him where she lives, however, and seems content just being with him. After taking her to various houses, thinking one might be

hers, he gives the little girl a quarter and flees, only to once again find himself in her company. She continues to follow Quentin as he crosses the river, where some boys are swimming. When the girl's brother JULIO and the town marshal ANSE catch up to them, Quentin is arrested on kidnapping charges and escorted to jail. When Quentin appears before a judge, he is ordered to pay six dollars in fines and one dollar to Julio, who is not pleased with the decision. Quentin's latest humiliation is witnessed by his friends Shreve, SPOADE, and Gerald BLAND. After the ordeal, Quentin and his friends meet with Gerald's mother, who has prepared a picnic for her son. With Mrs. BLAND are two younger women, Miss DAINGERFIELD and Miss HOLMES. At the picnic, Quentin confuses Gerald with Dalton Ames and starts a fight, which Gerald, who has been taking boxing lessons, easily wins. Bloodied and beaten, Quentin returns to his dorm room, where he attempts to clean the bloodstains on his clothes. He washes and dresses again before departing the room for the last time.

The third chapter of *The Sound and the Fury* is narrated by Jason COMPSON Jr., the resentful and hard-hearted son, and takes place on Good Friday, April 6, 1928. Jason is his mother's favorite, and like her, he is self-absorbed, but where her character plays the role of the suffering victim—hypochondriacal, put-upon, and weak—Jason snarls, bullies, and belittles. Jason does not dwell much upon the past to fuel his bitter hatred of his sister, whom he blames for his lost opportunity at the bank job Herbert had once promised him. Caddy's disgrace and divorce from Herbert meant the end of Jason's hopes, and her daughter, Quentin, who has lived in the Compson household since infancy to be reared by Mrs. Compson, is but a daily reminder of what was denied him. Named after her deceased uncle, Caddy's daughter Quentin is now 17 years old. Although she sends Quentin monthly checks, Caddy never sees her daughter. She once made arrangements with Jason to see her, then a toddler, after Mr. Compson's funeral. Jason agreed and was paid $100; he went to the designated spot, had the driver of the carriage slow down, lifted the child to the window and then, as Caddy came closer, told the driver to whip the horses and speed on. Jason's chapter clearly shows his relationship with his family and his attitude toward each member, dead or alive. Miss Quentin is despised and ostracized, and Benjy is an unnecessary burden whom Jason would like nothing better than to send to an asylum.

The final chapter is told in the third person and takes place on April 8, 1928. It is Easter morning, a day that begins badly for DILSEY, the Compsons' black servant. Her grandson Luster has not done his chores, so the house is cold and there is no firewood. Dilsey begins to make breakfast. Mrs. Compson repeatedly calls for a hot water bottle. Once breakfast is ready, Jason interrupts the meal to complain about the broken window in his bedroom, and assumes Luster did it. Fuming at his bad fortune, Jason is moved to insist that Quentin be awakened and told she must join the family for breakfast. While Dilsey is upstairs calling to Quentin, Jason, who knows that the window was broken the night before, suddenly realizes what might have happened. He rushes upstairs to Quentin's locked room and then turns to his mother and snatches a set of keys from her pocket in order to get in. When Jason discovers that Quentin is not in her room and has not slept there the night before, he rushes to his own room and discovers that his strongbox, hidden under a floorboard in his closet, has been pried open and the money taken. He calls the sheriff to tell him he has been robbed and to have a car ready by the time he gets there. When he arrives, Jason reports that Quentin stole and ran away with the money, but the sheriff wonders where Jason would have gotten the money and suspects that he was taking it from his niece all along. Though the amount is much more than $3,000, Jason could not admit to that without incriminating himself. The sheriff does not help Jason chase after Quentin and the pitchman from the carnival because the sheriff knows that Jason was partly the cause of her running away. He even questions Jason on what he expects to do with Quentin once he finds her. Jason says he will not do anything, but the sheriff hears the hatred in his voice and accuses Jason of driving Quentin away. Jason goes off on his own, but his attempt to find his niece and recover the money is unsuccessful.

Meanwhile, as Jason is meeting with the sheriff, Dilsey attends Easter services. Mrs. Compson had promised her time off. Dilsey takes with her her daughter FRONY, Frony's son LUSTER (1), and Benjy to the church, where they listen to a sermon by a visiting minister from St. Louis, Reverend SHEGOG. Although the preacher starts off slowly, he gradually builds to a crescendo that moves Dilsey to tears. As she leaves for home, Dilsey says to uncomprehending Frony: "I seed de beginin, en now I sees de endin" (p. 297). After lunch, Luster takes Benjy to the cellar and tries to perform a trick that he saw the night before at the carnival, but Dilsey has them go outside. At times, as is the case here, Luster can be impatient with and mean to Benjy. When Luster takes him to the fence by the golf course, Benjy starts moaning when he hears a golfer call for his caddie. For Benjy, the sound of the word reminds him of his absent sister. Dilsey tries unsuccessfully to quiet Benjy, then decides to let Luster take him for a ride in the carriage to the cemetery. She tells him to go the exact same route that T. P. always takes, but once in town by the monument of the Confederate soldier Luster decides to go left instead of their customary right turn, causing Benjy to start bellowing again. Jason, who is now in Jefferson after his futile attempt at finding Quentin and the carnival pitchman, hears Benjy's roaring and runs up to the carriage. With the back of his hand, he smacks Luster aside and takes control of the

reins so the horse can go to the right of the monument. Jason hits Luster over the head with his fist and scolds him for going left instead of right. He also strikes Benjy and tells him to shut up. He commands Luster to take Benjy home and warns him: "'If you ever cross that gate with him again, I'll kill you!'" (p. 320). The novel ends with the now quiescent Benjy returning to the Compson home, with serene and empty eyes looking upon each passing object "in its ordered place" (p. 321).

The Sound and the Fury was published to very favorable reviews. Lyle Saxon, for instance, in *New York Herald Tribune Books* on October 13, 1929, rightly observed that Faulkner "achieved a novel of extraordinary effect."

A story called "Twilight" begun by Faulkner in Paris in 1925 became the basis for the novel, which Faulkner earnestly started writing in early 1928. The narrative technique of the interior monologue prevalent throughout the novel is a clear influence of James JOYCE's *Ulysses*. The use of this narrative device, as Michael Gorden has pointed out in "Criticism in New Composition: *Ulysses* and *The Sound and the Fury*," published in *Twentieth Century Literature* 21 (October, 1975), provided Faulkner with "a solution to crucial problems in characterization that had plagued him in his first three novels" (p. 266).

Much of the last chapter of the novel, "April Eight, 1928," was published under the title "Dilsey" in *The PORTABLE FAULKNER* (1946); the first appearance of Faulkner's appendix to the novel, "1699–1945 The Compsons," also appeared in this volume (see Appendix IV). *The Sound and the Fury* was published together with *AS I LAY DYING* by the Modern Library, New York, in 1946; in this volume, the appendix appeared as a foreword, titled "Compson 1699–1945." The complete novel was also published with the appendix at the end in *The Faulkner Reader* (1954), and in 1984, a corrected text edited by Noel POLK was published by RANDOM HOUSE, New York. A film adaptation of *The Sound and the Fury*, with the screenplay by Irving Ravetch and Harriet Frank Jr., was released by Twentieth Century–Fox in March 1959; directed by Martin Ritt, the film starred Yul Brynner as Jason (Jr.), Joanne Woodward as (Miss) Quentin, Margaret Leighton as Caddy, Jack Warden as Benjy, and Ethel Waters as Dilsey. In 1957, Faulkner recorded two excerpts from *The Sound and the Fury* and two from *Light in August;* the recording is titled *William Faulkner Reads from His Works* (M-G-M E3617).

For further information regarding *The Sound and the Fury*, see *Faulkner in the University, Selected Letters of William Faulkner,* and *Faulkner at Nagano,* pp. 9, 69, 80, 103–106, 107, 142–44, and 162.

Spilner, Mr.   Minor character in *The TOWN* and "MULE IN THE YARD" (which Faulkner extensively revised for chapter 16 of the novel). Mr. Spilner is a farmer and one of Mrs. HAIT's neighbors. She ties a mule to a tree in a ravine behind his house.

Spoade A college student from Charleston, South Carolina, who was at HARVARD UNIVERSITY with Quentin COMPSON in 1910 (*The SOUND AND THE FURY*) and with Gavin STEVENS in 1909 (*The MANSION*). A senior when Quentin is a freshman, he is known for never missing chapel or his first lecture. Aware of Quentin's lack of interest in girls, Spoade humorously labels Quentin's roommate, Shreve MCKENZIE, Quentin's husband. Present at Quentin's hearing on the false kidnapping charges, Spoade, in Quentin's defense, says to the judge that Quentin's father is a congregational minister, which, of course, he is not.

Spoade's son, also referred to as Spoade in *The MANSION*, attends Harvard with Chick MALLISON, whom he invites to Charleston during a Christmas break.

Spoomer Character in "ALL THE DEAD PILOTS" (in *Collected Stories*). He is the nephew of a British army corps commander and thus a man of influence. The American Johnny SARTORIS, his rival for the affections of the French girl TOINETTE, manages to outwit Spoomer, however, and he is recalled to England and assigned to a ground school.

"Spotted Horses" *(Uncollected Stories)* Short story about wild ponies from Texas that Flem SNOPES transports to FRENCHMAN'S BEND, where he has his partner BUCK, "the Texas man," auction them off. Told from the first person singular point of view (see V. K. SURATT), "Spotted Horses" is a humorous tale about the sale and purchase of intractable horses impossible to catch and the damage they cause after they escape from Mrs. LITTLEJOHN's lot. A good portion of the story centers on the poor farmer Henry ARMSTID's obsession with buying a horse he cannot afford. Henry takes money from his wife and against her will bids on a horse, which the Texas man, who realizes Mrs. ARMSTID's predicament, refuses to sell to him. Determined to buy a horse, Henry hands the money to Flem, who keeps it even though Buck assures Mrs. Armstid that she can get it back. When Henry tries to capture the horse he thinks he bought, he breaks his leg and is knocked out. The next day, when Mrs. Armstid tries to get the money from Flem, he lies to her and says the Texan took it with him when he left.

"Spotted Horses" is more than just a story about a horse dealer who comes to the rural hamlet of Frenchman's Bend; under the tale of the humor and chicanery in duping unsuspecting farmers into bidding on wild ponies that are virtually impossible to catch lies the emergence of SNOPESISM in the unscrupulous figure of Flem.

In an August 1945 letter to Malcolm COWLEY, Faulkner mentioned that "Spotted Horses" created the character V. K. Suratt that he "fell in love with" (*Selected Letters of William Faulkner*, p. 197). The story's origin goes back to the 1926 novel fragment *FATHER ABRAHAM*; it was later revised several times with different titles: "As I Lay Dying," "Abraham's Children," "The Peasants," "Aria Con Amore" and "Horses." It was first published as "Spotted Horses" in the June 1931 issues of *SCRIBNER'S MAGAZINE* (139), 585–97. An expanded revision of the story is included in the first part of chapter 1 of book 4, "The Peasants," of *The HAMLET* (1940); it is reprinted as a novella in *The Faulkner Reader* (1954) and in *Three Famous Short Novels* (1958). The original version appears in *UNCOLLECTED STORIES OF WILLIAM FAULKNER* (1979).

For more information, see *Selected Letters of William Faulkner*, pp. 49–50, 115, 197, 202, 208, 233, 359; *Uncollected Stories of William Faulkner*, pp. 689–90; and *Faulkner in the University*, pp. 29–31 and 66.

Spratling Character in the short story "PETER" (in *Uncollected Stories*). An artist, he is sketching the mulatto boy PETER in a black-quarter brothel when the boy's mother objects and puts an end to the session. The character is named for Faulkner's NEW ORLEANS friend William SPRATLING.

Spratling, William (1900–1967) Artist, architect, and instructor. Born in New York State and reared in Atlanta, he befriended Faulkner in NEW ORLEANS in 1925, taking him into his apartment in Orleans Alley in the Vieux Carré. Faulkner worked on *SOLDIERS' PAY* there.

Faulkner and Spratling traveled to Europe together in the summer of 1925, landing at Genoa on August 2. Spratling became involved in a café fight and spent the night in a Genoese jail, an experience Faulkner borrowed for his unfinished novel *ELMER* and the short story "DIVORCE IN NAPLES."

Spratling returned to his teaching post at Tulane University in September. On the way home to New Orleans, he called on the publisher Horace LIVERIGHT; in October he wrote Faulkner with the news that Liveright had agreed to publish *Soldiers' Pay*.

Faulkner moved into Spratling's apartment on St. Peter Street when he returned to New Orleans in December 1925. They collaborated the following year on a book of sketches of Vieux Carré personalities called *Sherwood Anderson and Other Creoles:* Faulkner supplied the text, a parody of Sherwood ANDERSON's style. The authors paid a printer to strike off 400 copies, and sold every one at $1.50 each. The parody offended Anderson, however, and contributed to the chill that fell over his relationship with Faulkner.

Stallings, Lawrence (1894–1968) Georgia-born author and screenwriter. He served in France in World War I and was seriously wounded at Belleau Wood in 1918. His war experiences provided the background for his novel *Plumes* (1924) and for the bitter and highly successful play *What Price Glory?* (1924), written with Maxwell Anderson.

Stallings and Faulkner met in New York, where Stallings was a member of the writers' circle that gathered at the Algonquin Hotel, and in Hollywood. Faulkner credited him with helpful advice about dealing with movie people.

Stamper, Pat Character in *The* HAMLET, *The* MANSION, and "FOOL ABOUT A HORSE" (a short story Faulkner revised for *The Hamlet*). Stamper is a master horsetrader who outwits his rivals. In *The Hamlet* when Ab SNOPES realizes he has been duped in a trade, Stamper agrees to take back the worthless mules that Ab got in exchange for a horse. Finally, Stamper ends up with the mules and Mrs. Snopes's milk separator, while Ab unknowingly gets the same horse back, disguised.

Starnes, Mrs. Character in "HAIR" (in *Collected Stories*). She is Sophie STARNES's mother. Regarding her background as superior to that of her daughter's fiancé, the barber Henry STRIBLING, she allows Stribling to do her yardwork when he comes to visit each April on his vacation.

Starnes, Sophie Character in "HAIR" (in *Collected Stories*). She is engaged to the barber Henry STRIBLING (Hawkshaw), but dies before they can be married.

Starnes, Will Character in "HAIR" (in *Collected Stories*). He is the lazy, debt-ridden father of Sophie STARNES, Henry STRIBLING's fiancée. When he dies, Stribling pays off the mortgage on his house.

Stefan, Corporal Leader of a mutiny central to the plot in *A* FABLE. The mutiny involves a French regiment's refusal to make a foolhardy attack against the Germans. Corporal Stefan and his 12 followers attempt to bring about peace through a kind of civil disobedience in the army. The group—obviously reminiscent of Jesus and his 12 disciples—have visited widely on both the Allied and the German sides of the lines and have a following among common soldiers. The effect Stefan has had on both adversaries is evident in the Germans' puzzling refusal to take advantage of the French regiment's mutiny. This, too, is ascribed to Stefan and his affect on young soldiers of both sides. Stefan is betrayed by one of his own followers, arrested, and brought before the French supreme commander, who is, in fact, his father. The supreme commander offers Stefan wealth and power if he will renounce his mission of peace. Stefan refuses to turn on his followers, and the supreme commander orders his execution. Stefan thus becomes a martyr to peace, as is foretold, in a way, by his name. (St. Stephen was the first Christian martyr.) Faulkner uses a multitude of allusions and parallels to Christ and other ironic plot twists in creating Corporal Stefan. When Stefan is executed, for example, he is tied to a post

between two thieves who are being shot for crimes committed against civilians. Stefan's body is flung backward into a ditch where a rusty, discarded coil of barbed wire forms a crown of thorns on his head. Later, his half-sisters MARYA and Marthe (DEMONT) claim the body. He is buried in a makeshift sepulcher, but an artillery barrage causes the grave and the body to disappear. Later, PICKLOCK trades a dead German officer's watch for a body, presumably Stefan's, found by Marya and Marthe's neighbor. The body is transported to Paris, where it is given a full military burial as France's famous Unknown Soldier.

Stein, Jean (b. c. 1935) A companion and lover of Faulkner's in the mid-1950s, she was a 19-year-old student at the Sorbonne when they met in St. Mortiz, Switzerland, in the winter of 1953. Jean Stein seems to have restored Faulkner's morale, shattered by the end of his affair with Joan WILLIAMS. The novelist, working in Egypt with Howard HAWKS on the movie *Land of the Pharaohs*, saw Stein in Paris and Rome that winter. Despite the 37-year difference in their ages, the affair lasted four years.

Jean kept notes of their conversations and, with Faulkner's help, published them in a famous *PARIS REVIEW* interview in May 1956. She broke off the affair with the aging novelist in 1957. The action devastated Faulkner, touching off a serious drinking bout that landed him in the University of Virginia Medical Center in Charlottesville.

Steinbauer, Genevieve (Jenny) Character in *MOSQUITOES*. She and her boyfriend, Pete GINOTTA, are members of the *Nausikaa* yachting party, but do not fit in with the others. Pete is associated with bootleggers, and Jenny is neither artistic nor intelligent, though her sexual allure is disturbing to the men aboard the yacht, and to Patricia ROBYN and Dorothy JAMESON too.

Steinbauer, Miss Character in the short story "DON GIOVANNI." On a date with HERB, the main character of the story, she pushes him over for another man. (As Joseph BLOTNER and others have pointed out, Faulkner based the character Jenny STEINBAUER in *MOSQUITOES* on Miss Steinbauer; see *Uncollected Stories of William Faulkner*, p. 705.)

Stevens, Bucky In *REQUIEM FOR A NUN*, the young son and only surviving child of Gowan and Temple Drake STEVENS. While in California with his mother, who is escaping from the circumstances surrounding the death of her infant daughter, Bucky asks questions that cause Temple to return to JEFFERSON, MISSISSIPPI, and try to save from execution the convicted murderer of her daughter (pp. 68–69).

Stevens, Captain *See* STEVENS, JUDGE LEMUEL.

Stevens, Gavin A major character in several of Faulkner's important works: *KNIGHT'S GAMBIT, INTRUDER IN THE DUST, REQUIEM FOR A NUN, The TOWN* (in which he narrates chapters 2, 5, 8, 13, 15, 17, 20 and 22), and *The MANSION* (in which he narrates chapter 10). He also appears in *LIGHT IN AUGUST,* "HAIR," *GO DOWN, MOSES,* "THE TALL MEN," "HOG PAWN" (revised for chapter 14 of *The Mansion*), and "By the People" (revised for chapter 13 of *The Mansion*); he also is referred to in "A NAME FOR THE CITY" (revised for the prologue to act 1 of *Requiem for a Nun*).

Modeled partly on Faulkner's longtime friend Philip Avery STONE, Gavin Stevens is an attorney from a prominent family in JEFFERSON, MISSISSIPPI, Faulkner's fictional counterpart of Oxford, Mississippi. He is the son of Judge Lemuel STEVENS and twin of Margaret Stevens MALLISON; in *The Mansion,* he marries the widow Melisandre Backus Harriss (STEVENS), a childhood sweetheart and one of his sister's childhood friends. Gavin is a Don Quixote figure whose romantic idealism can appear as foolishness to others around him, in particular to his sister. When, for example, he defends the honor of the married Eula Varner SNOPES, whose dancing with Manfred DE SPAIN shocks onlookers, he gets his face bloodied by Manfred. What Gavin seems to be doing here, according to his nephew, Chick MALLISON, on whom Gavin has a considerable influence, is defending the ideal of women's chastity and virtue. Throughout *The Town* and *The Mansion,* Gavin is preoccupied with preventing the spread of SNOPSEISM. As part of this mission he takes an active interest in the education of Eula's teenage daughter Linda Snopes (KOHL) by discussing poetry with her and giving her catalogues of colleges she might like to attend. Although Gavin's interest in Linda may be an unconscious sublimation of his romantic feelings for her mother, he shows such genuine and singular kindness toward the daughter that after Eula's suicide, his friend and ally against Snopesism, V. K. RATLIFF, half-jokingly suggests that he marry Linda. Gavin, of course, declines (*The Town*, p. 351).

Gavin is Jefferson's "intellectual," a Phi Beta Kappa with a master's degree from HARVARD UNIVERSITY, a doctorate from Heidelberg University in Germany, and a law degree from the UNIVERSITY OF MISSISSIPPI. During World War I, he served in the American Field Service and YMCA in France from 1915 through 1918. His professional positions include county attorney, acting city attorney, and district attorney. In *Light in August,* Stevens, described as a tall and disheveled man, is the young district attorney who tells the sheriff that Joe CHRISTMAS will plead guilty to the murder of Joanna BURDEN. Stevens also reflects on the factors that lead up to Christmas's death and offers an interpretation that focuses on Christmas's inner struggles caused by the mixture of white and black blood flowing in his veins

(see especially pp. 448–49). Always thoughtful and humane, Stevens assures the elderly Mrs. HINES that her grandson Joe Christmas's body will be on the train to MOTTSTOWN in the morning to be buried there.

In *Intruder in the Dust,* after initial skepticism, Stevens becomes persuaded of Lucas BEAUCHAMP's innocence and defends him aggressively against a murder charge. He also delivers long, rambling soliloquies on race relations in the South. In *Requiem for a Nun,* Gavin takes his nephew's wife, Temple Drake STEVENS, to the governor's office in the middle of the night so the governor can hear Temple's plea for Nancy MANNIGOE, who is to be executed for having killed Temple's six-month-old baby.

Some readers see Gavin Stevens as Faulkner's mouthpiece, particularly in *Light in August* and *Intruder in the Dust,* but such an assumption cannot be justified. Faulkner was too skilled as an artist to identify with any of his characters, even though some of these characters may echo some of his sentiments. Faulkner does not intrude into his fictional works to present his opinions. (For more information, see *Faulkner in the University,* pp. 25, 72, 118, 140–41 and 201; and James Farnham's "Faulkner's Unsung Hero: Gavin Stevens" in *Arizona Quarterly* [summer 1965], 115–32, where Farnham discusses Stevens's significance in the SNOPES TRILOGY and how, by the end of *The Mansion,* he becomes a realist in his view of humanity). Horace BENBOW, a precursor of Gavin Stevens, shares a similar educational background and other personal characteristics.

Stevens, Gowan Character in *SANCTUARY, REQUIEM FOR A NUN,* and *The TOWN.* In *The Town,* Gowan is Chick MALLISON's first cousin once removed (their grandfathers are brothers) and Gavin STEVENS's 13-year-old cousin; in *Requiem for a Nun,* he is Gavin's nephew (Faulkner is not always consistent with some of his characters) and Temple Drake (STEVENS)'s husband.

For a time growing up, Gowan lived with the Mallisons and went to school in JEFFERSON, MISSISSIPPI, when his father, who worked for the State Department, was sent to the Far East. Gowan becomes one of the primary sources of information on the early events surrounding Flem SNOPES and his wife, Eula Varner SNOPES, that Chick retells in *The Town.* In the opening lines of *The Town,* Chick explains his indebtedness to him. It was Gowan who informed Chick of the events that took place before he was born.

In *Sanctuary,* Gowan is a college student at the University of Virginia who drinks heavily under the illusion that he can hold his liquor as a gentleman should. He comes back to Jefferson to see Narcissa Benbow SARTORIS (who, many years his senior, rejects his offer to marry him), and meets Temple Drake, a student at the state university in OXFORD, MISSISSIPPI, whom he takes to a dance. His plans to drive Temple to a baseball game in Starkville the next day are thwarted by his drinking, which sets in motion the theme of the novel: the materialization of evil. Instead of driving Temple directly to the game, Gowan first takes her to OLD FRENCHMAN PLACE to buy more liquor; as he approaches the property, his car crashes into a tree lying across the road and the two are stranded there until the following afternoon. The next morning, Gowan, ashamed of his drunkenness and severely beaten by VAN, one of the bootleggers, abandons Temple, whom POPEYE rapes with a corncob, and then drives to a Memphis brothel.

In *A Reader's Guide to William Faulkner*, Edmond L. Volpe observes that Gowan "represents the corruption of a social class whose moral code is nothing more than an empty concept of the gentleman. . . . His conscience responds only to his failure to live up to [that] code. . . ." (New York: Farrar, Straus & Giroux, 1965, p. 148). Gowan attempts to redeem himself by giving up drinking, and marries Temple a year or two later. In *Requiem for a Nun*, Gowan and Temple have two children, the younger of whom is killed by Nancy MANNIGOE.

Stevens, Judge   Eighty-year-old mayor of JEFFERSON, MISSISSIPPI, in "A ROSE FOR EMILY" who receives complaints about a smell coming from Miss Emily GRIERSON's property. Very much the gentleman, he sees to it that the actions taken to eliminate the odor do not publicly embarrass her. Judge Stevens arranges for a few men to spread lime in Miss Emily's property at night. (His relationship to the Stevens family and, in particular, to Judge Lemuel STEVENS and Gavin STEVENS is not certain; one commentator suggests that this 80-year-old mayor may be Gavin's grandfather.)

Stevens, Judge Lemuel   Father of the twins Gavin STEVENS, the YOKNAPATAWPHA COUNTY attorney, and Margaret (Maggie) Stevens MALLISON, the mother of Chick MALLISON, who is Gavin's young aide in *KNIGHT'S GAMBIT* ("Tomorrow"). Judge Stevens is a minor character in *The TOWN*, where Judge DUKINFIELD designates him to preside over the case of the missing brass fittings that Judge Stevens's son brings against Mayor Manfred DE SPAIN. (This episode is later referred to in *The MANSION*, the third volume of the SNOPES TRILOGY.) He appears in *The REIVERS*, where he advises Maury PRIEST after a shooting incident involving Boon HOGGANBECK, and as Captain Stevens in *Knight's Gambit* ("Tomorrow"). See also STEVENS, JUDGE.

Stevens, Melisandre Backus Harriss   Character in *The TOWN* (where she is identified by her maiden name, Melisandre Backus), *The MANSION*, and *KNIGHT'S GAMBIT* ("Knight's Gambit"). In 1942, as explained in *The Mansion* she marries her childhood friend Gavin STEVENS after the death of her husband, a wealthy New Orleans bootlegger. She has two children. Gavin's sister, Margaret MALLISON, had all along suggested to her brother that he marry her.

A Backus family to whom Melisandre may be related appears in the short story "MY GRANDMOTHER MILLARD AND GENERAL BEDFORD FORREST AND THE BATTLE OF HARRYKIN CREEK."

Stevens, Temple Drake   A 17-year-old college student in *SANCTUARY*, where she appears as Temple Drake, her maiden name, and the wife of Gowan STEVENS in *REQUIEM FOR A NUN*, where she is in her mid-20s and the mother of two children, one of whom is smothered to death by the maid, Nancy MANNIGOE. Temple has four brothers; her father is a judge in Jackson. Temple is a complex character, for in her discovery of evil—as frightening and painful as that discovery is—she also discovers in her nature an affinity to it.

In *Sanctuary*, Temple, a freshman at the state university at OXFORD, MISSISSIPPI, where she has a reputation as a loose young woman, meets Gowan Stevens. Their plans to go to a college baseball game are thwarted when Gowan wrecks his car at OLD FRENCHMAN PLACE, where he had planned to buy bootleg liquor from Lee GOODWIN. The next day, Temple, nervous and afraid of the bootleggers, hides in the barn with the feebleminded TOMMY, whom she asks to keep a lookout for Goodwin. The sexually impotent POPEYE sneaks in, shoots Tommy in the back of the head, and with a corncob sexually violates Temple. He then drives her to a Memphis brothel, where he introduces her to RED. A month later when Temple tries to run away with Red, with whom she has fallen in love, Popeye kills him.

During Temple's stay at the brothel, Goodwin is charged with Tommy's murder. When Goodwin's attorney, Horace BENBOW, interviews Temple, he expects her to testify on Goodwin's behalf at the trial, but when she appears, she perjures herself and identifies Goodwin as the murderer. At the end of *Sanctuary*, Temple, bored and sullen, is with her father in Paris.

In *REQUIEM FOR A NUN*, eight years after her return from Paris, Temple is married to Gowan Stevens, who has stopped drinking. But Temple's attempt at a conventional life as wife and mother of two children fails. Letters that she wrote to her lover Red (referred to as Alabama Red in *Requiem*), letters she does not want her husband to see, are being used by Red's brother, PETE, to blackmail her. Temple's plans to take her infant daughter and run away with Pete—her way of avoiding blackmail—are foiled when her maid Nancy kills the child to prevent Temple from running off. Temple wants Nancy saved from execution. Gowan's uncle, the attorney Gavin STEVENS, takes Temple to meet with the governor, to whom she recounts the events of *Sanctuary*, admits her past guilt, and tells of her attraction to evil. Her attempt, however, is futile; Nancy will be hanged. Among other issues, the problem of suffering and moral restitution plague Temple's thoughts and conversations throughout *Requiem*.

For further information, see *Faulkner in the University*, pp. 96 and 196.

Stillwell, Shuford H.   Mink SNOPES's fellow inmate at the Mississippi state penitentiary at PARCHMAN, in *The MANSION*. A gambler, he is in prison for having cut the throat of a Vicksburg prostitute. In 1943, Stillwell escapes and in the attempt another inmate, Jake BARRON, is killed by a guard. Because Mink did not go along with the plan, Stillwell blames him for Barron's death and threatens his life, forcing the warden not to consider parole for Mink. A few years later, however, Stillwell dies in a deconsecrated church when it collapses on him in the Mexican quarter of San Diego. Soon afterward, Mink goes free. As revealed in a conversation with the warden (p. 100), Stillwell's death seems to be an expected consequence of Mink's absolute confidence in the judgment of God.

Stokes, Mr.   Character in "A JUSTICE" (in *Collected Stories*). He is manager of the Compson farm four miles outside of JEFFERSON, MISSISSIPPI. Sam FATHERS works there as a carpenter.

Stone   Minor character in *The TOWN*. Stone is the OXFORD, MISSISSIPPI, attorney whom Linda Snopes (KOHL) consults to relinquish her inheritance to Flem SNOPES.

Stone, Philip Avery (1893–1967)   A member of a prominent OXFORD, MISSISSIPPI, law and banking family, Faulkner's friend, mentor and fiercely protective early supporter. He took bachelor's and law degrees from the UNIVERSITY OF MISSISSIPPI and Yale University and entered his father's law practice, but his first love was literature.

The Falkner and Stone families were acquainted, but Stone and Faulkner did not become close until 1914, when Phil Stone, older by four years and just returned from Yale, read some of Faulkner's early poetry. He encouraged Faulkner, talked to him in great detail about literature's aims and methods, loaned him books, and encouraged him in any way he could. Stone offered the apprentice artist a kind of conversation hard to find elsewhere in Oxford.

Stone filled Faulkner with anecdotes about Lafayette County hill people and with lore about hunting. At age 12, Stone had killed a bear at his father's camp in the MISSISSIPPI DELTA wilderness; Faulkner reworked Stone's experience in the novella "The Bear." Faulkner drew one of the themes of "The Bear," the timber companies' gradual destruction of the wilderness, from Stone's father's selling off portions of his hunting reserve to the clear-cutters.

Stone's uncles Theophilus and Amodeus Potts gave their first names and something of their experiences to the McCaslin twins, Theophilus and Amodeus MCCASLIN, respectively nicknamed Uncle Buck and Uncle Buddy, in GO DOWN, MOSES. Something of Stone himself went into the character of Gavin STEVENS, the JEFFERSON, MISSISSIPPI, lawyer of *INTRUDER IN THE DUST*. Stone also introduced Faulkner to the gambling, roadhouse, and bordello culture of northern Mississippi and MEMPHIS, Tennessee, raw material the novelist exploited for many works, from *SANCTUARY* (1931) to *The REIVERS* (1962). They used to tool around in a convertible Ford Stone dubbed "Drusilla," a name Faulkner chose for the redoubtable female cavalry trooper in *The UNVANQUISHED*.

Faulkner joined Stone in New Haven, Connecticut, in the spring of 1918, marking a new phase in his life. With Stone's encouragement and connivance he finagled his enlistment in the ROYAL AIR FORCE as a cadet. When he returned to Mississippi later in 1918, he and Stone were much together. Stone acted as his agent and promoter, having his poems and stories typed at his law office, fixing punctuation, sending manuscripts off to magazines, and negotiating with publishers on Faulkner's behalf.

To give Faulkner an income to support his writing, Stone in late 1921 used his influence to land him a job as postmaster of the University of Mississippi post office. In 1924, he oversaw the publication of Faulkner's first book, the collection of poems titled *The MARBLE FAUN*. Stone wrote a preface for the book, arranged for its promotion and sale, and may have paid for part of the $400 printing charge.

"This poet is my personal property," he wrote the Yale *Alumni Weekly*, "and I urge all my friends and classmates to buy the book."

By the late 1920s the relationship had begun to change. Faulkner evidently resented Stone's proprietorial attitude toward his work. A loan of several hundred dollars from Stone may have fueled the resentment. Whatever the cause, Faulkner no longer discussed everything he was working on with Stone, and he began typing out his own fair copies of manuscripts, beginning with *SARTORIS* (1929).

They drifted further apart during the Depression years of the 1930s. Beset with his own problems, Stone no longer seemed interested in Faulkner's literary work. When his father's bank failed, Stone took on $50,000 in family debt, vowing to pay it off. Faulkner loaned him $6,000 for this purpose in 1939. Increasingly hard up, Stone never paid the money back—a fresh cause of estrangement between the two old friends. During the 1950s Faulkner's comparatively liberal views on racial matters led to further alienation. Stone became increasingly critical, not to say dismissive, of Faulkner's oeuvre.

Stone claimed to have suggested to Faulkner the theme of the SNOPES TRILOGY, the rise and triumph of the rednecks at the expense of the old planter class. Faulkner dedicated all three of the Snopes novels—*The* HAMLET, *The* TOWN, and *The* MANSION—"To Phil Stone."

Stovall, Mr. Character in "THAT EVENING SUN" (in *Collected Stories*). A bank cashier and Baptist deacon, he is a sometime client of Nancy's (see MANNINGOE, NANCY). Stovall beats her when she accuses him in public of failing to pay for her services. Nancy is also pregnant, most certainly with his child. Stovall is referred to, but not by name, in *REQUIEM FOR A NUN*.

Stowers, Zack The friend who seeks Mr. BOWMAN's help in the short story "A DANGEROUS MAN" after Stowers's wife is supposedly insulted by a traveling salesman. Stowers beats the alleged offender with his fists while Mr. Bowman fights a second salesman, unfortunate enough to be with the first when Stowers and Mr. Bowman catch up to them.

Straud, Dr. Character in *SARTORIS*. Young Loosh PEABODY mentions him as an experimenter with electricity.

stream of consciousness A phrase that describes the fluency of conscious thoughts, perceptions, and sensations. It was first used by William James in *Principles of Psychology* (1890) and subsequently employed by writers and critics to describe a literary technique that expresses either the manner in which a character's thoughts are represented (directly or indirectly) to the reader or, less frequently, the manner an author uses to write a specific passage. Similar to but not identical with the INTERIOR MONOLOGUE, the stream-of-consciousness technique differs in that it normally adheres to syntactical and grammatical rules, whereas the interior monologue tends to disregard them. Faulkner is one of several writers associated with the stream-of-consciousness technique; others celebrated writers include Henry James, James JOYCE, and Virginia Woolf.

Stribling, Henry (Hawkshaw) Character in "HAIR" and "DRY SEPTEMBER" (in *Collected Stories*). The son of a tenant farmer, Hawkshaw learns barbering at a school in Birmingham, Alabama, saves money, rents a little place, and prepares to send for his fiancée, Sophie STARNES. She dies before they can be married.

Moving to JEFFERSON, MISSISSIPPI, where he finds work in Maxey's barbershop, he falls in love with the orphan girl Susan REED and eventually marries her.

In "Dry September," Hawkshaw tries to talk the leader of the lynch mob out of hanging Will MAYES, who is accused of attacking a White spinster.

Strother, Caspey Character in *SARTORIS*, son of Simon STROTHER. An African American, he returns from army service during World War I with ideas about racial equality that are taboo in JEFFERSON, MISSISSIPPI. As time passes, he comes to accept his subordinate station.

Strother, Euphrony Character in *SARTORIS*. She is Simon STROTHER's wife.

Strother, Joby Character in *SARTORIS*. A black servant of Colonel John SARTORIS, he was probably the grandfather of Simon STROTHER. The servant Joby Strother appears in *The UNVANQUISHED*.

Strother, Louvinia Character in *SARTORIS* and *The UNVANQUISHED*, the wife of Joby STROTHER. She equips Colonel John SARTORIS with his boots and pistols so he can escape from the Yankees.

In *The UNVANQUISHED*, the faithful Louvinia is mortified by the betrayal of her son LOOSH, who shows the Yankees where the Sartoris silver is hidden. She also appears in the short story "MY GRANDMOTHER MILLARD AND GENERAL BEDFORD FORREST AND THE BATTLE OF HARRYKIN CREEK."

Strother, Ringo (Marengo) Character in *The UNVANQUISHED*. One of the Sartoris slaves, he is the boyhood friend and companion of Bayard SARTORIS (3). They are inseparable in a series of adventures in northern Mississippi during the Civil War, among them an ambush of a Yankee patrol.

Ringo, resourceful and intelligent, is the first to recognize the money-making potential of a federal order for the restitution of stolen goods that Bayard's grandmother, Rosa MILLARD, extracts from Colonel Nathaniel DICK. With Ringo's canny advice, she develops the order into a lucrative scheme of selling the Yankees their own horses and mules.

Later, when the bushwhacker GRUMBY murders Miss Rosa over a question of stolen horses, Ringo helps Bayard track him down and exact his revenge. The boys nail Grumby's corpse to a cotton compress door and attach his severed hand to Miss Rosa's grave marker.

After the war, Ringo volunteers to help Bayard avenge his father's death at Ben REDMOND's hands. He is perplexed at first when Bayard allows Redmond to leave JEFFERSON, MISSISSIPPI, unscathed, but he accompanies Bayard home after the encounter and remains at his side in silent companionability through the long afternoon.

He also appears in the short story "MY GRANDMOTHER MILLARD AND GENERAL BEDFORD FORREST AND THE BATTLE OF HARRYKIN CREEK."

Strother, Simon Character in *SARTORIS*. The black coachman of old Bayard SARTORIS (3), he is the grandson of Joby STROTHER, a servant of Colonel John SARTORIS, and he still talks to the old colonel 40 years after his death.

Simon is found dead, his head bashed in, in the cabin of an attractive young woman, Meloney HARRIS, to whom he has been passing church money entrusted to him.

Strutterbuck, Captain In *The MANSION,* a patron at Miss Reba RIVERS's brothel in MEMPHIS, where he meets Montgomery Ward SNOPES. According to Reba, Strutterbuck is a veteran of two wars, the Spanish-American War and World War I. After his time with Thelma (2), one of the girls, Strutterbuck tries to skip out without paying but is stopped by MINNIE and Reba. He hands Reba a two-dollar money order, but before she lets him out she tells him to button himself up.

Strutterbuck, O'Milla The name that appears on the money order Captain STRUTTERBUCK uses at Miss Reba RIVERS's bordello in Memphis; it was issued at Lonoke, Arkansas. Reba thinks it is the name of Strutterbuck's sister or daughter. MINNIE believes it is his wife's name.

Stuart, James Ewell Brown (Jeb) (1833–1864) Virginia-born Confederate soldier. A flamboyant, gaudily attired cavalier, Robert E. Lee's "eyes of the army," he carried out a series of famous cavalry operations, including an 1862 ride around the Union army, that were sometimes more spectacular than productive. He was killed in action at Yellow Tavern in Virginia on May 11, 1864.

Bayard SARTORIS (2) of Faulkner's fictional clan rides with General Stuart in *SARTORIS.* Sartoris's fool-hardy behavior leads to his death: On a raid with Stuart, he rides into the Yankee General Pope's camp in search of anchovies and is shot for his trouble.

Studenmare, Captain Character in "A COURTSHIP" (in *Collected Stories*). He owns the steamboat that David HOGGANBECK pilots.

Sue Character in *SARTORIS.* HUB mentions her as having to take up his milking chores while he goes into JEFFERSON, MISSISSIPPI, with his drinking companions V. K. SURATT and young Bayard SARTORIS (3).

Summers, Paul D. Jr. (fl. 1950s) Faulkner's son-in-law. A 1951 West Point graduate from a well-to-do background, and a veteran of the Korean War, he met Jill FAULKNER at a wedding at Fort Leavenworth in March 1954.

They were married in OXFORD, MISSISSIPPI, in August 1954. Summers left the army for law school at the UNIVERSITY OF VIRGINIA and set up a practice in Charlottesville in 1957. He and Jill named the second of their three sons, William Cuthbert Faulkner Summers, for her father.

Suratt, V. K. An itinerant salesman in *SARTORIS, AS I LAY DYING,* and the short story "LIZARDS IN JAMSHYD'S COURTYARD"; in the last two works his initials are not used. In *As*

I Lay Dying, he offers Cash BUNDREN a gramophone for eight dollars. He is referred to in the short story "CENTAUR IN BRASS." Faulkner later changed his name to V. K. RATLIFF. Although not identified, Suratt is the narrator of the short story "SPOTTED HORSES."

For more information, see *Selected Letters of William Faulkner,* p. 197.

Susan Character in the short story "MOONLIGHT." A 16-year-old girl, she sends the unnamed protagonist a note saying that she will clandestinely meet him and be his for the night, but all she really wants to do is have him take her to the movies. Although she lets him kiss her, she rejects his sexual advances.

Sutpen, Clytemnestra (Clytie) Character in *ABSALOM, ABSALOM!* The daughter of Thomas SUTPEN and one of his slaves, she is the mainstay of the doomed household at SUTPEN'S HUNDRED.

While Thomas Sutpen is at war, Clytie and Sutpen's white daughter Judith SUTPEN take a subsistence from the land and keep the place intact. Clytie helps Judith fashion a wedding dress and veil out of rags and scraps. She takes responsibility for the orphaned Charles Etienne BON when his mother dies in New Orleans in 1871 and teaches him to farm. She risks her own life to nurse her half sister Judith and Charles Etienne during a yellow fever outbreak in 1884. Finally, she raises Charles Etienne's feebleminded son, Jim BOND.

In the end Clytie guards the last of the Sutpen secrets: Henry SUTPEN, who vanished after killing his sister Judith's suitor Charles BON (Charles Etienne's father) in 1865 and returned 40 years later to live as an invalid in his old home. Rosa COLDFIELD discovers him there in 1909, despite Clytie's frantic efforts to prevent Rosa from mounting the stairs to Henry's room.

Later, Miss Rosa sends for an ambulance to fetch Henry. Clytie panics, believing the authorities are about to arrest and hang him for shooting Charles Bon. She sets the house afire; she and Henry perish in the flames.

Sutpen, Ellen Coldfield Character in *ABSALOM, ABSALOM!* The older daughter of Goodhue COLDFIELD, she marries Thomas SUTPEN in 1838 and moves into the great house at SUTPEN'S HUNDRED even though she knows little or nothing about him and actually fears him.

Ellen bears two children conceived of the "demon," Henry (born 1839) and Judith (born 1841), and settles uneasily into the role of grand lady of the plantation.

Over time, Sutpen corrupts her. She stops going into town altogether, instead bidding the merchants and her social inferiors to wait upon her at Sutpen's Hundred. She becomes obsessed with the furnishings of the plantation house, with menus, even with how the elegant meals are prepared. She also welcomes Charles BON, the suave young man from New Orleans, as her daughter's suitor, as a model of comportment for her son, and as an ornament to her household.

Ellen's dreams are shattered on Christmas Eve, 1860, when her husband and son quarrel and Charles Bon abruptly leaves for New Orleans. She withdraws and sickens; only the bafflement in her eyes suggests anything of life. In 1862, she summons Miss Rosa, then 17, to her deathbed, asks her to look after Judith, and dies.

Sutpen, Eulalia Bon   Character in ABSALOM, ABSALOM! The daughter of a wealthy Haitian sugar planter, said to be part Spanish, she marries Thomas SUTPEN in 1827 and bears him a son. When Sutpen discovers that she is part black, he repudiates and divorces her.

Eulalia Bon resettles in New Orleans, where her son, Charles BON, matures into a suave and elegant young man. Plotting revenge, she arranges for him to attend the UNIVERSITY OF MISSISSIPPI. There he meets Sutpen's son (Henry SUTPEN) by his second wife, Ellen Coldfield SUTPEN.

Henry and Charles Bon become friends, as Eulalia had hoped, and Bon is taken to SUTPEN'S HUNDRED. There, according to her plan, Henry's sister, Judith SUTPEN, falls in love with him. When Sutpen learns his son with "a little spot of negro blood" hopes to marry his daughter, Eulalia has her revenge, although it is not clear whether she lives to savor it. She dies in New Orleans on a date unknown, possibly by the hand of her lawyer.

Sutpen, Henry   Character in ABSALOM, ABSALOM! The son of Thomas and Ellen Coldfield SUTPEN, he is a proud and sensitive rustic who falls under the sway of the cosmopolitan Charles BON at the university and takes him home to SUTPEN'S HUNDRED at the first opportunity.

There Bon meets Henry's sister, Judith SUTPEN, and they become engaged. On Christmas Eve 1860, Thomas Sutpen tells Henry that Bon is his half brother and that the marriage must be prevented. Henry refuses to accept this. He surrenders his home and birthright, even though he leaves Sutpen's Hundred knowing he has been told the truth.

When war breaks out, Henry and Charles enlist together in a Mississippi infantry regiment. Henry is wounded at SHILOH; Charles carries him off the battlefield and he recovers. He gradually comes to accept the notion of incest, wrestling with his conscience just as his father had done in Haiti 30 years before. Dukes and kings had married their sisters, Henry tells himself.

Toward war's end, with Johnston's army in North Carolina, Henry and his father cross paths. Colonel Sutpen summons Henry and informs him that Charles is part black. Henry will not accept miscegenation. After the war, he and Charles return to JEFFERSON, MISSISSIPPI. When Charles refuses to give up Judith, Henry shoots and kills him at the gates of Sutpen's Hundred and disappears.

Around 1905, ailing and elderly, Henry returns home to die. In 1909, fearing that Henry will be exposed, arrested, and hanged, the servant Clytemnestra SUTPEN (old Thomas Sutpen's daughter by one of his slaves) sets fire to the rotten, decrepit house. Henry and Clytie perish in the flames.

Sutpen, Judith   Character in ABSALOM, ABSALOM! The daughter of Thomas and Ellen Coldfield SUTPEN, she is her father's daughter: strong-willed, tough and determined to get what she wants.

Judith falls in love with her brother Henry SUTPEN's friend Charles BON and waits patiently for him through the Civil War, scratching a living out of the family place, SUTPEN'S HUNDRED, with the help of the servant, and her half sister, Clytemnestra SUTPEN. She seems barely aware of the havoc her choice has caused, for Bon, evidently unknown to her, is Sutpen's son (and thus her half brother) by his first wife, who has black blood. In any case, there is no evidence that she knows why her father and brother fall out on Christmas Eve 1860, or that she ever quarreled with her father over Bon.

Judith loses Bon when Henry shoots and kills him at the gate of Sutpen's Hundred on their return from North Carolina in 1865. In 1884, she helps Clytie nurse Bon's son (by a mistress or wife in New Orleans) through an attack of yellow fever, catches the disease herself, and dies.

The critic Cleanth BROOKS found Judith a sympathetic figure: "Judith is doomed by misfortunes not of her making, but she is not warped and twisted by them," Brooks observes. "Her humanity survives them."

Sutpen, Thomas   Character in ABSALOM, ABSALOM! The son of a poor white West Virginia farmer, he is the flawed, corrupt, doomed creator and master of SUTPEN'S HUNDRED, the plantation he hacks out of the YOKNAPATWAPHA COUNTY wilderness in the 1830s. In early youth, on his father's hardscrabble farm, he forms a design to build a dynasty of wealth and power, and he applies all his furious energies to the task.

Sutpen ventures to a Haiti sugar plantation and marries the wealthy planter's daughter; he casts her and their son aside when he learns she is part black. He rides into JEFFERSON, MISSISSIPPI, on a Sunday morning in June 1833, inveigles a hundred square miles of bottomland out of a Chickasaw chief, forces a captive French architect to design a mansion the size of a courthouse for him, and marries into a respectable Jefferson family. He and his wife, Ellen Coldfield SUTPEN, produce a son and dynastic heir, Henry SUTPEN, and a daughter, Judith SUTPEN.

In due course, the town of Jefferson accepts Sutpen. He gets richer and richer. He corrupts his wife; Ellen fills the mansion with fine things and takes on the airs of a great lady. Then Charles BON, Sutpen's son by his revenge-driven Haitian wife, arrives to threaten the design. Henry and Bon have become friends at the university; Henry brings him to Sutpen's Hundred during the holidays, and Judith falls in love with him almost at first sight. Sutpen then makes a grave miscalculation. Rather than acknowledge Bon openly as his son, he calls Henry into the library on Christmas Eve 1860 and reveals the relationship, with the expectation that Henry will resolve the matter for him.

War comes; Henry and Bon enlist together in a Mississippi regiment; Henry gradually learns to accept the notion of incest in the courtship of Charles and his sister. Sutpen too goes off to fight for the Confederacy. He is an excellent soldier, efficient and brave, and he has a citation for valor from the hand of General Lee himself to prove it. Toward war's end his path crosses Henry's in North Carolina, and he finally tells Henry that Bon has black blood. This Henry will never accept. When Bon refuses to repudiate Judith, Henry shoots and kills him at the gates of Sutpen's Hundred, and vanishes.

So Sutpen's design is in ruins. Nearing 60, a widower since 1863, he is forced to start over. The plantation is a wreck, but he takes this in hand with his usual fierce efficiency. His effort to establish a new dynasty leads, however, to disaster. Sutpen offers to marry his deceased wife's sister, Miss Rosa COLDFIELD, on the condition that she will first deliver him a son; outraged, she refuses and returns to her father's house in Jefferson. He then gets the adolescent granddaughter of his lackey Wash JONES with child, but when she delivers a girl he rejects and insults her. The betrayal enrages Jones. He attacks Sutpen with a rusted scythe and kills him.

Sutpen never knows where he failed. General Jason Lycurgus COMPSON II, to whom he confides, thinks his trouble was innocence. Sutpen believes he failed, not through moral retribution, not even through bad luck, but because he had made a miscalculation somewhere along the way.

Sutpen also appears in *The UNVANQUISHED, GO DOWN, MOSES, REQUIEM FOR A NUN* and *The REIVERS*.

Sutpen's Hundred   Fictional place in *ABSALOM, ABSALOM!*, Sutpen's Hundred is Thomas SUTPEN's plantation in YOKNAPATAWPHA COUNTY 12 miles northwest of JEFFERSON, MISSISSIPPI. Sutpen acquired the land from the CHICKASAW INDIANS in 1833, tore a plantation out of the wilderness and, with the unwilling assistance of a French architect, built an enormous house.

The mansion falls into disrepair after the Civil War. When Miss Rosa COLDFIELD takes Quentin COMPSON to Sutpen's Hundred in September 1910, the roofline sags, the chimneys are half-toppled, and the steps are rotting away. In December 1910, Clytemnestra SUTPEN, Sutpen's daughter by a slave woman, sets fire to the rotted shell, destroying Thomas Sutpen's creation utterly.

Sutterfield, Rev. Toby   An African-American stable hand in *A FABLE* who, with the British groom Mr. HARRY (which Sutterfield pronounces "Mistairy"), is traveling with a marvelously swift racehorse via railway through a Mississippi swamp when the train is derailed and one of the horse's legs is badly injured. Because both Sutterfield and Mr. Harry believe the horse should continue doing what it does best—racing and winning—rather than be destroyed or put out to stud, they steal the horse and doctor it as best they can. The horse then races at small tracks across the southeastern United States against competition which, for the most part, it can outrun on its three good legs. During this nomadic existence, Sutterfield, a self-ordained country minister, baptizes Mr. Harry, who in turn makes Sutterfield a Mason. This connection is important later in the novel when Mr. Harry returns to England to become a soldier known as the SENTRY. As a soldier, Mr. Harry has a kind of hypnotic hold over the men in his regiment who are willing to invest their pay with him. Sutterfield gains the confidence of a wealthy American woman whose son had been killed in the air war above France. He convinces her to support an organization, *Les Amis Myriades et Anonymes à la France de Tout le Monde* (The Many and Anonymous Friends of France throughout the World), that he creates to promote peace. While traveling in France, and now called Monsieur Tooleyman (a corruption of *Tout le Monde*), Sutterfield finds the sentry but is rebuffed by his former comrade. Another soldier, the RUNNER, discovers the connection between Sutterfield and the sentry and uses it to get the sentry's assistance in his campaign to turn the impromptu ceasefire, brought about by the French regiment's mutiny, into a permanent peace. Sutterfield, the sentry, and the runner lead a battalion of British troops into no-man's-land, where they lay down their weapons and are greeted by similarly disarmed German soldiers. The high commands on both sides, however, crush this peace movement by ordering a barrage on the unarmed men in no-man's-land, and both Sutterfield and the sentry are killed.

Sylvester's John   Character in "A COURTSHIP" (in *Collected Stories*). A young CHICKASAW INDIAN, he shows an interest in Herman BASKET's beautiful sister until the powerful IKKEMOTUBBE begins to court her.

Tallahatchie River The stream rises in southern Tippah County in northern Mississippi and flows 230 miles south and southwest, joining the Yalobusha to form the Yazoo River. The dark, slow-moving Tallahatchie forms all but a few miles of the northern border of LAFAYETTE COUNTY.

The Falkners and other families cooperatively shared a resort dubbed the "Club House," a large two-story cabin in the bottomlands where the Tippah River flows into the larger Tallahatchie. Faulkner used to hunt and fish there as a boy.

On Faulkner's hand-drawn map of his fictional Mississippi geography (see *Absalom, Absalom!*), the Tallahatchie forms the northern boundary of YOKNAPATAWPHA COUNTY. The BIG BOTTOM, the wilderness site of Major DE SPAIN's hunting camp in *GO DOWN, MOSES* and *The TOWN*, is in the Tallahatchie region.

Talliaferro, Ernest Character in *MOSQUITOES*. A northern Alabama native whose real name is Tarver, he is a 38-year-old widower and a former clerk in the women's clothing section of a department store. With a veneer of sophistication, he rises to the position of factotum to the wealthy Mrs. MAURIER. The novelist Dawson FAIRCHILD advises him mischievously about women.

"The Tall Men" *(Collected Stories)* Short story of an official who, seeking to arrest two young men for failing to register for the World War II draft, finds a family both opposed to the government and highly patriotic. Old Deputy Marshal GOMBAULT accompanies Mr. PEARSON, a young state draft investigator, who contemptuously assumes the McCallums are typical of those who take advantage of New Deal relief and farm subsidy programs.

When the two arrive to serve the warrant, they find a medical emergency. Buddy MCCALLUM, the boys' father, has mangled his leg in a mill accident. Attended by the doctor and surrounded by his older brothers, he orders his twins, Anse and Lucius MCCALLUM, to go to MEMPHIS to enlist. The two immediately leave to do so, ignoring Pearson's protests. Gombault helps him grasp the hard-working clan's strong individualism and sense of responsibility. After Buddy's leg is amputated, Gombault buries it and is himself revealed as one of the "tall" men.

The story first was published in the *SATURDAY EVENING POST* (May 31, 1941).

Tate One of the three flight commanders in the short story "WITH CAUTION AND DISPATCH."

Tennie *See* BEAUCHAMP, TENNIE.

Terrel *See* BEAUCHAMP, TOMEY'S TURL.

Terrel, Bill Character in *KNIGHT'S GAMBIT* ("Monk"). A convict serving a 20-year term for manslaughter, he incites the slow-witted Stonewall Jackson (Monk) ODLETHROP to murder Warden C. L. GAMBRELL in revenge for Gambrell's twice denying him parole.

"That Evening Sun" *(Collected Stories)* Short story about the Compsons' sometime black replacement cook, Nancy (MANNINGOE), who is neurotically frightened of the dark because she is convinced that her absent husband, JESUS, will come and kill her during the night for having been unfaithful to him. The story's title is taken from the first lines of W. C. HANDY's song "St. Louis Blues": "I hates to see that evening sun go down." Nancy has prostituted herself to Mr. STOVALL, a bank cashier and deacon in the Baptist Church, and is pregnant with his child. Knowing that she cannot sleep at the Compsons', where she will be out of danger, she talks the Compson children—Quentin, Caddy, and Jason (Richmond) COMPSON—into accompanying her to her cabin, where she nervously tries to entertain them with stories and popcorn. When Mr. (Jason Richmond) COMPSON realizes that his children are at Nancy's, he fetches them home and attempts to persuade Nancy to go to Aunt RACHEL's for the night, where she will be safe. She does not go.

The story is narrated 15 years later by Quentin, who was nine at the time. The Compson children were previously introduced in *The SOUND AND THE FURY* (1929). Although he and his seven-year-old sister, Caddy, sensed Nancy's fears and anxieties, they had only a vague idea of what was happening in Nancy's life and virtually no understanding of the details. The five-year-old Jason is even less aware. In the short story, Faulkner skillfully blends the children's younger personalities into the kind of adults they become. Their parents' personalities are also vividly drawn.

"That Evening Sun" is an adept and convincing presentation of the overwhelming effect of terror on a person troubled with guilt and convinced that she is about to be vindictively killed by her estranged husband. But despite the evocation of what Irving HOWE called "an aura of primitive fear," the story, according to Howe, is not ultimately about the drama between Nancy and her husband, but instead about "the moral stamina of the Compsons" and "their reactions to the closeness of death" (*William Faulkner: A Critical Study*, p. 266). "That Evening Sun" and "RED LEAVES," Howe suggests, are Faulkner's best stories and can arguably be called great.

"That Evening Sun" was first published under a slightly different title, "That Evening Sun Go Down," in the March 1931 issue of the *American Mercury* (22), 257–67; a revision titled "That Evening Sun" was reprinted in *These 13* (1931), *A Rose for Emily and Other Stories by William Faulkner* (1945), *The PORTABLE FAULKNER* (1946) *COLLECTED STORIES OF WILLIAM FAULKNER* (1950), *THE FAULKNER READER* (1954), *A Rose for Emily* (1956), and *Selected Short Stories of William Faulkner* (1962). For more information, see *Selected Letters of William Faulkner*, pp. 48–49, 91, 208, 278; *Faulkner in the University*, pp. 21, 79; and Diane Brown Jones, *A Reader's Guide to the Short Stories of William Faulkner*, pp. 267–316.

"That Will Be Fine" *(Collected Stories)* A short story that deals with the effects of Uncle RODNEY's womanizing and thievery. The story is narrated by Uncle Rodney's seven-year-old nephew, GEORGIE. Uncle Rodney has a reputation in his family for borrowing money he does not repay and for making promises he does not keep. He also has a reputation around MOTTSTOWN as a lady's man, which proves fatal by the end of the story. The family's Christmas holiday at Uncle Rodney's father's house in Mottstown is upset by the looming revelation of Uncle Rodney's misdeeds. Uncle Rodney's sister (Georgie's mother) and GEORGE (3) (Georgie's father) are all expected at Grandpa's home for the holiday. Uncle Rodney's other sister, Aunt LOUISA, and her husband, Uncle FRED, live with Grandpa. In the beginning of the story, Uncle Rodney has an urgent need to raise $2,000 to cover his theft of that amount from the Compress Association, where he has been working. Mr. PRUITT, president of the Association, comes with a sheriff to the household to have Uncle Rodney arrested on the charge of theft and forgery. The family persuades Pruitt to give them until Christmas to make good the theft.

Georgie, the narrator, is an ill-tempered and greedy boy who expects to earn something for every deed he does. His focus on making dimes, quarters, and multiples of quarters keeps him from noticing the ethics of what Uncle Rodney is paying him to do, making him a miniature of Uncle Rodney himself. Uncle Rodney has been paying Georgie to help him conduct an affair with Mrs. TUCKER by being the lookout for Mr. TUCKER. Uncle Rodney has also given Georgie money for helping him prize open Grandpa's desk to get whiskey. Georgie helps

his uncle to escape in the expectation of being paid 20 quarters. The boy is unaware of the gravity of the situation, and he unwittingly leads his uncle into an ambush at Mrs. Tucker's house. Uncle Rodney expects to leave town with Mrs. Tucker and her jewelry, but Mr. Tucker and five friends wait in the bushes outside the house. When Uncle Rodney goes to fetch her, the men shoot him dead and carry him off on a window shutter. Ironically, Georgie believes the body, covered with a quilt, is a side of beef intended as a present to his grandfather.

There is grotesque comedy or, more precisely, black humor in "That Will Be Fine." In his assessment of the story, James Ferguson comments: "Our laughter at the young narrator's unknowing allusion to the body of is uncle as 'a side of beef' . . . is hardly the laughter of delight; this is clearly an instance of very black humor. Moreover, the central ironies of the story derive from the appallingly mercenary and self-centered character of the narrator" (*Faulkner's Short Fiction*, p. 77). "That Will Be Fine" was first published in the July 1935 issue of the *American Mercury* (35), 264–76; it was later reprinted in *COLLECTED STORIES OF WILLIAM FAULKNER*. For further information, see *Selected Letters of William Faulkner*, pp. 91, 95–96, 274, 278; and Diane Brown Jones, *A Reader's Guide to the Short Stories of William Faulkner*, pp. 260–67.

Thelma **(1)** Character in *MOSQUITOES*. A friend of Jenny STEINBAUER, she witnesses a drowning at Mandeville. Jenny mentions her to Patricia ROBYN.

Thelma **(2)** In *The MANSION*, the new girl at Miss Reba RIVERS's brothel in Memphis. One of her first customers is Captain STRUTTERBUCK, who almost cheats her out of her fee.

Theodule A French soldier in *A FABLE* who was killed in 1916 somewhere near Fort Valaumont. His mother goes seeking his body in 1919 after the end of the war and encounters Sergeant LANDRY and his detail. They have been given orders to bring back to Paris the body of an unidentifiable Frenchman for burial in the Tomb of the Unknown Soldier. When she sees Landry's men carrying a body, Theodule's mother is certain it is her son, and she bribes the men with 100 francs to allow her to take the body for burial.

"There Was A Queen" *(Collected Stories)* Short story in which three generations of Sartoris women, white and black, consider the past and cope with disturbing events in the present (1929). The black cook and family pillar ELNORA reflects on those now dead and gone, and on those left in the big house—the wheelchair-bound 90-year-old Miss Jenny DU PRE; Narcissa Benbow SARTORIS, the widow of Miss Jenny's great grandnephew; and Narcissa's 10-year-old son, Benbow SARTORIS.

Elnora's usual contempt toward Narcissa is fueled by Narcissa's mysterious trip to Memphis. Later Elnora prepares supper while repeating the family history yet one more time to her daughter and son, who skeptically interrupts her. Meanwhile Narcissa tells Miss Jenny that she went to Memphis to buy back, with her body, anonymous letters that she had received before her marriage and which, if made public, might damage the family's reputation. Miss Jenny reacts nonjudgmentally, asking to be left alone. As Narcissa and her son dine, Elnora finds Miss Jenny dead by the library window.

Many readers resolve the story's ambiguities with the explanation that Narcissa's immoral, self-serving behavior has shocked Miss Jenny to death and has contributed to the final, irreversible decline of the Sartoris family. Attention to the story's rich symbolic subtext, both pagan and biblical, offers an alternative view. The imagery of rebirth and renewal suggests that Narcissa has passed a test of her resilience; Miss Jenny finally can pass on the torch to a new family guardian and die peacefully.

This first appeared in SCRIBNER'S MAGAZINE (January 1933) and in *Doctor Martino and Other Stories* (1934).

Thisbe, Aunt Character in GO DOWN, MOSES ("The Fire and the Hearth"). Molly BEAUCHAMP thinks of asking Aunt Thisbe to prepare a "sugar-tit" (a pacifier) for her child when she is away nursing one of the Edmonds infants.

Thomas, Son Character in *The REIVERS*. One of the drivers at Maury PRIEST's stable, he has the misfortune of being the one to whom LUDUS (2) confides his negative opinion of Boon HOGGANBECK. Boon shoots at Ludus but misses, and later tells Judge STEVENS that had he been in possession of a second pistol, he would have shot at Son too.

Thompson, Pappy Character in LIGHT IN AUGUST. Joe CHRISTMAS assaults him at a church service after Christmas murders Joanna BURDEN.

Thompson, Roz Character in LIGHT IN AUGUST. The grandson of Pappy THOMPSON, he wants to kill Pappy's assailant, Joe CHRISTMAS. But Christmas strikes first, fracturing Roz's skull with a bench leg as he enters the darkened church.

Thompson's In *The SOUND AND THE FURY*, the restaurant where SPOADE gets two cups of coffee in the morning and puts his socks on while the coffee cools.

Thorndyke, Mr. In *The TOWN,* an Episcopal clergyman in JEFFERSON, MISSISSIPPI. With three other preachers (a Methodist, a Baptist, and a Presbyterian), he visits Gavin STEVENS to suggest that either one or all four

ministers conduct Eula Varner SNOPES's funeral service. His offer, which angers Stevens, is turned down.

Thorpe A British aviator under Major BRIDESMAN's command in *A FABLE*.

Thorpe, Buck Character in KNIGHT'S GAMBIT ("Tomorrow"). A brawler, gambler, and moonshiner known to his friends as Bucksnorter, he comes to a violent end when he runs off with the 17-year-old daughter of a FRENCHMAN'S BEND farmer named BOOKWRIGHT. The outraged father shoots Thorpe, who is found with a half-drawn pistol in his hand.

Thoms, Captain Joe A Delta planter in "Mississippi." After a poor growing season, he pays his tenant farmers $200.

Three Basket Character in "RED LEAVES" (in *Collected Stories*). A CHICKASAW INDIAN, squat, paunchy, and approaching old age, he wears an enameled snuffbox clamped through one ear. Three Basket complains of having to supervise the chief's slaves at their work.

"Thrift" *(Uncollected Stories)* A short story concerning MACWYRGLINCHBEATH, a Scotsman of profound thriftiness, who decides early in his army career during World War I that he will make as good a profit as possible out of being a soldier. When he discovers that Royal Flying Corps personnel are paid a higher rate than infantrymen, he engineers a transfer into the flying corps by deliberately burning his foot. As a mechanic in the RFC, he learns that he can get additional pay by getting flight time, so he attempts to teach himself to fly, wrecking an aircraft in the process. He is so obdurate in his purpose that the RFC officers send him back to England to flight school. He becomes the pilot of an artillery observation airplane, and, in a device Faulkner later uses in the novel *A FABLE*, MacWyrglinchbeath also becomes a kind of insurance agent for another flyer. His pecuniary interest in keeping alive this other unnamed officer causes MacWyrglinchbeath to get into a dogfight with two German fighters; he shoots them down, but his own observer, ROBINSON, is killed. MacWyrglinchbeath becomes famous for his parsimony, which extends to his refusing a commission as a second lieutenant because he has figured out that he will make more money as a warrant officer. The story ends with MacWyrglinchbeath returning to his Highlands farm, where the bulk of his RFC pay awaits him.

The themes of shrewdness and avarice used by Faulkner here and elsewhere (in particular in some episodes dealing with Flem SNOPES) are often presented in a humorous or comic context; and often the humor is allied with the tall tale. "Thrift" was first published on September 6, 1930 in the SATURDAY EVENING POST 203, 16–17, 78, 82; it was reprinted in *O. Henry*

Memorial Award Prize Stories of 1931, edited by Blanche Colton Williams (Garden City: Doubleday, Doran & Co., 1931) and in *UNCOLLECTED STORIES OF WILLIAM FAULKNER.* For more information, see *Selected Letters of William Faulkner,* p. 274, and *Uncollected Stories of William Faulkner,* pp. 700–01. For further information about aircraft and flyers of World War I, see the website http://www.theaerodrome.com.

Thurmond, Richard J.   Business partner of Faulkner's great-grandfather, William C. FALKNER. Thurmond and the Old Colonel quarreled over management and ownership of railroads, and their collaboration broke up in enmity.

Falkner accused Thurmond of cheating him in various business deals; Thurmond hated the noisy and violent Old Colonel. On election day 1889, Thurmond approached him on the Square in OXFORD, MISSISSIPPI, aimed a .44 caliber pistol at his head, and fired. Falkner died the next night. A jury acquitted Thurmond on February 1890.

Thurmond appears as REDLAW in *SARTORIS* and as BEN REDMOND in *The UNVANQUISHED.* Faulkner fictionalizes the killing of the Old Colonel in both novels. In *The UNVANQUISHED,* young Bayard SARTORIS (3) agonizes over whether he should exact revenge for his father's death at Redmond's hands and finally confronts Redmond in his JEFFERSON, MISSISSIPPI, law office.

Till, Emmett   In August 1955, whites accused this 14-year-old black youth from Chicago, who was visiting relatives in Greenwood, Mississippi, of whistling at a white woman and making an obscene remark to her. When the boy disappeared, two male relatives of the woman were charged with his kidnapping and murder.

Faulkner read reports of the lynching while in Rome and immediately issued a statement condemning it.

Mississippi juries acquitted the two whites accused of Till's murder.

Faulkner later revised his attitude on the Till case, another example of his sometimes contradictory public pronouncements on racial issues. In a 1956 radio interview, he said, "The Till boy got himself into a fix, and he almost got what he deserved. But even so you don't murder a child."

Tobe (1)   Character in *SARTORIS.* He is the only man competent to handle the wild stallion that throws young Bayard *SARTORIS (4)* after a wild ride through JEFFERSON, MISSISSIPPI.

Tobe (2)   In *SOLDIERS' PAY,* the Saunderses' black servant.

Tobe (3)   In "A ROSE FOR EMILY," Miss Emily GRIERSON's black servant.

Toinette   Character in "ALL THE DEAD PILOTS" (in *Collected Stories*). A French girl, she is the object of affection of the rival ROYAL AIR FORCE flyers SPOOMER and Johnny SARTORIS.

Tom (1)   Character in *GO DOWN, MOSES* ("The Fire and the Hearth"). A JEFFERSON, MISSISSIPPI, sheriff's deputy, he helps make the case against Lucas BEAUCHAMP and George WILKINS for distilling illegal whiskey.

Tom (2)   A farmer referred to in *THE TOWN.* Legend has it that he gave the banker Colonel John SARTORIS an undecipherable note that the colonel had previously drawn up. Since neither one of them could read, the colonel ripped it up and wrote out another.

Tomey, Aunt (Tomasina)   Character in *GO DOWN, MOSES* ("The Fire and the Hearth" and "The Bear"). A slave, she is the mother of Tomey's Turl (BEAUCHAMP) by the old planter Lucius Quintus Carothers MCCASLIN, and the grandmother of Lucas BEAUCHAMP.

Tomey's Turl   *See* BEAUCHAMP, TOMEY'S TURL.

Tommy   A feebleminded man who works for the bootlegger Lee GOODWIN at OLD FRENCHMAN PLACE in *SANCTUARY.* Though he frightens Temple Drake (STEVENS) at first when she arrives at the hideout, he brings her food and later tries to protect her against the other men, but POPEYE shoots him in the back of the head.

"Tomorrow"   *See* KNIGHT'S GAMBIT.

Tom-Tom   *See* BIRD, TOM TOM.

Tooleyman (Monsieur Tooleyman)   In *A FABLE,* an English mispronunciation of the French expression "Tout le Monde" used by Rev. Toby SUTTERFIELD as a pseudonym while in France. It is derived from *Les Amis Myriades et Anonymes à la France de Tout le Monde,* an organization he heads.

The Town   The second novel of the SNOPES TRILOGY, published on May 1, 1957, 17 years after the first volume, *The HAMLET,* and two years before the third volume, *The MANSION.* As with the first and third volumes, *The Town* is dedicated to Faulkner's close friend Phil STONE, but here with the designation: "He did half the laughing for thirty years." Two of the novel's chapters (1 and 16) are revisions of two short stories Faulkner previously published. "CENTAUR IN BRASS," revised as chapter 1, first appeared in the *American Mercury* 25 (February 1932), 200–10; "MULE IN THE YARD," revised as chapter 16, was first published in *SCRIBNER'S MAGAZINE,* 96 (August 1934), 65–70. In Faulkner's original outline of the novel, this second volume of the trilogy was titled *Rus in Urbe* (see *Selected Letters of William Faulkner*, p. 107).

The early reviews of *The Town* that appeared in prominent journals were at best tepid. Alfred Kazin's assessment of the novel in the *New York Times Book Review* suggested that Faulkner was tired of the YOKNAPATAWPHA COUNTY chronicle, although Faulkner claimed otherwise (*Faulkner in the University*, p. 107).

Despite some critics' view that the novel's characters were more symbols than people, to Faulkner, the characters were real people who changed and grew as he grew older. At the University of Virginia in 1957, he said: "I know more about people than I knew when I first thought of them, and they have become more definite to me as people and that may be what seems like staleness gets into it" (*Faulkner in the University*, p. 108). Faulkner's emotional involvement in the novel is evident from his August 12, 1956, letter to Jean STEIN, in which he writes that he "almost cried" when he wrote one scene, presumably Eula SNOPES's suicide (*Selected Letters*, p. 402).

Whether Faulkner was tired of the Yoknapatawpha County chronicle or not is debatable. Of greater importance is the question of the novel's thematic unity. Although Faulkner's work can at times appear episodic, as in *LIGHT IN AUGUST*, his novels are thematically unified even when he uses the technique of multiple narrators, a device particularly characteristic of his fictional style. In *The Town*, the distinct perspectives the three narrators give on the events they relate also make the novel convincingly realistic. The diversity of seemingly unrelated incidents finds common ground in the narrators' opposition to the invasive force of SNOPESISM, but more significantly in their delineation of the effects of Flem SNOPES's character. Their concentration on his character and its impact on others provides a unity to the narrators' accounts and diversity of views. *The Town* is a novel of character, centered on Flem's and the ethics of greed. The novel also displays Flem's preoccupation with his attempt to gain respectability.

Although the locus of the work is the character of Flem as it is revealed through his schemes and dealings with others, the novel equally portrays the characters of others as they react to him—especially those of the narrators, whose knowledge of the events they retell is conditioned by hearsay, individual bias, and personal speculation. There are 24 chapters that cover a period from 1909—the year when Flem Snopes, his wife, Eula, and her daughter, Linda Snopes (KOHL), arrive in JEFFERSON, MISSISSIPPI,—to about a year after Eula shoots herself in 1927. The youngest narrator, Charles MALLISON, an attentive and imaginative child, is not born until 1915, but he narrates the majority of the chapters, 10 in all (1, 3, 7, 10, 12, 14, 16, 19, 21, 24). Most of the information he receives is from his cousin Gowan STEVENS, who is 13 years old at the beginning of the novel, and from the other two narrators, his uncle Gavin STEVENS and the observant sewing machine agent V. K. RATLIFF. In many respects, then, Mallison is closest to the collective impression of the town itself, as he himself says on the opening page: "So when I say 'we' and 'we thought' what I mean is Jefferson and what Jefferson thought." Gavin, who narrates eight chapters (2, 5, 8, 13, 15, 17, 20, 22), is a romantically idealistic attorney, quixotic in his defense of honor and decency, and engrossed in his opposition to Snopesism. With a Harvard M.A. and Heidelberg Ph.D., Gavin is the town intellectual—sensitive, analytic, and nurturing to Eula's teenage daughter, Linda. The discerning Ratliff, perhaps the most detached and objective of the three, narrates six chapters (4, 6, 9, 11, 18, 23). Together the three narrators provide the filters through which the events of *The Town* are retold and in some cases retold comically.

The plot of the novel is fairly simple. Flem and his family arrive in Jefferson, where, as Faulkner explained in a December 1938 letter to Robert K. HAAS, Flem exploits his wife's adultery to blackmail her lover. As Flem advances he leaves a position to be filled by another newcomer, Snopes. (*Selected Letters of William Faulkner*, p. 107). Flem, however, would just as soon rid Jefferson of any Snopeses who would impede his progress or expect assistance from him. In *The Hamlet*, Flem's indifference to the plight of Mink SNOPES for having murdered Jack HOUSTON is a calculated decision to avoid any contact with a relative charged with a crime. In chapter 10 of *The Town*, Flem goes one step further when he discovers that Montgomery Ward SNOPES's photography studio, the Atelier Monty, is a front for peep shows. For the sake of respectability and the Snopes name, Flem sees to it that Montgomery goes out of business by having him prosecuted for possessing bootleg whiskey, which Flem has planted in Montgomery's studio. This offense is less embarrassing to Flem than having his cousin arrested for showing slides of obscene French postcards. Flem returns Montgomery's studio key, which he took from sheriff Hub HAMPTON's desk drawer, to Gavin's office, and on his way out, the philosophic Gavin comments that Flem clearly cares about justice. But Flem's retort undercuts any virtuous motive behind his actions: "I'm interested in Jefferson. . . . We got to live here" (p. 176).

In accepting his wife's affair with the town's mayor, the bachelor Manfred DE SPAIN, the impotent Flem is attending not vicariously to his wife's sexual gratification but instead to his own exploitative intentions. The whole of Jefferson becomes spectator to a fate beyond its control and can do nothing to prevent the course of events, as Mallison explains midway through chapter 1.

Gavin Stevens, in his Don Quixote role as defender of woman's "virtue and chastity" (p. 76), unsuccessfully tries to protect Eula—whom he loves, without admitting it to himself—from de Spain at the Cotillion Ball. He is no match for de Spain, however, who bloodies his face. Earlier in this same chapter (3), his twin sister, Margaret Stevens MALLISON, sarcastically and almost prophetically remarks to Gowan: "You don't marry Semiramis: you just commit some form of suicide for her" (p. 50). Semiramis is the legendary founder and queen of Babylon, known for her beauty and sexuality. Gavin's romanticized love for Eula—he sees her as Helen of Troy, Venus, and Lilith all in one—becomes an obstacle to any sexual relationship they possibly could have had together, and when she offers her body to him in his office one night, he refuses. He does not want to be pitied, although at first he assumes her offer is a ploy to sway him as city attorney to drop the suit against de Spain and to stop investigating the theft of the brass safety valves at the city's power plant. During his superintendency (a position de Spain arranged while mayor), Flem stole these valves, but the scheme backfired. At the moment of Eula's seduction (and at other times throughout the novel), the emotionally complicated Gavin is a gallant knight in search of an idealized, virtuous love and, to use Cleanth BROOKS's phrase, is treated by Faulkner "as a figure of fun" (see "Passion, Marriage, and Bourgeois Respectability" in *William Faulkner: The Yoknapatawpha Country*, pp. 192–218).

The day after Eula's visit, Gavin withdraws the suit against de Spain and later on withdraws himself from Jefferson itself for several years to study at Heidelberg and to serve as a YMCA secretary during the First World War. After his return from Europe, Gavin's romanticized crusade continues by taking an active role in the education of Eula's 14-year-old daughter, Linda, and by protecting her against Snopesism. His love for Linda is avuncular, although those around him think otherwise, including Eula herself, who at her last meeting with Gavin has him promise that he will marry Linda. Her motive is not totally altruistic; she is also thinking of herself. By having Linda married, Eula would be free to leave Flem for de Spain; she would no longer need to maintain the appearance of a stable home life.

In the end, however, Eula kills herself, an act brutally practical for her. When Faulkner was asked his thoughts on Eula's suicide by a participant at one of the sessions at the University of Virginia, he said she did it for Linda's sake, that Eula believed that it was worse to run off with a lover than to kill herself (*Faulkner at the University*, p. 195). On the day of the funeral, de Spain leaves Jefferson for good.

Prior to Eula's death, Flem gains control over the Sartoris Bank by exposing the long-term affair between Eula and de Spain to Eula's father, Will VARNER. The outraged Varner rushes from his home in FRENCHMAN'S BEND to Jefferson at four A.M. to run them all out of town—de Spain, Eula, and Flem. However, Flem proposes a much different tactic, a self-rewarding one that fits his design. He prefers that Eula and her lover leave

Jefferson for good and that de Spain be forced to sell his bank stock to Flem so that Flem can take over as president. Reluctantly, Varner agrees to the deal. In between time, Flem, who all along had refused to send Linda away to college, fearing that she would get married and no longer be under his authority, eventually gives her his permission to attend the state university in nearby Oxford. Soon after, Linda, duped by Flem's apparent kindness, signs an agreement handing over to him any inheritance money she would get from her mother. "This act, which is crucial to the plot," Edmond L. Volpe writes, echoing the sentiments of many critics, "is contrived and implausible, but it is typical of the plot and character breakdowns in *The Town*" (*A Reader's Guide to William Faulkner*, p. 327). After her mother's suicide, Linda leaves for New York on her own. In the penultimate chapter to the novel, Ratliff offers an ironic commentary on the events in *The Town*. (Chapter 24 of the novel was reprinted as "The Waif" in the *Saturday Evening Post* on May 4, 1957.

For more details, see *Selected Letters of William Faulkner*, and *Faulkner in the University*.

T. P. *See* GIBSON, T. P.

Triplett, Earl Character who runs Uncle Ike MCCASLIN's hardware store in *The SOUND AND THE FURY* (where only his first name is used) and in *The MANSION*. Earl took over the business from McCaslin as Jason COMPSON IV, who started working there while in high school, would later take it over from Earl (*The Mansion*). Though his relationship with Jason is less than congenial, Earl does not divulge to Mrs. COMPSON that Jason used the money she thinks she invested in the hardware store to buy a car.

Trueblood, Ernest V. Pseudonym Faulkner used when he published "AFTERNOON OF A COW." Translation by Maurice Edgar COINDREAU, the short story was first published in French in *Fontaine* 27–28 (June/July 1943), 66–81. Trueblood is also the narrator of the short story.

Trumbull In *The HAMLET*, a blacksmith in FRENCHMAN'S BEND. He ran Will VARNER's blacksmith shop until it was taken over by I. O. SNOPES and his cousin Eck SNOPES. This episode is also referred to in *The TOWN*.

Tubbs, Euphus Character in *INTRUDER IN THE DUST*. The jailer in JEFFERSON, MISSISSIPPI, he reluctantly agrees to do his duty and protect his prisoner, Lucas BEAUCHAMP, a black man accused of killing a white man, should a lynch mob come for him.

In *REQUIEM FOR A NUN*, Tubbs reappears as the Jefferson jailer guarding Nancy MANNIGOE, who is accused of killing Temple Drake STEVENS's baby. In *The MANSION*, he schemes to release Montgomery Ward SNOPES before his bond is posted so he can collect his meal money.

Tubbs, Mrs. Character in INTRUDER IN THE DUST. She is the wife of Euphus TUBBS, the JEFFERSON, MISSISSIPPI, jailer. Mrs. Tubbs also appears in REQUIEM FOR A NUN and *The MANSION*. In *the MANSION*, Euphus has Montgomery Ward SNOPES, who is waiting to be sentenced, help Mrs. Tubbs either in her kitchen or with her vegetable garden.

Tucker, Mr. Character in "THAT WILL BE FINE" (in *Collected Stories*). A MOTTSTOWN man, he is the husband of one of the women with whom Uncle RODNEY has an affair. When he discovers that his wife is planning to run off with her lover, Uncle Rodney, Mr. Tucker and five of his friends ambush and kill him.

Tucker, Mrs. Character in "THAT WILL BE FINE" (in *Collected Stories*). She is one of Uncle RODNEY's amorous conquests.

Tull (1) Character in "TWO SOLDIERS" (in *Collected Stories*). He is the father of the girls in whom Pete GRIER is interested.

Tull (2) In SANCTUARY, a farmer two miles from OLD FRENCHMAN PLACE. Ruby LAMAR phones the sheriff from his house when TOMMY is murdered. See TULL, VERNON.

Tull (3) Referred to in *The MANSION* as one of the young men interested in courting Eula Varner (SNOPES).

Tull, Cora (Mrs. Vernon) Character in AS I LAY DYING (she narrates chapters 2, 6, and 39), *The HAMLET*, *The MANSION*, and the short story "SPOTTED HORSES" (which Faulkner revised for *The HAMLET*). She also is referred to in *The TOWN*. A pious woman who speaks her mind on religious matters, Cora is Vernon TULL's domineering wife. She is also an overbearing mother to her four daughters. In *As I Lay Dying*, Cora has been friendly with Addie BUNDREN for many years, although there is latent hostility between them. She and two of her daughters attend Addie on her deathbed. In the past, Cora has tried to get Addie to show a more religious spirit.

In *The Hamlet*, she unsuccessfully sues Eck SNOPES for the injuries her husband suffered from one of Eck's wild horses. The judge, however, dismisses the case because Eck was never given a bill of sale for the horse. In *The Town*, her sister's niece is I. O. SNOPES's illegal second wife, and in *The Mansion*, Mink SNOPES assumes that Mrs. Tull wrote the letter his wife sent to him in prison.

Tull, Eula One of Cora and Vernon TULL's daughters in AS I LAY DYING. Eula attends Addie BUNDREN in the last week of her life. It is implied that Eula hopes Darl BUNDREN will marry her.

Tull, Kate One of Cora and Vernon TULL's daughters in AS I LAY DYING. As with her sister Eula, Kate helps care for the dying Addie BUNDREN. Kate looks on Jewel BUNDREN as a potential mate.

Tull, Vernon A character in AS I LAY DYING (in which he narrates chapters 8, 16, 20, 31, 33 and 36), *The HAMLET*, *The TOWN*, and in the short stories "SPOTTED HORSES," "THE HOUND," "LIZARDS IN JAMSHYD'S COURTYARD" (all three revised by Faulkner for *The Hamlet*), "TWO SOLDIERS," and "SHINGLES FOR THE LORD." He also is referred to in *The MANSION*. A farmer in the vicinity of FRENCHMAN'S BEND, Tull is a kind, amiable and mild-mannered man dominated by his wife. He is a compassionate neighbor to the Bundrens and the Griers.

In *As I Lay Dying*, he aids the Bundrens in crossing the Yoknapatawpha River, but he is too shrewd to let them use his mules to ford the swollen river. He helps save Cash BUNDREN and Cash's tools when the Bundren wagon overturns in the water. In *The Hamlet*, he is injured by one of Eck SNOPES's wild ponies, severely enough to be out of work for a few days. In *The Town*, Deewit BINFORD borrows a flashlight from him. In "Shingles for the Lord," Tull is half owner with Pap GRIER of a hunting dog. He is one of the church members who help with the rebuilding of Reverend WHITFIELD's church. Pete GRIER courts his daughters in "Two Soldiers."

When Faulkner revised "Lizards in Jamshyd's Courtyard" for *The Hamlet*, he substituted Tull with Odum BOOKWRIGHT in reference to the men who foolishly dig for buried treasure at the Old Frenchman place.

Turl See BEAUCHAMP, TOMEY'S TURL.

"Turnabout" *(Collected Stories)* Short story of a World War I contest of combat in the air and on the sea. In a French port town (possibly Dunkirk), an American aviator, Captain BOGARD, encounters a young drunken British seaman, Claude HOPE, whom he takes to his air base. There the other Americans contemptuously judge Hope, who exhibits the breezy, self-effacing humor typical of his upper-class background, as weak and naive.

When Bogard takes him along as gunner on a bombing raid, Hope performs competently and is impressed by the coolness of the American crew as they safely land the plane with a bomb precariously dangling from a wing; the flyers had been unaware of this mishap. Hope returns the favor by inviting Bogard along on a daytime raid by his small torpedo boat. Bogard sees that this dangerous mission demands as much, if not more, courage and expertise as his own raids. He becomes sick when, under fire, the torpedo initially fails to disengage and the boat must keep circling its prey, an Argentine wheat freighter in a harbor protected by a German cruiser. At the very last moment, the British blow up the ship. Bogard comes to a disquieting truth:

Combatants are constantly at risk of being betrayed by mechanical malfunctions. A month later, Hope's torpedo boat is reported missing. Shortly afterward, Bogard and his crew are cited for valor for executing a daring daylight raid to destroy an ammunition depot and damage enemy headquarters. Perhaps inspired by Hope or perhaps avenging his death, Bogard imitates torpedo boat tactics in diving close to the target before releasing his bombs. As he does so, he fantasizes that all the military and political leaders from both sides are in the chateau he is attacking.

This story was first published in the SATURDAY EVENING POST (March 5, 1932) and later in *Doctor Martino and Other Stories* (1934). It also was the basis for the 1933 Howard HAWKS film, *Today We Live,* for which Faulkner was co-scriptwriter.

Turpin   In *The MANSION,* a young man in FRENCHMAN'S BEND. When he was trying to avoid the draft, Gavin STEVENS and V. K. RATLIFF looked for him at Mink SNOPES's abandoned and run-down house. On their way to find Mink hiding there years later, Stevens and Ratliff recall the Turpin episode.

Turpin, Buck   In *The SOUND AND THE FURY,* a person in JEFFERSON, MISSISSIPPI, who, according to Jason COMPSON IV is paid $10 from the traveling carnival for the privilege of putting the show on in town.

"Two Dollar Wife"   A short story that deals with irresponsible youth on a spree one New Year's Eve and the consequences of self-indulgent carelessness. Reminiscent of the flappers and swells of the Prohibition era, Doris HOUSTON and her date, Maxwell JOHNS, manage to get very drunk and carry out a wedding using a marriage license obtained sometime before on a dare. Coming back to the Houston house to announce their marriage, they discover that Doris's young brother has almost died from swallowing a needle they negligently left in a chair. The pair are part of a group of unlikable young people, and Faulkner seems to show a disgust with their moonshine- and gambling ways.

James Ferguson considers the story a failed potboiler, and "without question one of the worst pieces of fiction ever produced by a major American writer" (*Faulkner's Short Fiction,* p. 39). "Two Dollar Wife," originally titled "Christmas Tree," was first published in *College Life* 18 (January 1936), 8–10, 85, 86, 88, 90. It is reprinted in UNCOLLECTED STORIES OF WILLIAM FAULKNER. For more information, see *Selected Letters of William Faulkner,* p. 77, and *Uncollected Stories of William Faulkner,* pp. 701–02.

"Two Soldiers"   A short story set at the very beginning of World War II, concerning a young boy who refuses to be separated from his older brother, Pete GRIER, when Pete enlists in the army following the Japanese attack on Pearl Harbor. The boy, not quite nine years old, is the narrator of the story. Having no comprehension of the seriousness of war or the workings of the army, he understands only that his brother is gone, and that that is too much for him. The day after Pete leaves to join the army, the narrator makes his way from his home in FRENCHMAN'S BEND to Memphis, alone, with the intent of also enlisting so that he can act as his brother's helper. Finding the army enlistment office, the ingenuous narrator demands to be allowed to join his brother, but of course is prevented from doing so by the authorities. Pete is called into the office to talk to him, and he impresses upon his younger brother the need to take care of the farm and their parents. The narrator's earnestness touches everyone he meets. He is fed lunch by Mrs. MCKELLOGG, the wife of an army officer, and later in the day is driven back to Frenchman's Bend by a soldier. During the car ride, the young narrator breaks down and cries, without ever knowing quite why. (See the companion story, "SHALL NOT PERISH," in which the Grier family receives the news that Pete has been killed in the war.)

In "Two Soldiers," Faulkner undoubtedly was expressing some of his own sentiments about Pearl Harbor and the war effort to such an extent that some readers may consider the story too patently patriotic to be good literature and the young narrator's voice, as Joseph BLOTNER mentions, "overwrought and artificial" (*Faulkner: A Biography,* p. 436).

"Two Soldiers" was first published on March 28, 1942, in the SATURDAY EVENING POST 214, 9–11, 35–36, 38, 40; it was reprinted in COLLECTED STORIES OF WILLIAM FAULKNER and in *Selected Short Stories of William Faulkner.* For more information, see *Selected Letters of William Faulkner,* pp. 169, 184, 191–92, 274, 278, and Diane Brown Jones, *A Reader's Guide to the Short Stories of William Faulkner,* pp. 64–72.

U

"Uncle Willy" Short story in which Jefferson do-gooders try to reform the town ne'er-do-well, who is aided in his escape by a 14-year-old boy. Uncle Willy CHRISTIAN is a morphine addict who indulges his habit in front of the town boys he befriends. After church members force him to give up his addiction, he switches to alcohol. He returns from a MEMPHIS drinking spree with a prostitute as a wife.

After she is paid off and sent away, Uncle Willy is confined to an institution. While there, he manages to sell his holdings for cash, which he spends on an airplane. His plan is to set out for California with his black employees, the old handyman JOB and the driver SECRETARY. The flight instructor will not teach him without a medical certificate, so Uncle Willy has Secretary take the lessons in order to then teach him. Summoned by Uncle Willy, the boy runs away to join the trio as they set out from Memphis. Job, alarmed by the foolhardiness of the scheme, phones Jefferson for help to stop Uncle Willy. Before the rescuers arrive, Uncle Willy dies while trying to fly solo in the plane. This contest of small-town values with the individual rights of a resolute nonconformist yields no clear winner.

This story was first published in *American Mercury* (October 1935).

Uncollected Stories of William Faulkner A collection of 45 stories published by RANDOM HOUSE in 1979, and reissued as a centenary edition by Vintage International in 1997. Edited with an introduction, notes, and bibliography by Joseph BLOTNER, the volume contains uncollected stories (i.e., those not found in *COLLECTED STORIES OF WILLIAM FAULKNER*), never-before-published stories, and stories Faulkner revised for books (*The UNVANQUISHED, The HAMLET, GO DOWN, MOSES, BIG WOODS,* and *The MANSION*). (See Appendix I for titles and see entries for individual stories.)

In his introduction to the collection, Blotner rightly points out that the stories taken as a whole "present a view of Faulkner's developing art over a span of thirty years" (p. xv). Although some of the stories differ remarkably from one another and clearly show an apprentice at work, others clearly demonstrate Faulkner's strengths and success at writing short stories. The collection readily makes accessible to readers and students of Faulkner stories that would otherwise be difficult to track down.

United Daughters of the Confederacy An organization, still existant, of southern women formed to nurture memories of the Civil War. Local chapters sponsored aid programs for ex-soldiers and widows, arranged celebrations of Confederate heroes, and campaigned for memorial monuments.

Faulkner's grandmother, Sallie Murry FALKNER, served a term as president of the Albert Sidney Johnston Chapter. She quit the UDC in 1910 in a disagreement over the placement of the OXFORD, MISSISSIPPI, Confederate monument. Miss Sally favored the Courthouse Square; the committee opted for a site on the UNIVERSITY OF MISSISSIPPI campus.

University Greys A volunteer infantry company composed of students of the UNIVERSITY OF MISSISSIPPI, formed at the outset of the Civil War in 1861. In *ABSALOM, ABSALOM!*, Henry SUTPEN and Charles BON join the Greys after the first battle of BULL RUN.

The Confederate diehards of OXFORD, MISSISSIPPI, later boasted that the University Greys reached the high point of the Confederacy, about 50 yards beyond the advance of any other of General George C. PICKETT's troops at Gettysburg on July 3, 1863.

University of Mississippi A state university, founded in OXFORD, MISSISSIPPI, in 1848, known as Ole Miss, and a center of Faulkner scholarship. Falkners attended Ole Miss beginning with Faulkner's grandfather, J. W. T. FALKNER. Estelle Oldham (FAULKNER), the novelist's future wife, enrolled as a special student in 1915, and Faulkner attended classes sporadically in 1919–20.

Faulkner's father, Murry C. FALKNER, an Ole Miss dropout, became university secretary and business manager in December 1918. Faulkner's first published works—two drawings—appeared in the Ole Miss yearbook around that time. Faulkner himself enrolled as a nondegree student in English and foreign languages at age 22. There he acquired his Oxford nickname "Count No 'count," a reference to his notorious dandyism.

Faulkner's short story "Landing in Luck," about an air cadet's first solo flight, appeared in the student newspaper, *The MISSISSIPPIAN*, in November 1919, and he published critical articles there. But the university refused a copy of his first novel, *SOLDIERS' PAY*, in 1926.

Though Faulkner dropped out of Ole Miss for good in November 1920, his connection with the university did not cease. In the late 1920s, he worked the night shift in the university's power plant and wrote most of *AS I LAY DYING* (1930) on the job.

Faulkner reluctantly agreed in the spring of 1947 to address English classes at Ole Miss. On a promise that no faculty would be present and no notes would be taken, he spoke to six classes in April, talking about his writing and his contemporaries' achievement. In one session, he rated the leading writers of his generation, placing Ernest HEMINGWAY near the bottom of the list of five or six for an alleged lack of artistic courage. Faulkner's musings became public, deeply wounding Hemingway when they reached him.

Racial conflict convulsed Ole Miss during the Civil Rights era. Serious rioting erupted there in the autumn of 1962 when James Meredith, an African American, attempted to enroll. Two people were killed and more than 300 injured, and university buildings were damaged when white opponents of integration went on a rampage.

The university today maintains an important collection of Faulkner manuscripts and other material, and for more than a quarter century has been the site of an ANNUAL FAULKNER AND YOKNAPATAWPHA CONFERENCE. It owns and maintains ROMAN OAK.

University of Texas   A major research university in Austin, Texas. The university library built up a collection of Faulkner material in the 1950s at the instigation of James MERIWETHER, a faculty member and leading Faulkner textual scholar.

Faulkner on the campus of the University of Virginia. (William Faulkner Collection, Special Collections Department, Manuscripts Division, University of Virginia Library. Photo by Ralph Thompson.)

Faulkner made it clear, however, that he did not want his manuscripts to go to Texas, preferring HARVARD UNIVERSITY—as the country's oldest and most prestigious university—instead. Texas also houses the papers of Carvel Collins, one of the first Faulkner scholars, along with those of Joseph BLOTNER and James MERIWETHER.

University of Virginia   A state university and a major research center in Charlottesville, founded by Thomas Jefferson and others in 1825. Faulkner was writer in residence there in 1957–58, and the university maintains an important Faulkner archive.

Faulkner got his first view of the university in October 1931 at a southern writers conference, where he was treated as a major figure on the strength of *The SOUND AND THE FURY* (1929) and *SANCTUARY* (1931). Always ill at ease in such gatherings, he drank heavily through this one before his publisher, Harrison SMITH, could spirit him away to New York.

The university offered Faulkner the writer in residence post in 1956 with a salary of $2,500. He accepted at once, in part because his daughter, Jill FAULKNER, her husband, and their first child were established in Charlottesville. He arrived to take up his duties in February 1957.

Faulkner met with graduate and undergraduate classes, mostly in question-and-answer sessions. Asked at one session to describe his aims, he replied: "A writer wants to make something that he knows that a hundred or two hundred or five hundred, a thousand years later will make people feel what they feel when they read Homer, or read Dickens or Balzac, Tolstoy" (*Faulkner in the University,* 61).

Two University of Virginia faculty members, Frederick L. Gwynn and Joseph BLOTNER, recorded many of the sessions. Their edited transcripts were published as *Faulkner in the University* in 1959.

The Unvanquished   A novel in the YOKNAPATAWPHA COUNTY cycle, set in northern Mississippi during the Civil War and Reconstruction. Published in 1938, it fills out the Sartoris history that Faulkner sketched in *SARTORIS* (1930). Some critics dismiss *The Unvanquished* as a set of conventionally romantic Civil War tales peopled with stereotypical brave Confederate cavalrymen, indomitable women back home on the plantation, and loyal, self-sacrificing African-American servants.

The novel is the first of three—*The HAMLET* (1940) and *GO DOWN, MOSES* (1942) were to follow—to be spun out of material Faulkner had developed earlier. It consists of a sequence of six stories published in glossy magazines between September 1934 and December 1936, with a seventh, "An Odor of Verbena," written specifically to close out the volume. All seven sections are told from the point of view of young Bayard SARTORIS (3). Most commentators agree there is sufficient

Faulkner conducted a series of question-and-answer sessions at the University of Virignia, later collected in Faulkner in the University. (William Faulkner Collection, Special Collections Department, Manuscripts Division, University of Virginia Library. Photo by Ralph Thompson.)

continuity of characters, situations, and themes to classify *The Unvanquished* as a novel.

RANDOM HOUSE showed interest in publishing the Bayard-Ringo stories (so called after young Sartoris and his African-American childhood friend Ringo STROTHER) as a set in the spring of 1937. Two major thematic lines link the pieces: the war and its shattered aftermath, and the growing up of two boys. The publisher probably reasoned, too, that the stories would have broad appeal, since all but one of the first six had been published in the mass-circulation *SATURDAY EVENING POST*.

In Hollywood writing for films, Faulkner re-read the previously published stories and began the task of synthesis and revision, toning down comic or farcical elements and making other changes with a view to turning the collection into serious literature. The new story, "An Odor of Verbena," the longest of the seven at

12,500 words, carried the action into Reconstruction and the adulthood of Bayard and Ringo, tying the strands of the earlier stories together and providing the novel's climax. Faulkner continued the work on his return to OXFORD, MISSISSIPPI, in mid-August, and put his final touches on the manuscript in an office at Random House in New York in October.

The first story, "Ambuscade," published in the *Post* in September 1934, introduces Bayard and Ringo, both 12 years old, just after the fall of the strategic fortress of Vicksburg in July 1863. The setting is the SARTORIS plantation; Colonel John SARTORIS's mother-in-law, Rosa MILLARD, manages the place while he is off fighting in the war. The action involves the boys' firing at a Yankee officer, then hiding under the flowing skirts of Granny Millard when the enemy comes to investigate. For the novel, Faulkner added clarifying passages and

Faulkner at the University of Virginia, site of an important Faulkner archive. (William Faulkner Collection, Special Collections Department, Manuscripts Division, University of Virignia Library. Photo by Ralph Thompson.)

filled out the portrait of Colonel Sartoris, with the aim of building him into a more imposing figure.

In "Retreat," the second story, the Confederate cause is nearly lost, the Yankees are swarming, and Granny Rosa is worried about the family silver. A Union patrol confiscates two Sartoris mules, Old Hundred and Tinny; the boys help Colonel Sartoris's partisans capture some Yankees; the enemy in retribution burns the Sartoris plantation; the slave LOOSH leads the Yankees to the treasure and walks away from Sartoris a free man. In revising, Faulkner added six pages limning two characters who figure importantly in his later fiction, the twins Buck and Buddy MCCASLIN.

"Raid," the third story, finds Granny and the boys pursuing the federal troops into Alabama in search of compensation for the mules, the silver, and two "runaways," Loosh and PHILADELPHY. They stop over briefly at the Hawkhurst plantation, where cousin Drusilla Hawk (SARTORIS), whose fiancé has been killed at SHILOH, burns for revenge. Drusilla dresses like a man, rides well, and is willing to learn to shoot and wants to enlist in Colonel Sartoris's cavalry. Miss Rosa tracks

down the Union Colonel Nathaniel DICK, who agrees to provide compensation. Through a comedy of errors involving a play on the mules' names, he gives Miss Rosa a chit for 110 mules, 110 runaways, and 10 chests of silver. Here Granny, accepting the Yankees' overpayment, takes her first steps in straying from the strict code of behavior that has governed her life.

The first three stories appeared in the *Post* in the autumn of 1934. By then, Faulkner had written and sent on to the magazine the fourth and fifth stories in the series. The fourth, "Riposte in Tertio" (originally titled "The Unvanquished"), introduces Ab SNOPES, the father of the imperishable Flem SNOPES of the SNOPES TRILOGY. Ab sells the compensatory mules and horses back to the Federals, eventually turning a profit for Miss Rosa of nearly $7,000. Though Granny uses some of the money to help out those the war has made destitute, it has corrupted her and made her arrogant. Her explanation to God is more defiant than penitent as she explains that she has sinned to help the less fortunate.

Ab Snopes persuades Granny to use a forged federal order to seize four horses from a bushwhacker gang known as Grumby's Independents. Bayard and Ringo try to stop her, but she insists on going through with this last crooked deal. GRUMBY sees through the con and murders her at the appointed meeting place, an abandoned cotton compress.

Revenge is the theme and plot of the fifth story, "Vendée." Bayard and Ringo track down Grumby; Bayard shoots him. The boys stake his corpse to the door of the cotton compress, cut off his right hand, and nail it to Granny's wooden grave marker. Then the boys burst into tears.

"Skirmish at Sartoris" (originally titled "Drusilla" and first published in SCRIBNER'S MAGAZINE in 1935), the sixth story, recounts Colonel Sartoris's election-day shooting of the carpetbagger Calvin BURDEN and his grandson, a double homicide first related in *LIGHT IN AUGUST* (1932). By now, the ex-soldier Drusilla has come to live platonically at Sartoris and help the colonel restore the plantation. As a comic counterpoint, the ladies of JEFFERSON, MISSISSIPPI, believing Drusilla compromised, force her into marriage with the colonel. The ending is conventionally happy: the interfering carpetbaggers are confounded, and Drusilla and Sartoris are joined.

The mood darkens in the concluding story, "An Odor of Verbena," which recounts the killing of John Sartoris and the demand for revenge that falls on Bayard, now 24 years old. Ben REDMOND, Sartoris's business and political rival, shoots the colonel in the Jefferson square, an incident modeled on the murder in 1889 of Faulkner's grandfather, W. C. FALKNER.

Here Faulkner alludes to events in earlier stories and shows Bayard contemplating his violent, driven father's war career, his railroad-building, his forays into politics.

Right or wrong, Colonel Sartoris acts for the good of the community as he sees it, he and his admirers claim. But unlike Thomas SUTPEN, who makes a brief appearance in the story, Sartoris is no innocent; he recognizes he has done wrong to Redmond and others. Sensing the approach of death, he hints at as much to his son.

Drusilla, with her "rapport for violence," insists that Bayard kill his father's murderer, just as he had killed Grumby to revenge his grandmother; so too does George WYATT, one of his father's veterans and a sort of spokesman for Jefferson manhood. Even Aunt Jenny DU PRE, who rejects the old southern eye-for-an-eye code, understands finally that Bayard must face Redmond.

But he takes his revenge in his own way. Like his father, Bayard decides to approach Redmond unarmed. Like Aunt Jenny, he has rejected the code. He climbs the wooden stairs up to Redmond's second-floor office and stares him down. Redmond fires twice, missing intentionally, then rises, closes up the office, walks down to the depot, boards the southbound train, and leaves Jefferson forever. The widow Drusilla exits too, to live with relatives in Alabama. She leaves behind for Bayard a sprig of verbena, symbolic of optimism and renewal.

The critic Cleanth BROOKS characterized *The Unvanquished* as "a novel about growing up—it is the story of an education." The final story draws together the themes of the preceding ones and confirms Bayard's passage into adulthood. The confrontation with Redmond, in Brooks's words, "is the concluding act in his long initiation into the moral responsibility that goes with manhood."

Random House published *The Unvanquished,* with black-and-white drawings by Edward Shenton, in February 1938. The early notices were more favorable than usual with a new Faulkner work, perhaps because the book made fewer demands on the reviewer. *Time* saw in the novel "something of the air of Two Little Confederates as it might have been rewritten by an author aware of the race problem, economics and Freudian psychology." The reviewer for the hometown OXFORD EAGLE expressed undisguised relief: "Oxonians who . . . have found his writing too involved for their minds to follow or his subjects too revolting for them to stomach, will find here a book that they can understand, can enjoy, can leave lying on their living room tables," Dale Mullen wrote.

Brooks regarded the novel as undervalued, but most later critics grade *The Unvanquished* a minor work. Irving HOWE thought it betrayed its origin as a set of stories for glossy magazines, despite the undoubted power of some of the episodes: blacks trailing in the wake of the Union army in a mass movement toward freedom, for example, or Bayard's rejection of the southern code of violence. "When so much of the action is presented in a slick and jolly manner, no adequate treatment is possible of such themes as civil war, the disruption of a society, and the cost of immoral behavior in behalf of urgent human needs," Howe wrote.

Random House's hopes that *The Unvanquished* would have mass appeal were unrealized, at least initially. By June 1940, nearly two and a half years after its publication, the novel had earned Faulkner only $2,327.

Van One of the bootleggers at OLD FRENCHMAN PLACE in *SANCTUARY*. He badly beats up the drunken Gowan STEVENS and knocks him out; but when he tries to take sexual advantage of Temple Drake (STEVENS), Lee GOODWIN overpowers him.

Van Dyming Character in "FOX HUNT" (in *Collected Stories*). He is said to be interested in buying Steve GAWTREY's nonexistent horse; the valet ERNIE plants the notion on his boss, Harrison BLAIR.

Van Dyming, Carleton Character in "BLACK MUSIC" (in *Collected Stories*). A wealthy financier, he buys an estate in Virginia and indulges his wife Mattie's ambition to put up classical-style buildings modeled on the Acropolis and the Colisseum on the property.

Van Dyming, Matilda (Mattie) Character in "BLACK MUSIC" (in *Collected Stories*). The former Matilda Lumpkin of Poughkeepsie, New York, she marries the rich New York financier Carleton VAN DYMING and talks him into putting up classical-style buildings on their newly acquired Virginia estate.

Wilfred MIDGLESTON, a draftsman working for Van Dyming's architect, has a strange experience in which he imagines himself a faun. Naked and carrying a tin whistle that Mrs. Van Dyming mistakes for a knife, he chases her into the Virginia woods. She flees in terror, with the faun and her husband's prize bull in pursuit, and finally faints. The "madman" vanishes without a trace.

Van Tosch Character in *The REIVERS*. He owns Coppermine (Lightning), a race horse that refuses to run for him. Van Tosch's employee Bobo BEAUCHAMP steals the animal as part of an elaborate scheme to discharge his $128 debt to a White man.

Later, in PARSHAM, TENNESSEE, Van Tosch agrees to let Coppermine race a fourth heat in hopes of learning Ned MCCASLIN's secret for making him run.

Vardaman, James K. (1861–1930) Lawyer, newspaper editor, and politician. He led the "revolt of the rednecks" against Mississippi's planter-dominated Democratic Party machine during the first decade of the 20th century.

A flamboyant demagogue, Vardaman sprang from the small-farmer class of the Mississippi hill country. He had reforming instincts as governor from 1904 to 1908, but the reforms he supported were for whites only. He opposed even rudimentary state aid for black schools, saying education would "spoil a good field hand and make an insolent cook." He closed down the state's teacher training school for blacks, literally padlocking the doors.

An observer said of Vardaman, "He stood for the poor white against the 'nigger'—those were his qualifications as a stateman."

J. W. T. FALKNER Jr., Faulkner's paternal grandfather, supported Vardaman. Falkner headed OXFORD, MISSISSIPPI's, Vardaman Club and campaigned for him during his successful run for the U.S. Senate, where he served from 1913 to 1919. A Vardaman BURDEN appears in *AS I LAY DYING*, and the novelist names one of the extensive poor white Gowrie clan of *INTRUDER IN THE DUST* after Mississippi politician.

Varner, Eula *See* SNOPES, EULA VARNER.

Varner, Jody Character in *AS I LAY DYING*, *LIGHT IN AUGUST*, *The HAMLET*, *The TOWN*, *The MANSION*, and the short stories "FOOL ABOUT A HORSE" and "SPOTTED HORSES" (both of which were revised for *The Hamlet*). According to *As I Lay Dying*, Jody—Will VARNER's ninth of 16 children—was born in 1888, the year the bridge that is washed away was first built (p. 89). He is the only one of Varner's children to live at home as an adult, and helps in his father's business matters. In *Light in August*, Jody, clerking at his father's store, tells Lena GROVES that the fellow working at the planning mill is named Bunch, not Burch; he then sells her crackers, cheese, and a 15-cent box of "sour-deans" (sardines).

In *The Hamlet*, Jody is responsible for renting a farm to the tenant farmer (and reputed barn-burner) Ab SNOPES and for hiring his son Flem SNOPES as a clerk in the Varner store. Jody is also responsible for making sure that his sister Eula Varner (SNOPES), unlike their mother, gets at least some formal education. In one of the funnier passages in *The Hamlet*, when Eula is found to be pregnant, Jody becomes so irate about defending the honor of the Varner name that he has to be subdued by his father and his gun taken away. In *The Man-*

sion, Jody explains to his niece, Linda Snopes KOHL, Flem's scheme to have Montgomery Ward SNOPES sent to the state penitentiary at PARCHMAN and Flem's role in Mink SNOPES's futile attempt at escaping (p. 367).

Varner, Mrs. (Maggie) Minor character in *AS I LAY DYING, The HAMLET, The TOWN, The MANSION* and *FATHER ABRAHAM* (fragment of a novel Faulkner incorporated into *The Hamlet*). She is Will VARNER's wife, and mother of 16 children (including Jody and Eula). One of the finest housewives in the area, she wins prizes at the annual county fair for preserving fruits and vegetables. In *The Hamlet,* V. K. RATLIFF refers to her as Miss Maggie (86).

Varner, Will (Uncle Billy) Character in many of Faulkner's works: *LIGHT IN AUGUST, The HAMLET, INTRUDER IN THE DUST, The TOWN, The MANSION, FLAGS IN THE DUST,* and in the stories "SPOTTED HORSES," "THE HOUND," "LIZARDS IN JAMSHYD'S COURTYARD," "FOOL ABOUT A HORSE" (all four revised by Faulkner for *The Hamlet*), "Tomorrow" (in *Knight's Gambit*), "SHINGLES FOR THE LORD" and "By the People" (revised for *The Mansion*). Varner is also referred to in *AS I LAY DYING;* a neighbor of the Bundrens and a horse doctor, he sets Cash BUNDREN's broken leg after the Bundrens' wagon overturns as they attempt to cross the swollen Yoknapatawpha River.

Will is a robust and Rabelaisian man, father of 16 children, fountainhead of advice, and a practical-minded individual with diverse business interests. Of his 16 children, only Jody VARNER and his sister Eula Varner (SNOPES) (until her wedding midway through *The Hamlet*) remain at home. Although lazy by natural temperament, Varner is active in the life of the community at FRENCHMAN'S BEND. The 60-year-old Varner is identified in *The Hamlet* as a veterinarian, usurer, holder of mortgages, supervisor and largest landholder in one county, justice of the peace in another county, and election commissioner in both. In addition to owning the store in Frenchman's Bend, the cotton gin, and the combined grist mill and blacksmith shop, he held title to the OLD FRENCHMAN PLACE before signing it over to Flem SNOPES and his daughter Eula on the day of their wedding. In the second novel of the SNOPES TRILOGY, *The Town,* the reader learns that Varner owns one of the three biggest blocks of stock in Colonel Sartoris's bank in JEFFERSON, MISSISSIPPI, making it possible for his son-in-law Flem to become the bank's president when Manfred DE SPAIN is forced to resign. When Varner learns that Manfred and Eula have had a long-term affair and that his granddaughter Linda has signed over her inheritance to Flem (whom Varner has purposely kept out of his will), he becomes so enraged that he charges into Jefferson at four o'clock in the morning to have it out with Eula, Flem, and de Spain. Although Varner never forgave Flem for the large profit he made with the Old Frenchman Place, he accepts that Flem will become president

of the bank. Manfred's intention to leave Jefferson with Eula comes to naught when she commits suicide.

In *The Mansion,* the third novel of the Snopes trilogy, Varner (often referred to as Uncle Billy) privately appoints Clarence SNOPES as constable and then supervisor of Beat Two; later, through a talent for blackmail, Clarence becomes the county representative in Jackson, but loses Varner's support for Untied States Congress when V. K. RATLIFF engineers an embarrassing prank against him.

In "Tomorrow," Varner as justice of the peace and chief officer of the district is the one to whom BOOKWRIGHT surrenders himself for having killed THORPE. In "Shingles for the Lord," he is mentioned as having given Vernon TULL a puppy.

Varner's Store Fictional place, in southern YOKNAPATAWPHA COUNTY near FRENCHMAN'S BEND, 12 miles from JEFFERSON, MISSISSIPPI. Its porch is a gathering place for local men with time on their hands.

In *LIGHT IN AUGUST,* storekeeper Jody VARNER sells Lena GROVE crackers, cheese, and a 15-cent box of "sour-deans" (sardines). In Faulkner's hand-drawn map of Yoknapatawpha County in *ABSALOM, ABSALOM!,* Varner's Store is identified as the place "where Flem Snopes got his start."

Vatch Character in "MOUNTAIN VICTORY" (in *Collected Stories*). A young mountain man with an unappeasable hatred for Confederates, he ambushes Major Saucier WEDDEL, a returning soldier, and his servant JUBAL. Vatch kills his brother HULE, who tries to protect Weddel, by accident.

Velma Character in "A PORTRAIT OF ELMER" (in *Uncollected Stories*). She introduces the aspiring artist Elmer HODGE to sex when he is 15.

"Vendée" *See The UNVANQUISHED.*

Vera Character in *The REIVERS*. She is one of the girls in Miss REBA's brothel. Vera is on a visit to her family in Paducah, Kentucky, in May 1905, when Boon HOGGANBECK and his entourage visit Miss Reba's place.

Vernon **(1)** In *The SOUND AND THE FURY,* Myrtle's husband, the son-in-law of JEFFERSON, MISSISSIPPI's, sheriff. Vernon and his wife are present when Jason COMPSON Jr. arrives at the sheriff's house to report a theft and accuse his niece, Miss Quentin COMPSON, of running off with the money.

Vernon **(2)** Character in "DEATH DRAG" (in *Collected Stories*). He is a waiter in the restaurant where JOCK tells Captain WARREN about the ups and downs of his work as a stunt pilot.

Versh *See* GIBSON, VERSH.

Vickery, Olga W. (1925–1970) Polish-born American professor and critic. Vickery taught literature at several colleges and universities, including Mount Holyoke, Lake Forest, Purdue, and the University of Southern California. She received her doctorate from the University of Wisconsin in 1953. Among her better known contributions to Faulkner studies are her article on AS I LAY DYING in *Perspective* (1950); *The Novels of William Faulkner* (1959; 3d ed. 1995), based on her doctoral dissertation; and *William Faulkner: Three Decades of Criticism* (edited with Frederick J. Hoffman, 1960). *The Novels of William Faulkner* is an insightful and worthwhile study that preceded critical works by Cleanth BROOKS (*William Faulkner: The Yoknapatawpha Country*, 1963), Melvin Backman (*Faulkner: The Major Years*, 1966), and Michael MILLGATE (*The Achievement of William Faulkner*, 1966).

Vicksburg Campaign Union General Ulysses S. Grant carried out operations against this strategic Mississippi River fortress from October 1862 to July 1863. A series of battles and a six-month siege ended in the Confederate surrender of the city and fortress on July 4, 1863.

One of the decisive Union victories of the war, the Vicksburg campaign forms a backdrop to part of Faulkner's Civil War novel *The* UNVANQUISHED. The two young protagonists, Bayard SARTORIS (3) and Ringo STROTHER, execute their own military operations on a "living map" behind the smokehouse at Sartoris, the family plantation.

"Victory" *(Collected Stories)* Short story that follows a working-class Scot who fights bravely in World War I and believes his rise through the British ranks entitles him to become a gentleman, but who ends up unemployed and homeless.

When Alec GRAY revisits the French battlefields, people take him for an English lord. The tale shifts to Gray's early days as a soldier; he answers insolently to an officer and is charged with insubordination. A flashback to his God-fearing family reveals that his father opposed and his grandfather supported his enlistment. His initial revolt against the tyranny of tradition, family, and religion carries over as opposition to the army's petty regulations. Following his release from punishment, Gray takes revenge by brutally murdering his officer during trench warfare. Later he learns to play the military game by the rules. He fights heroically, trains as an officer, and is hospitalized. At war's end, he visits home but goes back to London to begin a gentleman's career. Civilian life in class-bound English society proves a difficult proposition: His accomplishments and new status can take him only so far. The eventual loss of his job starts a downward spiral that ends with him selling matches in the street. He rejects the idea of returning to Scotland or immigrating to Canada, and instead pathetically pursues the illusion of being a gentleman.

This story first was published in *These 13* (1931).

Vidal, François Character in "MOUNTAIN VICTORY" (in *Collected Stories*). A former general of Napoleon who migrates to NEW ORLEANS, he is the father (by a Choctaw woman) of Francis WEDDEL, and the grandfather of Major Saucier WEDDEL.

Viking Press Publishing firm, founded in 1925 by Harold Guinzburg and George Oppenheimer. In 1945, Viking contracted with Malcolm COWLEY to edit a collection of Faulkner's fiction for the Viking Portable Library series. At the time, all of Faulkner's books except *Sanctuary* were out of print, and Cowley suggested to the author that this project would be "a bayonet prick in the ass of Random House to reprint the others."

Cowley and Faulkner worked closely on the anthology. Viking published *The* PORTABLE FAULKNER in 1946 with an introduction by Cowley.

Vines, Deacon Character in LIGHT IN AUGUST. A deacon, he sends someone off on a mule to alert the sheriff when Joe CHRISTMAS begins to smash up the church.

Vinson, Mrs. Character in the short story "MISS ZILPHIA GANT" who tends bar in a tavern where stock traders gather. Mrs. Vinson induces the married Jim GANT to run off with her to Memphis. Jim's wife tracks the errant pair down and murders them both.

Virgil Character in *The* REIVERS. He is a desk clerk in the hotel at PARSHAM, TENNESSEE.

Vision in Spring A sequence of 14 love poems Faulkner wrote in 1921 and hand-bound to give to Estelle Franklin, whom he married in 1929 (see FAULKNER, LIDA ESTELLE OLDHAM). *Vision in Spring*, edited with an introduction by Judith L. Sensibar, was published posthumously in 1984. Though there is a single narrator of the poems named Pierrot, the sequence contains several distinct voices. In her introduction, Sensibar argues that in Faulkner's poems, and especially in *Vision in Spring*, Faulkner learned "ways to cast off the mask while retaining in his writing those qualities that made it so imaginatively compelling. . . . The protean poet-dreamer resurfaces in his tragic and comic fictional protagonists" (xiii–xiv). *Vision in Spring*, like Faulkner's poetry in general, is derivative and shows the influence of writers such as T. S. Eliot, Keats, Swinburne, and the symbolist poets.

Vitelli, Popeye *See* POPEYE.

Vladimir Kyrilytch   V. K. RATLIFF's patronymic ancestor who fought in General Burgoyne's army at the Revolutionary War battle of Saratoga in October 1777. He is referred to in *The MANSION*. Ratliff does not know his ancestor's last name. Ratliff explains to Gavin STEVENS that after the British defeat at Saratoga the army was abandoned in Virginia without money or food (p. 165). The first V. K., a Russian emigré, faced an additional difficulty because he did not know the language. He was hiding in a hayloft when Nelly RATCLIFFE came upon him and started feeding him. They married after she became pregnant. He took her last name, which eventually became Ratliff. The oldest son of each successive generation is named Vladimir Kyrilytch and "spends half his life trying to keep anybody from finding it out" (p. 166).

von Ploeckner   German amateur mountain climber who later becomes a general in the Nazi army during World War II. Von Ploeckner hires the guides BRIX and Emil HILLER for a two-day climb in the Swiss mountains. At von Ploechkner's insistence, Brix's fiancée accompanies the three men, and Brix and she are married in the mountains. Returning to the base village, however, Brix is killed in an accident. Von Ploeckner takes Mrs. BRIX with him back to Germany. Years later, Mrs. Brix stabs von Ploeckner to death.

Voss, Werner   A World War I German aviator referred to in *A FABLE*. See BALL, ALBERT.

Vynie   *See* SNOPES, VYNIE.

Wagner, Hal Pseudonym in *SARTORIS*. It is the name Byron SNOPES uses to disguise his identity as the author of a letter to Narcissa Benbow SARTORIS.

Waldrip Character in "HONOR" (in *Collected Stories*). A test pilot with Buck MONAGHAN, he teaches Monaghan the art of wing walking while they are in the air corps together.

Waldrip, Mrs. Vernon Character in *IF I FORGET THEE, JERUSALEM* ("The Old Man"). The CONVICT's former girlfriend, she dreams of being the consort of a successful criminal.

She visits the convict in prison once, and later sends him a postcard showing the hotel where she and her husband are spending their honeymoon.

Walker, Ed In *SANCTUARY*, Lee GOODWIN's jailor in JEFFERSON, MISSISSIPPI.

Walker, Mrs. In *SANCTUARY*, the JEFFERSON, MISSISSIPPI, jailor's wife who shelters Ruby LAMAR and her infant child at the jail when the hotel in town forces them to leave.

Walkley Character in "VICTORY" (in *Collected Stories*). A wartime officer acquaintance of Alec GRAY, he migrates to Canada after the war and becomes a successful wheat farmer. Walkley encounters Gray selling matches on a London sidewalk and tries to speak to him. Gray answers with a curse.

Wall An insurance salesman in the short story "A DANGEROUS MAN." Minnie Maude tells the narrator of the story that Wall is having an affair with the wife of the main character in the story, Mr. BOWMAN. Wall is described as a dapper-Dan type with a handsome but effeminate face.

Waller, Hamp Character in *LIGHT IN AUGUST*. He recovers Joanna BURDEN's nearly decapitated body from her burning house. His wife phones the sheriff to report the fire.

Waller, Mrs. Character in *LIGHT IN AUGUST*. The wife of Hamp WALLER, she telephones the sheriff to report the Burden house is on fire.

Walter (1) Character in *MOSQUITOES*. He is Patricia MAURIER's industrious African-American servant.

Walter (2) Character in *MOSQUITOES*. He is a member of the tugboat crew that pulls the grounded yacht *Nausikaa* off the mud.

Walthall, Parson In *The SOUND AND THE FURY*, the Methodist minister in JEFFERSON, MISSISSIPPI, who objects to the shooting of pigeons that flock around the courthouse. Seeing the pigeons as annoyances, Jason COMPSON Jr., and others want to rid the town of them, but Parson Walthall actively protests and prevents the men from further executing their plan.

Wardle, Mrs. In *SOLDIERS' PAY*, one of the townfolks of Charlestown, Georgia.

Warner, Jack (1892–1978) Born in Canada, the son of Polish immigrants named Eichelbaum, he and his three brothers built one of Hollywood's great movie empires after introducing sound to film with *The Jazz Singer* in 1927.

Faulkner went to work as a $300 a week contract scriptwriter for Warner Brothers in 1942. By then Jack handled the studio's "talent"—actors, directors, writers. There was mutual antipathy. The talent detested the bullying Jack Warner; he expressed his own views in a famous slur on writers. "You're all schmucks with Underwoods," he once said. (Underwood was a well-known brand of typewriter.) Faulkner's relations with Warner were difficult, and the studio head repeatedly denied his request for release from his contract in the later 1940s.

Warner Brothers (Warner Bros.) Hollywood movie studio, established in 1919 by Harry, Albert, Samuel, and Jack WARNER. The company emerged as a major studio with the release of the first feature movie with sound, *The Jazz Singer*, in 1927. All the same, Warner Brothers prided itself not on innovation but instead on turning out a steady stream of moderately budgeted, profitable movies.

Faulkner had a miserable career as a screenwriter for Warner Brothers in the 1940s. He blundered into an ironclad seven-year contract in 1942 for a pedestrian $300 a week at a time when top Hollywood writers were pulling down weekly wages of $2,500. Jack Warner reputedly boasted that he kept America's best writer on his payroll for $300 a week.

Faulkner worked on a succession of forgettable production-line films until his director friend Howard HAWKS rescued him to work on the war movie *Battle Cry* (later canceled) and the adaptation of Ernest HEMINGWAY's novel *To Have and Have Not,* starring Humphrey BOGART and Lauren Bacall. He also worked on the Bogart film *The Big Sleep,* an adaptation of Raymond Chandler's novel of the same title.

Warner routinely denied Faulkner's request to be let out of his long contract. Faulkner resisted passively, taking extended leaves from the studio. In November 1953, Hawks asked him to write the screenplay for *Land of the Pharaohs.* Faulkner agreed, but only to oblige Hawks. It was his last work for Warner Brothers.

Warren, Captain   Character in the short story "DEATH DRAG." He is a former member of the Royal Flying Corps who had trained as a pilot in Canada, where he met JOCK. He and Jock meet again in the small southern town when Jock and two friends, GINSFARB and JAKE, come to put on an air show. Captain Warren is very hospitable to Jock. He also appears in *Knight's Gambit* where Chick (Charles) MALLISON asks him how a 16-year-old can enlist to fight in World War II. Warren advises him to wait.

Warren, Robert Penn (1905–1989)   A Kentucky-born poet, novelist, and critic, he was associated with Allen Tate and other writers steeped in the issues and traditions of the South. A founder and editor of the *Southern Review* (1935–42), Warren taught at Yale (1961–73) and in 1986 became the first official poet laureate of the United States.

Warren's best-known work is the novel *All the King's Men* (1946), based on the career of the populist Louisiana politician Huey Long. In May 1946 HARCOURT, BRACE & COMPANY sent an advance copy of the novel to Faulkner, hoping for a comment suitable for the jacket blurb. Faulkner responded that he was not greatly impressed, although he found a relatively short historical sequence involving an ancestor of the narrator "beautiful and moving" (*Selected Letters,* p. 29).

Warren held Faulkner in high but not uncritical regard. "For range of effect, philosophical weight, originality of style, variety of characterization, humor and tragic intensity [Faulkner's works] are without equal in our time and country," he wrote. But he went on to assert that there are "grave defects" in Faulkner's fiction (Warren, *New and Selected Essays,* p. 197).

Warwick   Plantation of Hubert BEAUCHAMP in *GO DOWN, MOSES.* Miss Sophonsiba BEAUCHAMP, Beauchamp's spinster sister, rather pretentiously named the place after the English great house. Not everyone humored her whim.

"Was"   *See* GO DOWN, MOSES.

"Wash" (Collected Stories)   Short story of the extreme disillusionment of Wash JONES, a poor white man, by Thomas SUTPEN, his hero and benefactor, which results in violence and tragedy. In the opening scene, Wash's 17-year-old granddaughter MILLY gives birth to a baby fathered by the 60-year-old Sutpen; disappointed that the child is not a son, Sutpen speaks to her callously.

A flashback recalls how Sutpen fought in and lost his son in the Civil War, from which he returned to find his plantation in ruins. A squatter in Sutpen's old fishing shack, Wash is held in contempt by nearly everyone. Later he helps Sutpen in his store and the two drink together despite their social distance. When Sutpen becomes interested in Milly, Wash trusts that he will do right by her. Overhearing Sutpen's cruel remarks to Milly, he is enraged and slays Sutpen with a scythe. He then retreats to the cabin to tend to Milly and to await the law. When the sheriff finally arrives, Wash takes a butcher knife to Milly and the baby, sets the cabin on fire, and charges out with the scythe, ignoring the order to stop or to be shot.

Critics generally regard this as one of Faulkner's more powerful stories. For critic Jack F. Stewart, it is his "most concentrated parable of Southern degeneracy in the aftermath of the Civil War." For Neil Isaacs it represents a "mythic archetype of the death of the gods."

The story first appeared in HARPER'S (February 1934) and in *Doctor Martino and Other Stories* (1934). Faulkner reworked it for a key episode in the novel ABSALOM, ABSALOM!

Wasson, Ben (unknown)   Faulkner's friend and sometime agent and editor, born in Greenville, Mississippi. They met in OXFORD, MISSISSIPPI, where Wasson studied law at the UNIVERSITY OF MISSISSIPPI. An early admirer, Wasson sold handbound copies of The MARIONETTES, young Faulkner's poetic drama, for $5 apiece.

Wasson moved to New York City and entered the publishing world. In 1928, he placed *Flags in the Dust* with HARCOURT, BRACE & COMPANY, negotiating a $300 advance for Faulkner. With Wasson's extensive cuts, the novel was published as SARTORIS in 1929.

Wasson joined the firm of CAPE & SMITH in 1929 and became Faulkner's editor on The SOUND AND THE FURY. He helped the novelist land a screenwriting job with MGM in Hollywood in 1932.

Faulkner and Wasson saw each other frequently in Hollywood. The novelist arranged a bizarre episode in which Wasson escorted Faulkner's mistress, Meta CARPENTER, to dinner with Faulkner and his wife, Estelle. Faulkner pretended that Meta was Wasson's girlfriend, and his wife went along with the charade, but she later expressed her anger at Wasson.

Faulkner inexplicably cut Wasson in an encounter at RANDOM HOUSE in New York one day in 1957, abruptly ending 40 years of friendship. Wasson never learned why Faulkner had snubbed him, and they never saw each other again.

Watkins   One of the inmates in the clinic in the short story "MR. ACARIUS." His girlfriend, Miss Judy LESTER, smuggles booze to the patients by hiding half-pint bottles in her brassiere.

Wattman, Jakeleg   In *The MANSION,* a bootlegger who lives at Wyatt's Crossing, Gavin STEVENS and V. K. RATLIFF drive Linda Snopes KOHL to Jakeleg's so-called fishing camp for liquor so she will know the way next time.

Watts   (1) Character in *Sartoris*. He owns a hardware store in JEFFERSON, MISSISSIPPI.

Watts   (2) Character in "TURNABOUT" (in *Collected Stories*). He is an aerial gunner in Captain BOGARD's crew in France during World War I.

Watts, Birdie   Character in *The REIVERS*. She keeps the brothel on the opposite side of CATALPA STREET from Miss Reba RIVERS.

Watts, Mr.   Character in "THAT WILL BE FINE" (in *Collected Stories*). He is the JEFFERSON, MISSISSIPPI, sheriff.

Webb, James (unknown)   Chairman of the English department at the UNIVERSITY OF MISSISSIPPI, he persuaded the notoriously image-shy Faulkner to have his portrait painted in March 1962. The portrait would augment the expanding Faulkner collection at the university.

Faulkner agreed to sit for a series of photographs from which artist Murray Goldsborough would paint the portrait. Faulkner posed in a tweed jacket with a pipe. He admitted to Webb later that he liked Goldsborough's work.

Weddel, Francis (Vidal)   Character in "LO!" (in *Collected Stories*). He is chief of a tribe of CHICKASAW INDIANS that lives on land he inherited from his French father. When his nephew is accused of killing a white tollgate keeper, the tribe marches on Washington and demands a ceremonial trial. The nephew is acquitted.

Later, another tollkeeper is murdered; Weddel seeks a second trial for the nephew. This time, the president dispatches troops to halt the Choctaws before they can enter the capital.

Weddel appears in the short story "MOUNTAIN VICTORY" as the father of a Confederate soldier, Major Saucier WEDDEL.

Weddel, Grenier   In *The TOWN*, a bachelor whose marriage proposal is rejected by Sally Hampton (PARSONS). She marries Maurice PARSONS instead. Grenier, nonetheless, sends her a large corsage for the annual Christmas dance. Although she does not wear it, her husband is perturbed enough to give Grenier, and later his wife, a black eye.

Weddel, Major Saucier   Character in "MOUNTAIN VICTORY" (in *Collected Stories*). A Confederate soldier on his way home to Mississippi after the war, he and his servant JUBAL stay the night with a mountain family even though they have been warned not to tarry. Jubal, however, has breached a store of whiskey and is too drunk to travel, and Weddel refuses to abandon him.

When he sets out finally, the major is killed in an ambush by VATCH, who is jealous of his sister's infatuation for the major. Vatch also accidentally kills his brother HULE as Hule tries to save Weddel.

Wedlow, Mr.   The jeweler in the short story "SEPULTURE SOUTH: GASLIGHT" who inscribes the notice of the death of the unnamed narrator's grandfather.

West, David   Character in *MOSQUITOES*. A steward aboard the yacht *Nausikaa*, he falls in love with Patricia ROBYN after she half-consciously encourages him. They flee the yacht together but become lost and discouraged. When they return, David vanishes.

West, Doctor   Character in *KNIGHT'S GAMBIT* ("Smoke"). He owns the drugstore in JEFFERSON, MISSISSIPPI, where Judge DUKINFIELD's murderer buys a pack of rare cigarettes. The identification of the cigarettes helps Gavin STEVENS solve the Dukinfield murder.

West, Miss   Character in "HONOR" (in *Collected Stories*). The secretary for the car dealer REINHARDT, she befriends Buck MONAGHAN when he works on the lot as a salesman.

White   Character in "HONOR" (in *Collected Stories*). He is an army acquaintance of Buck MONAGHAN. In nighttime poker games, Monaghan reluctantly takes so much money off the stubborn White that White kills himself.

White, Hank   In *SOLDIERS' PAY*, one of the drunken men on the train with Joe GILLIGAN and Cadet Julian LOWE.

White, Hap   Minor character in the short story "TWO DOLLAR WIFE" who brings the Princeton man JORNSTADT to the New Year's Eve party at the club.

White, Jed   Character in *The UNVANQUISHED*. On George Wyatt's order, he rides out to SARTORIS plantation to report that young Bayard SARTORIS (3) is all right after his encounter with Ben REDMOND in Redmond's JEFFERSON, MISSISSIPPI, law office.

Whiteby Character in "VICTORY" (in *Collected Stories*). A former British officer and a veteran of World War I, he finds himself overwhelmed by postwar conditions and kills himself.

Whiteleaf Bridge Fictional place in southeastern YOKNAPATAWPHA COUNTY. It carries the road to FRENCHMAN'S BEND across fictional Whiteleaf Creek. The bridge figures in *The HAMLET* and *INTRUDER IN THE DUST*.

Whiteley An officer in the short story "THRIFT" who processes MACWYRGLINCHBEATH's transfer into the Royal Flying Corps. He is presented in a comic scene involving the spelling and pronunciation of the Scotsman MacWyrglinchbeath's name.

Whitfield (Rev.) Character in *AS I LAY DYING* (narrator of chapter 41), *The HAMLET*, "Tomorrow" (*KNIGHT'S GAMBIT*), and "SHINGLES FOR THE LORD." In *As I Lay Dying*, he had been Addie BUNDREN's lover in the past and fathered Jewel BUNDREN. When Addie is dying, his conscience bothers him and he decides to confess to Anse BUNDREN that he is Jewel's father. But when he finds out that Addie has died, he no longer sees the need to ask for forgiveness: Whitfield interprets the death as a clear sign from God that the affair is to be kept secret. He preaches at her funeral. In *The Hamlet*, Whitfield suggests to I. O. SNOPES and V. K. RATLIFF that the only way to cure Ike SNOPES of his sexual attraction for the cow is to kill the animal and make Ike eat some of the meat. In "Tomorrow," Whitfield marries S. J. FENTRY and his pregnant wife, who dies soon after giving birth. Whitfield helps Fentry bury her. In "Shingles for the Lord," Whitfield asks his congregation to help build a new church after the old one burns down.

Widrington Character in "BLACK MUSIC" (in *Collected Stories*). He manages a company that does business in a port town in a small Latin American country. His firm owns the cantina building in whose attic Wilfred MIDGLESTON finds shelter.

Widrington, Mrs. (1) Character in "BLACK MUSIC" (in *Collected Stories*). The wife of a company manager in the Latin American town where Wilfred MIDGLESTON turns up, she gives the fugitive Midgleston permission to sleep in the attic above the company-owned cantina.

Mrs. Widrington also appears in the short story "CARCASSONNE," where her husband is identified as the manager of a Standard Oil Company office.

Widrington, Mrs. (2) A minor character in *The TOWN*. She comes to JEFFERSON, MISSISSIPPI, with her wealthy contractor husband and an expensive Pekinese with a gold nameplate on its collar. When the dog is missing, Mrs. Widrington offers a reward in the newspapers. The dog is stolen and killed by Byron SNOPES's four half-breed Jircarill Apache Indian children.

Wilbourne, Dr. Character in *IF I FORGET THEE, JERUSALEM* ("The Wild Palms"). Harry WILBOURNE's father, he married Harry's much-younger mother late in life. Dr. Wilbourne died of toxemia from sucking a snake bite on a child's hand, leaving Harry an orphan at age 2. He provided $2,000 in his will for his son's medical education.

Wilbourne, Henry (Harry) Character in *IF I FORGET THEE, JERUSALEM* ("The Wild Palms"). A young, penniless, and pliant medical intern who lives a monastic life and has no experience of women, he falls deeply in love with Charlotte RITTENMEYER. After finding $1,278 in a New Orleans street, he quits his internship only a few months before he would have taken his medical degree and leaves for Chicago with Charlotte.

They exist precariously for the next two years. Charlotte's principles regarding love seem to bar security and routine. Harry finds a job doing laboratory work in a charity hospital in the black ghetto, but loses it after a few weeks. The two move from job to marginal job. Gradually their money runs out. They retire for a time to the lake cottage of their journalist friend MCCORD; then, against McCord's advice, Harry accepts an appointment as company physician at a spurious mine in the mountains of Utah.

Charlotte becomes pregnant in Utah and tries to talk Harry into performing an abortion on her. He resists and offers to make whatever sacrifices are necessary for the child. Charlotte is adamant. Children do not fit her notions of love; after all, she has left two daughters behind with her husband in New Orleans. Harry finally agrees to do the abortion but bungles the job, and Charlotte becomes seriously ill.

She dies in a Mississippi Gulf Coast hospital, and Harry is charged with manslaughter for her death. He pleads guilty and is sentenced to 50 years in prison. In jail, he refuses Charlotte's husband's offer to help him escape or, finally, to commit suicide. One must live to remember, he tells himself; he refuses to give up the memory of his life with Charlotte.

"Yes," he decides. "Between grief and nothing I will take grief" (*If I Forget Thee,* p. 273).

Wildermark A minor character in *The TOWN*. He owns a department store in JEFFERSON, MISSISSIPPI, where Gavin STEVENS buys a suitcase for Linda Snopes (KOHL), who is graduating from high school. Mrs. Mannie HAIT buys old-fashioned shoes from Wildermark, which he orders once a year for her.

Wildermark, Mr. (Senior)   Referred to in *The TOWN* as "the senior Mr. Wildermark" (p. 306) who was beaten in chess by Doctor Wyatt. The relationship between Wildermark and Wildermark Sr. is not specific in the novel.

"The Wild Palms"   *See IF I FORGET THEE, JERUSALEM.*

Wilkie   A servant (most likely a black man) of Gerald BLAND's grandfather referred to by Mrs. BLAND in *The SOUND AND THE FURY*. Very particular about his juleps, the grandfather would not allow Wilkie to pick the mint for them but instead gathered it himself before breakfast while the dew was still on it.

Wilkins, George   Character in *GO DOWN, MOSES* ("The Fire and the Hearth"). The husband of Lucas BEAUCHAMP's daughter Nathalie Beauchamp WILKINS, he secretly follows his father-in-law's example and sets up a still on Roth EDMOND's plantation. When Lucas reports him, both are caught and charged with making illegal whiskey.

Wilkins, Mary Holland Falkner (1872–1946)   Faulkner's aunt, the second child of John Wesley Thompson FALKNER and Sallie Murry FALKNER, known to the family as Huldy and to the novelist and his brothers as Auntee.

She introduced her brother Murry FALKNER to his future wife, Maud Butler (FALKNER), and Huldy and Miss Maud remained close friends all their lives. She married James Porter Wilkins, a physician, in 1898, and they settled in OXFORD, MISSISSIPPI. Their daughter Sallie Murry, a childhood playmate of the Falkner boys, was born in 1899.

Widowed in the early years of the new century, she took over the management of her parents' house, the Big Place, as her mother began to fail in health. Auntee often entertained the Falkner boys there. She took them all to the university observatory in 1910 to observe the transit of Halley's Comet.

In their later years, she and Faulkner's mother went to the movies together nearly every night, taking in the pictures at the Ritz and the Lyric on alternate evenings.

Brisk, outspoken, an accomplished horsewoman, and intensely family-proud, Auntee was a partial model for Granny Rosa MILLARD in *The UNVANQUISHED* and for Aunt Jenny DU PRE in *SARTORIS* and *The Unvanquished*.

Wilkins, Nathalie Beauchamp   Character in *GO DOWN, MOSES* ("The Fire and the Hearth"). The youngest child of Lucas and Molly BEAUCHAMP, at 17 she marries the rather simple George WILKINS in secret and takes his side when her father turns him in for making illegal whiskey.

Beauchamp has long been distilling whiskey discreetly himself, and both men end up being hauled into court. As the case is presented, Beauchamp learns that George and his daughter have been husband and wife for several months.

Wilkins, Mrs.   Character in *The UNVANQUISHED*. She is the wife of Professor WILKINS, one of Bayard SARTORIS (3)'s law teachers at the university in OXFORD, MISSISSIPPI, and an acquaintance of Bayard's grandmother, Rosa MILLARD. Bayard lives with the Wilkinses while he is studying law.

Wilkins, Professor   Character in *The UNVANQUISHED*. He is one of Bayard SARTORIS (3)'s law instructors at the university in OXFORD, MISSISSIPPI, and Bayard lives with the professor and his wife during the university term.

Ringo STROTHER carries word of Colonel John SARTORIS's killing to Wilkins, who interrupts Bayard at his law books to break the news of his father's death to him.

Willard   In *SOLDIERS' PAY*, Rector MAHON's neighbor, who, according to the rector, has good fruit in his orchard next to his small house.

William Faulkner: Early Prose and Poetry   A collection of poems, prose pieces, and pen-and-ink drawings that Faulkner published between 1917 and 1925, the early period of his literary career. Compiled with an introduction by Carvel COLLINS, the collection was published in 1962 by Little, Brown and Co., Boston. (For titles, see Appendix I.)

William Faulkner's University Pieces   A collection of Faulkner's poetry, prose, and drawings between 1916 and 1925 that first appeared in several UNIVERSITY OF MISSISSIPPI publications. Compiled with an introduction by Carvel COLLINS, *William Faulkner's University Pieces* was published in 1962 by Kendyusha Press in Japan to pay tribute to Faulkner's successful visit to Nagano (see FAULKNER AT NAGANO) and to the reception of his works by the Japanese academic community. The collection also contains Faulkner's first published short story, "Landing in Luck," a story about a cadet's first solo flight, which appeared in the November 1919 issue of the student newspaper, *The MISSISSIPPIAN*.

Williams, Joan (unknown)   In August 1949, Joan Williams turned up uninvited at ROWAN OAK for a glimpse of Faulkner, by then a famous author. A student at Bard College in New York, she was interested in Faulkner's work and wanted to become a writer herself.

Joan Williams was 20; Faulkner was 52. They exchanged letters and met surreptitiously in MEMPHIS in January 1950, where Faulkner made it evident he wished her to be his lover. She was not interested.

They continued to meet and correspond. Faulkner looked over Joan's short stories and encouraged her ambition. Estelle FAULKNER got wind of the relationship, met Joan at the PEABODY HOTEL in Memphis to discourage it, and afterward telephoned Joan's parents to enlist their help in breaking it off.

Faulkner and Joan Williams continued to see one another. He gave her the original manuscript of *The SOUND AND THE FURY*, which she did not keep. He asked his agent, Harold OBER, to place her short stories. She finally relented and slept with him, though she wrote later that she never felt comfortable with him as an older man—and married at that.

Joan drifted steadily away from Faulkner and in 1954 wrote that she intended to marry. They continued to correspond after her marriage to Ezra Bowen, son of the biographer Catherine Drinker Bowen.

Faulkner suggested *The Morning and the Evening* as the title for her first novel, finally accepted for publication in 1959. She visited Faulkner at Rowan Oak in late June 1962, only 10 days or so before his death.

Williams's second novel, *The Wintering*, appeared in 1971. It is a fictional account of her involvement with Faulkner, who is called Jeff Almoner in the novel.

Willow, Colonel Character in *ABSALOM, ABSALOM!* A Confederate officer, he tells Thomas SUTPEN of his son Henry's wounding at the battle of SHILOH in 1862.

Wilmoth Character in *GO DOWN, MOSES* ("Go Down, Moses"). The editor of the JEFFERSON, MISSISSIPPI, newspaper, he helps Gavin STEVENS bring the body of the killer Butch BEAUCHAMP, executed in Illinois, home for burial.

Wilson, Sergeant In *A FABLE*, an American sergeant referred to by an Iowan as the best in the army. See BUCHWALD.

Winbush, Fonzo Character who attends barber school in Memphis with Virgil SNOPES; he appears in *SANCTUARY* and *The MANSION*. (Fonzo is Grover Cleveland WINBUSH's nephew.) When the two country youths arrive in MEMPHIS, they stay at miss Reba RIVERS's brothel thinking it a boardinghouse. When the two intentionally go to another brothel, Fonzo worries that Miss Reba might find out and not let them "stay in the house with them ladies no more" (*Sanctuary*, p. 196). This episode provides a humorous aside to an otherwise violent novel. In *The Mansion*, Montgomery Ward SNOPES explains that Fonzo and Virgil heeded the advice of a Mrs. WINBUSH, who suggested that they stay at a house run by a Christian motherly type.

Winbush, Grover Cleveland In *The TOWN* and *The MANSION*, part owner, with Flem SNOPES, of a sidestreet restaurant in JEFFERSON, MISSISSIPPI. Winbush becomes Jefferson's night marshal after Snopes forces him out of the restaurant business, but when the town's drugstore is robbed he is fired for having been at one of Montgomery Ward SNOPES's peep shows instead of patrolling the streets. He later becomes a night watchman at a brick yard. See also RIDEOUT, AARON.

Winbush, Mack Character in *The REIVERS*. He owns the place eight miles out of JEFFERSON, MISSISSIPPI, from which Calvin BOOKWRIGHT sells his high-quality whiskey.

Winbush, Mrs. A woman in *The MANSION* who gives advice to Virgil SNOPES and Fonzo WINBUSH. According to Montgomery Ward SNOPES, she told Virgil and Fonzo before they left for barber school in MEMPHIS to rent a room from a mature, Christian, motherly woman. Unwittingly, the two naive youths ended up at Miss Reba RIVERS's brothel.

Winterbottom Character in *LIGHT IN AUGUST* and *The HAMLET*. In the former novel, he and ARMSTID take a break from negotiating the sale of a cultivator to gossip about the pregnant Lena GROVE as she passes on her way to JEFFERSON, MISSISSIPPI, in search of Lucas BURCH, the father of her unborn child. In *The Hamlet*, Winterbottom runs a boardinghouse in FRENCHMAN'S BEND where Launcelot SNOPES lives. Winterbottom also appears in the short story "SPOTTED HORSES," revised for *The Hamlet*.

Winterbottom, Mrs. Character in *SARTORIS*. Colonel John SARTORIS kills the two Burdens, carpetbaggers working for black suffrage, in her JEFFERSON, MISSISSIPPI, boardinghouse.

Wiseman, Eva Kauffman Character in *MOSQUITOES*. The elder sister of Julius KAUFFMAN, she has published a volume of verse titled *Satyricon in Starlight*, which Major AYERS derides as "the syphilis book" because he regards it as risqué. All the same, she seems a sensible woman, and the men of the *Nausikaa* yachting party are fond of her.

The Wishing Tree Posthumously published children's story, written in 1927 for Faulkner's stepdaughter, Victoria FRANKLIN. The author typed and bound the story and presented it to Victoria on her eighth birthday. "Bill he made this book," the inscription read.

The Wishing Tree is a fairy story that promises good things. For children who are good, though, the tree isn't necessary for good things to come to pass. Faulkner hand-produced at least two copies of the tale. *The Wishing Tree* was published posthumously in the *SATURDAY EVENING POST*, 240 (8 April 1967), 48–53, 57–58, 60–63. In April 1967, RANDOM HOUSE published the story in book form, with illustrations by Dan Bolognese.

"With Caution and Dispatch" *(Uncollected Stories)* A tall tale–like short story dealing with the misadventures of Second Lieutenant (Johnny) SARTORIS (1), a World War I aviator born in YOKNAPATAWPHA COUNTY, Mississippi. When Sartoris's squadron is ordered to fly their Sopwith Camel fighter planes to France, Sartoris manages to crash three times, destroying his aircraft but fortunately surviving each time. His first accident was the result of a mechanical malfunction caused by Sartoris's skylarking. This crash takes place in England. Sartoris is issued a second Camel, and he rushes to catch up with his group. While flying low over the English Channel, however, he manages to crash onto the deck of a supposedly neutral freighter. He is held a prisoner for a while, then taken off that ship and escorted onto a British man-of-war vessel, where he is told he has interfered with a top-secret operation and commanded to tell no one what he saw. In France, he is given a third Camel, which he crash-lands at his own aerodrome. Sartoris seems more afraid of being thought cowardly by his squadron mates than he is of his near-brushes with death.

In "With Caution and Dispatch"—one of several stories dealing with World War I and aviatorial courage (see also "ALL THE DEAD PILOTS" and "DEATH DRAG")—Faulkner mocks both the folly and courage of young aviators and the wastefulness and secretiveness of war. In the later novel *A FABLE,* he uses similar themes but to a much darker effect. Written sometime in the early 1930s, "With Caution and Dispatch" was first published posthumously in *UNCOLLECTED STORIES OF WILLIAM FAULKNER.*

For further information, see *Selected Letters of William Faulkner,* pp. 63, 274; *Uncollected Stories,* p. 711; and Diane Brown Jones, *A Reader's Guide to the Short Stories of William Faulkner,* pp. 210, 403, and 404. See also FAULKNER AND FLYING.

Witt A British flight commander in *A FABLE.*

the woman Character in *IF I FORGET THEE, JERUSALEM* ("The Old Man"). An unnamed victim of the Great Mississippi Flood of 1927, she takes refuge in a cypress tree when the waters rise and the CONVICT rescues her there. The floodwaters carry them far downstream; she gives birth; and after weeks of desperate effort, the convict returns her safely to dry land.

Wordwin Character in *The REIVERS.* The cashier in Grandfather PRIEST's Bank of Jefferson, he is entrusted with the task of going to MEMPHIS by train and driving Grandfather's new Winton Flyer to JEFFERSON, MISSISSIPPI.

Workitt, Uncle Sudley Character in *INTRUDER IN THE DUST.* A distant kinsman of the Gowries with the honorary title of "uncle," he is murder victim Vinson GOWRIE's partner in a lumber business.

Workman, Mr. Character in *KNIGHT'S GAMBIT* ("An Error in Chemistry"). He is an adjuster for the insurance company that underwrote a $500 policy for Ellie Pritchel FLINT.

Worsham, Belle Character in *GO DOWN, MOSES* ("Go Down, Moses"). A JEFFERSON, MISSISSIPPI, spinster, she is the granddaughter of the planter who owned the parents of Mollie (Molly) BEAUCHAMP and her brother HAMP.

Though she is poor, Miss Belle feels an obligation to bring Samuel BEAUCHAMP's body home from Chicago for a decent burial, whatever the cost.

Worsham, Dr. Character in *The UNVANQUISHED.* He is a preacher in Colonel John SARTORIS's church before the Civil War.

Worsham, Hamp Character in *GO DOWN, MOSES* ("Go Down, Moses"). The brother of Mollie (Molly) BEAUCHAMP, he and his wife live with Miss Belle WORSHAM, a penniless JEFFERSON, MISSISSIPPI, spinster, and help support her through the sale of chickens and vegetables.

Worsham, Samuel Character in *GO DOWN, MOSES* ("Go Down, Moses"). He is the father of Miss Belle WORSHAM. Mollie (Molly) BEAUCHAMP names her grandson for him.

Worthington, Mrs. In *SOLDIERS' PAY,* one of the townfolks in Charlestown, Georgia. A widow of some means, she has her driver take the suffering World War I veteran Donald MAHON to the dance she sponsors so he can listen to music, which he likes.

Wright, Doc In *The SOUND AND THE FURY,* one of the cotton speculators in the telegraph office in JEFFERSON, MISSISSIPPI. He and others are very curious about what Jason COMPSON Jr. buys and sells.

Wutherspoon, Jamie Character in "TURNABOUT" (in *Collected Stories*). An acquaintance of the British naval officer Midshipman HOPE, he uses a neighboring street in the French port town for his "home."

Wyatt Character in "A ROSE FOR EMILY" (in *Collected Stories*). An elderly woman, "crazy" by repute, Miss Emily GRIERSON's father fell out with his Alabama kin over a question of the old lady's estate.

Wyatt, Aunt Sally Character in *SARTORIS.* A spinster kinswoman of the Benbows, something of a busybody, she stays with Narcissa Benbow (SARTORIS) while her brother is in France with the YMCA during World War I.

Wyatt, George   Character in *The UNVANQUISHED*. He serves in Colonel John SARTORIS's troop during the war and afterward is an ally in Sartoris's schemes to suppress the black vote in JEFFERSON, MISSISSIPPI.

Wyatt attempts, through Drusilla Hawk SARTORIS, to persuade the colonel to leave off the taunting of Ben REDMOND that ultimately leads Redmond to shoot him. Wyatt gathers a group of six veterans to wait in the street as Bayard SARTORIS (3) mounts the steps to Redmond's law office to confront his father's killer. After the encounter, he orders Jed WHITE to ride out to SARTORIS plantation and report that Bayard is all right.

Wyatt, Henry   Character in *GO DOWN, MOSES* ("Delta Autumn"). A member of the MISSISSIPPI DELTA hunting party, he recalls a time when game was much more plentiful in the region.

Wyatt, Miss Sophie   Character in *SARTORIS*. She is one of two spinster sisters of Aunt Sally WYATT.

Wylie, Ash (1) (Uncle Ash)   Character in *GO DOWN, MOSES* ("The Old People," "The Bear") and the short story "A BEAR HUNT." He is a black cook in Major DE SPAIN's hunting camp in the big woods.

Wylie, Ash (2)   Character in "A BEAR HUNT" (in *Collected Stories*). The son of old Major DE SPAIN's camp cook, he arranges for John BASKET and his Indian associates to frighten Luke HOGGANBECK. Wylie seeks revenge for Hogganbeck's having burned a fine celluloid collar of Wylie's some 20 years before.

Wylie, Job   Character in "UNCLE WILLY" (in *Collected Stories*). He works in Uncle Willy CHRISTIAN's drugstore and refuses to leave when the clerk brought in to replace Willy fires him.

Wyott (1)   Character in *The REIVERS*. An early YOKNAPATAWPHA COUNTY settler, he built a store and ran a ferry at the crossing of the TALLAHATCHIE RIVER that later passed into BALLENBAUGH hands and became known as BALLENBAUGH'S FERRY.

Wyott (2)   Character in *The REIVERS*. He is a family friend of the Priests. Boon HOGGANBECK and Lucius (Loosh) PRIEST are near the Wyott place eight miles out of JEFFERSON, MISSISSIPPI, on the way to MEMPHIS when they discover the stowaway in the car, Ned MCCASLIN.

Wyott, Doctor   In *The TOWN*, the 80-year-old president emeritus of the Academy in JEFFERSON, MISSISSIPPI, which was founded by his grandfather. Doctor Wyott, who is able to read Greek, Hebrew, and Sanskrit, has been an atheist for more than 60 years and wears two foreign decorations to publicly display his beliefs.

Wyott, Miss Vaiden   A minor character in *The TOWN*. She is Wallstreet Panic SNOPES's teacher in JEFFERSON, MISSISSIPPI. Miss Vaiden helps the boy during the summer to pass the third grade, and at her suggestion, he changes his name to Wall Snopes upon entering the fourth grade. Grateful for her help, he asks her to marry him after he graduates from high school, but, sensitive to his feelings, she declines, telling him she is already engaged. Before she leaves to teach in a school in Bristol, Virginia, Miss Vaiden arranges for him to meet the girl he later marries.

Y

Yettie   *See* SNOPES, YETTIE.

Yocona River   Rising in western Pontotoc County, it flows westward for 130 miles, draining southern LAFAYETTE COUNTY, before emptying into the TALLA-HATCHIE RIVER in Quitman County. As a boy, Faulkner used to hunt in its bottoms.

The Yocona (pronounced Yock-nee) is shown on old maps as the Yocanapatafa. Faulkner used a version of the name for his fictional YOKNAPATAWPHA COUNTY. In the second decade of the 20th century, the state established the Yoknapatawpha Drainage District to control flooding in southern Lafayette County.

Yoknapatawpha County   Fictional place, Faulkner's "intact world" of north-central Mississippi, corresponding to the actual LAFAYETTE COUNTY, though differing in some details. Yoknapatawpha has given its name to a cycle of interconnected major novels (and some minor works) set there, beginning with *Sartoris* (1929) and continuing through *The SECOND AND THE FURY* (1929), *AS I LAY DYING* (1930), *LIGHT IN AUGUST* (1932), *ABSALOM, ABSALOM!* (1936), *The HAMLET* (1940), *GO DOWN, MOSES* (1942), *The TOWN* (1957), *The MANSION* (1959), and *The REIVERS* (1962).

Yoknapatawpha is a self-contained world of rich bottomlands, broad cotton fields, eroded hills, and pine barrens people by CHICKASAW INDIANS and African-American slaves, plantation masters, defeated Confederates, indomitable spinsters, and poor white hill farmers. Charlatans, thieves, and rascals jostle with honest, hard-working folk. In time, the Yoknapatawpha saga spans roughly 170 years, from the establishment of a Chickasaw agency and trading post on the future site of JEFFERSON, MISSISSIPPI, before 1800, to 1961. In content, it deals with the Native American tradition, early exploration and settlement, the rise of the plantation system, the Civil War, the emancipation of slaves and Reconstruction, the decline of the planter aristocracy, and the machine and commercial culture of the modern era—the transformation of the Compson Mile of the 1830s into the Eula Acres subdivision of the decade following World War II.

According to the critic Malcolm COWLEY, "Faulkner performed a labor of imagination that has not been equaled in our time, and a double labor: first, to invent a Mississippi county that was like a mythical kingdom, but was complete and living in all its details; second, to make his story of Yoknapatawpha stand as a parable or legend of all the Deep South."

Though Faulkner developed his grand design over 30 years, he sketched the outlines of his legendary place in *Sartoris,* his third novel. Signing himself "William Faulkner, sole owner and proprietor," the novelist drew a map of his fictional county for *Absalom, Absalom!* and prepared a second map for the Viking Press's *The PORTABLE FAULKNER* (1946). The *Absalom* sketch gives Yoknapatawpha County an area of 2,400 square miles, with a population of 6,298 whites and 9,313 Negroes. The fictional county is more than three times larger than Lafayette County, with only two-thirds of its model's population; nor did the real place ever have a black majority. The TALLA-HATCHIE RIVER forms the northern boundary of Faulkner's Yoknapatawpha; the Yoknapatawpha River (the original name of the YOCONA RIVER) delimits the county on the south. There are no formal eastern or western boundaries.

The geography of Yoknapatawpha is substantially consistent throughout the chronicle, with the exception of *As I Lay Dying.* For some reason, the routes the Bundrens follow and the landmarks they pass in that novel as they carry Addie BUNDREN's body to Jefferson for burial do not conform to those of the other novels. In other works, minor details do not always agree, a fact that troubled Faulkner's editors far more than it troubled Faulkner himself.

Faulkner's scratch maps place the county seat, Jefferson, near the center of Yoknapatawpha. "John Sartoris' railroad" bisects the county north and south. A road leads from Jefferson northwest 12 miles to the mansion of SUTPEN'S HUNDRED, set in "Issetibbeha's Chickasaw Grant." Just beyond, on the Tallahatchie, is the "fishing camp where Wash Jones killed Sutpen, later bought and restored by Major Cassius de Spain." The road out of Jefferson to the northeast passes "McCallum's [sic], where young Bayard Sartoris went when his grandfather's heart failed in the car wreck." Beyond the Mac-Callum farm is the large McCaslin plantation, which figures in *The Unvanquished, Go Down, Moses* and *Intruder in the Dust.* Southeast of the county seat, at a distance variously given as 12 or 20 or 22 miles, lies the hamlet of FRENCHMAN'S BEND, with VARNER'S STORE and the OLD FRENCHMAN PLACE.

Faulkner's Yoknapatawpha is a social microcosm of the American South; and it is far more than that. The novelist once called his imaginary Mississippi county "a kind of keystone of the universe." If it were taken away, he went on to say, "the universe itself would collapse."

Young, Stark (1881–1963) Poet, novelist, and critic. Born in OXFORD, MISSISSIPPI, he graduated from the UNIVERSITY OF MISSISSIPPI in 1901, published his first collection of verse in 1906, and taught drama and English at the University of Texas and Amherst College until 1921.

Faulkner first met Young in the summer of 1914, introduced by Philip STONE. Young encouraged and befriended Faulkner and read his poems.

Young invited Faulkner to come to New York and sleep on his sofa until he landed a job. In the autumn of 1921 Faulkner took him up on the offer, and Young found work for him at a bookshop.

Young and Faulkner continued to meet when Young returned to Oxford for visits with his family, but they followed divergent literary paths. Young's novel *So Red the Rose* (1934), a family chronicle set in Mississippi, is a conventional idealized account of the Old South in the Civil War, far different from the picture of the region Faulkner created in his YOKNAPATAWPHA COUNTY novels.

Z

Zilich, Sophie Character in "PENNSYLVANIA STATION" (in *Collected Stories*). She is Margaret GIHON's friend and next-door neighbor. Sophie writes letters for the illiterate Margaret.

Zsettlani In *A FABLE,* the name used to identify the four foreign members of the group of 13 soldiers in the French army who are led by Corporal STEFAN in a failed attempt to end World War I. The four include Stefan himself, POLCHEK, PIOTR (also called Pierre Bouc), and one other. Although its precise meaning is unclear, the word "Zsettlani" is apparently a collective noun referring to the common provenance of these men, perhaps connected to a Middle Eastern ethnic group or nationality or perhaps a dialect shared by these four (see *A Fable,* pp. 292, 301, and 361).

APPENDIX I

Chronology and Adaptations

1. Chronology of Faulkner's Writings, Interviews, Addresses, and Publications (Note: Roman numerals refer to volume numbers, Arabic numerals to page numbers.)

"L'Après-midi d'un Faune" (August 6, 1919; poem, first published in *New Republic,* XX, 24; reprinted in *Mississippian,* IX [October 29, 1919] 4, in *Salmagundi* [see below], and in *William Faulkner: Early Prose and Poetry* [see below]).

"Cathay" (November 12, 1919; poem, first published in *Mississippian,* IX, 8; reprinted in *William Faulkner: Early Prose and Poetry* [see below]).

"Sapphics" (November 26, 1919; poem, first published in *Mississippian,* IX, 3; reprinted in *William Faulkner: Early Prose and Poetry* [see below]).

"Landing in Luck" (November 26, 1919; short story, first published in *Mississippian,* IX, 2, 7; reprinted in *William Faulkner: Early Prose and Poetry* [see below]).

"After Fifty Years" (December 10, 1919; poem, first published in *Mississippian,* IX, 4; reprinted in "Faulkner Juvenilia" by Martha Mayes, *New Campus Writing No. 2,* edited by Nolan Miller [New York: Bantam, 1957], and in *William Faulkner: Early Prose and Poetry* [see below]).

"Moonlight" (c. 1919–21; short story published posthumously in *Uncollected Stories of William Faulkner* [see below]).

"Une Ballade des Femmes Perdues" (January 28, 1920; poem, first published in *Mississippian,* IX, 3; reprinted in "Faulkner Juvenilia" by Martha Mayes, *New Campus Writing No. 2,* edited by Nolan Miller [New York: Bantam, 1957], and in *William Faulkner: Early Prose and Poetry* [see below]).

"Naiad's Song" (February 4, 1920; poem, first published in *Mississippian,* IX, 3; reprinted in *William Faulkner: Early Prose and Poetry* [see below]).

"Fantouches" (February 25, 1920; poem, first published in *Mississippian,* IX, 3; reprinted in "Faulkner Juvenilia" by Martha Mayes, *New Campus Writing No. 2,* edited by Nolan Miller [New York: Bantam, 1957]; reprinted as "Fantoches" in *William Faulkner: Early Prose and Poetry* [see below]).

"Clair de Lune" (March 3, 1920; poem, first published in *Mississippian,* IX, 6; reprinted in *William Faulkner: Early Prose and Poetry* [see below]).

"Streets" (March 17, 1920; poem, first published in *Mississippian,* IX, 2; reprinted in *William Faulkner: Early Prose and Poetry* [see below]).

"The Ivory Tower" (March 17, 1920; critical essay, first published in *Mississippian,* IX, 4; reprinted with minor changes in "Faulkner Juvenilia" by Martha Mayes, *New Campus Writing No. 2,* edited by Nolan Miller [New York: Bantam, 1957]).

"A Poplar" (March 17, 1920; poem, first published in *Mississippian,* IX, 7; reprinted in "Faulkner Juvenilia" by Martha Mayes, *New Campus Writing No. 2,* edited by Nolan Miller [New York: Bantam, 1957], and in *William Faulkner: Early Prose and Poetry,* [see below]).

To the Editor (April 7, 1920; letter, first published in *Mississippian,* IX, 1; reprinted in "Faulkner Juvenilia" by Martha Mayes, *New Campus Writing No. 2,* edited by Nolan Miller [New York: Bantam, 1957].

"A Clymene" (April 14, 1920; poem, first published in *Mississippian,* IX, 3; reprinted in *William Faulkner: Early Prose and Poetry,* [see below]).

"Study" (April 24, 1920; poem, first published in *Mississippian,* IX, 4; reprinted in "Faulkner Juvenilia" by Martha Mayes, *New Campus Writing No. 2,* edited by Nolan Miller [New York: Bantam, 1957], and in *William Faulkner: Early Prose and Poetry* [see below]).

"Alma Mater" (May 12, 1920; poem, first published in *Mississippian,* IX, 3; reprinted in *William Faulkner: Early Prose and Poetry* [see below]).

The Marionettes (fall 1920; one-act verse play; published posthumously in 1977 [see below]).

Review of *In April Once* by W. A. Percy (November 10, 1920; book review, first published in *Mississippian,* IX, 5; reprinted in *William Faulkner: Early Prose and Poetry* [see below]).

"To a Co-ed" (1920; poem, first published in *Ole Miss, the Yearbook of the University of Mississippi,* XXIV [1919–20]; reprinted in *Memphis Commercial Appeal,* November 6, 1932 [Magazine Section], in *The Literary Career of William Faulkner* by James B. Meriwether [Princeton University Library, 1961], and in *William Faulkner: Early Prose and Poetry* [see below]).

Review of *Turns and Movies* by Conrad Aiken (February 16, 1921; book review, first published in *Mississip-*

pian, X, 5; reprinted in *William Faulkner: Early Prose and Poetry* [see below]).

"Co-Education at Ole Miss" (May 4, 1921; poem, first published in *Mississippian*, X, 5; reprinted in *William Faulkner: Early Prose and Poetry* [see below]).

"Nocturne" (1921; poem, first published in *Ole Miss, the Yearbook of the University of Mississippi*, XXV [1920–21]; facsimile published in *The Literary Career of William Faulkner* by James B. Meriwether [Princeton University Library, 1961], and in *William Faulkner: Early Prose and Poetry* [see below]).

Vision in Spring (1921–23; cycle of 14 love poems [earlier version contained eight poems]; posthumously published in 1984, edited by Judith L. Sensibar, University of Texas Press, Austin).

"Love" (fall 1921; short story unpublished and basis of film scenario *Manservant* [see below]).

"Adolescence" (c. 1922; short story published posthumously in *Uncollected Stories of William Faulkner* [see below]).

Review of *Aria da Capo* by Edna St. Vincent Millay (January 13, 1922; book review, first published in *Mississippian*, XI, 5; reprinted in *William Faulkner: Early Prose and Poetry* [see below]).

"American Drama: Eugene O'Neill" (February 3, 1922; article, first published in *Mississippian*, XI, 5; reprinted in *William Faulkner: Early Prose and Poetry* [see below]).

"The Hill" (March 10, 1922; prose poem, first published in *Mississippian*, XI, 1–2; reprinted in *William Faulkner: Early Prose and Poetry* [see below]).

"American Drama: Inhibitions" (March 17 and 24, 1922; article, first section published in *Mississippian*, XI, 5 [March 17, 1922], and second section in *Mississippian*, XI, 5 [March 24, 1922]; reprinted in *William Faulkner: Early Prose and Poetry*, [see below]).

"Portrait" (June 1922; poem, first published in *Double Dealer*, II, 337; reprinted in *Salmagundi* [see below], and in *William Faulkner: Early Prose and Poetry* [see below]).

Review of *Linda Condon, Cytherea*, and *The Bright Shawl* by Joseph Hergesheimer (December 15, 1922; review of 3 books, first published in *Mississippian*, XII, 5; reprinted in *William Faulkner: Early Prose and Poetry* [see below]).

"Mississippi Hills" (October 1924; poem, revised as "My Epitaph" [see below]; slightly altered and retitled as "Mississippi Hills: My Epitaph," reproduced in *William Faulkner: "Man Working," 1919–1962, A Catalogue of the William Faulkner Collections at the University of Virginia*, compiled by Linton R. Massey [Charlottesville: Bibliographical Society, University of Virginia, 1968]).

The Marble Faun (December 15, 1924; poem of 806 lines with prologue and epilogue; preface by Phil Stone; published by Four Seas Company, Boston; republished with *A Green Bough* [photographically reproduced from original editions], by Random House, New York, 1965).

Mississippi Poems (December 30, 1924; typescript of 12 poems presented by Myrtle Ramey; eight of which revised for *A Green Bough* [1933]; posthumously published in 1979 [see below]).

Helen: A Courtship (1925; poems for Helen Baird; published posthumously in 1981 [see below]).

"Mirrors of Chartres Street" (February–September 1925; 11 of 16 prose sketches appearing in the *New Orleans Times-Picayune*, with introduction by William Van O'Connor [Minneapolis: Faulkner Studies, 1953]; also see two separate references below titled *New Orleans Sketches*).

"Dying Gladiator" (January/February 1925; poem, first published in *Double Dealer*, VII, 85; reprinted in *Salmagundi* [see below] and in *William Faulkner: Early Prose and Poetry* [see below]).

"On Criticism" (January/February 1925; article, first published in *Double Dealer*, VII, 83–84; reprinted in *Salmagundi* [see below] and in *William Faulkner: Early Prose and Poetry* [see below]).

"New Orleans" (January/February 1925; prose sketch, first published in *Double Dealer*, VII, 102–07; reprinted in *Salmagundi* [see below] and in *New Orleans Sketches*, edited by Carvel Collins [see below]).

"Mirrors of Chartres Street" (February 8, 1925; sketch, first published in the *New Orleans Times-Picayune*, pp. 1, 6; reprinted in *Mirrors of Chartres Street* [Minneapolis: Faulkner Studies, 1953], in *New Orleans Sketches*, edited by Ichiro Nishizaki [see below], and in *New Orleans Sketches*, edited by Carvel Collins [see below]).

"Damon and Pythias Unlimited" (February 15, 1925; sketch, first published in the *New Orleans Times-Picayune*, p. 7; reprinted in *Mirrors of Chartres Street* [Minneapolis: Faulkner Studies, 1953], in *New Orleans Sketches*, edited by Ichiro Nishizaki [see below], and in *New Orleans Sketches*, edited by Carvel Collins [see below]).

"Home" (February 22, 1925; sketch, first published in the *New Orleans Times-Picayune*, p. 3; reprinted in *Mirrors of Chartres Street* [Minneapolis: Faulkner Studies, 1953], in *New Orleans Sketches*, edited by Ichiro Nishizaki [see below], and in *New Orleans Sketches*, edited by Carvel Collins [see below]).

"Nympholepsy" (1925; short story published posthumously in *Mississippi Quarterly*, XXVI (Summer 1973): 403–09, edited with an introduction by James B. Meriwether; reprinted in *Uncollected Stories of William Faulkner*, [see below]).

"Frankie and Johnny" (c. 1925; short story published posthumously in *Mississippi Quarterly*, XXXI (Summer 1978): 453–64, edited with an introduction by James B. Meriwether; reprinted in *Uncollected Stories of William Faulkner,* [see below]).

"Jealousy" (March 1, 1925; sketch, first published in the *New Orleans Times-Picayune,* p. 2; reprinted in *Faulkner Studies,* III (Winter 1954): 46–50; in *Jealousy and Episode: Two Stories by William Faulkner,* [Minneapolis: Faulkner Studies, 1955]; in *New Orleans Sketches,* edited by Ichiro Nishizaki [see below]; and in *New Orleans Sketches,* edited by Carvel Collins [see below]).

"The Priest" (1925; short story published posthumously in *Mississippi Quarterly,* XXIX (Summer 1976): 445–50, edited with an introduction by James B. Meriwether; reprinted in *Uncollected Stories of William Faulkner* [see below]).

"The Faun" (April 1925; poem, first published in *Double Dealer,* VII, 148; reprinted in *Salmagundi* [see below] and in *William Faulkner: Early Prose and Poetry* [see below]).

"Verse Old and Nascent: A Pilgrimage" (April 1925; article, first published in *Double Dealer,* VII, 129–31; reprinted in *Salmagundi* [see below] and in *William Faulkner: Early Prose and Poetry* [see below]).

"Cheest" (April 5, 1925; sketch, first published in the *New Orleans Times-Picayune,* p. 4; reprinted in *Mirrors of Chartres Street* [Minneapolis: Faulkner Studies, 1953]; in *New Orleans Sketches,* edited by Ichiro Nishizaki [see below]; and in *New Orleans Sketches,* edited by Carvel Collins [see below]).

"Out of Nazareth" (April 12, 1925; sketch, first published in the *New Orleans Times-Picayune,* p. 4; reprinted in *Mirrors of Chartres Street* [Minneapolis: Faulkner Studies, 1953]; in *New Orleans Sketches,* edited by Ichiro Nishizaki [see below]; and in *New Orleans Sketches,* edited by Carvel Collins [see below]).

"Sherwood Anderson" (April 26, 1925; article, first published in the *Dallas Morining News,* Part III, p. 7; reprinted in *Princeton University Library Chronicle,* XVIII (Spring 1957): 89–94, and in *William Faulkner: New Orleans Sketches* [1968 Random House edition, see below], edited by Carvel Collins).

"The Kingdom of God" (April 26, 1925; sketch, first published in the *New Orleans Times-Picayune,* p. 4; reprinted in *Mirrors of Chartres Street* [Minneapolis: Faulkner Studies, 1953]; in *New Orleans Sketches,* edited by Ichiro Nishizaki [see below]; and in *New Orleans Sketches,* edited by Carvel Collins [see below]).

"The Rosary" (May 3, 1925; sketch, first published in the *New Orleans Times-Picayune,* p. 2; reprinted in *Mirrors of Chartres Street* [Minneapolis: Faulkner Studies, 1953]; in *New Orleans Sketches,* edited by Ichiro Nishizaki [see below]; and in *New Orleans Sketches,* edited by Carvel Collins [see below]).

"The Cobbler" (May 10, 1925; sketch, first published in the *New Orleans Times-Picayune,* p. 7; reprinted in *Mirrors of Chartres Street* [Minneapolis: Faulkner Studies, 1953]; in *New Orleans Sketches,* edited by Ichiro Nishizaki [see below]; and in *New Orleans Sketches,* edited by Carvel Collins [see below]).

"Chance" (May 17, 1925; sketch, first published in the *New Orleans Times-Picayune,* p. 7; reprinted in *Mirrors of Chartres Street* [Minneapolis: Faulkner Studies, 1953]; in *New Orleans Sketches,* edited by Ichiro Nishizaki [see below]; and in *New Orleans Sketches,* edited by Carvel Collins [see below]).

"Sunset" (May 25, 1925; sketch, first published in the *New Orleans Times-Picayune,* p. 7; reprinted in *Mirrors of Chartres Street* [Minneapolis: Faulkner Studies, 1953]; in *New Orleans Sketches,* edited by Ichiro Nishizaki [see below]; and in *New Orleans Sketches,* edited by Carvel Collins [see below]).

"The Kid Learns" (May 31, 1925; sketch, first published in the *New Orleans Times-Picayune,* p. 2; reprinted in *Mirrors of Chartres Street* [Minneapolis: Faulkner Studies, 1953]; in *New Orleans Sketches,* edited by Ichiro Nishizaki [see below]; and in *New Orleans Sketches,* edited by Carvel Collins [see below]).

"The Lilacs" (June 1925; poem, first published in *Double Dealer,* VII, 185–87; reprinted in *Salmagundi* [see below], in *A Green Bough* [revised as I], and in *Anthology of Magazine Verse for 1925 and Yearbook of American Poetry,* edited by William Stanley Braithwaite [Boston: B. J. Brimmer Co., 1925]).

"The Liar" (July 26, 1925; sketch, first published in the *New Orleans Times-Picayune,* pp. 3, 6; reprinted in *New Orleans Sketches,* edited by Carvel Collins [see below]).

"Episode" (August 16, 1925; sketch, first published in the *New Orleans Times-Picayune,* p. 2; reprinted in *Eigo Seinen* [Tokyo] on December 1, 1954; in *Faulkner Studies,* III [Winter 1954], 51–53; in *Jealousy and Episode: Two Stories by William Faulkner* [Minneapolis: Faulkner Studies, 1955]; in *New Orleans Sketches,* edited by Ichiro Nishizaki [see below]; and in *New Orleans Sketches,* edited by Carvel Collins [see below]).

"Country Mice" (September 20, 1925; sketch, first published in the *New Orleans Times-Picayune,* p. 7; reprinted in *New Orleans Sketches,* edited by Carvel Collins [see below]).

"Yo Ho and Two Bottles of Rum" (September 27, 1925; sketch, first published in the *New Orleans Times-Picayune,* pp. 1–2; reprinted in *New Orleans Sketches,* edited by Carvel Collins [see below]).

Elmer (1925; unfinished novel; typescript posthumously published in *Mississippi Quarterly,* 36 [Summer 1983]: 343–447, and by Seajay Press, Northport, Alab., in 1983; see "A Portrait of Elmer" below).

"Al Jackson" (1925; short story published posthumously in *Uncollected Stories of William Faulkner* [see below]).

"Don Giovanni" (c. 1925; short story published posthumously in *Uncollected Stories of William Faulkner* [see below]).

"Peter" (c. 1925; short story published posthumously in *Uncollected Stories of William Faulkner* [see below]).

Mayday (January 27, 1926; fable [hand-lettered, illustrated, and bound by Faulkner] given to Helen Baird; facsimile reproduction with a companion essay by Carvel Collins published by University of Notre Dame Press, Notre Dame, Ind., 1977; published with text set in type and illustrations reproduced, with revised essay as an introduction, by University of Notre Dame Press, Notre Dame, Ind., 1980).

Soldiers' Pay (February 25, 1926; novel, first published by Boni & Liveright, New York; elsewhere since).

Foreword to *Sherwood Anderson & Other Famous Creoles: A Gallery of Contemporary New Orleans* by William Spratling (1926; published by Pelican Bookshop Press, New Orleans; reprinted in *The Tangled Fire of William Faulkner* by William Van O'Connor, Minneapolis: University of Minnesota Press, 1954).

Father Abraham (1926–27; unfinished story, edited and with an introduction and textual notes by James B. Meriwether and published posthumously by Red Ozier Press, New York, in 1983 [limited edition of 210 copies] and by Random House, New York, in 1984 [a facsimile edition]; forms the beginning of *The Hamlet* [see below]; also recast as "Spotted Horses" [see below]).

"The Wishing Tree" (c. January/February 1927; fairy tale, published posthumously in *Saturday Evening Post* 240 [April 8, 1967]: 48–53, 57–58, 60–63; and published in book form by Random House, New York, on April 10, 1967).

Mosquitoes (April 30, 1927; novel, first published by Boni & Liveright, New York; elsewhere since).

"Hermaphroditus" (April 1927; poem, first appeared in Faulkner's novel *Mosquitoes* [see above], p. 252; revision reprinted XXX in *A Green Bough* [see below]).

"The Big Shot" (c. 1929; short story, published posthumously in *Mississippi Quarterly*, XXVI (Summer 1973): 313–24, and in *Uncollected Stories of William Faulkner* [see below]).

"A Dangerous Man" (c. 1929; short story, published posthumously in *Uncollected Stories of William Faulkner* [see below]).

Sartoris (January 31, 1929; novel; published by Harcourt, Brace, New York; elsewhere since; also see below, *Flags in the Dust*).

The Sound and the Fury (October 7, 1929; novel, first published by Jonathan Cape and Harrison Smith, New York; elsewhere since; most of the last chapter, "April Eighth, 1928," published under the title "Dilsey" in *The Portable Faulkner* [see below]; published in 1946 by Modern Library, New York, with an appendix as a foreword titled "Compson 1699–1945" and together with *As I Lay Dying* [see below]; complete novel published with the appendix at the end in *The Faulkner Reader* [see below]; film adaptation with same title released in 1959 [see below]; corrected text by Noel Polk published by Random House, New York, in 1984).

"Dull Tale" (c. 1929–30; short story published posthumously in *Uncollected Stories of William Faulkner* [see below]).

"A Return" (c. 1929–30; short story, published posthumously in *Uncollected Stories of William Faulkner* [see below]).

As I Lay Dying (October 6, 1930; novel, first published by Jonathan Cape and Harrison Smith, New York; elsewhere since; published together with *The Sound and the Fury* [see below]; new edition published in 1964 by Random House, New York; corrected text by Noel Polk published in 1985 by the Library of America [volume 1 of Faulkner's collected works: *Novels 1930–1935*], New York, and by Vintage International, New York, in October 1990).

"A Rose for Emily" (April 1930; short story, first published in *Forum*, LXXXIII, 233–38; reprinted revision in *These 13*, in *A Rose for Emily and Other Stories* [see below], in *The Portable Faulkner* [see below], in *Collected Stories* [see below], in *The Faulkner Reader* [see below], in *A Rose for Emily* [see below], and in *Selected Short Stories of William Faulkner* [see below]).

To the editor (April 1930; letter, published in *Forum*, LXXXIII, lvi).

"Honor" (July 1930; short story, first published in *American Mercury*, XX, 268–74; reprinted in *Doctor Martino and Other Stories* [see below], in *Collected Stories* [see below], and in *Selected Short Stories of William Faulkner* [see below]).

"Thrift" (September 6, 1930; short story, first published in *Saturday Evening Post*, CCIII, 16–17, 78, 82; reprinted in *O. Henry Memorial Award Prize Stories of 1931*, edited by Blanche Colton Williams [Garden City: Doubleday, Doran, 1931] and in *Uncollected Stories of William Faulkner* [see below]).

"Red Leaves" (October 25, 1930; short story, first published in *Saturday Evening Post*, CCIII, 6–7, 54, 56, 58, 60, 62, 64; revision published in *These 13* [see below], in *The Portable Faulkner* [see below], in the edition of *A Rose for Emily and Other Stories* edited and annotated by Kenzaburo Ohashi [see below], in *Collected Stories of William Faulkner* [see below], and in *Selected Short Stories of William Faulkner* [see below]; a portion again revised and included in *Big Woods*, pp. 99–109 [see below]).

"Evangeline" (c. 1930–31; short story published posthumously in *Uncollected Stories of William Faulkner* [see below]).

"Dry September" (January 1931; short story, first published in *Scribner's Magazine*, LXXXIX, 49–56; reprinted revision in *These 13* [see below], in *A Rose for Emily and Other Stories by William Faulkner* [see below], in *Collected Stories of William Faulkner* [see below], in *The Faulkner Reader* [see below], and in *Selected Short Stories of William Faulkner* [see below]).

Sanctuary (February 9, 1931; novel, first published by Jonathan Cape and Harrison Smith, New York; elsewhere since; published with an introduction by Faulkner [see below] by Modern Library, New York, on March 25, 1932; film adaptation titled *The Story of Temple Drake* released in 1933 [see below]; chapter 25 published under the title "Uncle Blud and the Three Madams" in *The Portable Faulkner* [see below]; published together with *Requiem for a Nun* [see below]; film adaptation based on *Sanctuary* and *Requiem for a Nun* titled *Sanctuary* released in 1961 [see below]; corrected text by Joseph Blotner and Noel Polk published in 1985 by the Library of America [volume 1 of Faulkner's collected works: *Novels 1930–1935*], New York; the corrected text with Faulkner's introduction in the Editors' Note published by Vintage International, New York, in December 1993).

"That Evening Sun Go Down" (March 1931; short story, first published in *American Mercury*, XXII, 257–67; revision titled "That Evening Sun" reprinted *These 13* [see below], in *A Rose for Emily and Other Stories by William Faulkner* [see below], in *The Portable Faulkner* [see below], in *Collected Stories of William Faulkner* [see below], in *The Faulkner Reader* [see below], in *A Rose for Emily* [see below], and in *Selected Short Stories of William Faulkner* [see below]).

"Ad Astra" (March 27, 1931; short story, first published in *American Caravan*, IV, 164–81; reprinted revision in *These 13* [see below], in *The Portable Faulkner* [see below], and in *Collected Stories of William Faulkner* [see below]).

"Hair" (May 1931; short story, first published in *American Mercury*, XXIII, 53–61; reprinted revision in *These 13* [see below] and in *Collected Stories of William Faulkner* [see below]).

"Beyond the Talking" (May 20, 1931; review of *The Road Back* by Erich Maria Remarque, published in *New Republic*, LXVII, 23–24).

"Spotted Horses" (June 1931; short story, first published in *Scribner's Magazine*, LXXXIX, 585–97; expanded revision included in chapter 1 of book 4 of *The Hamlet* [see below], reprinted as a novella in *The Faulkner Reader* [see below], and in *Three Famous Short Novels* [see below]; original version reprinted in *Uncollected Stories of William Faulkner* [see below]).

"The Hound" (August 1931; short story, first published in *Harper's Magazine*, CLXIII, 266–74; reprinted in *Doctor Martino and Other Stories* [see below] and in *A Rose for Emily and Other Stories by William Faulkner* [see below]; revision included in book 3 of *The Hamlet* [see below]; original version reprinted in *Uncollected Stories of William Faulkner* [see below]).

"Fox Hunt" (September 1931; short story, first published in *Harper's Magazine*, CLXIII, 392–402; reprinted in *Doctor Martino and Other Stories* [see below] and in *Collected Stories of William Faulkner* [see below]).

"All the Dead Pilots" (September 21, 1931; short story, first published in *These 13* [see below]; reprinted in *Collected Stories of William Faulkner* [see below]).

"Carcassonne" (September 21, 1931; short story, first published in *These 13* [see below] and in *Collected Stories of William Faulkner* [see below]).

"Crevasse" (September 21, 1931; short story, first published in *These 13* [see below], in *Collected Stories of William Faulkner* [see below], and in *A Rose for Emily* [see below]).

"Divorce in Naples" (September 21, 1931; short story, first published in *These 13* [see below] and in *Collected Stories of William Faulkner* [see below]).

"A Justice" (September 21, 1931; short story, first published in *These 13* [see below]; reprinted in *The Portable Faulkner* [see below], in *Collected Stories of William Faulkner* [see below], and in *The Faulkner Reader* [see below]); revised portion included in *Big Woods*, pp. 139–42 [see below]).

"Mistral" (September 21, 1931; short story, first published in *These 13* [see below] and in *Collected Stories of William Faulkner* [see below]).

"Victory" (September 21, 1931; short story, first published in *These 13* [see below] and in *Collected Stories of William Faulkner* [see below]).

These 13 (September 21, 1931; collection of 13 short stories [see above]; published by Jonathan Cape and Harrison Smith, New York, 1931; stories reprinted in *Collected Stories of William Faulkner* [see below]).

"Doctor Martino" (November 1931; short story, first published in *Harper's Magazine*, CLXIII, 733–43; reprinted in *Doctor Martino and Other Stories* [see below] and in *Collected Stories of William Faulkner* [see below]).

Night Bird (c. November 1931; scenario of unwritten screenplay and basis of *The College Widow* [see below]; published posthumously in *Faulkner's MGM Screenplays*, pp. 32–33, edited with introduction and commentaries by Bruce F. Kawin, University of Tennessee Press, Knoxville, 1982).

Idyll in the Desert (December 1931; short story, first published separately by Random House, New York, in 1931; reprinted in *Uncollected Stories of William Faulkner* [see below]).

"With Caution and Dispatch" (c. 1932; short story, published posthumously in *Uncollected Stories of William Faulkner* [see below]).

"Death-Drag" (January 1932; short story, first published in *Scribner's Magazine*, XCI, 34–42; reprinted with minor revisions as "Death Drag" in *Doctor Martino and Other Stories* [see below], in *The Portable Faulkner* [see below], and in *Collected Stories of William Faulkner* [see below]).

"Centaur in Brass" (February 1932; short story, first published in *American Mercury*, XXV, 200–10; reprinted in *Collected Stories of William Faulkner* [see below]; revised for first chapter of *The Town* [see below]).

"Once Aboard the Lugger" (February 1, 1932; title for two short stories, the first of which was first published in *Contempo*, I, 1, 4, and reprinted in *Uncollected Stories of William Faulkner* [see below]; the second, first published in *Uncollected Stories of William Faulkner* [see below]).

"I Will Not Weep for Youth" (February 1, 1932; poem, first published in *Contempo*, I, 1; reprinted in *An Anthology of the Younger Poets*, edited by Oliver Wells and with a preface by Archibald MacLeish [Philadelphia: Centaur Press, 1932]).

"Knew I Love Once" (February 1, 1932; poem, first published in *Contempo*, I, 1; reprinted in *A Green Bough* [revised as XXXIII] and in *An Anthology of the Younger Poets*, edited by Oliver Wells [Philadelphia: Centaur Press, 1932]).

"Twilight" (February 1, 1932; poem, first published in *Contempo*, I, 1; reprinted in *A Green Bough* [revised as X], and in *An Anthology of the Younger Poets*, edited by Oliver Wells [Philadelphia: Centaur Press, 1932]).

"Visions in Spring" (February 1, 1932; poem, published in *Contempo*, I, 1).

"Spring" (February 1, 1932; poem, first published in *Contempo*, I, 2; reprinted in *A Green Bough* [revised as XXXVI]).

"April" (February 1, 1932; poem, published in *Contempo*, I, 2).

"To a Virgin" (February 1, 1932; poem, first published in *Contempo*, I, 2; reprinted in *A Green Bough* [revised as XXXIX], and in *An Anthology of the Younger Poets*, edited by Oliver Wells [Philadelphia: Centaur Press, 1932]).

"Winter Is Gone" (February 1, 1932; poem, first published in *Contempo*, I, 2; reprinted in *An Anthology of the Younger Poets*, edited by Oliver Wells [Philadelphia: Centaur Press, 1932]).

"My Epitaph" (February 1, 1932; poem, first published in *Contempo*, I, 2; revised and reprinted as *This Earth*, 1932 [see below]; reprinted in *A Green Bough* [revised as XLIV]; reprinted in *An Anthology of the Younger Poets*, edited by Oliver Wells [Philadelphia: Centaur Press, 1932]; retitled as "If There Be Grief"

and published in *Mississippi Verse*, edited by Alice James [Chapel Hill: University of North Carolina Press, 1934]; reprinted in *Life*, Llll [20 July 1952]: 42).

"Lizards in Jamshyd's Courtyard" (February 27, 1932; short story, first published in *Saturday Evening Post*, CCIV, 12–13, 52, 57; revision included in book 4 of *The Hamlet* [see below]; original version reprinted in *Uncollected Stories of William Faulkner* [see below]).

"Turn About" (March 5, 1932; short story, first published in *Saturday Evening Post*, CCIV, 6–7, 75–76, 81, 83; revision reprinted in *Doctor Martino and Other Stories* [see below] and in *A Rose for Emily and Other Stories by William Faulkner* [see below]; reprinted as "Turnabout" in *Collected Stories of William Faulkner* [see below], in *The Faulkner Reader* [see below], and in *Selected Short Stories of William Faulkner* [see below]; basis of screenplay of same title and film titled *Today We Live* [see below]).

"Introduction" to *Sanctuary* by William Faulkner (March 25, 1932; first published with the Modern Library edition of the novel [see above, *Sanctuary*]; reprinted in the editors' note of the Vintage International Edition, 1993 [see above, *Sanctuary*]).

"Smoke" (April 1932; short story, first published in *Harper's Magazine*, CLXIV, 562–78; reprinted with minor changes in *Doctor Martino and Other Stories* [see below] and in *Knight's Gambit* [see below]).

To Maurice Edgar Coindreau (April 14, 1932; letter, published in facsimile in *Princeton University Library Chronicle*, XVIII [Spring 1957], Plate 2).

Salmagundi (April 30, 1932; reprinted prose pieces and poems [see above]; edited with an introduction by Paul Romaine; published by Casanova Press, Milwaukee).

Manservant (May 24, 1932; scenario of unwritten screenplay based on the unpublished short story "Love" [see above]; published posthumously in *Faulkner's MGM Screenplays*, pp. 7–28, edited with introduction and commentaries by Bruce F. Kawin, University of Tennessee Press, Knoxville, 1982).

"A Child Looks for His Window" (May 25, 1932; poem, published in *Contempo*, II, 3).

The College Widow (May 26, 1932; scenario of unwritten screenplay based on *Night Bird* [see above]; published posthumously in *Faulkner's MGM Screenplays*, pp. 40–53, edited with introduction and commentaries by Bruce F. Kawin, University of Tennessee Press, Knoxville, 1982).

Absolution (June 1, 1932; scenario of unwritten screenplay; published posthumously in *Faulkner's MGM Screenplays*, pp. 60–69, edited with introduction and commentaries by Bruce F. Kawin, University of Tennessee Press, Knoxville, 1982).

Flying the Mail (June 3, 1932; scenario of unwritten screenplay; published posthumously in *Faulkner's*

MGM Screenplays, pp. 83–69, edited with introduction and commentaries by Bruce F. Kawin, University of Tennessee Press, Knoxville, 1982).

"Miss Zilphia Gant" (June 27, 1932; short story, first published separately by Book Club of Texas (Dallas), with a preface by Henry Smith; reprinted in *Uncollected Stories of William Faulkner* [see below]).

Light in August (October 6, 1932; novel; first published by Smith & Haas, New York; elsewhere since; excerpt from novel published under title of "Percy Grimm" in *The Faulkner Reader* [see below]; corrected text by Noel Polk published in 1985 by Library of America [volume 1 of Faulkner's collected works: *Novels 1930–1935*], New York, and in October 1990 by Vintage International, New York).

This Earth (December 1932; revision of poem "My Epitaph" [see above]; published by Equinox Cooperative Press, New York).

"A Mountain Victory" (December 3, 1932; short story, first published in *Saturday Evening Post,* CCV, 6–7, 39, 42, 44–46; reprinted revision as "Mountain Victory" in *Doctor Martino and Other Stories* [see below], in *Collected Stories of William Faulkner* [see below], and in *Selected Short Stories of William Faulkner* [see below]).

"There Was a Queen" (January 1933; short story, first published in *Scribner's Magazine,* XCIII, 10–16; reprinted in *Doctor Martino and Other Stories* [see below], in *Collected Stories of William Faulkner* [see below], and in *Selected Short Stories of William Faulkner* [see below]).

War Birds (January 12, 1933; screenplay unproduced, published posthumously in *Faulkner's MGM Screenplays,* pp. 275–420, edited with introduction and commentaries by Bruce F. Kawin, University of Tennessee Press, Knoxville, 1982).

Today We Live (April 12, 1933 [advance showing]; screenplay [originally titled "Turn About"] with Edith Fitzgerald and Dwight Taylor, based on Faulkner's short Story "Turn About" [see above]; directed by Howard Hawks and released on April 21, 1933 by MGM; original script titled "Turn About," published posthumously in *Faulkner's MGM Screenplays,* pp. 128–255, edited with introduction and commentaries by Bruce F. Kawin, University of Tennessee Press, Knoxville, 1982).

"The Race's Splendor (April 12, 1933; poem, first published in *New Republic,* LXXIV, 253; reprinted in *A Green Bough* [as XXXVII, and in *New Republic,* CXXXI [November 22, 1954]: 82).

"Night Piece" (April 12, 1933; poem, first published in *New Republic,* LXXIV, 253; reprinted in *A Green Bough* [as VII]).

"Gray the Day" (April 12, 1933; poem, first published in *New Republic,* LXXIV, 253; reprinted in *A Green Bough* [as XXX]).

"Over the World's Rim" (April 12, 1933; poem, first published in *New Republic,* LXXIV, 253; reprinted in *A Green Bough,* as XXVIII]).

"The Ship of Night" (April 19, 1933; poem, first published in *New Republic,* LXXIV, 272; reprinted in *A Green Bough* as XXXIV]).

A Green Bough (April 20, 1933; 44 poems [13 previously published; see above]; illustrations by Lynd Ward; published by Smith & Haas, New York; seven poems reprinted with titles—XIV ["Mother and Child"], XVI ["Mirror of Youth"], XVIII ["Boy and Eagle"], XIX ["Green Is the Water"], XX ["Here He Stands"], XXXV ["The Courtesan is Dead"], and XLIV ["If There Be Grief," also see above: "My Epitaph"]—in *Mississippi Verse,* edited by Alice James [Chapel Hill: University of North Carolina Press, 1934]; republished with *The Marble Faun* [photographically reproduced from original editions], by Random House, New York, 1965).

Louisiana Lou (April/May 1933; screenplay unproduced [later version without contribution from Faulkner was released by MGM in 1934 under the title *Lazy River*]).

"Man Comes, Man Goes" (May 3, 1933; poem, first published in *New Republic,* LXXIV, 338; reprinted in *A Green Bough* [as VI], in *The New Republic Anthology: 1915–1935,* edited by Groff Conklin [New York: Dodge, 1936], and in *Fiction Parade,* V [October 1937]: 740).

The Story of Temple Drake (May 12, 1933; film adaptation of the novel, *Sanctuary* [see above]; screenplay by Oliver H. P. Garret and directed by Stephen Roberts; released by Paramount).

"The Flowers That Died" (June 25, 1933; poem, published in *Contempo,* III, 1).

"Artist at Home" (August 1933; short story, first published in *Story,* III, 27–41; reprinted in *Collected Stories of William Faulkner* [see below]).

Mythical Latin-American Kingdom Story (August 26, 1933; tentative title of screenplay unproduced; published posthumously in *Faulkner's MGM Screenplays,* pp. 449–543, edited with introduction and commentaries by Bruce F. Kawin, University of Tennessee Press, Knoxville, 1982).

"Beyond" (September 1933; short story, first published in *Harper's Magazine,* CLXVII, 394–403; reprinted in *Doctor Martino and Other Stories* [see below], in *Collected Stories of William Faulkner* [see below], and in *Selected Short Stories of William Faulkner* [see below]).

"Elly" (February 1934; short story, first published in *Story,* IV, 3–15; reprinted in *Doctor Martino and Other Stories* [see below] and in *Collected Stories of William Faulkner* [see below]).

"Pennslyvania Station" (February 1934; short story, first published in *American Mercury,* XXXI, 166–74;

reprinted in *Collected Stories of William Faulkner* [see below]).

"Wash" (February 1934; short story, first published in *Harper's Magazine*, CLXVIII, 258–66; reprinted in *Doctor Martino and Other Stories* [see below], in *The Portable Faulkner* [see below], in *Collected Stories of William Faulkner* [see below], and in *The Faulkner Reader* [see below]; included, with major revisions, in the latter part of chapter 7 of *Absalom, Absalom!* [see below]).

"A Bear Hunt" (February 10, 1934; short story, first published in *Saturday Evening Post*, CCVI, 8–9, 74, 76; reprinted in *Collected Stories of William Faulkner* [see below]; reprinted, in revised version, in *Big Woods* [see below]).

"Black Music" (April 16, 1934; short story, first published in *Doctor Martino and Other Stories* [see below]; reprinted in *Collected Stories of William Faulkner* [see below]).

"Leg" (April 16, 1934; short story, first published in *Doctor Martino and Other Stories* [see below]; reprinted as "The Leg" in *Collected Stories of William Faulkner* [see below]).

Doctor Martino and Other Stories (April 16, 1934; collection of 14 stories [see above], published by Smith & Haas, New York).

"Mule in the Yard" (August 1934; short story, first published in *Scribner's Magazine*, XCVI, 65–70; reprinted in *Collected Stories of William Faulkner* [see below]; with major revisions incorporated in chapter 16 of *The Town* [see below]).

"Ambuscade" (September 29, 1934; short story, first published in *Saturday Evening Post*, CCVII, 12–13, 80–1; reprinted revision as chapter 1 of *The Unvanquished* [see below]; original version reprinted in *Uncollected Stories of William Faulkner* [see below]).

"Retreat" (October 13, 1934; short story, first published in *Saturday Evening Post*, CCVII, 16–17, 82, 84–85, 87, 89; reprinted revision as chapter 2 of *The Unvanquished* [see below]; original version reprinted in *Uncollected Stories of William Faulkner* [see below]).

"Lo!" (November 1934; short story, first published in *Story*, V, 5–21; reprinted in *Collected Stories of William Faulkner* [see below] and in *Selected Short Stories of William Faulkner* [see below]).

"Raid" (November 3, 1934; short story, first published in *Saturday Evening Post*, CCVII, 18–19, 72–73, 75, 77–78; reprinted revision as chapter 3 of *The Unvanquished* [see below]; original version reprinted in *Uncollected Stories of William Faulkner* [see below]).

"A Portrait of Elmer" (c. 1934–35; short story, posthumously published in *Uncollected Stories of William Faulkner* [see below]).

Pylon (March 25, 1935 [copyright page reads "First Printing, February, 1935"]; novel, first published by Smith & Haas, New York; elsewhere since; film adap-

tation titled *The Tarnished Angels* released in 1957 [see below]; corrected text by Noel Polk published in 1985 by Library of America [volume 1 of Faulkner's collected works: *Novels 1930–1935*], New York; corrected text by Noel Polk with illustrations by David Tamura published in February 1987 by Vintage, New York).

"Skirmish at Satoris" (April 1935; short story, first published in *Scribner's Magazine*, XCVII, 193–200; reprinted revision as chapter 6 of *The Unvanquished* [see below]; original version reprinted in *Uncollected Stories of William Faulkner* [see below]).

"Folklore of the Air" (November 1935; review of *Test Pilot* by Jimmy Collins, published in *American Mercury*, XXXVI, 370–72).

"Golden Land" (May 1935; short story, first published in *American Mercury*, XXXV, 1–14; reprinted in *Collected Stories of William Faulkner* [see below]).

"That Will Be Fine" (July 1935; short story, first published in *American Mercury*, XXXV, 264–76; reprinted in *Collected Stories of William Faulkner* [see below]).

"Uncle Willy" (October 1935; short story, first published in *American Mercury*, XXXVI, 156–68; reprinted in *Collected Stories of William Faulkner* [see below]).

"Lion" (December 1935; short story, first published in *Harper's Magazine*, CLXXI, 67–77; revised and included in "The Bear" in *Go Down, Moses and Other Stories* [see below]; original version reprinted in *Uncollected Stories of William Faulkner* [see below]).

"Two Dollar Wife" (1936; short story, first titled "Christmas Tree" and first published in *College Life*, XVIII (January 1936): 8–10, 85, 86, 88, 90; reprinted in *Uncollected Stories of William Faulkner* [see below]).

"The Brooch" (January 1936; short story, first published in *Scribner's Magazine*, XCIX, 7–12; reprinted in *Collected Stories of William Faulkner* [see below]).

The Road to Glory (June 1936; screenplay with Joel Sayre; directed by Howard Hawks and released by Twentieth Century–Fox).

"Fool About a Horse" (August 1936; short story, first published in *Scribner's Magazine*, C, 80–86; revision included in book 1 of *The Hamlet* [see below]; original version reprinted in *Uncollected Stories of William Faulkner* [see below]).

"Absalom, Absalom!" (August 1936; excerpt [chapter 1] from novel of same title [see below], published in *American Mercury*, XXXVIII, pp. 466–74).

Absalom, Absalom! (October 26, 1936; novel [with map of Yoknapatawpha County], first published by Random House, New York; elsewhere since; chapter 2 published in *The Portable Faulkner* [see below]; corrected text by Noel Polk published by Random House, New York, in 1986, and by Library of America [volume 2 of Faulkner's collected works: *Novels 1936–1940*], New York, in 1990).

"The Unvanquished" (November 14, 1936; short story, first published in *Saturday Evening Post,* CCIX, 12–13, 121–22, 124, 126, 128, 130; retitled and revised as "Riposte in Tertio," chapter 4 of *The Unvanquished* [see below]; original version and title reprinted in *Uncollected Stories of William Faulkner* [see below]).

"Vendée" (December 5, 1936; short story, first published in *Saturday Evening Post,* CCIX, 16–17, 86, 87, 90, 92, 93, 94; revised as chapter 5 in *The Unvanquished* [see below]; original version reprinted in *Uncollected Stories of William Faulkner* [see below]).

To Maurice Edgar Coindreau (February 26, 1937; letter, published in facsimile in *Princeton University Library Chronicle,* XVIII [spring 1957], plate 2).

"Monk" (May 1937; short story, first published in *Scribner's Magazine,* CL, 16–24; reprinted in *Knight's Gambit* [see below]).

Slave Ship (June 1937; screenplay with Sam Hellman, Lamar Trotti, and Gladys Lehman; directed by Tay Garnett and released by Twentieth Century–Fox).

To the President of the League of American Writers (1938; letter, published in *Writers Take Sides: Letters about the War in Spain from 418 American Authors* [New York: League of American Writers]).

"An Odor of Verbena" (February 15, 1938; short story, first published as chapter 7 of *The Unvanquished* [see below]; reprinted in *A Rose for Emily and Other Stories by William Faulkner* [see below] and in *The Faulkner Reader* [see below]).

The Unvanquished (February 15, 1938; series of seven interrelated stories, first published by Random House, New York; first six are revisions of previously published short stories [see above]; stories III, "Raid," and VII, "An Odor of Verbena," published in *The Portable Faulkner* [see below]; basis of unproduced screenplay of same title by Sidney Howard for MGM, 1938; corrected text by Noel Polk published in 1990 by Library of America [volume 2 of Faulkner's collected works: *Novels 1936–1940*], New York, and in October 1991 by Vintage International, New York).

The Wild Palms (January 19, 1939; novel with two interwoven narratives ("The Wild Palms" and "Old Man"), first published by Random House, New York; the parts designated "Old Man" published under the title "Old Man" in *The Portable Faulkner* [see below] and as a novella in *The Faulkner Reader* [see below]; elsewhere since; also see below: *The Wild Palms and The Old Man* and *The Old Man;* corrected text by Noel Polk published as *If I Forget Thee, Jerusalem* in 1990 by Library of America [volume 2 of Faulkner's collected works: *Novels 1936–1940*], New York, and by Vintage International in 1995).

"Barn Burning" (June 1939; short story, first published in *Harper's Magazine,* CLXXIX, 86–96; reprinted in *A Rose for Emily and Other Stories* [see below], in *Collected Stories of William Faulkner* [see below], in *The Faulkner Reader* [see below], and in *Selected Short Stories of William Faulkner* [see below]; revised portions included in book 1 of *The Hamlet* [see below]; television adaptation with same title telecast in 1954 and another in 1980; film version on videocassette released in 1985 [see below]).

"Hand Upon the Waters" (November 4, 1939; short story, first published in *Saturday Evening Post,* CCXII, 14–15, 75–76, 78–79; reprinted in *Knight's Gambit* [see below]).

The Hamlet (April 1, 1940; novel [first in the Snopes trilogy—see *The Town* and *The Mansion* below], first published by Random House, New York; chapter 1 of book 4, "The Peasants," published in *The Portable Faulkner* [see below; also see "Spotted Horses," above]; reset text published by Modern Library on March 20, 1950; film adaptation titled *The Long Hot Summer* released in 1958 [see below] and television adaptation titled *The Long Hot Summer* telecast in 1985 [see below]; corrected text by Noel Polk published in 1990 by Library of America [volume 2 of Faulkner's collected works: *Novels 1936–1940*], New York, and by Vintage International, New York, in October 1991).

"A Point of Law" (June 22, 1940; short story, first published in *Collier's Magazine,* CV, 20–21, 30, 32; reprinted revision included in "The Fire and the Hearth" in *Go Down, Moses and Other Stories* [see below]; original version reprinted in *The Uncollected Stories of William Faulkner* [see below]).

"Almost" (July 1940; short story, revised and retitled "Was"; first published in *Go Down, Moses and Other Stories* [see below]).

"The Old People" (September 1940; short story, first published in *Harper's Magazine,* CCXXXI, 418–25, revision included in *Go Down, Moses and Other Stories* [see below]) and reprinted in *Big Woods* [see below]; original version reprinted in *Uncollected Stories of William Faulkner* [see below]).

"Pantaloon in Black" (October 1940; short story, first published in *Harper's Magazine,* CLXXXI, 503–13, revised for *Go Down, Moses and Other Stories* [see below]; original version reprinted in *Uncollected Stories of William Faulkner* [see below]).

"Gold Is Not Always" (November 1940; short story, first published in *Atlantic Monthly,* CLXVI, 563–70; revision incorporated in "The Fire and the Hearth" in *Go Down, Moses and Other Stories* [see below]; original version reprinted in *Uncollected Stories of William Faulkner* [see below]).

"Tomorrow" (November 23, 1940; short story, first published in *Saturday Evening Post,* CCXIII, 22–23, 32, 35, 37, 38, 39; reprinted in *Knight's Gambit* [see below]; television adaptation with same title telecast in 1960 [see below] and film adaptation with same title released in 1972 [see below]).

"Go Down, Moses" (January 25, 1941; short story, first published in *Collier's Magazine*, CVII, 19–20, 45, 46; revision reprinted in *Go Down, Moses and Other Stories* [see below]; original version reprinted in *Uncollected Stories of William Faulkner* [see below]).

"The Tall Men" (May 31, 1941; short story, first published in *Saturday Evening Post*, CCXIII, 14–15, 95–96, 98–99; reprinted in *Collected Stories of William Faulkner* [see below]).

To the Editor (July 12, 1941; letter, published in *Memphis Commercial Appeal*, p. 4).

"Snow" (c. 1942; short story published posthumously in *Mississippi Quarterly*, XXVI (Summer 1973), 325–30, and in *Uncollected Stories of William Faulkner* [see below]).

"Two Soldiers" (March 28, 1942; short story, first published in *Saturday Evening Post*, CCXIV, 9–11, 35–36, 38, 40; reprinted in *Collected Stories of William Faulkner* [see below] and in *Selected Short Stories of William Faulkner* [see below]).

"The Bear" (May 9, 1942; short story, first published in *Saturday Evening Post*, CCXIV, 30–31, 74, 76–77; with major revisions included in "The Bear" in *Go Down, Moses and Other Stories* [see below], and reprinted in *The Portable Faulkner* [see below] and as a novella in *The Faulkner Reader* [see below]; reprinted without part 4 in *Big Woods* [see below]; the shorter first published version reprinted in *Uncollected Stories of William Faulkner* [see below]).

"Delta Autumn" (May/June 1942; short story, first published in *Story*, XX, 46–55; reprinted revision in *Go Down, Moses and Other Stories* [see below], in *A Rose for Emily and Other Stories by William Faulkner* [see below], and in *The Portable Faulkner* [see below]; section of reprinted revision again revised and included as epilogue in *Big Woods* [see below]; first version reprinted in *Uncollected Stories of William Faulkner* [see below]).

"Was" (May 11, 1942; short story, retitled revision of the story "Almost" [see above] and first published as the first story in *Go Down, Moses and Other Stories* [see below]; reprinted in *The Portable Faulkner* [see below]).

Go Down, Moses and Other Stories (May 11, 1942; novel containing seven interrelated stories, six of which previously published [see above], first published by Random House, New York; title changed for second edition published by Random House on January 26, 1949, and for all subsequent editions to *Go Down, Moses* [see below]).

"Shingles for the Lord" (February 13, 1943; short story, first published in *Saturday Evening Post*, CCXV, 14–15, 68, 70–71; reprinted in *Collected Stories of William Faulkner* [see below] and in *The Faulkner Reader* [see below]).

"My Grandmother Millard and General Bedford Forrest and the Battle of Harrykin Creek" (March/April 1943; short story, first published in *Story*, XXII, 68–86; reprinted in *Collected Stories of William Faulkner* [see below]).

"L'Après-midi d'une Vache" (June/July 1943; short story, French translation of "Afternoon of a Cow" [see below]; first published in Maurice Edgar Coindreau's French translation in *Fontaine*, pp. 27–28).

"Shall Not Perish" (July/August 1943; short story, first published in *Story*, XXIII, 40–47; reprinted in *Collected Stories of William Faulkner* [see below] and in *A Rose for Emily* [see below]).

Battle Cry (August 16, 1943; unproduced screenplay; edited by Louis Daniel Brodsky and Robert W. Hamblin; published in 1985 by University Press of Mississippi, Jackson).

To Have and Have Not (October 1944; screenplay with Jules Furthman; directed by Howard Hawks and released by Warner Brothers).

A Rose for Emily and Other Stories by William Faulkner (April 1945; eight selected stories [see above] with foreword by Saxe Commins, Editions for the Armed Services, New York; work with same title but containing only four stories [three of which appear in the Armed Services edition but here with "Red Leaves" as the fourth story; see above], edited with annotations by Kenzaburo Ohashi and published by Kairyudo, Tokyo, n.d.).

The Portable Faulkner (April 29, 1946; selection of Faulkner's work [see above] with a new map of Yoknapatawpha County [see above, *Absalom, Absalom!*] and first appearance of the appendix on the Compsons [see below]; edited by Malcolm Cowley; first published by Viking Press, New York).

"Compson: 1699–1945" (April 29, 1946; appendix to *The Sound and the Fury* first published as "1699–1945 The Compsons" in *The Portable Faulkner* [see above]).

"An Error in Chemistry" (June 1946; short story, first published in *Ellery Queen's Mystery Magazine*, VII, 5–19; reprinted in *Knight's Gambit* [see below]).

The Big Sleep (August 1946; screenplay adaptation (with Leigh Brackett and Jules Furthman) of novel by Raymond Chandler; directed by Howard Hawks and released by Warner Brothers).

"His Name Was Pete" (August 15, 1946; article, first published in *Oxford*, [Mississippi], *Eagle*, p. 1; reprinted with minor changes in *Oxford Eagle* December 21, 1950, p. 25, in *Magazine Digest*, XXVI (January 1953), 93–94, and in *Milwaukee Journal*, January 28, 1953, p. 24).

The Sound and the Fury and *As I Lay Dying* (December 20, 1946; two novels previously published separately [see above], published by Modern Library, New York, with a new appendix as a foreword by the author titled "Compson: 1699–1945" [see above]).

To the Editor (March 13, 1947; letter, first published in the *Oxford* [Mississippi] *Eagle,* p. 5; reprinted with minor changes in the *Oxford Eagle* [December 21, 1950], p. 25).

"Afternoon of a Cow" (Summer 1947; short story, first published in *Furioso,* II, 5–17; reprinted in *Parodies: An Anthology from Chaucer to Beerbohm—and After,* edited by Dwight Macdonald, published by Random House, New York, 1960; first published in 1943 in a French translation as "L'Après-midi d'une Vache" [see above]; reprinted in *Uncollected Stories of William Faulkner* [see below]).

"Lucas Beauchamp" (1948; short story, published posthumously with an introduction by Patrick Samway, S. J., in *Virginia Quarterly,* 75 (Summer 1999): 417–437; with slight changes extracted from the first two chapters of *Intruder in the Dust* [see below]).

Intruder in the Dust (September 27, 1948; novel, first published by Random House, New York; film adaptation with same title released in 1949 [see below]; elsewhere; by Vintage International in October of 1991, and by Library of America [volume 3 of Faulkner's collected works: *Novels 1942–1954*], New York, in 1994).

"A Courtship" (Autumn 1948; short story, first published in *Sewanee Review,* LVI, 634–53; reprinted in *Collected Stories Stories of William Faulkner* [see below]).

The Old Man (November 1948; reprint of the chapters designated "Old Man" from the novel *The Wild Palms* [see above], published by New American Library, New York [also see *The Wild Palms and The Old Man* and *If I Forget Thee, Jerusalem,* below]).

Go Down, Moses (January 26, 1949; novel containing seven interrelated stories, published by Random House, New York; previously published under the title *Go Down, Moses and Other Stories* [see above]; elsewhere; published in November 1990 by Vintage International, New York, and by Library of America [volume 3 of Faulkner's collected works: *Novels 1942–1954*], New York, in 1994).

Intruder in the Dust (October 11, 1949; film adaptation with same title [see above]; directed by Clarence Brown and released by MGM).

Knight's Gambit (November 27, 1949; six mystery stories [five of which previously published, see above], first published by Random House, New York; published by Vintage Books, New York, in October 1978, elsewhere).

"Knight's Gambit" (November 27, 1949; mystery story published in *Knight's Gambit* [see above]).

"To the Voters of Oxford" (1950; broadside, first printed in Oxford, Mississippi; reprinted with minor changes in *The New Yorker,* XXVI [November 25, 1950], 29; original reprinted in "Faulkner and His

Folk," by Hodding Carter, in *Princeton University Library Chronicle,* XVIII [Spring 1957], 98–99).

To the Editor (March 26, 1950; letter, published in *Memphis Commercial Appeal,* Section IV, p. 4).

To the Editor (April 9, 1950; letter, published in Memphis *Commercial Appeal,* Section IV, p. 4).

To the Secretary of the American Academy of Arts and Letters (June 12, 1950; letter, published in *Proceedings of the American Academy of Arts and Letters and the National Institute of Arts and Letters,* second series, no. 1, 1951).

Collected Stories of William Faulkner (August 21, 1950; 42 previously published stories [see above], Random House, New York; republished in November 1995 by Vintage International, New York).

To the Editor (September 14, 1950; letter, first published in *Oxford,* [Mississippi] *Eagle,* p. 13; reprinted in *Oxford Eagle* on December 21, 1950, p. 25, and in "Faulkner and His Folk," by Hodding Carter, in *Princeton University Library Chronicle,* XVIII [Spring 1957], 100—01).

"A Name for the City" (October 1950; fictional essay, first published in *Harper's Magazine,* CCI, 200–14; revision included in first section of the prologue to act 1 of *Requiem for a Nun* [see below]).

To the Editor (November 13, 1950; letter, published in *Time* LVI, 6).

Nobel Prize Acceptance Speech (December 10, 1950; address delivered in Stockholm, Sweden, upon receiving the Nobel Prize in literature; published in *Les Prix Nobel en 1950,* Stockholm, 1951; reprinted with minor changes as a pamphlet by Spiral Press, New York, 1951, and elsewhere; reprinted in *The Faulkner Reader* [see below], and in *Faulkner at Nagano* [see below]; recorded by Faulkner on Caedmon records [TC-1035]).

Notes on a Horsethief (February 1951 [though dated 1950]; novella with decorations by Elizabeth Calvert; published by Levee Press, Greenville, Mississippi; revised and incorporated into *A Fable* [see below]).

Address to graduating class of University High School (May 28, 1951; address delivered in Oxford, Mississippi; printed in *Oxford* [Mississippi], *Eagle,* May 31, 1951, p. 1; reprinted with minor changes as "Never Be Afraid" in *Harvard Advocate,* CXXXV [November 1951]: 7).

"An Interview with William Faulkner" (Summer 1951; interview with Lavon Rasco, published in *Western Review,* XV, 300–304).

Requiem for a Nun (September 27, 1951; novel in the form of a three-act play with a prose narrative preceding each act [sequel to *Sanctuary,* see above], first published by Random House, New York; excerpt from the novel, "The Courthouse (A Name for the City)" [act 1], published in *The Faulkner Reader* [see below]; also published by Vintage Books in April

1975, and by Library of America [volume 3 of Faulkner's collected works: *Novels 1942–1954*], New York, in 1994).

"The Jail" (September/October 1951; excerpt [preface to act 3, "The Jail" [from *Requiem for a Nun* [see above], published in *Partisan Review*, XVIII, pp. 496–515).

Address upon being made an Officer of the Legion of Honor (October 26, 1951; address delivered in New Orleans, Louisiana; facsimile of manuscript [in French] reproduced in *Princeton University Library Chronicle*, XVIII [Spring 1957]).

Address to the Annual Meeting of the Delta Council (May 15, 1952; address delivered in Cleveland, Mississippi; printed in the Greenville, Mississippi, *Delta Democrat-Times* [May 18, 1952], p. 9; reprinted in 1952 by the Delta Council in pamphlet form as *An Address Delivered by William Faulkner*, and as "Man's Responsibility to Fellow Man" in *Vital Speeches of the Day*, XVIII [September 15, 1952]: 728–30).

Review of Ernest Hemingway, *The Old Man and the Sea* (Autumn 1952; book review, published in *Shenandoah* III: 55).

"Mr. Acarius" (February 1953; short story posthumously published in *Saturday Evening Post*, CCXXXVIII (October 9, 1965): 26–27, 29, 31, and reprinted in *Uncollected Stories of William Faulkner* [see below]).

To Richard Walser (1953; letter, published in *The Enigma of Thomas Wolfe*, edited by Richard Walser, Cambridge: Harvard University Press, 1953, p. vii).

"Sherwood Anderson: An Appreciation" (June 1953; article, published in *Atlantic Monthly*, CXCI, 27–29).

Address to the graduating class of Pine Manor Junior College (June 8, 1953; addressed delivered in Wellesley, Massachusetts; printed as "Faith or Fear" in *Atlantic Monthly*, CXCII [August 1953]: 53–55).

"Conversation with William Faulkner" (January 1954; interview with Loic Bouvard, published in *Bulletin de l'association amicale universitaire France-Amérique*, pp. 23–29; translated from the French by Henry Dan Piper and published in *Modern Fiction Studies*, V [Winter 1959–60]: 361–364).

"An Interview with Faulkner" (February 14, 1954; interview with A. M. Dominicus, published in *La Fiera Letteria* [Rome]; translated from the Italian by Elizabeth Nissen and published in *Faulkner Studies*, III [Summer-Autumn 1954]: 33–37).

"A Guest's Impression of New England" (1954; article, first published in *New England Journeys* 2 (*Ford Times* special edition): 6–8; reprinted in *The Ford Times Guide to Travel in USA*, edited by C. H. Dykeman [New York: Golden Press, 1962]).

The Faulkner Reader (April 1, 1954; anthology containing a foreword by Faulkner, the Nobel Prize Address, the whole of *The Sound and the Fury*, three "novellas" from three novels; eight short stories, and excerpts

from three novels; Random House, New York; republished in 1959 by Modern Library, New York).

"Mississippi" (April 1954; article, first published in *Holiday*, XV, 33–47; excerpted in *Big Woods* [see below]).

"Foreword" to *The Faulkner Reader* (1954; published by Random House, New York; [see above]).

"Percy Grimm" (April 1, 1954; excerpt from *Light in August* [see above] reprinted in *The Faulkner Reader* [see above]).

"Notes on a Horsethief" (July 1954; excerpt from *A Fable* [see below], published in *Vogue*, CXXIV, pp. 46–51, 101–07; abbreviated version published with minor changes in *Perspectives USA* 9 [Autumn 1954]: 24–59; earlier 1951 version as novella with same title [see above]).

A Fable (August 2, 1954; novel, first published by Random House, New York; also published by New American Library in September 1958, Vintage in January 1978, and by Library of America [volume 3 of Faulkner's collected works: *Novels 1942–1954*] in 1994).

The Wild Palms and The Old Man (September 1954; novel, rearranged version of *The Wild Palms* [see above] dividing the originally intended interwoven narratives into two separate sections: "The Wild Palms" and "Old Man"; published by New American Library, New York [also see below, *If I Forget Thee, Jerusalem*]).

"Hog Pawn" (c. October 1954; short story, first published posthumously in *Uncollected Stories of William Faulkner* [see below]; refashioned and included in chapter 14 of book 3, "Flem," of *The Mansion* [see below]).

"Sepulture South: Gaslight" (December 1954; short story, published in *Harper's Bazaar*, LXXXVIII, 84–85, 140–41; reprinted in *Uncollected Stories of William Faulkner* [see below]).

To the Editor (December 26, 1954; letter, *New York Times*, Section IV, p. 6).

"To the Youth of Japan" (1955; pamphlet [text in English with Japanese translation], first published by the U.S. Information Service [Tokyo]; English text reprinted in *Faulkner at Nagano* [see below]).

"An Innocent at Rinkside" (January 24, 1955; article, published in *Sports Illustrated*, II, 15).

Address upon receiving the National Book Award for Fiction (January 25, 1955; address delivered in New York; printed in *New York Times Book Review* [February 6, 1955], pp. 2, 4).

"A Walk with Faulkner" (January 30, 1955; interview with Harvey Breit, published in *New York Times Book Review*, pp. 4, 12; reprinted in Harvey Breit's *The Writer Observed*, World, Cleveland, 1956, pp. 281–84).

To the Editor (February 20, 1955; letter, first published in the *Memphis Commercial Appeal*, Section V, p. 3; reprinted in *New York Times Book Review* [March 13, 1955], p. 8).

"Race at Morning" (March 5, 1955; short story, first published in *Saturday Evening Post*, CCXXVII, 26, 103–04, 106; revision reprinted in *Big Woods* [see below] and in *Selected Short Stories of William Faulkner* [see below]; original version reprinted in *Uncollected Stories of William Faulkner* [see below]).

To the Editor (March 20, 1955; letter, first published in the *Memphis Commercial Appeal*, Section V, p. 3; reprinted with changes in "On Fear: The South in Labor" [see below]; reprinted in full in "Faulkner and His Folk," by Hodding Carter, in *Princeton University Library Chronicle*, XVIII [Spring 1957]: 102–03).

To the Editor (March 25, 1955; letter, published in *New York Times*, p. 22).

New Orleans Sketches by William Faulkner (April 1, 1955; thirteen of sixteen prose sketches from the *New Orleans Times-Picayune* [see above], edited with notes in Japanese and English by Ichiro Nishizaki, Hokuseido Press, Tokyo; eleven reprinted in *Mirrors of Chartres Street* [see above]).

To the Editor (April 3, 1955; letter, first published in the *Memphis Commercial Appeal*, Section V, p. 3; reprinted in "Faulkner and His Folk," by Hodding Carter, in *Princeton University Library Chronicle*, XVIII [Spring 1957]: 103–04).

To the Editor (April 10, 1955; letter, published in the *Memphis Commercial Appeal*, Section V, p. 3).

Address at the University of Oregon (April 13, 1955; address delivered in Eugene, Oregon; printed as "On Privacy. The American Dream: What Happened to It" in *Harper's Magazine*, CCXI [July 1955]: 33–38).

To the Editor (April 17, 1955; letter, published in the *Memphis Commercial Appeal*, Section V, p. 3).

"Kentucky: May: Saturday" (May 16, 1955; article, first published in *Sports Illustrated*, II, 22–24, 26; reprinted in *Essays Today 2*, edited by Richard M. Ludwig [New York: Harcourt, Brace, 1956]).

Land of the Pharaohs (July 1955; screenplay with Harry Kurnitz and Harold Jack Bloom; directed by Howard Hawks and released by Warner Brothers).

"Impressions of Japan" (September 26 and October 2, 1955; article released by the United States Embassy in Tokyo, first part published in the *Memphis Commercial Appeal*, [September 1955], Section V, p. 14, and second part published in the *Memphis Commercial Appeal*, [October 2, 1955], Section V, p. 10; reprinted in *Faulkner at Nagano* [see below] and in *Esquire*, L [December 1958]: 140).

"By the People" (October 1955; short story, first published in *Mademoiselle*, XLI, 86–89, 130, 131, 132, 133, 134, 135, 136, 137, 138, 139; revision included in chapter 13 of *The Mansion* [see below]).

Address to the annual meeting of the Southern Historical Association (November 10, 1955; address delivered in Memphis, Tennessee; printed in the *Memphis Commercial Appeal*, [November 11, 1955], p. 8; reprinted as "To Claim Freedom Is Not Enough" in *Christian Century*, LXXII [November 30, 1955]: 1395–6; reprinted with additions as "American Segregation and the World Crisis" in the pamphlet, *Three Views of the Segregation Decisions*, pp. 9–12 [Atlanta, Georgia: Southern Regional Council, 1956]).

A Rose for Emily (1956; four stories [see above and also see *A Rose for Emily and Other Stories*], edited with notes by Naotaro Takiguchi and Masao Takahashi, published by Nan 'un-do, Tokyo; two of the stories—"Shall Not Perish" and "Crevasse"—do not appear in *A Rose for Emily and Other Stories*).

"Message Given at Nagano" (1956; statement, published in *Faulkner at Nagano* [see below]).

"A Letter to the North" (March 5, 1956; article, first published in *Life*, XL, 51–52; excerpt reprinted in *Readers' Digest*, LXVIII [May 1956]: 75–78).

"The Art of Fiction XII: William Faulkner" (Spring 1956; interview with Jean Stein, published in *Paris Review* 12: 28–52; reprinted in *Writers at Work: The Paris Review Interviews*, edited by Malcolm Cowley and published by Viking Press, New York, 1958, pp. 119–41).

"A Talk with William Faulkner" (March 22, 1956; interview with Russell Warren Howe, published in *Reporter*, XIV, pp. 18–20).

To the Editor (March 26, 1956; letter, published in *Life*, XL, 19 [also see above, "A Letter to the North"]).

To the Editor (April 19, 1956; letter, published in *Reporter*, XIV, 7).

To the Editor (April 23, 1956; letter, *Time*, LXVII, 12).

"On Fear: The South in Labor" (June 1956; article, published in *Harper's Magazine*, CCXII, 29–34).

"The Art of Fiction: An Interview with William Faulkner" (Summer 1956; interview with Cynthia Grenier, published in *Accent* XVI, pp. 167–77).

Faulkner at Nagano (July 15, 1956; interviews, short written statements and the Nobel Prize Address, edited with a preface by Robert A. Jelliffe; published by Kenyusha, Tokyo; many of the interviews reedited and rearranged, published in *Esquire*, L (December 1958): 139, 141–42).

"If I Were a Negro" (September 1956; article, published in *Ebony*, XI, 70–73).

Big Woods (October 14, 1955; four previously published hunting stories, revised with preludes and epilogue, published by Random House, New York; republished in 1994 by Vintage International, New York).

To the Editor (December 10, 1956; letter, *Time*, LXVIII, 6, 9).

To the Editor (December 16, 1956; letter, *New York Times*, section IV, p. 8).

To the Editor (February 11, 1957; letter, *Time,* LXIX, 8).

Address upon receiving the Silver Medal of the Athens Academy (March 28, 1957; address delivered in Athens, Greece; printed in *The Literary Career of William Faulkner* by James B. Meriwether [Princeton University Library, 1961]).

The Town (May 1, 1957; novel [second in the Snopes trilogy—see *The Hamlet,* above, and *The Mansion,* below], first published by Random House, New York; also published by Vintage Books in January 1961).

"The Waifs" (May 4, 1957; excerpt from *The Town* [see above], published in *Saturday Evening Post,* CCXXIX, pp. 27, 116, 118, and 120).

To the Editor (October 13, 1957; letter, published in *New York Times,* section IV, p. 10).

The Tarnished Angels (January 1958; film adaptation of *Pylon* [see above]; screenplay by George Zuckerman and directed by Douglas Sirk; released by Universal-International).

The Long Hot Summer (March 1958; film adaptation of *The Hamlet* [see above]; screenplay by Irving Ravetch and Harriet Frank Jr.; directed by Martin Ritt and released by Twentieth Century–Fox; television version with same title, see below).

Three Famous Short Novels (1958; excerpts from three novels: *The Hamlet* ["Spotted Horses"], *The Wild Palms* ["Old Man"], and *Go Down, Moses* ["The Bear"]; published by Random House, New York).

New Orleans Sketches (1958; sixteen prose sketches from the *Times-Picayune* [see above] and eleven short pieces titled "New Orleans" [see above] from the *Double Dealer;* edited with introduction by Carvel Collins; published by Rutgers University Press, New Brunswick, N.J.; republished in 1961 by Grove Press, New York; new edition with additional essay published in 1968 by Random House, New York).

Address to the Raven, Jefferson, and ODK Societies (February 20, 1958; address delivered in Charlottesville, Virginia; printed as "A Word to Virginians" in *University of Virginia Magazine,* II [Spring 1958]: 11–14; reprinted in *Faulkner in the University* [see below]).

Address to the English Club of the University of Virginia (April 24, 1958; printed as "A Word to Young Writers" in *Faulkner in the University* [see below]).

The Sound and the Fury (March 1959; film adaption of novel with same title [see above]; screenplay by Irving Ravetch and Harriet Frank Jr.; directed by Martin Ritt and released by Twentieth Century–Fox).

Faulkner in the University (1959; transcribed recordings of class conferences and addresses, edited by Frederick L. Gwynn and Joseph L. Blotner, Charlottesville: University Press of Virginia).

Note to *Requiem for a Nun: a Play* from the novel by William Faulkner, see above (1959; adapted to the stage by Ruth Ford; published by Random House, New York).

Address to the seventh national conference of the U.S. National Commission for UNESCO (October 2, 1959; address delivered in Denver, Colorado; printed as "From Yoknapatawpha to UNESCO, the Dream" in *Saturday Review,* XLII [November 14, 1959]: 21).

"Notice" (October 22, 1959; public notice (an appeal to hunters on Faulkner's land), first published in the *Oxford* [Mississippi] *Eagle,* p. 7; reprinted in *Time,* LXXIV [November 2, 1959]: 29).

The Mansion (November 13, 1959; novel [third in the Snopes trilogy—see *The Hamlet* and *The Mansion* above], first published by Random House, New York; also published by Vintage Books in September 1965).

Note to *The Mansion* by William Faulkner (November 13, 1959; note published with the novel, see above).

"Mink Snopes" (December 1959; excerpt [chapters 1 and 2] from *The Mansion* published in *Esquire,* LII, pp. 226–30, 247–64).

Tomorrow (March 7, 1960; television adaptation of short story of same title [see above]; telefilm by Horton Foote and directed by Robert Mulligan; telecast on CBS; for film version of short story, see below].

To the Editor (August 28, 1960; letter, published in *New York Times,* Section IV, p. 10).

To Sherwood Anderson (1961; letter [undated], facsimile reproduced in *The Literary Career of William Faulkner* by James B. Meriwether, Princeton University Library, plates 27, 28, and 29; also see Faulkner's novel *Mosquitoes* [pp. 277–8] where he incorporates material from this letter).

Sanctuary (February 1961; film adaptation based on novel of same title and *Requiem for a Nun* [see above]; screenplay by James Poe and directed by Tony Richardson; released by Twentieth Century–Fox).

"Albert Camus" (Spring 1961; homage to Albert Camus after his death [1960], published in *Transatlantic Review* 6: 5; French translation published a year earlier in the *Nouvelle Revue française*).

"Hell Creek Crossing" (March 31, 1962; excerpt from *The Reivers* [see below] with introductory, published in *Saturday Evening Post,* CCXXXV, pp. 22–25).

Selected Short Stories of William Faulkner (1962; thirteen short stories previously published [see above], Modern Library, New York).

The Reivers (June 4, 1962; novel, first published by Random House, New York; also published by Vintage Books in September 1966; film adaptation with same title released in 1969 [see below]).

William Faulkner: Early Prose and Poetry (1962; previously published poems, prose pieces, and pen-and-ink drawings [see above]; compiled with an introduction by Carvel Collins; published by Little, Brown, Boston).

"The Education of Lucius Priest" (May 1962; edited excerpt from *The Reivers* [see above] published in *Esquire*, LVII, pp. 109–16).

Address upon receiving the Gold Medal for Fiction of the National Institute of Arts and Letters (May 24, 1962; address delivered in New York; printed in *Proceedings of the American Academy of Arts and Letters and the National Institute of Arts and Letters*, Second Series, No. 13 [New York, 1963]: 226–27).

William Faulkner's University Pieces (1962; edited with an introduction by Carvel Collins, Kendyusha Press).

Essays, Speeches, and Public Lectures by William Faulkner (1966; collection of Faulkner's articles, speeches, forewords, book reviews, and public lectures; edited by James B. Meriwether and published by Random House, New York, 1966).

The Reivers (1969; film adaptation of novel of same title [see above]; screenplay by Irving Ravetch and Harriet Frank Jr.; directed by Mark Rydell and released by National General).

Tomorrow (1972; film adaptation of short story of same title [see above]; screenplay by Horton Foote; directed by Joseph Anthony and released by Filmgroup [for television adaptation of short story, see above]).

Flags in the Dust (August 22, 1973; novel [complete text of the novel *Sartoris*, see above]; edited with an introduction by Douglas Day and published posthumously by Random House, New York).

Uncollected Stories of William Faulkner (1979; forty-five stories [see above], some revised for books and others uncollected or unpublished; edited and notes by Joseph Blotner; first published by Random House, New York; republished in a centenary edition by Vintage International, New York, in September 1997).

The Marionettes: A Play in One Act (1977; edited with an introduction by Noel Polk; published by University Press of Virginia, Charlottesville).

Mississippi Poems (1979; poems published posthumously by Yoknapatawpha Press, Oxford, Miss.).

Barn Burning (March 17, 1980; television adaptation of short story of same title [see above]; telefilm by Horton Foote and directed by Peter Werner; telecast on PBS).

Helen: A Courtship (1981; poems for Helen Baird, published posthumously by Tulane University, New Orleans, and Yoknapatawpha Press, Oxford, Miss.).

The Long Hot Summer (October 6 and 7, 1985; television adaptation of *The Hamlet* [see above] and its film version titled *The Long Hot Summer* [see above]; telefilm by Rita Mae Brown and Dennis Turner; directed by Stuart Cooper; telecast by NBC).

If I Forget Thee, Jerusalem (1990; novel, original title of *The Wild Palms* [see above]; corrected text by Noel Polk published in 1990 by Library of America [volume 2 of Faulkner's collected works: *Novels 1936–1940*], New York, and in November 1995 by Vintage International, New York).

Old Man (1998; telefilm version of the "Old Man" section of the novel *Wild Palms* [see above]; telefilm by Horton Foote and directed by John Kent Harrison; telecast on CBS).

2. Categorical Chronology of Faulkner's Writings, Interviews, Addresses, and Publications

Addresses

Nobel Prize Acceptance Speech (December 10, 1950; address delivered in Stockholm, Sweden, upon receiving the Nobel Prize in literature; published in *Les Prix Nobel en 1950*, Stockholm, 1951; reprinted with minor changes as a pamphlet by Spiral Press, New York, 1951, and elsewhere; reprinted in *The Faulkner Reader* and in *Faulkner at Nagano*; recorded by Faulkner on Caedmon records [TC-1035]).

Address to graduating class of University High School (May 28, 1951, address delivered in Oxford, Mississippi; printed in the *Oxford, [Mississippi] Eagle*, May 31, 1951, p. 1; reprinted with minor changes as "Never Be Afraid" in *Harvard Advocate*, CXXXV [November 1951]: 7).

Address upon being made an Officer of the Legion of Honor (October 26, 1951; address delivered in New Orleans, Louisiana; facsimile of manuscript [in French] reproduced in *Princeton University Library Chronicle*, XVIII [Spring 1957]).

Address to the Annual Meeting of the Delta Council (May 15, 1952; address delivered in Cleveland, Mississippi; printed in the Greenville, Mississippi, *Delta Democrat-Times* [May 18, 1952], p. 9; reprinted in 1952 by the Delta Council in pamphlet form as *An Address Delivered by William Faulkner*, and as "Man's Responsibility to Fellow Man" in *Vital Speeches of the Day*, XVIII [September 15, 1952], 728–30).

Address to the graduating class of Pine Manor Junior College (June 8, 1953; addressed delivered in Wellesley, Massachusetts; printed as "Faith or Fear" in *Atlantic Monthly*, CXCII [August 1953]: 53–55).

Address upon receiving the National Book Award for Fiction (January 25, 1955; address delivered in New York; printed in *New York Times Book Review* [February 6, 1955], pp. 2, 4).

Address at the University of Oregon (April 13, 1955; address delivered in Eugene, Oregon; printed as "On Privacy. The American Dream: What Happened to It" in *Harper's Magazine*, CCXI [July 1955]: 33–38).

Address to the annual meeting of the Southern Historical Association (November 10, 1955; address delivered in

Memphis, Tennessee; printed in the Memphis *Commercial Appeal* [November 11, 1955], p. 8; reprinted as "To Claim Freedom Is Not Enough" in *Christian Century*, LXXII [November 30, 1955]: 1395–96; reprinted with additions as "American Segregation and the World Crisis" in the pamphlet *Three Views of the Segregation Decisions*, pp. 9–12 [Atlanta, Georgia: Southern Regional Council, 1956]).

Address upon receiving the Silver Medal of the Athens Academy (March 28, 1957; address delivered in Athens, Greece; printed in *The Literary Career of William Faulkner* by James B. Meriwether [Princeton University Library, 1961]).

Address to the Raven, Jefferson, and ODK Societies (February 20, 1958; address delivered in Charlottesville, Virginia; printed as "A Word to Virginians" in *University of Virginia Magazine*, II [Spring 1958]: 11–14; reprinted in *Faulkner in the University*).

Address to the English Club of the University of Virginia (April 24, 1958; printed as "A Word to Young Writers" in *Faulkner in the University*).

Address to the seventh national conference of the U.S. National Commission for UNESCO (October 2, 1959; address delivered in Denver, Colorado; printed as "From Yoknapatawpha to UNESCO, the Dream" in *Saturday Review*, XLII [November 14, 1959]: 21).

Address upon receiving the Gold Medal for Fiction of the National Institute of Arts and Letters (May 24, 1962; address delivered in New York; printed in *Proceedings of the American Academy of Arts and Letters and the National Institute of Arts and Letters*, Second Series, 13 [New York, 1963]: 226–27).

Articles and Essays

"The Ivory Tower" (March 17, 1920; critical essay, first published in *Mississippian*, IX, 4; reprinted with minor changes in "Faulkner Juvenilia" by Martha Mayes, *New Campus Writing No. 2*, edited by Nolan Miller [New York: Bantam, 1957]).

"American Drama: Eugene O'Neill" (February 3, 1922; article, first published in *Mississippian*, XI, 5; reprinted in *William Faulkner: Early Prose and Poetry*).

"American Drama: Inhibitions" (March 17 and 24, 1922; article, first section published in *Mississippian*, XI [March 17, 1922]: 5, and second section in *Mississippian*, XI [March 24, 1922]: 5; reprinted in *William Faulkner: Early Prose and Poetry*).

"On Criticism" (January/February 1925; article; first published in *Double Dealer*, VII, 83–84; reprinted in *Salmagundi* and in *William Faulkner: Early Prose and Poetry*).

"Verse Old and Nascent: A Pilgrimage" (April 1925; article, first published in *The Double Dealer*, VII, 129–31; reprinted in *Salmagundi* and in *William Faulkner: Early Prose and Poetry*).

"Sherwood Anderson" (April 26, 1925; article, first published in the *Dallas Morning News*, part 3, p. 7; reprinted in *Princeton University Library Chronicle*, XVIII (Spring 1957), 89–94, and in *William Faulkner: New Orleans Sketches* [1968 Random House edition], edited by Carvel Collins).

"His Name Was Pete" (August 15, 1946; article, first published in the *Oxford* [Mississippi] *Eagle*, p. 1; reprinted with minor changes in *Oxford Eagle* December 21, 1950, p. 25, in *Magazine Digest*, XXVI (January 1953): 93–94, and in the *Milwaukee Journal*, January 28, 1953, p. 24).

"Sherwood Anderson: An Appreciation" (June 1953; article, published in *Atlantic Monthly*, CXCI, 27–29).

"A Guest's Impression of New England" (1954; article, first published in *New England Journeys Number 2* (*Ford Times* special edition), 6–8; reprinted in *The Ford Times Guide to Travel in USA*, edited by C. H. Dykeman [New York: Golden Press, 1962]).

"Mississippi" (April 1954; article, first published in *Holiday*, XV, 33–47; excerpted in *Big Woods*).

"An Innocent at Rinkside" (January 24, 1955; article, published in *Sports Illustrated*, II, 15).

"Kentucky: May: Saturday" (May 16, 1955; article, first published in *Sports Illustrated*, II, 22–24, 26; reprinted in *Essays Today 2*, edited by Richard M. Ludwig [New York: Harcourt, Brace, 1956]).

"Impressions of Japan" (September 26 and October 2, 1955; article released by the United States Embassy in Tokyo, first part published in the *Memphis Commercial Appeal* [September 26, 1955], section V, p. 14, and second part published in the *Memphis Commercial Appeal*, [October 2, 1955], section V, p. 10; reprinted in *Faulkner at Nagano* and in *Esquire*, L [December 1958]: 140).

"A Letter to the North" (March 5, 1956; article, first published in *Life*, XL, 51–52; excerpt reprinted in *Readers' Digest*, LXVIII [May 1956]: 75–78).

"On Fear: The South in Labor" (June 1956; article, published in *Harper's Magazine*, CCXII, 29–34).

"If I Were a Negro" (September 1956; article, published in *Ebony*, XI, 70–73).

Collections

These 13 (September 21, 1931; collection of 13 short stories; published by Cape & Smith, New York, 1931; stories reprinted in *Collected Stories of William Faulkner* [see below]).

Doctor Martino and Other Stories (April 16, 1934; collection of 14 stories, published by Smith & Haas, New York).

The Portable Faulkner (April 29, 1946; selection of Faulkner's works with a new map of Yoknapatawpha County [see the novel *Absalom, Absalom!*] and first appearance of the appendix on the Compsons;

edited by Malcolm Cowley; first published by Viking Press, New York).

Knight's Gambit (November 27, 1949; six mystery stories [five of which previously published, see above], first published by Random House, New York; published by Vintage Books, New York, in October 1978, elsewhere).

Collected Stories of William Faulkner (August 21, 1950; 42 previously published stories, Random House, New York; republished in November 1995 by Vintage International, New York).

The Faulkner Reader (April 1, 1954; anthology containing a foreword by Faulkner, the Nobel Prize Address, the whole of *The Sound and the Fury,* three "novellas" from three novels; eight short stories, and excerpts from three novels; Random House, New York; republished in 1959 by Modern Library, New York).

Big Woods (October 14, 1955; four previously published hunting stories, revised with preludes and epilogue, published by Random House, New York; republished in 1994 by Vintage International, New York).

Three Famous Short Novels (1958; excerpts from three novels: *The Hamlet* ["Spotted Horses"], *The Wild Palms* ["Old Man"], and *Go Down, Moses* ["The Bear"]; published by Random House, New York).

Selected Short Stories of William Faulkner (1962; 13 short stories previously published, Modern Library, New York).

Uncollected Stories of William Faulkner (1979; 45 stories, some revised for books and others uncollected or unpublished; edited and notes by Joseph Blotner; first published by Random House, New York; republished in a centenary edition by Vintage International, New York, in September 1997).

Fable

Mayday (January 27, 1926; fable [hand-lettered, illustrated, and bound by Faulkner] given to Helen Baird; facsimile reproduction with a companion essay by Carvel Collins published by University of Notre Dame Press, Notre Dame, 1977; published with text set in type and illustrations reproduced, with revised essay as an introduction, by University of Notre Dame Press, Notre Dame, 1980).

Fairy Tale

"The Wishing Tree" (c. January/February 1927; posthumously published in *Saturday Evening Post* 240 [April 8, 1967]: 48–53, 57–58, 60–63; published in book form by Random House, New York, on April 10, 1967).

Forewords, Prefaces, Introductions, and Appendixes

"Foreword" to *Sherwood Anderson & Other Famous Creoles: A Gallery of Contemporary New Orleans* by William Spratling (1926; published by Pelican Bookshop Press, New Orleans; reprinted in *The Tangled Fire of William Faulkner* by William Van O'Connor, Minneapolis: University of Minnesota Press, 1954).

The Sound and the Fury and *As I Lay Dying* (December 20, 1946; two novels previously published separately, published by Modern Library, New York, with a new appendix as a foreword by the author titled "Compson: 1699–1945").

The Faulkner Reader (April 1, 1954; anthology containing a foreword by Faulkner, the Nobel Prize Address, the whole of *The Sound and the Fury,* three "novellas" from three novels; eight short stories, and excerpts from three novels; Random House, New York; republished in 1959 by Modern Library, New York).

"Foreword" to *The Faulkner Reader* (1954; published by Random House, New York).

Interviews

"An Interview with William Faulkner" (Summer 1951; interview with Lavon Rasco, published in *Western Review,* XV, pp. 300–304).

"Conversation with William Faulkner" (January 1954; interview with Loic Bouvard, published in *Bulletin de l'association amicale universitaire France-Amérique,* pp. 23–29; translated from the French by Henry Dan Piper and published in *Modern Fiction Studies,* V [Winter 1959–60]: 361–364).

"An Interview with Faulkner" (February 14, 1954; interview with A. M. Dominicus, published in *La Fiera Letteria* [Rome]; translated from the Italian by Elizabeth Nissen and published in *Faulkner Studies,* III (Summer-Autumn 1954]: 33–37).

"A Walk with Faulkner" (January 30, 1955; interview with Harvey Breit, published in *New York Times Book Review,* pp. 4, 12; reprinted in Harvey Breit's *The Writer Observed* [Cleveland: World 1956], pp. 281–284).

"The Art of Fiction XII: William Faulkner" (Spring 1956; interview with Jean Stein, published in *Paris Review* 12: 28–52; reprinted in *Writers at Work: The Paris Review Interviews,* edited by Malcolm Cowley and published by Viking Press, New York, 1958, pp. 119–141).

"A Talk with William Faulkner" (March 22, 1956; interview with Russell Warren Howe, published in *Reporter,* XIV, pp. 18–20).

"The Art of Fiction: An Interview with William Faulkner" (Summer 1956; interview with Cynthia Grenier, published in *Accent,* XVI, pp. 167–177).

Faulkner at Nagano (July 15, 1956; interviews, short written statements and the Nobel Prize Address, edited with a preface by Robert A. Jelliffe; published by Kenyusha, Tokyo; many of the interviews reedited and rearranged, published in *Esquire,* L (December 1958): 139, 141–42).

Letters

To the Editor (April 7, 1920; letter, first published in *Mississippian,* IX, 1; reprinted in "Faulkner Juvenilia" by Martha Mayes, *New Campus Writing No. 2,* edited by Nolan Miller [New York: Bantam, 1957]).

To the Editor (April 1930; letter, published in *Forum,* LXXXIII, lvi).

To Maurice Edgar Coindreau (April 14, 1932; letter, published in facsimile in *Princeton University Library Chronicle,* XVIII [Spring 1957]: plate 2).

To the President of the League of American Writers (1938; letter, published in *Writers Take Sides: Letters about the War in Spain from 418 American Authors* [New York: League of American Writers]).

To the Editor (July 12, 1941; letter, published in the *Memphis Commercial Appeal,* p. 4).

To the Editor (March 13, 1947; letter, first published in the *Oxford* [Mississippi] *Eagle,* p. 5; reprinted with minor changes in the *Oxford Eagle* [December 21, 1950], p. 25).

To the Editor (March 26, 1950; letter, published in the *Memphis Commercial Appeal,* section IV, p. 4).

To the Editor (April 9, 1950; letter, published in the *Memphis Commercial Appeal,* section IV, p. 4).

To the Secretary of the American Academy of Arts and Letters (June 12, 1950; letter, published in *Proceedings of the American Academy of Arts and Letters and the National Institute of Arts and Letters,* Second Series, 1, 1951).

To the Editor (September 14, 1950; letter, first published in the *Oxford* [Mississippi] *Eagle,* p. 13; reprinted in the *Eagle* on December 21, 1950, p. 25, and in "Faulkner and His Folk," by Hodding Carter, in *Princeton University Library Chronicle* XVIII [Spring 1957], 100–01).

To the Editor (November 13, 1950; letter, published in *Time,* LVI, 6).

To Richard Walser (1953; letter, published in *The Enigma of Thomas Wolfe,* edited by Richard Walser, Cambridge: Harvard University Press, 1953, p. vii).

To the Editor (December 26, 1954; letter, *New York Times,* Section IV, p. 6).

To the Editor (February 20, 1955; letter, first published in the *Memphis Commercial Appeal,* Section V, p. 3; reprinted in *New York Times Book Review* [March 13, 1955], p. 8).

To the Editor (March 20, 1955; letter, first published in the *Memphis Commercial Appeal,* Section V, p. 3; reprinted with changes in "On Fear: The South in Labor "; reprinted in full in "Faulkner and His Folk," by Hodding Carter, in *Princeton University Library Chronicle,* XVIII [Spring 1957]: 102–103).

To the Editor (March 25, 1955; letter, published in *New York Times,* p. 22).

To the Editor (April 3, 1955; letter, first published in the *Memphis Commercial Appeal,* Section V, p. 3; reprinted in "Faulkner and His Folk," by Hodding

Carter, in *Princeton University Library Chronicle,* XVIII [Spring 1957]: 103–104).

To the Editor (April 10, 1955; letter, published in the *Memphis Commercial Appeal,* Section V, p. 3).

To the Editor (April 17, 1955; letter, published in the *Memphis Commercial Appeal,* Section V, p. 3.).

To the Editor (March 26, 1956; letter, published in *Life,* XL, 19; [also see above, "A Letter to the North"]).

To the Editor (April 19, 1956; letter, published in *Reporter,* XIV, 7).

To the Editor (April 23, 1956; letter, *Time,* LXVII, 12).

To the Editor (December 10, 1956, letter, *Time,* LXVIII, 6, 9).

To the Editor (December 16, 1956, letter, *New York Times,* Section IV, p. 8).

To the Editor (February 11, 1957, letter, *Time,* LXIX, 8).

To the Editor (October 13, 1957, letter, published in *New York Times,* Section IV, p. 10).

To the Editor (August 28, 1960, letter, published in *New York Times,* Section IV, p. 10).

To Sherwood Anderson (1961; letter [undated], facsimile reproduced in *The Literary Career of William Faulkner* by James B. Meriwether, Princeton University Library, plates 27, 28, and 29; also see Faulkner's novel *Mosquitoes* [pp. 277–81] where he incorporates material from this letter).

Selected Letters of William Faulkner (1977; selected letters edited by Joseph Blotner, published by Random House, New York)

Novels

Elmer (1925; unfinished novel; typescript posthumously published in *Mississippi Quarterly* 36 [Summer 1983]: 343–447, and by Seajay Press of Northport, Alabama, in 1983; see the short story "A Portrait of Elmer," below).

Soldiers' Pay (February 25, 1926; novel, first published by Boni & Liveright, New York; elsewhere since).

Father Abraham (1926–27; an unfinished novel, edited with an introduction and textual notes by James B. Meriwether and published posthumously by Red Ozier Press, New York, in 1983 [limited edition of 210 copies] and by Random House, New York, in 1984 [facsimile edition]; forms the beginning of *The Hamlet;* recast as "Spotted Horses").

Mosquitoes (April 30, 1927; novel, first published by Boni & Liveright, New York; elsewhere since).

Sartoris (January 31, 1929; novel; published by Harcourt, Brace, New York; elsewhere since; also see below, *Flags in the Dust*).

The Sound and the Fury (October 7, 1929; novel, first published by Cape & Smith, New York; elsewhere since; most of the last chapter, "April Eighth, 1928," published under the title "Dilsey" in *The Portable Faulkner;* published in 1946 by Modern Library, New York, with an appendix as a foreword titled "Compson 1699–1945" and together with *As I Lay Dying;* complete novel published with the appendix at the end in *The Faulkner Reader;* film adaptation with same title released in 1959; corrected text by Noel Polk published by Random House, New York, in 1984).

As I Lay Dying (October 6, 1930; novel, first published by Cape & Smith, New York; elsewhere since; published together with *The Sound and the Fury;* new edition published in 1964 by Random House, New York; corrected text by Noel Polk published in 1985 by Library of America [volume 1 of Faulkner's collected works: *Novels 1930–1935*], New York, and by Vintage International, New York, in October 1990).

Sanctuary (February 9, 1931; novel, first published by Cape & Smith, New York; elsewhere since; published with an introduction by Faulkner by Modern Library, New York, on 25 March 1932; film adaptation titled *The Story of Temple Drake* released in 1933; chapter 25 published under the title "Uncle Bud and the Three Madams" in *The Portable Faulkner;* published together with *Requiem for a Nun;* film adaptation based on *Sanctuary* and *Requiem for a Nun,* titled *Sanctuary,* released in 1961; corrected text by Joseph Blotner and Noel Polk published in 1985 by Library of America [volume 1 of Faulkner's collected works: *Novels 1930–1935*], New York; the corrected text with Faulkner's introduction in the Editors' Note published by Vintage International, New York, in December 1993).

Light in August (October 6, 1932; novel; first published by Smith & Haas, New York; elsewhere since; excerpt from novel published under title of "Percy Grimm" in *The Faulkner Reader;* corrected text by Noel Polk published in 1985 by Library of America [volume 1 of Faulkner's collected works: *Novels 1930–1935*], New York, and in October 1990 by Vintage International, New York).

Absalom, Absalom! (October 26, 1936; novel [with map of Yoknapatawpha County], first published by Random House, New York; elsewhere since; chapter 2 published in *The Portable Faulkner;* corrected text by Noel Polk published by Random House, New York, in 1986, and by the Library of America [volume 2 of Faulkner's collected works: *Novels 1936–1940*], New York, in 1990).

The Unvanquished (February 15, 1938; series of seven interrelated stories, first published by Random House, New York; first six are revisions of previously published short stories; stories III, "Raid," and VII, "An Odor of Verbena," published in *The Portable Faulkner;* basis of unproduced screenplay of same title by Sidney Howard for MGM, 1938; corrected text by Noel Polk published in 1990 by the Library of America [volume 2 of Faulkner's collected works:

Novels 1936–1940], New York, and in October 1991 by Vintage International, New York).

The Wild Palms (January 19, 1939; novel with two interwoven narratives ("The Wild Palms" and "Old Man"), first published by Random House, New York; the parts designated "Old Man" published under the title "Old Man" in *The Portable Faulkner* and as a novella in *The Faulkner Reader;* elsewhere since; also see below: *The Wild Palms and The Old Man* and *The Old Man;* corrected text by Noel Polk published as *If I Forget Thee, Jerusalem* in 1990 by Library of America [volume 2 of Faulkner's collected works: *Novels 1936–1940*] and by Vintage International in 1995).

The Hamlet (April 1, 1940; novel [first in the Snopes trilogy—see *The Town* and *The Mansion,* below], first published by Random House, New York; chapter 1 of book 4, "The Peasants," published in *The Portable Faulkner* [also see "Spotted Horses" under *Short Stories* below]; reset text published by Modern Library on March 20, 1950; film adaptation titled *The Long Hot Summer* released in 1958; television adaptation titled *The Long Hot Summer* telecast in 1985; corrected text by Noel Polk published in 1990 by Library of America [volume 2 of Faulkner's collected works: *Novels 1936–1940*], New York, and by Vintage International, New York, in October 1991).

Go Down, Moses and Other Stories (May 11, 1942; novel containing seven interrelated stories, six of which previously published, first published by Random House, New York; title changed for second edition published by Random House on January 26, 1949 and for all subsequent editions to *Go Down, Moses*).

The Sound and the Fury and *As I Lay Dying* (December 20, 1946; two novels previously published separately, published by Modern Library, New York, with a new appendix as a foreword by the author titled "Compson: 1699–1945").

Intruder in the Dust (September 27, 1948; novel, first published by Random House, New York; film adaptation with same title released in 1949; elsewhere; by Vintage International in October of 1991, and by Library of America [volume 3 of Faulkner's collected works: *Novels 1942–1954*], New York, in 1994).

Go Down, Moses (January 26, 1949; novel containing seven interrelated stories, published by Random House, New York; previously published under the title *Go Down, Moses and Other Stories;* elsewhere; published in November 1990 by Vintage International, New York, and by Library of America [volume 3 of Faulkner's collected works: *Novels 1942–1954*], New York, in 1994).

Requiem for a Nun (September 27, 1951; novel in the form of a three-act play with a prose narrative preceding each act [sequel to *Sanctuary,* first published by Random House, New York; excerpt from the novel, "The Courthouse (A Name for the City)" [act 1], published in *The Faulkner Reader;* also published by Vintage Books in April 1975, and by Library of America [volume 3 of Faulkner's collected works: *Novels 1942–1954*], New York, in 1994).

A Fable (August 2, 1954; novel, first published by Random House, New York; also published by New American Library in September 1958, Vintage in January 1978, and by Library of America [volume 3 of Faulkner's collected works: *Novels 1942–1954*] in 1994).

The Wild Palms and The Old Man (September 1954; novel, rearranged version of *The Wild Palms* dividing the originally intended interwoven narratives into two separate sections: "The Wild Palms" and "Old Man"; published by New American Library, New York [also see below, *If I Forget Thee, Jerusalem*]).

The Town (May 1, 1957; novel [second in the Snopes trilogy—see *The Hamlet,* above, and *The Mansion,* below], first published by Random House, New York; also published by Vintage Books in January 1961).

The Mansion (November 13, 1959; novel [third in the Snopes trilogy—see *The Hamlet* and *The Mansion,* above], first published by Random House, New York; also published by Vintage Books in September 1965).

The Reivers (June 4, 1962; novel, first published by Random House, New York; also published by Vintage Books in September 1966; film adaptation with same title released in 1969).

Flags in the Dust (August 22, 1973; novel [complete text of the novel *Sartoris,* see above]; edited with an introduction by Douglas Day and published posthumously by Random House, New York).

If I Forget Thee, Jerusalem (1990; novel, original title of *The Wild Palms* [see above]; corrected text by Noel Polk published in 1990 by Library of America [volume 2 of Faulkner's collected works: *Novels 1936–1940*], New York, and in November 1995 by Vintage International, New York).

Poems and Verse Play

"L'Après-midi d'un Faune" (August 6, 1919; poem, first published in *New Republic,* XX, 24; reprinted in *Mississippian* IX [October 29, 1919]: 4, in *Salmagundi* and in *William Faulkner: Early Prose and Poetry*).

"Cathay" (November 12, 1919; poem, first published in *Mississippian,* IX, 8; reprinted in *William Faulkner: Early Prose and Poetry*).

"Sapphics" (November 26, 1919; poem, first published in *Mississippian,* IX, 3; reprinted in *William Faulkner: Early Prose and Poetry*).

"After Fifty Years" (December 10, 1919; poem, first published in *Mississippian,* IX, 4; reprinted in "Faulkner Juvenilia" by Martha Mayes, *New Campus Writing No.*

2, edited by Nolan Miller [New York: Bantam, 1957], and in *William Faulkner: Early Prose and Poetry*).

"Une Ballade des Femmes Perdues" (January 28, 1920; poem, first published in *Mississippian,* IX, 3; reprinted in "Faulkner Juvenilia" by Martha Mayes, *New Campus Writing No. 2,* edited by Nolan Miller [New York: Bantam, 1957], and in *William Faulkner: Early Prose and Poetry*).

"Naiad's Song" (February 4, 1920; poem, first published in *Mississippian,* IX, 3; reprinted in *William Faulkner: Early Prose and Poetry*).

"Fantouches" (February 25, 1920; poem, first published in *Mississippian,* IX, 3; reprinted in "Faulkner Juvenilia" by Martha Mayes, *New Campus Writing No. 2,* edited by Nolan Miller [New York: Bantam, 1957]; reprinted as "Fantoches" in *William Faulkner: Early Prose and Poetry*).

"Clair de Lune" (March 3, 1920; poem, first published in *Mississippian,* IX, 6; reprinted in *William Faulkner: Early Prose and Poetry*).

"Streets" (March 17, 1920; poem, first published in *Mississippian,* IX, 2; reprinted in *William Faulkner: Early Prose and Poetry*).

"A Poplar" (March 17, 1920; poem, first published in *Mississippian,* IX, 7; reprinted in "Faulkner Juvenilia" by Martha Mayes, *New Campus Writing No. 2,* edited by Nolan Miller [New York: Bantam, 1957], and in *William Faulkner: Early Prose and Poetry*).

"A Clymene" (April 14, 1920; poem, first published in *Mississippian,* IX, 3; reprinted in *William Faulkner: Early Prose and Poetry*).

"Study" (April 24, 1920; poem, first published in *Mississippian,* IX, 4; reprinted in "Faulkner Juvenilia" by Martha Mayes, *New Campus Writing No. 2,* edited by Nolan Miller [New York: Bantam, 1957], and in *William Faulkner: Early Prose and Poetry*).

"Alma Mater" (May 12, 1920; poem, first published in *Mississippian,* IX, 3; reprinted in *William Faulkner: Early Prose and Poetry*).

The Marionettes (fall 1920; verse play, published posthumously by University Press of Virginia in 1977, edited with an introduction by Noel Polk).

"To a Co-ed" (1920; poem, first published in *Ole Miss, the Yearbook of the University of Mississippi,* XXIV [1919–20]; reprinted in the *Memphis Commercial Appeal,* November 6, 1932 [magazine section], in *The Literary Career of William Faulkner* by James B. Meriwether [Princeton University Library, 1961], and in *William Faulkner: Early Prose and Poetry*).

"Co-Education at Ole Miss" (May 4, 1921; poem, first published in *Mississippian,* X, 5; reprinted in *William Faulkner: Early Prose and Poetry*).

"Nocturne" (1921; poem, first published in *Ole Miss, the Yearbook of the University of Mississippi,* XXV [1920–21]; facsimile published in *The Literary Career of William Faulkner* by James B. Meriwether [Princeton University Library, 1961], and in *William Faulkner: Early Prose and Poetry*).

Vision in Spring (1921–23; cycle of 14 love poems [earlier version contained eight poems]; posthumously published in 1984, edited by Judith L. Sensibar, University of Texas Press, Austin).

"The Hill" (March 10, 1922; prose poem, first published in *Mississippian*, XI, 1–2; reprinted in *William Faulkner: Early Prose and Poetry*).

"Portrait" (June 1922; poem, first published in *Double Dealer*, II, 337; reprinted in *Salmagundi* and in *William Faulkner: Early Prose and Poetry*).

"Mississippi Hills" (October 1924; poem, revised as "My Epitaph" [see below]; slightly altered and retitled as "Mississippi Hills: My Epitaph," reproduced in *William Faulkner: "Man Working," 1919–1962, A Catalogue of the William Faulkner Collections at the University of Virginia*, compiled by Linton R. Massey [Charlottesville: Bibliographical Society, University of Virginia, 1968]).

The Marble Faun (December 15, 1924; poem of 806 lines with prologue and epilogue; preface by Phil Stone; published by Four Seas Company, Boston; republished with *A Green Bough* [photographically reproduced from original editions] by Random House, New York, 1965).

Mississippi Poems (December 30, 1924; typescript of 12 poems presented to Myrtle Ramey; eight of which were revised for *A Green Bough* [1933]; posthumously published in 1979 [see below]).

Helen: A Courtship (1925; poems for Helen Baird, published posthumously in 1981 [see below]).

"Dying Gladiator" (January/February 1925; poem, first published in *Double Dealer*, VII, 85; reprinted in *Salmagundi* and in *William Faulkner: Early Prose and Poetry*).

"The Faun" (April 1925; poem, first published in *Double Dealer*, VII, 148; reprinted in *Salmagundi* and in *William Faulkner: Early Prose and Poetry*).

"The Lilacs" (June 1925; poem, first published in *Double Dealer*, VII, 185–87; reprinted in *Salmagundi*, in *A Green Bough* [revised as I], and in *Anthology of Magazine Verse for 1925 and Yearbook of American Poetry*, edited by William Stanley Braithwaite [Boston: B. J. Brimmer, 1925]).

"Hermaphroditus" (April 1927; poem, first appeared in Faulkner's novel *Mosquitoes*, p. 252; revision reprinted XXX in *A Green Bough*).

"I Will Not Weep for Youth" (February 1, 1932; poem, first published in *Contempo*, I, 1; reprinted in *An Anthology of the Younger Poets*, edited by Oliver Wells and with a preface by Archibald MacLeish [Philadelphia: Centaur Press, 1932]).

"Knew I Love Once" (February 1, 1932; poem, first published in *Contempo*, I, 1; reprinted in *A Green Bough* [revised as XXXIII], and in *Anthology of the Younger Poets*, edited by Oliver Wells [Philadelphia: Centaur Press, 1932]).

"Twilight" (February 1, 1932; poem, first published in *Contempo*, I, 1; reprinted in *A Green Bough* [revised as X], and in *An Anthology of the Younger Poets*, edited by Oliver Wells [Philadelphia: Centaur Press, 1932]).

"Visions in Spring" (February 1, 1932; poem, published in *Contempo*, I, 1).

"Spring" (February 1, 1932; poem, first published in *Contempo*, I, 2; reprinted in *A Green Bough* [revised as XXXVI]).

"April" (February 1, 1932; poem, published in *Contempo*, I, 2).

"To a Virgin" (February 1, 1932; poem, first published in *Contempo*, I, 2; reprinted in *A Green Bough* [revised as XXXIX], and in *An Anthology of the Younger Poets*, edited by Oliver Wells [Philadelphia: Centaur Press, 1932]).

"Winter Is Gone" (February 1, 1932; poem, first published in *Contempo*, I, 2; reprinted in *An Anthology of the Younger Poets*, edited by Oliver Wells [Philadelphia: Centaur Press, 1932]).

"My Epitaph" (February 1, 1932; poem, first published in *Contempo*, I, 2; revised and reprinted as *This Earth*, 1932; reprinted in *A Green Bough* [revised as XLIV]; reprinted in *An Anthology of the Younger Poets*, edited by Oliver Wells [Philadelphia: Centaur Press, 1932]; retitled as "If There Be Grief" and published in *Mississippi Verse*, edited by Alice James [Chapel Hill: University of North Carolina Press, 1934]; reprinted in *Life*, LIII [July 20, 1952]: 42).

Salmagundi (April 30, 1932; reprinted prose pieces and poems; edited with an introduction by Paul Romaine; published by Casanova Press, Milwaukee).

"A Child Looks from His Window" (May 25, 1932; poem, published in *Contempo*, II, 3).

This Earth (December 1932; revision of poem "My Epitaph"; published by Equinox Cooperative Press, New York).

"The Race's Splendor" (April 12, 1933; poem, first published in *New Republic*, LXXIV, 253; reprinted in *A Green Bough* [as XXXVII, and in *New Republic*, CXXXI [November 22, 1954]: 82).

"Night Piece" (April 12, 1933; poem, first published in *New Republic*, LXXIV, 253; reprinted in *A Green Bough* [as VII]).

"Gray the Day" (April 12, 1933; poem, first published in *New Republic*, LXXIV, 253; reprinted in *A Green Bough* [as XXX]).

"Over the World's Rim" (April 12, 1933; poem, first published in *New Republic*, LXXIV, 253; reprinted in *A Green Bough*, as XXVIII]).

"The Ship of Night" (April 19, 1933; poem, first published in *New Republic*, LXXIV, 272; reprinted in *A Green Bough* as XXXIV]).

A Green Bough (April 20, 1933; 44 poems [13 previously published; illustrations by Lynd Ward; published by Smith & Haas, New York; seven poems reprinted with titles—XIV ["Mother and Child"], XVI ["Mirror of Youth"], XVIII ["Boy and Eagle"], XIX ["Green Is the Water"], XX ["Here He Stands"], XXXV ["The Courtesan is Dead"], and XLIV ["If There Be Grief," also see above: "My Epitaph"]—in *Mississippi Verse*, edited by Alice James [Chapel Hill: University of North Carolina Press, 1934]; republished with *The Marble Faun* [photographically reproduced from original editions], by Random House, New York, 1965).

"Man Comes, Man Goes" (May 3, 1933; poem, first published in *New Republic*, LXXIV, 338; reprinted in *A Green Bough* [as VI], in *The New Republic Anthology: 1915–1935*, edited by Groff Conklin [New York: Dodge, 1936], and in *Fiction Parade*, V [October 1937]: 740).

"The Flowers That Died" (June 25, 1933; poem, published in *Contempo*, III, 1).

William Faulkner: Early Prose and Poetry (1962; previously published poems, prose pieces, and pen-and-ink drawings; compiled with an introduction by Carvel Collins; published by Little, Brown, Boston).

Mississippi Poems (1979; poems published posthumously by Yoknapatawpha Press, Oxford, Miss.).

Helen: A Courtship (1981; poems published posthumously by Tulane University, New Orleans, and by Yoknapatawpha Press, Oxford, Miss.).

Prose Sketches

"Mirrors of Chartres Street" (February–September 1925, 11 of 16 prose sketches appearing in the *New Orleans Times-Picayune*, with introduction by William Van O'Connor [Minneapolis: Faulkner Studies, 1953]; also see two separate references below titled *New Orleans Sketches*).

"New Orleans" (January/February 1925; prose sketch, first published in *Double Dealer*, VII, 102–07; reprinted in *Salmagundi* and in *New Orleans Sketches*, edited by Carvel Collins).

"Mirrors of Chartres Street" (February 8, 1925; sketch, first published in the *New Orleans Times-Picayune*, pp. 1, 6; reprinted in *Mirrors of Chartres Street* [Minneapolis: Faulkner Studies, 1953], in *New Orleans Sketches*, edited by Ichiro Nishizaki, and in *New Orleans Sketches*, edited by Carvel Collins).

"Damon and Pythias Unlimited" (February 15, 1925; sketch, first published in the *New Orleans Times-Picayune*, p. 7; reprinted in *Mirrors of Chartres Street* [Minneapolis: Faulkner Studies, 1953], in *New Orleans Sketches*, edited by Ichiro Nishizaki, and in *New Orleans Sketches*, edited by Carvel Collins).

"Home" (February 22, 1925; sketch, first published in the *New Orleans Times-Picayune*, p. 3; reprinted in *Mirrors of Chartres Street* [Minneapolis: Faulkner Studies, 1953], in *New Orleans Sketches*, edited by Ichiro Nishizaki, and in *New Orleans Sketches*, edited by Carvel Collins).

"Jealousy" (March 1, 1925; sketch, first published in the *New Orleans Times-Picayune*, p. 2; reprinted in *Faulkner Studies*, III (Winter 1954): 46–50; in *Jealousy and Episode: Two Stories by William Faulkner*, [Minneapolis: Faulkner Studies, 1955]; in *New Orleans Sketches*, edited by Ichiro Nishizaki; and in *New Orleans Sketches*, edited by Carvel Collins).

"Cheest" (April 5, 1925; sketch, first published in the *New Orleans Times-Picayune*, p. 4; reprinted in *Mirrors of Chartres Street* [Minneapolis: Faulkner Studies, 1953]; in *New Orleans Sketches*, edited by Ichiro Nishizaki; and in *New Orleans Sketches*, edited by Carvel Collins).

"Out of Nazareth" (April 12, 1925; sketch, first published in the *New Orleans Times-Picayune*, p. 4; reprinted in *Mirrors of Chartres Street* [Minneapolis: Faulkner Studies, 1953]; in *New Orleans Sketches*, edited by Ichiro Nishizaki; and in *New Orleans Sketches*, edited by Carvel Collins).

"The Kingdom of God" (April 26, 1925; sketch, first published in the *New Orleans Times-Picayune*, p. 4; reprinted in *Mirrors of Chartres Street* [Minneapolis: Faulkner Studies, 1953]; in *New Orleans Sketches*, edited by Ichiro Nishizaki; and in *New Orleans Sketches*, edited by Carvel Collins).

"The Rosary" (May 3, 1925; sketch, first published in the *New Orleans Times-Picayune*, p. 2; reprinted in *Mirrors of Chartres Street* [Minneapolis: Faulkner Studies, 1953]; in *New Orleans Sketches*, edited by Ichiro Nishizaki); and in *New Orleans Sketches*, edited by Carvel Collins).

"The Cobbler" (May 10, 1925; sketch, first published in the *New Orleans Times-Picayune*, p. 7; reprinted in *Mirrors of Chartres Street* [Minneapolis: Faulkner Studies, 1953]; in *New Orleans Sketches*, edited by Ichiro Nishizaki; and in *New Orleans Sketches*, edited by Carvel Collins).

"Chance" (May 17, 1925; sketch, first published in the *New Orleans Times-Picayune*, p. 7; reprinted in *Mirrors of Chartres Street* [Minneapolis: Faulkner Studies, 1953]; in *New Orleans Sketches*, edited by Ichiro Nishizaki; and in *New Orleans Sketches*, edited by Carvel Collins).

"Sunset" (May 25, 1925; sketch, first published in the *New Orleans Times-Picayune*, p. 7; reprinted in *Mirrors of Chartres Street* [Minneapolis: Faulkner Studies, 1953]; in *New Orleans Sketches*, edited by Ichiro Nishizaki; and in *New Orleans Sketches*, edited by Carvel Collins).

"The Kid Learns" (May 31, 1925; sketch, first published in the *New Orleans Times-Picayune*, p. 2; reprinted in *Mirrors of Chartres Street* [Minneapolis: Faulkner Studies, 1953]; in *New Orleans Sketches*, edited by Ichiro Nishizaki; and in *New Orleans Sketches*, edited by Carvel Collins).

"The Liar" (July 26, 1925; sketch, first published in the *New Orleans Times-Picayune*, pp. 3, 6; reprinted in *New Orleans Sketches*, edited by Carvel Collins).

"Episode" (August 16, 1925; sketch, first published in the *New Orleans Times-Picayune*, p. 2; reprinted in *Eigo Seinen* [Tokyo] on December 1, 1954; in *Faulkner Studies*, III [Winter 1954]: 51–53; in *Jealousy and Episode: Two Stories by William Faulkner* [Minneapolis: Faulkner Studies, 1955]; in *New Orleans Sketches*, edited by Ichiro Nishizaki; and in *New Orleans Sketches*, edited by Carvel Collins).

"Country Mice" (September 20, 1925; sketch, first published in the *New Orleans Times-Picayune*, p. 7; reprinted in *New Orleans Sketches*, edited by Carvel Collins).

"Yo Ho and Two Bottles of Rum" (September 27, 1925; sketch, first published in the *New Orleans Times-Picayune*, p. 1–2; reprinted in *New Orleans Sketches*, edited by Carvel Collins).

New Orleans Sketches by William Faulkner (April 1, 1955; 13 of 16 prose sketches from the *New Orleans Times-Picayune*, edited with notes in Japanese and English by Ichiro Nishizaki, Hokuseido Press, Tokyo; 11 reprinted in *Mirrors of Chartres Street*).

New Orleans Sketches (1958; 16 prose sketches from the *New Orleans Times-Picayune*, [see above]and 11 short pieces titled "New Orleans" [see above] from the *Double Dealer;* edited with introduction by Carvel Collins; published by Rutgers University Press, New Brunswick, N.J.; republished in 1961 by Grove Press, New York; new edition with additional essay published in 1968 by Random House, New York).

Short Stories

"Landing in Luck" (November 26, 1919; short story, first published in *Mississippian*, IX, 2, 7; reprinted in *William Faulkner: Early Prose and Poetry*).

"Moonlight" (c. 1919–21; short story published posthumously in *Uncollected Stories of William Faulkner*).

"Love" (fall 1921; short story unpublished and basis of film scenario titled *Manservant*).

"Adolescence" (c. 1922; short story published posthumously in *Uncollected Stories of William Faulkner*).

"Nympholepsy" (1925; short story published posthumously in *Mississippi Quarterly*, XXVI (Summer 1973): 403–09, edited with an introduction by James B. Meriwether; reprinted in *Uncollected Stories of William Faulkner*).

"Frankie and Johnny" (c. 1925; short story published posthumously in *Mississippi Quarterly*, XXXI (Summer 1978): 453–64, edited with an introduction by James B. Meriwether; reprinted in *Uncollected Stories of William Faulkner*).

"The Priest" (1925; short story published posthumously in *Mississippi Quarterly*, XXIX (Summer 1976): 445–50, edited with an introduction by James B. Meriwether; reprinted in *Uncollected Stories of William Faulkner*).

"Al Jackson" (1925; short story published posthumously in *Uncollected Stories of William Faulkner*).

"Don Giovanni" (c. 1925; short story published posthumously in *Uncollected Stories of William Faulkner*).

"Peter" (c. 1925; short story published posthumously in *Uncollected Stories of William Faulkner*).

"The Big Shot" (c. 1929; short story published posthumously in *Mississippi Quarterly*, XXVI (Summer 1973): 313–24, and in *Uncollected Stories of William Faulkner*).

"A Dangerous Man" (c. 1929; short story published posthumously in *Uncollected Stories of William Faulkner*).

"Dull Tale" (c. 1929–30; short story published posthumously in *Uncollected Stories of William Faulkner*).

"A Return" (c. 1929–30; short story published posthumously in *Uncollected Stories of William Faulkner*).

"A Rose for Emily" (April 1930; short story, first published in *Forum*, LXXXIII, 233–38; reprinted revision in *These 13*, in *A Rose for Emily and Other Stories*, in *The Portable Faulkner*, in *Collected Stories*, in *The Faulkner Reader*, in *A Rose for Emily*, and in *Selected Short Stories of William Faulkner*).

"Honor" (July 1930; short story, first published in *American Mercury*, XX, 268–74; reprinted in *Doctor Martino and Other Stories*, in *Collected Stories*, and in *Selected Short Stories of William Faulkner*).

"Thrift" (September 6, 1930; short story, first published in *Saturday Evening Post*, CCIII, 16–17, 78, 82; reprinted in *O. Henry Memorial Award Prize Stories of 1931*, edited by Blanche Colton Williams [Garden City: Doubleday, Doran, 1931] and in *Uncollected Stories of William Faulkner*).

"Red Leaves" (October 25, 1930; short story, first published in *Saturday Evening Post*, CCIII, 6–7, 54, 56, 58, 60, 62, 64; revision published in *These 13*, in *The Portable Faulkner*, in the edition of *A Rose for Emily and Other Stories* edited and annotated by Kenzaburo Ohashi, in *Collected Stories of William Faulkner*, and in *Selected Short Stories of William Faulkner;* a portion again revised and included in *Big Woods*, pp. 99–109).

"Evangeline" (c. 1930–31; short story published posthumously in *Uncollected Stories of William Faulkner*).

"Dry September" (January 1931; short story, first published in *Scribner's Magazine*, LXXXIX, 49–56; reprinted revision in *These 13*, in *A Rose for Emily and Other Stories by William Faulkner*, in *Collected Stories of William Faulkner*, in *The Faulkner Reader*, and in *Selected Short Stories of William Faulkner*).

"That Evening Sun Go Down" (March 1931; short story, first published in *American Mercury*, XXII, 257–67; revision entitled "That Evening Sun" reprinted in *These 13*, in *A Rose for Emily and Other Stories by William Faulkner*, in *The Portable Faulkner*, in *Collected Stories of William Faulkner*, in *The Faulkner Reader*, in *A Rose for Emily*, and in *Selected Short Stories of William Faulkner*).

"Ad Astra" (March 27, 1931; short story, first published in *American Caravan*, IV, 164–81; reprinted revision in *These 13,* in *The Portable Faulkner,* and in *Collected Stories of William Faulkner*).

"Hair" (May 1931; short story, first published in *American Mercury,* XXIII, 53–61; reprinted revision in *These 13* and in *Collected Stories of William Faulkner*).

"Spotted Horses" (June 1931; short story, first published in *Scribner's Magazine,* LXXXIX, 585–97; expanded revision included in chapter 1 of book 4 of *The Hamlet,* reprinted as a novella in *The Faulkner Reader* and in *Three Famous Short Novels;* original version reprinted in *Uncollected Stories of William Faulkner*).

"The Hound" (August 1931; short story, first published in *Harper's Magazine,* CLXIII, 266–74; reprinted in *Doctor Martino and Other Stories* and in *A Rose for Emily and Other Stories by William Faulkner;* revision included in book 3 of *The Hamlet;* original version reprinted in *Uncollected Stories of William Faulkner*).

"Fox Hunt" (September 1931; short story, first published in *Harper's Magazine,* CLXIII, 392–402; reprinted in *Doctor Martino and Other Stories* and in *Collected Stories of William Faulkner*).

"All the Dead Pilots" (September 21, 1931; short story, first published in *These 13;* reprinted in *Collected Stories of William Faulkner*).

"Carcassonne" (September 21, 1931; short story, first published in *These 13* and in *Collected Stories of William Faulkner*).

"Crevasse" (September 21, 1931; short story, first published in *These 13,* in *Collected Stories of William Faulkner,* and in *A Rose for Emily*).

"Divorce in Naples" (September 21, 1931; short story, first published in *These 13* and in *Collected Stories of William Faulkner*).

"A Justice" (September 21, 1931; short story, first published in *These 13;* reprinted in *The Portable Faulkner,* in *Collected Stories of William Faulkner,* and in *The Faulkner Reader;* revised portion included in *Big Woods,* pp. 139–42).

"Mistral" (September 21, 1931; short story, first published in *These 13* and in *Collected Stories of William Faulkner*).

"Victory" (September 21, 1931; short story, first published in *These 13* and in *Collected Stories of William Faulkner*).

These 13 (September 21, 1931; collection of 13 short stories; published by Cape & Smith, New York, 1931; stories reprinted *Collected Stories of William Faulkner*).

"Doctor Martino" (November 1931; short story, first published in *Harper's Magazine,* CLXIII, 733–43; reprinted in *Doctor Martino and Other Stories* and in *Collected Stories of William Faulkner*).

Idyll in the Desert (December 1931; short story, first published separately by Random House, New York, in 1931; reprinted in *Uncollected Stories of William Faulkner*).

"With Caution and Dispatch" (c. 1932; short story, published posthumously in *Uncollected Stories of William Faulkner*).

"Death-Drag" (January 1932; short story, first published in *Scribner's Magazine,* XCI, 34–42; reprinted with minor revisions as "Death Drag" in *Doctor Martino and Other Stories,* in *The Portable Faulkner,* and in *Collected Stories of William Faulkner*).

"Centaur in Brass" (February 1932; short story, first published in *American Mercury,* XXV, 200–10; reprinted in *Collected Stories of William Faulkner;* revised for first chapter of *The Town*).

"Once Aboard the Lugger" (February 1, 1932; title for two short stories, the first of which first published in *Contempo,* I, 1, 4, and reprinted in *Uncollected Stories of William Faulkner;* the second, first published in *Uncollected Stories of William Faulkner*).

"Lizards in Jamshyd's Courtyard" (February 27, 1932; short story, first published in *Saturday Evening Post,* CCIV, 12–13, 52, 57; revision included in book 4 of *The Hamlet;* original version reprinted in *Uncollected Stories of William Faulkner*).

"Turn About" (March 5, 1932; short story, first published in *Saturday Evening Post,* CCIV, 6–7, 75–76, 81, 83; revision reprinted in *Doctor Martino and Other Stories* and in *A Rose for Emily and Other Stories by William Faulkner;* reprinted as "Turnabout" in *Collected Stories of William Faulkner,* in *The Faulkner Reader,* and in *Selected Short Stories of William Faulkner;* basis of screenplay of same title and film titled *Today We Live*).

"Smoke" (April 1932; short story, first published in *Harper's Magazine,* CLXIV, 562–78; reprinted with minor changes in *Doctor Martino and Other Stories* and in *Knight's Gambit*).

"Miss Zilphia Gant" (June 27, 1932; short story, first published separately Book Club of Texas (in Dallas), with a preface by Henry Smith; reprinted in *Uncollected Stories of William Faulkner*).

"A Mountain Victory" (December 3, 1932; short story, first published in *Saturday Evening Post,* CCV, 6–7, 39, 42, 44–46; reprinted revision as "Mountain Victory" in *Doctor Martino and Other Stories,* in *Collected Stories of William Faulkner,* and in *Selected Short Stories of William Faulkner*).

"There Was a Queen" (January 1933; short story, first published in *Scribner's Magazine,* XCIII, 10–16; reprinted in *Doctor Martino and Other Stories,* in *Collected Stories of William Faulkner,* and in *Selected Short Stories of William Faulkner*).

"Artist at Home" (August 1933; short story, first published in *Story,* III, 27–41; reprinted in *Collected Stories of William Faulkner*).

"Beyond" (September 1933; short story, first published in *Harper's Magazine,* CLXVII, 394–403; reprinted in *Doctor Martino and Other Stories,* in *Collected Stories of William Faulkner,* and in *Selected Short Stories of William Faulkner*).

"Elly" (February 1934; short story, first published in *Story*, IV, 3–15; reprinted in *Doctor Martino and Other Stories* and in *Collected Stories of William Faulkner*).

"Pennsylvania Station" (February 1934; short story, first published in *American Mercury*, XXXI, 166–74; reprinted in *Collected Stories of William Faulkner*).

"Wash" (February 1934; short story, first published in *Harper's Magazine*, CLXVIII, 258–66; reprinted in *Doctor Martino and Other Stories*, in *The Portable Faulkner*, in *Collected Stories of William Faulkner*, and in *The Faulkner Reader*; with major revisions included in the latter part of chapter 7 of *Absalom, Absalom!*).

"A Bear Hunt" (February 10, 1934; short story, first published in *Saturday Evening Post*, CCVI, 8–9, 74, 76; reprinted in *Collected Stories of William Faulkner*; reprinted revision in *Big Woods*).

"Black Music" (April 16, 1934; short story, first published in *Doctor Martino and Other Stories*; reprinted in *Collected Stories of William Faulkner*).

"Leg" (April 16, 1934; short story, first published in *Doctor Martino and Other Stories*; reprinted as "The Leg" in *Collected Stories of William Faulkner*).

Doctor Martino and Other Stories (April 16, 1934; collection of 14 stories, published by Smith & Haas, New York).

"Mule in the Yard" (August 1934; short story, first published in *Scribner's Magazine*, XCVI, 65–70; reprinted in *Collected Stories of William Faulkner*; with major revisions incorporated in chapter 16 of *The Town*).

"Ambuscade" (September 29, 1934; short story, first published in *Saturday Evening Post*, CCVII, 12–13, 80–1; reprinted revision as chapter 1 of *The Unvanquished*; original version reprinted in *The Uncollected Stories of William Faulkner*).

"Retreat" (October 13, 1934; short story, first published in *Saturday Evening Post*, CCVII, 16–17, 82, 84–85, 87, 89; reprinted revision as chapter 2 of *The Unvanquished*; original version reprinted in *Uncollected Stories of William Faulkner*).

"Lo!" (November 1934; short story, first published in *Story*, V, 5–21; reprinted in *Collected Stories of William Faulkner* and in *Selected Short Stories of William Faulkner*).

"Raid" (November 3, 1934; short story, first published in *Saturday Evening Post*, CCVII, 18–19, 72–73, 75, 77–78; reprinted revision as chapter 3 of *The Unvanquished*; original version reprinted in *Uncollected Stories of William Faulkner*).

"A Portrait of Elmer" (c. 1934–35; short story, posthumously published in *Uncollected Stories of William Faulkner*).

"Skirmish at Satoris" (April 1935; short story, first published in *Scribner's Magazine*, XCVII, 193–200; reprinted revision as chapter 4 of *The Unvanquished*; original version reprinted in *Uncollected Stories of William Faulkner*).

"Golden Land" (May 1935; short story, first published in *American Mercury*, XXXV, 1–14; reprinted in *Collected Stories of William Faulkner*).

"That Will Be Fine" (July 1935; short story, first published in *American Mercury*, XXXV, 264–76; reprinted in *Collected Stories of William Faulkner*).

"Uncle Willy" (October 1935; short story, first published in *American Mercury*, XXXVI, 156–68; reprinted in *Collected Stories of William Faulkner*).

"Lion" (December 1935; short story, first published in *Harper's Magazine*, CLXXI, 67–77; revised and included in "The Bear" in *Go Down, Moses and Other Stories*; original version reprinted in *Uncollected Stories of William Faulkner*).

"Two Dollar Wife" (1936; short story first titled "Christmas Tree" and first published in *College Life*, XVIII (January 1936): 8–10, 85, 86, 88, 90; reprinted in *Uncollected Stories of William Faulkner*).

"The Brooch" (January 1936; short story, first published in *Scribner's Magazine*, XCIX, 7–12; reprinted in *Collected Stories of William Faulkner*).

"Fool About a Horse" (August 1936; short story, first published in *Scribner's Magazine*, C, 80–86; revision included in book 1 of *The Hamlet*; original version reprinted in *Uncollected Stories of William Faulkner*).

"The Unvanquished" (November 14, 1936; short story, first published in *Saturday Evening Post*, CCIX, 12–13, 121–22, 124, 126, 128, 130; retitled and revised as "Riposte in Tertio," chapter 4 of *The Unvanquished*; original version and title reprinted in *Uncollected Stories of William Faulkner*).

"Vendée" (December 5, 1936; short story, first published in *Saturday Evening Post*, CCIX, 16–17, 86, 87, 90, 92, 93, 94; revised as chapter 5 in *The Unvanquished*; original version reprinted in *Uncollected Stories of William Faulkner*).

"Monk" (May 1937; short story, first published in *Scribner's Magazine*, CL, 16–24; reprinted in *Knight's Gambit*).

"An Odor of Verbena" (February 15, 1938; short story, first published as chapter 7 of *The Unvanquished*; reprinted in *A Rose for Emily and Other Stories by William Faulkner* and in *The Faulkner Reader*).

The Unvanquished (February 15, 1938; series of seven interrelated stories, first published by Random House, New York; first six are revisions of previously published short stories; stories III, "Raid," and VII, "An Odor of Verbena," published in *The Portable Faulkner*; basis of unproduced screenplay of same title by Sidney Howard for MGM, 1938; corrected text by Noel Polk published in 1990 by Library of America [volume 2 of Faulkner's collected works: *Novels 1936–1940*], New York, and in October 1991 by Vintage International, New York).

"Barn Burning" (June 1939; short story, first published in *Harper's Magazine*, CLXXIX, 86–96; reprinted in *A Rose for Emily and Other Stories*, in *Collected Stories of*

William Faulkner, in *The Faulkner Reader*, and in *Selected Short Stories of William Faulkner;* revised portions included in book 1 of *The Hamlet;* television adaptation with same title telecast in 1954 and another in 1980; film version on videocassette released in 1985).

"Hand Upon the Waters" (November 4, 1939; short story, first published in *Saturday Evening Post*, CCXII, 14–15, 75–76, 78–79; reprinted in *Knight's Gambit*).

"A Point of Law" (June 22, 1940; short story, first published in *Collier's Magazine*, CV, 20–21, 30, 32; reprinted revision included in "The Fire and the Hearth" in *Go Down, Moses and Other Stories;* original version reprinted in *Uncollected Stories of William Faulkner*).

"Almost" (July 1940; short story, revised and retitled "Was"; first published in *Go Down, Moses and Other Stories*).

"The Old People" (September 1940; short story, first published in *Harper's Magazine*, CLXXXI, 418–25; revision included in *Go Down, Moses and Other Stories*) and reprinted in *Big Woods;* original version reprinted in *Uncollected Stories of William Faulkner*).

"Pantaloon in Black" (October 1940; short story, first published in *Harper's Magazine*, CLXXXI, 503–13; revised for *Go Down, Moses and Other Stories;* original version reprinted in *Uncollected Stories of William Faulkner*).

"Gold Is Not Always" (November 1940; short story, first published in *Atlantic Monthly*, CLXVI, 563–70; revision incorporated in "The Fire and the Hearth" in *Go Down, Moses and Other Stories;* original version reprinted in *Uncollected Stories of William Faulkner*).

"Tomorrow" (November 23, 1940; short story, first published in *Saturday Evening Post*, CCXIII, 22–23, 32, 35, 37, 38, 39; reprinted in *Knight's Gambit;* television adaptation with same title telecast in 1960 and film adaptation with same title released in 1972).

"Go Down, Moses" (January 25, 1941; short story, first published in *Collier's Magazine*, CVII, 19–20, 45, 46; revision reprinted in *Go Down, Moses and Other Stories;* original version reprinted in *Uncollected Stories of William Faulkner*).

"The Tall Men" (May 31, 1941; short story, first published in *Saturday Evening Post*, CCXIII, 14–15, 95–96, 98–99; reprinted in *Collected Stories of William Faulkner*).

"Snow" (c. 1942; short story published posthumously in *Mississippi Quarterly*, XXVI [Summer 1973]: 325–30, and in *Uncollected Stories of William Faulkner*).

"Two Soldiers" (March 28, 1942; short story, first published in *Saturday Evening Post*, CCXIV, 9–11, 35–36, 38, 40; reprinted in *Collected Stories of William Faulkner* and in *Selected Short Stories of William Faulkner*).

"The Bear" (May 9, 1942; short story, first published in *Saturday Evening Post*, CCXIV, 30–31, 74, 76–77; with major revisions included in "The Bear" in *Go Down, Moses and Other Stories*, and reprinted in *The Portable Faulkner* and as a novella in *The Faulkner Reader;* reprinted without part 4 in *Big Woods;* the shorter first published version reprinted in *Uncollected Stories of William Faulkner*).

"Delta Autumn" (May/June 1942; short story, first published in *Story*, XX, 46–55; reprinted revision in *Go Down, Moses and Other Stories*, in *A Rose for Emily and Other Stories by William Faulkner*, and in *The Portable Faulkner;* section of reprinted revision again revised and included as epilogue in *Big Woods;* first version reprinted in *Uncollected Stories of William Faulkner*).

"Was" (May 11, 1942; short story, retitled revision of the story "Almost" and first published as the first story in *Go Down, Moses and Other Stories;* reprinted in *The Portable Faulkner*).

"Shingles for the Lord" (February 13, 1943; short story, first published in *Saturday Evening Post*, CCXV, 14–15, 68, 70–71; reprinted in *Collected Stories of William Faulkner* and in *The Faulkner Reader*).

"My Grandmother Millard and General Bedford Foffest and the Battle of Harrykin Creek" (March/April 1943; short story, first published in *Story*, XXII, 68–86; reprinted in *Collected Stories of William Faulkner*).

"L'Après-midi d'une Vache" (June/July 1943; short story, French translation of "Afternoon of a Cow"; first published in Maurice Edgar Coindreau's French translation in *Fontaine*, pp. 27–28).

"Shall Not Perish" (July/August 1943; short story, first published in *Story*, XXIII, 40–47; reprinted in *Collected Stories of William Faulkner* and in *A Rose for Emily*).

A Rose for Emily and Other Stories by William Faulkner (April 1945; eight selected stories with foreword by Saxe Commins, Editions for the Armed Services, New York; work with same title but containing only four stories [three of which appear in the Armed Services edition, but here with "Red Leaves" as the fourth story], edited with annotations by Kenzaburo Ohashi and published by Kairyudo, Tokyo, n.d.).

"An Error in Chemistry" (June 1946; short story, first published in *Ellery Queen's Mystery Magazine*, VII, 5–19; reprinted in *Knight's Gambit*).

"Afternoon of a Cow" (Summer 1947; short story, first published in *Furioso*, II, 5–17; reprinted in *Parodies: An Anthology from Chaucer to Beerbohm—and After,* edited by Dwight Macdonald, published by Random House, New York, 1960; first published in 1943 in a French translation as "L'Après-midi d'une Vache"; reprinted in *Uncollected Stories of William Faulkner*).

"Lucas Beauchamp" (1948; short story, published posthumously with an introduction by Patrick Samway, S.J., in *Virginia Quarterly*, 75 (Summer 1999): 417–37; with slight changes extracted from the first two chapters of *Intruder in the Dust* [see below]).

"A Courtship" (Autumn 1948; short story, first published in *Sewanee Review*, LVI, 634–53; reprinted in *Collected Stories of William Faulkner*).

Knight's Gambit (November 27, 1949; six mystery stories [five of which previously published], first published by Random House, New York; published by Vintage Books, New York, in October 1978; elsewhere).

"Knight's Gambit" (November 27, 1949; mystery story published in *Knight's Gambit*).

Collected Stories of William Faulkner (August 21, 1950; 42 previously published stories, Random House, New York; republished in November 1995 by Vintage International, New York).

"A Name for the City" (October 1950; fictional essay, first published in *Harper's Magazine*, CCI, 200–14; revision included in first section of the prologue to act 1 of *Requiem for a Nun*).

"Mr. Acarius" (February 1953; short story, posthumously published in *Saturday Evening Post*, CCXXXVIII (October 9, 1965): 26–27, 29, 31, and reprinted in *Uncollected Stories of William Faulkner*).

"Hog Pawn" (c. October 1954; short story, first published posthumously in *Uncollected Stories of William Faulkner*; refashioned and included in chapter 14 of book 3, "Flem," of *The Mansion*).

"Sepulture South: Gaslight" (December 1954; short story, published in *Harper's Bazaar*, LXXXVIII, 84–85, 140–41; reprinted in *Uncollected Stories of William Faulkner*).

"Race at Morning" (March 5, 1955; short story, first published in *Saturday Evening Post*, CCXXVII, 26, 103–04, 106; revision reprinted in *Big Woods* and in *Selected Short Stories of William Faulkner*; original version reprinted in *Uncollected Stories of William Faulkner*).

"By the People" (October 1955; short story, first published in *Mademoiselle*, XLI, 86–89, 130, 131, 132, 133, 134, 135, 136, 137, 138, 139; revision included in chapter 13 of *The Mansion*).

A Rose for Emily (1956; four stories [see above; also see *A Rose for Emily and Other Stories*], edited with notes by Naotaro Takiguchi and Masao Takahashi, published by Nan 'un-do, Tokyo; two of the stories—"Shall Not Perish" and "Crevasse"—do not appear in *A Rose for Emily and Other Stories*).

Big Woods (October 14, 1955; four previously published hunting stories, revised with preludes and epilogue, published by Random House, New York; republished in 1994 by Vintage International, New York).

Selected Short Stories of William Faulkner (1962; 13 short stories previously published, Modern Library, New York).

Uncollected Stories of William Faulkner (1979; 45 stories, some revised for books and others uncollected or unpublished; edited and notes by Joseph Blotner; first published by Random House, New York; repub-

lished in a centenary edition by Vintage International, New York, in September 1997).

Reviews

Review of *In April Once*, by W. A. Percy (November 10, 1920; book review, first published in *Mississippian*, IX, 5; reprinted in *William Faulkner: Early Prose and Poetry*).

Review of *Turns and Movies*, by Conrad Aiken (February 16, 1921; book review, first published in *Mississippian*, X, 5; reprinted in *William Faulkner: Early Prose and Poetry*).

Review of *Aria da Capo*, by Edna St. Vincent Millay (January 13, 1922; book review, first published in *Mississippian*, XI, 5; reprinted in *William Faulkner: Early Prose and Poetry*).

Review of *Linda Condon, Cytherea*, and *The Bright Shawl*, by Joseph Hergesheimer (December 15, 1922; review of three books, first published in *Mississippian*, XII, 5; reprinted in *William Faulkner: Early Prose and Poetry*).

"Beyond the Talking" (May 20, 1931; review of *The Road Back*, by Erich Maria Remarque, published in *New Republic*, LXVII, 23–24).

"Folklore of the Air" (November 1935; review of *Test Pilot*, by Jimmy Collins, published in *American Mercury*, XXXVI, 370–72).

Review of *The Old Man and the Sea*, by Ernest Hemingway (Autumn 1952; book review, published in *Shenandoah*, III, 55).

Screenplays

Night Bird (c. November 1931; scenario of unwritten screenplay and basis of *The College Widow*; published posthumously in *Faulkner's MGM Screenplays*, pp. 32–33, edited with introduction and commentaries by Bruce F. Kawin, University of Tennessee Press, Knoxville, 1982).

Manservant (May 24, 1932; scenario of unwritten screenplay based on the unpublished short story "Love"; published posthumously in *Faulkner's MGM Screenplays*, pp. 7–28, edited with introduction and commentaries by Bruce F. Kawin, University of Tennessee Press, Knoxville, 1982).

The College Widow (May 26, 1932; scenario of unwritten screenplay based on *Night Bird*; published posthumously in *Faulkner's MGM Screenplays*, pp. 40–53, edited with introduction and commentaries by Bruce F. Kawin, University of Tennessee Press, Knoxville, 1982).

Absolution (June 1, 1932; scenario of unwritten screenplay; published posthumously in *Faulkner's MGM Screenplays*, pp. 60–69, edited with introduction and commentaries by Bruce F. Kawin, University of Tennessee Press, Knoxville, 1982).

Flying the Mail (June 3, 1932; scenario of unwritten screenplay; published posthumously in *Faulkner's*

MGM Screenplays, pp. 83–69, edited with introduction and commentaries by Bruce F. Kawin, University of Tennessee Press, Knoxville, 1982).

War Birds (January 12, 1933; screenplay unproduced, published posthumously in *Faulkner's MGM Screenplays,* pp. 275–420, edited with introduction and commentaries by Bruce F. Kawin, University of Tennessee Press, Knoxville, 1982).

Today We Live (April 12, 1933 [advance showing]; screenplay [originally titled "Turn About"] with Edith Fitzgerald and Dwight Taylor, based on Faulkner's short story "Turn About" [see above]; directed by Howard Hawks and released on April 21, 1933, by MGM; original script titled "Turn About," published posthumously in *Faulkner's MGM Screenplays,* pp. 128–255, edited with introduction and commentaries by Bruce F. Kawin, University of Tennessee Press, Knoxville, 1982).

Louisiana Lou (April/May 1933; screenplay unproduced [later version without contribution from Faulkner was released by MGM in 1934 under the title *Lazy River*]).

The Road to Glory (June 1936; screenplay with Joel Sayre; directed by Howard Hawks and released by Twentieth Century–Fox).

Slave Ship (June 1937; screenplay with Sam Hellman, Lamar Trotti, and Gladys Lehman; directed by Tay Garnett and released by Twentieth Century–Fox).

Battle Cry (August 16, 1943; unproduced screenplay; edited by Louis Daniel Brodsky and Robert W. Hamblin; published in 1985 by University Press of Mississippi, Jackson).

To Have and Have Not (October 1944; screenplay with Jules Furthman, adapted from the novel of the same title by Ernest Hemingway; directed by Howard Hawks and released by Warner Brothers).

The Big Sleep (August 1946; screenplay with Leigh Brackett and Jules Furthman, adapted from the novel of the same title by Raymond Chandler; directed by Howard Hawks and released by Warner Brothers).

Land of the Pharaohs (July 1955; screenplay with Harry Kurnitz and Harold Jack Bloom; directed by Howard Hawks and released by Warner Brothers).

The Tarnished Angels (January 1958; film adaptation of *Pylon* [see above]; screenplay by George Zuckerman and directed by Douglas Sirk; released by Universal-International).

Alessandro Fargnoli

APPENDIX II

Library Holdings; Bibliographies; Website; and Societies, Centers, and Conferences

1. Library Holdings and Manuscript Collections

Beinecke Rare Books and Manuscript Library, Yale University, New Haven, Connecticut

Berg Collection, New York Public Library

Louis Daniel Brodsky Collection, Kent Library, Southeastern Missouri State University, Cape Girardeau

Humanities Research Center, University of Texas, Austin

Lafayette County Courthouse, Oxford, Mississippi

Mississippi Department of Archives and History, Jackson

Princeton University Library, Princeton, New Jersey

Ripley Public Library, Ripley, Mississippi

Rowan Oak Papers, Special Collections Department, John Davis Williams Library, University of Mississippi, Oxford

Special Collections, University of Virginia, Charlottesville, Virginia

Tippah County Courthouse, Ripley, Mississippi

William B. Wisdom Collection, Howard-Tilton Memorial Library, Tulane University, New Orleans, Louisiana

2. Biographical References

Alexander, Sidney. "The Nobel Prize Comes to Mississippi: How Yoknapatawpha County Sees Its Author," *Commentary* 12 (Summer 1951): 176–80.

Bezzerides, A. I. *William Faulkner: A Life on Paper.* Ed. Ann Abadie. Jackson: University Press of Mississippi, 1980.

Blotner, Joseph. *Faulkner: A Biography.* 2 vols. New York: Random House, 1974. One vol. Rev. ed., 1984.

———, ed. *Selected Letters of William Faulkner.* New York: Random House, 1977.

Bouvard, Loic. "Conversation with William Faulkner." *Modern Fiction Studies* 5 (Winter 1959–60): 361–4.

Bradford, Roark. "The Private World of William Faulkner." *'48, the Magazine of the Year* 2 (May 1948): 83–4, 90.

Breit, Harvey. "A Walk with Faulkner." *New York Times Book Review* (January 30, 1955), 4, 12. Reprinted in *The Writer Observed.* Cleveland: World, 1956, 281–4.

Brennan, Dan. "Journey South." *University of Kansas City Review* 22 (Autumn 1955), 11–6.

Brodsky, Louis Daniel. *William Faulkner: Life Glimpses.* Austin: University of Texas Press, 1990.

Brodsky, Louis Daniel, and Robert W. Hamblin. *Faulkner and Hollywood: A Retrospective from the Brodsky Collection.* Cape Girardeau: Southeast Missouri State University, 1984.

Brodsky, Louis Daniel, and Robert W. Hamblin, eds. *The Brodsky Faulkner Collection, 1959–1989: The Collector's 101 Favorites.* Southeast Missouri State University: Center for Faulkner Studies, 1989.

———. *Country Lawyer and Other Stories for the Screen.* Jackson: University Press of Mississippi, 1987.

———. *Faulkner: A Comprehensive Guide to the Brodsky Collection. Vol. II: The Letters.* Jackson: University Press of Mississippi, 1984.

———. *Selections from the William Faulkner Collection of Louis Daniel Brodsky.* Charlottesville: University Press of Virginia, 1979.

———. *William Faulkner: A Perspective from the Brodsky Collection.* Cape Girardeau: Southeast Missouri State University, 1979.

Buttitta, Anthony. "William Faulkner: That Writin' Man of Oxford." *Saturday Review of Literature* 18 (May 21, 1938): 6–8.

Cantwell, Robert. "The Faulkners: Recollections of a Gifted Family." *New World Writings* 2 (November 1952), 300–15. Reprinted in *William Faulkner: Three Decades of Criticism,* edited by Frederick J. Hoffman and Olga W. Vickery. New York: Harcourt, Brace & World, 1963, pp. 51–66.

Carter, Hodding. "Faulkner and His Folk." *Princeton University Library Chronicle* 18 (Spring 1957): 95–107.

Chapsal, Madeleine. "A Lion in the Garden." *Reporter* 13 (November 3, 1955): 40.

Cofield, Jack. *William Faulkner: The Cofield Collection.* Oxford, Miss.: Yoknapatawpha Press, 1978.

Coughlan, Robert. *The Private World of William Faulkner.* New York: Harper, 1954.

Cowley, Malcolm. *The Faulkner-Cowley File: Letters and Memories, 1944–1962.* New York: Viking Press, 1966.

Cullen, John B., and Floyd C. Watkins. *Old Times in the Faulkner Country.* Chapel Hill: University of North Carolina Press, 1961.

Dain, Martin J. *Faulkner's County: Yoknapatawpha.* New York: Random House, 1964.

———. *Faulkner's World: The Photographs of Martin J. Dain.* Edited and with an introduction by Thomas S. Rankin. Jackson: University Press of Mississippi, 1997.

Dominicus, A. M. "An Interview with Faulkner." *Faulkner Studies* 3 (Summer-Autumn 1954): 33–37.

Evans, Medford. "Oxford, Mississippi." *Southwest Review* 15 (Winter 1929): 46–63.

Falkner, Murry C. *The Falkners of Mississippi: A Memoir.* Baton Rouge: Louisiana State University Press, 1967.

Fant, Joseph L., and Robert Ashley, eds. *Faulkner at West Point.* New York: Random House, 1964.

Faulkner, Jim. *Across the Creek: Faulkner Family Stories.* Jackson: University Press of Mississippi, 1986.

———. "Auntee Owned Two," *Southern Review* 8 (October 1972): 836–44.

Faulkner, John. *My Brother Bill: An Affectionate Reminiscence.* New York: Trident Press, 1963.

Franklin, Malcolm A. *Bitterweeds: Life with William Faulkner at Rowan Oak.* Irving, Tex.: Society for the Study of Traditional Culture, 1977.

———. "A Christmas in Columbus." *Mississippi Quarterly* 27 (Summer 1974): 319–22.

Gray, Richard. *The Life of William Faulkner: A Critical Biography.* Oxford, England: Blackwell, 1994.

Green, A. Wigfall. "William Faulkner at Home." *Sewanee Review* 40 (Summer 1932): 294–306. Reprinted in *William Faulkner: Two Decades of Criticism,* Frederick J. Hoffman and Olga W. Vickery (eds). East Lansing: Michigan State University Press, 1951, 33–47.

Grenier, Cynthia. "An Interview with William Faulkner—September, 1955." *Accent* 16 (Summer 1956): 167–77.

Gresset, Michel. *A Faulkner Chronology.* Jackson: University Press of Mississippi, 1985.

Gwynn, Frederick L., and Joseph Blotner, eds. *Faulkner in the University: Class Conferences at the University of Virginia, 1957–1958.* Charlottesville: University of Virginia Press, 1959.

———. "Faulkner in the University: A Classroom Conference." *College English* 19 (October 1957): 1–6.

———. "William Faulkner on Dialect." *University of Virginia Magazine* 2 (Winter 1958): 7–13; cont'd. in 2 (Spring 1958): 32–7.

Haynes, Jane Isbell. *William Faulkner: His Lafayette County Heritage.* Columbia, S.C.: Seajay Press, 1992.

———. *William Faulkner: His Tippah County Heritage.* Columbia, S.C.: Seajay Press, 1992.

Howe, Russell Warren. "A Talk with William Faulkner." *Reporter* 14 (March 22, 1956): 18–20.

Inge, M. Thomas, ed. *Conversations with William Faulkner.* Jackson: University Press of Mississippi, 1999.

Jelliffe, Robert A., ed. *Faulkner at Nagano.* Tokyo, Japan: Kenkyusha, 1956.

Karl, Frederick. *William Faulkner, American Writer: A Biography.* New York: Weidenfeld & Nicolson, 1989.

Lawrence, John, and Dan Hise. *Faulkner's Rowan Oak.* Jackson: University Press of Mississippi, 1995.

Meriwether, James B., and Michael Millgate, eds. *Lion in the Garden: Interviews with William Faulkner, 1926–1962.* New York: Random House, 1968.

Minter, David. *William Faulkner: His Life and Work.* Baltimore, Md.: Johns Hopkins University Press, 1980.

Morris, Willie. *Faulkner's Mississippi.* Birmingham, Ala.: Oxmoor House, 1990.

——— (with photos by William Albert Allard). "Faulkner's Mississippi." *National Geographic* 175 (March 1989): 313–39.

Oates, Stephen B. *William Faulkner: The Man and the Artist.* New York: Harper & Row, 1987.

Raimbault, R. N. *Faulkner.* Paris, France: Editions Universitaires, 1963.

Rascoe, Lavon. "An Interview with William Faulkner." *Western Review* 15 (Summer 1951): 300–4.

Richardson, H. Edward. *William Faulkner: The Journey to Self-Discovery.* Columbia: University of Missouri Press, 1969.

Smith, Bradley. "The Faulkner Country." *'48, the Magazine of the Year* 2 (May 1948): 85–9.

Smith, Marshall J. "Faulkner of Mississippi." *Bookman* 74 (December 1931): 411–7.

Snell, Susan. *Phil Stone of Oxford: A Vicarious Life.* Athens: University of Georgia Press, 1991.

Stein, Jean. "William Faulkner." *Paris Review,* 4 (Spring 1956): 28–52. Reprinted in *Writers at Work,* edited by Malcolm Cowley. New York: Viking, 1958: 119–41. Also reprinted in *William Faulkner: Three Decades of Criticism,* edited by Frederick J. Hoffman and Olga W. Vickery. New York: Harcourt, Brace & World, 1963, pp. 67–82.

Stone, Phil. "William Faulkner: The Man and His Work." *Oxford Magazine* (Oxford, Mississippi), copy 1 (1934): 13–14; continued in copies 2 and 3; unfinished. Reprinted in James B. Meriwether, "Early Notices of Faulkner by Phil Stone and Louis Cochran." *Mississippi Quarterly* 17 (Summer 1964): 136–64.

Sullivan, Frank. "A Distinguished Commuter." *Saturday Review* 34 (June 9, 1951): 4.

Taylor, Herman E. *Faulkner's Oxford: Recollections and Reflections.* Nashville, Tenn.: Rutledge Hill Press, 1990.

Wagner, Linda W. "William Faulkner." In *Dictionary of Literary Biography: American Novelists, 1910–1945,* Part 1: Louis Adamic—Vardis Fisher, vol. 9, edited by James J. Martine. Detroit: Gale, 1981, pp. 282–302.

Wasson, Ben. *Count No 'Count: Flashbacks to Faulkner.* Jackson: University Press of Mississippi, 1983.

Watson, James G., ed. *Thinking of Home: William Faulkner's Letters to His Mother and Father, 1918–1925.* New York: Norton, 1992.

Webb, James W., and A. Wigfall Green, eds. *William Faulkner of Oxford.* Baton Rouge: Louisiana State University Press, 1965.

Wilde, Meta Carpenter, and Orin Borsten. *A Loving Gentleman: The Love Story of William Faulkner and Meta Carpenter.* New York: Simon & Schuster, 1976.

Williamson, Joel. *William Faulkner and Southern History.* New York: Oxford University Press, 1993.

Wittenberg, Judith Bryant. *Faulkner: The Transfiguration of Biography.* Lincoln: University of Nebraska Press, 1979.

Wolff, Sally, with Floyd C. Watkins, eds. *Talking about William Faulkner: Interviews with Jimmy Faulkner and Others.* Baton Rouge: Louisiana State University Press, 1996.

Young, Stark. "New Year's Craw." *New Republic* 93 (January 12, 1938): 283–4.

3. Bibliographical References

Bassett, John E. *Faulkner: An Annotated Checklist of Recent Criticism.* Kent, Ohio: Kent State University Press, 1983.

———. *Faulkner in the Eighties: An Annotated Critical Bibliography.* Metuchen, N.J.: Scarecrow, 1991.

———. *William Faulkner: An Annotated Checklist of Criticism.* New York: David Lewis, 1972.

Beebe, Maurice. "Criticism of William Faulkner: A Selected Checklist with an Index to Studies of Separate Works." *Modern Fiction Studies* 2 (Autumn 1956): 150–64.

Blotner, Joseph. *William Faulkner's Library: A Catalogue.* Charlottesville: University Press of Virginia, 1964.

Blotner, Joseph, Thomas L. McHaney, Michael Millgate, Noel Polk, and James B. Meriwether, eds. *William Faulkner Manuscripts.* 44 vols. New York: Garland, 1985–87.

Bonner, Thomas, Jr., comp. *William Faulkner: The William B. Wisdom Collection: A Descriptive Catalogue.* New Orleans, La.: Tulane University Libraries, 1980.

Brodsky, Louis D., and Robert W. Hamblin, eds. *Faulkner: A Comprehensive Guide to the Brodsky Collection.* 5 vols. Jackson: University Press of Mississippi, 1982–88.

Butterworth, Keen. "A Census of Manuscripts and Typescripts of William Faulkner's Poetry." *Mississippi Quarterly* 26 (Summer 1973): 333–60.

Capps, Jack L., ed. *The Faulkner Concordances.* 34 vols. Ann Arbor, Mich.: UMI Research Press/The Faulkner Concordance Advisory Board, 1977–90.

Cox, Leland, ed. *William Faulkner: Biographical and Reference Guide: A Guide to His Life and Career.* Detroit, Mich.: Gale, 1982.

Daniel, Robert W. *A Catalogue of the Writings of William Faulkner.* New Haven: Yale University Library, 1942.

Hayhoe, George F. "Faulkner in Hollywood: A Checklist of His Film Scripts at the University of Virginia." *Mississippi Quarterly* 31 (Summer 1978): 407–19.

Howard, Peter. *William Faulkner: The Carl Peterson Collection.* Berkeley, Calif.: Serendipity Press, 1991.

Kawin, Bruce, ed. *Faulkner's MGM Screenplays.* Knoxville: University of Tennessee Press, 1982.

Massey, Linton, comp. *William Faulkner: "Man Working," 1919–1962: A Catalogue of the William Faulkner Collections at the University of Virginia.* Charlottesville: Bibliographical Society of the University of Virginia, 1968.

McHaney, Thomas. *William Faulkner: A Reference Guide.* Boston: G. K. Hall, 1976.

Meriwether, James B. *The Literary Career of William Faulkner: A Bibliographical Study.* Princeton, N.J.: Princeton University Library, 1961. Revised edition. Columbia, S.C.: University of South Carolina Press, 1972.

———, ed. *A Faulkner Miscellany.* Jackson: University Press of Mississippi, 1974.

Meriwether, James, B. *The Merrill Checklist of William Faulkner.* Columbus, Ohio: Merrill, 1970.

———. *William Faulkner: An Exhibit of Manuscripts* (Austin, Texas, 1959).

———. "The Short Fiction of William Faulkner: A Bibliography." *Proof* 1 (1971): 293–329.

———. "William Faulkner: A Check List." *Princeton University Library Chronicle* 18 (Spring 1957): 136–58. A bibliography of Faulkner's works.

Perry, Bradley T. "Faulkner Critics: A Bibliography Breakdown." *Faulkner Studies* 2 (Spring–Summer–Winter, 1953): 11–13, 30–32, 60–64.

———. "A Selected Bibliography of Critical Works on William Faulkner." *University of Kansas City Review* 18 (Winter 1951): 159–64.

Petersen, Carl. *Each in Its Ordered Place: A Faulkner Collector's Notebook.* Ann Arbor, Mich.: Ardis, 1975.

———. *On the Track of the Dixie Limited: Further Notes of a Faulkner Collector.* La Grange, Ill.: Colophon Book Shop, 1979.

Ricks, Beatrice. *William Faulkner: A Reference Guide.* Metuchen, N.J.: Scarecrow, 1981.

Runyan, Harry. "Faulkner's Non-Fiction Prose: An Annotated Checklist." *Faulkner Studies* 3 (Winter 1954): 67–9.

Sensibar, Judith. *Faulkner's Poetry: A Bibliographic Guide to Texts and Criticism.* Ann Arbor, Mich.: UMI Research Press, 1988.

Sleeth, Irene Lynn. "William Faulkner: A Bibliography of Criticism." *Twentieth Century Literature* 8 (April 1962): 18–43. Also published separately in *The Swallow Pamphlets,* Number 13. Denver: Alan Swalow, 1962.

Smith, Thelma M., and Ward L. Miner. "Faulkner Checklist and Bibliography." *Transatlantic Migration: The Contemporary American Novel in France.* Durham: Duke University Press, 1955, pp. 227–35.

Stallman, Robert W. "William Faulkner." In *Critiques and Essays on Modern Fiction, 1920–1951,* edited by John W. Aldridge. New York: Ronald Press, 1952, pp. 582–86.

Starke, Aubrey. "An American Comedy: An Introduction to a Bibliography of William Faulkner." *Colophon* 5 (1934), part 19.

Sweeney, Patricia. *William Faulkner's Women Characters: An Annotated Bibliography of Criticism, 1930–1983.* Santa Barbara, Calif.: ABC-Clio, 1985.

Vickery, Olga W. "A Selective Bibliography." *William Faulkner: Three Decades of Criticism.* East Lansing: Michigan State University Press, 1960, pp. 393–428. A bibliography of Faulkner criticism.

4. Reference Works, Guides, and Periodicals

Connolly, Thomas E. *Faulkner's World: A Directory of His People and Synopses of Actions in His Published Works.* Lanham, Md.: University Press of America, 1988.

Dasher, Thomas E. *William Faulkner's Characters: An Index to the Published and Unpublished Fiction.* New York: Garland, 1981.

English Institute Essays, 1952 (essays on *The Sound and the Fury*). New York: Columbia University Press, 1954.

The Faulkner Journal, 1985–1988, 1991–   (Dawn Trouard, managing editor, Humanities and Fine Arts Building, RM 405, University of Central Florida, Orlando, FL 32816-1346; Website: http://pegasus.cc.ucf.edu/~faulkner/).

The Faulkner Journal of Japan (see *Faulkner Studies*).

The Faulkner Newsletter & Yoknapatawpha Review, 1981 (Oxford, Mississippi; Website: http://www.watervalley.net/yoknapatawphapress/news.html).

Faulkner Studies (title given to three separate journals; the two that published in 1952–54 and 1980 are defunct; the third started publishing in 1991 in Japan, also *The Faulkner Journal of Japan*).

Ford, Margaret P., and Suzanne Kincaid. *Who's Who in Faulkner.* Baton Rouge: Louisiana State University Press, 1963.

Hamblin, Robert W., and Charles A. Peek, eds. *A William Faulkner Encyclopedia.* Westport, Conn.: Greenwood Press, 1999.

Harvard Advocate (William Faulkner issue) 135 (November 1951).

Hoffman, Frederick J. *William Faulkner.* 2nd ed. New York: Twayne, 1966.

Kirk, Robert W., with Marvin Klotz. *Faulkner's People: A Complete Guide and Index to Characters in the Fiction of William Faulkner.* Berkeley: University of California Press, 1963.

Mississippi Quarterly (summer issues devoted to Faulkner).

Modern Fiction Studies (William Faulkner special number) 2 (Autumn 1956). Essays by Melvin Backman, Robert Flynn, David L. Frazier, Roma A. King, W. R. Moses, Karl E. Zink.

Oxford American, 1992 (Website: http://www.oxfordamericanmag.com/).

Perspective (Faulkner) 2 (Summer 1949). Essays by Ruel E. Foster, Phyllis Hirshleifer, Sumner C. Powell, Russell Roth, Ray B. West.

Perspective (Faulkner, no. 2) 3 (Autumn 1950). Essays by Harry M. Campbell, Tommy Hudson, Olga Westland Vickery, Edgar W. Whan.

Princeton University Library Chronicle (William Faulkner) 18 (Spring 1957).

Runyan, Harry. *A Faulkner Glossary.* New York: Citadel, 1964.

Teaching Faulkner, edited by Robert W. Hamblin and Charles A. Peek, published by the Center for Faulkner Studies, Southeast Missouri State University (Website: http://www2.semo.edu/cfs/teach.html).

Tuck, Dorothy. *Crowell's Handbook of Faulkner.* New York: Crowell, 1964.

Volpe, Edmond L. *A Reader's Guide to William Faulkner.* New York: Noonday, 1964.

Weinstein, Philip, ed. *The Cambridge Companion to William Faulkner.* New York: Cambridge University Press, 1995.

5. Selected General Bibliography

Adam, Richard P. *Faulkner: Myth and Motion.* Princeton, N.J.: Princeton University Press, 1968.

Adams, Robert M. "Poetry in the Novel: or, Faulkner Esemplastic." *Virginia Quarterly Review* 29 (Summer 1953): 419–34.

D'Agostino, Nemi. "William Faulkner." *Studia Americani* 1 (1955): 257–308.

Aiken, Conrad. "'Mosquitoes,'" *New York Post* (June 11, 1927): 7. Reprinted in his *A Reviewer's ABC: Collected Criticism from 1916 to the Present.* New York: Meridian, 1958: 197–200.

———. "William Faulkner: The Novel as Form." *Atlantic Monthly* 164 (November 1939): 650–54. Reprinted in his *A Reviewer's ABC: Collected Criticism from 1916 to the Present.* New York: Meridian, 1958: 200–07; in *William Faulkner: Three Decades of Criticism,* edited by Frederick J. Hoffman and Olga W. Vickery. New York: Harcourt, Brace & World, 1963, 135–42; and also in *Faulkner A Collection of Critical Essays,* edited by Robert Penn Warren. Englewood Cliffs, N.J.: Prentice-Hall, Inc., 1966: 46–52.

Allen, Charles A. "William Faulkner's Vision of Good and Evil." *Pacific Spectator* 10 (Summer 1956): 236–41.

Altman, Meryl. "The Bug That Dare Not Speak Its Name: Sex, Art, Faulkner's Worst Novel, and the

Critics." *The Faulkner Journal* (Akron, Ohio; Fall 1993/Spring 1994) 9: 1–2, 43–68.

Anderson, Charles. "Faulkner's Moral Center." *Etudes Anglaises* 7 (January 1954): 48–58.

Anonymous. "The Worldwide Influence of William Faulkner: Reports from Six Capitols." *New York Times Book Review* 64 (November 15, 1959): 52–3. Statements by Walter Allen, Celia Bertin, Max Frankel, Flora Lewis, Masami Nishkawa, Emilio Cecchi.

Archer, H. Richard. "Collecting Faulkner Today." *Faulkner Studies* 1 (Fall 1952): 42–43.

———. "The Writings of William Faulkner: A Challenge to the Bibliographer." *Papers of the Bibliographical Society of America* 50 (3rd quart. 1956): 229–42.

Arnold, Edwin T. "Freedom and Stasis in Faulkner's Mosquitoes." *Mississippi Quarterly: The Journal of Southern Culture* (Mississippi State University), 1975, 28: 281–97.

Arthos, John. "Ritual and Humor in the Writing of William Faulkner." *Accent* 9 (Autumn 1948): 17–30. Reprinted in *William Faulkner: Two Decades of Criticism,* edited by Frederick J. Hoffman and Olga W. Vickery. East Lansing: Michigan State University Press, 1951: 101–18.

Aymé, Marcel. "What French Readers Find in William Faulkner's Fiction." *New York Times Book Review* (December 17, 1950): 4. Reprinted in *Highlights of Modern Literature,* edited by Francis Brown. New York: Mentor, 1954, pp. 103–06.

Bache, William B. "Moral Awareness in 'Dry September.'" *Faulkner Studies* 3 (Winter 1954): 53–57.

Backman, Melvin. *Faulkner: The Major Years: A Critical Study.* Bloomington: Indiana University Press, 1966.

———. "Faulkner's Sick Heroes: Bayard Sartoris and Quentin Compson." *Modern Fiction Studies* 2 (Autumn 1956): 95–108.

———. "Sickness and Primitivism: A Dominant Pattern in William Faulkner's Work." *Accent* 14 (Winter 1954): 61–73.

Backus, Joseph M. "Names of Characters in Faulkner's 'The Sound and the Fury.'" *Names* 6 (December 1958): 226–33.

Baker, Carlos. "Cry Enough!" *Nation* 179 (August 7, 1954): 115–18

———. "William Faulkner: The Doomed and the Damned." In *The Young Rebel in American Literature,* edited by Carl Bode. London: Heinemann, 1959, pp. 145–69..

Baker, James R. "Ideas and Queries." *Faulkner Studies* 1 (Spring 1952): 4–7.

———. "The Symbolic Extension of Yoknapatawpha County." *Arizona Quarterly* 8 (Autumn 1952): 223–8.

Baldanza, Frank. "Faulkner and Stein: A Study in Stylistic Intransigence." *Georgia Review* 13 (Fall 1959): 274–86.

Barth, J. Robert. "A Rereading of Faulkner's Fable." *America* 92 (October 9, 1954): 44–6.

Barth, J. Robert, ed. *Religious Perspectives in Faulkner's Fiction: Yoknapatawpha and Beyond.* Notre Dame, Ind.: University of Notre Dame Press, 1972.

Bassett, John Earl. *Vision and Revisions: Essays on Faulkner.* West Cornwall, Conn.: Locust Hill Press, 1989.

———. "Faulkner's *Mosquitoes:* Toward a Self-Image of the Artist." *Southern Literary Journal* 12, no. 2 (Chapel Hill, N.C., 1980): 49–64.

Beach, Joseph Warren. "William Faulkner." In *American Fiction, 1920–1940.* New York: Macmillan, 1941: 123–69.

Beck, Warren. *Faulkner: Essays.* Madison: University of Wisconsin Press, 1976.

———. *Man in Motion: Faulkner's Trilogy.* Madison: University of Wisconsin Press, 1961.

———. "Faulkner and the South." *Antioch Review* 1 (Spring 1941): 82–94.

———. "Faulkner's Point of View." *College English* 2 (May 1941): 736–49.

———. "A Note on Faulkner's Style," *Rocky Mountain Review* 6 (Spring–Summer 1942): 6–7, 14.

———. "William Faulkner's Style." *American Prefaces* 6 (Spring 1941): 195–211. Reprinted in *William Faulkner: Three Decades of Criticism,* edited by Frederick J. Hoffman and Olga W. Vickery. New York: Harcourt, Brace & World, 1963: 142–56. Also reprinted in *Faulkner A Collection of Critical Essays,* edited by Robert Penn Warren. Englewood Cliffs, N.J.: Prentice-Hall, Inc., 1966: 53–65.

Bergel, Lienhard. "Faulkner's 'Sanctuary.'" *Explicator* 6 (December 1947): item 20.

Birney, Earle. "The Two William Faulkners." *Canadian Forum* 18 (June 1938): 84–85.

Bledsoe, Erik. *Margaret Mitchell's Review of "Soldiers' Pay."* *Mississippi Quarterly: The Journal of Southern Culture* 49, no. 3 (Mississippi State University, Summer 1996): 591–93.

Bleikasten, Andre. *The Ink of Melancholy: Faulkner's Novels from "The Sound and the Fury" to "Light in August."* Bloomington: Indiana University Press, 1990.

Bloom, Harold, ed. *Modern Critical Views: William Faulkner.* New York: Chelsea House, 1986.

———. *William Faulkner's "Sanctuary": Modern Critical Interpretations.* New York: Chelsea House, 1988.

Blotner, Joseph L. "'As I Lay Dying': Christian Lore and Irony." *Twentieth Century Literature* 3 (April 1957): 14–9.

Blum, Irving D. "The Parallel Philosophy of Emerson's 'Nature' and Faulkner's 'The Bear.'" *Emerson Society Quarterly* 13 (4th quarter 1958): 22–5.

Bockting, Ineke. *Character and Personality in the Novels of William Faulkner: A Study in Psychostylistics.* Lanham, Md.: University Press of America, 1995.

Bosha, Francis. *The Textual History and Definitive Textual Apparatus for "Soldiers' Pay": A Bibliographic Study of William Faulkner's First Novel.* Dissertation Abstracts International (Ann Arbor, Mich.), 1979, 39: 5509 A.

Bowling, Lawrence E. "Faulkner: Technique of 'The Sound and the Fury.'" *Kenyon Review* 10 (Autumn 1948): 552–66. Reprinted in *William Faulkner: Two Decades of Criticism,* edited by Frederick J. Hoffman and Olga W. Vickery. East Lansing: Michigan State University Press, 1951, pp. 165–79.

———. "Faulkner and the Theme of Innocence." *Kenyon Review* 20 (Summer 1958): 466–87.

Boyle, Kay. "Tattered Banners." *New Republic* 94 (March 9, 1938): 136–37.

Boynton, Percy H. "The Retrospective South." In *America in Contemporary Fiction.* Chicago: University of Chicago Press, 1940, pp. 103–12.

Breaden, Dale G. "William Faulkner and the Land." *American Quarterly* 10 (Fall 1958): 344–57.

Breit, Harvey. "A Sense of Faulkner." *Partisan Review* 18 (January–February 1951): 88–94.

———. "William Faulkner." *Atlantic Monthly* 188 (October 1951): 53–6.

Brooks, Cleanth. *On the Prejudices, Predilections, and Firm Beliefs of William Faulkner.* Baton Rouge: Louisiana State University Press, 1987.

———. *William Faulkner: First Encounters.* New Haven, Conn.: Yale University Press, 1983.

———. *William Faulkner: Toward Yoknapatawpha and Beyond.* New Haven, Conn.: Yale University Press, 1978.

———. *William Faulkner: The Yoknapatawpha Country.* New Haven, Conn.: Yale University Press, 1963.

———. "'Absalom, Absalom!' The Definition of Innocence." *Sewanee Review* 59 (Autumn 1951): 543–58.

———. "Primitivism in 'The Sound and the Fury.'" In *English Institute Essays 1952,* edited by Alan S. Downer. New York: Columbia University Press, 1954, pp. 5–28.

Brooks, Cleanth, and Robert Penn Warren. *Understanding Fiction.* New York: F. S. Crofts, 1943: 409–14.

Broughton, Panthea Reid. *William Faulkner: The Abstract and the Actual.* Baton Rouge: Louisiana State University Press, 1974.

Brown, Calvin S. *A Glossary of Faulkner's South.* New Haven, Conn.: Yale University Press, 1976.

Brown, James. "Shaping the World of 'Sanctuary.'" *University of Kansas City Review* 25 (Winter 1958): 137–42.

Brumm, Ursula. "Wilderness and Civilization: A Note on William Faulkner." *Partisan Review* 22 (Summer 1955): 340–50. Reprinted in *William Faulkner: Three Decades of Criticism,* edited by Frederick J. Hoffman and Olga W. Vickery. New York: Harcourt, Brace & World, 1963, pp. 125–34.

Brylowski, Walter. *Faulkner's Olympian Laugh: Myth in the Novels.* Detroit, Mich.: Wayne State University Press, 1968.

Burgum, Edwin Berry. "William Faulkner's Patterns of American Decadence." *The Novel and the World's Dilemma.* New York: Oxford University Press, 1947: 205–22.

Butterworth, Nancy. *A Critical and Textual Study of Faulkner's "A Fable."* Ann Arbor, Mich.: UMI Research Press, 1983.

Campbell, Harry M. "Experiment and Achievement: 'As I Lay Dying' and 'The Sound and the Fury.'" *Sewanee Review* 51 (Spring 1943): 305–20.

———. "Faulkner's 'Absalom, Absalom!'" *Explicator* 7 (December 1948): item 24.

———. "Faulkner's 'Sanctuary.'" *Explicator* 4 (June 1946): item 61.

———. "Structural Devices in the Works of Faulkner," *Perspective* 3 (Autumn, 1950): 209–26.

Campbell, Harry M., and Ruel E. Foster. *William Faulkner: A Critical Appraisal.* Norman: Oklahoma University Press, 1951.

Canby, Henry Seidel. "The School of Cruelty." *Saturday Review of Literature* 7 (March 21, 1931): 673–74. Reprinted in *Seven Years' Harvest.* New York: Farrar & Rinehart, 1936, pp. 77–83.

Cantwell, Robert. "Faulkner's 'Popeye.'" *Nation* 186 (February 15, 1958): 140–41, 148.

Caraceni, Augusto. "William Faulkner." *Aretusa* 2 (November 1945): 23–28.

Carey, Glenn O., ed. *Faulkner: The Unappeased Imagination: A Collection of Critical Essays.* Troy, N.Y.: Whitston, 1980.

Cargill, Oscar. "The Primitivists." In *Intellectual America.* New York: Macmillan, 1941: 370–86.

Carothers, James B. *William Faulkner's Short Stories.* Ann Arbor, Mich.: UMI Research Press, 1985.

Carpenter, Lucas. "Faulkner's 'Soldiers' Pay': 'Yaphank' Gilligan." *Notes on Modern American Literature* 8, no. 3 (Jamaica, N.Y., Winter 1984): item 17.

Carpenter, Richard C. "Faulkner's 'Sartoris.'" *Explicator* 14 (April 1956): item 41.

Carter, Thomas H. "Dramatization of an Enigma." *Western Review* 19 (Winter 1955): 147–58.

Cash, W. J. *The Mind of the South.* New York: Knopf, 1941. Garden City, N.Y.: Doubleday, 1954.

Cecchi, Emilio. "William Faulkner." *Pan* 2 (May 1934): 64–70.

Chabrier, Gwendolyn. *Faulkner's Families: A Southern Saga.* New York: Gordian, 1993.

Chamberlain, John. "Dostoyefsky's Shadow in the Deep South." *New York Times Book Review* (February 15, 1931): 9.

Chamier, Suzanne. "Faulkner and Queneau: Raymond Queneau's Preface to 'Mosquitoes'." *The Faulkner*

Journal 13 (Orlando, Fla., Fall 1997/Spring 1998): 1–2, 15–36.

Chapman, Arnold. "Pampas and Big Woods: Heroic Initiation in Güiraldes and Faulkner." *Comparative Literature* 11 (Winter 1959): 61–77.

Chappell, Charles. *Detective Dupin Reads William Faulkner: Solutions to Six Yoknapatawpha Mysteries.* San Francisco: International Scholars Publications, 1997.

Chase, Richard. "Faulkner—The Great Years," *The American Novel and its Tradition.* Garden City: Doubleday Anchor Books, 1957. pp. 205–36.

Clarke, Deborah. *Robbing the Mother: Women in Faulkner.* Jackson: University Press of Mississippi, 1994.

Coanda, Richard. "'Absalom, Absalom!' The Edge of Infinity." *Renascence* 11 (Autumn 1958): 3–9.

Coffee, James M. *Faulkner's Un-Christlike Christians: Biblical Allusions in the Novels.* Ann Arbor: Michigan UMI Research Press, 1983.

Coindreau, Maurice E. *The Time of William Faulkner: A French View of Modern American Fiction.* Edited and translated by George M. Reeves. Columbia: South Carolina University Press, 1971.

———. "On Translating Faulkner." *Princeton University Library Chronicle* 18 (Spring 1957): 108–13.

———. "William Faulkner in France." *Yale French Studies* 10 (Fall 1952): 85–91.

Collins, Carvel. "Are These Mandalas?" *Literature and Psychology* 3 (November 1953): 3–6.

———. "A Conscious Literary Use of Freud?" *Literature and Psychology* 3 (June 1953): 2–3.

———. "Faulkner and Certain Earlier Southern Fiction." *College English* 16 (November 1954): 92–97.

———. "Faulkner's Reputation and the Contemporary Novel." In *Literature in the Modern World,* edited by William J. Griffin. Nashville: George Peabody College for Teachers, 1954, pp. 65–71.

———. "Faulkner's 'The Sound and the Fury.'" *Explicator* 17 (December 1958): item 19.

———. "The Interior Monologues of 'The Sound and the Fury.'" In *English Institute Essays 1952,* edited by Alan S. Downer. New York: Columbia University Press, 1954, pp. 29–56. Reprinted in *Massachusetts Institute of Technology Publications in the Humanities,* No. 6 (1954).

———. "Nathaniel West's 'The Day of the Locust' and 'Sanctuary.'" *Faulkner Studies* 2 (Summer 1953): 23–4.

———. "A Note on 'Sanctuary.'" *Harvard Advocate* 135 (November 1951): 16.

———. "A Note on the Conclusion of 'The Bear.'" *Faulkner Studies* 2 (Winter 1954): 58–60.

———. "The Pairing of 'The Sound and the Fury' and 'As I Lay Dying.'" *Princeton University Library Chronicle* 18 (Spring 1957): 114–23.

———. "War and Peace and Mr. Faulkner." *New York Times Book Review* (August 1, 1954): 1, 13.

Connolly, Cyril. "'Pylon.'" *New Statesman and Nation* 9 (April 13, 1935): 284–5.

Coughlan, Robert. *The Private World of William Faulkner.* New York: Harper, 1954.

Cowley, Malcolm. "Flem Snopes Gets his Come-Uppance." *New York Times Book Review* (November 15, 1959): 1, 18.

———. "Introduction," *The Portable Faulkner.* New York: Viking Press, 1946, pp. 1–24. Reprinted in *William Faulkner: Three Decades of Criticism,* edited by Frederick J. Hoffman and Olga W. Vickery. New York: Harcourt, Brace & World, 1963, pp. 94–109. Also reprinted in *Faulkner A Collection of Critical Essays,* edited by Robert Penn Warren. Englewood Cliffs, N.J.: Prentice-Hall, Inc., 1966, pp. 34–45.

———. "An Introduction to William Faulkner." In *Critiques and Essays on Modern Fiction, 1920–1951,* edited by John W. Aldridge. New York: Ronald Press, 1952, pp. 427–46.

———. "Poe in Mississippi." *New Republic* 89 (November 4, 1936): 22.

———. "Sanctuary." *New Republic* 97 (January 25, 1939): 349.

———. "William Faulkner's Human Comedy." *New York Times Book Review* (October 19, 1944): 4.

———. "William Faulkner's Legend of the South." *Sewanee Review* 53 (Summer 1945): 343–61. Reprinted in *A Southern Vanguard,* Allen Tate (ed). New York: Prentice-Hall, 1947, pp. 13–27.

———. "William Faulkner Revisited." *Saturday Review of Literature* 28 (April 14, 1945): 13–16.

———. "In Which Mr. Faulkner Translates Past into Present." *New York Herald Tribune* (Books) (September 30, 1951): 1, 14.

———. "Voodoo Dance." *New Republic* 82 (April 10, 1935): 284–5.

Coy, Javier, and Michel Gresset, eds. *Faulkner and History.* Salamanca, Spain: Universidad de Salamanca, 1986.

Cullen, John B. in collaboration with Floyd C. Watkins. *Old Times in the Faulkner Country.* Chapel Hill: University of North Carolina Press, 1961.

Dabney, Lewis M. *The Indians of Yoknapatawpha: A Study in Literature and History.* Baton Rouge: Louisiana State University Press, 1973.

Dain, Martin J. *Faulkner's County—Yoknapatawpha* (photos taken in and around Oxford, Mississippi). New York: Random House, 1964.

Dauffenbach, Claus. *A Portrait of the Modernist as a Young Aesthete: Faulkner's "Mosquitoes."* Amerikastudien—American Studies, Mainz, Germany (Amst). 1997, 42:4, 547–58.

Davis, Thadious M. *Faulkner's "Negro": Art and the Southern Context.* Baton Rouge: Louisiana State University Press, 1983.

De Voto, Bernard. "Faulkner's South." *Saturday Review of Literature* 17 (February 19, 1938): 5.

———. "Witchcraft in Mississippi." *Saturday Review of Literature* 15 (October 31, 1936): 3–4, 14. Reprinted in *Minority Report*. Boston: Little, Brown, 1940, pp. 209–18.

Doran, Leonard. "Form and the Story Teller." *Harvard Advocate* 135 (November, 1951): 12, 38–41.

Doster, William C. "The Several Faces of Gavin Stevens." *Mississippi Quarterly* 11 (Fall, 1958): 191–5.

Douglas, Harold J., and Robert Daniel. "Faulkner and the Puritanism of the South." *Tennessee Studies in Literature* 2 (1957): 1–13.

Dowling, David. *William Faulkner*. New York: St. Martin's Press, 1989.

Downing, Francis. "An Eloquent Man." *Commonweal* 53 (December 15, 1950): 255–58.

Duvall, John N. *Faulkner's Marginal Couple: Invisible, Outlaw, and Unspeakable Communities*. Austin: University of Texas Press, 1990.

Edel, Leon. *The Psychological Novel, 1900–1950*. New York: Lippincott, 1955, pp. 147–54.

Edgar, Pelham. "Four American Novelists." In *The Art of the Novel*. New York: Macmillan, 1933, pp, 338–51.

Edmonds, Irene C. "Faulkner and the Black Shadow." In *Southern Renascence: The Literature of the Modern South,* edited by Louis D. Rubin, Jr. and Robert D. Jacobs. Baltimore, Md: Johns Hopkins University Press, 1953, pp. 192–206.

Emerson, O. B. *Faulkner's Early Literary Reputation in America*. Ann Arbor, Mich.: UMI Research Press, 1984.

Emmanuel, Pierre. "Faulkner and the Sense of Sin." *Harvard Advocate* 135 (November, 1951): 20.

England, Martha Winburn. "Teaching 'The Sound and the Fury.'" *College English* 18 (January 1957): 221–24.

English, H. M. Jr. "'Requiem for a Nun.'" *Furioso* 7 (Winter 1952): 60–63.

Everett, Walter K. *Faulkner's Art and Characters*. Woodbury, N.Y.: Barron's Educational Series, 1969.

Fadiman, Clifton. "Mississippi Frankenstein." *The New Yorker* 14 (January 21, 1939): 60–62.

———. "William Faulkner." In *Party of One*. Cleveland: World, 1955, pp. 98–125.

———. "The World of William Faulkner." *Nation* 132 (April 15, 1931): 422–23.

Ferguson, James. *Faulkner's Short Fiction*. Knoxville: University of Tennessee Press, 1991.

Fiedler, Leslie A. "William Faulkner: An American Dickens." *Commentary* 10 (October 1950): 384–87.

Flint, R. W. "Faulkner as Elegist." *Hudson Review* 7 (Summer 1954): 246–57.

Flynn, Robert. "The Dialectic of 'Sanctuary.'" *Modern Fiction Studies* 2 (Autumn 1956): 109–13.

Ford, Dan, ed. *Heir and Prototype: Original and Derived Characterizations in Faulkner*. Conway: University of Central Arkansas Press, 1988.

Foster, Ruel E. "Dream as Symbolic Act in Faulkner." *Perspective* 2 (Summer 1949): 179–94.

———. "A Further Note on the Conclusion of 'The Bear.'" *Faulkner Studies* 3 (Spring 1954): 4–5.

Fowler, Doreen. *Faulkner: The Return of the Repressed*. Charlottesville: University Press of Virginia, 1997.

———. *Faulkner's Changing Vision: From Outrage to Affirmation*. Ann Arbor, Mich.: UMI Research Press, 1983.

Fowler, Doreen, and Ann J. Abadie, eds. *"A Cosmos of My Own": Faulkner and Yoknapatawpha, 1980*. Jackson: University Press of Mississippi, 1981.

———. *Faulkner: International Perspectives*. Jackson: University Press of Mississippi, 1980.

———. *Faulkner and the Craft of Fiction*. Jackson: University Press of Mississippi, 1989.

———. *Faulkner and Humor*. Jackson: University Press of Mississippi, 1986.

———. *Faulkner and Popular Culture*. Jackson: University Press of Mississippi, 1990.

———. *Faulkner and Race*. Jackson: University Press of Mississippi, 1987.

———. *Faulkner and Religion*. Jackson: University Press of Mississippi, 1991.

———. *Faulkner and the Southern Renaissance*. Jackson: University Press of Mississippi, 1982.

———. *Faulkner and Women*. Jackson: University Press of Mississippi, 1986.

———. *Fifty Years of Yoknapatawpha*. Jackson: University Press of Mississippi, 1980.

———. *New Directions in Faulkner Studies*. Jackson: University Press of Mississippi, 1984.

Frazier, David L. "Gothicism in 'Sanctuary': The Black Pall and the Crap Table." *Modern Fiction Studies* 2 (Autumn 1956): 114–24.

Frey, Leonard H. "Irony and Point of View in 'That Evening Sun.'" *Faulkner Studies* 2 (Autumn 1953): 33–40.

Friedman, Allen Warren. *William Faulkner*. New York: Ungar, 1984.

Frohock, W. M. "William Faulkner: The Private versus the Public Vision." *Southwest Review* 34 (Summer 1949): 281–94. Reprinted in *The Novel of Violence in America*. Dallas: Southern Methodist University Press, 1950, pp. 101–24.

———. "William Faulkner: The Private Vision." In *The Novel of Violence in America,* 2nd ed. Dallas: Southern Methodist University Press, 1957, pp. 144–65.

Galharn, Carl. "Faulkner's Faith: Roots from 'The Wild Palms.'" *Twentieth Century Literature* 1 (October 1955): 139–60.

Garrett, George P., Jr. "An Examination of the Poetry of William Faulkner." *Princeton University Library Chronicle* 18 (Spring 1957): 124–35.

———. "Faulkner's Early Literary Criticism." *Texas Studies in Literature and Language* 1 (Spring 1959): 3–10.

———. "Some Revisions in 'As I Lay Dying.'" *Modern Language Notes* 73 (June 1958): 414–17.

Geismar, Maxwell. "William Faulkner: Before and After the Nobel Prize." In *American Moderns: From Rebellion to Conformity*. New York: Hill and Wang, 1958, pp. 91–106.

———. "William Faulkner: The Negro and the Female." In *Writers in Crisis*. Boston: Houghton Mifflin, 1942, pp. 143–83.

Gérard, Albert. "Justice in Yoknapatawpha County: Some Symbolic Motifs in Faulkner's Later Writing." *Faulkner Studies* 2 (Winter 1954): 49–57.

Giles, Barbara. "The South of William Faulkner." *Masses and Mainstream* 3 (February 1950): 26–40.

Glicksberg, Charles I. "William Faulkner and the Negro Problem." *Phylon* 10 (June 1949): 153–60.

———. "The World of William Faulkner." *Arizona Quarterly* 5 (Spring 1949): 46–58.

Godden, Richard. *Fictions of Labor: William Faulkner and the South's Long Revolution*. Cambridge: Cambridge University Press, 1997.

Goellner, Jack. "A Closer Look at 'As I Lay Dying.'" *Perspective* 7 (Spring 1954): 42–54.

Going, William T. "Faulkner's 'A Rose for Emily.'" *Explicator* 16 (February 1958): item 27.

Gold, Joseph. *William Faulkner: A Study in Humanism: From Metaphor to Discourse*. Norman: Oklahoma University Press, 1966.

Gordon, Caroline. "Notes on Faulkner and Flaubert." *Hudson Review* 1 (Summer 1948), 222–31. Revised and reprinted in *The House of Fiction,* edited by Caroline Gordon and Allen Tate. New York: Scribner's, 1950, pp. 531–34.

Greene, Graham. "The Furies in Mississippi." *London Mercury* 35 (March 1937): 517–18.

Greet, T. Y. "The Theme and Structure of Faulkner's 'The Hamlet.'" *PMLA* 72 (September 1957): 775–90. Reprinted in *William Faulkner: Three Decades of Criticism,* edited by Frederick J. Hoffman and Olga W. Vickery. New York: Harcourt, Brace & World, 1963, pp. 330–47.

———. "Toward the Light: The Thematic Unity of Faulkner's 'Cycle.'" *Carolina Quarterly* 3 (Fall 1950): 38–44.

Gresset, Michel. *Fascination: Faulkner's Fiction, 1919–1936.* Durham, N.C.: Duke University Press, 1989.

Gresset, Michel, and Noel Polk, eds. *Intertextuality in Faulkner.* Jackson: University Press of Mississippi, 1985.

Gresset, Michel, and Patrick Samway, eds. *Faulkner and Idealism: Perspectives from Paris.* Jackson: University Press of Mississippi, 1983.

Griffin, William J. "How to Misread Faulkner: A Powerful Plea of Ignorance." *Tennessee Studies in Literature* 1 (1956): 27–34.

Grimwood, Michael. *Heart in Conflict: Faulkner's Struggles with Vocation.* Athens: University of Georgia Press, 1987.

Groden, Michael. "Criticism in New Composition: *Ulysses* and *The Sound and the Fury,*" *Twentieth Century Literature* 21 (October 1975): 266.

Guérard, Albert Jr. "'Requiem for a Nun': An Examination." *Harvard Advocate* 135 (November 1951): 19, 41–2.

Gutting, Gabriele. *The Function of Geographical and Historical Facts in William Faulkner's Fictional Picture of the Deep South.* New York: Lang, 1992.

Gwin, Minrose. *The Feminine in Faulkner: Reading (Beyond) Sexual Difference.* Knoxville: University of Tennessee Press, 1990.

Gwynn, Frederick L. "Faulkner's Prufrock—and Other Observations." *Journal of English and Germanic Philology* 52 (January 1953): 63–70.

———. "Faulkner's Raskolnikov." *Modern Fiction Studies* 4 (Summer 1958): 169–72.

Hahn, Stephen, and Robert W. Hamblin, eds. *Teaching Faulkner: Approaches and Methods.* Westport, Conn.: Greenwood Publishing, 2000.

Hamilton, Edith. "Faulkner: Sorcerer or Slave?" *Saturday Review* 35 (July 12, 1952): 8–10, 39–41.

Handy, William J. "'As I Lay Dying': Faulkner's Inner Reporter." *Kenyon Review* 21 (Summer 1959): 437–51.

Harder, Kelsie B. "Charactonyms in Faulkner's Novels." *Bucknell Review* 8 (May 1959): 189–211.

———. "Proverbial Snopeslore." *Tennessee Folklore Society Bulletin* 24 (September 1958): 89–95.

Hardwick, Elizabeth. "Faulkner and the South Today." *Partisan Review* 15, no. 10 (October 1948): 1130–35. Reprinted in *Faulkner A Collection of Critical Essays,* edited by Robert Penn Warren. Englewood Cliffs, N.J.: Prentice-Hall, Inc., 1966, pp. 226–30.

Hartwick, Harry. "The Cult of Cruelty." In *The Foreground of American Fiction.* New York: American Book Co., 1934, pp. 160–66.

Harrington, Evans B. "Technical Aspects of William Faulkner's 'That Evening Sun.'" *Faulkner Studies* 1 (Winter 1952): 54–59.

Harrington, Evans, and Ann J. Abadie, eds. *Faulkner, Modernism, and Film.* Jackson: University Press of Mississippi, 1979.

———. *Faulkner and the Short Story.* Jackson: University Press of Mississippi, 1992.

———. *The Maker and the Myth.* Jackson: University Press of Mississippi, 1978.

———. *The South and Faulkner's Yoknapatawpha: The Actual and the Apocryphal.* Jackson: University Press of Mississippi, 1977.

Harrington, Gary. *Faulkner's Fables of Creativity: The Non-Yoknapatawpha Novels*. Athens: University of Georgia Press, 1990.

Hatcher, Harlan. "Ultimate Extensions." In *Creating the Modern American Novel*. New York: Farrar and Rinehart, 1935, pp. 234–43.

Hayakawa, Hiroshi. "Negation in William Faulkner." In *Studies in English Grammar and Linguistics: A Miscellany in Honor of Takanobu Otsuka*. Edited by Kazuo Araki et al. Tokyo: Kenkyusha, 1958, pp. 103–13.

Heilman, Robert B. "Schools for Girls." *Sewanee Review* 60 (Spring 1952): 304–09.

Hepburn, Kenneth W. "Faulkner's 'Mosquitoes': A Poetic Turning Point." *Twentieth-Century Literature: A Scholary and Critical Journal* (Hempstead, N.Y. 1971): 17, 19–28.

Hettich, Blaise. "A Bedroom Scene in Faulkner." *Renascence* 8 (Spring 1956): 121–26.

Hickerson, Thomas Felix. *The Faulkner Feuds*. Chapel Hill;4.6.: Colonial Press, 1964.

Hicks, Granville. "Faulkner's South: A Northern Interpretation." *Georgia Review* 5 (Fall 1951): 269–84.

———. "The Last of the Snopeses." *Saturday Review* 42 (November 14, 1959): 20–21.

———. "The Past and the Future of William Faulkner." *Bookman* 74 (September 1931): 17–24.

Hines, Thomas S. *William Faulkner and the Tangible Past: The Architecture of Yoknapatawpha*. Berkeley: University of California Press, 1996.

Hoadley, Frank M. "Folk Humor in the Novels of William Faulkner." *Tennessee Folklore Society Bulletin* 23 (September 1957): 75–82.

Hoffman, A. C. "Faulkner's 'Absalom, Absalom!'" *Explicator* 10 (November 1951): item 12.

———. "Point of View in 'Absalom, Absalom!'" *University of Kansas City Review* 19 (Summer 1953): 233–39.

Hoffman, Daniel. *Faulkner's Country Matters: Folklore and Fable in Yoknapatawpha*. Baton Rouge: Louisiana State University Press, 1989.

———. "Violence and Rhetoric." In *The Modern Novel in America, 1900–1950*. Chicago: Henry Regnery, 1951, pp. 154–64.

Hoffman, Frederick J., and Olga W. Vickery, eds. *William Faulkner: Three Decades of Criticism*. East Lansing: Michigan State University Press, 1960.

Hogan, Patrick G., Jr. "Critical Misconceptions of Southern Thought: Faulkner's Optimism," *Mississippi Quarterly* 10 (January 1957): 19–28.

Holmes, Catherine Denham. *Annotations to William Faulkner's 'The Hamlet'*. Dissertation Abstracts International (Ann Arbor, Mich.) 1995 May, 55: 11.

Holmes, Edward M. *Faulkner's Twice-Told Tales: His Re-Use of Materials*. The Hague, Netherlands: Mouton, 1966.

Hönnighausen, Lothar. *Faulkner: Masks and Metaphors*. Jackson: University Press of Mississippi, 1997.

———. *William Faulkner: The Art of Stylization in His Early Graphic and Literary Work*. Cambridge, England: Cambridge University Press, 1987.

———, ed. *Faulkner's Discourse: An International Symposium*. Tubingen, Germany: Max Niemeyer Verlag, 1989.

Hopper, Vincent F. "Faulkner's Paradise Lost." *Virginia Quarterly Review* 23 (Summer 1947): 405–20.

Horton, Merrill. *Annotations to William Faulkner's "The Town"*. New York: Garland, 1996.

Howe, Irving. *William Faulkner: A Critical Study*. New York; Random House, 1952. Rev. ed. New York: Vintage Books, 1962.

———. "Faulkner: An Experiment in Drama." *Nation* 173 (September 29, 1951): 263–64.

———. "Faulkner: End of a Road." *New Republic* 141 (December 7, 1959): 17–21.

———. "The South and Current Literature." *American Mercury* 67 (October 1948): 494–503.

———. "The Southern Myth and William Faulkner." *American Quarterly* 3 (Winter 1951): 357–62.

———. "William Faulkner and the Negro." *Commentary* 12 (October 1951): 359–68.

———. "William Faulkner and the Quest for Freedom." *Tomorrow* 9 (December 1949): 54–56.

Howell, Elmo. "Colonel Sartoris Snopes and Faulkner's Aristocrats." *Carolina Quarterly* 11 (Summer 1959): 13–19.

———. "Faulkner's 'Sartoris.'" *Explicator* 17 (February 1959): item 33.

———. "A Note on Faulkner's Negro Characters." *Mississippi Quarterly* 11 (Fall 1958): 201–03.

———. "The Quality of Evil in Faulkner's 'Sanctuary.'" *Tennessee Studies in Literature* 4 (1959): 99–107.

Hudson, Tommy. "William Faulkner: Mystic and Traditionalist." *Perspective* 3 (Autumn 1950): 227–35.

Humphrey, Robert. "Faulkner's Synthesis." In *Stream of Consciousness in the Modern Novel*. Berkeley: University of California Press, 1954, pp. 17–21, 64–70, 104–11, *et passim*.

———. "Form and Function of Stream of Consciousness in William Faulkner's 'The Sound and the Fury.'" *University of Kansas City Review* 19 (Autumn 1952): 34–40.

Hunt, John W. *William Faulkner: Art in Theological Tension*. Syracuse, N.Y.: Syracuse University Press, 1965.

Hunter, Edwin R. *William Faulkner: Narrative Practice and Prose Style*. Washington, D.C.: Windhover, 1973.

Inge, M. Thomas, ed. *William Faulkner: The Contemporary Reviews*. Cambridge, England: Cambridge University Press, 1995.

Irwin, John T. *Doubling and Incest/Repetition and Revenge: A Speculative Reading of Faulkner*. Expanded edition Baltimore, Md.: Johns Hopkins University Press, 1996.

Izard, Barbara, and Hieronymous, Clara. *Requiem for a Nun: On Stage and Off.* Nashville and London: Aurora Pubs., 1970. 331 pp.

Jackson, James Turner. "Delta Cycle: A Study of William Faulkner." *Chimera* 5 (Autumn 1946): 3–14.

Jacobs, Robert D. "Faulkner and the Tragedy of Isolation." *Hopkins Review* 6 (Spring–Summer 1953): 162–83. Reprinted in *Southern Renascence: The Literature of the Modern South*, edited by Louis D. Rubin, Jr. and Robert D. Jacobs. Baltimore; Md.: Johns Hopkins University Press, 1953, pp. 170–91.

———. "How Do *You* Read Faulkner?" *Provincial* (April 1957): 3–5.

Jehlen, Myra. *Class and Character in Faulkner's South.* New York: Columbia University Press, 1976.

Jenkins, Lee Clinton. *Faulkner and Black-White Relations: A Psychoanalytic Approach.* New York: Columbia University Press, 1981.

Johnson, C. W. M. "Faulkner's 'A Rose for Emily.'" *Explicator* 6 (May 1948): item 45.

Jones, Diane Brown. *A Reader's Guide to the Short Stories of William Faulkner.* New York: G. K. Hall, 1994.

Jones, Leonidas M. "Faulkner's 'The Hound.'" *Explicator* 15 (March 1957): item 37.

Junior, Junius. *Pseudo-Realists.* New York: Outsider Press, 1931.

Kang, Hee. *The Snopes Trilogy: Reading Faulkner's Masculine and Feminine.* Ann Arbor, Mich: Dissertation Abstracts International. 53, 7 (January 1993).

Kartiganer, Donald M. *The Fragile Thread: The Meaning of Form in Faulkner's Novels.* Amherst: University of Massachusetts Press, 1979.

———, ed. *Faulkner and the Natural World.* Jackson: University of Mississippi Press, 1999.

Kartiganer, Donald M., and Ann J. Abadie, eds. *Faulkner and the Artist.* Jackson: University Press of Mississippi, 1996.

———. *Faulkner in Cultural Context.* Jackson: University Press of Mississippi, 1997.

———. *Faulkner and Gender.* Jackson: University Press of Mississippi, 1996.

———. *Faulkner and Ideology.* Jackson: University Press of Mississippi, 1995.

———. *Faulkner and Psychology.* Jackson: University Press of Mississippi, 1997.

Kawin, Bruce. *Faulkner and Film.* New York: Ungar, 1977.

Kazin, Alfred. "Faulkner: The Rhetoric and the Agony." *Virginia Quarterly Review* 18 (Summer 1942); 389–402. Reprinted in *On Native Grounds.* New York: Reynal & Hitchcock, 1942, pp. 453–70.

———. "Faulkner in His Fury." In *The Inmost Leaf.* New York: Harcourt, Brace, 1955, pp. 257–73.

———. "Faulkner's Vision of Human Integrity." *Harvard Advocate* 135 (November 1951): 8–9, 28–33.

———. "In the Shadow of the South's Last Stand." *New York Herald Tribune* (Books) February 20, 1938): 5.

———. "Mr. Faulkner's Friends, The Snopeses." *New York Times Book Review* (May 5, 1957): 1, 24.

———. "The Stillness of 'Light in August,'" *Partisan Review* 24 (Fall 1957): 519–38. Reprinted in *Twelve Original Essays on Great American Novels*, edited by Charles Shapiro. Detroit: Wayne State University Press, 1958, pp. 257–83; and in *William Faulkner: Three Decades of Criticism*, edited by Frederick J. Hoffman and Olga W. Vickery. New York: Harcourt, Brace & World, 1963, pp. 247–65; and also in *Faulkner A Collection of Critical Essays*, edited by Robert Penn Warren. Englewood Cliffs, N.J.: Prentice-Hall, Inc., 1966, pp. 147–62.

———. "A Study in Conscience." *New York Herald Tribune* (Books) (January 22, 1939): 2.

Kerr, Elizabeth M. *William Faulkner's Gothic Domain.* Port Washington, N.Y.: Kennikat Press, 1979.

———. *William Faulkner's Yoknapatawpha: "A Kind of Keystone in the Universe."* New York: Fordham University Press, 1976.

———. *Yoknapatawpha: Faulkner's "Little Postage Stamp of Native Soil."* Rev. ed. Amherst: University of Massachusetts Press, 1963.

King, Roma, Jr. "The Janus Symbol in 'As I Lay Dying.'" *University of Kansas City Review* 21 (Summer 1955): 287–90.

Kinney, Arthur F. *Critical Essays on William Faulkner: The Compson Family.* Boston: G. K. Hall, 1982.

———. *Faulkner's Narrative Poetics: Style as Vision.* Amherst: University of Massachusetts Press, 1978.

———. *Go Down, Moses: The Miscegenation of Time.* New York: Twayne, 1996.

Kirk, Robert W., and Marvin Klotz. *Faulkner's People.* Berkeley: University of California Press, 1963.

Knoll, Robert E. "'The Unvanquished' for a Start." *College English* 19 (May 1958): 338–43.

Kohler, Dayton. "William Faulkner and the Social Conscience." *College English* 11 (December 1949): 119–27. Also appeared in *English Journal* 38 (December 1949): 545–53.

Kreiswirth, Martin. *William Faulkner: The Making of a Novelist.* Athens: University of Georgia Press, 1983.

Kronenberger, Louis. "Faulkner's Dismal Swamp." *Nation* 146 (February 19, 1938): 212, 214.

Kubie, Lawrence S. "William Faulkner's 'Sanctuary': An Analysis," *Saturday Review of Literature* 11 (Ocotber 20, 1934): 218, 224–6. Reprinted in *Faulkner A Collection of Critical Essays*, edited by Robert Penn Warren. Englewood Cliffs, N.J.: Prentice-Hall, Inc., 1966, pp. 137–46.

Labor, Earle. "Faulkner's 'The Sound and the Fury.'" *Explicator* 17 (January 1959): item 29.

LaBudde, Kenneth. "Cultural Primitivism in William Faulkner's 'The Bear.'" *American Quarterly* 2 (Winter 1950): 322–8.

LaLonde, Christopher A. *William Faulkner and the Rites of Passage.* Macon, Ga.: Mercer University Press, 1996.

Leary, Lewis. *William Faulkner of Yoknapatawpha County.* New York: Crowell, 1973.

Leaver, Florence. "Faulkner: The Word as Principle and Power," *South Atlantic Quarterly* 57 (Autumn 1958): 464–76. Reprinted in *William Faulkner: Three Decades of Criticism,* edited by Frederick J. Hoffman and Olga W. Vickery. New York: Harcourt, Brace & World, 1963, pp. 199–209.

Leavis, F. R. "Dostoevsky or Dickens?" *Scrutiny* 2 (June 1933): 91–93.

Lee, Edwy B. "A Note on the Ordonnance of 'The Sound and the Fury.'" *Faulkner Studies* 3 (Summer–Autumn 1954): 37–39.

Lee, Robert, ed. *William Faulkner: The Yonapatawpha Fiction.* New York: St. Martin's, 1990.

Lemay, Harding. "Faulkner and his Snopes Family Reach the End of their Trilogy." *New York Herald Tribune* (Books) (November 15, 1959): 1, 14.

Levins, Lynn Gartrell. *Faulkner's Heroic Design: The Yoknapatawpha Novels.* Athens: University of Georgia Press, 1976.

Lewis, R. W. B. *The Picaresque Saint.* Philadelphia: J. B. Lippincott, 1958.

———. "The Hero in the New World: William Faulkner's 'The Bear.'" *Kenyon Review* 13 (Autumn 1951): 641–60. Reprinted in *Interpretations of American Literature,* edited by Charles Feidelson Jr. and Paul Brodtkorb Jr. New York: Oxford, 1959, pp. 332–48.

Lewis, Wyndham. "The Moralist with a Corn-cob: A Study of William Faulkner." *Life and Letters* 10 (June 1934): 312–28. Reprinted in *Men Without Art.* London: Cassell, 1934, pp. 42–64.

Lind, Ilse Dusoir. "The Design and Meaning of 'Absalom, Absalom!'" *PMLA* 70 (December 1955): 887–912. Reprinted in *William Faulkner: Three Decades of Criticism,* edited by Frederick J. Hoffman and Olga W. Vickery. New York: Harcourt, Brace & World, 1963, pp. 278–304.

———. "The Calvinistic Burden of "Light in August.'" *New England Quarterly* 30 (September 1957): 307–29.

———. "The Teachable Faulkner." *College English* 16 (February 1955): 284–87, 302.

Linn, James W., and Houghton W. Taylor. "Counterpoint: 'Light in August.'" In *A Foreword to Fiction.* New York: Appleton-Century, 1935, pp. 144–57.

Linn, Robert. "Robinson Jeffers and William Faulkner." *American Spectator* 2 (1933): 1. Reprinted in *The American Spectator Year Book,* edited by George Jean Nathan, Ernest Boyd, et al. New York: Frederick A. Stokes, 1934, pp. 304–07.

Lisca, Peter. "Some New Light on Faulkner's 'Sanctuary.'" *Faulkner Studies* 2 (Spring 1953): 5–9.

Litz, Walton. "William Faulkner's Moral Vision." *Southwest Review* 37 (Summer 1952): 200–09.

Lockyer, Judith. *Ordered by Words: Language and Narration in the Novels of William Faulkner.* Carbondale: Southern Illinois University Press, 1991.

Longley, John Lewis, Jr. *The Tragic Mask: A Study of Faulkner's Heroes.* Chapel Hill: University of North Carolina Press, 1963.

———. "Galahad Gavin and a Garland of Snopeses." *Virginia Quarterly Review* 33 (Autumn 1957): 623–28.

———. "Joe Christmas: the Hero in the Modern World." *Virginia Quarterly Review* 33 (Spring 1957): 233–49. Reprinted in *William Faulkner: Three Decades of Criticism,* edited by Frederick J. Hoffman and Olga W. Vickery. New York: Harcourt, Brace & World, 1963, pp. 265–78. Also reprinted in *Faulkner: A Collection of Critical Essays,* edited by Robert Penn Warren. Englewood Cliffs, N.J.: Prentice-Hall, Inc., 1966, pp. 163–74.

Lowrey, Perrin. "Concepts of Time in 'The Sound and the Fury.'" *English Institute Essays 1952,* edited by Alan S. Downer. New York: Columbia University Press, 1954, pp. 57–82.

Lydenberg, John. "Nature Myth in Faulkner's 'The Bear.'" *American Literature* 24 (March 1952): 62–72.

Lytle, Andrew. "Regeneration for the Man," *Sewanee Review* 57, no. 1 (Winter 1949): 120–27. Reprinted in *Faulkner A Collection of Critical Essays,* edited by Robert Penn Warren. Englewood Cliffs, N.J.: Prentice-Hall, Inc., 1966, pp. 231–37.

———. "'The Town': Helen's Last Stand." *Sewanee Review* 65 (Summer 1957): 475–84.

Machlachlan, John M. "William Faulkner and the Southern Folk." *Southern Folklore Quarterly* 9 (June 1945): 153–67.

MacLeish, Archibald. "Faulkner and the Responsibility of the Artist." *Harvard Advocate* 135 (November 1951): 18, 43.

MacLure, Millar. "William Faulkner: Soothsayer of the South." *Queen's Quarterly* 63 (Autumn 1956): 334–43.

Madge, Charles. "Time and Space in America." *London Mercury* 32 (May 1935): 83.

Malin, Irving. *William Faulkner: An Interpretation.* Stanford, Calif.: Stanford University Press, 1957.

Marcus, Steven. "Faulkner's Town: Mythology as History." *Partisan Review* 24 (Summer 1957): 432–41. WF III.

Marvin, John R. "'Pylon': The Definition of Sacrifice." *Faulkner Studies* 1 (Summer 1952): 20–23.

Massey, Linton. "Notes on the Unrevised Galleys of Faulkner's 'Sanctuary.'" *Studies in Bibliography* 8 (1956): 195–208.

Matthews, John T. *The Play of Faulkner's Language.* Ithaca, N.Y.: Cornell University Press, 1982.

Maxwell, Allen. "'The Wild Palms.'" *Southwest Review* 24 (April 1939): 357–60.

Mayes, Martha. "Faulkner Juvenalia." In *New Campus Writing, No. 2.* New York: Bantam, 1957, pp. 135–44.

McCamy, Edward. "Byron Bunch." *Shenandoah* 3 (Spring 1952): 8–12.

McClennan, Joshua. "'Absalom, Absalom!" and the Meaning of History." *Papers of the Michigan Academy of Science, Arts, and Letters* 42 (1956), 357–69.

———. "William Faulkner and Christian Complacency." *Papers of the Michigan Academy of Science, Arts, and Letters* 41 (1956): 315–22.

McCole, Camille J. "The Nightmare Literature of William Faulkner." *Catholic World* 141 (August 1935): 576–83.

———. "William Faulkner: Cretins, Coffinworms, and Cruelty." In *Lucifer at Large.* New York: Longmans, 1937, pp. 203–28.

McCorquodale, Marjorie K. "Alienation in Yoknapatawpha County." *Forum* (Houston) 1 (January 1957): 4–8.

McDonald, Hal. *Faulkner's* Sanctuary. *Explicator* (Washington, D.C.) 1997 Summer, 55:4, 222–23.

McElderry, B. R. Jr. "The Narrative Structure of 'Light in August.'" *College English* 19 (February 1958): 200–7. Reprinted in *Mississippi Quarterly* 11 (Fall 1958): 177–87.

McGrew, Julia. "Faulkner and the Icelanders." *Scandinavian Studies* 31 (February 1959): 1–14.

McIlwaine, Shields. "Naturalistic Modes: The Gothic, The Ribald, and the Tragic." *The Southern Poor-White from Lubberland to Tobacco Road.* Norman: University of Oklahoma Press, 1939, pp. 217–40.

McLaughlin, Richard. "Requiem for Temple Drake." *Theatre Arts* 35 (October 1951): 50, 77.

Meriwether, James B., ed. *A Faulkner Miscellany.* Jackson: University Press of Mississippi, 1974.

Meriwether, James B. "Snopes Revisited." *Saturday Review* 40 (April 27, 1957): 12–3.

———. "William Faulkner." *Shenandoah* 10 (Winter 1959): 18–24.

Merwin, W. S. "William Faulkner." In *Nobel Prize Winners,* edited by L. J. Ludovici. Westport, Conn.: Associated Booksellers, 1957, pp. 43–60.

Millgate, Michael. *The Achievement of William Faulkner.* New York: Random House, 1966.

———. *Faulkner's Place.* Athens: University of Georgia Press, 1997.

———. *New Essays on "Light in August."* New York: Cambridge University Press, 1987.

———. *William Faulkner.* New York: Grove, 1961.

Miner, Ward L. *The World of William Faulkner.* Durham, N.C.: Duke University Press, 1952.

Moloney, Michael F. "The Enigma of Time: Proust, Virginia Woolf, and Faulkner." *Thought* 32 (Spring 1957): 69–85.

Monteiro, George. "Bankruptcy in Time: A Reading of William Faulkner's 'Pylon,'" *Twentieth Century Literature* 4 (April–July 1958): 9–20.

———. "Initiation and the Moral Sense in Faulkner's 'Sanctuary.'" *Modern Language Notes* 73 (November 1958): 500–4.

Moreland, Richard C. *Faulkner and Modernism: Rereading and Rewriting.* Madison: University of Wisconsin Press, 1990.

Morris, Welsey, and Barbara Alverson Morris. *Reading Faulkner.* Madison: University of Wisconsin Press, 1990.

Morris, Wright. "The Function of Rage: William Faulkner." In *The Territory Ahead.* New York: Harcourt, Brace, 1958, pp. 171–84.

———. "The Violent Land: Some Observations on the Faulkner Country." *Magazine of Art* 45 (March 1952): 99–103.

Mortimer, Gail L. *Faulkner's Rhetoric of Loss: A Study in Perception and Meaning.* Austin: University of Texas Press, 1983.

Moseley, Edwin M. "Christ as Social Scapegoat: Faulkner's *Light in August.*" In Edwin M. Moseley, *Pseudonyms of Christ in the Modern Novel: Motifs and Methods.* Pittsburgh: University of Pittsburgh Press, 1962.

Moses, W. R. "The Unity of 'The Wild Palms.'" *Modern Fiction Studies* 2 (Autumn 1956): 125–31.

———. "Water, Water Everywhere: 'Old Man' and 'A Farewell to Arms.'" *Modern Fiction Studies* 5 (Summer 1959): 172–74.

———. "Where History Crosses Myth: Another Reading of 'The Bear.'" *Accent* 13 (Winter 1953): 21–33.

Mueller, W. R. "The Theme of Suffering: William Faulkner's 'The Sound and the Fury.'" In *The Prophetic Voice in Modern Fiction.* New York: Association Press, 1959, pp. 110–35.

Mumbach, Mary Katherine. *"Remaining Must Remain": Patterns of Christian Comedy in Faulkner's "The Mansion".* Dissertation Abstracts International (Ann Arbor, Mich.) 1981 October 42–44.

Neville, Helen. "The Sound and the Fury." *Partisan Review* 5 (June 1938): 53–55.

Nicholson, Norman. "William Faulkner." *Man and Literature.* London: SCM Press, 1943, pp. 122–38.

———. "William Faulkner." In *The New Spirit,* edited by E. W. Martin. London: Dobson, 1946, pp. 32–41.

Nilon, Charles H. *Faulkner and the Negro.* New York: Citadel, 1965.

Nordanberg, Thomas. *Cataclysm as Catalyst: The Theme of War in William Faulkner's Fiction.* Uppsala, Sweden: Almqvist, 1983.

O'Connor, William Van. *The Tangled Fire of William Faulkner.* Minneapolis: University of Minnesota Press, 1954.

———. *William Faulkner.* (Pamphlets on American Writers, No. 3), Minneapolis: University of Minnesota Press, 1959.

———. "Faulkner's Legend of the Old South." *Western Humanities Review* 7 (Autumn 1953): 293–301.

———. "Hawthorne and Faulkner: Some Common Ground." *Virginia Quarterly Review* 33 (Winter 1957): 105–123.

———. "The Old Master, the Sole Proprietor." *Virginia Quarterly Review* 36 (Winter 1960): 147–51.

———. "Protestantism in Yoknapatawpha County." *Hopkins Reviews* 5 (Spring 1952): 26–42. Reprinted in *Southern Renascence: The Literature of the Modern South,* edited by Louis D. Rubin Jr. and Robert D. Jacobs. Baltimore: Johns Hopkins University Press, 1953, pp. 153–69.

———. "Rhetoric in Southern Writing: Faulkner." *Georgia Review* 12 (Spring 1958): 83–86.

———. "A Short View of Faulkner's 'Sanctuary.'" *Faulkner Studies* 1 (Fall 1952): 33–39.

———. "'The Sound and the Fury' and the Impressionistic Novel." *Northern Review* 6 (June–July 1953): 17–22.

———. "The Wilderness Theme in Faulkner's 'The Bear.'" *Accent* 13 (Winter 1953): 12–20. Reprinted in *William Faulkner: Three Decades of Criticism,* edited by Frederick J. Hoffman and Olga W. Vickery. New York: Harcourt, Brace & World, 1963, pp. 322–30.

———. "William Faulkner's Apprenticeship." *Southwest Review* 38 (Winter 1953): 1–14.

O'Donnell, George Marion. "Faulkner's Mythology." *Kenyon Review* 1 (Summer, 1939): 285–99. Reprinted in *William Faulkner: Three Decades of Criticism,* edited by Frederick J. Hoffman and Olga W. Vickery. New York: Harcourt, Brace & World, 1963, pp. 82–93. Also reprinted in *Faulkner A Collection of Critical Essays,* edited by Robert Penn Warren. Englewood Cliffs, N.J.: Prentice-Hall, Inc., 1966, pp. 23–33.

O'Faolain, Sean. "William Faulkner: More Genius than Talent." In *The Vanishing Hero: Studies in Novelists of the Twenties.* Boston: Little, Brown, 1956, pp. 73–111.

Page, Sally. *Faulkner's Women: Characterization and Meaning.* Deland, Fla.: Everett/Edward, 1972.

Parker, Robert Dale. *Faulkner and the Novelistic Imagination.* Urbana: University of Illinois Press, 1985.

Pearson, Norman Holmes. "Faulkner's Three 'Evening Suns.'" *Yale University Library Gazette* 29 (October 1954): 61–70.

———. "Lena Grove." *Shenandoah* 3 (Spring 1952): 3–7.

Peavy, Charles. *Go Slow Now: Faulkner and the Race Question.* Eugene: University of Oregon Press, 1971.

Penick, Edwin A., Jr. "The Testimony of William Faulkner." *Christian Scholar* 38 (June 1955): 121–33.

Perdeck, A. "William Faulkner." *Critisch Bulletin* (1934): 209–13.

Peters, Erskine. *William Faulkner: The Yoknapatawpha World and Black Being.* Darby, Penn.: Norwood, 1983.

Peyre, Henri. "American Literature through French Eyes." *Virginia Quarterly Review* 23 (Summer 1947): 421–37.

Phillips, Gene D. *Fiction, Film, and Faulkner: The Art of Adaptation.* Knoxville: University of Tennessee Press, 1988.

Pilkington, James Penn. "Faulkner's 'Sanctuary.'" *Explicator* 4 (June 1946): item 61.

Podhoretz, Norman. "William Faulkner and the Problem of War: His Fable of Faith." *Commentary,* 18, no. 3 (September 1954): 227–32. Reprinted in *Faulkner: A Collection of Critical Essays,* edited by Robert Penn Warren. Englewood Cliffs, N.J.: Prentice-Hall, Inc., 1966, pp. 243–50.

Poirier, William R. "'Strange Gods' in Jefferson, Mississippi: Analysis of 'Absalom, Absalom!'" In *William Faulkner: Two Decades of Criticism,* edited by Frederick J. Hoffman and Olga W. Vickery. East Lansing: Michigan State University Press, 1951, pp. 217–43.

Polk, Noel. *Children of the Dark House: Text and Context in Faulkner.* Jackson: University Press of Mississippi, 1996.

———. *An Editorial Handbook for William Faulkner's "The Sound and the Fury".* New York: Garland Publishers, 1985.

———. *Faulkner's "Requiem for a Nun": A Critical Study.* Bloomington: Indiana University Press, 1981.

———, ed. *"Intruder in the Dust": A Concordance to the Novel.* West Point, N.Y.: Faulkner Concordance Advisory Board, 1983.

———. *New Essays on "The Sound and the Fury."* New York: Cambridge University Press, 1993.

———. *"Requiem for a Nun": A Concordance to the Novel.* Ann Arbor, Mich.: UMI Research Press, 1979.

Polk, Noel, and John D. Hart, eds. *"Absalom, Absalom!": A Concordance to the Novel.* 2 vols. Ann Arbor, Mich.: UMI Research Press, 1989.

———. *"The Hamlet": A Concordance to the Novel.* 2 vols. Ann Arbor, Mich.: UMI Research Press, 1990.

———, eds. *The Mansion: A Concordance to the Novel.* 2 vols. Ann Arbor, Mich.: UMI Research Press, 1988.

———. *"Pylon": A Concordance to the Novel.* Ann Arbor, Mich.: UMI Research Press, 1989.

———. *"The Reivers": A Concordance to the Novel.* Ann Arbor, Mich.: UMI Research Press, 1990.

———. *"The Unvanquished": A Concordance to the Novel.* Ann Arbor, Mich.: UMI Research Press, 1990.

Polk, Noel, and Kenneth L. Privratsky, eds. *"A Fable": A Concordance to the Novel.* 2 vols. Ann Arbor, Mich.: UMI Research Press, 1981.

———. *"The Sound and the Fury:" A Concordance to the Novel.* 2 vols. Ann Arbor, Mich.: UMI Research Press, 1980.

Polk, Noel, and Lawrence Z. Pizzi, eds. *"The Town": A Concordance to the Novel*. Ann Arbor, Mich.: UMI Research Press, 1985.

Poster, Herbert. "Faulkner's Folly." *American Mercury* 73 (December 1951): 106–12.

Powell, Sumner C. "William Faulkner Celebrates Easter, 1928." *Perspective* 2 (Summer 1949): 195–218.

Powers, Lyall H. *Faulkner's Yoknapatawpha Comedy*. Ann Arbor: University of Michigan Press, 1980.

Prescott, Orville. "The Eminently Obscure: Mann, Faulkner." In *In My Opinion*. Indianapolis: Bobbs-Merrill, 1952, pp. 75–91.

Pritchett, V. S. "Books in General." *New Statesman and Nation* 41 (June 2, 1951): 624, 626.

———. "The Hill-Billies." In *Books in General*. New York: Harcourt, Brace, 1953, pp. 242–47.

———. "Time Frozen: *A Fable*." *Partisan Review* 21, no. 5 (September–October 1954): 557–61. Reprinted in *Faulkner A Collection of Critical Essays*, edited by Robert Penn Warren. Englewood Cliffs, N.J.: Prentice-Hall, 1966, pp. 238–42.

Pusey, William Webb III. "William Faulkner's Works in Germany to 1940: Translations and Criticism." *Germanic Review* 30 (October 1955): 211–26.

Putzel, Max. *Genius of Place: William Faulkner's Triumphant Beginnings*. Baton Rouge: Louisiana State University Press, 1985.

Randall, Julia. "Some Notes on 'As I Lay Dying.'" *Hopkins Review* 4 (summer 1951): 47–51.

Ransom, John Crowe. "William Faulkner: An Impression." *Harvard Advocate* 135 (November 1951): 17.

Rascoe, Burton. "Faulkner's New York Critics." *American Mercury* 50 (June 1940): 243–47.

Reaver, J. Russell. "This Vessel of Clay: A Thematic Comparison of Faulkner's 'As I Lay Dying' and Latorre's 'The Old Woman of Peralillo.'" *Florida State University Studies* 14 (1954): 131–40.

Redman, Ben Ray. "Faulkner's Double Novel." *Saturday Review of Literature* 19 (January 21, 1939): 5.

———. "Flights of Fancy." *Saturday Review of Literature* 11 (March 30, 1935): 577, 581.

Reed, John Q. "Theme and Symbol in Faulkner's 'Old Man.'" *Educational Leader* 21 (January 1958): 25–31.

Reed, Joseph W., Jr. *Faulkner's Narrative*. New Haven, Conn.: Yale University Press, 1973.

Rice, Philip Blair. "Faulkner's Crucifixion." *Kenyon Review* 16 (Autumn 1954): 661–70. Reprinted in *William Faulkner: Three Decades of Criticism*, edited by Frederick J. Hoffman and Olga W. Vickery. New York: Harcourt, Brace & World, 1963, pp. 373–81.

Richardson, H. Edward. "The 'Hemingwaves' in Faulkner's 'Wild Palms.'" *Modern Fiction Studies* 4 (Winter 1958–1959): 357–60.

Richardson, Kenneth E. *Force and Faith in the Novels of William Faulkner*. The Hague, Netherlands: Mouton, 1967.

Riedel, F. C. "Faulkner as Stylist." *South Atlantic Quarterly* 56 (Autumn 1957): 462–79.

Robb, Mary Cooper. *William Faulkner: An Estimate of His Contribution to the American Novel*. Pittsburgh: University of Pittsburgh Press, 1957.

Roberts, Diane. *Faulkner and Southern Womanhood*. Athens: University of Georgia Press, 1994.

Rolle, Andrew F. *"William Faulkner: An Inter-disciplinary Examination."* Mississippi Quarterly 11 (Fall 1958): 157–59.

Rollyson, Carl E. *Uses of the Past in the Novels of William Faulkner*. Ann Arbor, Mich.: UMI Research Press, 1984.

Ross, Stephen M. *Fiction's Inexhaustible Voice: Speech and Writing in Faulkner*. Athens: University of Georgia Press, 1983.

Ross, Stephen M., and Noel Polk. *Reading Faulkner: "The Sound and the Fury."* Jackson: University Press of Mississippi, 1996.

Roth, Russell. "The Brennan Papers: Faulkner in Manuscript." *Perspective* 2 (Summer 1949): 219–24.

———. "The Centaur and the Pear Tree." *Western Review* 16 (Spring 1952): 199–205.

———. "Ideas and Queries." *Faulkner Studies* 1 (Summer 1952): 23–26.

———. "William Faulkner: The Pattern of Pilgrimage." *Perspective* 2 (Summer 1949): 246–54.

Rousselle, Melinda McLeod. *Annotations to William Faulkner's "Sanctuary."* New York: Garland, 1989.

Rubin, Louis D. Jr. "Snopeslore: Or, Faulkner Clears the Deck." *Western Review* 22 (Autumn 1957): 73–76.

Rugoff, Milton. "Faulkner's Old Spell in a New Novel of Yoknapatawpha." *New York Herald Tribune* (Books) (May 5, 1957): 1.

Runyan, Harry. "Faulkner's Poetry." *Faulkner Studies* 3 (Summer-Autumn 1954): 23–29.

Ruppersburg, Hugh M. *Voice and Eye in Faulkner's Fiction*. Athens: University of Georgia Press, 1983.

Ruzicka, William T. *Faulkner's Fictive Architecture: The Meaning of Place in the Yoknapatawpha Novels*. Ann Arbor, Mich.: UMI Research Press, 1987.

Ryan, Marjorie. "The Shakespearian Symbolism in 'The Sound and the Fury.'" *Faulkner Studies* 2 (Autumn 1953): 40–44.

Sandeen, Ernest. "William Faulkner: Tragedian of Yoknapatawpha." In *Fifty Years of the American Novel*, edited by Harold C. Gardiner. New York: Scribners, 1952, pp. 165–82.

Sartre, Jean-Paul. *Literary and Philosophical Essays*. Translated by Annette Michelson. London: Rider & Co., 1955.

Sawyer, Kenneth B. "Hero in 'As I Lay Dying,'" *Faulkner Studies* 3 (Summer–Autumn 1954): 30–33.

Schappes, Morris U. "Faulkner as Poet." *Poetry: A Magazine of Verse* 43 (October 1933): 48–52.

Schwartz, Delmore. "The Fiction of William Faulkner." *Southern Review,* 7 (Summer 1941): 145–60.

Schwartz, Lawrence H. *Creating Faulkner's Reputation: The Politics of Modern Literary Criticism.* Knoxville: University of Tennessee Press, 1988.

Scott, Arthur L. "The Faulknerian Sentence." *Prairie Schooner* 27 (Spring 1953): 91–98.

———. "The Myriad Perspectives of 'Absalom, Absalom!'" *American Quarterly* 6 (Fall 1954): 210–20.

Scott, Evelyn. *On William Faulkner's "The Sound and the Fury."* New York: Cape & Smith, 1929.

Scott, Nathan A. Jr. "The Vision of William Faulkner." *Christian Century* 74 (September 18, 1957): 1104–6.

Sensibar, Judith L. *The Origins of Faulkner's Art.* Austin: University of Texas Press, 1984.

Serafin, Joan M. *Faulkner's Uses of the Classics.* Ann Arbor, Mich.: UMI Research Press, 1983.

Sewall, Richard B. "'Absalom, Abasalom!'" In *The Vision of Tragedy.* New Haven: Yale University Press, 1959, pp. 133–47.

Sherwood, John C. "The Traditional Element in Faulkner." *Faulkner Studies* 3 (Summer–Autumn 1954): 17–23.

Singal, Daniel J. *William Faulkner: The Making of a Modernist.* Chapel Hill: University of North Carolina Press, 1997.

Slatoff, Walter J. *Quest for Failure: A Study of William Faulkner.* Ithaca, N.Y.: Cornell University Press, 1960.

———. "The Edge of Order: The Pattern of Faulkner's Rhetoric." *Twentieth Century Literature* 3 (October 1957): 107–27. Reprinted in *William Faulkner: Three Decades of Criticism,* edited by Frederick J. Hoffman and Olga W. Vickery. New York: Harcourt, Brace & World, 1963, pp. 173–98.

Smith, Hallett. "Summary of a Symposium on 'Light in August.'" *Mississippi Quarterly* 11 (Fall 1958): 188–90.

Smith, Henry Nash. "William Faulkner and Reality." *Faulkner Studies* 2 (Summer 1953): 17–19.

Smith, Thelma M., and Ward L. Miner. "Faulkner." In *Transatlantic Migration.* Durham: Duke University Press, 1955, pp. 122–45.

Snead, James A. *Figures of Division: William Faulkner's Major Novels.* New York: Methuen, 1986.

Snell, George. "The Fury of William Faulkner." *Western Review* 11 (Autumn 1946): 29–40. Reprinted in *The Shapers of American Fiction.* New York: E. P. Dutton, 1947, pp. 87–104.

Spiller, R. E. "The Uses of Memory: Eliot, Faulkner." *The Cycle of American Literature.* New York: Macmillan, 1955, pp. 291–300.

Stallings, Lawrence. "Gentleman from Mississippi." *American Mercury* 34 (April 1935): 499–501.

Stavrou, C. N. "Ambiguity in Faulkner's Affirmation." *The Personalist* 40 (Spring 1959): 169–77.

Stewart, George R., and Joseph M. Backus. "Each in Its Ordered Place: Structure and Narrative in 'Benjy's Section' of 'The Sound and the Fury.'" *American Literature* 29 (January 1958): 440–56.

Stewart, James T. "Miss Havisham and Miss Grierson." *Furman Studies* 6 (Fall 1958): 21–23.

Stewart, Randall. *American Literature and Christian Doctrine.* Baton Rouge: Louisiana State University Press, 1958, pp. 136–42.

———. "Hawthorne and Faulkner." *College English* 17 (February 1956): 258–62.

Stone, Geoffrey. "'Light in August.'" *Bookman* 75 (November 1932): 736–38.

Stonesifer, Richard J. "In Defense of Dewey Dell." *Educational Leader* 22 (July 1958): 27–33.

———. "Faulkner's 'Old Man' in the Classroom." *College English* 17 (February 1956): 254–57.

Stonum, Gary Lee. *Faulkner's Career: An Internal Literary History.* Ithaca, N.Y.: Cornell University Press, 1979.

Sullivan, Walter. "The Tragic Design of 'Absalom, Absalom!'" *South Atlantic Quarterly* 50 (October 1951): 552–66.

Sundquist, Eric. *Faulkner: The House Divided.* Baltimore, Md.: Johns Hopkins University Press, 1983.

Swallow, Alan. "A General Introduction to 'Faulkner Studies.'" *Faulkner Studies* 1 (Spring 1952): 1–3.

Swiggart, Peter. *The Art of Faulkner's Novels.* Austin: University of Texas Press, 1962.

———. "Moral and Temporal Order in 'The Sound and the Fury.'" *Sewanee Review* 61 (Spring 1953): 221–37.

———. "Time in Faulkner's Novels." *Modern Fiction Studies* 1 (May 1955): 25–29.

Swisher, Clarice, ed. *Readings on William Faulkner.* San Diego, Calif.: Greenhaven Press, 1997.

Taylor, W. F. "A Wider Range." In *The Story of American Letters.* Chicago: Henry Regnery, 1956, pp. 471–81.

Taylor, Walter. *Faulkner's Search for a South.* Urbana: University of Illinois Press, 1983.

Thomas, Douglas M. "Memory-Narrative in 'Absalom, Absalom!'" *Faulkner Studies* 2 (Summer 1953): 19–22.

Thompson, Alan R. "The Cult of Cruelty." *Bookman* 74 (January–February 1932): 477–87.

———. "'Sanctuary.'" *Bookman* 73 (April 1931): 188–89.

Thompson, Lawrence. *William Faulkner: An Introduction and Interpretation.* New York: Barnes & Noble, 1963.

———. "Mirror Analogues in 'The Sound and the Fury.'" In *English Institute Essays 1952,* edited by Alan S. Downer. New York: Columbia University Press, 1954, pp. 83–106. Reprinted in *William Faulkner: Three Decades of Criticism,* edited Frederick J. Hoffman and Olga W. Vickery. New York: Harcourt, Brace & World, 1963, pp. 211–225. Also reprinted in *Faulkner A Collection of Critical Essays,* edited by Robert Penn Warren. Englewood Cliffs, N.J.: Prentice-Hall, Inc., 1966, pp. 109–21.

Thorp, Willard. "Four Times and Out?" *Scrutiny* 1 (September 1932): 172–73.

Tilley, Winthrop. "The Idiot Boy in Mississippi: Faulkner's 'The Sound and the Fury.'" *American Journal of Mental Deficiency* 59 (January 1955): 374–77.

Torchiana, Donald T. "Faulkner's 'Pylon' and the Structure of Modernity." *Modern Fiction Studies* 3 (Winter 1957–58): 291–308.

———. "The Reporter in Faulkner's 'Pylon.'" *History of Ideas News Letter* 4 (Spring 1958): 33–39.

Tritschler, Donald. "The Unity of Faulkner's Shaping Vision." *Modern Fiction Studies* 5 (Winter 1959–60): 337–43.

Troy, William. "The Poetry of Doom." *Nation* 143 (October 31, 1936): 524–25.

———. "And Tomorrow." *Nation* 140 (April 3, 1935): 393.

Urgo, Joseph R. *Faulkner's Apocrypha: "A Fable," Snopes, and the Spirit of Human Rebellion.* Jackson: University Press of Mississippi, 1989.

Utley, Francis Lee, Lynn Z. Bloom, and Arthur F. Kinney, eds. *Bear, Man, and God: Seven Approaches to William Faulkner's "The Bear."* New York: Random House, 1964.

Vanderwerken, David L. *Faulkner's Literary Children: Patterns of Development.* New York: Peter Lang, 1997.

Van Doren, Mark. "'Pylon.'" *New York Herald Tribune* (Books) (March 24, 1935), 3.

Vickery, John B. "William Faulkner and Sir Philip Sidney?" *Modern Language Notes* 70 (May 1955): 349–50.

Vickery, Olga W. *The Novels of William Faulkner: A Critical Interpretation.* Baton Rouge: Louisiana State University Press, 1959; 3rd ed.

———. "'As I Lay Lying.'" *Perspective* 3 (Autumn 1950): 179–91.

———. "Faulkner and the Contours of Time." *Georgia Review* 12 (Summer 1958): 192–201.

———. "Faulkner's First Novel." *Western Humanities Review* 11 (Summer 1957): 251–56.

———. "Faulkner's Mosquitoes.'" *University of Kansas City Review* 24 (Spring 1958): 219–24.

———. "Gavin Stevens: From Rhetoric to Dialectic." *Faulkner Studies* 2 (Spring 1953): 1–4.

———. "The Making of a Myth: 'Sartoris.'" *Western Review* 22 (Spring 1958): 209–19.

———. "'The Sound and the Fury': A Study in Perspective." *PMLA* 69 (December 1954): 1017–37.

Visser, Irene. *Compassion in Faulkner's Fiction.* Lewiston, N.Y.: Edwin Mellen, 1996.

Wadlington, Warwick. *Reading Faulknerian Tragedy.* Ithaca, N.Y.: Cornell University Press, 1987.

Wagenknecht, Edward. "Erskine Caldwell and William Faulkner." *Cavalcade of the American Novel.* New York: Henry Holt, 1952, pp. 417–25.

Waggoner, Hyatt H. *William Faulkner: From Jefferson to the World.* Lexington: University of Kentucky Press, 1959.

———. "William Faulkner: The Definition of Man." *Books at Brown* 18 (March 1958): 116–22.

———. "William Faulkner's Passion Week of the Heart." *The Tragic Vision and the Christian Faith,* edited by Nathan A. Scott Jr. New York: Association Press, 1957, pp. 306–23.

Wagner, Linda W., ed. *William Faulkner: Four Decades of Criticism.* East Lansing: Michigan State University Press, 1973.

Wagner-Martin, Linda, ed. *New Essays on "Go Down, Moses."* New York: Cambridge University Press, 1996.

Warren, Robert Penn, ed. *Faulkner: A Collection of Critical Essays.* Englewood Cliffs, N.J.: Prentice-Hall, 1966.

———. "Cowley's Faulkner." *New Republic* 115 (August 12, 1946): 176–80; continued (August 26, 1946): 234–37.

———. "Faulkner: The South, the Negro, and Time." *Southern Review* 1 (Summer 1965): 501–29. Reprinted in *Faulkner A Collection of Critical Essays,* edited by Robert Penn Warren. Englewood Cliffs, N.J.: Prentice-Hall, Inc., 1966, pp. 251–71.

———. "William Faulkner." *Selected Essays.* New York: Random House, 1958, pp. 59–79. Reprinted in *William Faulkner: Three Decades of Criticism,* edited by Frederick J. Hoffman and Olga W. Vickery. New York: Harcourt, Brace & World, 1963, pp. 109–24.

Wasiolek, Edward. "'As I Lay Dying': Distortion in the Slow Eddy of Current Opinion," *Critique* 3 (Spring–Fall 1959): 15–23.

———. "Dostoevsky and 'Sanctuary.'" *Modern Language Notes* 74 (February 1959): 114–17.

Watkins, Floyd C. "The Gentle Reader and Mr. Faulkner's Morals." *Georgia Review* 13 (Spring, 1959): 68–75.

———. "The Structure of 'A Rose for Emily.'" *Modern Language Notes* 69 (November 1954): 508–10.

Watson, Jay. *Forensic Fictions: The Lawyer Figure in Faulkner.* Athens: University of Georgia Press, 1993.

Weinstein, Philip. *Faulkner's Subject: A Cosmos No One Owns.* New York: Cambridge University Press, 1992.

———. *What Else But Love: The Ordeal of Race in Faulkner and Morrison.* New York: Columbia University Press, 1996.

Wells, Dean Faulkner. *The Ghosts of Rowan Oak: William Faulkner's Ghost Stories for Children.* Oxford, Miss.: Yoknapatawpha Press, 1980.

Wells, Dean Faulkner, and Lawrence Wells, "The Trains Belonged to Everybody: Faulkner as Ghost Writer." *Southern Review* 12 (Autumn 1976): 864–71.

West, Anthony. "A Dying Fall." *New Yorker* 35 (December 5, 1959): 236–43.

West, Ray B., Jr. "Hemingway and Faulkner." In *The Short Story in America, 1900–1950*. Chicago: Henry Regnery, 1952, pp. 85–106.

———. "Atmosphere and Theme in Faulkner's 'A Rose for Emily.'" *Perspective* 2 (Summer 1949): 239–45. Reprinted in *William Faulkner: Two Decades of Criticism,* edited by Frederick J, Hoffman and Olga W. Vickery. East Lansing: Michigan State University Press, 1951, pp. 259–67.

———. "Faulkner's 'A Rose for Emily.'" *Explicator* 7 (October 1948): item 8.

———. "William Faulkner: Artist and Moralist." *Western Review* 16 (Winter 1952): 162–67.

West, Ray B., Jr., and R. W. Stallman. "Theme through Atmosphere." *The Art of Modern Fiction.* New York: Rinehart, 1949, pp. 270–75.

Whan, Edgar W. "'Absalom, Absalom!' as Gothic Myth." *Perspective* 3 (Autumn 1950), 192–201.

Wheeler, Otis B. "Faulkner's Wilderness." *American Literature* 31 (May 1959): 127–36.

Whicher, Stephen E. "The Compsons' Nancies—A Note on 'The Sound and the Fury' and 'That Evening Sun.'" *American Literature* 26 (May 1954): 253–55.

White, William. "One Man's Meat: Societies and Journals Devoted to a Single Author." *The American Book Collector* 8 (November 1957): 22–24.

Whittemore, Reed. "Notes on Mr. Faulkner." *Furioso* 2 (Summer 1947): 18–25.

Wilder, Amos N. "Faulkner and Vestigial Moralities." *Theology and Modern Literature.* Cambridge: Harvard University Press, 1958, pp. 113–31.

William, Cecil B. "William Faulkner and the Nobel Prize Awards." *Faulkner Studies* 1 (Summer 1952): 17–19.

Williams, David. *Faulkner's Women: The Myth and the Muse.* Montreal, Canada: McGill Queen's University Press, 1977.

Wilson, Paul A. *Faulkner and Camus: Requiem for a Nun: Odyssey: A Journal of the Humanities* (Rochester, Mich.) 1979, 3:2, 3–9.

Woodward, C. Vann. *The Burden of Southern History.* Baton Rouge: Louisiana State University Press, 1960.

———. *Origins of the New South, 1877–1913.* Baton Rouge: Louisiana State University Press, 1951.

Wykes, Alan "The Perceptive Few and the Lost Generation." In *A Concise Survey of American Literature.* London: Arthur Baker, 1955, pp. 165–74.

Young, T. D., and Floyd C. Watkins. "Faulkner's Snopeses." *Mississippi Quarterly* 11 (Fall 1958): 196–200.

Zender, Karl F. *The Crossing of the Ways: William Faulkner, the South, and the Modern World.* New Brunswick, N.J.: Rutgers University Press, 1989.

Zink, Karl E. "Faulkner's Garden: Woman and the Immemorial Earth." *Modern Fiction Studies* 2 (Autumn 1956): 139–49.

———. "Flux and the Frozen Moment: The Imagery of Stasis in Faulkner's Prose." *PMLA* 71 (June 1956): 285–301.

———. "William Faulkner: Form as Experience." *South Atlantic Quarterly* 53 (July 1954): 384–403.

Zoellner, Robert H. "Faulkner's Prose Style in 'Absalom, Absalom!'" *American Literature,* 30 (January 1959): 486–502.

6. Website
William Faulkner on the Web. Available online. URL:http://www.mcsr.olemiss.edu/~egjbp/faulkner/faulkner.html (From this website, there will be links to others including the Center for Faulkner Studies at http://www2.semo.edu/cfs.)

7. Societies, Centers, and Conferences
Center for Faulkner Studies, Southeast Missouri State University, One University Plaza, Cape Girardeau, MO 63701–4799. The center possesses the Louis Daniel Brodsky collection of Faulkner material and promotes educational and research projects relating to Faulkner's work and life. It also publishes twice annually the very useful pamphlet *Teaching Faulkner,* edited by Robert W. Hamblin, the Center's director. Website: http://www2.semo.edu/cfs/ and E-mail:cfs@semovm.semo.edu

Faulkner E-mail discussion group. To subscribe, send the message "subscribe faulkner" to md@listserv.olemiss.edu

Faulkner and Yoknapatawpha Conference, a week-long conference sponsored by the English Department and the Center for the Study of Southern Culture at the University of Mississippi, Oxford, Mississippi. It is usually held during the last week of July. Website: http://www.mcsr.olemiss.edu/~egibp/faulkner/fyconference.html

William Faulkner Foundation, Rennes University, Rennes, France, is the major European center for Faulkner studies and research. It is located at 6, avenue Gaston Berger, 3500 Rennes France. Website: http://www.uhb.fr/faulkner/WF/index.htm and E-mail: Foundation Faulkner@uhb.fr

The William Faulkner Society promotes Faulkner scholarship and the critical study of his works. Its annual meeting is held at the American Literature Association Convention; this society is affiliated with *The Faulkner Journal.* For membership contact Evelyn Jaffe Schreiber, 5508 Devon Road, Bethesda, MD 20814. Website: http://www.acad.swarthmore.edu/faulkner/

The William Faulkner Society of Japan, contact Professor Yamashita, Faculty of Humanities, Soai University 4–4–1 Nankou-naka, Suminoe-ku, Osaka City, 559–0033 Japan; E-mail: yamasita@soai.ac.jp

APPENDIX III

Family Trees

GENEALOGY OF WILLIAM FAULKNER*

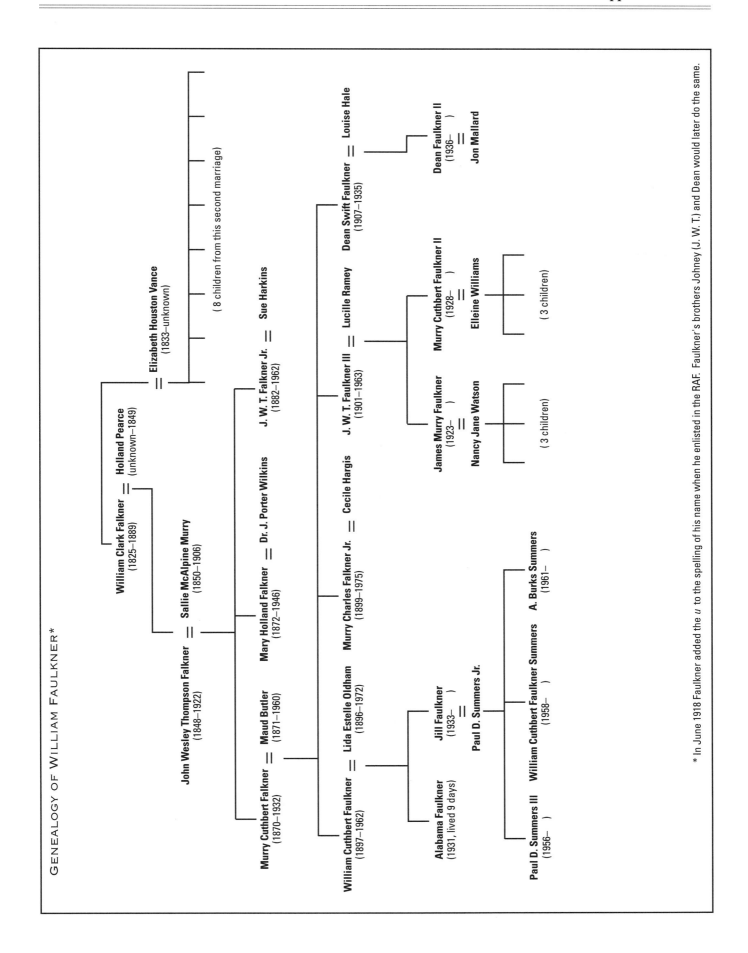

* In June 1918 Faulkner added the *u* to the spelling of his name when he enlisted in the RAF. Faulkner's brothers Johney (J. W. T.) and Dean would later do the same.

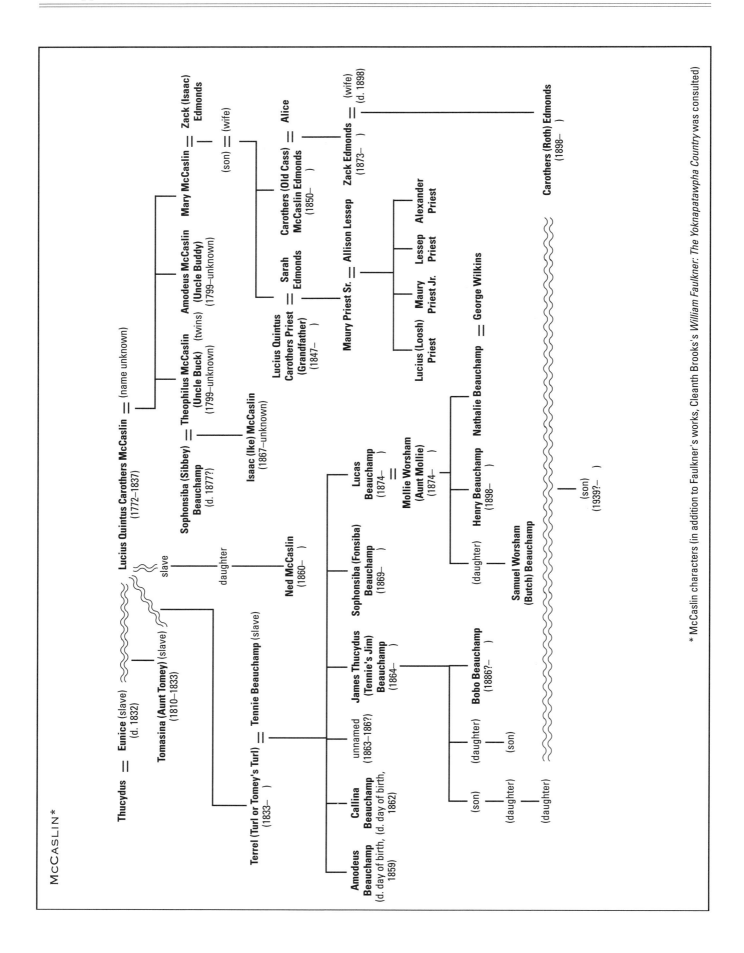

MCCASLIN*

* McCaslin characters (in addition to Faulkner's works, Cleanth Brooks's *William Faulkner: The Yoknapatawpha Country* was consulted)

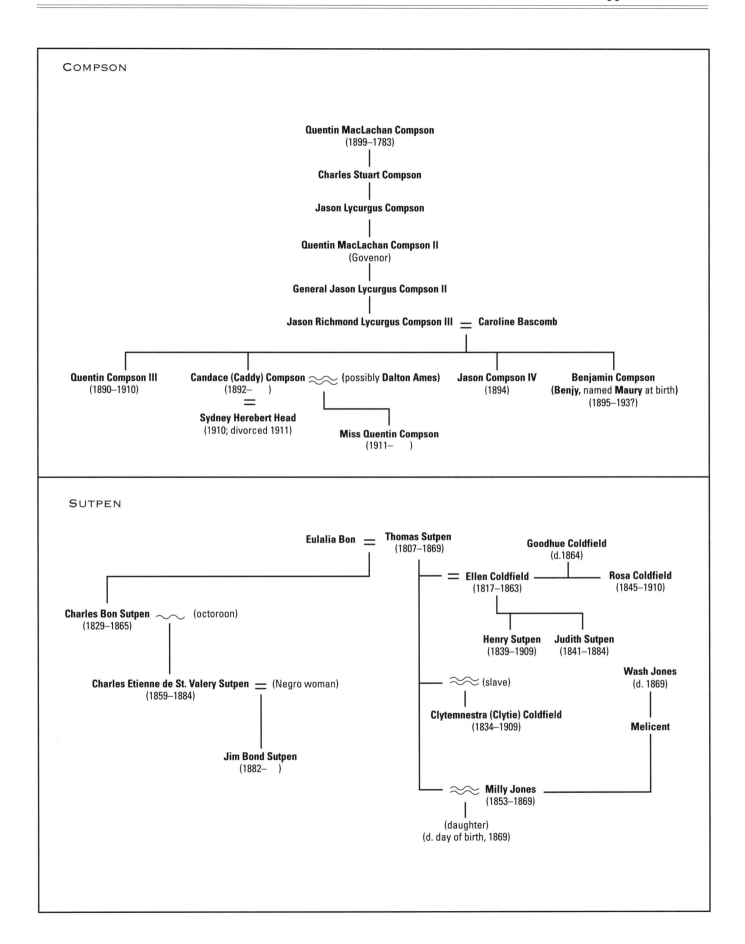

COMPSON

Quentin MacLachan Compson
(1899–1783)

Charles Stuart Compson

Jason Lycurgus Compson

Quentin MacLachan Compson II
(Govenor)

General Jason Lycurgus Compson II

Jason Richmond Lycurgus Compson III — Caroline Bascomb

Quentin Compson III
(1890–1910)

Candace (Caddy) Compson — (possibly Dalton Ames)
(1892–   )
=
Sydney Herebert Head
(1910; divorced 1911)

Miss Quentin Compson
(1911–   )

Jason Compson IV
(1894)

Benjamin Compson
(Benjy, named Maury at birth)
(1895–193?)

SUTPEN

Eulalia Bon — Thomas Sutpen
(1807–1869)

Goodhue Coldfield
(d.1864)

= Ellen Coldfield ———— Rosa Coldfield
(1817–1863)   (1845–1910)

Charles Bon Sutpen ∼∼ (octoroon)
(1829–1865)

Henry Sutpen   Judith Sutpen
(1839–1909)   (1841–1884)

Charles Etienne de St. Valery Sutpen — (Negro woman)
(1859–1884)

∼∼ (slave)

Clytemnestra (Clytie) Coldfield
(1834–1909)

Wash Jones
(d. 1869)

Melicent

Jim Bond Sutpen
(1882–   )

∼∼ Milly Jones
(1853–1869)

(daughter)
(d. day of birth, 1869)

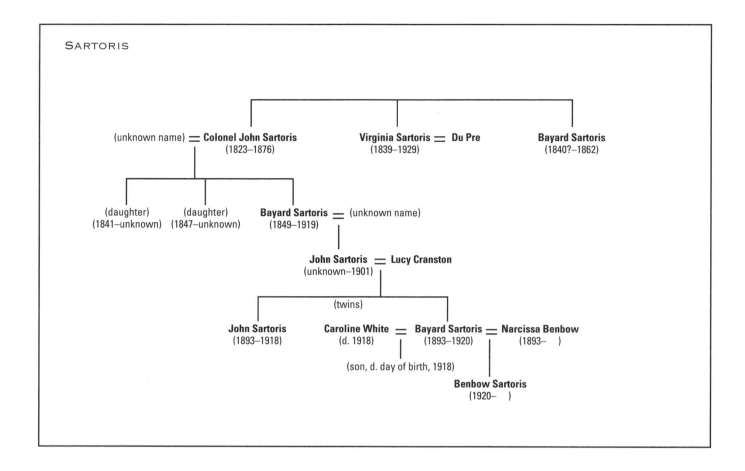

SARTORIS

(unknown name) = **Colonel John Sartoris**
(1823–1876)

Virginia Sartoris = **Du Pre**
(1839–1929)

Bayard Sartoris
(1840?–1862)

(daughter)
(1841–unknown)

(daughter)
(1847–unknown)

Bayard Sartoris = (unknown name)
(1849–1919)

John Sartoris = **Lucy Cranston**
(unknown–1901)

(twins)

John Sartoris
(1893–1918)

Caroline White = **Bayard Sartoris** = **Narcissa Benbow**
(d. 1918)   (1893–1920)   (1893–   )

(son, d. day of birth, 1918)

Benbow Sartoris
(1920–   )

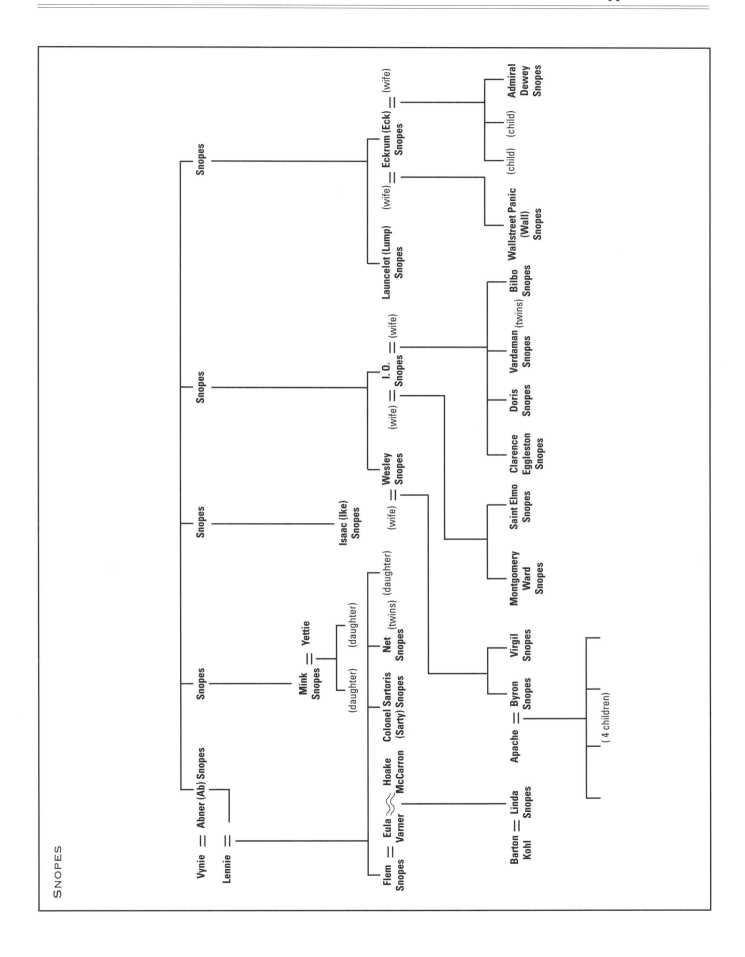

APPENDIX IV

I Faulkner's Appendix to
The Sound and the Fury

In an interview at the University of Virginia, Faulkner explained that the appendix to *The Sound and the Fury* was written about 20 years after the novel was published in 1929 as another attempt at trying "to make that book . . . match the dream" (*Faulkner in the University*, p. 84). Entitled "1699–1945 The Compsons," the appendix first appeared in *The Portable Faulkner* (1946). When *The Sound and the Fury* was published together with *As I Lay Dying* by The Modern Library in 1946, the appendix appeared as a foreword entitled "Compson 1699–1945."

1699–1945 THE COMPSONS

IKKEMOTUBBE. A dispossessed American king. Called *l'Homme* (and sometimes *de l'Homme*) by his fosterbrother, a Chevalier of France, who, had he not been born too late, could have been among the brightest in that glittering galaxy of knightly blackguards who were Napoleon's marshals, who thus translated the Chickasaw title meaning "The Man"; which translation Ikkemotubbe, himself a man of wit and imagination as well as a shrewd judge of character, including his own, carried one step further and anglicized it to "Doom." Who granted out of his vast lost domain a solid square mile of virgin north Mississippi dirt as truely angled as the four corners of a cardtable top (forested then because these were the old days before 1833 when the stars fell and Jefferson, Mississippi, was one long rambling one-storey mudchinked log building housing the Chickasaw Agent and his trading-post store) to the grandson of a Scottish refugee who had lost his own birthright by casting his lot with a king who himself had been dispossessed. This in partial return for the right to proceed in peace, by whatever means he and his people saw fit, afoot or ahorse provided they were Chickasaw horses, to the wild western land presently to be called Oklahoma: not knowing then about the oil.

JACKSON. A Great White Father with a sword. (An old duellist, a brawling lean fierce mangy durable imperishable old lion who set the well-being of the nation above the White House, and the health of his new political party above either, and above them all set, not his wife's honor, but the principle that honor must be defended whether it was or not because defended it was whether or not.) Who patented, sealed, and countersigned the grant with his own hand in his gold tepee in Wassi Town, not knowing about the oil either: so that one day the homeless descendants of the dispossessed would ride supine with drink and splendidly comatose above the dusty allotted harborage of their bones in specially built scarlet-painted hearses and fire-engines.

These were Compsons:
QUENTIN MacLACHAN. Son of a Glasgow printer, orphaned and raised by his mother's people in the Perth highlands. Fled to Carolina from Culloden Moor with a claymore and the tartan he wore by day and slept under by night, and little else. At eighty, having fought once against an English king and lost, he would not make that mistake twice and so fled again one night in 1779, with his infant grandson and the tartan (the claymore had vanished, along with his son, the grandson's father, from one of Tarleton's regiments on a Georgia battlefield about a year ago) into Kentucky, where a neighbor named Boon or Boone had already established a settlement.

CHARLES STUART. Attained and proscribed by name and grade in his British regiment. Left for dead in a Georgia swamp by his own retreating army and then by the advancing American one, both of which were wrong. He still had the claymore even when on his homemade wooden leg he finally overtook his father and son four years later at Harrodsburg, Kentucky, just in time to bury the father and enter upon a long period of being a split personality while still trying to be the schoolteacher which he believed he wanted to be, until he gave up at last and became the gambler he actually was and which no Compson seemed to realize they all were, provided the gambit was desperate and the odds long enough. Succeeded at last in risking not only his neck but the security of his family and the very integrity of the name he would leave behind him, by joining the confederation headed by an acquaintance named

Wilkinson (a man of considerable talent and influence and intellect and power) in a plot to secede the whole Mississippi Valley from the United States and join it to Spain. Fled in his turn when the bubble burst (as anyone except a Compson schoolteacher should have known it would), himself unique in being the only one of the plotters who had to flee the country: this not from the vengeance and retribution of the government which he had attempted to dismember, but from the furious revulsion of his late confederates now frantic for their own safety. He was not expelled from the United States; he talked himself countryless, his expulsion due not to the treason but to his having been so vocal and vociferant in the conduct of it, burning each bridge vocally behind him before he had even reached the place to build the next one: so that it was no provost marshal nor even a civic agency but his late coplotters themselves who put afoot the movement to evict him from Kentucky and the United States and, if they had caught him, probably from the world too. Fled by night, running true to family tradition, with his son and the old claymore and the tartan.

JASON LYCURGUS. Who, driven perhaps by the compulsion of the flamboyant name given him by the sardonic embittered woodenlegged indomitable father who perhaps still believed with his heart that what he wanted to be was a classicist schoolteacher, rode up the Natchez Trace one day in 1820 with a pair of fine pistols and one meagre saddlebag on a small light-waisted but stronghocked mare which could do the first two furlongs in definitely under the halfminute and the next two in not appreciably more, though that was all. But it was enough: who reached the Chickasaw Agency at Okatoba (which in 1860 was still called Old Jefferson) and went no further. Who within six months was the Agent's clerk and within twelve his partner, officially still the clerk though actually halfowner of what was now a considerable store stocked with the mare's winnings in races against the horses of Ikkemotubbe's young men which he, Compson, was always careful to limit to a quarter or at most three furlongs; and in the next year it was Ikkemotubbe who owned the little mare and Compson owned the solid square mile of land which some day would be almost in the center of the town of Jefferson, forested then and still forested twenty years later, though rather a park than a forest by that time, with is slave quarters and stables and kitchen gardens and the formal lawns and promenades and pavilions laid out by the same architect who built the columned porticoed house furnished by steamboat from France and New Orleans, and still the square intact mile in 1840 (with not only the little white village called Jefferson beginning to enclose it but an entire white county about to surround it, because in a few years now Ikkemotubbe's descendants and people

would be gone, those remaining living not as warriors and hunters but as white men—as shiftless farmers or, here and there, the masters of what they too called plantations and the owners of shiftless slaves, a little dirtier than the white man, a little lazier, a little crueller—until at last even the wild blood itself would have vanished, to be seen only occasionally in the noseshape of a Negro on a cottonwagon or a white sawmill hand or trapper or locomotive fireman); known as the Compson Domain then, since now it was fit to breed princes, statesmen and generals and bishops, to avenge the dispossessed Compsons from Culloden and Carolina and Kentucky; then known as the Governor's house because sure enough in time it did produce or at least spawn a governor—Quentin MacLachan again, after the Culloden grandfather—and still known as the Old Governor's even after it had spawned (1861) a general—(called so by predetermined accord and agreement by the whole town and county, as though they knew even then and beforehand that the old governor was the last Compson who would not fail at everything he touched save longevity or suicide)—the Brigadier Jason Lycurgus II who failed at Shiloh in '62 and failed again, though not so badly, at Resaca in '64, who put the first mortgage on the still intact square mile to a New England carpetbagger in '66, after the old town had been burned by the Federal General Smith and the new little town, in time to be populated mainly by the descendants not of Compsons but of Snopeses, had begun to encroach and then nibble at and into it as the failed brigadier spent the next forty years selling fragments of it off to keep up the mortgage on the remainder: until one day in 1900 he died quietly on an army cot in the hunting and fishing camp in the Tallahatchie River bottom where he passed most of the end of his days.

And even the old governor was forgotten now; what was left of the old square mile was now known merely as the Compson place—the weedchoked traces of the old ruined lawns and promenades, the house which had needed painting too long already, the scaling columns of the portico where Jason III (bred for a lawyer, and indeed he kept an office upstairs above the Square, where entombed in dusty filingcases some of the oldest names in the county—Holston and Sutpen, Grenier and Beauchamp and Coldfield—faded year by year among the bottomless labyrinths of chancery: and who knows what dream in the perennial heart of his father, now completing the third of his three avatars—the one as son of a brilliant and gallant statesman, the second as battleleader of brave and gallant men, the third as a sort of privileged pseudo Daniel Boone-Robinson Crusoe, who had not returned to juvenility because actually he had never left it—that that lawyer's office might again be the anteroom to the governor's mansion and the old splendor) sat all day long with a decanter of whiskey and a litter of dogeared Horaces and Livys and Catulluses, composing (it was said) caustic and satiric eulogies on both his dead and his living fellowtownsmen, who sold the last of the property, except that fragment containing the house and the kitchengarden and the collapsing stables and one servant's cabin in which Dilsey's family lived, to a golfclub for the ready money with which his daughter Candace could have her fine wedding in April and his son Quentin could finish one year at Harvard and commit suicide in the following June of 1910; already known as the Old Compson place even while Compsons were still living in it on that spring dusk in 1928 when the old governor's doomed lost nameless seventeen-year-old great-greatgranddaughter robbed her last remaining sane male relative (her uncle Jason IV) of his secret hoard of money and climbed down a pear tree and ran off with a pitchman in a travelling streetshow, and still known as the Old Compson place long after all traces of Compsons were gone from it: after the widowed mother died and Jason IV, no longer needing to fear Dilsey now, committed his idiot brother, Benjamin, to the State Asylum in Jackson and sold the house to a countryman who operated it as a boarding house for juries and horse- and muletraders; and still known as the Old Compson place even after the boardinghouse (and presently the golfcourse too) had vanished and the old square mile was even intact again in row after row of small crowded jerrybuilt individually owned demiurban bungalows.

And these:

QUENTIN III. Who loved not his sister's body but some concept of Compson honor precariously and (he knew well) only temporarily supported by the minute fragile membrane of her maidenhead as a miniature replica of all the whole vast globy earth may be poised on the nose of a trained seal. Who loved not the idea of the incest which he would not commit, but some presbyterian concept of its eternal punishment: he, not God, could by that means cast himself and his sister both into hell, where he could guard her forever and keep her forevermore intact amid the eternal fires. But who loved death above all, who loved only death, loved and lived in a deliberate and almost perverted anticipation of death, as a lover loves and deliberately refrains from the waiting willing friendly tender incredible body of his beloved, until he can no longer bear not the refraining but the restraint, and so flings, hurls himself, relinquishing, drowning. Committed suicide in Cambridge Massachusetts, June 1910, two months after his sister's wedding, waiting first to complete the current academic year and so get the full value of his paid-in-advance tuition, not because he had his old Culloden and Carolina and Kentucky grandfathers in him but because the remaining piece of the old Compson mile which had been sold to pay for his sister's wedding and his year at Harvard had been the one thing, excepting that same sister and the sight of an open fire, which his youngest brother, born an idiot, had loved.

CANDACE (CADDY). Doomed and knew it; accepted the doom without either seeking or fleeing it. Loved her brother despite him, loved not only him but loved in him that bitter prophet and inflexible corruptless judge of what he considered the family's honor and its doom, as he thought he loved, but really hated, in her what he considered the frail doomed vessel of its pride and the foul instrument of its disgrace; not only this, she loved him not only in spite of but because of the fact that he himself was incapable of love, accepting the fact that he must value above all not her but the virginity of which she was custodian and on which she placed no value whatever: the frail physical stricture which to her was no more than a hangnail would have been. Knew the brother loved death best of all and was not jealous, would have handed him (and perhaps in the calculation and deliberation of her marriage did hand him) the hypothetical hemlock. Was two months pregnant with another man's child, which regardless of what its sex would be she had already named Quentin after the brother whom they both (she and the brother) knew was already the same as dead, when she married (1910) an extremely eligible young Indianian she and her mother had met while vacationing at French Lick the summer before. Divorced by him 1911. Married 1920 to a minor moving picture magnate, Hollywood, California. Divorced by mutual agreement, Mexico 1925. Vanished in Paris with the German occupation, 1940, still beautiful, and probably still wealthy too, since she did not look within fifteen years of her actual forty-eight, and was not heard of again. Except there was a woman in Jefferson, the county librarian, a mouse-sized and -colored woman who had never married, who had passed through the city schools in the same class with Candace Compson and then spent the rest of her life trying to keep *Forever Amber*, in its orderly overlapping avatars, and *Jurgen* and *Tom Jones* out of the hands of the highschool juniors and seniors who could reach them down, without even having to tiptoe, from the back shelves where she herself would have to stand on a box to hide them. One day in 1943, after a week of a distraction bordering on disintegration almost, during which those entering the library would find her always in the act of hurriedly closing her desk drawer and turning the key in it (so that the matrons, wives of the bankers and doctors and lawyers, some of whom had also been in that old highschool class, who came and went in the afternoons with the copies of the *Forever Ambers* and the volumes of Thorne Smith carefully wrapped from view in sheets of Memphis and Jackson newspapers, believed she was on the verge of illness or perhaps even loss of mind), she closed and locked the library in the middle of the afternoon and with her handbag clasped tightly under her arm and two feverish spots of determination in her ordinarily colorless cheeks, she entered the farmers' supply store where Jason IV had started as a clerk and where he now owned his own business as a buyer of and dealer in cotton, striding on through that gloomy cavern which only men ever entered—a cavern cluttered and walled and stalag-mite-hung with plows and discs and loops of tracechain and singletrees and mulecollars and side-meat and cheap shoes and horse linament and flour and molasses, gloomy because the goods it contained were not shown but hidden rather since those who supplied Mississippi farmers, or at least Negro Missis-sippi farmers, for a share of the crop did not wish, until that crop was made and its value approximately computable, to show them what they could learn to want, but only to supply them on specific demand with what they could not help but need—and strode on back to Jason's particular domain in the rear: a railed enclosure cluttered with shelves and pigeonholes bear-ing spiked dust-and-lint-gathering gin receipts and ledgers and cotton samples and rank with the blended smell of cheese and kerosene and harness oil and the tremendous iron stove against which chewed tobacco had been spat for almost a hundred years, and up to the long high sloping counter behind which Jason stood, and, not looking again at the overalled men who had quietly stopped talking and even chewing when she entered, with a kind of fainting desperation she opened the handbag and fumbled something out of it and laid it open on the counter and stood trem-bling and breathing rapidly while Jason looked down at it—a picture, a photograph in color clipped obvi-ously from a slick magazine—a picture filled with lux-ury and money and sunlight—a Riviera backdrop of mountains and palms and cypresses and the sea, an open powerful expensive chromium-trimmed sports car, the woman's face hatless between a rich scarf and a seal coat, ageless and beautiful, cold serene and damned; beside her a handsome lean man of mid-dleage in the ribbons and tabs of a German staff-gen-eral—and the mouse-sized mouse-colored spinster trembling and aghast at her own temerity, staring across it at the childless bachelor in whom ended that long line of men who had had something in them of decency and pride, even after they had begun to fail at the integrity and the pride had become mostly vanity and selfpity: from the expatriate who had to flee his native land with little else except his life, yet who still refused to accept defeat, through the man who gam-bled his life and his good name twice and lost twice and declined to accept that either, and the one who with only a clever small quarterhorse for tool avenged

his dispossessed father and grandfather and gained a principality, and the brilliant and gallant governor, and the general who, though he failed at leading in battle brave and gallant men, at least risked his own life too in the failing, to the cultured dipsomaniac who sold the last of his patrimony, not to buy drink but to give one of his descendants at least the best chance in life he could think of.

"It's Caddy!" the librarian whispered. "We must save her!"

"It's Cad, all right," Jason said. Then he began to laugh. He stood there laughing above the picture, above the cold beautiful face now creased and dogeared from its week's sojourn in the desk drawer and the handbag. And the librarian knew why he was laughing, who had not called him anything but Mr. Compson for thirty-two years now, ever since the day in 1911 when Candace, cast off by her husband, had brought her infant daughter home and left the child and departed by the next train, to return no more, and not only the Negro cook, Dilsey, but the librarian too, divined by simple instinct that Jason was somehow using the child's life and its illegitimacy to blackmail the mother not only into staying away from Jefferson for the rest of her life, but into appointing him sole unchallengeable trustee of the money she would send for the child's maintenance, and had refused to speak to him at all since that day in 1928 when the daughter climbed down the pear tree and ran away with the pitchman.

"Jason!" she cried. "We must save her! Jason! Jason!"—and still crying it even when he took up the picture between thumb and finger and threw it back across the counter toward her.

"That Candace?" he said. "Don't make me laugh. This bitch ain't thirty yet. The other one's fifty now."

And the library was still locked all the next day too when at three o'clock in the afternoon, footsore and spent yet still unflagging and still clasping the handbag tightly under her arm, she turned into a neat small yard in the Negro residence section of Memphis and mounted the steps of the neat small house and rang the bell and the door opened and a black woman of about her own age looked quietly out at her. "It's Frony, isn't it?" the librarian said. "Don't you remember me—Melissa Meek, from Jefferson—"

"Yes," the Negress said. "Come in. You want to see Mama." And she entered the room, the neat yet clut-tered bedroom of an old Negro, rank with the smell of old people, old women, old Negroes, where the old woman herself sat in a rocker beside the hearth where even though it was June a fire smoldered—a big woman once, in faded clean calico and an immaculate turban wound round her head above the bleared and now apparently almost sightless eyes—and put the dogeared clipping into the black hands which, like those of the women of her race, were still as supple and delicately shaped as they had been when she was thirty or twenty or even seventeen.

"It's Caddy!" the librarian said. "It is! Dilsey! Dilsey!"

"What did he say?" the old Negress said. And the librarian knew whom she meant by "he"; nor did the librarian marvel, not only that the old Negress would know that she (the librarian) would know whom she meant by the "he," but that the old Negress would know at once that she had already shown the picture to Jason.

"Don't you know what he said?" she cried. "When he realized she was in danger, he said it was her, even if I hadn't even had a picture to show him. But as soon as he realized that somebody, anybody, even just me, wanted to save her, would try to save her, he said it wasn't. But it is! Look at it!"

"Look at my eyes," the old Negress said. "How can I see that picture?"

"Call Frony!" the librarian cried. "She will know her!" But already the old Negress was folding the clipping carefully back into its old creases, handing it back.

"My eyes ain't any good any more," she said. "I can't see it."

And that was all. At six o'clock she fought her way through the crowded bus terminal, the bag clutched under one arm and the return half of her roundtrip ticket in the other hand, and was swept out onto the roaring platform on the diurnal tide of a few middle-aged civilians, but mostly soldiers and sailors enroute either to leave or to death, and the homeless young women, their companions, who for two years now had lived from day to day in pullmans and hotels when they were lucky, and in daycoaches and busses and stations and lobbies and public restrooms when not, pausing only long enough to drop their foals in charity wards or policestations and then move on again, and fought her way into the bus, smaller than any other there so that her feet touched the floor only occasionally, until a shape (a man in khaki; she couldn't see him at all because she was already crying) rose and picked her up bodily and set her into a seat next the window, where still crying quietly she could look out upon the fleeing city as it streaked past and then was behind, and presently now she would be home again, safe in Jefferson, where life lived too with all its incomprehensible passion and turmoil and grief and fury and despair, but there at six o'clock you could close the covers on it and even the weightless hand of a child could put it back among its unfeatured kindred on the quiet eternal shelves and turn the key upon it for the whole and dreamless night. *Yes* she thought, crying quietly, *that was it; she didn't want to see it know whether it was Caddy or not because she knows Caddy doesn't want to be saved hasn't anything any more worth being saved for nothing worth being lost that she can lose.*

JASON IV. The first sane Compson since before Culloden and (a childless bachelor) hence the last. Logical, rational, contained and even a philosopher in the old stoic tradition: thinking nothing whatever of God one way or the other, and simply considering the police and so fearing and respecting only the Negro woman who cooked the food he ate, his sworn enemy since his birth and his mortal one since that day in 1911 when she too divined by simple clairvoyance that he was somehow using his infant niece's illegitimacy to blackmail her mother. Who not only fended off and held his own with Compsons, but competed and held his own with the Snopeses, who took over the little town following the turn of the century as the Compsons and Sartorises and their ilk faded from it (no Snopes, but Jason Compson himself, who as soon as his mother died—the niece had already climbed down the pear tree and vanished, so Dilsey no longer had either of these clubs to hold over him—committed his idiot younger brother to the state and vacated the old house, first chopping up the vast once splendid rooms into what he called apartments and selling the whole thing to a countryman who opened a boardinghouse in it), though this was not difficult since to him all the rest of the town and the world and the human race too except himself were Compsons, inexplicable yet quite predictable in that they were in no sense whatever to be trusted. Who, all the money from the sale of the pasture having gone for his sister's wedding and his brother's course at Harvard, used his own niggard savings out of his meagre wages as a storeclerk to send himself to a Memphis school where he learned to class and grade cotton, and so established his own business, with which, following his dipsomaniac father's death, he assumed the entire burden of the rotting family in the rotting house, supporting his idiot brother because of their mother, sacrificing what pleasures might have been the right and just due and even the necessity of a thirty-year-old bachelor, so that his mother's life might continue as nearly as possible to what it had been; this not because he loved her but (a sane man always) simply because he was afraid of the Negro cook whom he could not even force to leave, even when he tried to stop paying her weekly wages; and who despite all this, still managed to save $2840.50 (three thousand, as he reported it on the night his niece stole it) in niggard and agonized dimes and quarters and halfdollars, which hoard he kept in no bank because to him a banker too was just one more Compson, but hid in a locked steel box beneath a sawn plank in the floor of his locked clothes closet in the bedroom whose bed he made each morning himself, since he kept the room's door locked all the time save for a half hour each Sunday morning when, himself present and watching, he permitted his mother and Dilsey to come in long enough to change the bedlinen and sweep the floor.

Who, following a fumbling abortive attempt by his idiot brother on a passing female child, had himself appointed the idiot's guardian without letting their mother know and so was able to have the creature castrated before the mother even knew it was out of the house, and who following the mother's death in 1933 was able to free himself forever not only from the idiot brother and the house but from the Negro woman too, moving into a pair of offices up a flight of stairs above the supplystore containing his cotton ledgers and samples, which he had converted into a bedroom-kitchen-bath, in and out of which on weekends there would be seen a big, plain, friendly, brazenhaired pleasantfaced woman no longer very young, in round picture hats and in its season an imitation fur coat, the two of them, the middleaged cottonbuyer and the woman whom the town called, simply, his friend from Memphis, seen at the local picture show on Saturday night and on Sunday morning mounting the apartment stairs with paper bags from the grocer's containing loaves and eggs and oranges and cans of soup, domestic, uxorious, connubial, until the late afternoon bus carried her back to Memphis. He was emancipated now. He was free. "In 1865," he would say, "Abe Lincoln freed the niggers from the Compsons. In 1933, Jason Compson freed the Compsons from the niggers."

BENJAMIN. Born Maury, after his mother's only brother: a handsome flashing swaggering workless bachelor who borrowed money from almost anyone, even Dilsey although she was a Negro, explaining to her as he withdrew his hand from his pocket that she was not only in his eyes the same as a member of his sister's family, she would be considered a born lady anywhere in any eyes. Who, when at last even his mother realized what he was and insisted weeping that his name must be changed, was rechristened Benjamin by his brother Quentin (Benjamin, our lastborn, sold into Egypt). Who loved three things: the pasture which was sold to pay for Candace's wedding and to send Quentin to Harvard, his sister Candace, firelight. Who lost none of them, because he could not remember his sister but only the loss of her, and firelight was the same bright shape as going to sleep, and the pasture was even better sold than before, because now he and Luster could not only follow timeless along the fence the motions which it did not even matter to him were human beings swinging golfsticks, Luster could lead the to clumps of grass or weeds where there would appear suddenly in Luster's hand, small white spherules which competed with and even conquered what he did not even know was gravity and all the immutable laws, when released from the hand toward plank floor of smokehouse wall or concrete sidewalk. Gelded 1913. Committed to the State Asylum, Jackson, 1933. Lost nothing then either

because, as with his sister, he remembered not the pasture but only its loss, and firelight was still the same bright shape of sleep.

QUENTIN. The last. Candace's daughter. Fatherless nine months before her birth, nameless at birth and already doomed to be unwed from the instant the dividing egg determined its sex. Who at seventeen, on the one thousand eight hundred ninetyfifth anniversary of the day before the resurrection of Our Lord, swung herself by a rainpipe from her window to the locked window of her uncle's locked and empty bedroom and broke a pane and entered the window, and with the uncle's firepoker ripped off the locked hasp and staple of the closet door and prized up the sawn plank and got the steel box (and they never did know how she had broken the lock on it, how a seventeen-year-old girl could have broken that lock with anything, let alone a poker) and rifled it (and it was not $2840.50 or three thousand dollars either, it was almost seven thousand. And this was Jason's rage, the red unbearable fury which on that night and at intervals recurring with little or no diminishment for the next five years, made him seriously believe it would at some unwarned instant destroy him, kill him as instantaneously dead as a bullet or a lightningbolt: that although he had been robbed not of a mere petty three but of almost seven, he couldn't even report it; he could not only never receive justification—he did not want sympathy—from other men unlucky enough to have one bitch for a sister and another for a niece, he couldn't even demand help in recovering it. Because he had lost four thousand dollars which did not belong to him he couldn't even recover the three thousand which did, since those first four thousand dollars were not only the legal property of his niece as a part of the money supplied for her support and maintenance by her mother over the last sixteen years, they did not exist at all, having been officially recorded as expended and consumed in the annual reports he submitted to the district Chancellor, as required of him as guardian and trustee by his bondsmen: so that he had been robbed not only of his thievings but his savings too, and by his own victim; he had been robbed not only of the four thousand dollars which he had risked jail to acquire, but of the three thousand which he had hoarded at the price of sacrifice and denial, almost a nickel and a dime at a time, over a period of almost twenty years: and this not only by his own victim but by a child who did it at one blow, without premeditation or plan, not even knowing or even caring how much she would find when she broke the drawer open; and now he couldn't even go to the police for help: he who had considered the police always, never given them any trouble, had paid the taxes for years which supported them in parasitic and sadistic idleness; not only that, he didn't dare pursue the girl himself because he might catch her and she would talk, so that his only recourse was a vain dream which kept him tossing and sweating on nights two and three and even four years after the event, when he should have forgotten about it: of catching her without warning, springing on her out of the dark, before she had spent all the money, and murdering her before she had time to open her mouth) and climbed down the pear tree in the dusk and ran away with the pitchman who was already under sentence for bigamy. And so vanished; whatever occupation overtook her would have arrived in no chromium Mercedes; whatever snapshot would have contained no general of staff.

And that was all. These others were not Compsons. They were black:

TP. Who wore on Memphis' Beal Street the fine bright cheap intransigent clothes manufactured specifically for him by the owners of Chicago and New York sweatshops.

FRONY. Who married a pullman porter and went to Saint Louis to live and later moved back to Memphis to make a home for her mother since Dilsey refused to go further than that.

LUSTER. A man, aged 14. Who was not only capable of the complete care and security of an idiot twice his age and three times his size, but could keep him entertained.

DILSEY.

They endured.

II Faulkner's Introduction to *Sanctuary*

In his introduction to the edition of Sanctuary *published by The Modern Library in 1932, Faulkner gave a misleading explanation of his intentions in writing the novel. He withdrew it from later editions.*

This book was written three years ago. To me it is a cheap idea, because it was deliberately conceived to make money. I had been writing books for about five years, which got published and not bought. But that was all right. I was young then and hard-bellied. I had never lived among nor known people who wrote novels and stories and I suppose I did not know that people got money for them. I was not very much annoyed when publishers refused the mss. now and then. Because I was hard-gutted then. I could do a lot of things that could earn what little money I needed, thanks to my father's unfailing kindness which supplied me with bread at need despite the outrage to his principles at having been of a bum progenitive.

Then I began to get a little soft. I could still paint houses and do carpenter work, but I got soft. I began to think about making money by writing. I began to be concerned when magazine editors turned down short stories, concerned enough to tell them that they would buy these stories later anyway, and hence why not now. Meanwhile, with one novel completed and consistently refused for two years, I had just written my guts into *The Sound and the Fury* though I was not aware until the book was published that I had done so, because I had done it for pleasure. I believed then that I would never be published again. I had stopped thinking of myself in publishing terms.

But when the third mss., *Sartoris*, was taken by a publisher and (he having refused *The Sound and the Fury*) it was taken by still another publisher, who warned me at the time that it would not sell, I began to think of myself again as a printed object. I began to think of books in terms of possible money. I decided I might just as well make some of it myself. I took a little time out, and speculated what a person in Mississippi would believe to be current trends, chose what I thought was the right answer and invented the most horrific tale I could imagine and wrote it in about three weeks and sent it to Smith, who had done *The Sound and the Fury* and who wrote me immediately, "Good God, I can't publish this. We'd both be in jail." So I told Faulkner, "You're damned. You'll have to work now and then for the rest of your life." That was in the summer of 1929. I got a job in the power plant, on the night shift, from 6 P.M. to 6 A.M., as a coal passer. I shoveled coal from the bunker into a wheelbarrow and wheeled it in and dumped it where the fireman could put it into the boiler. About 11 o'clock the people would be going to bed, and so it did not take so much steam. Then we could rest, the fireman and I. He would sit in a chair and doze. I had invented a table out of a wheelbarrow in the coal bunker, just beyond a wall from where a dynamo ran. It made a deep, constant humming noise. There was no more work to do until about 4 A.M., when we would have to clean the fires and get up steam again. On these nights, between 12 and 4, I wrote *As I Lay Dying* in six weeks, without changing a word. I sent it to Smith and wrote him that by it I would stand or fall.

I think I had forgotten about *Sanctuary,* just as you might forget about anything made for an immediate purpose, which did not come off. *As I Lay Dying* was published and I didn't remember the mss. of *Sanctuary* until Smith sent me the galleys. Then I saw that it was so terrible that there were but two things to do: tear it up or rewrite it. I thought again, "It might sell; maybe 10,000 of them will buy it." So I tore the galleys down and rewrote the book. It had been already set up once, so I had to pay for the privilege of rewriting it, trying to make out of it something which would not shame *The Sound and the Fury* and *As I Lay Dying* too much and I made a fair job and I hope you will buy it and tell your friends and I hope they will buy it too.

III Faulkner's Nobel Prize Acceptance Speech
Stockholm, December 10, 1950

I feel that this award was not made to me as a man but to my work—a life's work in the agony and sweat of the human spirit, not for glory and least of all for profit, but to create out of the materials of the human spirit something which did not exist before. So this award is only mine in trust. It will not be difficult to find a dedication for the money part of it commensurate with the purpose and significance of its origin. But I would like to do the same with the acclaim too, by using this moment as a pinnacle from which I might be listened to by the young men and women already dedicated to the same anguish and travail, among whom is already that one who will some day stand here where I am standing.

Our tragedy today is a general and universal physical fear so long sustained by now that we can even bear it. There are no longer problems of the spirit. There is only the question: When will I be blown up? Because of this, the young man or woman writing today has forgotten the problems of the human heart in conflict with itself which alone can make good writing because only that is worth writing about, worth the agony and the sweat.

He must learn them again. He must teach himself that the basest of all things is to be afraid; and teaching himself that, forget it forever, leaving no room in his workshop for anything but the old verities and truths of the heart, the old universal truths lacking which any story is ephemeral and doomed—love and honor and pity and pride and compassion and sacrifice. Until he does so, he labors under a curse. He writes not of love but of lust, of defeats in which nobody loses anything of value, of victories without hope and, worst of all, without pity or compassion. His griefs grieve on no universal bones, leaving no scars. He writes not of the heart but of the glands.

Until he relearns these things, he will write as though he stood among and watched the end of man. I decline to accept the end of man. It is easy enough to say that man is immortal simply because he will endure; that when the last ding-dong of doom has clanged and faded from the last worthless rock hanging tideless in the last red and dying evening, that even then there will still be one more sound: that of his puny inexhaustible voice, still talking. I refuse to accept this. I believe that man will not merely endure: he will prevail. He is immortal, not because he alone among creatures has an inexhaustible voice but because he has a soul, a spirit capable of compassion and sacrifice and endurance. The poet's, the writer's, duty is to write about these things. It is his privilege to help man endure by lifting his heart, by reminding him of the courage and honor and hope and pride and compassion and pity and sacrifice which has been the glory of his past. The poet's voice need not merely be the record of man, it can be one of the props, the pillars to help him endure and prevail.

APPENDIX V

Dateline

1897

William Cuthbert Falkner born (in New Albany, Mississippi, September 25)

Havelock Ellis publishes *Studies in the Psychology of Sex*

H. G. Wells publishes *The Invisible Man*

1902

The Falkner family moves to Oxford, Mississippi

John Steinbeck is born

Emile Zola dies

Beatrix Potter publishes *Peter Rabbit*

1905

Falkner enters the first grade on his eighth birthday

First movie theatre opens in Pittsburgh, Pennsylvania

Edith Wharton publishes *The House of Mirth*

The Bloomsbury Group is founded

1911

Falkner enters the eighth grade (September)

Marie Curie awarded Nobel Prize in chemistry

Roald Amundsen reaches South Pole

1914

Falkner begins long-lasting friendship with Phil Stone

Archduke Francis Ferdinand is assassinated in Sarajevo and World War I begins

James Joyce publishes *Dubliners*

Tennessee Williams is born

1915

Falkner drops out of school

Franz Kafka publishes *Der Verwandlung* (*The Metamorphosis*)

Germany sinks *Lusitania*

D. W. Griffith's film *The Birth of a Nation* opens

1916

James Joyce publishes *A Portrait of the Artist as a Young Man*

1917

Falkner drawings appear in *Ole Miss* yearbook

United States declares war on Germany

T. S. Eliot publishes *Prufrock and Other Observations*

C. G. Jung publishes *Psychology of the Unconscious*

1918

Falkner is rejected by the U.S. Army; in June changes spelling of his name to *Faulkner* when enlisting in the Royal Air Force; attends School of Military Aeronautics in Toronto; is discharged when World War I ends (November 11); returns to Oxford, Mississippi

Irving Berlin's *Yip Yip Yaphank* opens on Broadway

James Joyce's *Ulysses* begins serialization in the *Little Review*

Willa Cather publishes *My Antonía*

World War I ends

1919

Faulkner's first publication, the poem "L'Après-midi d'un Faune," appears in *The New Republic* (reprinted in *The Mississippian*)

Racehorse Man o' War loses only race

Sherwood Anderson publishes *Winesburg, Ohio*

1921

John Dos Passos publishes *Three Soldiers*

1922

James Joyce publishes *Ulysses*

1924

Faulkner publishes *The Marble Faun*

Ottoman Empire ends

André Breton publishes *Manifeste de surréalisme* (*Manifesto of Surrealism*)

1925

Faulkner travels in Europe

The Charleston becomes a popular dance

Hitler publishes volume one of *Mein Kampf*

Scopes "Monkey Trial" takes place

F. Scott Fitzgerald publishes *The Great Gatsby*

1926

Faulkner's first novel, *Soldiers' Pay,* is published

Magician Harry Houdini dies

1927

Faulkner publishes *Mosquitoes*

Sinclair Lewis publishes *Elmer Gantry*

1929

Faulkner publishes *Sartoris;* marries Estelle Franklin; publishes *The Sound and the Fury*

Thomas Wolfe publishes *Look Homeward, Angel*

Ernest Hemingway publishes *A Farewell to Arms*

1930

Faulkner buys Rowan Oak; publishes *As I Lay Dying*

Noël Coward publishes *Private Lives*

Dashiell Hammett publishes *The Maltese Falcon*

D. H. Lawrence dies

Sinclair Lewis wins the Nobel Prize in literature

1931

Faulkner and Estelle's daughter Alabama is born; she dies nine days later. Faulkner publishes *Sanctuary* and *These 13* (a collection of short stories)

Robert Frost wins Pulitzer Prize for *Collected Poems*

Salvador Dali paints "Persistence of Memory"

1932

Faulkner writes for Metro-Goldwyn-Mayer (MGM); publishes *Salmagundi* (prose and poetry) and *Light in August*

Franklin Delano Roosevelt elected president of the United States

Adolf Hitler becomes German citizen

Amelia Earhart is first woman to make transatlantic solo flight

Aldous Huxley publishes *Brave New World*

1933

Faulkner publishes *A Green Bough* (collection of poems); works as scriptwriter in New Orleans; daughter Jill is born

Hitler comes to power in Germany; first concentration camps built

C. G. Jung publishes *Modern Man in Search of a Soul*

1934

Faulkner publishes *Doctor Martino and Other Stories;* works for Universal Studios

F. Scott Fitzgerald publishes *Tender is the Night*

Luigi Pirandello wins Nobel Prize in literature

1935

Faulkner publishes *Pylon;* works for Twentieth Century–Fox; begins affair with Meta Dougherty Carpenter

Alcoholic Anonymous starts in New York City

Persia is renamed Iran

1936

Faulkner publishes *Absalom, Absalom!*

King Edward VIII abdicates

Margaret Mitchell publishes *Gone With the Wind*

Baseball Hall of Fame opens in Cooperstown, New York

Eugene O'Neill wins Nobel Prize in literature

1937

Faulkner returns to Oxford, Mississippi, from California

John Steinbeck publishes *Of Mice and Men*

Amelia Earhart is lost in the Pacific

1938

Faulkner publishes *The Unvanquished;* buys Greenfield Farm

Kristallnacht

Eddie Arcaro wins his first Kentucky Derby

Thornton Wilder wins Pulitzer Prize for *Our Town*

1939

Faulkner is elected to the National Institute of Arts and Letters; publishes *The Wild Palms*

James Joyce publishes *Finnegans Wake*

World War II begins

1940

Faulkner publishes *The Hamlet* (the first of the Snopes trilogy)

F. Scott Fitzgerald dies

1941

James Joyce dies

Joe DiMaggio sets major league record by hitting safely in 56 consecutive games

1942

Faulkner publishes *Go Down, Moses;* writes for Warner Brothers

Enrico Firmi splits atom

1945

First atomic bomb is detonated in New Mexico

United States drops atomic bombs on Hiroshima and Nagasaki, Japan

1946

The Portable Faulkner is published

Victor Emmanuel III abdicates as King of Italy

1948

MGM buys screen rights to *Intruder in the Dust,* two months before novel is published in September; Faulkner is elected to the American Academy of Arts and Sciences

Indian nationalist leader Mohandas Gandhi is assassinated

Babe Ruth dies

1949

Faulkner publishes *Knight's Gambit*

Arthur Miller receives Pulitzer Prize for *Death of a Salesman*

1950

Faulkner is awarded the American Academy's Howells Medal for Fiction; *Collected Stories of William Faulkner* is published; Faulkner wins the 1949 Nobel Prize in literature

George Bernard Shaw dies

Alger Hiss convicted of perjury

1951

In Hollywood, Faulkner writes scripts for Howard Hawks; publishes novella *Notes on a Horsethief;* wins National Book Award for Fiction (for *Collected Stories*); publishes *Requiem for a Nun*

J. D. Salinger publishes *The Catcher in the Rye*

James Jones publishes *From Here to Eternity*

Rachel Carson publishes *The Sea Around Us*

1954

Faulkner publishes *A Fable*

Ernest Hemingway wins Nobel Prize in literature

Charles A. Lindbergh wins Pulitzer Prize for *The Spirit of St. Louis*

1955

Faulkner receives the National Book Award for *A Fable* (novel also wins the Pulitzer Prize); on invitation of State Department participates in Nagano Seminar, Japan; publishes *Big Woods*

James Agee dies

Vladimir Nabokov publishes *Lolita*

Thomas Mann dies

Albert Einstein dies

1957

Faulkner begins Writer-in-Residence at the University of Virginia (1957–1958); travels to Athens on invitation of State Department; awarded the Silver Medal of Greek Academy; publishes *The Town* (the second novel of the Snopes trilogy)

Jack Kerouac publishes *On the Road*

Dr. Seuss publishes *The Cat in the Hat*

Bernard Malamud publishes *The Assistant*

1958

Faulkner participates in Council on Humanities at Princeton University

John Kenneth Galbraith publishes *The Affluent Society*

1959

Requiem for a Nun opens on Broadway; Faulkner publishes *The Mansion* (the third of the Snopes trilogy)

De Gaulle becomes president of the Fifth Republic in France

Hawaii becomes fiftieth state

1960

Faulkner appointed to University of Virginia faculty

John F. Kennedy–Richard Nixon presidential debates are televised

Students conduct nonviolent sit-ins at all-white lunch counters in Greensboro, North Carolina

Harper Lee publishes *To Kill a Mockingbird*

1961

Faulkner travels to Venezuela on invitation of State Department

Ernest Hemingway dies

Soviet cosmonaut Uri Gagarin orbits Earth

Alan Shepard flies in first United States space flight

Civil rights Freedom Riders in Alabama are beaten

1962

Faulkner receives the Gold Medal for Fiction of the National Institute of Arts and Letters; publishes *The Reivers;* dies of heart attack

John Steinbeck wins Nobel Prize in literature

Alexander Solzhenitsyn publishes *One Day in the Life of Ivan Denisovich*

Adolf Eichmann is hanged

Hermann Hesse dies

e. e. cummings dies

Eleanor Roosevelt dies

Rachel carson publishes *Silent Spring*

Black student James Meredith is escorted to the University of Mississippi by federal marshals

INDEX

Note: **Boldface** numbers indicate primary discussions of a topic. *Italic* numbers indicate illustrations.

Britt, Commander **26**
Brix **26–27,** 115, 217, 247
Brix, Mrs. **27,** 217, 247
Brodsky, Louis Daniel **27,** 107, 160
"The Brooch" (short story) 26, **27,** 196
Brooks, Cleanth **27**
    on *Absalom, Absalom!* 3
    on "Barn Burning" 13
    on *A Fable* 57
    on Faulkner's poetry 103, 155
    on *Flags in the Dust* 89
    on *Light in August* 31, 141, 142
    on *Mosquitoes* 163, 164
    on "Pantaloon in Black" 98
    on "A Rose for Emily" 195
    on *Sartoris* 202, 203
    on *The Sound and the Fury* 41, 220
    on time, concept of 86–87
    on *The Town* 236
    on *The Unvanquished* 243
Broun, Heywood 6
Broussard **27**
Brown, Joe *See* Burch, Lucas
Brownlee, Percival (Spintrius) **27**
Brummage, Judge **27**
Brzewski **27**
Brzonyi **27**
Buchwald 17, **27**
Buck **28** *See also* Hipps, Buck
Buck, Pearl S. 168
Buckner (Buck) **28,** 123
Buckner, Billie **28,** 123
Buckworth **28**
Bud, Uncle **28**
Buffaloe, Mr. **28**
Buford **28**
Bull Run, first battle of **28,** 63, 67, 82,
    208
Bullitt, Bob (R. Q.) **28**
Bullitt, Mrs. **28**
Bunch, Byron **28,** 105, 114, 140
Bunden, Bud 5, **28**
Bunden, Joe 4, **28–29**
Bunden, Juliet 4–5, **29,** 102, 117
Bundren, Addie 5, 9–10, **29,** 251
Bundren, Anse 9, 10, **29,** 199
Bundren, Cash 9, 10, **29**
Bundren, Darl 9, 10, **29,** 30, 96
Bundren, Dewey Dell 9, 10, **29–30,** 138,
    163
Bundren, Jewel 9, 10, **30,** 96, 104
Bundren, Mrs. **30**
Bundren, Vardaman 9, 10, **30,** 244
Burch, Lucas (Joe Brown) 28, **30,** 50,
    105, 140, 141, 142
Burchett **30,** 162, 188
Burchett, Mrs. **30**
Burden, Beck **30**
Burden, Calvin (elder) **31,** 242
Burden, Calvin (younger) **31**
Burden, Evangeline **31**
Burden, Joanna 30, **31,** 38, 140, 141
Burden, Juana **31**
Burden, Nathaniel **31**

Burden, Sarah **31**
Burden, Vangie **31**
Burgess **31**
Burgess, Mrs. **31**
Burk **31**
Burke **31**
Burney, Dewey **31,** 181
Burney, Mr. **32**
Burney, Mrs. **32**
Burnham, Lieutenant Frank **32**
Burrington, Nathaniel **32**
Burt **32**
Bush, Lem **32**
Butch **32**
Butler, Burlina 82
Butler, Charles Edward **32,** 60, 67, 68
Butler, Joe **32**
Butler, Lelia Dean Swift **32,** 60, 67
Butler, Maud *See* Falkner, Maud Butler
Byhalia, Mississippi **32,** 66, 73, 77
By Their Fruits (Falkner III) 111
"By the People" (short story) 25, **32–33,**
    153

C

Caddy *See* Compson, Candace
Cain **34**
Cajan, the **34,** 123
Caldwell, Sam **34,** 116
Caledonia Chapel **34,** 126
Callaghan **34**
Callaghan, Miss **34**
Callicoat, Buster **34**
Callicoat, David **34**
Callie, Aunt **34**
Calvert, Elizabeth 169
Camus, Albert **34–35**
Canby, Henry Seidel 78, 199
Canova, Signor (Joel Flint) **34,** 89–90
Cantwell, Robert 123
Cape, Jonathan 35, 210
Cape & Smith 10, **35,** 72, 110, 210, 219
Carberry, Dr. **35**
"Carcassonne" (short piece) **35,** 146,
    251
Carl **35,** 49–50
Carpenter, Meta **35–36,** 66, 73, 77, 80,
    249
Carruthers, Miss **36**
Carter **36**
Casanova Press 199
Case, Frank 6
Caspey **36**
Casse-tête **36,** 58
Catalpa Street **36,** 250
Cavalcanti **36**
Cayley, Hence **36**
Cayley, Miss **36**
"Centaur in Brass" (short story) **36**
    characters in 18, 21, 44, 111,
      120–121
    revision of 234
Cerf, Bennett **36–37,** 135, 136, 186, 189

Chance, Vic **37**
Chandler, Ramond 73
Charleston, Georgia 217
Charley **37**
Charley, Uncle **37**
Charlie **37**
Chatto & Windus 37
Chickasaw Indians **37,** 45, 124, 129, 132,
    143, 149, 162, 178, 188, 233, 250, 256
Chlory **37**
Christ-figure
    Benjy Compson as 41
    Colonel Stefan as 36, 57–58, 172,
      223
Christian, Mrs. **37**
Christian, Uncle Willy **37–38,** 120, 206,
    207, 239
Christian, Walter **38**
Christmas, Joe 11, 18, 30, 31, 37, **38,** 84,
    104, 114, 115, 140–141, 142, 151, 224
Church, Mrs. **38**
Cinthy **38**
Civil Rights movement 75, 83, 126
Civil War
    Bull Run **28,** 63, 67, 82, 208
    commanders in 90, 102, 208, 210,
      228
    Confederate States of America **44**
    Falkner family in 8, 63, 67, 82, 152,
      208
    in Faulkner's fiction 1, 24, 82–83,
      166, 193, 240
    Oxford, Mississippi, during 173,
      210
    Pickett's charge 179
    Shiloh 90, 205, **208**
    Vicksburg campaign 102, 177, 208,
      246
The Clansman (Dixon) 84
Clapp, Walter **38**
Clay, Sis Beulah **38**
Clefus **38**
Clytemnestra *See* Sutpen, Clytemnestra
Cochrane, Dr. Ab **38–39,** 165
Cofer **39**
Coindreau, Maurice Edgar 5, **39,** 74, 78,
    94, 236
Colbert, David **39**
Coldfield, Ellen *See* Sutpen, Ellen
    Coldfield
Coldfield, Goodhue 2, 19, **39,** 228
Coldfield, Rosa (Miss Rosa) 1, 2, 3, 19,
    39, 42, 228, 230
Coleman, Mrs. **39**
Collected Stories of William Faulkner **39–40,**
    74
Collier **40**
Collins, Carvel **40,** 112, 157, 168, 240,
    252
Collyer **40**
Commercial Hotel **40**
Commins, Saxe 39, **40,** 55, 77, *79,* 88,
    190, 196–197
Compson **40**

New Criticism 27
New Hope Church **167**
New Orleans, Louisiana **167–168**
    Faulkner in 6, 7, 12, 71, 81, 144, 222
    in Faulkner's fiction 164, 178, 194
New Orleans Sketches 6, 164, **168**
New Orleans Times-Picayune (newspaper) 71, 167, **168**
New York City
    Algonquin Hotel 6, 77, 223
    Faulkner's trips to 72, 76–77, 136, 223, 257
    short story set in 177–178
Nightingale, Mr. **168**
Nightingale, Tug 151, **168**
Nine-Mile Branch **168**
Nobel Prize in literature 74–75, 77, 113, **168–169**, 197
    acceptance speech 55, 58–59, 74, 88, 169, 208
Nordell, Roderick 190
Notes on a Horsethief (novella) **169**
    characters in 126
    revision of 57
Nunnery, Cedric **169**, 212
"Nympholepsy" (short story) **169–170**

O

Ober, Harold 125, 145, 158, **171**, 189, 253
Odlethrop, Mrs. **171**
Odlethrop, Stonewall Jackson (Monk) 94, 136, **171**, 231
O'Donnell, George Marion 78
"An Odor of Verbena" (short story) 19, 240, 241, **242**
Odum, Cliff **171**
Okatoba County **171**
Okatoba Hunting and Fishing Club **171**
Old Ben 64, 99, 116, 149
Old Frenchman place 8, 25, 93, 103, 104, 108, 110, 143, **171**, 187, 200, 213, 225
Old General (the Generalissimo; the marshal; the old marshal) 48, 57, **171–172**, 197
Oldham, Dorothy (Dot) 92, **172**
Oldham, Lemuel Earl 65, 66, 70, **172**
Oldham, Lida Allen 65, **172**
"The Old Man" (short story) **122–123**
    characters in 22, 28, 34, 44, 110, 248, 254
"The Old People" (short story) **98**
    characters in 16, 49, 64, 116, 124, 127, 129, 149, 162
    Chickasaw history and culture in 37
    writing history of 97
Oliver 5, **172**
Omlie, Vernon C. 81, **172**
"Once Aboard the Lugger" (I and II) (short stories) **173**
    characters in 53, 130, 178
    reviews of 206–207
"On Fear: The South in Labor" (essay) 111, 158

O'Neill, Eugene 40, 168
Ord, Matt **173**, 183
Ord, Mrs. **173**
Oscar **173**
Osgood, Captain **173**
Otis 21, 116, 159, **173**, 182, 189
Ott, Jimmy **173**
Owl-by-Night **173**
Oxford, Mississippi 72, 102, 138, **173–174**
    during Civil War 173, 210
    conference in 7
    dances in 110
    Falkner family in 59, 60, *62*, 67, 69, 83
    fictional place based on 128–129
    filming of *Intruder in the Dust* in 126, 158
    racial relations in 83–84, 124
    response to Faulkner's works in 188, 243
    statue of Faulkner in *174*
Oxford Eagle (newspaper) 81, **174–175**, 243

P

pacifism, Faulkner's 59
Painter **176**
"Pantaloon in Black" (short story) **98**
    characters in 4, 6, 21, 53, 135, 147, 153, 157, 193
    writing history of 97
Paoli **176**
Pap *See also* Grier, Res (Pap)
    in "Fool About a Horse" 90, **176**, 216
    in *Sanctuary* **176**, 200
Paralee **176**
Parchman 154, **176**, 215
Paris Review (journal) 77, 123, **176**, 202, 223
Parker, Dorothy 6
Parker's **176**, 220
Parsham, Tennessee 119, **176**, 182, 189, 194
Parsons, Maurice **176**, 250
Parsons, Sally Hampton **176**, 250
Pascagoula, Mississippi 12, 66, 71, 122, 163, **176–177**
Pate, Lucy *See* Houston, Lucy Pate
Patterson **177**
Patterson, Mrs. 15, **177**
Patterson boy **177**
Paul **177**
Peabody, Doctor **177**
Peabody, Doctor Lucius Quintus **177**
Peabody, Lucius ("Loosh") 1, **177**
Pearson, Mr. **177**, 231
Peebles, E. E. **177**
Pemberton, John C. **177**
"Pennsylvania Station" (short story) **177–178**
    characters in 96, 179, 258

Pete
    in *If I Forget Thee, Jerusalem* **178**
    in "Once Aboard the Lugger" 130, 173, **178**
    in *Requiem for a Nun* **178**, 191, 225
Peter **178**
"Peter" (short story) **178**, 222
Peters, Erskine 165
Pettibone **178**
Pettigrew **178**
Pettigrew, Thomas Jefferson **178**
Peyton, George **178**
Philadelphia (Philadelphy) **178–179**, 242
Philip 54, **179**
Phoebe (Fibby) **179**
Pickett, George C. **179**, 239
Picklock 58, **179**, 223
Pinkie **179**
Pittsburgh Landing **179**
Plimpton, George 190
Ploeckner **179**, 193
poetic truth 1
poetry, Faulkner's 5, 71, 103, 113, 155, 160
"A Point of Law" (short story) 97, 114
Polchek 58, **179**
Poleymus **179**
political satire 33
Polk, Noel 80, 124, 156, **179**, 184, 191, 199, 221
Pomp **179**
Pontotoc, Mississippi **179**
Popeye **180**
    in "The Big Shot" 20, 52
    model for 158
    in *Requiem for a Nun* 192
    in *Sanctuary* 19, 100, 191, 200–201, 225
The Portable Faulkner 74, 77, 78, 81, **180**, 221, 246
"A Portrait of Elmer" (short story) **180**
    characters in 7, 55, 115, 162, 245
    material for 54
Pose **181**
postmodernism xi, 5, 131, **181**
Pound, Ezra 51, 162
Powell, John **181**
Powell, Summer 78
Powers, Mrs. Margaret 32, 96, 145, 152, **181**, 206, 218
Powers, Richard (Dick) 32, **181**
Prall, Elizabeth (Elizabeth Prall Anderson) 7, 71, **181**
Price **181**
"The Priest" (short story) **181–182**
Priest, Allison Lessep **182**
Priest, Lessep **182**
Priest, Lucius (Boss Priest; Grandfather) **182**, 189
Priest, Lucius (Loosh) 53, 116, 119, 139, 148, 150, **182–183**, 189, 193
Priest, Maurice *See* Parsons, Maurice
Priest, Maury, Jr. **183**
Priest, Maury, Sr. 62, 181, **183**

S

Saddie **199**
Sales, Mac **199**
Salmagundi (collection) **199**
Salmon **199**
Sam **199**
Samson **199**
Samson, Rachel **199**
Samson's Bridge **199**
Samuel **199**
Samway, Patrick 145
Sanctuary (novel) **199–202**
 adaptations of 80, 201
 characters in 18, 19, 50, 51, 52, 91,
  95, 100, 102, 111, 126, 130, 138,
  166, 176, 180, 185, 187, 194, 207,
  212, 216, 224–225, 234, 248, 253
 geographical references in 155, 171
 material for 70, 158, 226
 publication history of 72
 response to 61, 74, 76, 175, 188,
  199
 sequel to 191
Sander, Aleck 17, 101, 106, 125, 126,
 152, **202**
Sander, Big Top **202**
Sander, Guster **202**
Sander, Little Top **202**
Sarah **202**
Sardis Lake 20, **202**
Sartoris (novel) **202–203**
 characters in 1, 6, 15, 18, 19, 21, 26,
  32, 44, 52, 54, 55, 63, 91, 102,
  111, 114, 120, 121, 126, 130, 147,
  148, 153, 155, 161, 162, 163, 166,
  177, 179, 186, 187, 190, 192, 193,
  195, 203–205, 209, 210, 212, 217,
  227, 228, 234, 250, 254
 dedication of 7, 203
 geographical references in 256
 material for 81, 89
 publication history of 72, 89, 110,
  143, 210, 249
 reviews of 203
 writing history of 177
Sartoris (place) **203**
Sartoris, Bayard 52, **204,** 228
Sartoris, Bayard (infant) **203**
Sartoris, Bayard (old) **204**
 character resembling 125
 model for 60, 204
 in "My Grandmother Millard" 166
 in *Sartoris* 202, 203
 in *The Town* 214
 in *The Unvanquished* 49, 83, 105,
  205, 227, 240–243, 255
Sartoris, Bayard (young) 4, 18, 130,
 202–203, **204,** 205, 212
Sartoris, Benbow (Bory) **204,** 232
Sartoris, Caroline White **204**
Sartoris, Colonel John 31, 83, 106, 112,
 187, 188, **204–205,** 211, 241, 242–243,
 255
 model for 62, 63, 67, 128

Sartoris, Drusilla Hawk 112, **205,** 242,
 243, 255
Sartoris, John **205**
Sartoris, John (Johnny) 7, 26, 121, 202,
 203, 204, **205,** 222, 234, 254
Sartoris, Lucy Cranston **205**
Sartoris, Narcissa Benbow **205**
 in *Sanctuary* 224
 in *Sartoris* 6, 15, 18, 19, 28, 32, 200,
  202, 203, 204
 in "There Was a Queen" 232–233
Sartoris, Virginia *See* Du Pre, Virginia
Sartoris Station **205**
Sartre, Jean-Paul 11, 74, 78, 87
Sarty *See* Snopes, Colonel Sartoris
Saturday Evening Post (magazine) 15, 60,
 73, 99, 189, 193, **206,** 241
Saunders, Cecily (Cecily Saunders Farr)
 55, 96, 152, 181, **206,** 217, 218
Saunders, Minnie **206**
Saunders, Robert, Jr. (Bob) **206**
Saunders, Robert, Sr. **206**
Saxon, Lyle 72, 221
scapegoat ritual 52
Schluss **206**
Schofield, Dr. **206**
Schultz, Reverend **206**
Schultz, Sister **206**
Schwartz, Delmore 57, 58
Scott, Evelyn 78
Scribner's Magazine 27, **206–207**
Secretary **207,** 239
Selby, Claude 92
Seminary Hill **207**
Semmes **207**
Sensibar, Judith L. 246
The sentry 112, 230
"Sepulture South: Gaslight" (short story)
 207
 characters in 9, 140, 195, 250
Sewanee Review (journal) **207**
Shack **207**
Shakespeare, William 184, 219
"Shall Not Perish" (short story)
 207–208, 238
 characters in 49, 104, 135, 185
shame, theme of 1
Shegog, Judith 210
Shegog, Reverend **208,** 221
Shegog, Robert 37, 196
Shenton, Edward 20, 243
Sherman, William Tecumseh 90, **208,** 210
"Sherwood Anderson: An Appreciation"
 (essay) 11
Sherwood Anderson and Other Creoles
 (parody) 222
Shiloh, battle of 90, 205, **208**
"Shingles for the Lord" (short story)
 208–209
 characters in 8, 9, 104, 135, 185,
  211, 251
Ship Island, Ripley & Kentucky Railroad
 105, **209**
Short, Herman **209**

Shreve *See* MacKenzie, Shrevlin
Shumann, Dr. Carl 183–184, **209**
Shumann, Jack 183, 190, **209**
Shumann, Laverne 118, 183–184, 190,
 209
 model for 81, 172
Shumann, Roger 89, 106, 118, 129, 173,
 183, 190, **209**
 model for 81, 172
Sibleigh **209**
Sickymo **209**
Sienkiewicz, Henryk 88
Simmons **209**
Simms **210**
Simon 14, **210**
Skeet **210**
Skei, Hans 52
Skipworth **210**
"Skirmish at Sartoris" (short story) 118,
 207, **242**
Smith, Andrew J. 173, 193, 208, **210**
Smith, Essie Meadowfill 115, 117, 157,
 210
Smith & Haas 3, 35, 37, 103, 106, 186,
 210–211
Smith, Harrison (Hal) 2, 3, 10, 35, 37,
 103, 106, 110, 142, 184, **210,** 240
Smith, Henry Nash 203
Smith, Lieutenant **210**
Smith, McKinley 115, **210,** 215
Smith, Miss **210**
Smith, Mrs. **210**
Smith, R. Boyce (Ronnie) **210**
"Smoke" (short story) 135, **136**
 characters in 50, 52, 117, 129, 250
Snopes **211**
Snopes, Ab(ner) 13, 48, 107, 108, 111,
 117, 150, 159, **211,** 213, 223, 242
Snopes, Admiral Dewey **211–212**
Snopes, Bilbo **212,** 214
Snopes, Byron 15, 32, 106, 185, 202,
 212, 248
Snopes, Clarence Eggleston 33, 152,
 200, **212,** 214, 216, 245
Snopes, Colonel Sartoris (Sarty) 13,
 211, **212**
Snopes, Doris **212**
Snopes, Eckrum (Eck) 109, 110, 169,
 190, 211, **212,** 214, 216
Snopes, Eula Varner **213**
 in "Centaur in Brass" 121
 in *The Hamlet* 108, 138, 148, 244
 in *The Mansion* 25, 185, 224
 in *The Town* 49, 235–236
Snopes, Flem 82, 211, **213–214,** 216–217
 in "Centaur in Brass" 18, 36, 121
 character prefiguring 20
 in *The Hamlet* 8, 107, 108, 110, 115
 in "Lizards in Jamshyd's Courtyard"
  143
 in *The Mansion* 6, 20–21, 42, 137,
  154, 155, 215
 model for 21
 in *Sartoris* 212